Lecture Notes in Computer Science

Lecture Notes in Artificial Intelligence **14325**

Founding Editor

Jörg Siekmann

The series Lecture Notes in Artificial Intelligence (LNAI) was established in 1988 as a topical subseries of LNCS devoted to artificial intelligence.

The series publishes state-of-the-art research results at a high level. As with the LNCS mother series, the mission of the series is to serve the international R & D community by providing an invaluable service, mainly focused on the publication of conference and workshop proceedings and postproceedings.

Fenrong Liu · Arun Anand Sadanandan ·
Duc Nghia Pham · Petrus Mursanto ·
Dickson Lukose
Editors

PRICAI 2023: Trends in Artificial Intelligence

20th Pacific Rim
International Conference on Artificial Intelligence, PRICAI 2023
Jakarta, Indonesia, November 15–19, 2023
Proceedings, Part I

Editors
Fenrong Liu
Tsinghua University
Beijing, China

Duc Nghia Pham
MIMOS (Malaysia)
Kuala Lumpur, Malaysia

Dickson Lukose
Tabcorp Holdings Limited
Melbourne, VIC, Australia

Arun Anand Sadanandan
SEEK Limited
Cremorne, NSW, Australia

Petrus Mursanto
Universitas Indonesia
Depok, Indonesia

ISSN 0302-9743 ISSN 1611-3349 (electronic)
Lecture Notes in Artificial Intelligence
ISBN 978-981-99-7018-6 ISBN 978-981-99-7019-3 (eBook)
https://doi.org/10.1007/978-981-99-7019-3

LNCS Sublibrary: SL7 – Artificial Intelligence

This Springer imprint is published by the registered company Springer Nature Singapore Pte Ltd.
The registered company address is: 152 Beach Road, #21-01/04 Gateway East, Singapore 189721, Singapore

Paper in this product is recyclable.

Preface

Greetings and welcome to 20th Pacific Rim International Conference on Artificial Intelligence (PRICAI 2023). It was an honor to convene this significant event in a hybrid format in Jakarta, Indonesia. It was indeed a privilege for the Faculty of Computer Science at Universitas Indonesia to undertake the role of hosting these pivotal discussions that reach beyond the academic realm, advancing societies and economies across the Pacific Rim and Oceania.

This year, we received a remarkable 422 submissions: 354 for the Main track and 68 for the AI-Impact track. Every submission underwent a rigorous double-blind review process, receiving a minimum of 3 reviews, and in some cases up to 6. Throughout the process, the program committee (PC) members engaged in discussions, with additional reviews sourced as needed, prior to finalizing recommendations. The program chairs then assessed the reviews and comments, calibrating discrepancies in individual reviews and ratings to maintain decision consistency. The collective effort of the entire program committee, including chairs, 409 PC members, and 91 external reviewers, was monumental in ensuring a fair and consistent selection process. We ultimately accepted 95 regular papers and 36 short papers for oral presentation, resulting in a 22.51% acceptance rate for regular papers and an overall acceptance rate of 31.04%. Additionally, a comprehensive quality control procedure was introduced for camera-ready papers. The aim was to prompt authors to incorporate the feedback provided by PC members and reviewers into their final submissions. Content similarity checks were also performed to ensure that the similarity rate did not exceed 15%.

The technical program was comprehensive and intellectually engaging, featuring five workshops, nine tutorials, two panel discussions, and the main conference sessions. All regular and short papers were orally presented over three days in parallel and in topical program sessions. We were honored to have some of the brightest minds in AI to share their insights and enrich our collective understanding: Thomas Anton Kochan (Massachusetts Institute of Technology, USA), Hanna Kurniawati (Australian National University, Australia), Anand Rao (Carnegie Mellon University, USA), and Geoff Webb (Monash University, Australia).

A heartfelt thanks was expressed towards the organizing committee for their tireless and unwavering efforts that facilitated the success of this event. A special recognition to Adila Alfa Krisnadhi for his leadership on local arrangements. We would also like to acknowledge our workshop and tutorial organizers, who formed the core of our technical program. These dedicated individuals brought a diverse range of expertise that promised to deepen our exploration of AI technologies.

We would like to thank our advisory board members for their invaluable guidance during the planning stages. A special recognition to Abdul Sattar for his extraordinary contribution towards planning, execution, and a conference site visit that contributed to the success of PRICAI 2023. Furthermore, we extend our gratitude to the PRICAI Steering Committee for entrusting us with the privilege of hosting this impactful conference.

We would not have been here without the support of our sponsors, whose commitment enabled us to keep pushing boundaries. To them, as well as all participants in this event, thank you.

As we delved into the various topics that PRICAI 2023 had to offer, let us remind ourselves that our deliberations have a lasting impact on the future of AI in the Pacific Rim and beyond. We genuinely hope that our time spent at PRICAI 2023 will pave the way for innovations that are both groundbreaking and beneficial.

November 2023

Fenrong Liu
Arun Anand Sadanandan
Duc Nghia Pham
Dickson Lukose
Petrus Mursanto

Organization

PRICAI Steering Committee

Steering Committee

Quan Bai	University of Tasmania, Australia
Tru Hoang Cao	University of Texas Health Science Center at Houston, USA
Xin Geng	Southeast University, China
Guido Governatori	Reasoning Research Institute, Australia
Takayuki Ito	Kyoto University, Japan
Byeong-Ho Kang	University of Tasmania, Australia
M. G. M. Khan	University of the South Pacific, Fiji
Sankalp Khanna	CSIRO Australian e-Health Research Centre, Australia
Fenrong Liu	Tsinghua University, China
Dickson Lukose	Tabcorp Holdings Ltd., Australia
Hideyuki Nakashima	Sapporo City University, Japan
Abhaya Nayak	Macquarie University, Australia
Seong Bae Park	Kyung Hee University, South Korea
Duc Nghia Pham	MIMOS Berhad, Malaysia
Abdul Sattar	Griffith University, Australia
Alok Sharma	RIKEN, Japan & University of the South Pacific, Fiji
Thanaruk Theeramunkong	Thammasat University, Thailand
Zhi-Hua Zhou	Nanjing University, China

Honorary Members

Randy Goebel	University of Alberta, Canada
Tu-Bao Ho	Japan Advanced Institute of Science and Technology, Japan
Mitsuru Ishizuka	University of Tokyo, Japan
Hiroshi Motoda	Osaka University, Japan
Geoff Webb	Monash University, Australia
Albert Yeap	Auckland University of Technology, New Zealand
Byoung-Tak Zhang	Seoul National University, South Korea
Chengqi Zhang	University of Technology Sydney, Australia

Conference Organizing Committee

General Chairs

Dickson Lukose	Tabcorp Holdings Ltd., Australia
Petrus Mursanto	Universitas Indonesia, Indonesia

Program Chairs

Fenrong Liu	Tsinghua University, China
Arun Anand Sadanandan	SEEK, Australia
Duc Nghia Pham	MIMOS Berhad, Malaysia

Local Organizing Chair

Adila Alfa Krisnadhi	Universitas Indonesia, Indonesia

Workshop Chairs

Evi Yulianti	Universitas Indonesia, Indonesia
Takahiro Uchiya	Nagoya Institute of Technology, Japan

Tutorial Chairs

Fariz Darari	Universitas Indonesia, Indonesia
M. A. Hakim Newton	University of Newcastle, Australia

Publicity Chairs

Panca Hadi Putra	Universitas Indonesia, Indonesia
Md Khaled Ben Islam	Griffith University, Australia

Advisory Board

Abdul Sattar	Griffith University, Australia
Hammam Riza	KORIKA; University of Syiah Kuala, Indonesia
Patricia Anthony	Lincoln University, New Zealand
Jirapun Daengdej	Merlin's Solutions International, Thailand
Seong Bae Park	Kyung Hee University, South Korea
M. G. M. Khan	University of the South Pacific, Fiji

Qingliang Chen	Jinan University, China
Takayuki Ito	Kyoto University, Japan
Tru Hoang Cao	University of Texas Health Science Center at Houston, USA
Sankalp Khanna	CSIRO Australian e-Health Research Centre, Australia
Stéphane Bressan	National University of Singapore, Singapore
Hideyuki Nakashima	Sapporo City University, Japan

Program Committee

Tooba Aamir	Data61, CSIRO, Australia
Azizi Ab Aziz	Universiti Utara Malaysia, Malaysia
Taufik Abidin	Universitas Syiah Kuala, Indonesia
Kiki Adhinugraha	La Trobe University, Australia
Martin Aleksandrov	Freie Universität Berlin, Germany
Hissah Alotaibi	University of Melbourne, Australia
Sagaya Amalathas	University of Southampton, Malaysia
Galia Angelova	Bulgarian Academy of Sciences, Bulgaria
Patricia Anthony	Lincoln University, New Zealand
Ryuta Arisaka	Kyoto University, Japan
Mohammad Arshi Saloot	MIMOS Berhad, Malaysia
Siti Liyana Azman	International Islamic University Malaysia, Malaysia
Mohamed Jaward Bah	Zhejiang Lab, China
Quan Bai	University of Tasmania, Australia
Thirunavukarasu Balasubramaniam	Queensland University of Technology, Australia
Arishnil Kumar Bali	University of the South Pacific, Fiji
Vishnu Monn Baskaran	Monash University, Malaysia
Chutima Beokhaimook	Rangsit University, Thailand
Pascal Bercher	Australian National University, Australia
Ateet Bhalla	Independent Technology Consultant, India
Hanif Bhuiyan	Monash University, Australia
Ran Bi	Dalian University of Technology, China
Thomas Bolander	Technical University of Denmark, Denmark
Chih How Bong	Universiti Malaysia Sarawak, Malaysia
Aida Brankovic	CSIRO, Australia
Chenyang Bu	Hefei University of Technology, China
Agus Buono	Bogor Agriculture University, Indonesia
Xiongcai Cai	University of New South Wales, Australia

Jian Cao	Shanghai Jiao Tong University, China
Tru Cao	University of Texas Health Science Center at Houston, USA
Sixian Chan	Zhejiang University of Technology, China
Narayan Changder	National Institute of Technology Durgapur, India
Hutchatai Chanlekha	Kasetsart University, Thailand
Kaylash Chaudhary	University of the South Pacific, Fiji
Bincai Chen	Dalian University of Technology, China
Gang Chen	Victoria University of Wellington, New Zealand
Liangyu Chen	East China Normal University, China
Qi Chen	Victoria University of Wellington, New Zealand
Rui Chen	Nankai University, China
Siqi Chen	Tianjin University, China
Songcan Chen	Nanjing University of Aeronautics and Astronautics, China
Tingxuan Chen	Central South University, China
Weitong Chen	University of Adelaide, Australia
Weiwei Chen	Sun Yat-sen University, China
Wu Chen	Southwest University, China
Yakun Chen	University of Technology Sydney, Australia
Yingke Chen	Northumbria University, UK
Wai Khuen Cheng	Universiti Tunku Abdul Rahman, Malaysia
Yihang Cheng	Tianjin University, China
Boonthida Chiraratanasopha	Yala Rajabhat University, Thailand
Cody Christopher	Data61, CSIRO, Australia
Jinmiao Cong	Dalian University of Technology, China
Dan Corbett	University of Sydney, Australia
Zhihong Cui	Shandong University, China
Jirapun Daengdej	Assumption University of Thailand, Thailand
Li Dai	Zaozhuang University, China
Fariz Darari	Universitas Indonesia, Indonesia
Iman Dehzangi	Rutgers University, USA
Zelin Deng	Changsha University of Science and Technology, China
Chandra Kusuma Dewa	Universitas Islam Indonesia, Indonesia
Sarinder Kaur Dhillon	Universiti Malaya, Malaysia
Shiyao Ding	Kyoto University, Japan
Zheng Dong	Baidu, China
Shyamala Doraisamy	University Putra Malaysia, Malaysia
Ellouze Ellouze	University of Sfax, Tunisia
Uzoamaka Ezeakunne	Florida State University, USA
Lei Fan	University of New South Wales, Australia

Chastine Fatichah	Institut Teknologi Sepuluh Nopember, Indonesia
Shanshan Feng	Shandong Normal University, China
Xiao Feng	University of Electronic Science and Technology of China, China
Valnir Ferreira Jr.	Independent Consultant, Australia
Muhammad Firoz-Mridha	American International University-Bangladesh, Bangladesh
Tim French	University of Western Australia, Australia
Xiaoxuan Fu	China University of Political Science and Law, China
Somchart Fugkeaw	Thammasat University, Thailand
Katsuhide Fujita	Tokyo University of Agriculture and Technology, Japan
Naoki Fukuta	Shizuoka University, Japan
Hua Leong Fwa	Singapore Management University, Singapore
Marcus Gallagher	University of Queensland, Australia
Dragan Gamberger	Ruđer Bošković Institute, Croatia
Jian Gao	Northeast Normal University, China
Xiaoying Gao	Victoria University of Wellington, New Zealand
Xin Geng	Southeast University, China
Yasmeen George	Monash University, Australia
Sujata Ghosh	Indian Statistical Institute, India
Michael Granitzer	University of Passau, Germany
Alban Grastien	Australian National University, Australia
Charles Gretton	Australian National University, Australia
Wen Gu	Japan Advanced Institute of Science and Technology, Japan
Jiawei Guo	Shenzhen Institute of Artificial Intelligence and Robotics for Society, China
Avisek Gupta	TCG CREST, India
Fikret Gurgen	Boğaziçi University, Turkey
Julian Gutierrez	Monash University, Australia
Rafik Hadfi	Kyoto University, Japan
Misgina Tsighe Hagos	University College Dublin, Ireland
Mourad Hakem	Université de Franche-Comté, France
Bavly Hanna	University of Technology Sydney, Australia
Jawad Ahmad Haqbeen	Kyoto University, Japan
Md Mahmudul Hasan	University of New South Wales, Australia
Mehedi Hasan	BRAC University, Bangladesh
David Hason Rudd	University of Technology Sydney, Australia
Hamed Hassanzadeh	CSIRO, Australia
Tessai Hayama	Nagaoka University of Technology, Japan

Jane Jean Kiam	Universität der Bundeswehr München, Germany
Huan Koh	Monash University, Australia
Kazunori Komatani	Osaka University, Japan
Sébastien Konieczny	French National Centre for Scientific Research, France
Harindu Korala	Monash University, Australia
Fajri Koto	Mohamed bin Zayed University of Artificial Intelligence, United Arab Emirates
Adila A. Krisnadhi	Universitas Indonesia, Indonesia
Alfred Krzywicki	University of Adelaide, Australia
Charles Kuan	Tabcorp Holdings Limited, Australia
Li Kuang	Central South University, China
Dinesh Kumar	University of the South Pacific, Fiji
Shiu Kumar	Fiji National University, Fiji
Young-Bin Kwon	Chung-Ang University, South Korea
Ho-Pun Lam	Independent Researcher, Australia
Davide Lanti	Free University of Bozen-Bolzano, Italy
Roberto Legaspi	KDDI Research, Japan
Dazhu Li	Chinese Academy of Sciences, China
Gang Li	Deakin University, Australia
Guangliang Li	Ocean University of China, China
Guoqiang Li	Shanghai Jiao Tong University, China
Ren Li	Chongqing Jiaotong University, China
Tianrui Li	Southwest Jiaotong University, China
Weihua Li	Auckland University of Technology, New Zealand
Yicong Li	University of Technology Sydney, Australia
Yuan-Fang Li	Monash University, Australia
Xiubo Liang	Zhejiang University, China
Ariel Liebman	Monash University, Australia
Alan Wee-Chung Liew	Griffith University, Australia
Donghui Lin	Okayama University, Japan
Chanjuan Liu	Dalian University of Technology, China
Di Liu	Inner Mongolia University, China
Fenrong Liu	Tsinghua University, China
Guanfeng Liu	Macquarie University, Australia
Hao Liu	Hong Kong University of Science and Technology, China
Jinghui Liu	University of Melbourne, Australia
Kangzheng Liu	Huazhong University of Science and Technology, China
Xinpeng Liu	Dalian University of Technology, China
Yang Liu	Dalian University of Technology, China

Yue Liu	Data61, CSIRO, Australia
Sin Kit Lo	Data61, CSIRO, Australia
Emiliano Lorini	French National Centre for Scientific Research, France
Qinghua Lu	Data61, CSIRO, Australia
Dickson Lukose	Tabcorp Holdings Limited, Australia
Jieting Luo	Zhejiang University, China
Sreenivasan M.	International Institute of Information Technology, India
Chuan Ma	Zhejiang Lab, China
Hui Ma	Victoria University of Wellington, New Zealand
Pathum Chamikara Mahawaga Arachchige	Data61, CSIRO, Australia
Michael Maher	Reasoning Research Institute, Australia
Vikash Maheshwari	Universiti Teknologi PETRONAS, Malaysia
Rohana Mahmud	Universiti Malaya, Malaysia
Eric Martin	University of New South Wales, Australia
Sanparith Marukatat	National Electronics and Computer Technology Center, Thailand
Atiya Masood	Iqra University, Pakistan
Nur Ulfa Maulidevi	Bandung Institute of Technology, Indonesia
Alan Mccabe	Griffith University, Australia
Md Humaion Kabir Mehedi	BRAC University, Bangladesh
Qingxin Meng	University of Nottingham - Ningbo, China
Jian Mi	Yangzhou University, China
Lynn Miller	Monash University, Australia
Muhammad Syafiq Mohd Pozi	Universiti Utara Malaysia, Malaysia
Kristen Moore	Data61, CSIRO, Australia
Fernando Mourao	SEEK, Australia
Lailil Muflikhah	Universitas Brawijaya, Indonesia
Ganesh Neelakanta Iyer	National University of Singapore, Singapore
M. A. Hakim Newton	University of Newcastle, Australia
Phi Le Nguyen	Hanoi University of Science and Technology, Vietnam
Thanh Thi Nguyen	Deakin University, Australia
Nianwen Ning	Henan University, China
Hussain Nyeem	Military Institute of Science and Technology, Bangladesh
Kouzou Ohara	Aoyama Gakuin University, Japan
Nurul Aida Osman	Universiti Teknologi PETRONAS, Malaysia
Takanobu Otsuka	Nagoya Institute of Technology, Japan
Abiola Oyegun	Birmingham City University, UK

Maurice Pagnucco	University of New South Wales, Australia
Shirui Pan	Griffith University, Australia
Anum Paracha	Birmingham City University, UK
Anand Paul	Kyungpook National University, South Korea
Pengfei Pei	Chinese Academy of Sciences, China
Shengbing Pei	Anhui University, China
Songwen Pei	University of Shanghai for Science and Technology, China
Tao Peng	UT Southwestern Medical Center, USA
Arif Perdana	Monash University, Indonesia
Laurent Perrussel	University of Toulouse, France
Duc Nghia Pham	MIMOS Berhad, Malaysia
Ioannis Pierros	Aristotle University of Thessaloniki, Greece
Chiu Po Chan	Universiti Malaysia Sarawak, Malaysia
Thadpong Pongthawornkamol	Kasikorn Business-Technology Group, Thailand
Surya Prakash	University of the South Pacific, Fiji
Mauridhi Hery Purnomo	Institut Teknologi Sepuluh Nopember, Indonesia
Ayu Purwarianti	Bandung Institute of Technology, Indonesia
Qi Qi	Hainan University, China
Shiyou Qian	Shanghai Jiao Tong University, China
Jianglin Qiao	Western Sydney University, Australia
Chuan Qin	Baidu, China
Lyn Qiu	Shanghai Jiao Tong University, China
Joel Quinqueton	Laboratoire d'Informatique, de Robotique et de Microélectronique de Montpellier, France
Teeradaj Racharak	Japan Advanced Institute of Science and Technology, Japan
Jessica Rahman	CSIRO, Australia
Mohammad Shahriar Rahman	United International University, Bangladesh
Srikari Rallabandi	Vidya Jyothi Institute of Technology, India
Tian Ran	Northwest Normal University, China
Annajiat Alim Rasel	BRAC University, Bangladesh
Mahmood Rashid	Griffith University, Australia
Md Saifullah Razali	University of Wollongong, Australia
Farid Razzak	New York University, USA
Karuna Reddy	University of the South Pacific, Fiji
Fenghui Ren	University of Wollongong, Australia
Jiankang Ren	Dalian University of Technology, China
Yongli Ren	RMIT University, Australia
Yuheng Ren	Jimei University, China
Mark Reynolds	University of Western Australia, Australia
Jia Rong	Monash University, Australia

Yi Rong	Wuhan University of Technology, China
Liat Rozenberg	Griffith University, Australia
Ji Ruan	Auckland University of Technology, New Zealand
Filip Rusak	CSIRO, Australia
Arun Anand Sadanandan	SEEK Limited, Australia
Khairun Saddami	Universitas Syiah Kuala, Indonesia
Payel Sadhukhan	TCG CREST, India
Sofia Sahab	Kyoto University, Japan
Chiaki Sakama	Wakayama University, Japan
Ario Santoso	Independent, The Netherlands
Muhamad Saputra	Monash University, Indonesia
Yunita Sari	Universitas Gadjah Mada, Indonesia
Anto Satriyo Nugroho	National Research and Innovation Agency, Indonesia
Abdul Sattar	Griffith University, Australia
Thanveer Shaik	University of Southern Queensland, Australia
Lin Shang	Nanjing University, China
Nandita Sharma	Australian Government, Australia
Dazhong Shen	University of Science and Technology of China, China
Yifan Shen	University of Illinois Urbana-Champaign, USA
Chenwei Shi	Tsinghua University, China
Kaize Shi	University of Technology Sydney, Australia
Xiaolong Shi	Guangzhou University, China
Zhenwei Shi	Beihang University, China
Kazutaka Shimada	Kyushu Institute of Technology, Japan
Yanfeng Shu	CSIRO, Australia
Harvinder Singh	Torrens University, Australia
Ronal Singh	Data61, CSIRO, Australia
Patrick Chin Hooi Soh	Multimedia University, Malaysia
Chattrakul Sombattheera	Mahasarakham University, Thailand
Insu Song	James Cook University, Australia
Xin Song	Hebei University, China
Pokpong Songmuang	Thammasat University, Thailand
Lay-Ki Soon	Monash University Malaysia, Malaysia
Bela Stantic	Griffith University, Australia
Markus Stumptner	University of South Australia, Australia
Guoxin Su	University of Wollongong, Australia
Ruidan Su	Shanghai Jiao Tong University, China
Xingchi Su	Zhejiang Lab, China
Jie Sun	Nanjing Xiaozhuang University, China
Xin Sun	Zhejiang Lab, China

Ying Sun	Hong Kong University of Science and Technology, China
Yongqian Sun	Nankai University, China
Boontawee Suntisrivaraporn	DTAC, Thailand
Thepchai Supnithi	National Electronics and Computer Technology Center, Thailand
Chang Wei Tan	Monash University, Australia
David Taniar	Monash University, Australia
Thitipong Tanprasert	Assumption University of Thailand, Thailand
Xiaohui Tao	University of Southern Queensland, Australia
Sotarat Thammaboosadee	Mahidol University, Thailand
Truong Thao Nguyen	National Institute of Advanced Industrial Science and Technology, Japan
Bui Thi-Mai-Anh	Institut de la Francophonie pour l'Informatique, Vietnam
Michael Thielscher	University of New South Wales, Australia
Hung Nghiep Tran	National Institute of Informatics, Japan
Jarrod Trevathan	Griffith University, Australia
Bambang Riyanto Trilaksono	Institut Teknologi Bandung, Indonesia
Bayu Trisedya	SEEK, Australia
Eric Tsui	Hong Kong Polytechnic University, China
Shikui Tu	Shanghai Jiao Tong University, China
Ayad Turky	University of Sharjah, United Arab Emirates
Takahiro Uchiya	Nagoya Institute of Technology, Japan
Khimji Vaghjiani	Torrens University, Australia
Hans van Ditmarsch	University of Toulouse, France
Miroslav Velev	Aries Design Automation, USA
Agustinus Waluyo	La Trobe University, Australia
Biao Wang	Zhejiang Lab, China
Chao Wang	HKUST Fok Ying Tung Research Institute, China
Chen Wang	National Institute of Water and Atmospheric Research, New Zealand
Hao Wang	Monash University, Australia
Hao Wang	Nanyang Technological University, Singapore
Li Wang	Henan University, China
Shuxia Wang	Northwestern Polytechnical University, China
Weiqing Wang	Monash University, Australia
Xiangmeng Wang	University of Technology Sydney, Australia
Xinxhi Wang	Shanghai University, China
Yuxin Wang	Dalian University of Technology, China
Zhen Wang	Zhejiang Lab, China
Ian Watson	University of Auckland, New Zealand

Jingwen Zhu	Nankai University, China
Liang Zhu	Hebei University, China
Nengjun Zhu	Shanghai University, China
Xingquan Zhu	Florida Atlantic University, USA
Yanming Zhu	Griffith University, Australia

Additional Reviewers

Angelov, Zhivko
Azam, Basim
Burgess, Mark
Cao, Xuemei
Chan, Chee-Yong
Chandra, Abel
Chen, Xiaohong
Clifton, Ava
Duan, Jiaang
Ebrahimi, Ali
Fang, Han
Fei, Wu
Fodor, Gabor Adam
Folkman, Lukas
Geng, Chuanxing
Guo, Ruoyu
Guo, Siyuan
Hammond, Lewis
Han, Xin
Hao, Chen
Haruta, Shuichiro
He, Haoyu
He, Tao
He, Zhengqi
Hu, Han Wen
Hua, Qin
Hua, Yuncheng
Huang, Renhao
Hung, Nguyen
Jiang, Zhaohui
Li, Jingyang
Li, Xiang
Liga, Davide
Lin, Songtuan
Liu, Chuan
Liu, Hongquan
Liu, Yongchang
Liu, Yutao
Liu, Zhaorui
Ma, Jiaxuan
Mataeimoghadam, Fereshteh
Mayer, Wolfgang
Mezza, Stefano
Mohamed Muzammil, Mohamed Mufassirin
Mu, Chunjiang
Nikafshan Rad, Hima
Nwe, Hlaing Myat
Pan, Chaofan
Peng, Lilan
Perera, Isuri
Rahman, Julia
Reddy, Emmenual
Ren, Siyue
Ren, Yixin
Schwenker, Friedhelm
Selway, Matt
Semenov, Ivan
Shiri, Fatemeh
Singh, Priyanka
Singh, Satyanand
Smith, Jeff
Song, Zhihao
Soni, Bhanu Pratap
Tan, Hongwei
Tang, Jiaqi
Viriyavisuthisakul, Supatta
Wang, Luzhi
Wang, Mengyan
Wang, Xiaodan

Wang, Yunyun
Wei, Tianpeng
Wu, Lingi
Wu, Shixin
Xia, Boming
Xu, Dalai
Xu, Rongxin
Xu, Weilai
Yang, Yikun
Yao, Naimeng
Yin, Yifan
Yuan, Zixuan
Zaman, Rianon
Zhang, Denghui
Zhang, Junyu
Zhang, Lin
Zhang, Yunfei
Zhang, Zhenxing
Zhao, Zijun
Zheng, Xin
Zheng, Yizhen
Zhou, Zheng

Contents – Part I

Agents/Decision Theory

Data Mining and Knowledge Discovery

(Deep) Reinforcement Learning

Generative AI

Graph Learning

Knowledge Representation and Reasoning

Contents – Part II

Machine Learning/Deep Learning

Natural Language Processing

Contents – Part III

Vision and Perception

AI Impact

Agents/Decision Theory

DAGE: Dropout with Action Gradient Estimator for Continuous Control

Zhongjian Qiao(✉) and Kechen Jiao

Tsinghua Shenzhen International Graduate School, Tsinghua University, Beijing, China
{qzj22,jkc22}@mails.tsinghua.edu.cn

Abstract. For actor-critic algorithms in reinforcement learning, the policy update is guided by a Q function, so the quality of the policy is largely affected by the quality of the Q function. Most work has focused on how to estimate a more accurate Q function, such as using a dropout operator. However, we show that for continuous control scenarios using deterministic policy gradient algorithms, the quality of the Q function does not depend on the accuracy of the Q function itself, but on the accuracy of the action gradient of the Q function. Motivated by this observation, we propose Dropout with Action Gradient Estimator (DAGE), which aims at estimating the action gradient of the Q function accurately instead of the Q function itself. We conduct sufficient experiments on PyBullet Control Suite, and empirically show that DAGE can estimate a more accurate action gradient and achieve better performance than baselines.

Keywords: action gradient · dropout operator · continuous control

1 Introduction

In reinforcement learning [19], actor-critic [14] algorithms are one of the most commonly used algorithms. In actor-critic algorithms, there is a critic which estimates a Q-value, and an actor for policy learning based on the Q-value provided by the critic. Therefore, the quality of the learned policy is largely determined by the quality of the Q-value provided by the critic. There has been lots of work aiming at improving the quality of the critic by estimating a more accurate Q-value. Among these methods, ensemble [21] is commonly used. For example, REDQ [4] uses Q-ensemble to reduce the standard deviation of Q-value estimation, REM [1] weights the outputs of multiple Q-networks to estimate a more accurate Q-value. However, compared to using a single network, ensemble methods have too much computational burden since there are multiple networks to update. The dropout operator [18], which has ensemble nature, can achieve similar performance to ensemble, while the computational cost is much lower. Therefore, the dropout operator has been applied to replace ensemble. For example, DroQ [10] uses a small ensemble of Q networks to achieve much higher sample efficiency than REDQ; MEPG [9] leverages the dropout operator, also greatly reducing

Z. Qiao and K. Jiao—Equal Contribution.

F. Liu et al. (Eds.): PRICAI 2023, LNAI 14325, pp. 3–14, 2024.
https://doi.org/10.1007/978-981-99-7019-3_1

the computation cost. Those methods all aim at estimating a more accurate Q-value, just replacing ensemble with a dropout operator. However, we point out that in continuous control tasks where deterministic policy gradient is leveraged, the quality of the critic does not depend on the accuracy of the Q function itself, but on the accuracy of the action gradient of the Q function. Hence, to guide policy update better, we should focus on estimating the action gradient of the Q function accurately.

To that end, we propose Dropout with Action Gradient Estimator (DAGE), which aims at estimating a more accurate action gradient by utilizing a dropout operator. DAGE can be seen as a framework and used for any deterministic policy gradient algorithm, such as DDPG [15], TD3 [7], etc. We conduct experiments on a set of continuous control tasks on open-source PyBullet Suite [5], which is more challenging than MuJoCo [20]. We show that DPG algorithms (such as DDPG, TD3) combined with our framework results in better performance than vanilla algorithms.

Our contributions can be summarized as follows.

- We give an insight into the role of the action gradient in DPG algorithms;
- As far as we know, we are the first to utilize a dropout operator to estimate an accurate action gradient.
- On PyBullet Suite, DAGE achieves better overall performance compared against popular baseline methods.

2 Related Work

Action Gradient Estimation. Deterministic Policy Gradient (DPG) [17] is widely applied in continuous control tasks. Some early work [11,16] explored the role of the action gradient and involved the gradient of the value function in backpropagation process. However, they do not apply function approximation so there are no performance guarantees on DPG algorithms with neural networks. As far as we know, MAGE [6] is the closet to our work, which also utilizes the action gradient to guide policy update. However, MAGE learns the action gradient in a model-based scheme [13], which greatly increases computational burden. We learn the action gradient in the context of model-free scenarios instead.

Dropout Operator in RL. Dropout is a technique to avoid overfitting in deep learning [18]. It has been applied to RL to improve the performance of DRL algorithms. DRL algorithms use the dropout operator for different purposes: [12] introduce dropout to model-based algorithms to replace ensemble models. [8] apply dropout to a Q function to estimate uncertainty to encourage exploration. In our work, we introduce consistent dropout operator similar to [9] to a Q function, aiming to estimate the action gradient more accurately, which is different from other work.

3 Background

We consider a Markov Decision Process (MDP), which can be formulated by tuple $(\mathcal{S}, \mathcal{A}, r, p, \gamma, \mu)$, where $\mathcal{S}$ is state space, $\mathcal{A}$ is action space, r is reward function, p is state transition probability, γ is discount factor and μ is initial state distribution. For actor-critic algorithms, the critic tries to estimate a Q function, defined as $Q(s,a) = \mathbb{E}\left[\sum_{t=0}^{\infty} \gamma^t r(s_t, a_t) | s_0 = s, a_0 = a\right]$. And the actor aims to find the optimal policy:

$$\pi^* = \arg\max_{\pi} \left[Q(s_0, a_0) | s_0 \sim \mu, a_0 \sim \pi(s_0)\right] \tag{1}$$

For deterministic policy gradient algorithms, we denote $J(\theta) = \mathbb{E}\left[Q(s_0, \pi_\theta(s_0))\right]$, then the goal of reinforcement learning is to maximize $J(\theta)$. According to Deterministic Policy Gradient (DPG) theorem [17]:

$$\nabla_\theta J(\theta) = \mathbb{E}_s \left[\nabla_a Q_\phi(s,a)|_{a=\pi_\theta(s)} \nabla_\theta \pi_\theta(s)\right] \tag{2}$$

where $\nabla_a Q_\phi(s,a)$ is the action gradient of the Q function. Equation 2 shows that policy gradient is only related to the action gradient of the Q function, instead of the Q function itself. Therefore, to better guide policy update, it is necessary to estimate a more accurate action gradient.

4 Estimate Action Gradient Accurately

4.1 You Need to Minimize Action Gradient Error

In this subsection, we formalize the concept of action gradient error and demonstrate why it is necessary to minimize action gradient error for DPG algorithms. In general policy evaluation process, critic aims to learn a Q function as accurate as possible, that is:

$$\phi^* = \arg\max_{\phi} \mathbb{E}_{s,a\sim\pi} \left[\left(Q^\pi_\phi(s,a) - Q^\pi(s,a)\right)^2\right] \tag{3}$$

where $Q^\pi(s,a)$ is ground-truth and $Q^\pi_\phi(s,a)$ is a parametrized network. In practice, $Q^\pi(s,a)$ is hard to get, so we use target Q-value $Q_{target}(s,a) = r(s,a) + \gamma Q_\phi(s',a')$ to approximate $Q^\pi(s,a)$. Then the target is to minimize TD-error:

$$\phi^* = \arg\max_{\phi} \mathbb{E}_{(s,a,s',a')\sim\pi} \left[\left(Q^\pi_\phi(s,a) - \left(r(s,a) + \gamma Q^\pi_\phi(s',a')\right)\right)^2\right] \tag{4}$$

where TD-error is denoted as $\delta_\phi = \left(Q^\pi_\phi(s,a) - \left(r(s,a) + \gamma Q^\pi_\phi(s',a')\right)\right)^2$. Proposition 1 shows that bounding TD-error is beneficial for estimating a more accurate objective function $J(\theta)$:

Proposition 1. *Let π_θ be policy to be optimized, $J(\theta)$ be objective function estimated by Q_ϕ, $J^*(\theta)$ be ground-truth, then the difference between $J(\theta)$ and $J^*(\theta)$ is bounded by TD-error:*

$$|J(\theta) - J^*(\theta)| \leq \delta_\phi^{\frac{1}{2}} \tag{5}$$

Proof.

$$\begin{aligned} |J(\theta) - J^*(\theta)|^2 &= \left|\mathbb{E}_\pi \left[Q_\phi^\pi(s,a) - Q^\pi(s,a)\right]\right|^2 \\ &\leq \mathbb{E}_\pi \left|Q_\phi^\pi(s,a) - Q^\pi(s,a)\right|^2 \\ &\approx \mathbb{E}_\pi \left|Q_\phi^\pi(s,a) - \left(r(s,a) + \gamma Q_\phi^\pi(s',a')\right)\right|^2 \\ &= \delta_\phi \end{aligned}$$

so $|J(\theta) - J^*(\theta)| \leq \delta_\phi^{\frac{1}{2}}$. □

But is that enough? Even if bounding TD-error can estimate a more accurate objective function, it does not guarantee that a better policy will be learned, because the direction of policy update, that is, policy gradient, is not guaranteed. We denote the norm of TD-error to the gradient of action as action gradient error: $\|\nabla_a \delta_\phi\|$. According to Proposition 2, we show that if we want to get a better policy gradient, we need to bound action gradient error:

Proposition 2. *Let $\nabla_\theta J(\theta)$ be policy gradient to be optimized, $\nabla_\theta J^*(\theta)$ be ground-truth, and we further hypothesize π is L_π – Lipschitz continuous differentiable deterministic policy, then the difference between $\nabla_\theta J(\theta)$ and $\nabla_\theta J^*(\theta)$ is bounded by action gradient error $\|\nabla_a \delta_\phi\|$:*

$$\|\nabla_\theta J(\theta) - \nabla_\theta J^*(\theta)\| \leq L_\pi \|\nabla_a \delta_\phi\|^{\frac{1}{2}} \tag{6}$$

Proof.

$$\begin{aligned} \|\nabla_\theta J(\theta) - \nabla_\theta J^*(\theta)\| &= \left\|\mathbb{E}_\pi \left[\nabla_a \left(Q_\phi^\pi(s,a) - Q^\pi(s,a)\right)|_{a=\pi_\theta(s)} \nabla_\theta \pi_\theta(s)\right]\right\| \\ &\leq \mathbb{E}_\pi \left\|\nabla_a \left(Q_\phi^\pi(s,a) - Q^\pi(s,a)\right)|_{a=\pi_\theta(s)}\right\| \|\nabla_\theta \pi_\theta(s)\| \\ &\leq L_\pi \|\nabla_a \delta_\phi\|^{\frac{1}{2}} \end{aligned}$$

□

Proposition 2 shows that minimizing action gradient error can estimate a more accurate policy gradient, thereby learning a better policy. To ensure the accuracy of $J(\theta)$ and $\nabla_\theta J(\theta)$, we add action gradient error into the process of policy evaluation as a regularizer:

$$\begin{aligned} &\min\nolimits_\phi \mathbb{E}_\pi |\delta_\phi| \\ &\text{s.t.} \mathbb{E}_\pi \|\nabla_a \delta_\phi\| \leq \eta \end{aligned} \tag{7}$$

In practice, we use the Lagrange multiplier method to transform the optimization objective into:

$$\min_\phi \mathcal{L}(\phi) = \mathbb{E}_\pi \left[|\delta_\phi| + \lambda \|\nabla_a \delta_\phi\|\right] \tag{8}$$

where λ is a hyperparameter.

4.2 Dropout Operator for Consistent Bellman Update

The dropout operator is often added to a Q function structure to achieve a similar effect to ensemble. In fact, each update process with a dropout operator can be seen as updating a sub-network of Q network, therefore the dropout operator has ensemble nature. Previous work has focused on using the dropout operator to estimate a more accurate Q-value, we use the dropout operator to estimate a more accurate action gradient instead. However, since the dropout operator randomly discards different neurons each time, applying regular dropout operator directly into Q-network introduces source-target inconsistency, that is, online Q-network and target Q-network are not the same sub-Q network(different neurons are dropped). And it may cause Q-function to not converge, resulting in failure of training. Therefore, we introduce the consistent dropout operator similar to MEPG [9], but we further apply it in action gradient update process.

For a neural network, feed-forward process of layer l can be described as:

$$z^l = w^l x^l + b^l, x^{l+1} = f(z^l)$$

where x is the input at layer l, w and b are weights and bias respectively, and f is the activation function. If we apply dropout operator into layer l:

$$\hat{x}^l = x^l \odot m^l, z^l = w^l \hat{x}^l + b^l \tag{9}$$

where $m \sim Bernoulli(1-p)$ is dropout mask, p is dropout rate, $\odot$ is element-wise product. We denote this dropout operator as $\mathcal{D}^l_m$, which means applying dropout with mask m at layer l. To avoid source-target inconsistency, we use the same mask m on online Q-network and target Q-network:

$$\mathcal{D}^l_m J^Q(\phi) = \mathbb{E}_{(s,a)\sim\mathcal{B}}\left[\left(\mathcal{D}^l_m Q(s,a) - \left(r + \gamma\mathcal{D}^l_m \bar{Q}(s',a')\right)\right)^2\right] \tag{10}$$

where we apply the same dropout operator $\mathcal{D}^l_m$ on Q and $\bar{Q}$. Similarly, we apply it on action gradient error:

$$\nabla_a \mathcal{D}^l_m J^Q(\phi) = \mathbb{E}_{(s,a)\sim\mathcal{B}}\left[\nabla_a \left(\mathcal{D}^l_m Q(s,a) - \left(r + \gamma\mathcal{D}^l_m \bar{Q}(s',a')\right)\right)^2\right] \tag{11}$$

Thus consistent dropout operator can eliminate the problem of inconsistency while preserving Q diversity.

5 DAGE Framework

In this section, we propose Dropout with Action Gradient Estimator(DAGE). DAGE realizes an accurate estimation of the action gradient through action gradient estimator and consistent dropout operator. In the policy evaluation process, a dropout operator mask m is sampled, then we apply $\mathcal{D}^l_m$ on Eq. 10 11 to update Q-function. In the policy improvement process, the complete Q-network which doesn't apply the dropout operator is used to train the policy network, equivalent to using the entire ensemble for policy improvement. DAGE is summarized in Algorithm 1. Since DAGE is a framework for any DPG rl algorithms, so we apply DAGE to DDPG and TD3 algorithm, called DE-DDPG and DE-TD3. For DE-DDPG, there is one online Q-network and one target Q-target, we apply the consistent dropout operator on both online and target Q-network. For DE-TD3, there are two online Q-networks and two target Q-networks. During forward propagation, we apply the same dropout operator on both online networks and target networks, online networks are then updated by min target.

Algorithm 1 Dropout with Action Gradient Estimator (DAGE)

Initialize: critic network Q_ϕ, actor network π_θ parameterized by ϕ and θ; target critic network $Q_{\phi'}$; replay buffer $\mathcal{B}$; Initial state s_0.

Parameters: dropout rate p, regularization coefficient λ.

for $t = 1$ to T **do**
  Perform action $a \sim \pi_\theta(s)$, observe the reward r and the next state s'.
  Update replay buffer $\mathcal{B} \leftarrow \mathcal{B} \cup (s, a, r, s')$
  Sample N transitions $\{(s, a, r, s')\}_N$ from $\mathcal{B}$.
  Sample $m \sim Bernoulli(1-p)$
  Calculate target value $y = r(s, a) + \gamma \mathcal{D}_m^l Q_{\phi'}(s', \pi_\theta(s'))$
  Calculate TD-error $\mathcal{L}_\phi^{TD} = \frac{1}{N} \sum \left(y - \mathcal{D}_m^l Q_\phi(s, a)\right)^2$
  Calculate action gradient error $\mathcal{L}_\phi^{AG} = \frac{1}{N} \sum \nabla_a \left(y - \mathcal{D}_m^l Q_\phi(s, a)\right)^2$
  Update critic $\phi \leftarrow \arg\min_\phi \mathcal{L}_\phi^{TD} + \lambda \mathcal{L}_\phi^{AG}$
  Update actor parameter θ by: $\nabla_\theta J(\theta) = \frac{1}{N} \sum \nabla_a Q_\phi(s, a)|_{a=\pi_\theta(s)} \nabla_\theta \pi_\theta(s)$
  Update target network: $\phi' \leftarrow \tau\phi + (1-\tau)\phi'$
end for

6 Experiment

In this section, we aim to answer the following questions: (1) Does DAGE perform better than baseline methods on PyBullet Suite? (2) Does DAGE estimate a more accurate action gradient? (3) What is the contribution of each component of DAGE to the performance? (4) Is DAGE sensitive to the main hyper-parameters? We conduct sufficient experiments on PyBullet Suite and compare our method to common baselines. It is worth mentioning that PyBullet suite is considered more challenging than Mujoco suite.

6.1 Overall Performance

We evaluate DAGE on four PyBullet tasks: HopperPyBulletEnv-v0, Walker2D-PyBulletEnv-v0, AntPyBulletEnv-v0, HalfCheetahPyBulletEnv-v0. We implement DDPG, TD3 and DE-DDPG, DE-TD3. We run each algorithm under 5 different seeds, and the learning curves are presented in Fig. 1. Regarding the selection of hyper-parameters of each algorithm in the experiment, we list them in Table 1. In particular, for DE-DDPG and DE-TD3, we set the hyper-parameter λ to 0.1 and the dropout rate p to 0.1, other hyper-parameters are consistent with DDPG and TD3. Learning curves in Fig. 1 shows that the application of the DAGE framework to a vanilla DPG algorithm can significantly improve sample efficiency and final performance on all four PyBullet tasks. To show the aggregate performance of DAGE algorithm on these tasks, we compute SAC Normalized Score of each algorithm as $\frac{agent\_score - random\_score}{SAC\_score - random\_score}$, where agent score represents the score of the corresponding algorithm on a given task; random score represents the score of the random policy; SAC score represents the score of SAC algorithm. Figure 2 shows the results aggregated over 4 tasks of PyBullet Control Suite according to the metrics presented in [2]. IQM drops 25% of the highest and lowest scores in all runs, and calculates the average of the rest. Optimality Gap measures the performance gap between the estimated algorithm and SAC. From Fig. 2, we can clearly see that DE-DDPG and DE-TD3 outperform DDPG and TD3 in all four aggregated metrics.

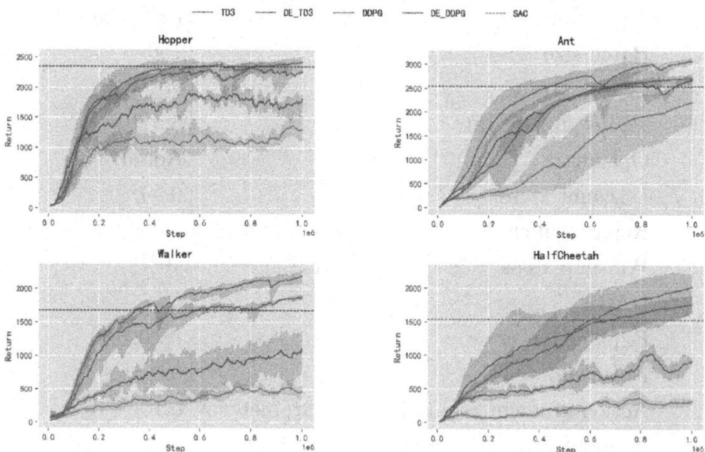

Fig. 1. Learning curves for four different tasks in PyBullet Control Suite for DAGE and vanilla DPG algorithms (5 runs, averaged return ± standard deviation). DE-TD3 and DE-DDPG are vanilla TD3 and DDPG algorithms after using DAGE framework. As a reference, we use dotted lines to show the final performance of SAC algorithm on each task (run and average with five different seeds).

6.2 Does DAGE Estimate Action Gradient More Accurately?

The core idea of DAGE is to estimate a more accurate action gradient. In this subsection, we explore whether the action gradient estimated by DAGE

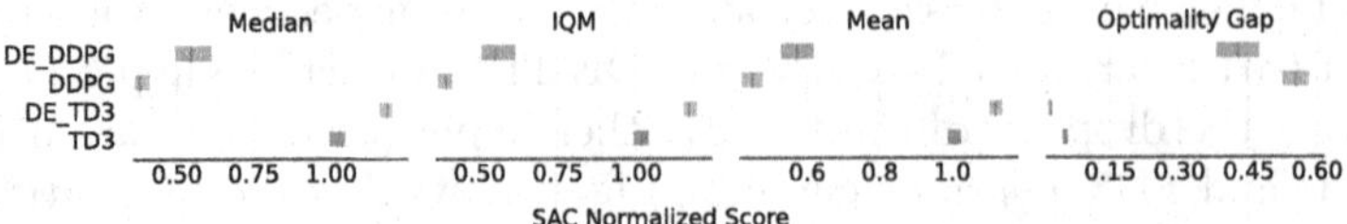

Fig. 2. Aggregated metrics over 5 runs on 4 tasks of PyBullet Control Suite with 95% confidence intervals. The mean and intervals of metrics are estimated by percentile bootstrap with statified sampling according to [2]. The short black vertical lines represent the mean of metrics and the shaded sections represent the 95% confidence intervals. Higher Median, Mean, IQM and lower Optimality Gap, better the aggregated performance.

Table 1. Hyper-parameters setup for experiment

Hyper-parameter	Value
Shared	
Actor network	$(256, 256)$
Critic network	$(256, 256)$
Batch size	256
Learning rate	10^{-3}
Target update rate	5×10^{-3}
Optimizer	Adam
Discount factor	0.99
Replay buffer size	10^6
Warmup steps	10^4
DAGE	
Exploration noise	$\mathcal{N}(0, 0.1)$
Noise clip	0.5
Action gradient regularization parameter λ	0.1
Dropout rate p	0.1
DDPG	
Exploration noise	$\mathcal{N}(0, 0.1)$
Noise clip	0.5
TD3	
Exploration noise	$\mathcal{N}(0, 0.1)$
Noise clip	0.5
Policy update frequency	2
SAC	
Entropy weight	0.2
Maximum log std	2
Minimum log std	-20

is more accurate. To verify this, we compare the estimation of action gradient by TD3 and DE-TD3. To get true action gradient, we follow the definition of action gradient and use Monte Carlo method to estimate it. Specifically, $\nabla_a Q(s,a) := \lim_{\Delta a \to 0} \frac{Q(s,a+\Delta a)-Q(s,a)}{\Delta a}$, we use Monte Carlo method to estimate the true Q-value, then we set Δa a small value so we can get an estimation of the true action gradient. For ease of calculation, we conduct experiments on MountainCarContinuous-v0 task on gym [3], where action-dim is 1. Figure 3 shows our experimental results. We can see that DE-TD3 estimates a more accurate action gradient than TD3, which verifies our idea.

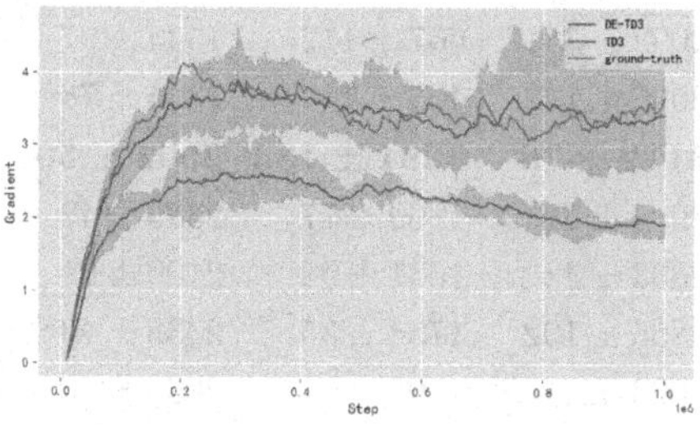

Fig. 3. Comparison of DE-TD3 and TD3 for estimation of action gradient. The solid purple line is true action gradient.

6.3 Ablation Study

In this section, we aim to demonstrate how each component of DAGE contributes to final performance improvement. We conduct ablation study on the same four tasks of PyBullt Control Suite and show the ablation results of DE-DDPG and DE-TD3 in Table 2. DAGE has two essential components: the action gradient regularizer and the consistent dropout operator. We first remove the action gradient regularizer and keep the consistent dropout operator, resulting in D-DDPG and D-TD3. Then we only apply the action gradient regularizer and remove the consistent dropout operator, resulting in AG-DDPG and AG-TD3. To further verify the superiority of the consistent dropout operator over the regular dropout operator, we replace the consistent dropout operator in DE-DDPG, DE-TD3 and D-DDPG, D-TD3 with the regular dropout operator, named DE-DDPG-R, DE-TD3-R and D-DDPG-R, D-TD3-R respectively.

Table 2 shows that both the action gradient regularizer and the consistent dropout operator are essential components for DAGE, and without either component, the performance of the algorithm will decline. More specifically, we can see D-DDPG-R(D-TD3-R) outperforms vanilla DDPG(TD3) while DE-DDPG(DE-TD3) and D-DDPG(D-TD3) outperforms DE-DDPG-R(DE-TD3-R) and D-DDPG-R(D-TD3-R) respectively, which shows that consistency is critical for the dropout operator. AG-DDPG(AG-TD3) also outperforms vanilla DDPG(TD3), showing that a more accurate action gradient is beneficial for DPG algorithms.

Table 2. The average and std of the final returns over five runs for each algorithm (mean ± std). We run each algorithm for 1M steps and take the return of the last step as final return. The maximum average return for each task is bolded. Ant, Half, Hopper, Walker are shorthands for AntPyBulletEnv-v0, HalfCheetahPyBulletEnv-v0, HopperPyBulletEnv-v0, Walker2DPyBulletEnv-v0, respectively.

Algorithm	Ant	Half	Hopper	Walker
DE-DDPG	**2531 ± 197**	**1064 ± 70**	**1879 ± 109**	**997 ± 49**
DE-DDPG-R	2109 ± 207	894 ± 69	1655 ± 88	906 ± 32
AG-DDPG	2218 ± 117	871 ± 42	1520 ± 77	778 ± 44
D-DDPG	2290 ± 132	944 ± 55	1777 ± 91	824 ± 79
D-DDPG-R	2092 ± 341	667 ± 112	1544 ± 97	630 ± 64
DDPG	2006 ± 122	408 ± 11	1344 ± 78	474 ± 31
DE-TD3	**3112 ± 78**	**2091 ± 133**	**2502 ± 50**	**2289 ± 211**
DE-TD3-R	2984 ± 51	1809 ± 77	2335 ± 42	1893 ± 133
AG-TD3	2633 ± 43	1651 ± 98	2109 ± 21	1707 ± 132
D-TD3	2865 ± 102	1794 ± 35	2332 ± 43	1877 ± 88
D-TD3-R	2503 ± 51	1703 ± 44	2066 ± 56	1730 ± 10
TD3	2413 ± 197	1576 ± 23	2080 ± 74	1904 ± 22

6.4 Parameter Sensitivity

In this section, We study the effect of the main hyper-parameters on the performance of DAGE algorithm. There are two main hyper-parameters of DAGE: the action gradient regularization coefficient λ and the dropout rate p. We adjust λ on HopperPyBulletEnv-v0 task and p over four PyBullet tasks. We use DE-TD3 to perform parameter sensitivity experiments. The original parameters of DE-TD3 are consistent with Table 1, $\lambda = 0.1$, $p = 0.1$. First keep $\lambda = 0.1$, take the following values for p respectively: [0.2, 0.1, 0.05, 0.01], draw the corresponding heat map. Then keep $p = 0.1$, take the following values for lambda respectively: [0.1, 0.5, 1, 5], draw the corresponding performance curve. As shown in Fig. 4, DE-TD3 is robust to dropout rate p, which means we do not need to spend time tuning the value of p. For λ, we observe that when λ is relatively small, as the value of λ increases, the performance of the algorithm will improve because action gradient guides the actor to update, but when λ is relatively large (like 5), the performance of the algorithm will be greatly reduced. In further exploration, we found that too large λ will cause the actor to fall into local optimum, that is, the action gradient quickly decays to 0, and the actor stops updating. We leave more in-depth exploration of this phenomenon for future work.

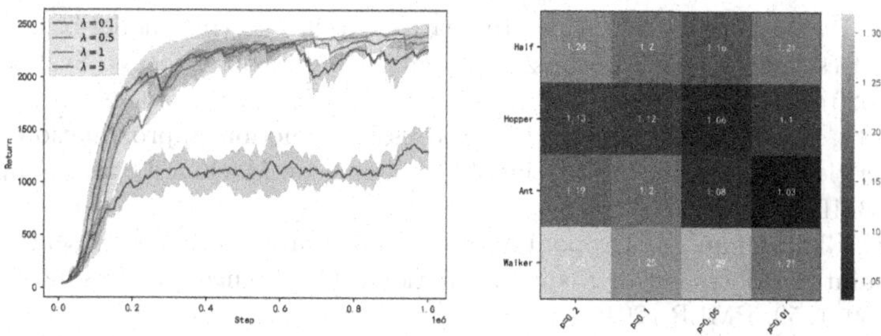

Fig. 4. (a) Learning curves for HopperPyBulletEnv-v0 task in PyBullet Control Suite for DE-TD3 with different λ. (b) Heat map for four different tasks in PyBullet Control Suite for DE-TD3 with different p. The numbers in the heat map are Mean SAC Normalized Score.

7 Conclusion

In this work, We show that for DPG algorithms, it is beneficial to use the action gradient to guide the policy update, since policy gradient is only concerned with the action gradient. Further, we use the consistent dropout operator to estimate a more accurate action gradient and achieve improved performance than baselines. We hope that our work sheds light on how to use the action gradient to guide policy updates, and how to estimate the action gradient more accurately. For future work, we first want to explore why the local optimum phenomenon mentioned in Sect. 6.4 occurs, and we want to extend the use of action gradient to the general policy gradient algorithms, through techniques such as reparameterization.

Acknowledgements. This work was supported in part by the Science and Technology Innovation 2030-Key Project under Grant 2021ZD0201404.

References

1. Agarwal, R., Schuurmans, D., Norouzi, M.: An optimistic perspective on offline reinforcement learning. In: International Conference on Machine Learning, pp. 104–114. PMLR (2020)
2. Agarwal, R., Schwarzer, M., Castro, P.S., Courville, A.C., Bellemare, M.: Deep reinforcement learning at the edge of the statistical precipice. Adv. Neural. Inf. Process. Syst. **34**, 29304–29320 (2021)
3. Brockman, G., Cheung, V., Pettersson, L., Schneider, J., Schulman, J., Tang, J., Zaremba, W.: Openai gym. arXiv preprint arXiv:1606.01540 (2016)
4. Chen, X., Wang, C., Zhou, Z., Ross, K.W.: Randomized ensembled double q-learning: learning fast without a model. In: International Conference on Learning Representations (2020)
5. Coumans, E., Bai, Y.: Pybullet, a python module for physics simulation for games, robotics and machine learning (2016)

6. D'Oro, P., Jaśkowski, W.: How to learn a useful critic? model-based action-gradient-estimator policy optimization. Adv. Neural. Inf. Process. Syst. **33**, 313–324 (2020)
7. Fujimoto, S., Hoof, H., Meger, D.: Addressing function approximation error in actor-critic methods. In: International Conference on Machine Learning, pp. 1587–1596. PMLR (2018)
8. Gal, Y., Ghahramani, Z.: Dropout as a bayesian approximation: representing model uncertainty in deep learning. In: International Conference on Machine Learning, pp. 1050–1059. PMLR (2016)
9. He, Q., Su, H., Chen, G., Hou, X.: MEPG: a minimalist ensemble policy gradient framework for deep reinforcement learning. In: Decision Awareness in Reinforcement Learning Workshop at ICML 2022 (2022)
10. Hiraoka, T., Imagawa, T., Hashimoto, T., Onishi, T., Tsuruoka, Y.: Dropout q-functions for doubly efficient reinforcement learning. In: International Conference on Learning Representations (2021)
11. Jordan, M., Jacobs, R.: Learning to control an unstable system with forward modeling. In: Advances in Neural Information Processing Systems, vol. 2 (1989)
12. Kahn, G., Villaflor, A., Pong, V., Abbeel, P., Levine, S.: Uncertainty-aware reinforcement learning for collision avoidance. arXiv preprint arXiv:1702.01182 (2017)
13. Kaiser, Ł., et al.: Model based reinforcement learning for Atari. In: International Conference on Learning Representations (2019)
14. Konda, V., Tsitsiklis, J.: Actor-critic algorithms. In: Advances in Neural Information Processing Systems, vol. 12 (1999)
15. Lillicrap, T.P., et al.: Continuous control with deep reinforcement learning. arXiv preprint arXiv:1509.02971 (2015)
16. Prokhorov, D.V., Wunsch, D.C.: Adaptive critic designs. IEEE Trans. Neural Networks **8**(5), 997–1007 (1997)
17. Silver, D., Lever, G., Heess, N., Degris, T., Wierstra, D., Riedmiller, M.: Deterministic policy gradient algorithms. In: International conference on machine learning, pp. 387–395. PMLR (2014)
18. Srivastava, N., Hinton, G., Krizhevsky, A., Sutskever, I., Salakhutdinov, R.: Dropout: a simple way to prevent neural networks from overfitting. J. Mach. Learn. Res. **15**(1), 1929–1958 (2014)
19. Sutton, R.S., Barto, A.G.: Reinforcement Learning: An introduction. MIT press (2018)
20. Todorov, E., Erez, T., Tassa, Y.: Mujoco: A physics engine for model-based control. In: 2012 IEEE/RSJ International Conference on Intelligent Robots and Systems, pp. 5026–5033. IEEE (2012)
21. Wiering, M.A., Van Hasselt, H.: Ensemble algorithms in reinforcement learning. IEEE Trans. Syst. Man Cybern. B Cybern **38**(4), 930–936 (2008)

Conditional Variational Inference for Multi-modal Trajectory Prediction with Latent Diffusion Prior

Lyn Qiu[1], Xu Li[2], Mingming Sun[2], and Junchi Yan[1](✉)

[1] MoE Key Lab of Artificial Intelligence, Shanghai Jiao Tong University, Shanghai, China
{lyn_qiu,yanjunchi}@sjtu.edu.cn

[2] Cognitive Computing Lab, Baidu Research, Beijing, China
{lixu13,sunmingming01}@baidu.com

Abstract. Predicting pedestrian trajectories is vital for improving safety and efficiency in human-robot interaction within traffic systems. However, this task is inherently challenging due to the unpredictable nature of human behavior. We present MotDiff, a method based on Variational Auto-encoders with a diffusion prior, which synthesizes latent variables to capture the unobserved uncertainty and complex relation among agents. We provide a comprehensive theoretical background of our approach and evaluate it with various generative modeling methods using three public pedestrian datasets, showing its effectiveness in achieving both accuracy and diversity.

Keywords: Generative Models · Motion Prediction · Probabilistic Inference

1 Introduction

Accurate forecasting of pedestrian trajectories is essential for ensuring traffic safety, yet the inherent stochastic nature of pedestrian motion behaviors significant challenges for prediction. Many deep generative models [3,9] have shown great promise for this task by capturing multi-modal distributions of pedestrian motion and enabling diverse trajectory generation. Specially, previous CVAE based models [1,11] about to modeling the multi-modal distribution of future trajectories, which usually requires an standard Gaussian prior on the latent variables. Obviously, such convention often limiting the overall performance for modelling complex and high-dimensional data tasks [19].

Denoising diffusion probabilistic models (DDPMs) [6] have showcased superior performances in various data generation tasks. To address this, we propose

L. Qiu—Work partly done during internship at Cognitive Computing Lab, Baidu Research.

J. Yan—The SJTU authors were supported by NSFC (61972250, U19B2035), Shanghai Municipal Science and Technology Major Project (2021SHZDZX0102).

F. Liu et al. (Eds.): PRICAI 2023, LNAI 14325, pp. 15–22, 2024.
https://doi.org/10.1007/978-981-99-7019-3_2

MotDiff, a variational Auto-Encoder based model for pedestrian motion prediction with a latent diffusion prior. Besides, We design an attention-based diffusion network for this prior module, which utilizes past routines and environmental maps as conditions for classifier-free guidance. Experimental results confirm the effectiveness of our framework design and demonstrate the efficacy of MotDiff in three datasets.

2 Methodology

2.1 Preliminaries and Definitions

In each scene, the observable history states of agents are given by a tensor $\mathbf{X} \in \mathbb{R}^{N \times T_h \times D}$, where N is the agent number in the scene, T_h is the history time steps, D is the number of features of a agent (e.g. position, heading, speed). The future trajectories of agents are given by a tensor $\mathcal{Y} \in \mathbb{R}^{N \times T_f \times 2}$, where T_f is the future time steps. Despite of the agents stats, the road map features captured from a bird-eye view [15] are also considered as context conditions, represented by $\boldsymbol{M} \in \mathbb{R}^{L \times D_l}$, where L is the number of lane segments and D_l is the feature number of each lane segment (e.g. position, type).

Our task is to generate plausible future trajectories based on the past observation history states and the road map information, $p(\mathcal{Y}|\mathbf{X}, \boldsymbol{M})$. For simplicity, we absorb $\boldsymbol{M}$ to $\mathbf{X}$ as they both play as conditions in the distribution in further expression, then the likelihood need to be maximize is $p(\mathcal{Y} \mid \mathbf{X})$.

2.2 Conditional Variational Inference with Latent Diffusion Prior

In our approach, a discrete latent variable of hidden size d_K is adopted to capture the unobserved features like pedestrains' intention and driving habits, where $Z \in \mathbb{R}^{N \times T_h \times d_K}$ represent the hidden states for each agent in the scene.

$$p(\mathcal{Y}|\mathbf{X}) = \sum_{Z} p(\mathcal{Y}|\mathbf{X}, Z) p(Z|\mathbf{X}). \tag{1}$$

If we set a distribution over the latent variables, the likelihood gradient $\log p_\phi(\mathcal{Y} \mid \mathbf{X})$ can be formed as:

$$\sum_{Z} q(Z) \log \frac{p_\theta(\mathcal{Y}, Z \mid \mathbf{X})}{q(Z)} + D_{KL}(q(Z) \| p_\phi(Z \mid \mathcal{Y}, \mathbf{X})) \tag{2}$$

Here we choose $q(Z) = q_\psi(Z \mid \mathcal{Y}, \mathbf{X})$ as approximating distribution to $p_\phi(\mathcal{Y}, Z \mid \mathbf{X})$ [4], and the associated evidence lower bound could be finally expressed as [22]:

$$\mathbb{E}_q[\log p_\phi(\mathcal{Y} \mid Z, \mathbf{X}) - \log q_\psi(Z \mid \mathcal{Y}, \mathbf{X})] + \log \mathbb{E}_q[p(Z \mid \mathbf{X})] \tag{3}$$

Inspired by of DDPMs [6], the forward process could be fixed to a markov chain gradually added a variance schedule $\beta_1, \ldots, \beta_K$:

$$q_\psi(Z_{\mathbf{1:K}} \mid Z_0) := \prod_{k=1}^{K} q_\psi(\mathbf{Z}_k \mid \mathbf{Z}_{k-1}), \quad q_\psi(Z_k \mid Z_{k-1}) := \mathcal{N}\left(Z_k; \sqrt{1-\beta_k} Z_{k-1}, \beta_k \mathbf{I}\right) \tag{4}$$

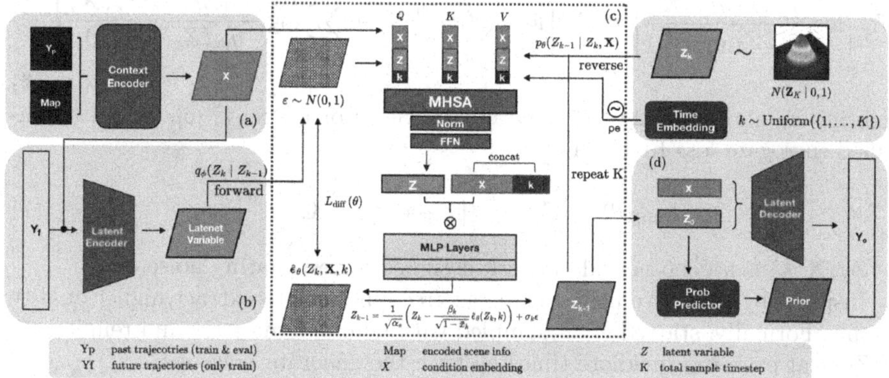

Fig. 1. Approach overview: (a) shows the context encoding module, which processes the past trajectories and available maps into a comprehensive condition embedding $\mathbf{X}$. This embedding is passed to the Latent Encoder (b) and Diffusion module (c) for further processing. **(b)** shows the generation of latent variables Z. During training, Z is produced through interactions between condition and past trajectories. During sampling, Z is acquired from a normal Gaussian. Both processes require a uniformly sampled time embedding k. **(c)** depicts the transformation of latent compound variable Z_k, which, after a forward diffusion process with the successive addition of Gaussian noise, ultimately becomes close to pure Gaussian noise. For K sampling loops, Z first interacts with the condition embedding and time embedding in a Multi-Head Self-Attention module, followed by interactions with a concatenation of these two variables through three MLP-based coupled layers. **(d)** the final output Z_0 is then combined with the past and background conditions to generate the predicted trajectories $\mathcal{Y}_0$ and priors $p_\theta(Z_0 \mid \mathbf{X})$.

Then the ELBO could be expressed as $\mathbb{E}_q\left[\log \frac{p_\theta(\mathbf{x}_{0:\mathbf{K}})}{q(\mathbf{x}_{1:\mathbf{K}}|\mathbf{x}_0)}\right] \leq \log p_\theta(\mathbf{x}_0)$, we can replace the last term of Eq. (3) and leads to the expression:

$$\mathbb{E}_q\left[\log p_\phi(\mathcal{Y} \mid Z_0, \mathbf{X}) - \log q_\psi(Z_0 \mid \mathcal{Y}, \mathbf{X})\right] + \mathbb{E}_q\left[\log \frac{p_\theta(Z_{0:\mathbf{K}} \mid \mathbf{X})}{q_\psi(Z_{1:\mathbf{K}} \mid Z_0)}\right] \leq \log p_\theta(\mathcal{Y} \mid \mathbf{X}) \tag{5}$$

2.3 Sampling with Classifier-Free Guidance

During inference, we add sufficient past trajectory and map as condition $\mathbf{X}$ for prediction task. The reverse diffusion process can be fixed to a Markov chain, and the last term of Eq. (5) could be further decomposed as:

$$\mathbb{E}_q\left[\log \frac{p_\theta\left(Z_{\mathbf{0:K}} \mid \mathbf{X}\right)}{q_\psi\left(Z_{\mathbf{1:K}} \mid Z_0\right)}\right]=\mathbb{E}_q\left[\log q_\psi\left(Z_K \mid \mathbf{X}\right)+\sum_{k \geq 1} \log \frac{p_\theta\left(Z_{k-1} \mid Z_k, \mathbf{X}\right)}{q_\psi\left(Z_k \mid Z_{k-1}\right)}\right] \tag{6}$$

Ignoring $\mathbb{E}_q$ and applying the reparameterization of $\boldsymbol{\mu}_\theta\left(\mathbf{x}_t, t\right)$ [6], we get a simplified surrogate loss function :

$$L_{\text{diff}}(\theta):=\mathbb{E}_{k, Z_0, \epsilon}\left[\left\|\boldsymbol{\epsilon}-\hat{\epsilon}_\theta\left(Z_k ; \mathbf{X}, k\right)\right\|^2\right] \tag{7}$$

$\hat{\epsilon}_\theta\left(\mathbf{Z}_k ; \mathbf{X}, k\right)$ is a deep neural network designed for estimating noise ϵ.

Inspired by [7,8], We utilize classifier-free guidance to extract higher quality sample. Formally, started Z_k is sampled with Gaussian noise ϵ_k and refining Z_k to Z_{k-1} at each intermediate timestep with the generate noise $\hat{\boldsymbol{\epsilon}}_\theta$:

$$\hat{\epsilon}:=\hat{\boldsymbol{\epsilon}}_\theta\left(Z_k, \varnothing, k\right)+\omega\left(\hat{\boldsymbol{\epsilon}}_\theta\left(Z_k, \mathbf{X}, k\right)-\hat{\boldsymbol{\epsilon}}_\theta\left(Z_k, \varnothing, k\right)\right) \tag{8}$$

where ω is the guidance scalar to control the strength of guidance.

Table 1. Comparison on ETH/UCY dataset in ADE/FDE metric. For those that simultaneously leverage multiple modes, we designate them with symbol †.

	ETH	HOTEL	UNIV	ZARA1	ZARA2	AVG
Social-GAN [5]	0.81/1.52	0.72/1.61	0.60/1.26	0.34/0.69	0.42/0.84	0.58/1.18
SoPhie [16]	0.70/1.43	0.76/1.67	0.54/1.24	0.30/0.63	0.38/0.78	0.54/1.15
†Goal-GAN [3]	0.59/1.18	0.19/0.35	0.60/1.19	0.43/0.87	0.32/0.65	0.43/0.85
†MG-GAN [2]	0.47/0.91	0.14/0.24	0.54/1.07	0.36/0.73	0.29/0.60	0.36/0.71
†Social-Ways [1]	0.39/0.64	0.39/0.66	0.55/1.31	0.44/0.64	0.51/0.92	0.44/0.83
†PECNet [11]	0.54/0.87	0.18/0.24	0.35/0.60	0.22/0.39	0.17/0.30	0.29/0.48
†Trajectron++ [17]	0.39/0.83	0.12/0.21	0.20/0.44	0.15/0.33	0.15/0.33	0.19/0.41
MotDiff (ddpm)	0.40/0.82	0.12/0.32	0.28/0.54	0.26/0.37	0.29/0.37	0.27/0.48
MotDiff (ddim)	**0.36**/0.74	**0.11/0.21**	0.24/0.47	0.18/**0.32**	0.23/**0.32**	0.22/**0.41**

Table 2. Evaluating MotDiff on the Stanford Drone Dataset in ADE/FDE metrics.

	Social-GAN [5]	†DESIRE [9]	SoPhie [16]	†Goal-GAN [3]	†PECNet [11]	MotDiff(ddpm)	MotDiff(ddim)
minADE	27.23	19.3	16.2	12.2	9.96	9.92	**8.92**
minFDE	41.44	34.1	29.3	22.1	15.88	19.64	**13.61**

2.4 Training Objective and Model Design

The overall objective function is designed as follows:

$$L := \underbrace{\mathbb{E}_q[\log p_\phi(\mathcal{Y} \mid Z_0, \mathbf{X})]}_{L_{recon}} - \underbrace{D_{KL}(q_\psi(Z_0 \mid \mathcal{Y}, \mathbf{X}) \| p_\theta(Z_0 \mid \mathbf{X}))}_{L_{KL}} + w_{diff} * L_{\text{diff}}(\theta) \tag{9}$$

Finally, the diffusion prior p_θ is trained jointly with the reconstruction loss of the likelihood p_ϕ and KL divergence between the approximate posterior q_ψ and prior p_θ, which aims to help regularize the normalization of prior generation. Besides, we find it's beneficial to set the diffusion loss weight w_{diff} be 10 through experiments.

Figure 1 shows the overall architecture and diffusion module. MotDiff mainly has three models, the latent encoder $q_\psi(Z \mid \mathbf{X}, \mathcal{Y})$, Conditional prior diffusion network $p_\phi(Z \mid \mathbf{X})$, and latent decoder $p_\theta(\mathcal{Y} \mid \mathbf{X}, Z)$. For diverse temporal sequential generation, we adopt a transformer [21] that facilitates interaction with latent variables.

3 Experiments

We evaluate our approach on widely-used pedestrian motion forecasting datasets: ETH/UCY [10,13], Stanford Drone [14] and TrajNet++ Challenge [15]. Our evaluation metrics include Minimum Average Displacement Error (minADE) and Final Displacement Error (minFDE). All experiments were conducted on a single NVIDIA V100 Tensor Core GPU with 32GB memory, utilizing the PyTorch 1.12.1 framework [12].

3.1 Benchmark Results

As shown in Tabel 1 and Tabel 2, we perform quantitative comparison between MotDiff and a diverse set of existing generative modeling methods on ETH/UCY and SDD datasets. We apply DDIM [18] to expedited sampling with superior quality for MotDiff. Experimental results show that MotDiff achieves an average ADE/FDE of 0.22/0.41 in ETH/UCY with DDIM sampling, which surpasses most of the past methods. Meanwhile, MotDiff achieves better performance in larger dataset SDD with an average ADE/FDE of 8.92/13.61, which outperforms all the multi-modal methods.

3.2 Ablation Study

We conduct ablation studies to evaluate the contributions of critical components, specifically the diffusion prior and the architecture or hyperparameters of the diffusion model.

Table 3 shows that the use of latent diffusion prior is effective over the normal Gaussian prior and the relaxed Boltzmann prior [20] in ETH and TrajNet++ datasets.

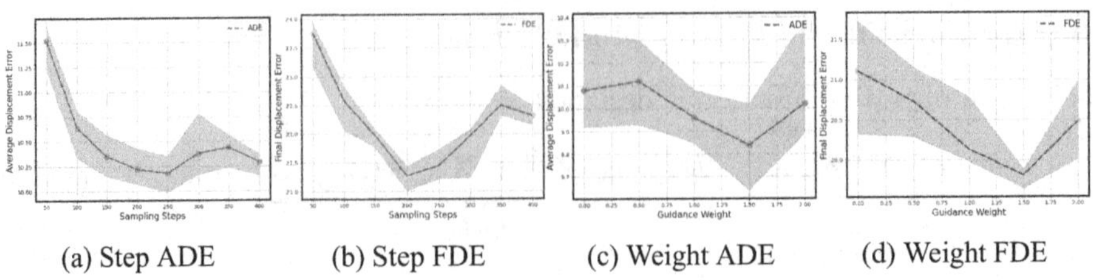

(a) Step ADE (b) Step FDE (c) Weight ADE (d) Weight FDE

Fig. 2. Influence of varying DDPM sampling steps and distinct guidance weights.

Table 3. MotDiff with different prior on ETH and TrajNet++ in ADE/FDE metrics.

Prior Type	ETH		TrajNet++	
	minADE	minFDE	minADE	minFDE
Normal Guassian	0.82	1.44	0.128	0.234
Boltzmann [20]	0.52	1.09	0.125	0.228
Latent Diffusion	**0.47**	**0.96**	**0.118**	0.229

As shown in Fig. 2a and 2b, employing the ddpm sampling technique, across a range of diffusion timesteps (50–400) in the SDD dataset, the ADE/FDE metric scores initially decreased and reached a minimum at 250 timesteps, followed by a slight increase. This phenomenon is likely attributed to overfitting, where the diffusion model failed to enhance its performance beyond a particular point. As shown in Fig. 2c and 2d, we perform a comparative analysis of Motdiff's performance under various guidance weights (0–2.0) in SDD dataset. Results indicate this approach generally improves MotDiff's performance, and the optimal classifier scale is approximately 1.50. These insights emphasize the importance of carefully considering and calibrating the guidance weight to achieve optimal performance.

4 Conclusion

We have developed a variational inference model with latent diffusion prior, named MotDiff, which adeptly processes input data of heterogeneous structures and generates intricate dynamic future trajectories conditioned on the input data. The novel diffusion prior excels at learning latent variables enriched with high semantic and geographical context information. The effectiveness of our proposed method is substantiated via comprehensive experimental results on three pedestrian datasets.

References

1. Amirian, J., Hayet, J.B., Pettré, J.: Social ways: Learning multi-modal distributions of pedestrian trajectories with GANs. In: CVPR Workshops (2019)
2. Dendorfer, P., Elflein, S., Leal-Taixé, L.: Mg-gan: A multi-generator model preventing out-of-distribution samples in pedestrian trajectory prediction. In: ICCV (2021)
3. Dendorfer, P., Osep, A., Leal-Taixé, L.: Goal-GAN: multimodal trajectory prediction based on goal position estimation. In: ACCV (2020)
4. Girgis, R., et al.: Latent variable sequential set transformers for joint multi-agent motion prediction. arXiv preprint arXiv:2104.00563 (2021)
5. Gupta, A., Johnson, J., Fei-Fei, L., Savarese, S., Alahi, A.: Social GAN: socially acceptable trajectories with generative adversarial networks. In: CVPR, pp. 2255–2264 (2018)
6. Ho, J., Jain, A., Abbeel, P.: Denoising diffusion probabilistic models. In: NeurIPS (2020)
7. Ho, J., Salimans, T.: Classifier-free diffusion guidance. arXiv preprint arXiv:2207.12598 (2022)
8. Janner, M., Du, Y., Tenenbaum, J.B., Levine, S.: Planning with diffusion for flexible behavior synthesis. arXiv preprint arXiv:2205.09991 (2022)
9. Lee, N., Choi, W., Vernaza, P., Choy, C.B., Torr, P.H., Chandraker, M.: Desire: distant future prediction in dynamic scenes with interacting agents. In: CVPR, pp. 336–345 (2017)
10. Lerner, A., Chrysanthou, Y., Lischinski, D.: Crowds by example. In: Computer graphics forum, vol. 26, pp. 655–664. Wiley Online Library (2007)
11. Mangalam, K., et al.: It is not the journey but the destination: Endpoint conditioned trajectory prediction. In: ECCV, pp. 759–776 (2020)
12. Paszke, A., Gross, S., Massa, F., Lerer, A., Bradbury, J., Chanan, G., Killeen, T., Lin, Z., Gimelshein, N., Antiga, L., et al.: Pytorch: An imperative style, high-performance deep learning library. Advances in neural information processing systems 32 (2019)
13. Pellegrini, S., Ess, A., Van Gool, L.: Improving data association by joint modeling of pedestrian trajectories and groupings. In: ECCV. pp. 452–465 (2010)
14. Robicquet, A., Sadeghian, A., Alahi, A., Savarese, S.: Learning social etiquette: human trajectory understanding in crowded scenes. In: ECCV, pp. 549–565 (2016)
15. Sadeghian, A., Kosaraju, V., Gupta, A., Savarese, S., Alahi, A.: TrajNet: towards a benchmark for human trajectory prediction. arXiv preprint (2018)
16. Sadeghian, A., Kosaraju, V., Sadeghian, A., Hirose, N., Rezatofighi, H., Savarese, S.: Sophie: an attentive gan for predicting paths compliant to social and physical constraints. In: CVPR, pp. 1349–1358 (2019)
17. Salzmann, T., Ivanovic, B., Chakravarty, P., Pavone, M.: Trajectron++: dynamically-feasible trajectory forecasting with heterogeneous data. In: ECCV, pp. 683–700 (2020)
18. Song, J., Meng, C., Ermon, S.: Denoising diffusion implicit models. arXiv preprint arXiv:2010.02502 (2020)
19. Tomczak, J., Welling, M.: VAE with a vampprior. In: AISTATS (2018)
20. Vahdat, A., Andriyash, E., Macready, W.: Dvae#: Discrete variational autoencoders with relaxed boltzmann priors. In: Advances in Neural Information Processing Systems, vol. 31 (2018)

21. Vaswani, A., et al.: Attention is all you need. In: NeurIPS, vol. 30 (2017)
22. Wehenkel, A., Louppe, G.: Diffusion priors in variational autoencoders. arXiv preprint arXiv:2106.15671 (2021)

Egalitarian Price of Fairness for Indivisible Goods

Karen Frilya Celine, Muhammad Ayaz Dzulfikar, and Ivan Adrian Koswara(✉)

School of Computing, National University of Singapore, Singapore, Singapore
{karen.celine,ayaz.dzulfikar}@u.nus.edu, ivanak@comp.nus.edu.sg

Abstract. In the context of fair division, the concept of price of fairness has been introduced to quantify the loss of welfare when we have to satisfy some fairness condition. In other words, it is the price we have to pay to guarantee fairness. Various settings of fair division have been considered previously; we extend to the setting of indivisible goods by using egalitarian welfare as the welfare measure, instead of the commonly used utilitarian welfare. We provide lower and upper bounds for various fairness and efficiency conditions such as envy-freeness up to one good (EF1) and maximum Nash welfare (MNW).

Keywords: Fair division · Price of fairness · Egalitarian welfare

1 Introduction

Fair division is the problem of allocating scarce resources to agents with possibly differing interests. It has many real world applications, such as the distribution of inheritance, divorce settlements and airport traffic management. Economists have studied fair division as far back as the 1940 s [8,11]. Recently, the problem of fair division has also received significant interest in artificial intelligence [1,4, 6,9,10].

In a fair division problem, there are several possible goals to strive for. One goal is *fairness*, where each individual agent should feel they get a fair allocation; another is *social welfare*, where the goal is to optimize the welfare of all agents as a whole. These goals are not always aligned. For example, to maximize the sum of utilities of the agents (i.e. utilitarian welfare), the optimal allocation is to assign each item to the agent that values it the most. Clearly this allocation can be far from fair, as an agent might be deprived of every item. However, making the allocation fairer comes at the cost of decreasing the total welfare. In other words, there is a price to pay if we want a division to be fair.

The notion of *price of fairness* was introduced independently by Bertsimas et al. [5] and Caragiannis et al. [7] to capture this concept. Initially, the setting was for utilitarian welfare on divisible goods. Since then, there have been other works discussing the setting of utilitarian welfare with indivisible goods [3,4], as well as the setting of egalitarian welfare with divisible goods [2,7]. Since the same cannot be said for egalitarian welfare with indivisible goods, our paper completes the picture by investigating this setting.

F. Liu et al. (Eds.): PRICAI 2023, LNAI 14325, pp. 23–28, 2024.
https://doi.org/10.1007/978-981-99-7019-3_3

One problem with investigating fairness conditions is that they might not have a satisfying allocation for some instances, especially when the goods are indivisible. We follow Bei et al. [4]'s method of handling this problem by considering only fairness conditions which can always be satisfied in all instances for any number of agents. As such, we do not investigate properties such as envy-freeness and proportionality, which are not guaranteed to be satisfiable. Special cases such as envy-freeness up to any good (EFX) which has been shown to be satisfiable for $n \leq 3$ agents can be considered for future works.

We study the price of fairness of three fairness properties: envy-freeness up to one good (EF1), balancedness, and round-robin. Not only are these properties always satisfiable, but an allocation which has all three properties can be easily found by the round-robin algorithm. Furthermore, these fairness notions are widely studied in the literature. In particular, tight bounds for the utilitarian price of fairness of these properties have been found [4], which allows for comparison between the utilitarian and egalitarian prices of fairness.

Moreover, we also study the price of fairness of two welfare maximizers: maximum utilitarian welfare (MUW) and maximum Nash welfare (MNW). While these are efficiency notions instead of fairness notions, they are crucial to the study of resource allocation. Studying their prices of fairness helps us compare between the different types of welfare maximizers, and might shed light on if and when one type of welfare function would best quantify social welfare.

Preliminaries. We first define the terms used in this paper. An **instance** $\mathcal{I}$ consists of the agents $N = \{1, 2, \dots, n\}$, the goods $M = \{1, 2, \dots, m\}$, and each agent's utility function u_i. We assume $n \geq 2$. The utility function is nonnegative, additive, and *normalized*, i.e. $u_i(M) = 1$ for each i. An **allocation** $\mathcal{A}$ for an instance is a partition $(A_1, \dots, A_n)$ of the goods M; agent i receives bundle A_i. A **property** P is a Boolean predicate on the allocations.

The **egalitarian welfare** of an allocation $\mathcal{A}$ of an instance $\mathcal{I}$ is $\mathsf{EW}(\mathcal{I}, \mathcal{A}) := \min_{i \in N} u_i(A_i)$. We denote the **maximum egalitarian welfare (MEW)** of an instance as $\mathsf{MEW}(\mathcal{I})$, where the maximum is taken over all allocations. For a property P, we denote $\mathsf{MEW}_P(\mathcal{I})$ as the maximum taken over allocations with property P. The **price of fairness (POF)** of a property P for instance $\mathcal{I}$ is $\mathsf{POF}_P(\mathcal{I}) := \mathsf{MEW}(\mathcal{I})/\mathsf{MEW}_P(\mathcal{I})$. The price of fairness of a property P over a family of instances is the supremum of the price of fairness over those instances.

For price of fairness, we use the convention $0/0 = 1$ and $x/0 = \infty$ for $x > 0$. Price of fairness is traditionally represented as a function in terms of the number of agents n. We follow this convention in this paper. In this case, for any fixed n, the price of fairness for that n is the supremum over all instances with n agents.

An allocation $\mathcal{A}$ is **envy-free up to one good (EF1)** if, for any pair of agents i, j, there exists $G \subseteq A_j$ with $|G| \leq 1$ such that $u_i(A_i) \geq u_i(A_j \setminus G)$. An allocation $\mathcal{A}$ is **balanced (Ba)** if, for any pair of agents i, j, we have $|A_i| - |A_j| \in \{-1, 0, 1\}$. An allocation is **round-robin (RR)** if it is produced by the round-robin algorithm for some ordering of agents and tiebreak choices. Note that a RR allocation is also EF1 and balanced [4]. As a result, since RR is always satisfiable, EF1 and balancedness are also always satisfiable. Lastly, the **utilitarian (resp. Nash) welfare** of an allocation A is the sum (resp. product) of utilities $\sum_i u_i(A_i)$ (resp. $\prod_i u_i(A_i)$). An allocation is **MUW (resp. MNW)** if it achieves the maximum possible utilitarian (resp. Nash) welfare for its instance.

Our Results. We investigate the upper and lower bounds of the price of fairness for five fairness and efficiency properties described above. Letting n be the number of agents in the instance, we show that EF1, balancedness, and round-robin have price of fairness $\Theta(n)$. Meanwhile, MUW and MNW have infinite price of fairness, except for the case of MNW with $n = 2$ where the price of fairness is finite. Our results are summarized in Table 1. We have also included the utilitarian prices of fairness found by Bei et al. [4] for comparison. We restrict our attention to the general instances for any fixed n; future work can be done on specializing to, say, instances with identical ordering, or some other constraint, in case it can bring down the price of fairness for some of the properties.

Table 1. Summary of results

Property		Price of fairness: Egalitarian	Price of fairness: Utilitarian [3,4]
Envy-free up to one good (EF1)		$\Theta(n)$	$\Theta(\sqrt{n})$
Balanced		n	$\Theta(\sqrt{n})$
Round-robin algorithm (RR)		$\Theta(n)$	n
Maximum Nash welfare (MNW)	$(n = 2)$	≈ 2	≈ 1.2
	$(n \geq 3)$	∞	$\Theta(n)$
Maximum utilitarian welfare (MUW)		∞	1
Maximum egalitarian welfare (MEW)		1	$\Theta(n)$

In a way, our results are surprising compared to the utilitarian results. Utilitarian welfare is purely an efficiency notion, while egalitarian welfare captures some sort of "fairness", since maximizing the utility of the poorest agent means that every agent's utility is taken into consideration and no agent's poverty can be ignored. However, the egalitarian price of fairness for the properties are actually worse (higher) than the utilitarian price of fairness. Despite appearing "fairer", egalitarian welfare turns out to be less fair when we impose other fairness conditions.

2 Results

We provide the bounds of price of fairness along with their proofs. For space reasons, these proofs are only sketched out; the reader is invited to fill in the details.

Theorem 1. $\mathsf{POF}_{\mathsf{EF1}} \geq n-1$ *and* $\mathsf{POF}_{\mathsf{RR}}, \mathsf{POF}_{\mathsf{Ba}} \geq n$.

Proof. Let $m \gg n$ and $\varepsilon \ll 1/m$. Consider the instance $\mathcal{I}$ with following utilities:

- $u_1(1) = 1$ and $u_1(j) = 0$ for $2 \leq j \leq m$.
- For $i = 2, \ldots, n-1$: $u_i(1) = 1-(m-1)\varepsilon$ and $u_i(j) = \varepsilon$ for $2 \leq j \leq m$.
- $u_n(1) = 1-(m-1)\varepsilon^2$ and $u_n(j) = \varepsilon^2$ for $2 \leq j \leq m$.

It can be shown that,

$$\mathsf{MEW} = (m-(n-1))\cdot\varepsilon^2, \qquad \mathsf{MEW}_{\mathsf{EF1}} = \left\lceil \frac{m-1}{n-1} \right\rceil \cdot \varepsilon^2, \qquad \mathsf{MEW}_{\mathsf{Ba}} = \left\lceil \frac{m}{n} \right\rceil \cdot \varepsilon^2.$$

Therefore, as $m \to \infty$,

$$\mathsf{POF}_{\mathsf{EF1}}(\mathcal{I}) = \frac{\mathsf{MEW}}{\mathsf{MEW}_{\mathsf{EF1}}} \to n-1 \qquad \text{and} \qquad \mathsf{POF}_{\mathsf{Ba}}(\mathcal{I}) = \frac{\mathsf{MEW}}{\mathsf{MEW}_{\mathsf{Ba}}} \to n.$$

Since any RR allocation is balanced, $\mathsf{POF}_{\mathsf{RR}}(\mathcal{I}) \geq \mathsf{POF}_{\mathsf{Ba}}(\mathcal{I}) \geq n$. □

Theorem 2. $\mathsf{POF}_{\mathsf{Ba}} \leq n$.

Proof. For simplicity, assume n divides m; the proof can be modified for the general case. Consider any MEW allocation $\mathcal{A}$ for an instance $\mathcal{I}$ with n agents and m goods. For each agent, let them keep the most valuable m/n goods from their bundle in $\mathcal{A}$; distribute all excess goods so that each agent receives m/n goods exactly. Then each agent keeps at least $\frac{m/n}{m} = \frac{1}{n}$ of the value of their bundle, and so $\mathsf{MEW}_{\mathsf{Ba}} \geq \frac{1}{n} \cdot \mathsf{MEW}$. Therefore,

$$\mathsf{POF}_{\mathsf{Ba}}(\mathcal{I}) \leq \frac{\mathsf{MEW}}{\mathsf{MEW}_{\mathsf{Ba}}} = n.$$ □

Theorem 3. $\mathsf{POF}_{\mathsf{RR}} \leq 2n-1$, *and so,* $\mathsf{POF}_{\mathsf{EF1}} \leq 2n-1$.

Proof. Consider an instance $\mathcal{I}$ with n agents and a MEW allocation $\mathcal{A}$. Now remove all goods except for the best good in each agent's bundle. Call this reduced instance $\mathcal{I}'$, and the restriction of $\mathcal{A}$ into the reduced instance to be $\mathcal{A}'$.

We can find an allocation $\mathcal{B}$ on $\mathcal{I}'$ which is RR and weakly dominates $\mathcal{A}'$. First, find any Pareto-optimal balanced allocation that weakly dominates $\mathcal{A}'$; this will be our $\mathcal{B}$. It can be shown that the envy-graph of $\mathcal{B}$ is acyclic and thus admits a topological ordering. The desired round-robin ordering of $\mathcal{B}$ can be obtained by reversing the topological order of the envy-graph.

We now apply this round-robin ordering to the original instance $\mathcal{I}$. For our analysis, we follow an agent and compare the goods chosen using the round-robin ordering to the goods in their bundle in $\mathcal{A}$. On her first turn, she takes a good g_1 that is at least as valuable as the best good in her $\mathcal{A}$ bundle, by construction of $\mathcal{B}$. On her k-th turn for $k \geq 2$, she takes a good g_k that is at least as valuable as the (kn)-th good in her $\mathcal{A}$ bundle, simply because it hasn't been chosen by anyone.

Therefore, g_1 has value at least the mean of the $2n-1$ most valuable goods in the $\mathcal{A}$ bundle, and g_k has value at least the mean of the next n most valuable goods in the bundle (i.e. the (kn)-th to $(kn+n-1)$-th most valuable goods). It follows that the goods $\{g_1, g_2, \ldots\}$ have total value at least $\frac{1}{2n-1}$ times the value of their $\mathcal{A}$ bundle, giving $\mathsf{POF}_{\mathsf{RR}} \leq 2n-1$.

Since an RR allocation is EF1, it follows $\mathsf{POF}_{\mathsf{EF1}} \leq \mathsf{POF}_{\mathsf{RR}} \leq 2n-1$. □

Theorem 4. $\mathsf{POF}_{\mathsf{MUW}} = \infty$.

Proof. Let $\varepsilon \ll 1$. Take the instance with $n=2$, $m=3$ and the utilities below:

- $u_1(1) = u_1(2) = 1/2$ and $u_1(3) = 0$.
- $u_2(1) = u_2(2) = 1/2 - \varepsilon$ and $u_2(3) = 2\varepsilon$.

It can be shown that, as $\varepsilon \to 0$,

$$\mathsf{MEW} = \frac{1}{2}, \qquad \mathsf{MEW}_{\mathsf{MUW}} = 2\varepsilon, \qquad \text{and so} \quad \mathsf{POF}_{\mathsf{MUW}}(\mathcal{I}) = \frac{\mathsf{MEW}}{\mathsf{MEW}_{\mathsf{MUW}}} \to \infty.$$

For larger n, simply add additional goods; each agent exclusively desires one new good. This does not influence the $n=2$ instance above. □

Theorem 5. *Consider instances with $n = 2$ agents. Let $\lambda = 1.324\ldots$ be the real number satisfying $\lambda^3 - \lambda - 1 = 0$. Then,*

$$\mathsf{POF}_{\mathsf{MNW}} \geq \lambda^2 = 1.754\ldots$$

Proof. Let x, y be positive real numbers satisfying $x > 1$ and

$$\frac{1}{x+\sqrt{x}} < y < \frac{1}{x^2}. \tag{1}$$

Consider an instance $\mathcal{I}$ with $n=2$ and $m=3$, with the following utilities:

- $u_1(1) = xy$, and $u_1(2) = 1 - xy$, and $u_1(3) = 0$.
- $u_2(1) = 1 - xy$, and $u_2(2) = (x-1)y$, and $u_2(3) = y$.

Given that the inequalities in (1) hold, it can be shown that $\mathsf{MEW} = xy$ but $\mathsf{MEW}_{\mathsf{MNW}} = y$, giving $\mathsf{POF}_{\mathsf{MNW}}(\mathcal{I}) = x$.

However, y in (1) can exist if and only if the gap is non-empty, and this happens if and only if $x < \lambda^2$. Therefore

$$\mathsf{POF}_{\mathsf{MNW}} \geq \sup x = \lambda^2 \approx 1.754\ldots.$$ □

Theorem 6. *For $n = 2$ agents,* $\mathsf{POF}_{\mathsf{MNW}} \leq 2$.

Proof. Consider an instance with $n = 2$ agents. In a MEW allocation, the agent with greater utility gets $\geq 1/2$ utility; otherwise the bundles can be swapped to strictly improve both agents. Suppose the agent with lower utility gets utility x; then the Nash welfare is $\geq x/2$.

Since the MNW allocation must have Nash welfare $\geq x/2$ and an agent can have utility ≤ 1, then in a MNW allocation, the agent with lower utility must still get $\geq x/2$ utility. So $\mathsf{POF}_{\mathsf{MNW}}(\mathcal{I}) \leq \frac{x}{x/2} = 2$. □

Theorem 7. *For $n \geq 3$ agents,* $\mathsf{POF}_{\mathsf{MNW}} = \infty$.

Proof. Let $\varepsilon \ll 1$. Take the instance with $n = m = 3$ and the following utilities:

- $u_1(1) = 1$ and $u_1(2) = u_1(3) = 0$.
- $u_2(1) = 1/3 - \varepsilon/2$, $u_2(2) = \varepsilon/2$, and $u_2(3) = 2/3$.
- $u_3(1) = 1 - \varepsilon/2 - \varepsilon^2/2$, $u_3(2) = \varepsilon^2/2$, and $u_3(3) = \varepsilon/2$.

It can be shown that, as $\varepsilon \to 0$,

$$\mathsf{MEW} = \frac{\varepsilon}{2}, \qquad \mathsf{MEW}_{\mathsf{MNW}} = \frac{\varepsilon^2}{2}, \qquad \text{and so} \quad \mathsf{POF}_{\mathsf{MNW}}(\mathcal{I}) = \frac{\mathsf{MEW}}{\mathsf{MEW}_{\mathsf{MNW}}} \to \infty.$$

For larger n, simply add additional goods; each agent exclusively desires one new good. This does not influence the $n = 3$ instance above. □

Acknowledgements. The authors would like to thank their lecturer Warut Suksompong for his valuable contributions.

References

1. Amanatidis, G., Birmpas, G., Markakis, E.: Comparing approximate relaxations of envy-freeness. In: Proceedings of the 27th International Joint Conference on Artificial Intelligence (IJCAI), pp. 42–48 (2018)
2. Aumann, Y., Dombb, Y.: The efficiency of fair division with connected pieces. ACM Trans. Econ. Comput. **3**(4), 23:1–23:16 (2015)
3. Barman, S., Bhaskar, U., Shah, N.: Optimal bounds on the price of fairness for indivisible goods. In: Proceedings of the 16th International Conference on Web and Internet Economics (WINE), pp. 356–369 (2020)
4. Bei, X., Lu, X., Manurangsi, P., Suksompong, W.: The price of fairness for indivisible goods. In: Proceedings of the 28th International Joint Conference on Artificial Intelligence (IJCAI), pp. 81–87 (2019)
5. Bertsimas, D., Farias, V., Trichakis, N.: The price of fairness. Oper. Res. **59**(1), 17–31 (2011)
6. Biswas, A., Barman, S.: Fair division under cardinality constraints. In: Proceedings of the 27th International Joint Conference on Artificial Intelligence (IJCAI), pp. 91–97 (2018)
7. Caragiannis, I., Kaklamanis, C., Kanellopoulos, P., Kyropoulou, M.: The efficiency of fair division. Theor. Comput. Syst. **50**(4), 589–610 (2012)
8. Dubins, L.E., Spanier, E.H.: How to cut a cake fairly. Amer. Math. Monthly **68**(1), 1–17 (1961)
9. Michorzewski, M., Peters, D., Skowron, P.: Price of fairness in budget division and probabilistic social choice. In: Proceedings of the 34th AAAI Conference on Artificial Intelligence (AAAI), pp. 2184–2191 (2020)
10. Oh, H., Procaccia, A.D., Suksompong, W.: Fairly allocating many goods with few queries. In: Proceedings of the 33rd AAAI Conference on Artificial Intelligence (AAAI), pp. 2141–2148 (2019)
11. Steinhaus, H.: The problem of fair division. Econometrica **16**(1), 101–104 (1948)

Intelligent Network Intrusion Detection and Situational Awareness for Cyber-Physical Systems in Smart Cities

Shouliang Song[1,2], Anming Dong[1,2(✉)], Honglei Zhu[1,2], Shuai Wang[1,2], and Jiguo Yu[3]

[1] Key Laboratory of Computing Power Network and Information Security, Ministry of Education, Shandong Computer Science Center (National Supercomputer Center in Jinan), Qilu University of Technology (Shandong Academy of Sciences), Jinan 250353, China

[2] School of Information Science and Technology, Qilu University of Technology (Shandong Academy of Sciences), Jinan 25353, China
anmingdong@qlu.edu.cn

[3] Big Data Institute, Qilu University of Technology (Shandong Academy of Sciences), Jinan 25353, China

Abstract. Smart cities are enabled by cyber-physical systems (CPS) which leverage the Internet of Things (IoT) to connect the physical world and information systems. Due to lack of security protection, IoT systems are vulnerable to various cyber attacks. In this paper, we investigate the network intrusion detection method for the security protection of loT edge servers or gateways in CPS of smart cities. We develop an abnormal flow detection algorithm based on deep learning (DL), where a Long Short Term Memory (LSTM) model is utilized to identify abnormal flows, followed by a Convolutional Neural Network (CNN) model to distinguish the malicious flow. Based on this framework, we construct a situational awareness system that consists of a real-time flow monitoring module running on IoT edge servers, and a situation visualization module deployed at a cloud server. The flow monitoring module is responsible for capturing, parsing, and identifying the flow of the edge server, while the situation visualization module demonstrates the security situations with charts and curves in real-time. The experimental results show that high recognition accuracy of 99.2% for the LSTM model and 97.4% for the CNN model.

This work was supported in part by the National Key R&D Program of China under Grant 2019YFB2102600, the Shandong Provincial Natural Science Foundation (No. ZR2021MF026 and ZR2023MF040), the Innovation Team Cultivating Program of Jinan under Grant 202228093, and the Piloting Fundamental Research Program for the Integration of Scientific Research, Education and Industry of Qilu University of Technology (Shandong Academy of Sciences) under Grants 2021JC02014 and 2022XD001, the Talent Cultivation Promotion Program of Computer Science and Technology in Qilu University of Technology (Shandong Academy of Sciences) under Grants 2021PY05001 and 2023PY059.

F. Liu et al. (Eds.): PRICAI 2023, LNAI 14325, pp. 29–35, 2024.
https://doi.org/10.1007/978-981-99-7019-3_4

Keywords: Smart cities · IoT · cyber-physical systems · Situational awareness · Deep learning · Network attacks

1 Introduction

The cyber-physical system (CPS) integrates computing and physical processes by organically combining computing, communication, and control. Smart cities use the Internet of Things (IoT) to connect the digital and physical realms, process data and provide management and decision-making services with artificial intelligence and cloud computing to improve urban governance and resident satisfaction. However, smart city CPS faces the challenges of security and vulnerability of IoT devices. Recently, attacks against smart city CPS have become increasingly sophisticated, including DDoS and code injection, and traditional security measures are struggling to cope with such evolutionary attacks. Proactive security systems are critical for CPS in smart cities, and situational awareness can detect cyber-attacks in real time, alerting, protecting and tracking them in a timely manner. Using machine learning and big data analysis [1], CPS network attacks can be identified in real-time to ensure the security of smart city information systems. Real-time identification of CPS network attacks and perception of network posture are key ways to ensure the security of smart city information fusion systems and are of great significance.

2 Related Work

Network Intrusion Detection (NID) is an important technical component of network situational awareness [8]. The traditional network intrusion detection system mainly takes two approaches feature-based detection methods and anomaly-based detection methods. The former compares new data with known intrusion features [5]. It cannot detect unknown attacks but is characterized by ease of deployment. The latter compares new data with normal user behavior models [4] and is able to detect unknown attacks.

Machine-learning-based anomaly detection techniques include support vector machine (SVM), K-approximation (KNN), decision trees, artificial neural networks, etc. Ali [2] proposed a model based on FLN and Particle Swarm Optimization (PSO-FLN) [3] to solve the IDS problem. Yao [10] proposed a modeling framework called Multi-level semi-supervised ML (MSML) to solve the intrusion detection problem. Its main shortcoming is the low detection rate for fewer attack categories. The common techniques of intrusion detection based on deep learning include convolution neural network (CNN), self-encoder, recurrent neural network(RNN), depth neural network (DNN) and so on. Shone [7] proposed an intrusion detection method based on deep automatic encoder and decision tree. Jiang [6] proposed an efficient IDS system by combining CNN and Bidirectional Long Short-Term Memory (BiLSTM). Yin [11] proposed an RNN-based intrusion detection method for multi-class classification on NSL-KDD dataset. These methods show good results overall, but perform poorly with small amounts of data.

To address the above issues, this paper designs and implements a complete network security situational awareness system. The contributions of this paper mainly include the following aspects:

1) Realize real-time capturing and parsing of network streams so that our system can perceive the current status of the network in time.
2) In this paper, we propose two model algorithms: LSTM-based network traffic attack identification algorithm and CNN-based malicious traffic classification algorithm, which are used serially to enable our system to detect and react to network attacks in a timely manner.
3) In this paper, we design a complete situational awareness system, which includes flow capture module, flow parsing module, intelligent perception module, and visualization module.

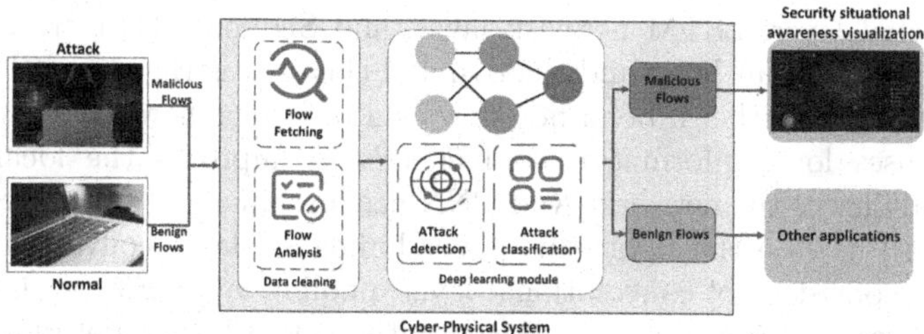

Fig. 1. Framework of Network Situation Awareness System

3 Construction of Network Situation Awareness System

3.1 Overall System Architecture

As shown in Fig. 1, the system is mainly composed of a real-time flow capture module, a flow parsing module, and a deep learning flow monitoring module. Flow capture is realized by the traffic tool that comes with the server operating system itself. The flow data is further analyzed by the flow parsing algorithm. The parsed flow data is sent to the deep learning algorithm module to determine the flow status in real time. For normal flow, the system releases it; for malicious flow, the system filters it, and uploads the traffic identification results to the cloud platform and displays them on the Security Situational Awareness visualization interface.

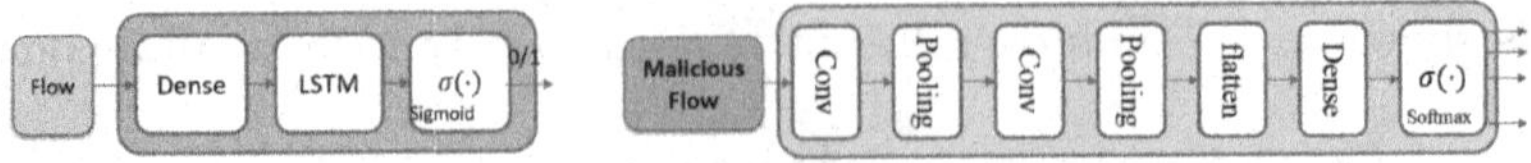

Fig. 2. On the left is our LSTM model structure, on the right is our CNN model structure

3.2 Intelligent Sense Module Construction

The intelligent Sense module is an important module for network situational awareness. It is responsible for detecting the flow from the data cleaning module. The intelligent sensing module uses two models, the long short-term memory neural network (LSTM) model and the convolutional neural network (CNN) model. The LSTM model is used to identify malicious and benign flows, and the malicious flow is fed into the CNN model for attack classification.

LSTM filters are suitable for the detection of attack flow containing session flow characteristics. The structure of the LSTM model implemented in this paper is shown in Fig. 2 on the left, and the LSTM model consists of three parts: Dense fully connected layer, LSTM network layer, and Sigmoid classifier, where the Dense layer is the input layer and the Sigmoid classifier is the output layer, and the output result is either a bona fide flow or a malicious flow.

CNN senses local information and effectively improves the local feature extraction ability of the network. And CNN has low time and space complexity. As shown in Fig. 2 on the right, this paper builds a 7-layer convolutional neural network, consisting of convolutional layer, pooling layer, Flatten layer, fully connected layer and Softmax layer. Because the network is to determine which category the network flow belongs to, which is a multi-classification problem, the Softmax layer is used in the last layer.

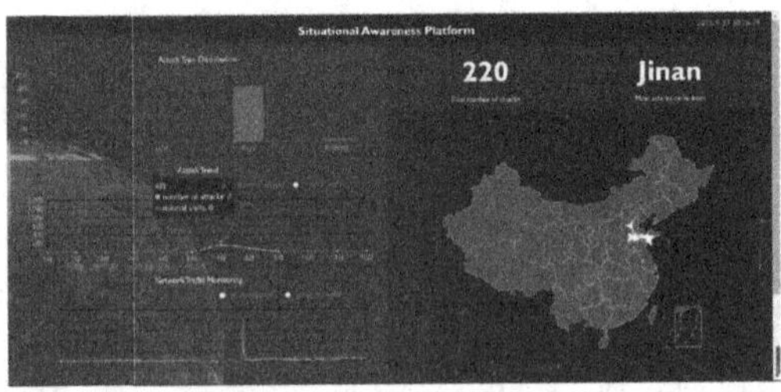

Fig. 3. Network situational awareness visualization interface

3.3 Flow Packet Capture and Parsing

The establishment of a network security situational awareness system first requires the detection of flow that affects the security of the system to be acquired. In this system we use tcpdump to capture flow packets.

After capturing the packets, we extract the required feature attributes. There are 41 of these feature attributes. Through the description related to feature attributes in the literature [9], this paper is divided into two steps in extracting features. The first step is to extract the basic network connection features. The second step extracts the time-based and host-based network flow statistics features.

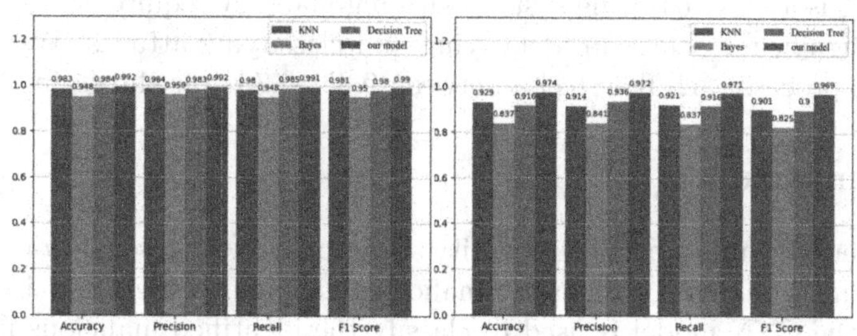

Fig. 4. Accuracy evaluation results of four models with KDDCUP99. On the left is our LSTM model, and on the right is our CNN model.

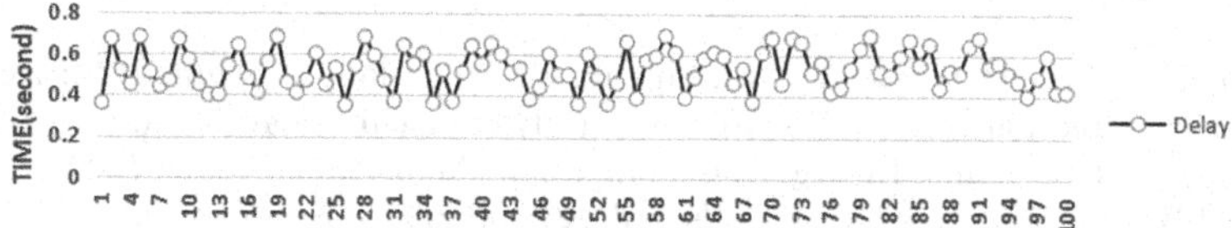

Fig. 5. Delay result of the System

3.4 System Visualization

The designed situational awareness visualization interface, shown in Fig. 3, is used to display information such as threat type distribution, attack posture, flow status, and attack sources in real time. The threat types mainly include DOS, Probing, R2L, and U2R. The attack source is shown in the form of a map showing the region from which the attacker comes.

4 Experiment Results and Analysis

The recognition accuracy of our LSTM model, compared with three machine learning models(KNN, Bayes, ID3), was compared on the KDDCup99 dataset. The results show that the average accuracy of our LSTM model is 99.2%, which is better than the highest accuracy of 98.3% of the compared machine learning models. The detailed comparison results are shown in Fig. 4 on the left.

The recognition accuracy of our CNN model, compared with the three machine learning models, was also compared on the KDDCUP99 dataset. The results show that our CNN model has a classification accuracy of 97.4%, which is better than the highest accuracy of 92.9% of the compared machine learning models. The detailed comparison results are shown in Fig. 4 on the right. Because IoT is a very real-time system with high latency requirements, it should not cause significant delays in identifying and classifying attacks. We calculate the time to process each flow to be between 0.35~0.70 s, as shown in Fig. 5.

5 Summarize

In this paper, we built a network security situational awareness platform. Where the LSTM model is used to identify malicious flow and benign flow in the network, and the CNN model is used to classify the identified malicious flow. The results of identification and classification are then sent to the cloud for visualization and display. In future work, advanced deep neural networks should be studied to predict attack behaviors that threaten IoT edge servers, such as the Transformer structures and the attention mechanism.

References

1. Ahmad, Z., Shahid Khan, A., Wai Shiang, C., Abdullah, J., Ahmad, F.: Network intrusion detection system: A systematic study of machine learning and deep learning approaches. Trans. Emerg. Telecommun. Technol. **32**(1), e4150 (2021)
2. Ali, M.H., Al Mohammed, B.A.D., Ismail, A., Zolkipli, M.F.: A new intrusion detection system based on fast learning network and particle swarm optimization. IEEE Access **6**, 20255–20261 (2018). https://doi.org/10.1109/ACCESS.2018.2820092
3. Bai, Q.: Analysis of particle swarm optimization algorithm. Comput. Inf. Sci. **3**(1), 180 (2010)
4. Chung, C.J., Khatkar, P., Xing, T., Lee, J., Huang, D.: Nice: network intrusion detection and countermeasure selection in virtual network systems. IEEE Trans. Dependable Secure Comput. **10**(4), 198–211 (2013). https://doi.org/10.1109/TDSC.2013.8
5. Eskandari, M., Janjua, Z.H., Vecchio, M., Antonelli, F.: Passban ids: an intelligent anomaly-based intrusion detection system for IoT edge devices. IEEE Internet Things J. **7**(8), 6882–6897 (2020). https://doi.org/10.1109/JIOT.2020.2970501
6. Jiang, K., Wang, W., Wang, A., Wu, H.: Network intrusion detection combined hybrid sampling with deep hierarchical network. IEEE Access **8**, 32464–32476 (2020). https://doi.org/10.1109/ACCESS.2020.2973730
7. Shone, N., Ngoc, T.N., Phai, V.D., Shi, Q.: A deep learning approach to network intrusion detection. IEEE Trans. Emerging Top. Comput. Intell. **2**(1), 41–50 (2018). https://doi.org/10.1109/TETCI.2017.2772792
8. Tang, T.A., Mhamdi, L., McLernon, D., Zaidi, S.A.R., Ghogho, M.: Deep learning approach for network intrusion detection in software defined networking. In: 2016 International Conference on Wireless Networks and Mobile Communications (WINCOM), pp. 258–263. IEEE (2016)

9. Tavallaee, M., Bagheri, E., Lu, W., Ghorbani, A.A.: A detailed analysis of the kdd cup 99 data set. IEEE (2009)
10. Yao, H., Fu, D., Zhang, P., Li, M., Liu, Y.: MSML: a novel multilevel semi-supervised machine learning framework for intrusion detection system. IEEE Internet Things J. **6**(2), 1949–1959 (2018)
11. Yin, C., Zhu, Y., Fei, J., He, X.: A deep learning approach for intrusion detection using recurrent neural networks. IEEE Access **5**, 21954–21961 (2017). https://doi.org/10.1109/ACCESS.2017.2762418

Data Mining and Knowledge Discovery

A Dynamic Linear Bias Incorporation Scheme for Nonnegative Latent Factor Analysis

Yurong Zhong, Zhe Xie, Weiling Li(✉), and Xin Luo

School of Computer Science and Technology, Dongguan University of Technology, Dongguan 523808, China
weilinglicq@outlook.com

Abstract. High-Dimensional and Incomplete (HDI) data is commonly encountered in big data-related applications like social network services systems, which are concerning limited interactions among numerous nodes. Knowledge discovery from HDI data is a vital issue in the domain of data science due to their embedded rich patterns like node behaviors, where the fundamental task is to perform HDI data representation learning. Nonnegative Latent Factor Analysis (NLFA) models have proven to possess the superiority to address this issue, where a Linear Bias Incorporation (LBI) scheme is effective in preventing the model from the training overshooting and fluctuation for good convergence. However, existing LBI schemes are all statistic ones where the linear biases are fixed, which significantly restricts the scalability of the resultant NLFA model and results in loss of representation learning ability to HDI data. Motivated by the above discoveries, this paper innovatively presents a Dynamic Linear Bias Incorporation (DLBI) scheme. It firstly extends the linear bias vectors into matrices, and then builds a binary weight matrix to switch from the linear biases' active states to their inactive states. The weight matrix's each entry is manipulated between the binary states dynamically according to variation of the linear bias value, thereby establishing the dynamic linear biases for an NLFA model. Empirical studies on three HDI datasets from real applications indicate that the proposed DLBI-based NLFA outperforms state-of-the-art models in representation accuracy.

Keywords: Nonnegative Latent Factor Analysis · Knowledge Discovery from High-Dimensional and Incomplete Data · Linear Bias · Missing Data Estimation

1 Introduction

With the burgeoning amount of data that is being generated every day, High-Dimensional and Incomplete (HDI) data is becoming increasingly common in big data-related applications like recommender systems [3, 4, 28] and Quality-of-Service (QoS) predictor in web service [6, 7, 29]. Note that HDI data is typically characterized by: 1) High-Dimensionality, i.e., its large number of entities; and 2) Incompleteness, i.e., its interactions among a large number of entities can be fully observed. Moreover, HDI data are commonly filled with nonnegative values like user-service QoS data [6, 7]. Despite its incompleteness, valuable knowledge like user-item preferences [3, 4] can be achieved.

F. Liu et al. (Eds.): PRICAI 2023, LNAI 14325, pp. 39–51, 2024.
https://doi.org/10.1007/978-981-99-7019-3_5

Hence, an analysis model should well represent HDI data for discovering such hidden knowledge.

The development of sophisticated models has been a notable focus in terms of well-representing HDI data. Among them, first of all, by taking interaction behavior among many entities as a graph, recent years have witnessed well accuracy performance of a Graph Convolutional Network (GCN) model in various applications like recommender systems [3, 4, 28], social discovery [9] and bioinformatics [11]. A GCN model is able to capture the node information from the graph and extract nonlinear features from HDI data. However, it cannot represent HDI data filled with nonnegative values precisely. Moreover, in spite of GPU acceleration, complex designs concerning network structure and learning strategy make GCN models suffer high computational complexity. In comparison, a Nonnegative Matrix Factorization (NMF) model factorizes nonnegative HDI data into nonnegative Latent Factor (LF) matrices in a low-rank way, which is iteratively solved by a Nonnegative and Multiplicative Update (NMU) algorithm for discovering valuable knowledge, such as Yang *et al.*'s B-NMF [13] and Cai *et al.*'s ANMF [14]. Note that NMF is a linear single-layered auto-encoder in nature [13–15], which achieves lower computational complexity than GCN does when representing nonnegative HDI data. In spite of their effectiveness and efficiency, HDI data's incompleteness is not taken into consideration, i.e., HDI data's missing values are desired to be prefilled before their training, which leads to unnecessary computational costs and the loss of information. For fully considering inherent characteristics of HDI data, a Nonnegative Latent Factor Analysis (NLFA) model is proposed [16]. Its modeling is similar to NMF, but takes incompleteness into consideration, i.e., its learning objective is defined on observed interactions only. Then, a Single LF-dependent Nonnegative and Multiplicative Update (SLF-NMU) algorithm is designed for efficiently solving such a learning objective. Hence, NLFA achieves lower computational complexity than NMF does, as well as the great representation accuracy.

Furthermore, a Linear Bias Incorporation (LBI) scheme has proven to be effective in preventing NLFA from the training overshooting and fluctuation for good convergence [2, 17]. For example, Luo *et al.*'s BNLFA [17] assigns a single linear bias vector for each user/item of HDI data for describing the significant tendencies that some users give higher ratings than others for certain items in recommendations. Chen *et al.* further assign multiple linear bias vectors to each entity for achieving higher recommendation accuracy [2]. Note that these LBI schemes are all statistic ones where the linear biases are fixed, which significantly restricts the scalability of the resultant NLFA model and results in loss of representation learning ability to HDI data. Motivated by the above discoveries, this paper innovatively presents a Dynamic Linear Bias Incorporation (DLBI) scheme. It firstly extends the linear bias vectors into matrices, and then builds a binary weight matrix to switch from some linear biases' active states to their inactive states. The weight matrix's each entry is manipulated between the binary states dynamically according to variation of the linear bias value, thereby establishing the dynamic linear biases for an NLFA model.

Hence, the main contribution of this paper includes:

1. It innovatively presents the DLBI scheme, thereby achieving a DLBI-based NLFA (DNLFA) model;

2. The proposed DNLFA's algorithm design and analysis is presented in detail; and
3. Extensive experiments are performed on three real-world nonnegative HDI data to indicate that the proposed DNLFA model outperforms state-of-the-art models in representation accuracy.

2 Methodology

2.1 Problem Formulation

Definition 1. *(Nonnegative HDI data)*: Given U and I, ($|U|\times|I|$)-size Y describes user-item interactions among them and these interactions are weighted. Given Y's known entry set Λ and unknown one Γ, then Y is nonnegative HDI data if $|\Lambda| \ll |\Gamma|$.

Definition 2. *(The NLFA problem)*: When Y and Λ are taken as the input, NLFA [16] minimizes a learning objective defined on Λ only for acquiring rank-f approximation $\hat{y}_{u,i} = \sum_{d=1}^{f_1} p_{u,d} q_{i,d}$, where $p_{u,d} \in P \geq 0$ and $q_{i,d} \in Q \geq 0$. For avoiding the model's overfitting, an L_2-norm-based regularization [1, 12, 23] is adopted in NLFA. Hence, NLFA's learning objective g with Euclidean distance [14, 18, 19, 24–27] is given as:

$$\begin{gathered} \underset{P,Q}{\arg\min} g = \underset{P,Q}{\arg\min} \frac{1}{2} \sum_{y_{u,i} \in \Lambda} \left(\left(y_{u,i} - \hat{y}_{u,i}\right)^2 + \lambda \sum_{d=1}^{f_1} \left(\left(p_{u,d}\right)^2 + \left(q_{i,d}\right)^2 \right) \right), \\ s.t. \forall u \in \{1, 2, \ldots, |U|\}, i \in \{1, 2, \ldots, |I|\}, d \in \{1, 2, \ldots, f_1\} : p_{u,d} \geq 0, q_{i,d} \geq 0, \end{gathered} \tag{1}$$

where regularization coefficient $\lambda > 0$.

Definition 3. *(The BNLFA problem)*: According to previous studies [17], nonnegative HDI data generated from recommender systems exhibits significant tendencies that some users prefer to give higher ratings than others for certain items. For well describing such bias effects, two linear bias vectors N and M are assigned for NLFA's P and Q, respectively. Hence, $\forall n_u \in N$ and $m_i \in M$, (1) can be extended as follows:

$$\begin{gathered} \underset{P,Q,N,M}{\arg\min}\ g = \underset{P,Q,N,M}{\arg\min} \frac{1}{2} \sum_{y_{u,i} \in \Lambda} \left(\left(y_{u,i} - \hat{y}_{u,i}\right)^2 + \lambda \left((n_u)^2 + (m_i)^2 \right) + \sum_{d=1}^{f_1} \left(\left(p_{u,d}\right)^2 + \left(q_{i,d}\right)^2 \right) \right), \\ s.t. \forall u \in \{1, 2, \ldots, |U|\}, i \in \{1, 2, \ldots, |I|\}, d \in \{1, 2, \ldots, f_1\} : \\ p_{u,d} \geq 0, q_{i,d} \geq 0, n_u \geq 0, m_i \geq 0, \end{gathered} \tag{2}$$

where $\hat{y}_{u,i}$ in (2) becomes $\sum_{d=1}^{f_1} p_{u,d} q_{i,d} + n_u + m_i$.. Hence, with (2), a BNLFA model is achieved.

2.2 The Proposed Dynamic Linear Biases

First of all, we extend linear bias vectors $|U|$-length N and $|I|$-length M adopted in (2) into matrix forms, i.e. ($|U|\times f_2$)-size B and ($|I|\times f_2$)-size C. Then, two weighted matrices ($|U|\times f_2$)-size W and ($|I|\times f_2$)-size Z are introduced for B and C, respectively. For well understanding them, the evolution from N and M to B, C, W and Z are described in Fig. 1. Then the problem arises: "*How to dynamically set the values of optimized parameters in W and Z as zeroes?*" Hence, W and Z are manipulated with the following principle:

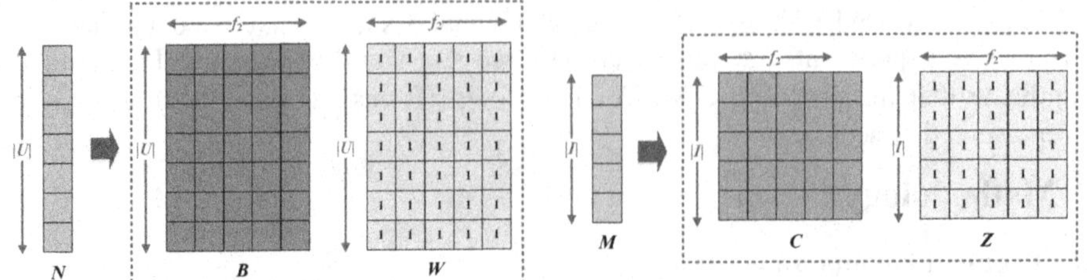

Fig. 1. Evolution from N and M to B, C, W and Z.

1. Values of W and Z are all initialized as ones, i.e. $\forall\, w_{u,d} = 1$ and $z_{i,d} = 1$; and
2. While the model iteratively updates optimized parameters in B/C, the rules at each iteration for setting values of the corresponding optimized parameters in W/Z as zeroes are: if $\forall b_{u,d} \geq \varepsilon$ ($c_{i,d} \geq \varepsilon$), $w_{u,d}$ ($z_{i,d}$) keeps unchanged, otherwise $w_{u,d} = 0$ ($z_{i,d} = 0$), where $u \in \{1,2,\ldots,|U|\}$, $i \in \{1,2,\ldots,|I|\}$, $d \in \{1,2,\ldots,f_2\}$ and $\varepsilon > 0$.

Note that a small example of dynamic linear biases is described in Fig. 2. With such a design, DLBI is compatible for an NLFA model.

2.3 The Proposed DNLFA Model

With DLBI, (1) can be reformulated as:

$$\begin{gathered}\underset{P,Q,B,C}{\arg\min}\ g = \underset{P,Q,B,C}{\arg\min}\ \frac{1}{2}\sum_{y_{u,i}\in\Lambda}\left(\left(y_{u,i}-\hat{y}_{u,i}\right)^2 + \lambda\sum_{d_1=1}^{f_1}\left(\left(p_{u,d_1}\right)^2 + \left(q_{i,d_1}\right)^2 + \sum_{d=1}^{f_2}\left(\left(w_{u,d_2}b_{u,d_2}\right)^2 + \left(z_{i,d_2}c_{i,d_2}\right)^2\right)\right)\right), \\ s.t.\ \forall u \in \{1,2,\ldots,|U|\}, i \in \{1,2,\ldots,|I|\}, d_1 \in \{1,2,\ldots,f_1\}, d_2 \in \{1,2,\ldots,f_2\}: \\ p_{u,d_1} \geq 0, q_{i,d_1} \geq 0, b_{u,d_2} \geq 0, c_{i,d_2} \geq 0, w_{u,d_2} = \{0,1\}, z_{i,d_2} = \{0,1\},\end{gathered} \tag{3}$$

where $\hat{y}_{u,i}$ in (3) becomes $\sum_{d_1=1}^{f_1} p_{u,d_1}q_{i,d_1} + \sum_{d_2=1}^{f_2}\left(w_{u,d_2}b_{u,d_2} + z_{i,d_2}c_{i,d_2}\right)$. With (3), a DNLFA model is achieved.

To efficiently solve DNLFA's learning objective, an SLF-NMU algorithm is adopted [16, 17]. First of all, an additive gradient descent (AGD) algorithm is applied to (3). Hence, learning rules of LFs $p_{u,d1}$, $q_{i,\,d1}$, $b_{u,d2}$ and $c_{i,d2}$ are given as:

$$\begin{gathered}\underset{P,Q,B,C}{\arg\min}\ g \overset{AGD}{\Rightarrow} \\ \forall u \in \{1,2,\ldots,|U|\}, i \in \{1,2,\ldots,|I|\}, d_1 \in \{1,2,\ldots,f\}, d_2 \in \{1,2,\ldots,f_2\}: \\ \begin{cases} p_{u,d_1} \leftarrow p_{u,d_1} + \eta_{u,d_1}\sum_{i\in\Lambda(u)}\left(q_{i,d_1}\left(y_{u,i}-\hat{y}_{u,i}\right) - \lambda p_{u,d_1}\right), \\ q_{i,d_1} \leftarrow q_{i,d_1} + \eta_{i,d_1}\sum_{u\in\Lambda(i)}\left(p_{u,d_1}\left(y_{u,i}-\hat{y}_{u,i}\right) - \lambda q_{i,d_1}\right), \\ b_{u,d_2} \leftarrow b_{u,d_2} + \eta_{u,d_2}\sum_{i\in\Lambda(u)}\left(w_{u,d_2}\left(y_{u,i}-\hat{y}_{u,i}\right) - \lambda b_{u,d_2}\right), \\ c_{i,d_2} \leftarrow c_{i,d_2} + \eta_{i,d_2}\sum_{u\in\Lambda(i)}\left(z_{i,d_2}\left(y_{u,i}-\hat{y}_{u,i}\right) - \lambda c_{i,d_2}\right), \end{cases}\end{gathered} \tag{4}$$

where $\eta_{u,d1}$, $\eta_{i,d1}$, $\eta_{u,d2}$ and $\eta_{i,d2}$ denote the learning rate for LFs $p_{u,d1}$, $q_{i,\,d1}$, $b_{u,d2}$ and $c_{i,d2}$, respectively. With (4), LFs $p_{u,d1}$, $q_{i,\,d1}$, $b_{u,d2}$ and $c_{i,d2}$

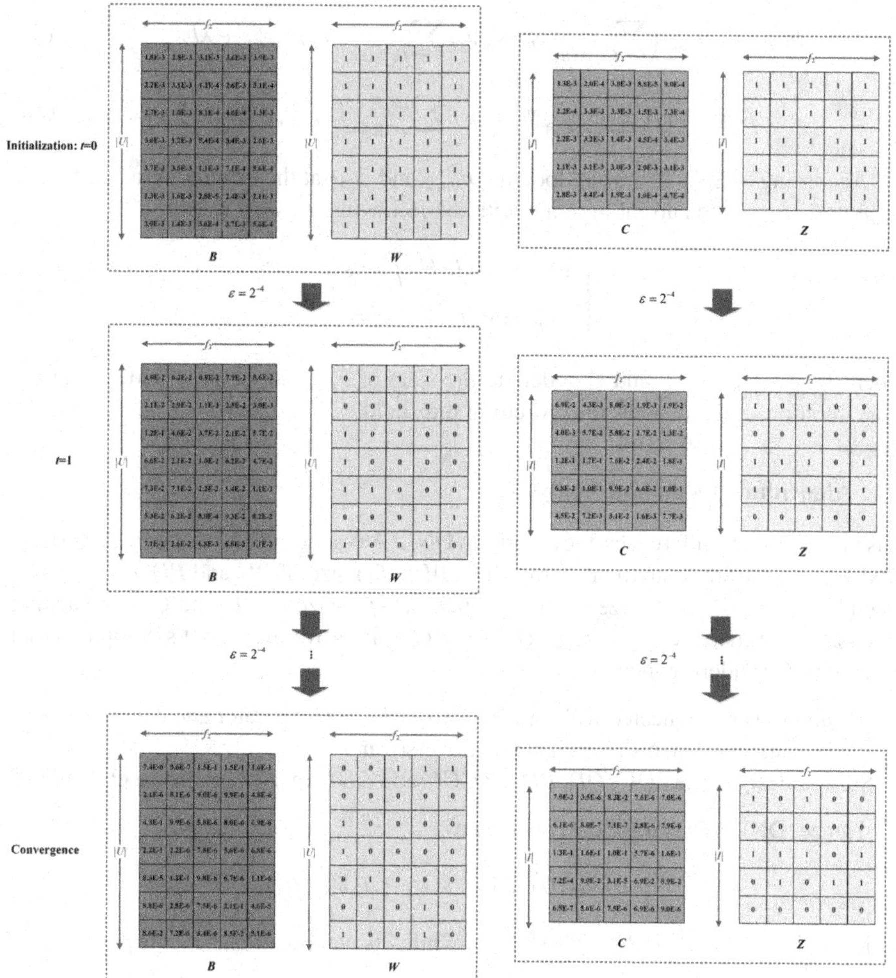

Fig. 2. A small example of dynamic linear biases.

might become negative owing to the negative terms $-\eta_{u,d_1}\sum_{i\in\Lambda(u)}\left(q_{i,d_1}\hat{y}_{u,i}+\lambda p_{u,d_1}\right)$, $-\eta_{i,d_1}\sum_{u\in\Lambda(i)}\left(p_{u,d_1}\hat{y}_{u,i}+\lambda q_{i,d_1}\right)$, $-\eta_{u,d_2}\sum_{i\in\Lambda(u)}\left(w_{u,d_2}\hat{y}_{u,i}+\lambda b_{u,d_2}\right)$ and $-\eta_{i,d_2}\sum_{u\in\Lambda(i)}\left(z_{i,d_2}\hat{y}_{u,i}+\lambda c_{i,d_2}\right)$. For canceling these negative terms, then we set $\eta_{u,d_1}=p_{u,d_1}/\sum_{i\in\Lambda(u)}\left(q_{i,d_1}\hat{y}_{u,i}+\lambda p_{u,d_1}\right)$, $\eta_{i,d_1}=q_{i,d_1}/\sum_{u\in\Lambda(i)}\left(p_{u,d_1}\hat{y}_{u,i}+\lambda q_{i,d_1}\right)$, $\eta_{u,d_2}=b_{u,d_2}/\sum_{i\in\Lambda(u)}\left(w_{u,d_2}\hat{y}_{u,i}+\lambda b_{u,d_2}\right)$ and $\eta_{i,d_2}=c_{i,d_2}/\sum_{u\in\Lambda(i)}\left(z_{i,d_2}\hat{y}_{u,i}+\lambda c_{i,d_2}\right)$, thereby reformulating (4) as follows:

$$p_{u,d_1}\leftarrow p_{u,d_1}\left(\sum\nolimits_{i\in\Lambda(u)}\left(y_{u,i}q_{i,d_1}\right)/\sum\nolimits_{i\in\Lambda(u)}\left(\hat{y}_{u,i}q_{i,d_1}+\lambda p_{u,d_1}\right)\right), \tag{5a}$$

$$q_{i,d_1}\leftarrow q_{i,d_1}\left(\sum\nolimits_{u\in\Lambda(i)}\left(y_{u,i}p_{u,d_1}\right)/\sum\nolimits_{u\in\Lambda(i)}\left(\hat{y}_{u,i}p_{u,d_1}+\lambda q_{i,d_1}\right)\right), \tag{5b}$$

$$b_{u,d_2} \leftarrow b_{u,d_2}\left(\sum_{i\in\Lambda(u)} y_{u,i}w_{u,d_2} / \sum_{i\in\Lambda(u)} \left(\hat{y}_{u,i}w_{u,d_2} + \lambda b_{u,d_2}\right)\right), \tag{5c}$$

$$c_{i,d_2} \leftarrow c_{i,d_2}\left(\sum_{u\in\Lambda(i)} y_{u,i}z_{i,d_2} / \sum_{u\in\Lambda(i)} \left(\hat{y}_{u,i}z_{i,d_2} + \lambda c_{i,d_2}\right)\right), \tag{5d}$$

According to Sect. 3.1, after updating $b_{u,d2}$ and $c_{i,d2}$ at the t-th iteration, we update $w_{u,d2}$ and $z_{i,d2}$ at the current iteration with the following learning rules:

$$\begin{cases} w_{u,d_2}^t = 0 \ if \ b_{u,d_2}^t < \varepsilon, \\ z_{i,d_2}^t = 0 \ if \ c_{i,d_2}^t < \varepsilon. \end{cases} \tag{6}$$

where b_{u,d_2}^t, c_{i,d_2}^t, w_{u,d_2}^t and z_{i,d_2}^t denote the state of $b_{u,d2}$, $c_{i,d2}$, $w_{u,d2}$ and $z_{i,d2}$ at the t-the iteration, and ε denotes the presetting threshold.

2.4 Algorithm Design and Analysis

Based on the above inferences, the algorithm DNLFA is achieved. As shown in Algorithm DNLFA, we introduce auxiliary arrays, i.e., ($|U|\times f_1$)-size of *PU* and *PD*, ($|I|\times f_1$)-size of *QU* and *QD*, ($|U|\times f_2$)-size of *BU* and *BD*, ($|I|\times f_2$)-size of *CU* and *CD* for caching necessary intermediate status of *P*, *Q*, *B* and *C* to improve the model's computational efficiency. Considering them,

1. *PU* and *PD* are connected with $\forall y_{u,i} \in \Lambda$ to cache the numerator and denominator of *P*'s learning increments in each single traverse; and
2. Similar designs (i.e., *QU*, *QD*, *BU*, *BD*, *CU* and *CD*) are also applied to *Q*, *B* and *C*.

Hence, DNLFA's storage cost is given as:

$$S = \Theta((|U| + |I|) \times (f_1 + f_2) + |\Lambda|), \tag{7}$$

which is linear with ($|U|+|I|$) and $|\Lambda|$. Meanwhile, its computational cost is given as:

$$T = \Theta(|\Lambda| \times (f_1 + f_2) \times K), \tag{8}$$

which is linear with $|\Lambda|$ under the condition of $|\Lambda| \gg (|U|+|I|)$. Following Algorithm DNLFA's *S* and *T*, the proposed DNLFA model is highly efficient.

3 Experiments

3.1 Experimental Setup

Tasks. This paper is concerned with the estimation of missing values from HDI data. The performance of involved models is assessed based on the Root Mean Squared Error (RMSE) [2, 5, 20–22], which serves as a metric for evaluating the prediction accuracy of the model. Note that a low RMSE value implies a high prediction accuracy of the model for missing values of HDI data. Additionally, each model's total time cost is recorded to evaluate its computational efficiency.

Algorithm DNLFA

Input: Λ, U, I, f_1, f_2, λ, ε, K

Operation

Initialize $P, Q, B, C, PU, PD, QU, QD, BU, BD, CU, CD$
Initialize W, Z **with ones**
for t=1 to K:
  set $PU, PD, QU, QD, BU, BD, CU, CD$ **with zeroes**
  for $y_{u,i} \in \Lambda$:
    $\hat{y}_{u,i} = \sum_{d_1=1}^{f_1} p_{u,d_1} q_{i,d_1} + \sum_{d_2=1}^{f_2} \left(w_{u,d_2} b_{u,d_2} + z_{i,d_2} c_{i,d_2} \right)$
    for d_1=1 to f_1:
      $PU_{u,d1}=PU_{u,d1}+y_{u,i}q_{i,d1}$, $PD_{u,d1}=PD_{u,d1}+\hat{y}_{u,i}q_{i,d1}+\lambda p_{u,d1}$
      $QU_{i,d1}=QU_{i,d1}+y_{u,i}p_{u,d1}$, $QD_{i,d1}=QD_{i,d1}+y_{u,i}p_{u,d1}+\lambda q_{i,d1}$
    end for
    for d_2=1 to f_2:
      $BU_{u,d2}=BU_{u,d2}+y_{u,i}w_{u,d2}$, $BD_{u,d2}=BD_{u,d2}+\hat{y}_{u,i}w_{u,d2}+\lambda b_{u,d2}$
      $CU_{i,d2}=CU_{i,d2}+y_{u,i}z_{i,d2}$, $CD_{i,d2}=CD_{i,d2}+y_{u,i}z_{i,d2}+\lambda c_{i,d2}$
    end for
  end for
  for $u \in \{1,2,\ldots,|U|\}$:
    for d_1=1 to f_1:
      $p_{u,d1}=p_{u,d1}(PU_{u,d1}/PD_{u,d1})$
    end for
    for d_2=1 to f_2:
      $b_{u,d2}=b_{u,d2}(BU_{u,d2}/BD_{u,d2})$
      if $b_{u,d2}<\varepsilon$: $w_{u,d2}=0$
    end for
  end for
  for $i \in \{1,2,\ldots,|I|\}$:
    for d_1=1 to f_1:
      $q_{i,d1}=q_{i,d1}(QU_{i,d1}/QD_{i,d1})$
    end for
    for d_2=1 to f_2:
      $c_{i,d2}=c_{i,d2}(CU_{i,d2}/CD_{i,d2})$
      if $c_{i,d2}<\varepsilon$: $z_{i,d2}=0$
    end for
  end for
end for

Output: P, Q, B, C, W, Z

Table 1. HDI data.

No	Name	$\lvert\Lambda\rvert+\lvert\Gamma\rvert$	$\lvert U\rvert$	$\lvert I\rvert$	Density	Source
D1	EM	2,811,718	61,265	1,623	2.83%	EachMovie
D2	Flixter	8,196,077	147,612	48,794	0.11%	[8]
D3	Douban	16,830,839	129,490	58,541	0.22%	[10]

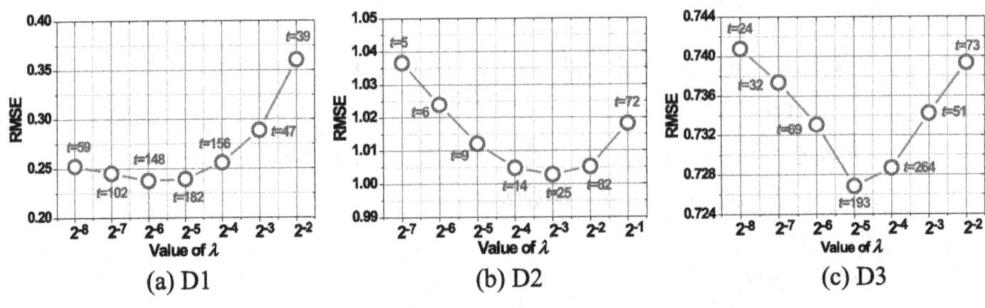

(a) D1 (b) D2 (c) D3

Fig. 3. Effects of λ.

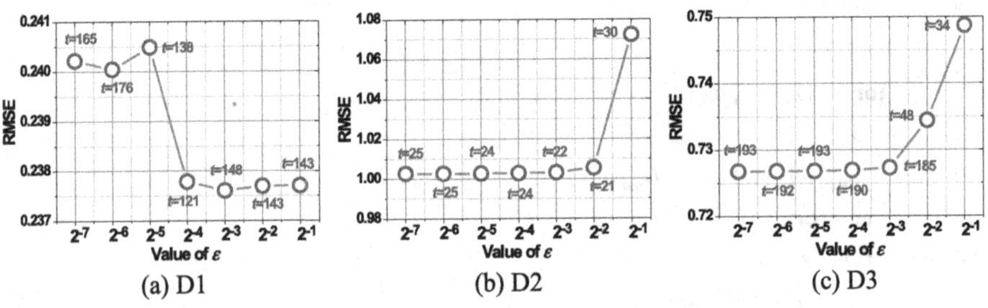

(a) D1 (b) D2 (c) D3

Fig. 4. Effects of ε.

Datasets. Three HDI data in real big data-related applications are adopted in our experiments, and their details are given in Table 1. Each dataset's Λ is randomly divided into ten disjoint subsets for tenfold cross-validation: each time 70% known data serve as the training set, 10% known data serve as the validation set, and 20% known data serve as the test set. The finally averaged results is obtained by repeating the process ten times.

Termination Condition. Each model's training process terminates if: 1) iteration count $t = 1000$; and 2) The RMSE gap in two consecutive iterations gets smaller than 10^{-5}.

3.2 Effects of Hyper-Parameter on DNLFA's Performance

As demonstrated in Sect. 2, it is necessary to test DNLFA's performance sensitivity with its λ and ε. DNLFA's performances as one hyper-parameter varies with another fixed on D1–3 are respectively described in Figs. 3–4, where t denotes DNLFA's converging iteration count. From these results, we find that:

1. **DNLFA's representation accuracy heavily depends on λ.** When λ becomes inappropriate, i.e. too large or too small value is adopted for λ, DNLFA suffers considerable accuracy loss. For example, as shown in Fig. 3(a), RMSE of DNLFA on D1 with $\lambda = 2^{-8}, 2^{-7}, 2^{-6}, 2^{-5}, 2^{-4}, 2^{-3}$ and 2^{-2} is 0.2524, 0.2451, 0.2376, 0.2393, 0.2559, 0.2887 and 0.3604, respectively. The gap between $\lambda = 2^{-2}$ and $\lambda = 2^{-6}$ is 34.07%;
2. **Optimal ε for DNLFA varies on different datasets.** This finding can be supported by Fig. 4. Moreover, when the value of ε is set in an appropriate range, RMSE and convergence rate of DNLFA tends to saturate.

3.3 Comparison Results

The proposed DNLFA is compared with the following state-of-the-art models: ANMF [14], NLFA [16], NIR [5], BNLFA [17], EBNL [2], LightGCN [3] and HMLET [4], where EBNL's f_1 and f_2 are also set at 20 and 5, respectively, and other compared models' f_1 is set at 20 uniformly (f_1 only for them). Note that the above compared models are chosen with the following considerations:

1. ANMF is a recent NMF model, and NIR is a recent NLFA model. On the other hand, BNLFA incorporates linear bias vectors into NLFA for HDI data's each user/item, and EBNL further extends BNLFA's linear bias vectors into linear bias matrices;

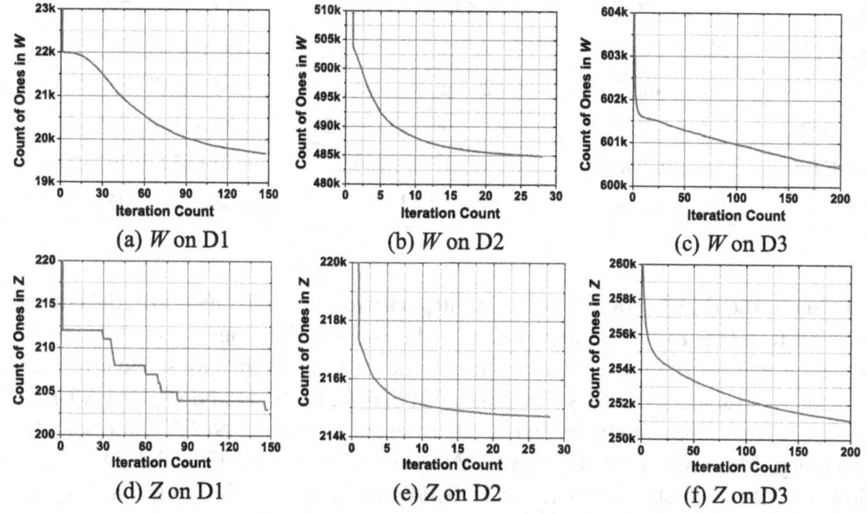

Fig. 5. Count of ones in DNLFA's W and Z on D1–3.

2. LightGCN is a commonly-adopted GCN model, and HMLET is a recent GCN model.

Figure 5 gives the count of ones in DNLFA's W and Z on D1–3. RMSE and total time cost of involved models on D1–3 are recorded in Tables 2–3. Note that "Intractable" in Tables 2–3 denotes ANMF fails to achieve the final results owing to consuming over one hour at each iteration on D3. From these results, we have the following findings:

Table 2. RMSE of involved models on D1–3.

No	D1	D2	D3
ANMF	0.2972 ± 1.3E-2	1.8235 ± 1.1E-2	Intractable
NLFA	0.2352 ± 9.3E-5	0.9619 ± 3.5E-4	0.7285 ± 2.8E-4
NIR	0.2404 ± 9.0E-3	0.9592 ± 7.4E-4	0.7284 ± 2.6E-4
BNLFA	0.2345 ± 6.5E-4	0.9502 ± 4.9E-4	0.7256 ± 8.1E-4
EBNL	0.2369 ± 6.8E-4	0.9422 ± 1.1E-5	0.7286 ± 1.1E-5
LightGCN	0.2433 ± 3.7E-4	1.0216 ± 9.5E-4	0.7681 ± 5.1E-4
HMLET	0.2495 ± 9.3E-4	1.0422 ± 4.9E-3	0.8405 ± 2.6E-3
DNLFA	**0.2339 ± 5.4E-5**	**0.9268 ± 5.7E-5**	**0.7207 ± 2.5E-4**

Table 3. Total time cost (Sec.) of involved models on D1–3.

No	D1	D2	D3
ANMF	12,317 ± 1,015.97	318,016 ± 16,928.33	Intractable
NLFA	127 ± 19.65	840 ± 73.65	1,890 ± 211.32
NIR	**96 ± 9.87**	1,624 ± 165.64	1,941 ± 182.61
BNLFA	223 ± 24.16	123 ± 15.12	840 ± 78.36
EBNL	314 ± 46.92	293 ± 26.37	**195 ± 17.45**
LightGCN	2,795 ± 218.37	17,506 ± 1529.95	32,857 ± 2295.36
HMLET	7,527 ± 696.51	34,817 ± 2766.24	159,832 ± 7926.51
DNLFA	171 ± 14.19	**89 ± 9.44**	884 ± 101.06

1. **Owing to the DLBI scheme, DNLFA outperforms state-of-the-art models in representation accuracy.** As shown in Fig. 5, during DNLFA's convergence process, the count of ones in W or Z decreases, i.e., its count of zeroes increases. Meanwhile, as recorded in Table 2, DNLFA's RMSE is lower than that of NLFA/NIR/BNLFA/EBNL. Hence, we have the conclusion that the DLBI scheme can boost NLFA's representation accuracy. Moreover, compared with ANMF/LightGCN/HMLET, DNLFA achieves lower RMSE, which contributes to DNLFA's full consideration to the nonnegativity and incompleteness of HDI data or overly-complicated designs in terms of their modeling.
2. **DNLFA's computational efficiency is promising.** As recorded in Table 3, DNLFA's total time cost is the least on D2, and it has the third least total time cost on D1 and D3. More specifically, total time cost of NLFA, NIR, BNLFA, EBNL and the proposed DNLFA is close, since their computational complexity is linear with $|\Lambda|$. Meanwhile, they are much lower than that of ANMF, LightGCN and HMLET, since 1) ANMF does not consider the incompleteness of HDI data, i.e., its computational complexity is linear with $(|U|\times|I|)$; and 2) Note that LightGCN and HMLET are implemented

with GPU acceleration. Their high total time cost is caused by multi-layered nonlinear computation. Hence, DNLFA's computational efficiency is promising.

4 Conclusion

This paper proposes the DLBI scheme that dynamically manipulates the corresponding weighted matrix's each entry between the binary states according to variation of the linear bias value. With the proposed DLBI scheme, a DNLFA model is achieved for attaining the highly-accurate representation to HDI data. Based on extensive experiment results on three real-world HDI data, we have the conclusions that: 1) Owing to the DLBI scheme, DNLFA outperforms state-of-the-art models in representation accuracy; and 2) DNLFA's computational efficiency is promising. Note that a DNLFA model's performance depends on the choice of its hyper-parameters, i.e., λ and ε. Hence, in the future, it is highly necessary to investigate computing intelligence approaches for making them self-adaptive.

Acknowledgments. This work was supported by the Guangdong Basic and Applied Basic Research Foundation under Grant 2022A1515110579 and 2021B1515140046.

References

1. Wu, D., Luo, X.: Robust latent factor analysis for precise representation of high-dimensional and sparse data. IEEE/CAA J. Automatica Sinica. **8**(4), 796–805 (2021)
2. Chen, J., Luo, X., Yuan, Y., Shang, M., Zhong, M., Xiong, Z.: Performance of latent factor models with extended linear biases. Knowl.-Based Syst..-Based Syst. **123**, 128–136 (2017)
3. He, X., Deng, K., Wang, X., Li, Y., Zhang, Y., Wang, M.: LightGCN: simplifying and powering graph convolution network for recommendation. In: Proceedings of the 43rd International ACM SIGIR Conference on Research and Development in Information Retrieval, pp. 639–648 (2020)
4. Kong, T., et al.: Linear, or non-linear, that is the question. In: Proceedings of the 15th ACM International Conference on Web Search and Data Mining, pp. 517–525 (2022)
5. Luo, X. Wang, Z., Shang, M.: An instance-frequency-weighted regularization scheme for non-negative latent factor analysis on high-dimensional and sparse data. IEEE Trans. on Systems, Man, and Cybernetics: Systems **51**(6), 3522–3532 (2021)
6. Wu, D., Zhang, P., He, Y., Luo, X.: A double-space and double-norm ensembled latent factor model for highly accurate web service QoS prediction. IEEE Trans. on Services Computing (2022). https://doi.org/10.1109/TSC.2022.3178543
7. Luo, X., Chen, M., Wu, H., Liu, Z., Yuan, H., Zhou, M.: Adjusting learning depth in non-negative latent factorization of tensors for accurately modeling temporal patterns in dynamic QoS data. IEEE Trans. on Automation Science and Eng. **8**(4), 2142–2155 (2021)
8. Goldberg, K., Roeder, T., Gupta, D., Perkins, C.: Eigentaste: a constant time collaborative filtering algorithm. Inf. Retrieval **4**(2), 133–151 (2001)
9. Yu, K., Jiang, H., Li, T., Han, S., Wu, X.: Data fusion oriented graph convolution network model for rumor detection. IEEE Trans. on Network and Service Manage. **17**(4), 2171–2181 (2020)
10. Ma, H., Zhou, D., Liu, C., Lv, M., King, I.: Recommender systems with social regularization. Proceedings of the 4th International Conference Web Search and Data Mining, pp. 287–296 (2011)

11. Xiong, W., Li, F., Yu, Hong, Ji, D.: Extracting drug-drug interactions with a dependency-based graph convolution neural network. Proceedings of 2019 IEEE International Conference on Bioinformatics and Biomedicine, pp. 755–759 (2019)
12. Li, Z., Li, S., Bamasag, O., Alhothali, A., Luo, X.: Diversified regularization enhanced training for effective manipulator calibration. IEEE Trans. on Neural Networks and Learning Systems (2022). https://doi.org/10.1109/TNNLS.2022.3153039
13. Yang, Z., Chen, W., Huang, J.: Enhancing recommendation on extremely sparse data with blocks-coupled non-negative matrix factorization. Neurocomputing **278**, 126–133 (2018)
14. Cai, T., Tan, V., Févotte, C.: Adversarially-trained nonnegative matrix factorization. IEEE Signal Process. Lett. **28**, 1415–1419 (2021)
15. Sedhain, S., Menon, A., Sanner, S., Xie, L.: AutoRec: Autoen-coders meet collaborative filtering. In: Proceedings of the 24th International Conference World Wide Web, pp. 111–112 (2015)
16. Luo, X., Zhou, M., Xia, Y., Zhu, Q.: An efficient non-negative matrix-factorization-based approach to collaborative filtering for recommender systems. IEEE Trans. on Industrial Informatics. **10**(2), 1273–1284 (2014)
17. Luo, X., Zhou, M., Xia, Y., Zhu, Q., Ammari, A., Alabdulwahab, A.: Generating highly accurate predictions for missing QoS data via aggregating nonnegative latent factor models. IEEE Trans. on Neural Networks and Learning Syst. **27**(3), 524–537 (2016)
18. Shang, M., Yuan, Y., Luo, X., Zhou, M.: An α-β-divergence-generalized recommender for highly accurate predictions of missing user preferences. IEEE Transactions on Cybernetics. **52**(8), 8006–8018 (2022)
19. Wu, D., Luo, X., He, Y., Zhou, M.: A prediction-sampling-based multilayer-structured latent factor model for accurate representation to high-dimensional and sparse data. IEEE Trans. on Neural Networks and Learning Systems (2022). https://doi.org/10.1109/TNNLS.2022.3200009
20. Liu, Z., Luo, X., Wang, Z.: Convergence analysis of single latent factor-dependent, nonnegative, and multiplicative update-based nonnegative latent factor models. IEEE Trans. on Neural Networks and Learning Syst. **32**(4) 1737–1749 (2020)
21. Luo, X., Zhou, Y., Liu, Z., Zhou, M.: Fast and accurate non-negative latent factor analysis on high-dimensional and sparse matrices in recommender systems. IEEE Transactions on Knowledge and Data Engineering (2021). https://doi.org/10.1109/TKDE.2021.3125252
22. Yuan, Y., He, Q., Luo, X., Shang, M.: A multilayered-and-randomized latent factor model for high-dimensional and sparse matrices. IEEE Trans. on big data. **8**(3), 784–794 (2022)
23. Yu, Z., et al.: Semisupervised classification with novel graph construction for high-dimensional data. IEEE Trans. on Neural Networks and Learning Syst. **33**(1), 75–88 (2022)
24. Wu, H., Luo, X., Zhou, M., Rawa, M., Sedraoui, K., Albeshri, A.: A PID-incorporated latent factorization of tensors approach to dynamically weighted directed network analysis. IEEE/CAA Journal of Automatica Sinica. **9**(3), 533–546 (2021)
25. Chen, J., Luo, X., Zhou, M.: Hierarchical particle swarm optimization-incorporated latent factor analysis for large-scale incomplete matrices. IEEE Trans. on Big Data. **8**(6), 1524–1536 (2022)
26. Luo, X., Zhou, Y., Liu, Z., Zhou, M.: Generalized nesterov's acceleration-incorporated non-negative and adaptive latent factor analysis. IEEE Trans. on Services Computing (2022). https://doi.org/10.1109/TSC.2021.3069108
27. Luo, X., Wu, H., Li, Z.: NeuLFT: a novel approach to nonlinear canonical polyadic decomposition on high-dimensional incomplete tensors. IEEE Trans. on Knowledge and Data Engineering (2022). https://doi.org/10.1109/TKDE.2022.3176466

28. Wang, X., He, X., Wang, M., Feng, F., Chua, T.: Neural graph collaborative filtering. Proceedings of the 42nd International ACM SIGIR Conference on Research and Development in Information Retrieval, pp. 165–174 (2019)
29. Chen, Z., Shen, F., You, D.: Your neighbors alleviate cold-start: on geographical neighborhood influence to collaborative web service QoS prediction. Knowl.-Based Syst..-Based Syst. **138**, 188–201 (2017)

An Anomaly Detection Framework for System Logs Based on Ensemble Learning

Wenjing Xiong[1], Wu Chen[2(✉)], Jiamou Liu[3], and Kaiqi Zhao[3]

[1] College of Computer and Information Science, Southwest University, Chongqing, China
[2] School of Software, Southwest University, Chongqing, China
chenwu@swu.edu.cn
[3] The University of Auckland, Auckland, New Zealand

Abstract. Logs offer vital insights into system states and contextual details, crucial for identifying anomalies. Numerous machine learning and deep learning approaches have been proposed for log anomaly detection. Recent studies reveal that distinct software systems tend to generate a substantial volume of complexity and diversity of logs that exhibit considerable discrepancies in class distribution. In this paper, we introduce IELog, a framework for anomaly detection. IELog employs DSS (Denoise Selection Sampling) to oversample the minority class, mitigating imbalanced data impact. Subsequently, IELog proposes the AW (Anomaly Weighting) ensemble rule to effectively combine the prediction outcomes of individual base models, leveraging their distinct strengths. Extensive experiments have been performed on four different public log datasets, which demonstrate the validity of the proposed framework IELog.

Keywords: Log anomaly detection · Ensemble learning · Imbalanced data

1 Introduction

As systems grow in scale and complexity, system anomalies are bound to occur, posing a major challenge for maintainers due to their impact on system performance and availability [1]. Hence, efficiently identifying anomalies is vital, enhancing software quality, system reliability, and reducing maintenance costs [2].

Recent studies underscores system log importance in monitoring and troubles- hooting [3–6]. These logs provide crucial historical insights into system behavior and evolution. Initially, researchers primarily employ machine learning to mine the relationships among logs to detect anomalies [7,8]. These methods analyze quantitative event relationships to detect log sequence anomalies. Subsequently, more focus turned to the sequential event connections in log sequences,

F. Liu et al. (Eds.): PRICAI 2023, LNAI 14325, pp. 52–65, 2024.
https://doi.org/10.1007/978-981-99-7019-3_6

using sequence models like LSTM or Transformer to detect anomalies [2,3]. Recently, some studies have transformed log sequences into graphs, using Graph Neural Networks for anomaly detection [5,6].

Despite fantastic advances in log-based anomaly detection, there are still several aspects that are rarely taken into account:

Imbalanced Log Dataset. Data imbalance is a common issue in system logs, with normal logs far outnumbering anomalous logs [9]. This is due to anomalies' infrequent occurrence in contrast to the system's normal operation. For instance, HDFS dataset's anomalous logs make up only 2.93%. Yet, in log anomaly detection, rare anomalous logs are crucial indicators for identifying and addressing potential issues [4]. The excess of normal logs can result in anomalous logs being overlooked or misunderstood as noise. Thus, focusing on these anomalies is vital for comprehensive detection. Unfortunately, existing methods often overlook data imbalance, favoring the majority class in learning process and introducing detection biases. In consequence, how to mitigate the effect of data imbalance on anomaly detection when monitoring and troubleshooting the system by utilizing logs present a relatively major challenge.

Complexity and Diversity of Log Anomalies. The complexity and diversity of log anomalies stem from the heterogeneous nature of anomalous behaviors within software systems, resulting in a broad spectrum of anomalous behaviors present in logs, which can manifest distinct underlying patterns [10]. Additionally, log data is voluminous and exhibits variations in terms of format, structure, and level of detail. A universal model excelling in identifying diverse log anomalies is challenging due to different models' distinct, strengths, weaknesses, and applicability [1]. Given the intricate types and anomalous patterns of real-world logs, a singular model isn't universally applicable to detect all log anomalies. Henceforth, how to combine the strengths of diverse models in enhancing the performance of log anomaly detection remains a challenge.

To tackle the above challenges, we introduce IELog, a log anomaly detection framework. It addresses data imbalance by innovatively generating refined anomalous samples through noise reduction, enhancing the performance by effectively resolving class overlapping in imbalanced data. Additionally, IELog utilizes a novel ensemble learning approach, synergizing the capabilities of base models. This enhances performance beyond what individual models can achieve and yields heightened result reliability.

The main contributions of our work are as follows:

- A data balancing method DSS (Denoise Selection Sampling) is proposed to effectively alleviate the impact of imbalanced data for anomaly detection.
- A new ensemble rule AW (Anomaly Weighting) is proposed to combine the strengths of multiple models in detecting complex and diverse anomalous log patterns, thereby improving the performance of anomaly detection.
- A comprehensive series of experimental studies are conducted on four different public log datasets for validating the effectiveness of IELog.

2 Related Work

Log-Based Anomaly Detection. Researchers extensively study logs to detect anomalies. Liang et al. [8] adopt SVM to find the inherent relationships to detect anomalies. Liu et al. [7] construct Isolation Trees for isolating anomalies. Various approaches rely on deep learning to facilitate the identification of log anomalies. For example, DeepLog [3] and LogRobust [4] employ an LSTM to detect the anomalies. Wang et al. [5] transform log sequences into graphs, using Position Aware Weighted Graph Attention Layer for detecting anomalies.

Ensemble Learning. Several studies demonstrated that ensemble learning is an effective strategy for enhancing log anomaly detection. Wang et al. [11] use spectral clustering for data balancing and propose an NW (Neighbor Weighting) ensemble rule by considering the relationship between the tested samples and historical samples. Pal et al. [12] predict faults in network systems using weighted combination of block-divided data. Sun et al. [13] use SplitBal or ClusterBal to balance the datasets and adopt ensemble rules to combine base classifiers' results.

Imbalanced Data. High log imbalance has emerged as a prominent challenge in anomaly detection. Sun et al. [14] incorporate the semantics of events and the semantics of the region where each word is located through the Adaptive Region embedding. Wang et al. [15] adopt the mean-shift clustering to calculate samples' weights thus reducing the effect of imbalance. Studiawan et al. [9] detect anomalies based on the sentiment analysis, employing Tomek-Link to address the imbalance and identify anomalies through the Gated Recurrent Unit.

While these methods have shown effectiveness in detecting log anomalies, they often overlook the essential characteristics of imbalanced log datasets and diverse log anomalies. On one hand, in order to mitigate the overlook of anomalous logs due to data imbalance, we introduce a data balancing approach to stress anomalous logs. On the other hand, for improved identification of diverse anomalous logs, a novel ensemble rule is devised to combine multiple models, thereby enhancing the performance of log anomaly detection.

3 Approach

3.1 Overall Framework

Given any system-generated logs, IELog serves as a tool to detect log anomalies for aiding development and operations personnel in system maintenance. Figure 1 presents IELog's overview, comprising two phases: training and testing. In the training phase, **Data Preprocessing** is focused on processing raw logs into vector representations. Then, calculate the weights of base model using AW (Anomaly Weighting). In the testing phase, the processed logs are fed to the framework, with each base model providing a result. **Anomaly Detection with Ensemble**, through AW, IELog predicts the anomalies of log samples.

3.2 Data Preprocessing

Data preprocessing comprises three steps: log parsing, log grouping, and event embedding. (1)Log parsing converts the raw log messages into structured events, removing irrelevant data like parameters. For example, a log message <*2013-8-21 15:04:54, INFO dfs.Responder: Responder 596 for block blk_388 terminating*> can be parsed into event <*Responder * for block * terminating*> and parameters (e.g. <*596*>). In research, we utilize the state-of-the-art log parsing method Drain [16]. (2)Log grouping divides logs into distinct groups, known as log sequences (or graphs), serving as fundamental components for feature extraction during the pre-construction of log anomaly detection models. (3)Event embedding generates semantic representation vectors for log events. This representation distinguishes the events, despite the dissimilar syntaxes of the various event types but similar semantics [10]. Following prior work [6], we adopt a renowned word embedding model Glove [17] and the TF-TDF [18] for this purpose.

3.3 Models Training

In this stage, considering the main log anomaly detection classifications of machine learning, sequence-based, and graph-based models, we incorporate the strengths each category in our model selection. This leads to the meticulous choice of representative models from each category to be incorporated into our ensemble framework. Eventually, we select 6 supervised models with distinct traits as base models: SVM [8], IsolationForest [7], DeepLog [3], LogRobust [4], CNN [19] and GLAD-PAW [5]. As previously mentioned, these models excel at capturing various log features and displaying unique differences, making them suitable for an ensemble learning framework and enhancing the performance of log anomaly detection. Specifically, SVM and IsolationForest effectively identify

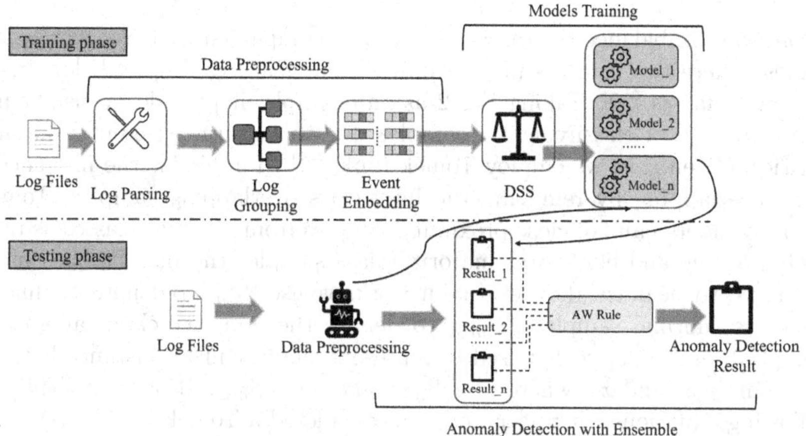

Fig. 1. An overview of IELog.

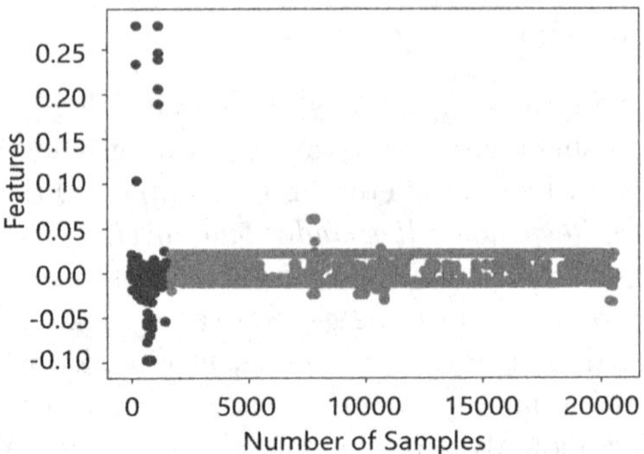

Fig. 2. Visualization of samples' features on BGL. The blue dots represent the features of anomalous samples and the red dots represent the normal ones. (Color figure online)

event count anomalies by utilizing log event count vectors. DeepLog and LogRobust employ LSTM to recognize sequence anomalies via event sequential vectors or event semantic vectors as model inputs. CNN and GLAD-PAW detect anomalies by capturing relationships in the context of log sequences and topology in log graphs, respectively. Both models have demonstrated promising outcomes in identifying sequential or structural anomalies within event sequences or graphs.

The mentioned models are trained using balanced data allocated to each of them, which is obtained through the following designed method.

DSS. To mitigate the bias and issues stemming from data imbalance in the log dataset, we devise a data balancing method termed DSS(Denoise Selection Sampling), tailored to the characteristics of logs. DSS consists of three steps:*Denoising*, *Selecting*, and *Sampling*.

- *Denoising.* Imbalanced datasets are often accompanied by class overlapping issues, where two samples may exhibit similar features despite belonging to different classes [20]. Taking Fig. 2 as an example, it provides a insight into the challenge of classifying log samples due to feature representation similarities. Given this, we employ Tomek-Link [21] to minimize the influence of class overlapping by removing the inter-class overlapping samples. Tomek-Link considers pairs of close proximity samples from different classes as noisy or borderline and eliminates majority class samples (normal samples in log datasets) to clean the dataset. In our work, we use S_{max} to denote the majority class (normal samples), S_{min} to denote the minority class (anomalous samples), and $d\ (x_i,\ x_j)$ is used to represent the Euclidean distance between the sample x_i and x_j, where $x_i \in S_{max}$ and $x_j \in S_{min}$. If no x_k satisfies the following equations, then $< x_i, x_j >$ is considered a Tomek-Link:

$$d(x_i, x_k) < d(x_i, x_j) \quad or \quad d(x_j, x_k) < d(x_i, x_j) \tag{1}$$

by following the procedures above, we obtain the cleaned datasets by removing the $x_i \in S_{max}$ in $< x_i, x_j >$.

- *Selecting.* After data denoising, the next step involves generating new samples. To achieve this, we prioritize selecting samples with similarity to the anomalous center rather than those situated at the boundary. K-Means [22] is a powerful clustering algorithm that utilizes a rigorous distance metric to achieve superior clustering performance, especially on datasets where samples have relatively small distances between them, such as log datasets exhibiting high similarity after feature representation. Additionally, K-Means demonstrates remarkable efficiency in processing large-scale datasets. Hench, K-Means is used to cluster the data and ascertain the center of anomalous samples. Further, the cosine similarity metric is implemented to evaluate the similarity between the samples and the anomalous center. Following this, we select samples that closely resemble the anomalous center to generate new samples.
- *Sampling.* Then, we refer to the generation formula suggested in [23], denoted as Eq. 2. This formula will be employed to generate a new sample by utilizing the feature of the chosen sample:

$$F_{new} = F_i * (V_i * \alpha + 1) \tag{2}$$

where F_i is the feature of the selected sample according to the previous steps, while in [23] is a random selection from the minority class, V_i is a random vector with values between 0 and 1, and α is a coefficient.

3.4 Anomaly Detection with Ensemble

We design an ensemble rule AW(Anomaly Weighting), shown in Algorithm 1, to enhance the performance of log anomaly detection by integrating diverse base

Algorithm 1: Ensemble Rule

Input: Balanced log dataset $X = \{x_1, x_2, x_3, ..., x_n\}$
Output: Ensemble result $Y = \{y_1, y_2, y_3, ..., y_n\}$
Require: Given a set with m models $Model\_set = \{M_1, M_2, M_3, ..., M_m\}$, the prediction probability of each model for input data x_i is $Prediction\_set_i = \{pred_{i1}, pred_{i2}, pred_{i3}, ..., pred_{im}\}$, the set of model's overall discriminative ability is $W\_set = \{W_1, W_2, W_3, ..., W_m\}$, and the set of weights for model's distinctive discriminative ability is $D\_set = \{D_1, D_2, D_3, ..., D_m\}$.

for *each* $x_i \in X$ **do**
  $\text{sum\_pred}_i = \sum_{j=1}^{m} \text{pred}_{ij} * \text{W}_j * \text{D}_j$
  if $sum\_pred_i > threshold$ **then**
    $y_i = 1$;
  else
    $y_i = 0$;
  end
end
return $Y = \{y_1, y_2, y_3, ..., y_n\}$

models for stable and accurate results. Existing ensemble rules treat positive and negative samples equally in terms of importance. However, in log anomaly detection, the accurate judgment of anomalous logs holds greater importance, due to the potential consequences of missed anomalies. In light of this, AW assigns weights to the base models, favoring those with stronger capabilities in identifying anomalous logs. When assigning weights to base models, AW focuses on combining two metrics: (1) the overall discriminative ability, denoted as W; (2) the distinctive discriminative ability for the anomaly, denoted as D.

Given m base models for AW, denoted as $Model\_set = \{M_1, M_2, M_3, ..., M_m\}$, each of these models produces a prediction result for each sample x_i in the training dataset $X = \{x_1, x_2, x_3, ..., x_n\}$. For each base model j, its overall discriminative ability is reflected in

$$W_j = \frac{1}{2}\ln(\frac{num(all)}{num(error)} - 1) \tag{3}$$

where *num(error)* is the number of samples that the model does not correctly classify, *num(all)* is the number of samples. Here,n, m, j are positive integers.

Additionally, we aim to capture the differences among base models in recognizing anomalous logs through D. Specifically, from the perspective of log anomaly detection, making accurate judgments on anomalous logs is more crucial than on normal logs, as missing anomalous logs can potentially lead to significant incidents or accidents. Furthermore, the ability of a base model is particularly highlighted when it can identify anomalous logs that other base models cannot recognize. As a result, we use D_j to represent the distinctive discriminative ability of a model j for the anomalous logs.

$$D_j = \frac{\sum_{t=1}^{m} num(Distinct_{tj})}{num(Correct_j)}(t \neq j) \tag{4}$$

where $num(Correct_j)$ is the number of anomalous logs that base model j can correctly identify, $num(Distinct_{tj})$ is the number of anomalous logs that model j can correctly identify but not by model t. Here, m, j, t are positive integers.

At last, AW incorporates a threshold that assists in determining the presence of anomalies. Specifically, the final outcome for a given sample x_i, denoted as sum_pred_i, is derived by combining the predictions from base models. Depending on whether sum_pred_i exceeds the predefined threshold, x_i is classified as anomalous or normal, respectively.

Theorem 1. *For binary classification, consider a set of trained base models* $\mathrm{Model\_set} = \{M_1, M_2, M_3, ..., M_m\}$*, combined with weighted averaging* ($\mathrm{sum\_pred} = \sum_{j=1}^{m} \mathrm{pred}_j * \omega_j$)*. Here,* $\mathrm{pred}_j = \mathrm{M}_j(\mathbf{x})$ *is the prediction of base model* j *for sample* $\mathbf{x}$ *and* $\sum_{j=1}^{m}\omega_j = 1$*. In our study,* ω_j *is* W_j *and* D_j*. Then, for any second-order differentiable function, the error of the ensemble model can be decomposed as*

$$E = \bar{E} - \bar{A} \tag{5}$$

where

$$E = E_D\{\zeta(sum\_pred, y)\} \tag{6}$$

$$\bar{E} = \sum_{j=1}^{m} \omega_j E_D\{\zeta(pred_j, y)\} \tag{7}$$

$$\bar{A} = \frac{1}{2}\sum_{j=1}^{m} \omega_j E_D\{\zeta''(pred_j^*, y)pred_j{}^2 - \zeta''(sum\_pred^*, y)sum\_pred^2\} \tag{8}$$

in the above equations, E_D $\{\bullet\}$ *represents the expectation within sample space* D *and* y *is the actual value of the sample. The variable* pred_j^* *assumes a real value between 0 and* pred_j*, while* sum_pred* *takes a real value ranging from 0 to* sum_pred. *Analogous to the Lagrange Median Theorem, the values of* pred_j^* *and* sum_pred* *depend on the specific form of the loss function* ζ(pred,y)*, and the exact numerical values of* pred_j *and* sum_pred.

4 Experiment and Analysis

In this section, experiments are designed to answer the following questions:

- **RQ1. Whether the proposed AW ensemble rule improves the performance of log anomaly detection?**
- **RQ2. Whether the proposed data balancing method DSS is conducive to the performance of log anomaly detection?**
- **RQ3. Whether the framework proposed is conducive to the performance of log anomaly detection?**

4.1 Experimental Setup

Log Datasets. In experiments, we select four public log datasets[1] shown in Table 1: HDFS, BGL, Hadoop, and TrainTicket. They are derived from real-world and widely utilized in diverse studies on log analysis [3,4,6,11,15].

Ensemble Rule. Two ensemble rules are selected: voting and weighting. The voting rule adheres to the principle of majority rule. The weighting incorporates classifiers' error rates using a weighted alpha for the final prediction.

Data Balancing Method. Two oversampling algorithms are chosen for comparison. One is SMOTE [24], generating new samples by randomly selecting a sample from the neighboring classes of certain samples. Another is NAO [23], generating new samples based on selected sample features (formula 2).

[1] https://github.com/DeepTraLog/DeepTraLog/tree/main/TraceLogData https://github.com/logpai/loghub.

Table 1. Log Datasets

Datasets	Log lines	Anomalies	Percentage of anomalies (%)
HDFS	11175629	16838 (blocks)	2.93%
BGL	4747963	348460	7.34%
Hadoop	21579470	1177062	5.45%
TrainTicket	9528670	6154083	64.5% ⋆

⋆ It has a high proportion of anomalies, as all logs within the anomalous folder are treated as anomalous due to the absence of individual labels.

Baseline. Seven commonly used models and an ensemble method are as baselines. SVM [8] and IsolationForest [7] are traditional machine learning approaches. DeepLog [3] and LogRobust [4], employ LSTM to identify anomalous log sequences. CNN [19] utilizes filters to capture relationships in the context of log sequences. GLAD-PAW [5] transforms log sequences into graphs for detecting. NeuralLog [2] introduces an approach based on the Transformer without log parsing. NW [11] employs spectral clustering and introduces an ensemble rule that leverages the relationship between test samples and historical data.

Performance Metrics. We use four metrics to measure the effectiveness of log anomaly detection: (1) $Precision = \frac{TP}{TP+FP}$; (2) $Recall = \frac{TP}{TP+FN}$; (3) $F1\text{-}Score = \frac{2*precision*recall}{precision+recall}$; (4) $Accuracy = \frac{TP+TN}{TP+TN+FP+FN}$

TP(True Positive) denotes correctly detected anomalies. FP(False Positive) represents normal samples misidentified. FN(False Negative) is the undetected anomalies. TN(True Negative) represents anomalies wrongly classified.

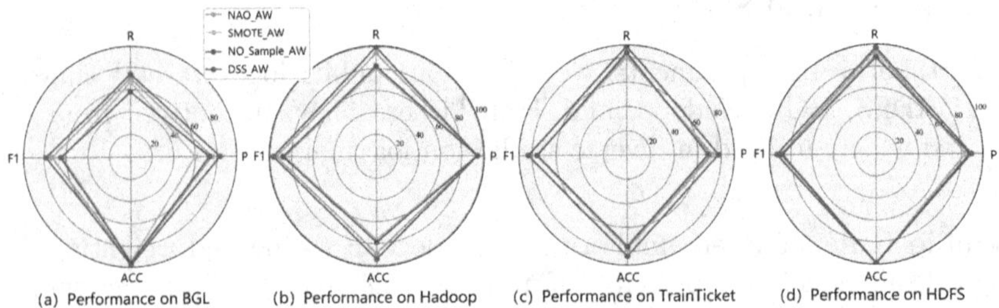

Fig. 3. Performance comparison of AW under different sampling methods.

Settings. For the models with existing public implementations[2], such as SVM, Isolation Forest, DeepLog, LogRobust, NeuralLog, and CNN, we use their predefined parameters of the existing implementations. For models lacking publicly implementations, like GLAD-PAW, we meticulously develop our implementations based on their papers, following their parameter values. Experiments are

[2] https://github.com/LogIntelligence/LogADEmpirical.

conducted on a system with 16GB RAM and RTX 3070 with 8GB GPU memory. The setup includes Windows 11, Python 3.7, and PyTorch 1.11.0. Log grouping uses *block_id* for HDFS and a fixed window of 300 for other datasets. Each dataset is randomly split into 20% training and 80% testing sets. To improve the overall generalization performance, 50% of training set are randomly sampled for base model to be used for training. Following thorough experimental validation, AW's threshold is set to 0.3 and α in formula 2 is set to 0.05.

Table 2. F1-Score and Acc comparison of log anomaly detection, with NS representing No Sample.

Models	BGL		Hadoop		TrainTicket		HDFS	
	F1(%)	Acc(%)	F1(%)	Acc(%)	F1(%)	Acc(%)	F1(%)	Acc(%)
DeepLog	54.02	90.80	59.57	44.20	56.34	55.65	36.91	96.30
LogRobust	72.25	94.97	68.61	53.43	65.73	52.82	54.70	98.11
NeuralLog	74.21	96.08	86.27	76.10	79.52	78.90	88.77	99.44
GLAD-PAW	35.40	78.44	67.92	52.84	66.12	66.68	70.84	98.63
CNN	72.56	95.51	60.50	45.09	55.97	45.61	51.13	97.80
SVM	73.50	96.06	65.25	49.66	73.85	71.70	81.70	99.03
IsolationForest	45.71	89.83	64.70	49.27	59.04	62.54	66.63	98.21
NS_Vote	57.66	93.61	85.72	75.31	72.92	74.46	83.10	98.98
NS_Weight	59.53	94.72	87.01	77.24	74.26	75.50	84.67	99.04
NS_AW	64.78	94.86	88.05	78.86	75.92	75.68	88.19	99.29
SMOTE_Vote	61.64	94.48	75.68	61.64	62.39	71.30	82.71	98.93
SMOTE_Weight	62.81	93.79	77.81	64.33	76.28	76.00	85.75	99.23
SMOTE_AW	72.62	95.96	86.59	76.61	76.69	77.74	87.55	99.21
NAO_Vote	66.29	94.62	86.44	76.38	74.39	74.87	82.51	99.08
NAO_Weight	70.23	95.03	88.81	80.05	74.17	74.19	85.30	99.15
NAO_AW	72.84	95.73	94.57	89.19	76.46	76.98	89.29	99.30
DSS_Vote	72.62	95.96	87.30	77.68	77.55	78.69	86.46	99.13
DSS_Weight	77.15	96.52	92.21	85.61	79.12	78.91	88.38	99.37
DSS_AW	**78.21**	**96.65**	**97.07**	**94.32**	**83.39**	**83.78**	**93.23**	**99.57**

4.2 Results and Analysis

For **RQ1**, we compare three ensemble rules under a consistent data-balancing approach. AW outperforms other ensemble rules and base models (Table 2). For instance, in the BGL dataset, AW achieves F1-Score of 78.21% and Acc of 96.65%, an improvement of 1.06%–42.81% and 0.13%–18.21% over base models and other ensemble rules. Notably, HDFS results show 93.23% F1-Score and 99.57% Acc. Overall, AW excels in F1-Score and Acc compared to existing ensemble rules under the same data balancing strategy or without sampling.

Unlike prevailing ensemble rules, AW introduces a novel method using two model weights. These weights not only comprehensively evaluate each model's anomaly detection ability but also consider disparities in the ability of detecting anomalous samples across the base models. By synthesizing the distinct recognition prowess of individual models, AW significantly boosts log anomaly detection performance, surpassing the capabilities of existing ensemble rules.

To answer **RQ2**, we compare three distinct data balancing methods while using a consistent ensemble rule. The results show that DSS outperforms other methods across all metrics, as shown in Table 2 and Fig. 3.

In contrast to baselines, DSS exhibits the potential to generate more meaningful samples. Figure 2 depicts similar features between numerous normal and anomalous ones after semantic extraction, causing indistinct class boundaries. As shown in Fig. 4 (a), the presence of samples located at the boundary and class overlapping can confuse and impede the model's ability to accurately classify.

Table 3. Performance of anomaly detection with IELog and NW on four datasets

Datasets	NW				IELog			
	P(%)	R(%)	F1(%)	Acc(%)	P(%)	R(%)	F1(%)	Acc(%)
BGL	80.00	69.31	74.27	96.10	**82.93**	**74.00**	**78.22**	**96.65**
HDFS	87.93	96.09	91.53	99.48	**89.44**	**97.37**	**93.23**	**99.57**
Hadoop	94.49	83.64	88.74	79.93	**94.49**	**99.80**	**97.07**	**94.32**
TrainTicket	71.09	83.17	76.66	77.08	**77.67**	**90.01**	**83.39**	**83.78**

Repeated generation of minority samples by SMOTE or NAO may exacerbate overfitting, impeding the performance of log anomaly detection. Besides, it is essential to note that selecting boundary samples for generation will diminish the disparity between the classes as the number of boundary samples increases. For DSS, it extends the distinction between normal and anomalous samples. DSS utilizes the Tomek-Link to clean the dataset, removing the normal sample in the overlapping pairs (Fig. 4(a) to (b)). To avoid introducing extraneous data, DSS selects samples similar to the anomalous center for generating new samples, enhancing the distinction between classes, ultimately yielding more precise classification results. The marked distribution difference between the two classes after sampling in Fig. 4 (b) highlights DSS's effectiveness.

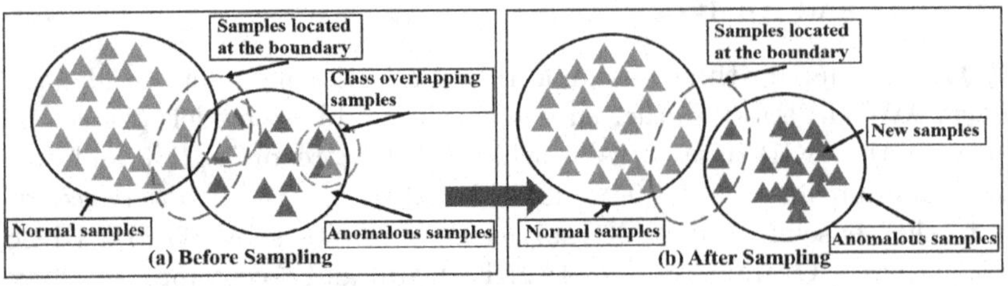

Fig. 4. Examples of DSS. (a) and (b) show data distributions before and after sampling. Blue triangles represent normal samples, green indicates anomalies, and orange indicates newly generated DSS samples. Additionally, Dashed red boxes denote samples at the boundary, while those in the orange dashed box signify overlapping classes. (Color figure online)

Regarding **RQ3**, it pertains to the performance of IELog when compared to alternative methods. Specifically, we compare IELog with NW [11], implementing NW with the same classifiers. Results in Table 3 illustrate that IELog yields superior results for all metrics. IELog particularly excels in Hadoop dataset, with a 8.33% increase in F1-Score and a 14.39% increase in Acc. NW combines base model's prediction using k-nearest neighbors of test samples. Yet, as seen in Fig. 2, numerous log dataset samples display similar features. In instances where test samples are located at the boundary, they might share the same k-nearest neighbors, which is a challenge in accurately classifying test samples via NW.

5 Conclusion

In this paper, we propose a framework for log anomaly detection, IELog. IELog is designed to address the issue of data imbalance and the complex and diverse nature of log anomalies. IELog introduces the DSS for generating samples that are more conducive to anomaly detection to balance datasets. Additionally, an ensemble rule AW is used to combine the predictions of base models and provide more accurate results for anomaly detection. Through extensive experiments on four public datasets, we demonstrate the superior performance of IELog in log anomaly detection and highlight the importance of parts in IELog.

References

1. Zhao, N., et al. An empirical investigation of practical log anomaly detection for online service systems. In: Proceedings of the 29th ACM Joint Meeting on European Software Engineering Conference and Symposium on the Foundations of Software Engineering, pp. 1404–1415 (2021)
2. Le, V.-H., Zhang, H.: Log-based anomaly detection without log parsing. In: 2021 36th IEEE/ACM International Conference on Automated Software Engineering (ASE), pp. 492–504. IEEE (2021)
3. Du, M., Li, F., Zheng, G., Srikumar, V.: DeepLog: anomaly detection and diagnosis from system logs through deep learning. In: Proceedings of the 2017 ACM SIGSAC Conference on Computer and Communications Security, pp. 1285–1298 (2017)
4. Xu Zhang, et al.: Robust log-based anomaly detection on unstable log data. In: Proceedings of the 2019 27th ACM Joint Meeting on European Software Engineering Conference and Symposium on the Foundations of Software Engineering, pp. 807–817 (2019)
5. Wan, Y., Liu, Y., Wang, D., Wen, Y.: GLAD-PAW: graph-based log anomaly detection by position aware weighted graph attention network. In: Karlapalem, K., et al. (eds.) PAKDD 2021. LNCS (LNAI), vol. 12712, pp. 66–77. Springer, Cham (2021). https://doi.org/10.1007/978-3-030-75762-5_6
6. Zhang, C., et al.: DeepTraLog: trace-log combined microservice anomaly detection through graph-based deep learning. In: 2022 IEEE/ACM 44th International Conference on Software Engineering (ICSE), pp. 623–634 (2022)
7. Liu, F.T., Ting, K.M., Zhou, Z.-H.: Isolation forest. In: 2008 Eighth IEEE International Conference on Data Mining, pp. 413–422. IEEE (2008)

8. Liang, Y., Zhang, Y., Xiong, H., Sahoo, R.: Failure prediction in IBM bluegene/l event logs. In: Seventh IEEE International Conference on Data Mining (ICDM 2007), pp. 583–588. IEEE (2007)
9. Studiawan, H., Sohel, F., Payne, C.: Anomaly detection in operating system logs with deep learning-based sentiment analysis. IEEE Trans. Dependable Secure Comput. **18**(5), 2136–2148 (2020)
10. Chen, R., et al.: LogTransfer: cross-system log anomaly detection for software systems with transfer learning. In: 2020 IEEE 31st International Symposium on Software Reliability Engineering (ISSRE), pp. 37–47. IEEE (2020)
11. Wang, B., Ying, S., Cheng, G., Li, Y.: A log-based anomaly detection method with the NW ensemble rules. In: 2020 IEEE 20th International Conference on Software Quality, Reliability and Security (QRS), pp. 72–82. IEEE (2020)
12. Pal, A., Kumar, M.: DLME: distributed log mining using ensemble learning for fault prediction. IEEE Syst. J. **13**(4), 3639–3650 (2019)
13. Sun, Z., Song, Q., Zhu, X., Sun, H., Baowen, X., Zhou, Y.: A novel ensemble method for classifying imbalanced data. Pattern Recogn. **48**(5), 1623–1637 (2015)
14. Sun, P., et al.: Context-aware learning for anomaly detection with imbalanced log data. In: 2020 IEEE 22nd International Conference on High Performance Computing and Communications; IEEE 18th International Conference on Smart City; IEEE 6th International Conference on Data Science and Systems (HPCC/SmartCity/DSS), pp. 449–456. IEEE (2020)
15. Wang, B., Ying, S., Cheng, G., Wang, R., Yang, Z., Dong, B.: Log-based anomaly detection with the improved k-nearest neighbor. Int. J. Software Eng. Knowl. Eng. **30**(02), 239–262 (2020)
16. He, P., Zhu, J., Zheng, Z., Lyu, M.R.: Drain: an online log parsing approach with fixed depth tree. In: 2017 IEEE International Conference on Web Services (ICWS), pp. 33–40. IEEE (2017)
17. Pennington, J., Socher, R., Manning, C.D.: Glove: global vectors for word representation. In: Proceedings of the 2014 Conference on Empirical Methods in Natural Language Processing (EMNLP), pp. 1532–1543 (2014)
18. Salton, G., Buckley, C.: Term-weighting approaches in automatic text retrieval. Inf. Process. Manage. **24**(5), 513–523 (1988)
19. Lu, S., Wei, X., Li, Y., Wang, L.: Detecting anomaly in big data system logs using convolutional neural network. In: 2018 IEEE 16th International Conference on Dependable, Autonomic and Secure Computing, 16th International Conference on Pervasive Intelligence and Computing, 4th International Conference on Big Data Intelligence and Computing and Cyber Science and Technology Congress (DASC/PiCom/DataCom/CyberSciTech), pp. 151–158. IEEE (2018)
20. Vuttipittayamongkol, P., Elyan, E., Petrovski, A.: On the class overlap problem in imbalanced data classification. Knowl.-Based Syst. **212**, 106631 (2021)
21. Tomek, I.: Two modifications of CNN (1976)
22. Hartigan, J.A., Wong, M.A.: Algorithm as 136: a k-means clustering algorithm. J. Roy. Stat. Soc.: Ser. C (Appl. Stat.) **28**(1), 100–108 (1979)

23. Chen, X., Liu, S., Zhang, W.: Predicting coding potential of RNA sequences by solving local data imbalance. IEEE/ACM Trans. Comput. Biol. Bioinf. **19**(2), 1075–1083 (2020)
24. Chawla, N.V., Bowyer, K.W., Hall, L.O., Kegelmeyer, W.P.: Smote: synthetic minority over-sampling technique. J. Artif. Intell. Res. **16**, 321–357 (2002)

Be Informed of the Known to Catch the Unknown

Payel Sadhukhan[1(✉)] and Sarbani Palit[2]

[1] Institute for Advancing Intelligence, TCG CREST, Kolkata, India
payel0410@gmail.com

[2] Computer Vision and Pattern Recognition Unit, Indian Statistical Institute, Kolkata, India

Abstract. Many real-world applications are perturbed by the misprediction of the unknown instances into the known or seen domain. The issue is more compounded when we have to recognize the unknowns as well as correctly classify the knowns in a mixed bag of known and unknown instances. In this article, we present a scheme that can efficiently classify instances from the seen classes and can also detect instances coming from unseen (unknown) classes. We have integrated the principles of reverse nearest neighborhood and the principles of intuitionistic fuzzy sets for this purpose. Reverse nearest neighborhood provides a natural and elegant way of tackling the issue of unknown class without incommoding the known class classifications. Further, we incorporate intuitionistic fuzzy sets to infer the unknown class memberships of the instances from the reverse nearest neighbor information of the known classes. Empirical evidence on five real-world datasets indicates the improved efficaciousness of the proposed method over six state-of-the-art competing methods.

Keywords: open set classification · intuitionistic fuzzy · reverse nearest neighborhood · openness

1 Introduction

Since the primal days of the development of machine intelligence, a machine has been taught to efficiently carry out the tasks which it has been 'taught'. However intelligent a machine is, it can only *carry out* a task in which it has been trained. It can rarely have some perception and behave logically in circumstances of which it is uninformed [22]. To develop an automated and self-sufficient system, we must focus on filling this critical gap. In machine learning context, unknown class detection is the detection of unknown (unseen during training) class instances in an open world of known and unknown classes. Fraud detection [5], fingerprint spoof detection [15], impostor detection [10], and genre identification [14] are some domains that constitute a pertinent context for unknown class detection in the real-world domain. To tackle this issue, we need to work on and address unknown class detection. Unknown class detection is different from outlier detection [1], the latter is focused on detecting stray elements of one

F. Liu et al. (Eds.): PRICAI 2023, LNAI 14325, pp. 66–78, 2024.
https://doi.org/10.1007/978-981-99-7019-3_7

given class. Detecting the unknown class is significantly different from anomaly detection also. In anomaly detection [4], one decides whether a test element is an outlier from a given set of known classes. The task of unknown class detection along with the traditional classification of known class instances is termed open set recognition (OSR). The task of open set recognition (OSR) is much more complicated than simply rejecting the uncertain test points. In OSR, one has to correctly classify the known class points besides detecting the unknown instances. In unknown class detection, a significant fraction of points can come from the unseen class/es. In such a scenario, for efficacious performance, one needs to balance and do well in both unknown class detection and known class classification. A scheme addressing this task should be self-contained, and be able to decide what it does not know, more favorably without any human intervention. In recent years, the machine learning community has given considerable attention to this particular aspect. As a result, developments in the domain of open set recognition have been significant in terms of both quantity and quality [6].

In this paper, we propose a novel scheme of simultaneous known class classification and unknown class detection. In the training phase, we will have instances from a certain number of known classes (seen during training). Let that number be c and let us have instances from these particular c classes only at training. During the test phase, the classifier can encounter instances from these c classes or from some other class/es also to which the classifier is not exposed in the training phase. We denote the unknown class by c+1. We may note that there can be more than one unseen class, which we should not know because technically that information should be unknown also. Hence, we consider exactly one unknown class which we consider as $(c+1)$. Hence, at training, we do not have instances from $(c+1)^{th}$ class. The classifier has to correctly classify the instances from the seen c classes and also detect the instances which belong to the unknown class. In our scheme, we integrate two existing techniques to facilitate open set recognition. The two techniques are i]. principles of reverse nearest neighborhood and ii]. principles of intuitionistic fuzzy sets. k-nearest neighborhood of a query point $\mathbf{p}$ identifies the points lying closest to $\mathbf{p}$ as the neighbors of $\mathbf{p}$. On the contrary, following principles of the reverse k-nearest neighborhood (RkNN), the neighbors of $\mathbf{p}$ are those points to whose nearest neighborhood $\mathbf{p}$ lies. We may note that in a search space with cardinality n, the reverse nearest neighbor count of $\mathbf{p}$ can range from 0 to n. Unlike kNN, RkNN possesses an intrinsic capability to handle unknown class detection through its zero neighbor count. The non-zero neighbor count of 1 to n can accommodate the known class classifications. The zero neighborhood property of RkNN gives the backbone for unknown class detection. The other technique of intuitionistic fuzzy technique allows us to have a three-way membership of instances to a certain class. The first two elements are the membership and non-membership of an instance to a particular class. In addition to that, the third component of intuitionistic fuzzy gives a measure of the uncertainty or vagueness of the membership and non-memberships with respect to that class. We associate the zero RkNN count of a test instance with this third element of uncertainty of class membership. This information on the uncertainty of class memberships helps us in detecting unknown class instances. In this work, we do not use the uncertainty in class membership (w.r.t. intuitionistic fuzzy) to fine-tune the known class memberships. In an open world, the presence of unknown class/es primarily accounts for the uncertainty of class membership to a considerable extent. Hence, we use the uncertainty in class membership to resolve the issue of unknown class prediction.

Our technique can be summarized as follows.

- We build an ensemble of three-way decision-making. In each element (classifier) of the ensemble, the first two classes are represented by two random and mutually exclusive partitions of the given known classes. The unknown class (class/es not belonging to either of the first two) accounts for the third component of this three-way decision-making.
- Ensemble size depends on and is proportional to the number of known classes involved.
- Reverse nearest neighborhood coupled with intuitionistic fuzzy principles allow us to make a three-way decision using two known class partitions only.
- Empirical results on five real-world datasets and three metrics manifest the competence of the proposed method over a number of (six) state-of-the-art openset classifiers.

The rest of this article is organized as follows. In the next section, we briefly overview the existing works on Open Set Recognition. In Sect. 3 and Sect. 4, we describe our approach and present the Experimental Setup respectively. In Sect. 5 we demonstrate the results and conclude the paper in Sect. 6.

2 Extant Works

Open set recognition (OSR) in a mixed bag of seen and unseen classes has acquired the interest of the machine learning community for quite some time [13]. The primary reason is the application of this learning in real-world domains. Several diversified techniques have been applied to tackle OSR [13]. [7] implemented unknown class recognition through estimation of the prior probability of the known classes and posterior probabilities for the known as well as unknown classes. One class classifier representing a class through its positive instances has been one of the primal solutions for dealing with the open-world problem. Though it is sufficient to deal with a setup having one known class and the rest as an unknown class, the need for a more refined scheme that can handle more than two known classes along with the unknown is only natural. [19] addressed this issue by implementing open set recognition in the context of two known and the remaining as an unknown class. They modified the conventional SVM for this. Besides drawing a decision boundary separating the two known classes, [19] considers one more hyperplane which separates the unknown class from the known subspace. The learning of the classifier model followed by incorporating Compact Abating Probability (CAP) is another solution. An amalgamation of the extreme value theory and the probabilistic CAP model is implemented in [18] to classify the instances from the known class/es and subsequently recognize the unknowns. CAP model considers decreasing confidence of class membership as one moves away from a known class instance into the unmarked space. Regions beyond a thresholded radius are subsequently categorized as unknown or open space. In [8], a posterior probability estimator is implemented for each training class. A test instance is predicted into a known class only if the maximum probability surpasses the threshold. If none is found, the point is recognized as unknown. Distribution learning of the known classes through Extreme Value Theory (EVT) and incremental learning are incorporated in [16] to implement open set classification. A few recent schemas have incorporated neural networks to recognize samples from unseen classes along with the classification of samples into seen or known classes. Open set recognition through a weightless neural network is used in [3]. In [2], a neural network-based classifier detects the unknown samples through comparison and computation of the similarity between the unknown data and the known or bounded knowledge. A recent scheme uses fake data generated from GAN to identify the rightful training instances [9]. [21] uses latent representations to reconstruct, thereby facilitating the detection of the instances belonging to the unknown class without deteriorating the known-class performance. [12] has tweaked traditional k-NN based classifier to facilitate open set recognition. It has proposed two schemes. In the first variant, an instance is classified as unknown on non-agreement in class labels of its first two neighbors, agreement assigns the instance to its first (as well second) neighbor's class. The second considers the test instance's distance from its two nearest neighbors and calculates their ratio (nearer/ farther). If the ratio is beyond a threshold and the two nearest neighbors are from different classes, the instance is classified as unknown and vice versa. A recent work [17] has used a naive classifier based on reverse nearest neighbor principles to facilitate open set classification.

In recent years, a number of works have explored domain-specific open set classification [11,20].

3 Approach

Open set recognition is the process of simultaneous unknown class detection and known class classification in a mixed bag of known and unknown instances. Regular classification paradigms restrict their choices and predictions within one of the known classes. To achieve a noteworthy performance in the context of open set recognition, we have to devise a scheme that provides an open-ended answer. We integrate the principles of reverse nearest neighborhood and intuitionistic fuzzy for the same.

In a given search space with cardinality n, the reverse nearest neighbor cardinality of a query point $\mathbf{p}$ can be anything between 0 and n. Let us assume that the points in a given search space come from different classes. A query point $\mathbf{p}$ is more similar to the class from which it has the highest number of reverse nearest neighbors. If it does not get any reverse nearest neighbor in the given space, it is probably dissimilar and does not belong to any of the existing (known) classes in the search space. Though reverse nearest neighbor principles provide the fundamental framework for open set recognition, it alone may not be sufficient for an efficacious solution. Reverse nearest neighborhood scores should be indicative of the uncertainty in the known class memberships of the classes. In order to materialize the known class uncertainties into unknown class membership, we involve the principles of intuitionistic fuzzy in our scheme. We describe our approach in the following paragraph.

Dataset Partition: We partition the set of known classes into two non-overlapping sets. Let the training and test sets be denoted by $\mathrm{D_{tr}}$ and $\mathrm{D_{te}}$. We denote the set of known classes (seen classes) with K. $\mathrm{K} = \{1, 2, \ldots, , \mathrm{c}\}$. The unknown class is denoted as $c+1$. We randomly partition K into two sets $\mathrm{K_1}$ and $\mathrm{K_2}$ such that $\mathrm{K_1} \cap \mathrm{K_2} = \phi$. We randomly select $\mathrm{K_1}$ from K such that $|\mathrm{K_1}| = \lceil \mathrm{c}/2 \rceil$ and $\mathrm{K_2} = \mathrm{K} \setminus \mathrm{K_1}$. Hence $|\mathrm{K_2}| = \lfloor \mathrm{c}/2 \rfloor$. It ensures that the size of $\mathrm{K_1}$ and $\mathrm{K_2}$ are equal if the size of K is even, differs by exactly 1 otherwise. So, a class i, $i = 1, 2, \ldots, c$ belongs to any one of $\mathrm{K_1}$ or $\mathrm{K_2}$. **Reverse k-nearest neighbor search**: We perform the Reverse nearest search of a test point, $\mathbf{p}$ in the context of these two class sets $\mathrm{K_1}$ and $\mathrm{K_2}$ and accumulate the results. We obtain the RkNN data of test point $\mathbf{p}$ in context of these two known sets $\mathrm{K_1}$ and $\mathrm{K_2}$. RkNN search is always performed with respect to the neighborhood size, k. Its value has to be determined empirically through parameter optimization.

Integrating RkNN and Intuitionistic Fuzzy Scores: Let the number of RkNNs of $\mathbf{p}$ from $\mathrm{K_1}$ and $\mathrm{K_2}$ be a_1 and a_2 respectively. This signifies that $\mathbf{p}$ has got a_1 neighbors from the classes (seen) belonging to $\mathrm{K_1}$. The same figure with respect to classes belonging to $\mathrm{K_2}$ is a_2.

We obtain the intuitionistic membership scores of $\mathbf{p}$ with respect to individual classes 1, 2, $\ldots$, c+1 from a_1 and a_2. Let $\mu_i(\mathbf{p})$, $\nu_i(\mathbf{p})$ and $\pi_i(\mathbf{p})$ be the intuitionistic membership, non-membership and uncertainty scores of $\mathbf{p}$ with respect to class i. Note that, the unknown class (instances of which are unseen at the training phase) does not have any active component like a_1 or a_2. But that does not prevent us from computing the unknown class scores, which are circumstantially determined from the uncertainty of the known classes, $\pi_i(\mathbf{p})$, $i = 1, 2, \cdots, c$. The number of RkNNs from a class is an indicator of the instance's proximity to that class. If between two classes (known), the instance has more RkNNs from one class than the other, the instance is likely to belong to the former class. $\mu_i(\mathbf{p})$ indicates $\mathbf{p}$'s likelihood of belonging to class i. It is made proportional to the RkNN count of $\mathbf{p}$ from the known class set to which class i belongs. Following the same logic, the non-membership score of class i, $\nu_i(\mathbf{p})$ is made proportional to the RkNN count of the other class.

A positive RkNN count from either (or both of) the known class ensemble/s is indicative of $\mathbf{p}$'s membership to a known class. To do the needful, on getting a positive RkNN count from the known classes ($a_1 + a_2 \neq 0$), we assign 0 to the uncertainty component of the known classes. On the contrary, a zero RkNN count of $\mathbf{p}$ from both $\mathrm{K_1}$ and $\mathrm{K_2}$ indicates positive uncertainty of $\mathbf{p}$'s membership to both known classes $\mathrm{K_1}$ and $\mathrm{K_2}$. We assign 0 to the membership and non-membership scores to both sets of known classes when $a_1 + a_2 = 0$. The technical foundation is—K_1 *and* K_2 *because* **p** *cannot gather any evidence of membership to the component of these two classes.* Consequently, we will have 1 as the uncertainty of both K_1 and K_2.

$$\mu_{\mathrm{i}}(\mathbf{p}) = \begin{cases} \frac{a_1}{a_1+a_2}, & \text{if } \mathrm{i} \in \mathrm{K}_1 \text{ and } a_1 + a_2 \neq 0 \\ \frac{a_2}{a_1+a_2}, & \text{if } \mathrm{i} \in \mathrm{K}_2 \text{ and } a_1 + a_2 \neq 0 \\ 0, & \text{if } a_1 + a_2 = 0 \end{cases}$$

$$\nu_{\mathrm{i}}(\mathbf{p}) = \begin{cases} \frac{a_2}{a_1+a_2}, & \text{if } \mathrm{i} \in \mathrm{K}_1 \text{ and } a_1 + a_2 \neq 0 \\ \frac{a_1}{a_1+a_2}, & \text{if } \mathrm{i} \in \mathrm{K}_2 \text{ and } a_1 + a_2 \neq 0 \\ 0, & \text{if } a_1 + a_2 = 0 \end{cases}$$

Consequently,

$$\pi_{\mathrm{i}}(\mathbf{p}) = 1 - \mu_{\mathrm{i}}(\mathbf{p}) - \nu_{\mathrm{i}}(\mathbf{p})$$

$\pi_{\mathrm{i}}(\mathbf{p})$ denotes the uncertainty associated with the memberships and non memberships of class i. In a similar fashion, we calculate $\mu_{\mathrm{i}}(\mathbf{p})$, $\nu_{\mathrm{i}}(\mathbf{p})$ and $\pi_{\mathrm{i}}(\mathbf{p})$ for all known classes i=1, 2, …, c. Now, we obtain the membership score for the unknown class, $\mu_{\mathrm{c+1}}(\mathbf{p})$ from the uncertainty scores $\pi_{\mathrm{i}}(\mathbf{p})$'s of all the known classes. We compute $\mu_{\mathrm{c+1}}(\mathbf{p})$ as the average of the uncertainty scores from the c known classes. We do not calculate the non-membership $\nu_{\mathrm{c+1}}(\mathbf{p})$ and uncertainty $\pi_{\mathrm{c+1}}(\mathbf{p})$ because $\mu_{\mathrm{c+1}}(\mathbf{p})$ is sufficient for our prediction.

$$\mu_{\mathrm{c+1}}(\mathbf{p}) = \frac{\sum_{i=1}^{c} \pi_{\mathrm{i}}(\mathbf{p})}{c}$$

Classification Performance from the Ensemble: It is interesting to note that the same membership scores will be given to all known classes belonging to a partition. **p** will have same will have same $\mu_{(\cdot)}(\mathbf{p})$ values for classes belonging to K_1 and the same happens for K_2 also. Because of the same $\mathrm{R}_i(\mathbf{p})$ across a number of classes, $\mu_i(\mathbf{p})$ alone gives a lesser discriminating power among the known classes. In order to remedy this, we use an ensemble of such classifiers and accumulate the results. Let the ensemble size be denoted by N. For N times, we randomly partition K set into two sets K_1 and K_2 and repeat the experiment and gather the results. Let $\mathrm{M}_{(\cdot)}(\mathbf{p})$ be the variable where we will accumulate the membership scores from the ensemble of classifiers. Let $\mu_i(\mathbf{p}^n)$ be the $\mu_i(\mathbf{p})$ membership scores of **p** w.r.t. class i at n^{th} classification (n^{th} iteration of the ensemble), $n = 1, 2, \cdots, N$, $i = 1, 2, \cdots, c+1$. (***We compute the membership scores for the individual known classes as well as the unknown class, as we are in the final phase of prediction.)

$$M_{\mathrm{i}}(\mathbf{p}) = \sum_{n=1}^{N} \mu_i(\mathbf{p}^n), \qquad \text{for i=1, 2,} \cdots \text{, c, c+1}$$

To maintain the integrity of the fuzzy membership scores ($0 \leq M_{\mathrm{i}}(\mathbf{p} \leq 1)$, we have to divide $M_{\mathrm{i}}(\mathbf{p})$ by N.

$$M_{\mathrm{i}}(\mathbf{p}) = \frac{M_{\mathrm{i}}(\mathbf{p})}{N}, \qquad \text{for i=1, 2, } \cdots \text{, c, c+1}$$

For the test point $\mathbf{p}$, the memberships values $M_{\text{i}}(\mathbf{p})$, $i = 1, 2, \ldots, c+1$ quantifies $\mathbf{p}$'s association with each known class. Consequently, we classify $\mathbf{p}$ to the class from which it has the highest membership score. Let $\text{Pred}(\mathbf{p})$ be the predicted class of instance $\mathbf{p}$.

$$\text{Pred}(\mathbf{p}) = \arg\max_{i} M_{\text{i}}(\mathbf{p})$$

Hence, our scheme allows a test point $\mathbf{p}$ to be classified into any one of the given known classes or to the unknown class. This decision-making is facilitated without any human or empirical intervention.

Essential Remark on a Limitation of the Scheme and Its Redressal: The proposed scheme involves reverse-nearest neighborhood search and intuitionistic fuzzy principles. For high-dimensional real-world datasets, it is likely to suffer from the curse of dimensionality. So we suggest a reduction in the features using extraction or selection before proceeding with the learning for high-dimensional datasets.

4 Empirical Setup

Datasets: We have employed five real-world datasets to assess the efficacy of the proposed method with respect to *six* state-of-the-art methods in the field of open-set recognition. These datasets are obtained in closed form—that is they do not possess any openness and the class information of all the instances is known. In order to accommodate them for the purpose of open set recognition, we have generated the open version of each dataset following the same protocol as done by [18]. In each dataset, we have kept $\lfloor 50\% \rfloor$ of the total classes as the known set and varied the cardinality of the unknown class set from 1 to $\lceil 0.5 * |\text{total classes}| \rceil$ to vary the openness. A brief description of these datasets is given in Table 1. We believe that openness cannot be quantified because we don't know the unknown. But [19] is a state-of-the-art method in OSR that has proposed a formula for the quantification of openness. The formula is given as follows.

$Openness = 1 - \sqrt[2]{\frac{2*|Training\ classes|}{|Target\ classes| + |Test\ classes|}}$. Target class consists of all the training and test classes as well as the leftover unknown classes that do not participate in the training and testing.

Evaluating Metrics: We have used three metrics, namely—*accuracy, average* F_1 *over known and unknown classes* (AKUF_1) [12] and F_1 *for known classes* to measure the performance of the schemes.

Comparing Methods and Parameter Optimization: We have used six competing methods, namely, *1-vs-set* [19], *WSVM* [18], *PI-SVM* [8], two variants of *Nearest neighbor distance-ratio open set classifier* [12] (OSNN-CV and OSNN-NDR) and *reverse-nearest neighbor based naive open-set classifier* (Naive-RkNN) [17] in the comparative study. The proposed method and each of the

Table 1. Description of datasets. N, f, and C denote the number of instances, features, and the total number of classes respectively. c_k and c_u denote the cardinalities of the known and unknown classes respectively.

Datasets	N	f	C	c_k	c_u
Optdigits	5620	64	10	5	1–5
Penbased	10992	16	10	5	1–5
Segment	2310	19	7	3	1–4
Vehicle	846	18	4	2	1–2
Vowel	990	13	11	5	1–6

comparing methods involve parameters whose values have to be fixed empirically through parameter optimization. The parameter optimization is performed on a validation set that is carved out of the training set. This is done to maintain the integrity of openness for the test dataset. The proposed method involves two parameters, neighborhood search size k and ensemble size N. For each dataset, a single k value is used and it is obtained through parameter-optimization on the training and validation set. Ensemble size N of a dataset is equal to twice the number of known classes present in the dataset. The optimized value of k for a dataset is determined via cross-validation on the training set. We carve out a cross-validation training set, T, and validation set V from the training set $\mathbf{D}_{\text{tr}}$ only. For open set classification, we introduce openness in V following the same protocol as described in the above section. If m is the number of classes in D_{tr}, we fix the known class and unknown class cardinalities at $\lfloor 0.5 \times m \rfloor$ and $\lceil 0.5 \times m \rceil$ respectively.

5 Results and Analysis

We present the performance of the proposed and competing methods in terms of the three evaluating metrics in Tables 2 and 3. We obtained the results for 20 independent runs and reported the mean score. For each of the metrics, the range of scores is between 0 and 1 and the higher the score better is the performance.

Dataset Specific Analysis: In Optdigits, we have considered 5 openness values. Hence, for each method, there are 15 scores (5 opennesses $\times$ 3 metrics). The proposed scheme has delivered the best scores in 13 out of 15 cases. Naive-RkNN has given the best scores on the remaining cases. The cardinality of the unknown classes is same for Penbased dataset, resulting in 15 scores. Similar to the previous case, the proposed method has achieved 14 out of 15 best scores on this dataset and Naive-RkNN has emerged as the best scorer for the remaining case. The superiority of the proposed method prevails on Segment and Vehicle datasets, where it achieves the best scores on 11 out of 12 and 3 out of 4 cases respectively. The performance of the proposed method is slightly subdued in Vowel dataset, where it achieves the best scores in 9 out of 18 cases only. Naive-RkNN has achieved the remaining 9 out of 18 best scores of Vowel dataset.

Table 2. Performance of the methods on three metrics across various opennesses. Results from two datasets – Optdigits and Penbased are given in this table. The background of the best score at each openness is highlighted in blue.

	Proposed method	Naive-RkNN	1-vs-set	WSVM	PI-SVM	OSNN-CV	OSNN-NDR
Optdigits							
	Accuracy						
Unknown class = 1	0.928	0.882	0.164	0.901	0.869	0.878	0.806
Unknown class = 2	0.904	0.880	0.256	0.884	0.793	0.865	0.708
Unknown class = 3	0.904	0.885	0.313	0.876	0.758	0.851	0.631
Unknown class = 4	0.894	0.881	0.424	0.878	0.736	0.843	0.602
Unknown class = 5	0.902	0.884	0.508	0.869	0.678	0.828	0.502
	AKU F_1						
Unknown class = 1	0.879	0.817	0.163	0.825	0.684	0.798	0.446
Unknown class = 2	0.884	0.829	0.208	0.823	0.667	0.794	0.401
Unknown class = 3	0.898	0.854	0.234	0.812	0.638	0.793	0.388
Unknown class = 4	0.892	0.840	0.301	0.822	0.636	0.791	0.360
Unknown class = 5	0.901	0.855	0.318	0.824	0.604	0.789	0.312
	Known F_1						
Unknown class = 1	0.956	0.926	0.005	0.921	0.922	0.924	0.898
Unknown class = 2	0.932	0.919	0.012	0.914	0.896	0.903	0.854
Unknown class = 3	0.924	0.920	0.009	0.906	0.872	0.900	0.802
Unknown class = 4	0.892	0.916	0.004	0.902	0.835	0.891	0.787
Unknown class = 5	0.901	0.918	0.006	0.896	0.797	0.884	0.769
Penbased							
	Accuracy						
Unknown class = 1	0.894	0.832	0.215	0.804	0.812	0.724	0.767
Unknown class = 2	0.865	0.786	0.312	0.795	0.752	0.712	0.688
Unknown class = 3	0.878	0.812	0.385	0.725	0.702	0.701	0.614
Unknown class = 4	0.872	0.732	0.426	0.692	0.682	0.713	0.582
Unknown class = 5	0.838	0.749	0.515	0.694	0.654	0.713	0.567
	AKU F_1						
Unknown class = 1	0.824	0.747	0.208	0.581	0.605	0.618	0.423
Unknown class = 2	0.834	0.689	0.285	0.716	0.562	0.625	0.394
Unknown class = 3	0.867	0.875	0.301	0.625	0.559	0.619	0.385
Unknown class = 4	0.870	0.682	0.336	0.605	0.551	0.634	0.361
Unknown class = 5	0.838	0.701	0.415	0.617	0.534	0.636	0.343
	Known F_1						
Unknown class = 1	0.935	0.902	0.137	0.896	0.904	0.818	0.864
Unknown class = 2	0.905	0.862	0.143	0.880	0.859	0.799	0.830
Unknown class = 3	0.904	0.875	0.126	0.840	0.829	0.776	0.777
Unknown class = 4	0.886	0.812	0.127	0.815	0.814	0.770	0.735
Unknown class = 5	0.844	0.792	0.151	0.805	0.777	0.775	0.714

Evaluating Metric Specific Analysis: Our method has achieved the best *accuracy* score on 17 out of 22 cases (all five datasets and their opennesses taken together). Naive-RkNN has achieved the remaining five best scores (all on Vowel dataset). On $AKUF_1$, the proposed method has emerged as the top scorer in 17

Table 3. Performance of the methods on three metrics across various opennesses. Results from three datasets – Segment, Vehicle, and Vowel are given in this table. The background of the best score at each openness is highlighted in blue.

	Proposed method	Naive-RkNN	1-vs-set	WSVM	PI-SVM	OSNN-CV	OSNN-NDR
Segment							
	Accuracy						
Unknown class = 1	0.885	0.823	0.467	0.752	0.757	0.758	0.734
Unknown class = 2	0.845	0.834	0.579	0.667	0.652	0.669	0.626
Unknown class = 3	0.858	0.829	0.614	0.589	0.578	0.602	0.541
Unknown class = 4	0.929	0.834	0.609	0.550	0.551	0.596	0.487
	AKU F_1						
Unknown class = 1	0.821	0.783	0.354	0.521	0.510	0.615	0.424
Unknown class = 2	0.812	0.804	0.488	0.475	0.572	0.398	402
Unknown class = 3	0.857	0.800	0.531	0.488	0.460	0.584	0.386
Unknown class = 4	0.925	0.801	0.499	0.480	0.462	0.579	0.374
	Known F_1						
Unknown class = 1	0.927	0.886	0.275	0.876	0.879	0.877	0.863
Unknown class = 2	0.875	0.880	0.309	0.789	0.778	0.773	0.752
Unknown class = 3	0.865	0.863	0.316	0.705	0.689	0.693	0.672
Unknown class = 4	0.919	0.851	0.200	0.685	0.680	0.686	0.654
Vehicle							
	Accuracy						
Unknown class = 1	0.626	0.527	0.384	0.521	0.490	0.461	0.407
Unknown class = 2	0.557	0.534	0.447	0.492	0.472	0.504	0.395
	AKU F_1						
Unknown class = 1	0.485	0.511	0.382	0.425	0.447	0.452	0.401
Unknown class = 2	0.545	0.534	0.427	0.446	0.452	0.576	0.403
	Known F_1						
Unknown class = 1	0.754	0.585	0.446	0.684	0.612	0.500	0.389
Unknown class = 2	0.649	0.573	0.400	0.621	0.572	0.465	0.377
Vowel							
	Accuracy						
Unknown class = 1	0.859	0.863	0.616	0.615	0.718	0.201	0.458
Unknown class = 2	0.875	0.862	0.618	0.617	0.669	0.281	0.402
Unknown class = 3	0.829	0.860	0.670	0.666	0.603	0.313	0.388
Unknown class = 4	0.821	0.863	0.689	0.689	0.590	0.438	0.384
Unknown class = 5	0.810	0.862	0.698	0.695	0.576	0.512	0.382
Unknown class = 6	0.809	0.871	0.714	0.710	0.555	0.510	0.362
	AKU F_1						
Unknown class = 1	0.805	0.792	0.560	0.561	0.530	0.200	0.312
Unknown class = 2	0.837	0.805	0.602	0.600	0.528	0.267	0.304
Unknown class = 3	0.807	0.809	0.641	0.638	0.498	0.285	0.289
Unknown class = 4	0.817	0.814	0.662	0.663	0.497	0.341	0.286
Unknown class = 5	0.808	0.813	0.664	0.662	0.491	0.402	0.280
Unknown class = 6	0.804	0.817	0.681	0.679	0.488	0.413	0.279
	Known F_1						
Unknown class = 1	0.874	0.828	0.713	0.714	0.824	0.129	0.620
Unknown class = 2	0.913	0.821	0.698	0.699	0.789	0.146	0.592
Unknown class = 3	0.868	0.800	0.701	0.703	0.757	0.099	0.547
Unknown class = 4	0.826	0.802	0.697	0.696	0.702	0.141	0.538
Unknown class = 5	0.798	0.795	0.690	0.687	0.692	0.143	0.525
Unknown class = 6	0.782	0.789	0.693	0.693	0.685	0.167	0.505

out of 22 cases. The remaining four best scores are obtained by Naive-RkNN—one on Penbased, one on Vehicle, and the remaining three on Vowel. On *Known class* F_1, the proposed method has rendered the top score on 18 out of 22 cases. Naive-RkNN has achieved the remaining four best scores—two on Optdigits, one on Vowel, and one on Segment. These findings manifest the competency of the proposed method in handling both known class classification and unknown class detection under open set constraints.

Robustness: The proposed scheme delivers a fairly constant performance (with respect to the three metrics) across varying opennesses. The change in performance scores of the proposed method is less than 7% across different openness values (on over 90% of the cases). On the contrary, the six competing methods show variations in performance (more than 10% change) across the openness ranges. The second aspect indicates the robustness of the proposed method in tackling different openness values (which is a characteristic of the real world) and maintaining its performance. The proposed method maintains its superiority on datasets with few classes (Vehicle, Segment) and more classes (Optdigits, Penbased).

6 Conclusion

In this paper, we have presented an open-set classifier by integrating the concepts of RkNN and intuitionistic fuzzy principles. RkNN based neighborhood identification coupled with the 3-way decision making of intuitionistic fuzzy aids the task of unknown class detection besides the regular known class classification. A unique attribute of the proposed scheme is its implicit estimation of the sampling window of the training data. The RkNN process adaptively adjusts the class boundaries, depending on the local sparseness of the training data. The outcomes of the empirical study demonstrate the capability of the proposed classifier to efficiently classify the instances belonging to the known class and also the unknown class. The findings of the empirical study demonstrate the capability of the proposed method to withstand varying levels of openness, thereby maintaining its performance. Like any k-nearest neighborhood-based scheme, the proposed scheme has an intrinsic multi-class framework. It is a favorable characteristic for dealing with datasets with a variable number of classes. In this paper, the results of the empirical study on five datasets establish the intrinsic ability of the proposed scheme in addressing open set classification. In future work, we aim to refine the proposed scheme further and also include more datasets (possibly high-dimensional and multi-media data like images) in our study.

References

1. Boukerche, A., Zheng, L., Alfandi, O.: Outlier detection: methods, models, and classification. ACM Comput. Surv. (CSUR) **53**(3), 1–37 (2020)
2. Cardoso, D.O., França, F., Gama, J.: A bounded neural network for open set recognition. In: 2015 International Joint Conference on Neural Networks (IJCNN), pp. 1–7, July 2015
3. Cardoso, D.O., Gama, J.a., França, F.M.: Weightless neural networks for open set recognition. Mach. Learn. **106**(9–10), 1547–1567 (2017)
4. Chandola, V., Banerjee, A., Kumar, V.: Anomaly detection: a survey. ACM Computing Surveys (CSUR) **41**(3), 1–58 (2009)
5. Di Martino, M., Decia, F., Molinelli, J., Fernández, A.: Improving electric fraud detection using class imbalance strategies. In: ICPRAM (2), pp. 135–141 (2012)
6. Geng, C., Huang, S.J., Chen, S.: Recent advances in open set recognition: a survey. IEEE Trans. Pattern Anal. Mach. Intell. **43**(10), 3614–3631 (2020)
7. Gorte, B., Gorte-Kroupnova, N.: Non-parametric classification algorithm with an unknown class. In: Proceedings of International Symposium on Computer Vision - ISCV, pp. 443–448, November 1995
8. Jain, L.P., Scheirer, W.J., Boult, T.E.: Multi-class open set recognition using probability of inclusion. In: Fleet, D., Pajdla, T., Schiele, B., Tuytelaars, T. (eds.) ECCV 2014. LNCS, vol. 8691, pp. 393–409. Springer, Cham (2014). https://doi.org/10.1007/978-3-319-10578-9_26
9. Jo, I., Kim, J., Kang, H., Kim, Y.D., Choi, S.: Open set recognition by regularising classifier with fake data generated by generative adversarial networks. In: 2018 IEEE International Conference on Acoustics, Speech and Signal Processing (ICASSP), pp. 2686–2690. IEEE (2018)
10. Li, F., Wechsler, H.: Open set face recognition using transduction. IEEE Trans. Pattern Anal. Mach. Intell. **27**(11), 1686–1697 (2005)
11. Liu, S., Shi, Q., Zhang, L.: Few-shot hyperspectral image classification with unknown classes using multitask deep learning. IEEE Trans. Geosci. Remote Sens. **59**(6), 5085–5102 (2020)
12. Mendes Júnior, P.R., et al.: Nearest neighbors distance ratio open-set classifier. Mach. Learn. **106**(3), 359–386 (2017)
13. Perera, P., Oza, P., Patel, V.M.: One-class classification: a survey. arXiv preprint arXiv:2101.03064 (2021)
14. Pritsos, D.A., Stamatatos, E.: Open-set classification for automated genre identification. In: Serdyukov, P., et al. (eds.) ECIR 2013. LNCS, vol. 7814, pp. 207–217. Springer, Heidelberg (2013). https://doi.org/10.1007/978-3-642-36973-5_18
15. Rattani, A., Scheirer, W.J., Ross, A.: Open set fingerprint spoof detection across novel fabrication materials. IEEE Trans. Inf. Forensics Secur. **10**(11), 2447–2460 (2015)
16. Rudd, E.M., Jain, L.P., Scheirer, W.J., Boult, T.E.: The extreme value machine. IEEE Trans. Pattern Anal. Mach. Intell. **40**(3), 762–768 (2018)
17. Sadhukhan, P.: Can reverse nearest neighbors perceive unknowns? IEEE Access **8**, 6316–6343 (2020). https://doi.org/10.1109/ACCESS.2019.2963471
18. Scheirer, W.J., Jain, L.P., Boult, T.E.: Probability models for open set recognition. IEEE Trans. Pattern Anal. Mach. Intell. **36**(11) (2014)
19. Scheirer, W., Rocha, A., Sapkota, A., Boult, T.: Toward open set recognition. IEEE Trans. Pattern Anal. Mach. Intell. **35**(7), 1757–1772 (2013)

20. Scherreik, M.D., Rigling, B.D.: Open set recognition for automatic target classification with rejection. IEEE Trans. Aerosp. Electron. Syst. **52**(2), 632–642 (2016)
21. Yoshihashi, R., Shao, W., Kawakami, R., You, S., Iida, M., Naemura, T.: Classification-reconstruction learning for open-set recognition. In: Proceedings of the IEEE/CVF Conference on Computer Vision and Pattern Recognition, pp. 4016–4025 (2019)
22. Zhao, P., Zhang, Y.J., Zhou, Z.H.: Exploratory machine learning with unknown unknowns. In: Proceedings of the AAAI Conference on Artificial Intelligence, vol. 35, pp. 10999–11006 (2021)

Network Structure Embedding Method Based on Role Domain Feature

Liang Ge(✉), Haifeng Li, Yiping Lin, and Junwei Xie

College of Computer Science, Chongqing University, Chongqing 400030, China
{geliang,yplin}@cqu.edu.cn, {lihaifeng,xiejunwei}@stu.cqu.edu.cn

Abstract. Network structure is formed by intricate connections between nodes, exploring and learning the network topological structural features has a profound impact in the field of network representation learning. Role refers to a collection of nodes with similar structural features in the network. So network representation learning that preserves node structure in a low-dimensional vector representation space is also known as role discovery, which focuses on partitioning the network into different sets of roles based on structural features. Although existing methods for network structure embedding have made some progress in role discovery tasks, most of them focus on the local structural features to generate node representations, resulting in the inability to learn multiaspect structural features of roles. Therefore, we propose a network structure embedding model URold, which uses role domain feature to enhance node structure representation capabilities and learn the proximity between roles. We conduct role discovery experiments on six real-world networks, and compare with eight state-of-the-art network structure embedding algorithms. The results show that our method URold achieves the best performance and demonstrates excellent role discovery ability.

Keywords: Network structure embedding · Role domain feature · Role discovery

1 Introduction

There are widespread networks around us, such as social networks, where nodes represent users and edges represent social relationships. The network topological structure is of great research significance. For instance, the interactions between proteins and nucleic acids is beneficial for us to understand biological activities. By constructing graphs based on the structural contexts of target residues and their spatial neighborhood, nucleic-acid-binding residues on proteins can be effectively identified [26].

Network structure embedding(also known as network role discovery) is an important research field in data analysis and mining. There are differences in the structural features of nodes, and role refers to a set of nodes with similar structural features. Community discovery is similar to role discovery, they both

F. Liu et al. (Eds.): PRICAI 2023, LNAI 14325, pp. 79–91, 2024.
https://doi.org/10.1007/978-981-99-7019-3_8

use the equivalence rule to divide the nodes. Community discovery emphasizes the close connection of nodes in the same community [8], while role discovery is to divide the network with equivalent structure, independent of the distance between nodes.

Although some network structure embedding models have made progress in role discovery tasks, they ignore the proximity between the roles represented by the nodes. For example, HORD [21] only learns node structure similarity based on the local structure and high-order features of nodes and the consistency between them, making the node representation unable to find the logical correlation between roles. There are certain differences in the strength of associations between roles in the real world, like the association between students and teachers is stronger than that between students and singers. In view of the shortcomings of the current models, we propose a novel network embedding model to effectively integrate role domain features into role discovery, which can effectively learn the structural embedding representation of nodes. Role domain describes the role probability distribution of nodes in the network.

In this paper, the main contributions of our work can be summarized as follows:

- Improve the representation learning module by introducing deep clustering layer, which can learn global network topological features.
- By considering the role distribution of neighborhood nodes, learning the proximity between different roles.
- We experiment on role discovery tasks in several real-world networks, the results show that our model URold achieves significant improvements compared to other state-of-the-art methods.

The rest of paper is organized as follows: Sect. 2 introduces some mainstream frameworks in network structure embedding. Section 3 introduces the detail of our model URold. Section 4 shows the performance of models in role discovery tasks. Finally, we summarize the paper and propose future research on our work in Sect. 5.

2 Related Work

With the continuous generation of network data, exploring network structure is helpful for us to better explore the hidden important information. Network representation learning develops rapidly. Generally speaking, according to the different ways of learning embedding, the current network structure embedding algorithms can be divided into three categories: based on matrix factorization [10], random walk [1,19], and deep learning [23].

Matrix factorization refers to the generation of node embeddings by decomposing feature matrices or similarity matrices, among which representative algorithms are: GraRep [3] considers the high-order similarity between nodes, and combines the decomposition of high-order adjacency matrix to obtain node embedding. XNetMF [9] uses the singular value decomposition to obtain the final embedding based on the similarity between K-degree vectors. AROPE [29] proposes an embedding algorithm of any order of proximity, which requires less resources for switching between different orders of proximity for different downstream tasks. Lemane [28] trains different proximity for different downstream tasks, which improves the practical application ability of the model.

With the rise of Deepwalk [18] in the field of network embedding, random walk has gradually been introduced into network structure embedding. For example, struct2vec [19] constructs a multi-layer structure graph based on structural similarity, and then uses random walk on it to learn node representation. Node2vec [5] considers the neighborhood and structural similarity of nodes at the same time, using two hyperparameters control the random walk to bias the width search and depth search. Role2vec [1] combines the subgraph obtained by using motif features to establish a connection between the node and its corresponding role attribute.

In order to obtain deeper nonlinear structural features, using deep learning methods for network structure representation has gradually become popular. Among them, SDNE [25] proposed to use supervised and unsupervised models to reconstruct the first-order and second-order neighborhood features. DRNE [23] aims to learn the rule equivalence between nodes, and combine node degree information to learn node embedding. VERSE [22] uses three different node similarities and combines single-layer neural networks for role embedding. GAS [6] uses graph convolutional layers to obtain structural features, and then uses this feature as input information to train graph autoencoders. MSVGAE [7] learns the mixed probability distribution of the original feature space from multiple dimensions, and then obtains node embedding by reconstructing graph features.

The existing network structure embedding algorithms are only suitable for shallow role discovery. The learned embedding representations can only infer the corresponding role categories of nodes, while neglecting to preserve the inherent correlation between roles in the original network. Our model URold is committed to exploring deeper role features, further capturing logical correlation between roles in real-world networks.

3 Methodology

3.1 Notions

In this article, we learn the structural embedding of undirected and unweighted graph G. Generally, we set $G = (V, E)$, where $V = \{v_1, v_2, ..., v_n\}$ is the node set, $E = \{e_1, e_2, ..., e_n\}$ is the edge set, and $n = |V|$ represents the total number of nodes in the network. For node $v_i \in V$, its neighborhood $N_i = \{v_j | (i, j) \in E\}$, the first-order egonet of node v_i is represented as $\xi(v_i)$. The goal of our model is to learn a mapping $M : X \in R^{n \times f} \to Z \in R^{n \times d}$, where X represents the vector space composed of node structural features, Z represents the embedded representation of the network, f represents the dimension of each original node feature, and d represents the embedded dimension.

3.2 Overall Framework

The overall framework of our model URold is shown in Fig. 1. Firstly, the structural features of nodes are extracted from the original network. Then we perform node embedding representation learning. Specifically, we use an autoencoder to reconstruct the initial feature space for reducing the impact of noise. At the same time, unsupervised deep clustering algorithm is used to capture high-order role domain features, and combine node neighborhood features to learn the proximity between roles.

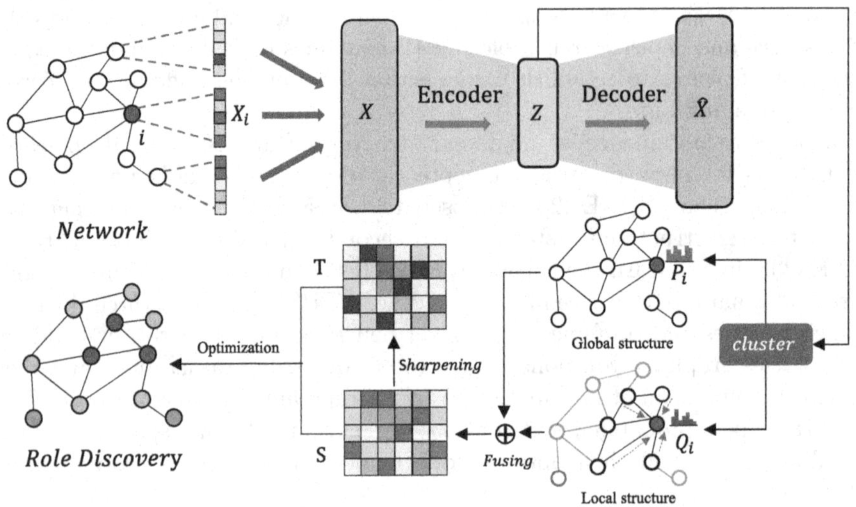

Fig. 1. Illustration of the proposed framework URold.

3.3 Feature Extraction

The adjacency matrix is usually used to describe the network topology, but due to its sparsity, the nodes with similar structural may be far away from each other and have no direct connection. Relying solely on the adjacency matrix is not enough to obtain deeper structural information of nodes, so it is essential to extract high-quality structural features from the original network. Refer to ReFeX [11], we first extract the egonet-based infrastructure feature representation X_a, which contains six variables and is described as follows:

- The number of edges in the egonet of node $v : x_{a_1} = |E_{\xi(v)}|$
- The degree of node $v : x_{a_2} = |N(v)|$
- The sum of node's degree in the egonet of node $v : x_{a_3} = \sum_{u \in \xi(v)} d(u)$
- The proportion of within-egonet edges to all edges within and leaving the egonet of node $v : x_{a_4} = x_{a_1}/x_{a_3}$

- The proportion of non-egonet edges to all edges within and leaving the egonet of node $v : x_{a_5} = (x_{a_3} - x_{a_1})/x_{a_3}$
- The clustering coefficient for node $v : x_{a_6} = 2|T(v)|/(x_{a_2}(x_{a_2} - 1))$

Then we calculate the low-order role domain features X_b to further learn the role features of nodes in the global network. The specific calculation process is as Algorithm 1. In lines 1–2 of Algorithm 1, we normalize X_a and use K-Means algorithm to compute cluster centroids. In lines 3–7, we calculate the distance from each node to all cluster centroids and convert it into probabilities. In line 8, we obtain X_b by weighted aggregate neighborhood role domain features, where $D_{ii} = \sum_j A_{ij}$ represents the degree matrix.

Algorithm 1. Process of extracting low-order role domain features

Input: The network $G = (V, E)$, the adjacency matrix A, the egonet basic structure matrix X_a
Output: The low-order role domain features X_b
1: H_{Norm}= MinMaxNorm(X_a)
2: H_c = KMEANS(H_{Norm})
3: **for** all $u \in V$ **do**
4: $dis(u) = CalcDist(H_{Norm}, H_c)$
5: $X_b(u) = (Max(dis(u))$ - $dis(u))/(Max(dis(u))$ - $Min(dis(u)))$
6: $X_b(u) = X_b(u)/Sum(X_b(u))$
7: **end for**
8: $X_b = D^{-1} AX_b$
9: return X_b

Finally, we use $X_a \circ X_b$ to represent the initial structural features, where $\circ$ represents connection. We define $X_{out} = Rec(X_{in})$ as the aggregation operation, which calculates the sums and means of neighborhood structural features of X_{in}. Specifically, X_{in} represents the initial node features and we use the aggregation result X_{out} to update node features. We compute the feature space X through multiple iterations of aggregation, where $X_{in} = X_a \circ X_b$ in the first iteration, and the input of each subsequent iteration is the output of the previous iteration.

3.4 Representation Learning

Code Reconstruction Layer. We use an autoencoder to further capture the non-linear relationship between node feature representations. We choose the multi-layer perceptron model as the encoder, which is defined as follows:

$$Z_v = f(X_v|W_i, b_i) = f(W_i X_v + b_i) \tag{1}$$

where Z_v represents the embedding of node v, and $f(\cdot)$ represents the activation function, here we choose $tanh(\cdot)$ as the activation function. W_i, b_i are the weight and bias of the ith layer network, respectively. The decoding process is:

$$\hat{X}_v = g(Z_v|\hat{W}_i, \hat{b}_i) = g(\hat{W}_i Z_v + \hat{b}_i) \tag{2}$$

In order to guide the autonomous learning process of the autoencoder, we reconstruct the feature space X as follows:

$$L_r = \min_{\Phi} ||X - \hat{X}||_F^2 \tag{3}$$

where Φ represents the parameters that need to be learned. X contains more zero elements, if only the Eq. (3) is the target optimization function of the autoencoder, our model will focus on learning the zero elements in the feature space. So we make a little change to the objective optimization function as follows:

$$L_r = \min_{\Phi} ||(X - \hat{X}) \odot B||_F^2 \tag{4}$$

where $\odot$ means the Hadamard product, and if $X_{ij} = 0, B_{ij} = 1$, else $B_{ij} = 3$. The reason for this is the reconstruction of non-zero elements in the feature space imposes a greater penalty than zero elements, forcing the model to learn the high-dimensional features of non-zero elements, so that model can capture structural differences between different nodes.

Deep Clustering Layer. Inspired by [2], we introduced the deep clustering loss into role discovery task for learn high-order role domain features. First, we cluster the node representation $z_i \in Z$, and get the centroid representation $\psi \in R^{k \times d}$ in each cluster, where k represents the number of clusters. Then we use the student distribution to calculate the probability distribution P between nodes and cluster in the network:

$$p_{ij} = \frac{(1 + ||z_i - \psi_j||^2)^{-1}}{\sum_j (1 + ||z_i - \psi_j||^2)^{-1}} \tag{5}$$

Then we combine the role distribution of the node neighborhood to learn the proximity features that exist between roles. Specifically, we calculate the role distribution Q of the node's neighborhood:

$$q_{ij} = \frac{|y_{u \in N(v_i)} = l_j|}{\sum_j |y_{u \in N(v_i)} = l_j|} \tag{6}$$

where l_j represents the label corresponding to the cluster centroid ψ_j, and y_u represents the potential label learned by node u. Combining the high-order role domain features P and the neighborhood role distribution Q, that is, $S = P + Q$, and then normalize it to obtain the final node role domain S. In order to improve the cohesion between clusters and the differences among different clusters, we construct the target distribution T by sharpening S to guide the entire model learning process:

$$t_{ij} = \frac{s_{ij}^2 / \sum_i s_{ij}}{\sum_j s_{ij}^2 / \sum_i s_{ij}} \tag{7}$$

By training the network parameters, we use the KL-divergence between S and T to define the optimization objection is:

$$L_a = KL(T||S) = \sum_i \sum_j t_{ij} \log(\frac{t_{ij}}{s_{ij}}) \tag{8}$$

Finally, we use the node degree information to modify the embedding representation [23]. The modification process is expressed as follows:

$$L_d = \sum_{i=1}^{n}(MLP(z_i) - log(d(v_i) + 1)) \tag{9}$$

Among them, we use a multi-layer perceptron to reduce the dimensionality of z_i. In summary, we use L_c to represent the loss of the clustering layer:

$$L_c = L_a + \gamma L_d \tag{10}$$

Training Strategy. The final optimization function of URold is as follows:

$$L = L_r + \beta L_c \tag{11}$$

where L_r represents the loss of the reconstructed feature matrix, and L_c represents the loss of the deep cluster layer. We update the model parameters by backpropagation.

4 Experiments

4.1 Datasets and Baselines

We select several real-world networks as datasets, and list it as follows:

(1) Air-traffic networks [10]: There are three air-traffic networks, including European, Brazilian, and American air-traffic networks (Europe, Brazil, and USA for short). In these networks, nodes represent airports and edges represent existing flights between airports.
(2) Actor co-occurrence network [15]: In the network, nodes represent actors and edges between actors represent their presence in the same wiki page. The labels of the nodes are based on the influence of the actors. We use Actor to represent this network.
(3) English-language movie network [13]: It's a film-director-actor-writer network (Film for short). In the network, nodes represent four types of identities: film, director, actor, and writer.

Table 1 shows the details of the real-world networks, including the number of nodes, edges, classes, transitivity, and density. We choose 8 state-of-the-art role discovery algorithms to compare with our model URold, including GraphWave [4], RDAA [12], RESD [27], Role2vec [1], RolX [10], SEGK [17], ripple2vec [14], struc2vec [19].

Table 1. The statistical information of several real-world networks.

Dataset	Nodes	Edges	Classes	Transitivity	Density (%)
Brazil	131	1,074	4	0.4497	12.613
Europe	399	5,995	4	0.3337	7.5503
USA	1,190	13,599	4	0.4263	1.9222
Actor	7,779	26,733	4	0.0156	0.0888
Film	27,312	122,706	4	0.0278	0.329

4.2 Experiment Settings

In the feature extraction module, we set the number of feature aggregation iterations to 3 and the number of bins to 4. In the representation learning module, the encoder and decoder in the autoencoder have three-layer networks respectively. In the joint optimization objective function of the model, we set $\beta = 0.8$, and $\gamma = 0.7$. During the experiment, we used the default parameters in the corresponding papers when running the baseline method, and the embedding dimension was set to 128 unless otherwise specified. During model training, set epoch to 100 and batchsize to 32.

4.3 Experiments on Role Classification

We use role classification tasks to measure the ability of algorithms to extract structural roles from the network. Specifically, 70% of the embedded representation obtained from model learning is randomly selected as the training set, which is used as input to train a simple linear regression classifier. The remaining 30% of the embedded data is used as the test set. We set up 20 random samples each time and calculate the average of the 20 test results and report their F1-micro(F1 for short) and F1-macro(F2 for short) scores. The results are shown in Table 2. In real-world networks, roles are not isolated, and there are differences in their logical correlations. Learning only the similarity of structural features is not sufficient. It is also necessary to learn the proximity between roles, which is conducive to preserve the logical correlation between roles in embedding representation. From Table 2, our model URold achieves the best scores in five datasets. URold performs most prominently in the Brazil dataset, compared with the second-ranked RESD, the F1 and F2 scores have increased by 5.68% and 6.65% respectively. Both GraphWave and SEGK have memory overflow when embedding Film dataset. The reason is that the former needs to continuously simulate the graph wavelet diffusion process, and the latter needs to calculate a graph kernel matrix containing global node similarity. Role2vec has the lowest F1 and F2 scores of all datasets, indicating that its embedding does not accurately identify the role represented by the node. ripple2vec constructs a context graph with ripple distance to capture neighborhood structure features, and performs better than other baselines in the Film dataset, second only to URold.

Table 2. The results of role classification on five datasets, we report the average F1 and F2 scores from 20 experiments. In the table, OM means that it cannot be calculated in fixed memory, OT means that the result cannot be calculated within 12 h, and the bold fonts indicate best results.

Method	Brazil		Europe		USA		Actor		Film	
	F1	F2	F1	F2	F1	F2	F1	F2	F1	F2
GraphWave	0.758	0.751	0.518	0.488	0.521	0.469	0.472	0.457	OM	OM
RDAA	0.791	0.772	0.459	0.431	0.648	0.638	0.480	0.466	0.499	0.396
RESD	0.792	0.781	0.557	0.545	0.639	0.628	0.471	0.458	0.497	0.405
Role2vec	0.363	0.322	0.358	0.341	0.442	0.438	0.311	0.294	0.308	0.292
RolX	0.746	0.743	0.551	0.543	0.628	0.617	0.467	0.451	0.487	0.383
SEGK	0.723	0.716	0.536	0.524	0.615	0.607	0.479	0.459	OM	OM
ripple2vec	0.755	0.748	0.563	0.553	0.618	0.613	0.470	0.463	0.511	0.391
struc2vec	0.768	0.747	0.578	0.562	0.627	0.614	0.463	0.451	OT	OT
URold	**0.837**	**0.833**	**0.591**	**0.586**	**0.663**	**0.653**	**0.487**	**0.468**	**0.517**	**0.411**

4.4 Visualization

Here we choose Brazil network for the visualization experiment. We use the t-SNE [24] algorithm to project the embedded representation into a two dimensional plane space. The similarity between nodes can be more intuitively observed in low-dimensional space, and closer nodes are more similar. Nodes of the same color indicate that they belong to the same class of roles. The results are shown in Fig. 2. ripple2vec can learn to capture the (dis)similarities of the local neighborhood structures by constructing ripple vectors, but different color node regions are very close together. GraphWave projects linearly in two-dimensional space, but does not make clear distinctions between different roles. Role2vec has the worst visualization effect, with nodes of different colors randomly interlaced together. RESD relies on reconstruction features and neglects to learn more distinguishable structural features, making it difficult to distinguish between green and purple nodes in the graph. RDAA learns the similarity between neighboring nodes, but is not effective in structural similarity. UNRold is a variant of URold that does not consider the distribution of neighborhood roles in deep clustering layers. Although UNRold successfully divides the nodes by color, it ignores the proximity between different colors, such as it is difficult to know which green or yellow node is more similar to blue node. URold can not only partition nodes of different colors, but also learn about the proximity between roles. For example, the green nodes are more closely related to the yellow nodes, but the association between them and the blue is weaker.

4.5 Case Study: Role Discovery

We conduct a case study of role discovery in the Ca-Netscience network [16, 20]. This network is mainly used to describe collaborations between scientists working on network theory and experiments. In the network, nodes represent

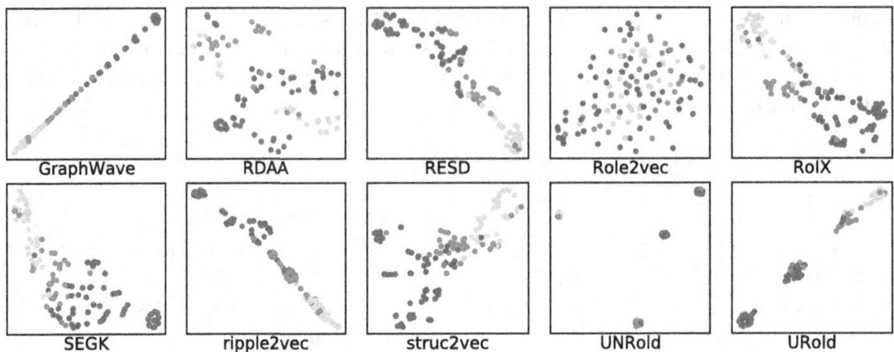

Fig. 2. Visualization of node representations on the Brazil network. (Color figure online)

authors, and edges represent cooperation between nodes. Then we use K-Means algorithm to assign roles by clustering the low dimensional embedding. The role feature learning ability of model is reflected by analyzing whether the embedding reflects the structural similarity. The results are shown in Fig. 3. In order to better observe the experimental results, we use black boxes to select three types of representative nodes in the network, respectively using squares, pentagons and hexagons to represent the real node types. The color of nodes is obtained by embedding through clustering. Role2vec and ripple2vec have the worst role discovery performance, with the former tending to identify neighboring nodes as the same role and the latter being very cluttered, especially with the complete inability to correctly identify roles in complex structures. SEGK and struc2vec correctly identify only three different types of roles in the left part of the black box, indicating that they can only learn shallow structural similarity. Although RESD can recognize both square and pentagon, it is easy to label nodes with the same degree and the same color. RDAA depicts the different dependencies between each node and its neighbors through the role attention mechanism, which makes it easier for nodes in the same neighborhood to be labeled with the same color. While both RolX and URold label the three roles with the correct colors, RolX is unstable, such as assigning multiple colors to star subgraphs across the global network. URold is robust and can also learn the proximity between roles, such as red and blue nodes being more likely to appear together.

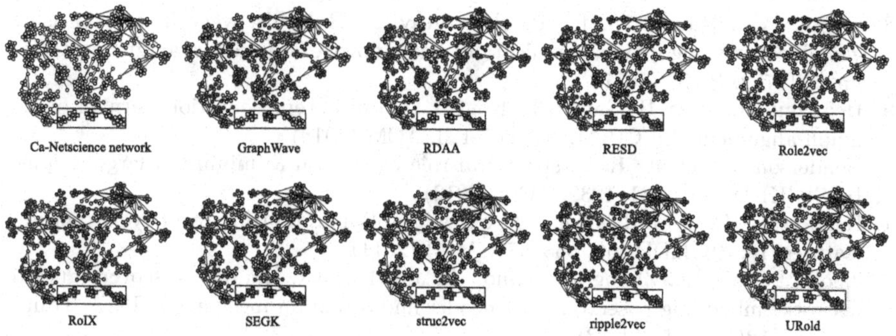

Fig. 3. Case study of role discovery on the Ca-Netscience network.

5 Conclusion and Further Discussion

In this paper, we propose a network structure embedding model URold, which based on role domain features for role discovery. We use the low-order role domain features to enhance the ability of node structural feature representation. We introduce deep clustering algorithm into the representation learning module, which captures the high-order role domain features in the network. In addition, we also consider the distribution of roles in the neighborhood to learn the proximity between roles. The experimental results show that our model URold has achieved excellent results in role discovery tasks such as role classification and visualization. In future work, we will further explore the node structure representation in dynamic graphs.

References

1. Ahmed, N.K., et al.: Role-based graph embeddings. IEEE Trans. Knowl. Data Eng. **34**(5), 2401–2415 (2022)
2. Cai, J., Wang, S., Xu, C., Guo, W.: Unsupervised deep clustering via contractive feature representation and focal loss. Pattern Recogn. **123**, 108386 (2022)
3. Cao, S., Lu, W., Xu, Q.: Grarep: learning graph representations with global structural information. In: Proceedings of the 24th ACM International on Conference on Information and Knowledge Management, vol. 19–23-, pp. 891–900. ACM (2015)
4. Donnat, C., Zitnik, M., Hallac, D., Leskovec, J.: Learning structural node embeddings via diffusion wavelets. In: SIGKDD, pp. 1320–1329. ACM (2018)
5. Grover, A., Leskovec, J.: node2vec: Scalable feature learning for networks. In: Proceedings of the 22nd ACM SIGKDD International Conference on Knowledge Discovery and Data Mining, vol. 13–17-, pp. 855–864. ACM (2016)
6. Guo, X., Zhang, W., Wang, W., Yu, Y., Wang, Y., Jiao, P.: Role-oriented graph auto-encoder guided by structural information. In: DASFAA, vol. 12113, pp. 466–481 (2020)
7. Guo, Z., Wang, F., Yao, K., Liang, J., Wang, Z.: Multi-scale variational graph autoencoder for link prediction. In: WSDM, pp. 334–342 (2022)

8. Gupte, P.V., Ravindran, B., Parthasarathy, S.: Role discovery in graphs using global features: algorithms, applications and a novel evaluation strategy. In: ICDE, pp. 771–782. IEEE (2017)
9. Heimann, M., Shen, H., Safavi, T., Koutra, D.: Regal: representation learning-based graph alignment. In: CIKM, pp. 117–126. ACM (2018)
10. Henderson, K., et al.: Rolx: structural role extraction & mining in large graphs. In: SIGKDD, pp. 1231–1239. ACM (2012)
11. Henderson, K., et al.: It's who you know: graph mining using recursive structural features. In: SIGKDD, pp. 663–671. ACM (2011)
12. Jiao, P., Tian, Q., Zhang, W., Guo, X., Jin, D., Wu, H.: Role discovery-guided network embedding based on autoencoder and attention mechanism. IEEE Trans. Cybern. **53**(1), 1–14 (2023)
13. Leskovec, J., Huttenlocher, D., Kleinberg, J.: Predicting positive and negative links in online social networks. In: Proceedings of the 19th International Conference on World Wide Web. WWW '10, pp. 641–650. Association for Computing Machinery, New York (2010). https://doi.org/10.1145/1772690.1772756
14. Luo, J., Xiao, S., Jiang, S., Gao, H., Xiao, Y.: ripple2vec: Node embedding with ripple distance of structures. Data Sci. Eng. **7**(2), 156–174 (2022)
15. Ma, X., Qin, G., Qiu, Z., Zheng, M., Wang, Z.: Riwalk: fast structural node embedding via role identification. In: ICDM, vol. 2019-, pp. 478–487 (2019)
16. Newman, M.E.J.: Finding community structure in networks using the eigenvectors of matrices. Phys. Rev. E **74**(3), 036104–036104 (2006)
17. Nikolentzos, G., Vazirgiannis, M.: Learning structural node representations using graph kernels. IEEE Trans. Knowl. Data Eng. **33**(5), 2045–2056 (2021)
18. Perozzi, B., Al-Rfou, R., Skiena, S.: Deepwalk: online learning of social representations. In: Proceedings of the 20th ACM SIGKDD International Conference on Knowledge Discovery and Data Mining, pp. 701–710. ACM (2014)
19. Ribeiro, L., Saverese, P., Figueiredo, D.: struc2vec: Learning node representations from structural identity. In: Proceedings of the 23rd ACM SIGKDD International Conference on Knowledge Discovery and Data Mining, vol. 129685, pp. 385–394. ACM (2017)
20. Rossi, R.A., Ahmed, N.K.: The network data repository with interactive graph analytics and visualization. In: Proceedings of the National Conference on Artificial Intelligence, vol. 6, pp. 4292–4293 (2015)
21. Tian, Q., Zhang, W., Jiao, P., Zhong, K., Wu, N., Pan, L.: Integrating higher-order features for structural role discovery. In: LNICST, vol. 451, pp. 244–258 (2022)
22. Tsitsulin, A., Mottin, D., Karras, P., Müller, E.: Verse: versatile graph embeddings from similarity measures. In: WWW, pp. 539–548 (2018)
23. Tu, K., Cui, P., Wang, X., Yu, P., Zhu, W.: Deep recursive network embedding with regular equivalence. In: KDD, pp. 2357–2366. ACM (2018)
24. Van Der Maaten, L., Hinton, G.: Visualizing data using t-SNE. J. Mach. Learn. Res. **9**, 2579–2625 (2008)
25. Wang, D., Cui, P., Zhu, W.: Structural deep network embedding. In: Proceedings of the 22nd ACM SIGKDD International Conference on Knowledge Discovery and Data Mining, vol. 13–17-, pp. 1225–1234. ACM (2016)
26. Xia, Y., Xia, C.Q., Pan, X., Shen, H.B.: Graphbind: protein structural context embedded rules learned by hierarchical graph neural networks for recognizing nucleic-acid-binding residues. Nucleic Acids Res. **49**(9), e51–e51 (2021)
27. Zhang, W., Guo, X., Wang, W., Tian, Q., Pan, L., Jiao, P.: Role-based network embedding via structural features reconstruction with degree-regularized constraint. Knowl.-Based Syst. **218**, 106872 (2021)

28. Zhang, X., Xie, K., Wang, S., Huang, Z.: Learning based proximity matrix factorization for node embedding. In: SIGKDD, pp. 2243–2253 (2021)
29. Zhang, Z., Cui, P., Wang, X., Pei, J., Yao, X., Zhu, W.: Arbitrary-order proximity preserved network embedding. In: SIGKDD, pp. 2778–2786. ACM (2018)

Machine Learning-Driven Reactor Pressure Vessel Embrittlement Prediction Model

Pin Jin[1], Liang Chen[1(✉)], Haopeng Chen[2(✉)], Lingti Kong[3], and Zhengcao Li[4]

[1] SJTU Paris Elite Institute of Technology, Shanghai Jiao Tong University, Shanghai 200240, China
{liang.chen,18858594080}@sjtu.edu.cn

[2] School of Software, Shanghai Jiao Tong University, Shanghai 200240, China
chen-hp@sjtu.edu.cn

[3] School of Materials Science and Engineering, Shanghai Jiao Tong University, Shanghai 200240, China
konglt@sjtu.edu.cn

[4] School of Materials Science and Engineering, Tsinghua University, Beijing 100084, China
zcli@tsinghua.edu.cn

Abstract. The application of machine learning in the nuclear field has been considered for the prediction of neutron irradiation embrittlement of reactor pressure vessel (RPV) steels in recent years. In this study, the RPV irradiation surveillance data are summarized and the integration of physical mechanisms with machine learning is investigated. It is found that the experimental results of the fusion model outperform the single machine learning models or physics formulas. In addition, the data amount of the RPV dataset is enhanced using the variational auto-encoder (VAE) model. Then a combined model of VAE and physical formula guided multilayer perceptron (VPMLP) is proposed, and its advantages in terms of prediction accuracy and generalization ability are experimentally demonstrated.

Keywords: Reactor pressure vessel · Irradiation embrittlement prediction · Multilayer perceptron · Physical mechanisms · Data enhancement

1 Introduction

Machine learning has been receiving increasing attention from researchers related to engineering, including the nuclear field for its powerful ability to analyze the intrinsic connections between data [9]. Nuclear reactor pressure vessel (RPV)

This work was supported by National Natural Science Foundation of China (No. 12205188), Natural Science Foundation of Shanghai (No. 22ZR1428700), and China National Nuclear Corporation (No. CNNC-LCKY-202236).

F. Liu et al. (Eds.): PRICAI 2023, LNAI 14325, pp. 92–97, 2024.
https://doi.org/10.1007/978-981-99-7019-3_9

is one of the most important safety barriers in light-water reactors [11], and its neutron irradiation embrittlement is of crucial concern for the safe long-term operation of reactors [7]. Therefore, it's imperative to develop an accurate prediction model for the irradiation embrittlement of RPV steels.

Since the 1980s, based on a gradual understanding of physical mechanisms, RPV embrittlement prediction models have been largely developed, such as FIS/FIM [1], JEAC4201-2007 [10], EONY [2], and ASTM E900-15 [5]. Machine learning is now emerging as a new approach for the prediction. Morgan et al. [8] pioneered the use of Gaussian kernel ridge regression to investigate the IVAR+ dataset. Diego Ferreño et al. [3] selected the best-performing gradient boosting model. Kirk et al. [6] combined a K-nearest neighbor model with empirical equation parameters. Tang et al. [4] constructed a neural network model. Xu et al. [12] used the XGBoost method to construct a prediction model.

However, decades of research on the traditional embrittlement prediction formulas developed with physical mechanisms have not been combined with machine learning. To tackle this issue, a combined model of variational auto-encoder and physical formula guided multilayer perceptron (VPMLP) is proposed in this work. To verify its effectiveness, the proposed model and several typical models are experimented on the RPV irradiation surveillance dataset. The experiments show that the proposed model produces more accurate results and obtains an improvement in the generalization ability.

The rest of this paper is organized as follows. In Sect. 2, the proposed model and its components are described. Experimental results and analysis are presented in Sect. 3. Finally, conclusions are drawn in Sect. 4.

2 Methodology

2.1 Proposed VPMLP Model

The structure of the proposed model is shown in Fig. 1. The VAE model is first fit with the original data to generate new valid data. The newly generated data are mixed with the original dataset to increase the training volume, and the prediction effect is compared and analyzed using a physical formula guided multilayer perceptron.

2.2 Framework of VAE Model

In order to investigate whether the VAE can play a role in supplementing additional data, we construct a VAE generation model applicable to the dataset in this study, as shown in Fig. 1. We choose 15-dimensional input vectors, including reactor type, product form, material composition, and irradiation condition for the RPV steels. The selection of these variables is consistent with the traditional embrittlement prediction formulas. Based on the basic symmetry, we set the number of hidden layers and the number of neurons for the encoder and decoder to be the same. The single hidden layer structure is adopted for its

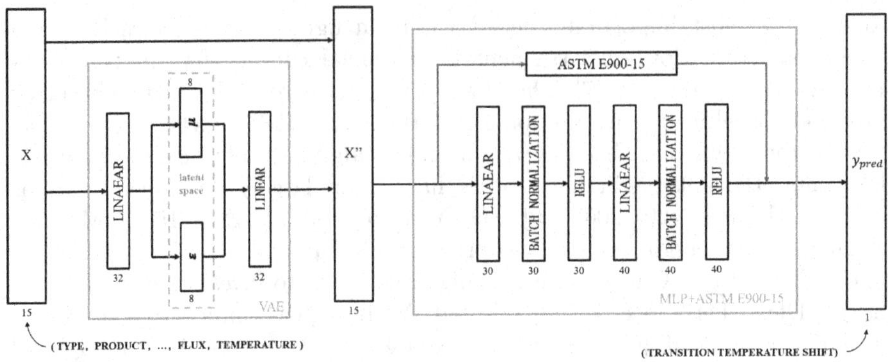

Fig. 1. Schematic diagram of the structure of our proposed VPMLP model.

faster convergence. By means of grid search, the final hyperparameters of the model are set to Batch Size 16, number of neurons in the linear hidden layer 32, potential space dimension 8, and activation function sigmoid.

2.3 Physical Formula Guided Multilayer Perceptron

The 15-dimensional input vector is chosen as in the VAE model. The output vector of the model is set to a one-dimensional ductile-to-brittle transition temperature shift (TTS) which represents the degree of irradiation embrittlement of RPV steels. The Batch Normalization layer speeds up the training process and normalizes the weights. Too deep MLP networks tend to lead to more serious overfitting, thus the two linear hidden layers achieve a relative balance between the training speed, prediction performance, and generalization ability of the model. The remaining hyperparameters are selected by grid search: RELU activation function, Adam optimizer, L2 regularization factor of 0.1, and number of neurons 30 and 40, respectively.

To better integrate the physical formula with machine learning, through experimental analysis, we choose to fuse the ASTM E900-15 model with the multilayer perceptron by combining the loss function. We first choose squared loss as the loss function: $J_{MSE} = \frac{1}{N}\sum_{i=1}^{N}(y_i - g(x_i;\theta))^2$. And we use the L2 regular term to mitigate overfitting, based on the premise of computational efficiency, where $L2 = \alpha\sum_{j=1}^{n} w_j^2$. The current objective function takes the following form: $L(\theta) = \frac{1}{N}\sum_{i=1}^{N}(y_i - g(x_i;\theta))^2 + \alpha\sum_{j=1}^{n} w_j^2$. Similarly, we pass the constraints of the physical formula to the model by adding a "physical formula regular term". The formula of ASTM E900-15 can be essentially reduced to a multivariate function, i.e., there is a corresponding function f with material type t, alloy chemical composition (Cu, Ni, Mn, P), neutron flux ϕ and irradiation temperature T as variables, while satisfying: $f(t, Cu, Ni, Mn, P, \phi, T) = 0$. The corresponding regularization term R_{phy} for one sample can be expressed as: $R_{phy}(t, Cu, Ni, Mn, P, \phi, T) = \lambda f^2(t, Cu, Ni, Mn, P, \phi, T)$. Adding this physical term results in an objective function of the following form: $Loss = J_{MSE} + L2 + R_{phy}$, whose specific expression is: $L(\theta, \alpha, \lambda) = \frac{1}{N}\sum_{i=1}^{N}(y_i - g(x_i;\theta))^2 + \alpha\sum_{j=1}^{n} w_j^2 + \lambda\sum_{k=1}^{N} f^2((t, Cu, Ni, Mn, P, \phi, T)_k)$, where θ denotes the hyperparameters of the model; α and λ denote the regularization coefficients; N denotes the number of samples; y_i and x_i denote the label and characteristics of the ith sample, respectively, where some of the dimensional characteristics in x_i contain the parameters required for the physical formula of $t, Cu, Ni, Mn, P, \phi, T$; w_j is the weight of the fitting process; g denotes the multiple regression function fitted by the model. The predictive performance of the model after incorporating the physical formulations is higher than the baselines, as demonstrated by the final experiments, which are described in Sect. 3.2.

3 Experiments

3.1 Dataset, Evaluation Metrics and Baselines

Dataset. The RPV irradiation surveillance dataset achieves a total of about 1800 data. Based on statistical analysis, the structure of the dataset is highly heterogeneous, caused by the design specifications of RPV steels and reactors.

Evaluation Metrics. The coefficient of determination (R^2), root mean square error (RMSE), and mean absolute error (MAE) are adopted to evaluate the prediction performance. R^2 is defined as the ratio of the dispersion between predicted and true values. The RMSE and MAE are used to measure the difference between the prediction and their true values. Here, the higher value of R^2 and the lower values of RMSE and MAE indicate the better model prediction accuracy.

Baselines. Two advanced methods are selected as the baselines to compare with our proposed model. The first one is EONY [2], which is incorporated in current U.S. NRC Regulations on Pressurized Thermal Shock. The second one is RPV-GB [3], a gradient boosting model developed by Ferreño et al.

3.2 Experimental Results

For the accurate prediction of the RPV embrittlement, in addition to the fit of the overall data, the extrapolation capability from the low-fluence irradiation data to the high-fluence irradiation prediction requires consideration, which is because the main cause of RPV embrittlement at the end of service is the accumulation of large amounts of neutron irradiation.

Table 1 shows the performance of all experiment models. Our method outperforms all baselines in all cases except on the high-fluence test set, where the prediction accuracy is lower than ASTM E900-15. It can be seen that all models show some prediction performance degradation in the high-fluence region. The degradation is relatively small for ASTM E900-15 and EONY, while it's much larger for the model containing machine learning, which proves that the

Table 1. Prediction evaluation results. The best results are in **bold**.

Model	Test Set			High Fluence Test Set		
	R^2	RMSE(°C)	MAE(°C)	R^2	RMSE(°C)	MAE(°C)
E900-15	0.7981	13.96	10.9	**0.6827**	**15.96**	**13.6**
MLP	0.831	13.33	9.98	0.5095	23.73	19.91
MLP + E900-15	**0.8391**	**13.02**	**9.57**	0.6178	19.25	16.86
EONY	0.4603	23.34	20.06	0.3202	26.46	22.94
RPV-GB	0.7948	14.69	10.71	0.5215	23.38	19.29

two physical formulas have stronger generalization ability. In addition, the fusion model of E900-15 and MLP actually improves the prediction accuracy compared to the single MLP or GB model, suggesting that incorporating suitable physical formula into machine learning can improve the prediction ability of the models even under high neutron fluence conditions. Considering the test metrics of these models together, it can be seen that the integrated model fusing physical formula and machine learning can achieve a balance between the prediction accuracy and the extrapolation ability to high-fluence region.

Table 2. Prediction evaluation results. The best results are in **bold**.

New Data Percentage(%)		0	5	10	15	20	25	30	35	40	45
Train Set	R^2	**0.827**	0.726	0.686	0.607	0.501	0.458	0.397	0.344	0.356	0.280
	RMSE(°C)	**11.82**	18.53	19.20	24.28	28.66	32.33	35.85	39.52	41.49	43.89
	MAE(°C)	**9.15**	11.76	12.81	14.02	16.16	18.30	20.13	22.10	23.63	25.14
Test Set	R^2	0.839	**0.846**	0.825	0.804	0.756	0.693	0.645	0.589	0.516	0.413
	RMSE(°C)	13.02	**12.64**	13.33	14.04	15.68	17.51	18.78	20.27	21.95	24.15
	MAE(°C)	9.57	**9.35**	9.81	10.42	11.78	12.81	13.90	14.69	15.96	17.46

Table 2 shows the change in the evaluation metrics of the fusion model on the dataset as new data generated by VAE model is added. It is found that the prediction effectiveness of the model generally shows a decreasing trend with the gradual increase of new data. However, it should be noted that when the new data occupies 5% of the original volume, the model has a better prediction on the test set for all three metrics, R^2, RMSE, and MAE. This indicates that the newly generated data effectively complement the original dataset in the sparse part and improve the prediction accuracy. Nuclear power data are relatively scarce. The experimental results demonstrate the potential of data enhancement through VAE modeling in this field.

4 Conclusion

In this paper, a combined model of variational auto-encoder and physical formula guided multilayer perceptron (VPMLP) is proposed for the prediction of

RPV neutron irradiation embrittlement. The fused physical formula enables the neural network to better utilize the physical information for prediction, and the model can alleviate the problem of insufficient training data for RPV embrittlement prediction and improve the prediction accuracy. The experimental results demonstrate the advantages of the proposed VPMLP model in terms of prediction accuracy and generalization ability.

References

1. Brillaud, C., Hedin, F., Houssin, B.: A comparison between French surveillance program results and predictions of irradiation embrittlement. In: Stoller, R.E., Garner, F.A., Henager, C.H., Iagata, N. (eds.) Effects of Radiation on Materials: 13th International Symposium, ASTM STP 956, Philadelphia, PA, pp. 420–447. American Society for Testing and Materials (1987)
2. Eason, E.D., Odette, G.R., Nanstad, R.K., et al.: A physically-based correlation of irradiation-induced transition temperature shifts for RPV steels. J. Nucl. Mater. **433**(1–3), 240–254 (2013)
3. Ferreño, D., Serrano, M., Kirk, M., et al.: Prediction of the transition-temperature shift using machine learning algorithms and the plotter database. Metals **12**(2), 186 (2022)
4. Jing, K., Kai, S., Xiaoxi, M., et al.: Research on prediction model of irradiation embrittlement of RPV materials based on artificial neural network. Nucl. Power Eng. **41**(6), 92–95 (2020)
5. Kirk, M.: Summary of work to develop the transition temperature shift equation used in ASTM standard guide e900–15. In: International Review of Nuclear Reactor Pressure Vessel Surveillance Programs, West Conshohocken, PA, pp. 432–456. ASTM International (2018)
6. Kirk, M., Hashimoto, Y., Nomoto, A.: Application of a machine learning approach based on nearest neighbors to extract embrittlement trends from RPV surveillance data. J. Nucl. Mater. **568**, 153886 (2022)
7. Kolluri, M., Martin, O., Naziris, F., et al.: Structural materias research on parameters influencing the material properties of RPV steels for safe long-term operation of PWR NPPs. Nucl. Eng. Des. **406**, 112236 (2023)
8. Liu, Y.C., Wu, H., Mayeshiba, T., et al.: Machine learning predictions of irradiation embrittlement in reactor pressure vessel steels. NPJ Comput. Mater. **8**(1), 85 (2022)
9. Montáns, F.J., Chinesta, F., Gómez-Bombarelli, R., et al.: Data-driven modeling and learning in science and engineering. Comptes Rendus Mécanique **347**(11), 845–855 (2019)
10. Soneda, N., Nomoto, A.: Characteristics of the new embrittlement correlation method for the Japanese reactor pressure vessel steels. J. Eng. Gas Turbines Power **132**(10), 102918 (2010)
11. Wang, H., Villanueva, W., Chen, Y., et al.: Thermo-mechanical behavior of an ablated reactor pressure vessel wall in a nordic BWR under in-vessel core melt retention. Nucl. Eng. Des. **379**, 111196 (2021)
12. Xu, C., Liu, X., Wang, H., et al.: A study of predicting irradiation-induced transition temperature shift for RPV steels with xgboost modeling. Nucl. Eng. Technol. **53**(8), 2610–2615 (2021)

Mitigating Misinformation Spreading in Social Networks via Edge Blocking

Ahad N. Zehmakan[1] and Khushvind Maurya[2(✉)]

[1] The Australian National University, Canberra, Australia
ahadn.zehmakan@anu.edu.au

[2] Indian Institute of Technology (IIT) Delhi, New Delhi, India
khushvind.iitd@gmail.com

Abstract. We study the problem of mitigating the spread of misinformation in social networks, simulated by the Independent Cascade model. We propose an intuitive community-based algorithm, which aims to detect well-connected communities in the network and disconnect the inter-community edges. Our experiments on real-world social networks demonstrate that the proposed algorithm significantly outperforms the prior methods, which mostly rely on centrality measures.

1 Introduction

The widespread adoption of social media platforms has undeniably resulted in a significant increase in the dissemination of misinformation. This issue permeates various domains such as politics, economics, and sociology [5].

One commonly employed strategy to contain the misinformation spreading is edge blocking. Blocking an edge implies that the connection between the two nodes connected by the edge is suspended, for example by not exposing posts from one user to another. Edge blocking has garnered greater attention recently (in comparison to node blocking), cf. [21,22], since it is less intrusive and provides controlling power in a more granular level.

In the present work, we focus on designing an effective and efficient source-agnostic edge-blocking strategy. To model the spread of misinformation, we exploit the popular Independent Cascade model [9]. We investigate the problem of minimizing the expected number of nodes that will be exposed to a piece of misinformation when we are allowed to block k edges for some given integer k.

We propose a community-based algorithm, which partitions the nodes into communities. Then, we try to slow down the flow of misinformation between these communities by disconnecting the inter-community edges. We provide our experimental findings on several real-world graph data. We observe that our proposed algorithm significantly outperforms the existing algorithms.

An extended version of this paper can be found in [23].

F. Liu et al. (Eds.): PRICAI 2023, LNAI 14325, pp. 98–103, 2024.
https://doi.org/10.1007/978-981-99-7019-3_10

1.1 Preliminaries

Graph Definitions. Let $G = (V, E, \omega)$ be a weighted graph, where function $\omega : E \rightarrow [0, 1]$ assigns a value between 0 and 1 to each edge in the graph. Let us define $n := |V|$ and $m := |E|$. For a node $v \in V$, $N(v) := \{v' \in V : (v, v') \in E\}$ is the *neighborhood* of v. Furthermore, $\hat{N}(v) := N(v) \cup \{v\}$ is the *closed neighborhood* of v. Let $d(v) := |N(v)|$ be the *degree* of v in G. The *girth* of a graph G is the length of the shortest cycle contained in the graph. If G has no cycle, then the girth is defined to be infinity.

Independent Cascade Model [6,9]**.** Each node can have one of the following three states: *Ignorant (white)*: a node which has not heard of the misinformation, *Spreader (red)*: a spreader is a node who has heard the misinformation and spreads it, *Stifler (orange)*: a node who has heard the misinformation but does not spread it. Let a coloring $\mathcal{C}$ be a function $\mathcal{C} : V \rightarrow \{w, r, o\}$, where w, r, and o correspond to white, red, and orange, respectively. The process starts from an initial coloring $\mathcal{C}_0$. Then, in each round $t \in N$, all nodes simultaneously update their state according to following updating rules: (i) a white node v becomes red with probability $p^*(v) := 1 - \prod_{v' \in N(v) \& \mathcal{C}_{t-1}(v') = r} (1 - \omega((v, v')))$, (ii) a red node becomes orange, (iii) an orange node remains orange.

1.2 Prior Work

The countermeasure of edge blocking has gained significant popularity, cf. [14, 18, 21, 22]. Kimura et al. [13] introduced a method of efficiently estimating the influence of nodes using bond percolation. This bond percolation method then was used in [11,12] to identify a set of edges which, when blocked, maximize the contamination degree of the network. Yan et al. [19] proposed a greedy method to identify the most critical edges among a set of candidate edges to minimize the spread of a misinformation. Pagerank centrality [2] is used in [19] as a criterion for blocking the edges to minimize the spread of misinformation. The susceptibility of a graph to diffusion is defined in [10] as the sum of the expected influence of each node when it is the single source for a cascade. Further, a greedy method is proposed that minimizes the spread susceptibility of the network. Finally, Zareie and Sakellariou [22] took into account additional features of edges (beyond centrality), such as entropy, to determine what edges to block. Some more results on edge blocking problems are discussed in, [3,20].

2 Proposed Algorithm

We rely on Louvain community detection algorithm [1]. It is used by our algorithm to first find a set of communities such that the number of inter-community edges is at most k, the budget for the number of edges to be blocked. Then, we simply block all these edges. The Louvain algorithm receives a graph G and a resolution parameter r. The value of r controls the number of communities (and consequently, the number of inter-community edges) the algorithm will output. Our goal is to generate a set of communities such that the number of inter-community edges is smaller than k but as close as possible to it.

To achieve this, we employ a multi-step process, which is described in Algorithm 1. This essentially follows a hit-and-trial process by updating the resolution parameter. In addition to graph G and budget k, it also receives an initial resolution parameter r, two repetition parameters h_1 and h_2, and an increasing factor $f > 1$. It initially sets $S = \emptyset$ and $count = 0$. Then, it runs in a **while** loop until *count* is larger than the number of repetitions h_1. Inside this, it first runs a **for** loop for h_2 times. Each time, it runs the Louvain algorithm and finds the inter-community edges. Then, for each of these edge sets $\mathcal{E}$, if the size of $\mathcal{E}$ is smaller than k, but larger than current S, then we update $S = \mathcal{E}$. This way, the size of S gets closer to the budget k, but it does not exceed it. Note that we run the **for** loop h_2 times, since the Louvain algorithm is nondeterministic. Once the **for** loop is over, we update the resolution factor to $r = r * f$, where f is the increasing factor. Furthermore, if $|\mathcal{E}| > k$, we increment *count*. Note that at the beginning, *count* might remain zero until r is large enough such that $\mathcal{E}$ (the number of inter-community edges) becomes large. Then, *count* will increase until it exceeds h_1 and then the **while** loop is over. We then return the set S.

Algorithm 1 Pseudocode for our proposed algorithm

Input: $G(V, E, \omega)$, r, Increasing Factor f, Repetitions h_1 and h_2, and Budget k
Output: Set of edges S of size at most k to be blocked.

```
procedure ALGORITHM(G, r, f, h1, h2, k)
    S = ∅
    count = 0
    while (count <= h1) do
        for i from 1 to h2 do
            C = set of communities returned by the Louvain algorithm for G, r
            ℰ = set of inter-community edges for C
            if |ℰ| > |S| and |ℰ| <= k then
                S = ℰ
            end if
        end for
        update r = r * f
        if |ℰ| > k then
            count++
        end if
    end while
    return S
end procedure
```

3 Evaluation

Social Networks. For our experiments, we use three subgraphs of Facebook, namely Facebook from SNAP dataset [15] and Facebook-Politician and Facebook-Govt from Network Repository [17].

Edge Weights. Most real-world networks are unweighted, and one needs to introduce a meaningful procedure for weight assignment. There is a strong correlation between the number of shared friends of two individuals and their level of communication [7,16]. Therefore, we assign the edge weights according to the Jaccard index [8] in our set-up. More precisely, for each edge $(v, u) \in E$, we set $\omega((v, u)) = \frac{|\hat{N}(v) \cap \hat{N}(u)|}{N(v) \cup N(v)}$. We use $|\hat{N}(v) \cap \hat{N}(u)|$ instead of $|N(v) \cap N(u)|$ in the numerator to ensure that the weight of an edge is never equal to zero.

Some of the prior algorithms that we discuss in Sect. 3.1 rely on a measure of distance between two nodes. Since the edge weights represent the strength of the relations, it is conventional to use their "opposite" form when calculating distance. More precisely, for an edge (v, u), we use $1 - \omega((v, u))$.

Algorithm Parameters. For our algorithm, as discussed in Sect. 2, we need to set the initial resolution parameter r, the repetitions h_1 and h_2, and increasing factor $f > 1$. In our experiments, we set $r = 0.01$ for Facebook and Facebook-Politician and $r = 0.05$ for Facebook-Govt, $f = 1.05$, and $h_1 = h_2 = 5$. Note that the closer f is to 1 and the larger h_1 and h_2 are, the more precise our algorithm would be. There is nothing specifically unique about these choices. They are just some reasonable choices that allow our algorithm to perform well on the datasets used, as will be discussed in Sect. 3.1.

Containment Factor. To measure the effectiveness of an edge blocking algorithm that blocks edges in a set S, we rely on *containment factor* $cf = 100 \cdot \frac{\phi(G(V,E,\omega),R) - \phi(G(V,E \setminus S,\omega),R)}{\phi(G(V,E,\omega),R)}$.

Here $\phi(G(V, E, \omega), R)$ and $\phi(G(V, E \setminus S, \omega), R)$ denote the expected final number of orange nodes (when initially nodes in R are red) before and after blocking edges in S. (Note that we focus on orange nodes, since all red nodes eventually become orange.) Thus, $\phi(G(V, E, \omega), R)$ is the number of nodes that become orange before blocking any edges, and cf measures what percentage of them will remain white once edges in S are blocked. To be consistent with prior work, cf. [22], we use cf in our evaluations to compare the algorithms.

3.1 Comparison of Algorithms

We compare our proposed algorithm against algorithms from prior work.

- **RNDM:** A set of edges is randomly selected to be blocked.
- **HWT:** Edges with the largest weight are blocked.
- **DEG** [9,19]**:** The edges for which the sum of the degree of their two endpoints are the largest are blocked.
- **WDEG:** This is the same as DEG, except the weighted degrees (the sum of the weight of adjacent edges for each node) are considered.
- **CLO:** The edges for which the sum of the closeness of their two endpoints are the largest are blocked.

- **WCLO:** This is the same as CLO, except the edge weights (their "opposite" actually, as explained) are considered when calculating closeness.
- **BET** [4]**:** The edges with the highest betweenness centrality are blocked.
- **WBET:** The edges with the highest weighted betweenness are blocked.
- **PGRK** [2,19]**:** The edges for which the sum of the PageRank centrality of their two endpoints are the largest are blocked.
- **IEED** [22]**:** In each iteration, a "critical" edge is determined and blocked from the network. Criticality is determined using nodes' influence and edges' blocking efficiency, weighed using a notion of entropy. (Please refer to [22] for more details on this algorithm.)

For each of our three networks, we select a randomly chosen set R of nodes of size $|R| = 0.001n$ to be red initially (and the rest white). We let the number of blocked edges to range from 0.01 m to 0.2 m. Then, we compute the containment factor cf for all the algorithms by blocking the corresponding edges and running the Independent Cascade model. For each experiment, we select $|R|$ nodes to be red, and then run the Independent Cascade Model 10 times to obtain the cf for the same set of initial red nodes. We run each of these experiments 10 times for different sets of initial red nodes and report the average value of cf.

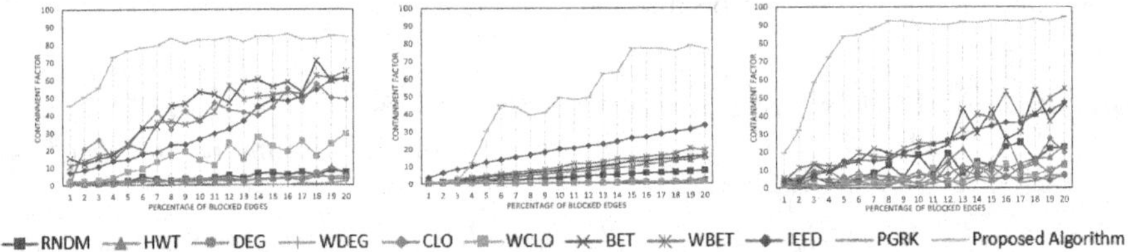

Fig. 1. The containment factor for different algorithms on Facebook (top-left), Facebook-Govt (top-right), and Facebook-Politician (bottom) networks. (Color figure online)

The outcomes of our experiments are provided in Fig. 1. We observe that our proposed algorithm consistently outperforms all other algorithms, especially by a significant margin for higher percentages of blocked edges. The only case where our algorithm does not perform better than the other algorithms is for small percentages of blocked edges on the Facebook-Govt dataset.

References

1. Blondel, V.D., Guillaume, J.L., Lambiotte, R., Lefebvre, E.: Fast unfolding of communities in large networks. J. Stat. Mech. Theor. Exp. **2008**(10), P10008 (2008)
2. Brin, S., Page, L.: The anatomy of a large-scale hypertextual web search engine. Comput. Netw. ISDN Syst. **30**(1–7), 107–117 (1998)
3. Burzyn, P., Bonomo, F., Durán, G.: Np-completeness results for edge modification problems. Discret. Appl. Math. **154**(13), 1824–1844 (2006)

4. Dey, P., Roy, S.: Centrality based information blocking and influence minimization in online social network. In: ANTS, pp. 1–6. IEEE (2017)
5. Eismann, K.: Diffusion and persistence of false rumors in social media networks: implications of searchability on rumor self-correction on Twitter. J. Bus. Econ. **91**(9), 1299–1329 (2021)
6. Goldenberg, J., Libai, B., Muller, E.: Talk of the network: a complex systems look at the underlying process of word-of-mouth. Mark. Lett. **12**(3), 211–223 (2001)
7. Goyal, A., Bonchi, F., Lakshmanan, L.V.: Learning influence probabilities in social networks. In: Third ACM International Conference on Web Search and Data Mining (2010)
8. Jaccard, P.: Étude comparative de la distribution florale dans une portion des alpes et des jura. Bull. Soc. Vaudoise Sci. Nat. **37**, 547–579 (1901)
9. Kempe, D., Kleinberg, J., Tardos, É.: Maximizing the spread of influence through a social network. In: Ninth ACM SIGKDD International Conference on Knowledge Discovery and Data Mining (2003)
10. Khalil, E., Dilkina, B., Song, L.: CuttingEdge: influence minimization in networks. In: Proceedings of Workshop on Frontiers of Network Analysis: Methods, Models, and Applications at NIPS (2013)
11. Kimura, M., Saito, K., Motoda, H.: Minimizing the spread of contamination by blocking links in a network. In: AAAI, vol. 8, pp. 1175–1180 (2008)
12. Kimura, M., Saito, K., Motoda, H.: Blocking links to minimize contamination spread in a social network. ACM Trans. Knowl. Disc. Data (TKDD) **3**(2), 1–23 (2009)
13. Kimura, M., Saito, K., Nakano, R.: Extracting influential nodes for information diffusion on a social network. In: AAAI, vol. 7, pp. 1371–1376 (2007)
14. Kuhlman, C.J., Tuli, G., Swarup, S., Marathe, M.V., Ravi, S.: Blocking simple and complex contagion by edge removal. In: IEEE 13th International Conference on Data Mining. IEEE (2013)
15. Leskovec, J., Krevl, A.: SNAP Datasets: Stanford large network dataset collection, June 2014. https://snap.stanford.edu/data
16. Onnela, J.P., et al.: Structure and tie strengths in mobile communication networks. Nat. Acad. Sci. **104**, 7332–7336 (2007)
17. Rossi, R.A., Ahmed, N.K.: The network data repository with interactive graph analytics and visualization. In: AAAI (2015). https://networkrepository.com
18. Tong, G., et al.: An efficient randomized algorithm for rumor blocking in online social networks. Trans. Netw. Sci. Eng. **7**, 845–854 (2017)
19. Yan, R., Li, Y., Wu, W., Li, D., Wang, Y.: Rumor blocking through online link deletion on social networks. ACM Trans. Knowl. Disc. Data (TKDD) **13**(2), 1–26 (2019)
20. Yannakakis, M.: Node-and edge-deletion NP-complete problems. In: Proceedings of the Tenth Annual ACM Symposium on Theory of Computing, pp. 253–264 (1978)
21. Yao, Q., Zhou, C., Xiang, L., Cao, Y., Guo, L.: Minimizing the negative influence by blocking links in social networks. In: Lu, Y., Wu, X., Zhang, X. (eds.) ISCTCS 2014. CCIS, vol. 520, pp. 65–73. Springer, Heidelberg (2015). https://doi.org/10.1007/978-3-662-47401-3_9
22. Zareie, A., Sakellariou, R.: Rumour spread minimization in social networks: a source-ignorant approach. Online Soc. Netw. Media **29**, 100206 (2022)
23. Zehmakan, A.N., Maurya, K.: Mitigating misinformation spreading in social networks via edge blocking. arXiv preprint arXiv:2308.08860 (2023)

Multi-modal Component Representation for Multi-source Domain Adaptation Method

Yuhong Zhang[1,2(✉)], Zhihao Lin[1], Lin Qian[1], and Xuegang Hu[1]

[1] School of Computer and Information Engineering, Hefei University of Technology, Hefei 230601, China
zhangyh@hfut.edu.cn

[2] Institute of Artificial Intelligence, Hefei Comprehensive National Science Center, Hefei 230088, China

Abstract. Multi-source domain adaptation aims to leverage multiple labeled source domains to train a classifier for an unlabeled target domain. Existing methods address the domain discrepancy by learning the invariant representation. However, due to the large difference in image style, image occlusion and missing, etc., the invariant representation tends to be inadequate, and some components tend to be lost. To this end, a multi-source domain adaptation method with multi-modal representation for components is proposed. It learns the multi-modal representation for missing components from an external knowledge graph. First, the semantic representation of the class subgraph, including not only the class but also rich class components, is learned from knowledge graph. Second, the semantic representation is fused with the visual representations of each domain respectively. Finally, the multi-modal invariant representations of source and target domains are learned. Experiments show the effectiveness of our method.

Keywords: Domain adaptation · Multi-modal representation · Knowledge graph

1 Introduction

Domain adaptation (DA) aims to leverage a labeled-rich source domain to train a model on an unlabeled target domain, where the distributions of the two domains are different but related. In some applications, source training data is collected from multiple domains, which leads to Multi-Source Domain Adaptation (MSDA).

The existing MSDAs mainly fall into two categories. The first is weighting on the individual alignment of each domain, such as ABMSDA [1], BSA [2]. The

Supported by the National Natural Science Foundation of China under grant 61976077, the Natural Science Foundation of Anhui Province under grant 2208085MF170 and the University Synergy Innovation Program of Anhui Province under grant GXXT-2022-040.

F. Liu et al. (Eds.): PRICAI 2023, LNAI 14325, pp. 104–109, 2024.
https://doi.org/10.1007/978-981-99-7019-3_11

second is alignment on merged multiple source domains, such as M^3SDA [3]. In applications, there are large gaps in image style among different domains, image occlusion, or insufficient image. These will lead to the invariant features being incomplete during alignment, and some class components are easily lost. DAC [4] riches the representation of class prototype by fusing the visual representation of components. LTC-MSDA [5] learns the class prototype with the visual and semantic features, in which the semantic features are learned based on the semantic similarity of the class prototype. Although these methods can supplement the missing feature representations to a certain extent, they still need to be further improved in terms of the missing components.

To this end, this paper introduces the knowledge graph as an external resource to obtain more components and enriches the representations by fusing the multi-modal component representations to improve multi-source domain adaptation. The contributions are summarized as follows. (1) To address the missing of the class components, a multi-modal representation for class components is proposed. And it uses semantics of class components to compensate for the lack of existing visual representations due to discrepancies of domains and the occlusions in images. (2) With various structural relationships in the external resource KG, some class components that are not present in the images can also be captured to complement the component features.

2 Proposed Method

Given multiple labeled source domains $X^S = \{(x_i^S, w_i^S)\}_{i=1}^{n_s}$, and unlabeled target domain $X^T = \{(x_j^T)\}_{j=1}^{n_t}$, the labels of all domains are expressed as $W = \{w_i\}_{i=1}^{n}$, where n is the number of labels, and n_s and n_t are the number of samples in multiple source and target domain. An knowledge graph KG = (E, R, T), $(W \subset E)$ is treated as an external resource to capture class components. Our task is to train a well-performing classifier for target domain. Figure 1 shows the framework of our proposed method.

2.1 Semantic Representation of Class Components

We use KG as an external resource to obtain semantic representations of class related components to enrich the representations.

The Class Subgraph. We capture the related components related to class w_i of the image from the external KG. Here a popular KG, ConceptNet [6] is adopted. Specifically, the class label w_i is treated as the key to query the corresponding node and its neighbors and relationships in ConceptNet. The queried result is regarded as class subgraph G, and it contains rich components and the structural relationships between class and components, which will compensate the missing of some features in the images. It is noted that the number of relationships of class-subgraph is decided by the external KG. The specific process of subgraph division is as follows: (1) G is initialized to empty. (2) For each class label

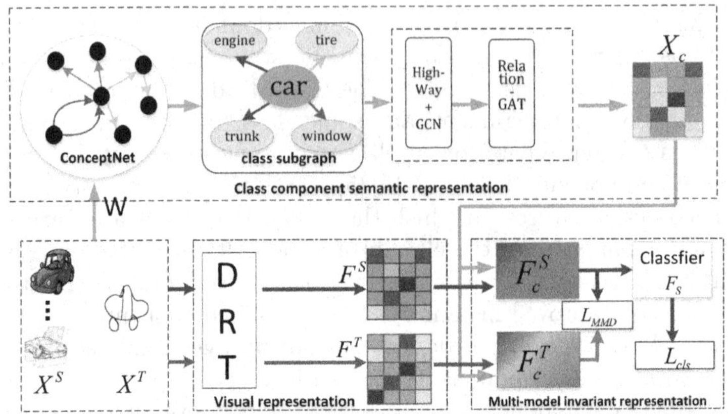

Fig. 1. The framework of our method.

$w_i \in W$, the corresponding node is queried from the knowledge graph, and then its k-hop neighbors, and the corresponding relationships between them are extracted together to form the class subgraph G.

Semantic Representation of Class Components. The semantic representation of the class subgraph, $G = \{E', R', T'\}$ is performed. First, the component nodes are initialized to a 100-dimensional vector with glove [7], and the relations are initialized randomly. The class nodes are initialized to a 100-dimensional vector with all zeros, and then aggregates its neighborhoods to obtain its representation Secondly, the representation of class nodes, component nodes and relations are concatenated into the triples, and then they are optimized together in an attention way. The attention of the triple $(w_i \|r_h\| c_k)$ to the class node w_i is calculated as follows:

$$\alpha_{ihk} = \frac{\exp\left(a^T \left[w_i \|r_h\| c_k\right]\right)}{\sum_{c_k \in N_i} \sum_{r_h \in R_{w_i, c_k}} \exp\left(a^T \left[w_i \|r_h\| c_k\right]\right)} \tag{1}$$

From this, the representation of class components after aggregating the triples can be expressed as:

$$x_c = \mathrm{ReLU}\left(\sum_{c_k \in N_i} \sum_{r_h \in R_{w_i c_k}} \alpha_{ihk} \left[w_i \|r_h\| c_k\right]\right) \tag{2}$$

where $(w_i \|r_h\| c_k)$ represents the semantic representation of the triplet (class node, relation, component node), where w_i, r_h, c_k represent class node, relation and component node respectively, and $\|$ is the splicing operation. N_i is the set of component nodes of class node w_i, and R_{w_i,c_k} is the set of all relations between class node w_i and all component nodes c_k. Finally, we get the vector representation of the class components X_c after the aggregating relationship.

2.2 Multi-modal Invariant Representation Learning

In this subsection, the component semantic representation is fused with the visual representation to complement the possible missing component features. Secondly, invariant feature representations are learned based on the multi-modal representations with MMD.

First, the semantic representation of class component, X_c, is fused with the visual features of the source and target domains, F^S and F^T, to obtain the source multi-modal representation F_c^S and the target multi-modal representation F_c^T. The fusion formula is as follows:

$$F_c^S = \left[F^S \| X_c\right], F_c^T = \left[F^T \| X_c\right] \tag{3}$$

Second, the multi-modal invariant representations is learned with MMD and the cross-entropy loss is used to train the classifier. Thus, overall objective function is shown as follows:

$$L\left(\theta_{cls}, \theta_D\right) = \frac{1}{n_s} \sum_{i=1}^{n_s} L\left(F_s\left(F_c^S\right)\right) + MMD\left(F_c^S, F_c^T\right) \tag{4}$$

3 Experiments

3.1 Datasets and Baselines

Two popular datasets, DomainNet [3] and Office-Home [8], are used to validate the effectiveness of our method. Three types of baselines are compared with our method, including **1) Single-best** means performing the single source domain adaptation, and selecting the best single-source result as the result of multi-source domain adaptation. It includes DAN [9], DANN [10] and MCD [11]. **2) Source-combine** combines all source domains as a single domain to perform single-source domain adaptation. It also includes DAN [9], DANN [10] and MCD [11]. **3) Multi-source** means that the knowledge learned from multiple source domains is transferred to the target domain. It includes M^3SDA [3], DRT [12], SPS [13], DAC [4] and LTC-MSDA [5]. The results of most baselines come from their original paper [13,14].

In the training, the labels in target is unavailable and only labels in source domains are fed. In addition, the epoch is 15, the initial learning rate is 0.001, the batch size is 64, and the learning rate decays by 0.1 every five cycles.

3.2 The Performance

Overall Performance. The overall performance of all methods are in Table 1. 1) Compared with the single-source DA, MSDA methods perform better. 2) Compared with methods based on visual representation, multi-modal methods perform better generally. It indicates that the semantic information is helpful for the learning of invariant representation of multiple domains. 3) Compared with

Table 1. Overall performance (accuracy %) on DomainNet and Office-home dataset

Standard	Models	DomainNet						Ofiice-home			
		clp	inf	pnt	qdr	rel	skt	Ar	Pr	Cl	Rw
Single Best	DANN	37.9	11.4	33.9	13.7	41.5	28.6	67.9	80.4	55.9	75.8
	DAN	39.5	14.5	29.1	14.9	41.9	30.7	68.2	80.3	56.5	75.9
	MCD	42.6	19.6	42.6	3.8	50.5	33.8	69.1	79.6	52.2	75.1
Source Combine	DANN	45.5	13.1	37	13.2	48.9	31.8	68.4	79.5	59.1	82.7
	DAN	47.3	11.4	36.7	14.7	49.1	33.5	68.5	79.0	59.4	82.5
	MCD	54.3	22.1	45.7	7.6	58.4	43.5	67.8	79.2	59.9	80.9
Multi-Source	M^3SDA	58.6	26	52.3	6.3	62.7	49.5	67.2	79.1	63.5	79.4
	DRT	71	31.6	61	12.3	71.4	60.7	72.6	68.5	54.6	75.4
	SPS	70.8	24.6	55.2	19.4	67.5	57.6	75.1	84.4	66	84.2
	LTC-MSDA	63.1	28.7	56.1	16.3	66.1	53.8	67.4	79.2	64.1	80.1
	DAC	72.5	27.6	57.8	23	66.7	59.5	-	-	-	-
	Ours	**74.3**	**37.2**	**67.2**	**34.8**	**73.4**	**63.6**	**80.1**	**85.6**	**67**	**86.6**

other semantic-visual fusion methods, our method improves the performance by 9.2% and 2.4%. It shows that our capturing the components from external KG can strengthen the missing components and enrich the representations. 4) Compared with DAC, which uses the visual representation of class components, our method can classify better. It indicates that the semantic representation of class component can enrich the insufficient visual representation when there are large difference of image style and occlusion in each source domain, it also complements relevant components that do not occur in the images. 5) When the multiple source and target domains have large differences of style and occlusions, our method outperforms more obviously. As for the difficult tasks, such as qdr and inf, our method outperforms the best baseline by 11.8% and 5.6%, respectively. As for easy tasks, such as clp and rel, our method outperforms the best baseline by 3.3% and 2%, respectively.

Table 2. Ablation of our method on DomainNet and Office-home dataset

Models	DomainNet						Ofiice-home			
	clp	inf	pnt	qdr	rel	skt	Ar	Pr	Cl	Rw
Only-Vision	71.0	31.8	61.0	12.5	71.4	60.7	72.6	68.5	54.6	75.4
Vision+similar attribute	73.2	36.4	65.8	23.7	72.3	63.2	75.3	77.1	56.6	76.9
Ours	**74.3**	**37.2**	**67.2**	**34.8**	**73.4**	**63.6**	**80.1**	**85.6**	**67.0**	**86.6**

Ablation. It can be seen from Table 2: 1) Compared with Only-vision, the other two variants improve the performance by 5.7% and 7.9%. This indicates that component-based semantic representations can supplement partly the class components, thereby helping to learn more transferable features. 2) Our method performs better than vision+similar attribute. This shows that considering the complex relations between components and classes, GAT can obtain a better component semantic representation by considering the different importance of these relations.

4 Conclusion

In this paper, we explore the role of component semantics in MSDA. We introduce the multi-modal class components from an external KG to learn the semantic representation of class components, which is integrated with the original visual representation to perform MSDA. Extensive experiments validate that our method can complement the missing representation of class components and then improve the performance of MSDA. In the near future, we will further focus on the domain generalization methods when the target is unknown.

References

1. Zuo, Y., Yao, H., Xu, C.: Attention-based multi-source domain adaptation. IEEE Trans. Image Process. **30**, 3793–3803 (2021)
2. Kang, G., Jiang, L., Wei, Y., Yang, Y., Hauptmann, A.: Contrastive adaptation network for single- and multi-source domain adaptation. IEEE Trans. Pattern Anal. Mach. Intell. **44** 1793–1804 (2022)
3. Peng, X., Bai, Q., Xia, X., Huang, Z., Saenko, K., Wang, B.: Moment matching for multi-source domain adaptation. In: ICCV, pp. 1406–1415 (2019)
4. Deng, Z., Zhou, K., Yang, Y., Xiang, T.: Domain attention consistency for multi-source domain adaptation. In: BMVC, p. 4 (2021)
5. Wang, H., Xu, M., Ni, B., Zhang, W.: Learning to Combine: Knowledge Aggregation for Multi-source Domain Adaptation. In: Vedaldi, A., Bischof, H., Brox, T., Frahm, J.-M. (eds.) ECCV 2020. LNCS, vol. 12353, pp. 727–744. Springer, Cham (2020). https://doi.org/10.1007/978-3-030-58598-3_43
6. Speer, R., Chin, J., Havasi, C.: Conceptnet 5.5: an open multilingual graph of general knowledge. In: AAAI, pp. 4444–4451 (2017)
7. Pennington, J., Socher, R., Manning, C.D.: Glove: global vectors for word representation. In: EMNLP, pp. 1532–1543 (2014)
8. Venkateswara, H., Eusebio, J., Chakraborty, S., Panchanathan, S.: Deep hashing network for unsupervised domain adaptation. In: CVPR, pp. 5385–5394 (2017)
9. Long, M., Cao, Y., Wang, J., Jordan, M. I.: Learning transferable features with deep adaptation networks. In: ICML, pp. 97–105 (2015)
10. Ganin, Y.: Domain-adversarial training of neural networks. J. Mach. Learn. Res. **17**, 1–35 (2016)
11. Saito, K., Watanabe, K., Ushiku, Y., Harada, T.: Maximum classifier discrepancy for unsupervised domain adaptation. In: CVPR, pp. 3723–3732 (2018)
12. Li, Y., Yuan, L., Chen, Y., Wang, P., Vasconcelos, N.: Dynamic transfer for multi-source domain adaptation. In: CVPR, pp. 10998–11007 (2021)
13. Wang, Z., Zhou, C., Du, B., He, F.: Self-paced supervision for multi-source domain adaptation. In: Raedt, L.D. (eds)., IJCAI, pp. 3551–3557 (2022)
14. Dong, J., Fang, Z., Liu, A., Sun, G., Liu, T.: Confident anchor-induced multi-source free domain adaptation. In: NeurIPS, pp. 2848–2860 (2021)

(Deep) Reinforcement Learning

Abbreviated Weighted Graph in Multi-Agent Reinforcement Learning

Siying Wang, Hongfei Du, Wenyu Chen, and Hong Qu(✉)

School of Computer Science and Engineering, University of Electronic Science and Technology of China, Chengdu, China
siyingwang@std.uestc.edu.cn, duhongfei@ydnkj.com, {cwy,hongqu}@uestc.edu.cn

Abstract. The cooperation phenomenon in real life can often be viewed as an interaction between multiple agents. The exchange of unstructured information between agents is usually abstracted as the transmission of node information in a graph. Various approaches have been proposed to build graph models and fuse the information of agents in their observation range. However, it is inefficient to directly apply the related algorithms of graph neural networks to integrate the information of each agent, which can not effectively use the observation features of the dominant agent in cooperation, and it may also be overly focused on the weight of the edges. In this paper, we propose AWGmix, which is an abbreviated weighted graph information-enhanced algorithm for multi-agent reinforcement learning. Specifically, we propose a simple and convenient method to calculate the weight of edges between graph nodes modeled from agent connections, and design an attribution module based on attention mechanism to find the dominant agents and enrich the representation of observations. Experimental results demonstrate the superiority and effectiveness of our proposed method on Starcraft II micromanagement benchmark tasks.

Keywords: Reinforcement Learning · Multi-Agent Reinforcement Learning · Partial Observable Markov Decision Process · Cooperative Game · Graph Neural Network

1 Introduction

Cooperation is common from viruses, bacteria to social animals and humans [10]. Numerous cooperative issues in human society generally take the form of multi agent cooperative systems where the goal is to maximize the team reward. Multi-Agent Reinforcement Learning (MARL), which utilizes Reinforcement Learning (RL) methods to co-train a group of agents, can be used to solve these cooperative problems. However, many MARL approaches still struggle with the sample-inefficiency and high-dimensional state-action spaces. Still, the joint state-action space expands exponentially with the increasing number of agents, which is

F. Liu et al. (Eds.): PRICAI 2023, LNAI 14325, pp. 113–124, 2024.
https://doi.org/10.1007/978-981-99-7019-3_12

called the curse of dimensionality, will further deteriorate the training efficiency of agents. One of the keys to solving this problem is to find a way to effectively extract and fuse the information of agents and train the joint policy.

Recently, the mainstream algorithms have introduced the specific training pattern named *Centralized-Training with Decentralized-Execution* (CTDE), which enables agents to get the global state information and opponents' actions during the training stage, to ease the non-stationarity and sample-inefficiency in multi-agent systems. This framework enables some successful developments of methods that directly extend some efficient single-agent algorithms to multi-agent realm, for example, replacing the deep deterministic policy gradient (DDPG) estimate with a multi agent style counterpart [8], or designing a precise neural network structure to ensure *Individual-Global-Max* (IGM) principle [18]. However, it is ineffective to search for the optimal cooperative policy directly in the joint state-action space, and this issue will get worse as this combined space expands as the number of agents rises [8].

On the other side, the interactions for cooperation between agents are also crucial to the training of joint policy, while this process is usually modeled as the information exchange in a graph. Some researchers try to extend existing approaches of Graph Convolutional Network (GCN) by extracting the features from observations of agents to enrich the representation of joint value function [4]. Generally, these approaches reckon that all agents share equal importance with the same weighted value of edge in the modeled graph [4], or equip the attention mechanism to integrate the observations of various agents more effectively [11]. In addition, Graph indeed provides a good medium for information fusion, but current methods either crudely simplify the connection relations among all agents to be equal and do not take the connection relationship and information outside the field of view into account, or just roughly calculate the connection weights of agents, which consume a large amount of computation. However, some attention-based strategies ignore the role of the dominant agents and their behavior in collaboration in favor of concentrating simply on the agents' observations.

To address the problems above, we propose an abbreviated weighted graph information-enhanced algorithm, named AWGmix, for multi-agent reinforcement learning. Specifically, AWGmix contains an attribution module based on the attention module to determine the dominant agents, which should be paid more attention to training. Then a convenient and clean method is proposed to calculate the edge weight of agents based on the Floyd hop-counting (FHC) in the modeled graph through the relationship between the observation range and relative location.

We briefly summarize the main contributions of AWGmix as follows:

- We propose an attribution module to determine the dominant agents in the cooperative scenarios, which will boost the whole training.
- We abandon the complex attention-based mechanism of calculating the weight of edges in vanilla Graph Neural Network (GNN), and then propose a simple method based on Floyd hop-counting concerning the relationship between the observation range and relative location of agents.

- The Hypernetwork is implemented to mix all the individual utility of agents together to improve the training efficiency, and we evaluate and demonstrate the effectiveness of our method on the challenging StarCraft II micromanagement benchmark tasks.

For the following components of this paper, we firstly present related works about GNNs or attention based multi-agent algorithms, and other value decomposition approaches in Sect. 2. Then the background of MARL is formulated in Sect. 3. The novel Abbreviated Weighted Graph Information Enhanced algorithm is introduced and illustrated in Sect. 4. Then the experiments and ablations are described in Sect. 5, as well as the experiment description and parameters setup. We also analyze the reasons for the effectiveness of our proposed method, and then conclude it in Sect. 6.

2 Related Works

The simplest solution to the MARL problem is to extend the single agent RL algorithm to the field of MARL [25]. However, such an approach may cause non-stationarity due to the update of the policies during the training process [2]. Part of the solution to this problem is to improve the representation of the policies by considering the actions taken by other agents during training [8]. In addition, the CTDE paradigm is widely applied in value-based MARL [8,14,15,18,20]. This framework assigns centralized critics to each agent instance, which alleviates the non-stationarity of cooperation. Qatten [26] analyzes the relationship between Q_{tot} of VDN and $Q_i(\tau_i, u_i)$, then assembles the utilities through the multi-head attention structure. WQMIX [13] then reduces the weight of suboptimal joint actions while maintaining the representativeness of the joint Q_{tot}. QPLEX [21] creates a unique network that factorizes the Q_{tot} with the dueling structure. ROMA [22] assigns similar roles to agents with the same trajectories to enhance cooperation. ResQ [17] extends Qtran [18] with other joint-actions based on the residual model[19]. VMIX [19] added an A2C framework to QMIX, and SMIX [27] balanced variance and bias by incorporating λ-return into the Q_{tot}. On the other hand, such as HAPPO/HATRPO [5], all the information of the agent is taken into account to consider the influence of the sequence of agents' actions. MAT [24] goes a step further, adding the Transformer architecture to HAPPO to focus on the effect of observations on each agent.

In addition, many researchers have modeled and abstracted the cooperation of agents into the information transfer between graph nodes in order to better simulate interactions and enrich the representation of features in training. G2ANet [7] aims to abstract the game during training to simulate the interaction. Meanwhile, the multi-actor-attention-critic (MAAC) [3] enhances the representation of values in MADDPG by using an attention mechanism to enrich state information. ATT-MADDPG uses attention modules [9] to gather information about teammates and ensure effective training of agents. VGN [23] takes into account the influence of agents with the minimal Q-values and enriches the policy by applying double attention GCN. The DGN [4] approximates the interaction between agents as a fully-connected GCN and uses a multi-layer GCN to integrate information from agents out of sight. GraphMIX [11] takes into account situations where agents may have limited direct observations of each other, and incorporates GCN into QMIX [15] for effective information fusion. DVD [6] improves the joint value function by separating the confusing path from the global state and instead enriches it with a fully connected graph of the history of action-observation.

Throughout these approaches, there were two common ways to handle interactions between agents. One way is to use GCN directly to integrate the agent's observations, while another requires designing a complex attention module to obtain edge weights in the modeled graph. These methods do not effectively capture interactions among agents beyond the observable range, nor do they identify the key agents in the cooperation. In this paper, we explore a weight calculation technique that makes it easy to abstract the relationships between agents into weighted factors and examine the effect of dominant agents on cooperative behavior, to improve sample efficiency and training performance.

3 Background

3.1 Decentralized POMDP

The cooperative task in multi agent setting is usually described as a *decentralized partially observable Markov decision process* (Decentralized POMDP) [12], which is depicted with a tuple $< S, U, P, r, Z, O, n, \gamma >$ where n means the number of agents with $n \in N$. The state $s \in S$ indicates the global state of environment. An action $u_i \in U$ is chosen at each time step t to integrate into a joint action $\mathbf{u} \in \mathbf{U} \equiv U^n$, which leads to a transition of the environment state that follows the transition function $P(s' \mid s, \mathbf{u}) : S \times \mathbf{U} \times S \rightarrow [0,1]$. The reward function $r(s, \mathbf{u}) : S \times \mathbf{U} \rightarrow \mathbf{R}$ is shared among all agents. Each agent i receives an partial observation value $z_i \in Z$ based on $O(z_i|s, u_i) : S \times U \rightarrow Z$ and tracks its action-observation history $\tau_i \in \mathcal{T} \equiv (Z \times U)^*$, and their respective strategies $\pi_i(u|\tau_i) : \mathcal{T} \times U \rightarrow [0,1]$ form a joint state action value function $Q^\pi(s_t, \mathbf{u}_t) = \mathbb{E}_{s_{t+1:\infty}, \mathbf{u}_{t+1:\infty}}[R_t \mid s_t, \mathbf{u}_t]$, to collectively optimize total performance, where $R_t = \sum_{i=0}^{T} \gamma^i r_{t+i}$.

3.2 Value Decomposition and CTDE Paradigm

Our primary focus revolves around the *Centralized-Training* with *Decentralized-Execution* paradigm in MARL, where the learning algorithm is granted access to s and τ of all agents to facilitate centralized policy training. However, agents only make decisions based on their local observations during execution stage. Most value-based algorithms implemented within CTDE adopt the IGM principle to ensure consistency between the joint state action value function $Q_{tot}(\tau, \mathbf{u})$ and the utilities $[Q_i(\tau_i, u_i)]_{i=1}^n$:

$$\underset{\mathbf{u}}{\operatorname{argmax}}\, Q_{tot}(\boldsymbol{\tau}, \mathbf{u}) = (\underset{u_1}{\operatorname{argmax}}\, Q_1(\tau_1, u_1), \ldots, \underset{u_n}{\operatorname{argmax}}\, Q_n(\tau_n, u_n)). \quad (1)$$

Following the IGM principle, we can ensure that the same set of maximum actions is guaranteed between $[Q_i(\tau_i, u_i)]_{i=1}^n$ and $Q_{tot}(\tau, \mathbf{u})$. Therefore, if there is a function $f_s(Q_1(\tau_1, u_1), \ldots, Q_n(\tau_n, u_n), s) = Q_{tot}(s, \mathbf{u})$, the $\frac{\partial f_s}{\partial Q_u} \geq 0, \forall u \in U \equiv (1, \ldots, n)$ is all that is required. So far, VDN [20] and QMIX [15] have emerged as two exemplary paradigms in this context. VDN factorizes Q_{tot} into a sum of utilities $Q_{tot}^{\text{VDN}}(\boldsymbol{\tau}, \boldsymbol{u}) = \sum_{i=1}^n Q_i(\tau_i, u_i)$, while QMIX combines a state-dependent continuous monotone function, $Q_{tot}^{\text{QMIX}}(\boldsymbol{\tau}, \boldsymbol{u}) = \sum_{i=1}^n |w_i| Q_i(\tau_i, u_i)$, with the utility of each agent. Here $|\cdot|$ is an absolute function ensuring the monotonicity between Q_{tot} and $[Q_i(\tau_i, u_i)]_{i=1}^n$.

3.3 GCN and Its Attentional Applications in MARL

GCN - Graph Convolutional Network. When cooperation between agents is modeled as the interaction between GNN nodes, we can use GNN approaches to deal with the information propagation process. The most straightforward approach to fuse the information is GCN, which performs convolutional operations on the nodes with connected relations, .i.e, the adjacent matrix as:

$$\mathbf{H}^{l+1} = \sigma\left(\mathbf{P}\mathbf{H}^l\mathbf{W}^l\right), \tag{2}$$

where σ indicates the ReLU activation function, $\mathbf{P}$ is symmetric normalization of the adjacency matrix, expressed as $\mathbf{D}^{-\frac{1}{2}}\mathbf{A}\mathbf{D}^{-\frac{1}{2}}$.

Attention Mechanism in MARL. Attention mechanisms have garnered considerable interest in various domains of AI. The general idea of MARL is to utilize the soft-attention to determine the important relationship of all other agents to the present one as follows:

$$w_k = \frac{\exp\left(f\left(\Omega, e_k\right)\right)}{\sum_{i=1}^K \exp\left(f\left(\Omega, e_i\right)\right)}; \tag{3}$$

where, e_k represents the agent k's feature vector, w_k denotes the importance weights of agent k, and Ω represents the feature vector of the current agent, typically referring to its observation o.

4 Methods

We begin by constructing the agent relationship as a specific graph, with each node representing an individual agent and all nodes connected in pairs. The graph is also known as the Agent Coordination Graph [7]:

Definition 1. *(Agent Coordination Graph) The agent-agent relationship is specified as an undirected graph $G = (N, V)$, which consists of the set of nodes N and the set of edges V, which are unordered pairs of N components. Each node represents an agent's entry, while the edge shows the link between two agents.*

In this component, we will present our model AWGmix, an abbreviated weighted graph information-enhanced algorithm for MARL, which can better integrate the information of agents outside the visual field and rely on the dominant agents to make better decisions. Figure 1 presents the overview of our model. The entire model is mainly made up of two modules (1) Attribution module (2) Abbreviated weighted graph module. The first module reacts to the role of the dominant agents for cooperation; while the second module considers the information of the agents outside the visual with the help of Floyd hop-counting.

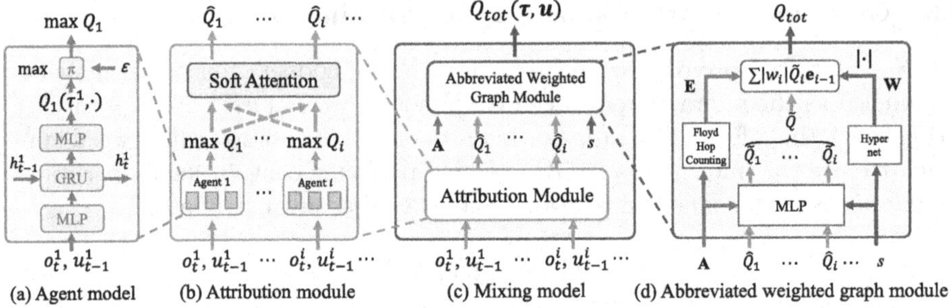

Fig. 1. General schematic diagram of AWGmix's model, which contains 4 parts: (a) policy network of agents, (b) attribution module, (c) mixing network, (d) abbreviated weighted graph module.

4.1 Attribution Module

This module is mainly based on the attention module, fusing the observation and action of other agents to enrich the representative capability of the policy network. This module consists of the policy networks of agents and the soft-attention part to obtain the information-enhanced utilities $[\hat{Q}_i(\tau_i, u_i)]_{i=1}^n$.

We consider the same policy network structure of agents as in QMIX [15], which uses the GRU layer to generate the state-action Q_i. As shown in part (a) of Fig. 1, the agent model encodes the current observation o_t and the last taken action u_{t-1} as inputs through the feedforward network, and then the encoding result and the GRU hidden embedding vector of the previous step are put into the GRU layer to obtain the Q-value output vector. For value-based MARL algorithms, the policy network generally computes the Q-values of all actions and then uses the ϵ-greedy mechanism to get the final output utility [13,15,18,26].

Once the vanilla utilities Q_i are obtained, they are fed into a self attention module to fuse the state-action information of agents with the soft attention mechanism. This module will make the agents pay more attention to the allies with **larger** Q-values, which are the dominant agents, and then focus on the impact of their actions in cooperation [23]. Here the self-attention in this module follows Eq. (3) as:

$$w_k = \frac{\exp\left(f\left(Q_i, Q_k\right)\right)}{\sum_{j=1}^{n} \exp\left(f\left(Q_i, Q_j\right),\right)}, \tag{4}$$

and the enhanced $\hat{Q}_i$ of agents can be obtained as in the (b) part of Fig. 1.

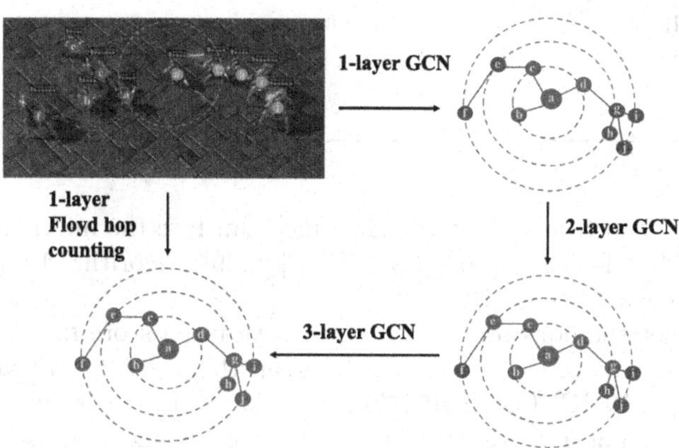

Fig. 2. Comparison of FHC and vanilla GCN in information propagation in MARL. If agent a wants to get information from agent i, it needs 3-layers of GCN network for information fusion, while FHC can achieve the same effect with only 1-layer.

4.2 Abbreviated Weighted Graph Module

Floyd Hop-Counting Part. In large cooperation scenarios, agents that are too far away will not be able to observe each other and cannot collaborate better to accomplish the cooperative tasks. As shown in Fig. 2, the typical 2s3z cooperation scenario in StarCraft Multi-Agent Challenge (SMAC). The ally agents are marked in red and enemies are marked in purple, and the dotted cycles depict their observation range, respectively. Since we consider the partial observability of agents, which means each agent i only receives a local observation o_t^i at each step t, it can only observe the agents in its sight range. Take the agent a as an example, it can only observe the information of agent b, agent c and agent d at the current moment, and if it needs to fuse the information of agents outside of the field of view, it needs to use a multi-layer GCN network for information transfer, which is time-consuming.

To avoid the limitation and to achieve information transfer and fusion outside the field of view in a single-layer GNN approach, a weighted hop counting method based on the Floyd shortest path calculation is proposed in AWGmix, named Floyd hop-counting (FHC). The FHC constructs the virtual edges based on the adjacent matrix of agents, and can calculate the hops between any agents pair

Algorithm 1. Obtain Floyd Hop Counting Matrix

Input: A: adjacent matrix of agents; N: the number of all the agents;
Initial: $M \in \mathbb{R}^{N \times N}$, $M = A + I$ with I the identity matrix;
for agent $k = 1$ to n **do**
  for agent $i = 1$ to n **do**
    for agent $j = 1$ to n **do**
      if $M_{ij} > M_{ik} + M_{kj}$ **then**
        $M_{ij} = M_{ik} + M_{kj}$
      end if
    end for
  end for
end for

based on Floyd shortest path approach, which can fuse the information of k-th order neighborhood with only one layer FHC [28,29]. Algorithm 1 represents the algorithm for constructing FHC.

When we get the hops of any two agents, we use a score function as (5) to calculate the weight of the connection between them and get Floyd Weighted Hop-Counting (FWHC) from FHC. The intuition of this score function is that the closer the two agents are, the greater the weight, and vice versa. Thus the information of the agents outside the field of view can also be fused using a single layer of FWHC, and we can obtain the weight matrix $\mathbf{E}$

$$\mathbf{E}_{ij} = Score(M_{ij}) = \frac{1}{e^{M_{ij}-1}}. \tag{5}$$

Graph Structure and State Information Augmentation Part. This part mainly focuses on the state and graph structure information augmentation for the enhanced utilities obtained by the attribution module. We concatenate the adjacency matrix $\mathbf{A}$, enhanced utilities $[\hat{Q}_i(\tau_i, u_i)]_{i=1}^n$, and state information s to obtain the augmented $[\tilde{Q}_i(\tau_i, u_i)]_{i=1}^n$ as

$$\tilde{\boldsymbol{Q}} = \mathrm{MLP}(\mathbf{A}; \hat{Q}_1, \cdots, \hat{Q}_n; s). \tag{6}$$

At this point, the embedding $\tilde{\boldsymbol{Q}} = (\tilde{Q}_1, \tilde{Q}_2, \ldots, \tilde{Q}_n)$ incorporates the structural information of the graph composed by the agents and also the global state information, which enables them to work better with each other.

Mixing Part via Hypernetwork. The role of the mixing part is the same as that in QMIX [15], i.e., we input the state s into a hypernetwork [1] to generate the vector $\mathbf{W}$ which is consistent with the dimension of $\tilde{\boldsymbol{Q}}$, and then to integrate the Q_{tot}. To ensure the continuity of the IGM, we also perform the absolute operation $|\cdot|$ on the generated $\mathbf{W}$ vector. So far, we are able to integrate the augmented $\tilde{\boldsymbol{Q}}$ with the help of $\mathbf{W}$ to obtain Q_{tot} and weigh the contribution made by each $\tilde{Q}_i$ with the weight matrix $\mathbf{E}$ as follows:

$$Q_{tot} = \mathbf{W} \cdot \tilde{\boldsymbol{Q}} \cdot \mathbf{E} = \sum_{i=1}^{n} |w_i| \tilde{Q}_i \mathbf{e}_{i-1}, \tag{7}$$

where $\mathbf{e}_{i-1}$ indicates the (i-1)th column vector of $\mathbf{E}$. Then Q_{tot} can be updated in a manner similar to DQN with the targets as $Q_{tot} \leftarrow r + \gamma Q'_{tot}(\tilde{Q}'_1, \cdots, \tilde{Q}'_n; s'; \mathbf{A}')$.

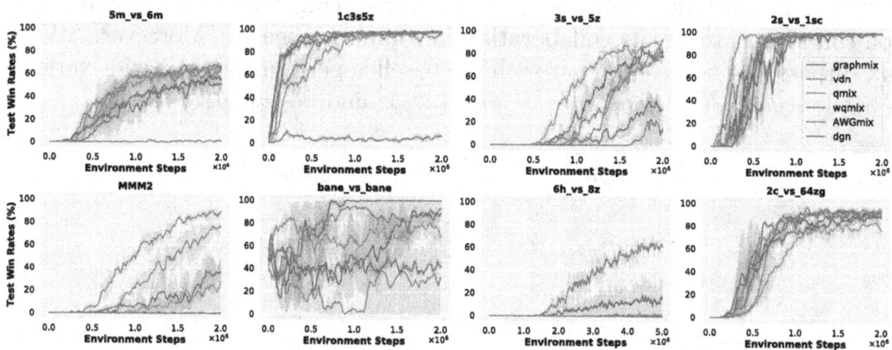

Fig. 3. Training curves of AWGmix and other baselines. The solid lines reflect the median values, and the shadowed zone represents the 25%–75% quartile results.

5 Experiments

In this part, we perform the experiments of AWGmix on the SMAC, which provides a rich range of hard cooperative scenarios. Our focus is on addressing micromanagement issues, in which each controlled unit is handled by an independent learnable agent with limited local observation. The objective is to train groups of units to engage in battles against the opposing units controlled by the game's built-in programmed AI. All approaches are executed in the PyMARL framework [16], we run the experiments with 5 random seeds and plot the training results by shading the 25%–75% quartile range. In all the experiments, the learning rate of AWGmix is set to 0.0005, the update interval of the target network is 200 steps, the hyper-network has 2 hidden layers with 64 neurons and $\gamma = 0.99$. We set the sampling batch size to 32 and the size of replay buffer to 5000, all the other parameters are the same as those of Qmix.

5.1 Results

SMAC provides a range of scenarios that serve as standard training experiments for agent cooperation, providing an in-depth assessment of the cooperative characteristics of trained agents. All of 8 battle scenarios are considered and grouped into **Easy** (*1c3s5z*, *2s_vs_1sc*), **Hard** (*5m_vs_6m*, *3s_vs_5z*, *2c_vs_64zg*, *bane_vs_bane*) and **Super-Hard** (*6h_vs_8z*, *MMM2*). By default, the game AI difficulty level in SMAC is configured to **Very Difficult** to ensure a challenging environment for cooperation.

We consider GraphMIX, DGN, VDN, QMIX, and WQMIX as baseline algorithms for comparison and evaluation. As shown in Fig. 3, the performance improvement of our AWGmix is particularly noticeable in some super-hard scenarios requiring complicated cooperation between the agents, such as *6h_vs_8z* and *MMM2*, which fully demonstrates that introducing graph structure information contributes to agents collaboration in complex scenarios. Moreover, AWGmix surpasses or achieves on par with the baseline performance in a wide variety of battle scenarios, such as *5m_vs_6m*, *1c3s5z* and *2c_vs_64zg*.

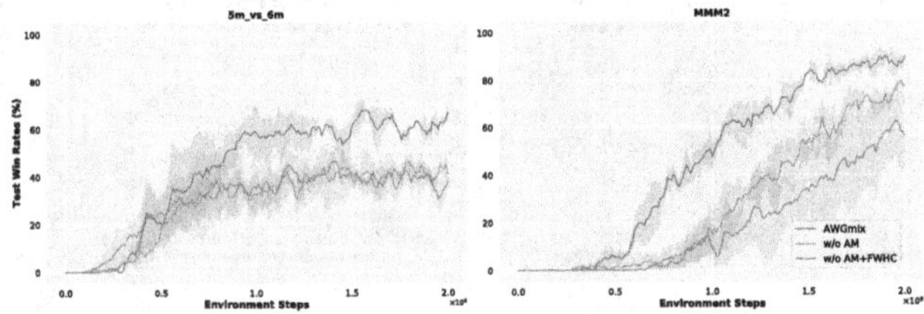

Fig. 4. Training curves of AWGmix and other baselines. The solid lines reflect the median values, and the shadowed zone represents the 25%–75% quartile results.

However, our AWGmix method is not perfect and even fails to outperform VDN in some scenarios such as the *3s_vs_5z*. One possible explanation for this could be the relatively small number of agents involved in simpler tasks, resulting in less expressive power in terms of the graph structure information they form. Consequently, the inclusion of parameters associated with the graph structure may not significantly enhance the representation of policies. Moreover, this introduction of additional parameters related to the graph structure could potentially lead to a decrease in training efficiency.

5.2 Ablations

To test the impact of the attribution module and FWHC in AWGmix, we remove the attribution module and FWHC part from AWGmix and conduct the experiments on the *MMM2* and *5m_vs_6m*, respectively. As shown in Fig. 4, the training performance of AWGmix after removing these two modules was significantly reduced. In particular, in the *MMM2* scenario, AWGmix can reach about 90% win rate, but only 60% after removing these modules, indicating that both the graph structure information and the attribution module have a greater impact on the collaborative ability of agents.

6 Conclusion

In this paper we present AWGmix, a MARL approach based on the agent modeled graph information. AWGmix builds an agent-coordination graph and calculates the number of hops between agent pairs based on Floyd's shortest path method, and uses this to build the specific weights of the edges in a graph. In addition, AWGmix contains an attribution module to integrate the Q-values, which enables the agents to consider the action information of others and cooperate more efficiently when making decisions. For work in future, we may consider encoding the changing information of the graph structure and feeding it into the policy network to test its effect on the actions and cooperation of agents.

References

1. Ha, D., Dai, A., Le, Q.V.: Hypernetworks. arXiv preprint arXiv:1609.09106 (2016)
2. Hernandez-Leal, P., Kaisers, M., Baarslag, T., Cote, E.M.d.: A survey of learning in multiagent environments: dealing with non-stationarity. CoRR abs/1707.09183, https://arxiv.org/abs/1707.09183 (2017)
3. Iqbal, S., Sha, F.: Actor-attention-critic for multi-agent reinforcement learning. In: Proceedings of the 36th International Conference on Machine Learning, pp. 2961–2970. PMLR (2019)
4. Jiang, J., Dun, C., Huang, T., Lu, Z.: Graph convolutional reinforcement learning. In: International Conference on Learning Representations (2020), https://openreview.net/forum?id=HkxdQkSYDB
5. Kuba, J.G., et al.: Trust region policy optimisation in multi-agent reinforcement learning. In: International Conference on Learning Representations (2022), https://openreview.net/forum?id=EcGGFkNTxdJ
6. Li, J., et al.: Deconfounded value decomposition for multi-agent reinforcement learning. In: International Conference on Machine Learning, pp. 12843–12856. PMLR (2022)
7. Liu, Y., Wang, W., Hu, Y., Hao, J., Chen, X., Gao, Y.: Multi-agent game abstraction via graph attention neural network. In: Proceedings of the AAAI Conference on Artificial Intelligence, vol. 34, pp. 7211–7218 (2020)
8. Lowe, R., Wu, Y., Tamar, A., Harb, J., Abbeel, P., Mordatch, I.: Multi-agent actor-critic for mixed cooperative-competitive environments. In: Proceedings of the 31st International Conference on Neural Information Processing Systems, NeurIPS, pp. 6382–6393 (2017)
9. Mao, H., Zhang, Z., Xiao, Z., Gong, Z.: Modelling the dynamic joint policy of teammates with attention multi-agent DDPG. In: Proceedings of the 18th International Conference on Autonomous Agents and MultiAgent Systems, pp. 1108–1116 (2019)
10. Melis, A.P., Semmann, D.: How is human cooperation different? Philos. Trans. Roy. Soc. B: Biol. Sci. **365**(1553), 2663–2674 (2010)
11. Naderializadeh, N., Hung, F.H., Soleyman, S., Khosla, D.: Graph convolutional value decomposition in multi-agent reinforcement learning. arXiv preprint arXiv:2010.04740 (2020)
12. Oliehoek, F.A., Amato, C.: A Concise Introduction to Decentralized POMDPs. Springer Briefs in Intelligent Systems, Springer (2016). https://doi.org/10.1007/978-3-319-28929-8

13. Rashid, T., Farquhar, G., Peng, B., Whiteson, S.: Weighted QMIX: expanding monotonic value function factorisation for deep multi-agent reinforcement learning. In: Proceedings of the 34th International Conference on Neural Information Processing Systems, NeurIPS, vol. 33, pp. 10199–10210 (2020)
14. Rashid, T., Samvelyan, M., De Witt, C.S., Farquhar, G., Foerster, J., Whiteson, S.: Monotonic value function factorisation for deep multi-agent reinforcement learning. J. Mach. Learn. Res. **21**(178), 1–51 (2020)
15. Rashid, T., Samvelyan, M., Witt, C.S.d., Farquhar, G., Foerster, J.N., Whiteson, S.: QMIX: monotonic value function factorisation for deep multi-agent reinforcement learning. In: Proceedings of the 35th International Conference on Machine Learning, pp. 4292–4301. PMLR (2018)
16. Samvelyan, M., et al.: The starcraft multi-agent challenge. In: Proceedings of the 18th International Conference on Autonomous Agents and MultiAgent Systems, AAMAS, pp. 2186–2188 (2019)
17. Shen, S., et al.: Resq: a residual q function-based approach for multi-agent reinforcement learning value factorization. Adv. Neural. Inf. Process. Syst. **35**, 5471–5483 (2022)
18. Son, K., Kim, D., Kang, W.J., Hostallero, D., Yi, Y.: QTRAN: learning to factorize with transformation for cooperative multi-agent reinforcement learning. In: Proceedings of the 36th International Conference on Machine Learning, pp. 5887–5896. PMLR (2019)
19. Su, J., Adams, S., Beling, P.: Value-decomposition multi-agent actor-critics. In: Proceedings of the AAAI Conference on Artificial Intelligence, vol. 35, pp. 11352–11360 (2021)
20. Sunehag, P., et al.: Value-decomposition networks for cooperative multi-agent learning based on team reward. In: Proceedings of the 17th International Conference on Autonomous Agents and MultiAgent Systems, AAMAS, pp. 2085–2087 (2018)
21. Wang, J., Ren, Z., Liu, T., Yu, Y., Zhang, C.: QPLEX: duplex dueling multi-agent q-learning. In: International Conference on Learning Representations (2020)
22. Wang, T., Dong, H., Lesser, V., Zhang, C.: Roma: multi-agent reinforcement learning with emergent roles. In: International Conference on Machine Learning, pp. 9876–9886. PMLR (2020)
23. Wei, Q., Li, Y., Zhang, J., Wang, F.Y.: VGN: value decomposition with graph attention networks for multiagent reinforcement learning. IEEE Trans. Neural Networks Learn. Syst. (2022)
24. Wen, M., et al.: Multi-agent reinforcement learning is a sequence modeling problem. Adv. Neural. Inf. Process. Syst. **35**, 16509–16521 (2022)
25. de Witt, C.S., et al.: Is independent learning all you need in the starcraft multi-agent challenge? arXiv preprint arXiv:2011.09533 (2020)
26. Yang, Y., et al.: Qatten: a general framework for cooperative multiagent reinforcement learning. arXiv preprint arXiv:2002.03939 (2020)
27. Yao, X., Wen, C., Wang, Y., Tan, X.: Smix (λ): enhancing centralized value functions for cooperative multiagent reinforcement learning. IEEE Trans. Neural Networks Learn. Syst. (2021)
28. Zeng, D., Chen, W., Liu, W., Zhou, L., Qu, H.: Rethinking random walk in graph representation learning. In: IEEE International Conference on Acoustics, Speech and Signal Processing (ICASSP), pp. 1–5. IEEE (2023)
29. Zhou, L., Wang, T., Qu, H., Huang, L., Liu, Y.: A weighted GCN with logical adjacency matrix for relation extraction. In: ECAI 2020, pp. 2314–2321. IOS Press (2020)

Diverse Policies Converge in Reward-Free Markov Decision Processes

Fanqi Lin[1(✉)], Shiyu Huang[2(✉)], and Wei-Wei Tu[2]

[1] Tsinghua University, Beijing 100084, China
lfq20@mails.tsinghua.edu.cn
[2] 4Paradigm Inc., Beijing 100084, China
{huangshiyu,tuweiwei}@4paradigm.com

Abstract. Reinforcement learning has achieved great success in many decision-making tasks, and traditional reinforcement learning algorithms are mainly designed for obtaining a single optimal solution. However, recent works show the importance of developing diverse policies, which makes it an emerging research topic. Despite the variety of diversity reinforcement learning algorithms that have emerged, none of them theoretically answer the question of how the algorithm converges and how efficient the algorithm is. In this paper, we provide a unified diversity reinforcement learning framework and investigate the convergence of training diverse policies. Under such a framework, we also propose a provably efficient diversity reinforcement learning algorithm. Finally, we verify the effectiveness of our method through numerical experiments.

Keywords: Reinforcement learning · Diversity Reinforcement Learning · Bandit

1 Introduction

Reinforcement learning (RL) shows huge advantages in various decision-making tasks, such as recommendation systems [20,23], game AIs [3,10] and robotic controls [17,24]. While traditional RL algorithms can achieve superhuman performances on many public benchmarks, the obtained policy often falls into a fixed pattern. For example, previously trained agents may just overfit to a determined environment and could be vulnerable to environmental changes [6]. Finding diverse policies may increase the robustness of the agent [12,16]. Moreover, a fixed-pattern agent will easily be attacked [21], because the opponent can find its weakness with a series of attempts. If the agent could play the game with different strategies each round, it will be hard for the opponent to identify the upcoming strategy and it will be unable to apply corresponding attacking tactics [13]. Recently, developing RL algorithms for diverse policies has attracted the attention of the RL community for the promising value of its application and also for the challenge of solving a more complex RL problem [4,7,11].

Current diversity RL algorithms vary widely due to factors like policy diversity measurement, optimization techniques, training strategies, and application

F. Liu et al. (Eds.): PRICAI 2023, LNAI 14325, pp. 125–136, 2024.
https://doi.org/10.1007/978-981-99-7019-3_13

scenarios. This variation makes comparison challenging. While these algorithms often incorporate deep neural networks and empirical tests for comparison, they typically lack in-depth theoretical analysis on training convergence and algorithm complexity, hindering the development of more efficient algorithms.

To address the aforementioned issues, we abstract various diversity RL algorithms, break down the training process, and introduce a unified framework. We offer a convergence analysis for policy population and utilize the contextual bandit formulation to design a more efficient diversity RL algorithm, analyzing its complexity. We conclude with visualizations, experimental evaluations, and an ablation study comparing training efficiencies of different methods. We summaries our contributions as follows: (1) We investigate recent diversity reinforcement learning algorithms and propose a unified framework. (2) We give out the theoretical analysis of the convergence of the proposed framework. (3) We propose a provably efficient diversity reinforcement learning algorithm. (4) We conduct numerical experiments to verify the effectiveness of our method.

2 Related Work

Diversity Reinforcement Learning. Recently, many researchers are committed to the design of diversity reinforcement learning algorithms [4,7,11,19]. DIYAN [7] is a classical diversity RL algorithm, which learns maximum entropy policies via maximizing the mutual information between states and skills. Besides, [19] trains agents with latent conditioned policies which make use of continuous low-dimensional latent variables, thus it can obtain infinite qualified solutions. More recently, RSPO [26] obtains diverse behaviors via iteratively optimizing each policy. DGPO [4] then proposes a more efficient diversity RL algorithm with a novel diversity reward via sharing parameters between policies.

Bandit Algorithms. The challenge in multi-armed bandit algorithm design is balancing exploration and exploitation. Building on ϵ-greedy [22], UCB algorithms [1] introduce guided exploration. Contextual bandit algorithms, like [14,18], improve modeling for recommendation and reinforcement learning. They demonstrate better convergence properties with contextual information [5,14]. Extensive research [2] provides regret bounds for these algorithms.

3 Preliminaries

Markov Decision Process. We consider environments that can be represented as a Markov decision process (MDP). An MDP can be represented as a tuple $(\mathcal{S}, \mathcal{A}, P_T, r, \gamma)$, where $\mathcal{S}$ is the state space, $\mathcal{A}$ is the action space and $\gamma \in [0, 1)$ is the reward discount factor. The state-transition function $P_T(s, a, s') : \mathcal{S} \times \mathcal{A} \times \mathcal{S} \mapsto [0, 1]$ defines the transition probability over the next state s' after taking action a at state s. $r(s, a) : \mathcal{S} \times \mathcal{A} \rightarrow \mathbb{R}$ is the reward function denoting the immediate reward received by the agent when taking action

a in state s. The discounted state occupancy measure of policy π is denoted as $\rho^\pi(s) = (1-\gamma)\sum_{t=0}^{\infty} \gamma^t P_t^\pi(s)$, where $P_t^\pi(s)$ is the probability that policy π visit state s at time t. The agent' objective is to learn a policy π to maximize the expected accumulated reward $J(\theta) = \mathbb{E}_{z\sim p(z), s\sim\rho^\pi(s), a\sim\pi(\cdot|s,z)}[\sum_t \gamma^t r(s_t, a_t)]$. In diversity reinforcement learning, the latent conditioned policy is widely used. The latent conditioned policy is denoted as $\pi(a|s,z)$, and the latent conditioned critic network is denoted as $V^\pi(s,z)$. During execution, the latent variable $z \sim p(z)$ is randomly sampled at the beginning of each episode and keeps fixed for the entire episode. When the latent variable z is discrete, it can be sampled from a categorical distribution with N_z categories. When the latent variable z is continuous, it can be sampled from a Gaussian distribution.

Table 1. Comparison of different diversity algorithms.

Method	Citation	Policy Selection	Reward Calculation
RSPO	[26]	Iteration Fashion	Behavior-driven / Reward-driven exploration
SIPO	[9]	Iteration Fashion	Behavior-driven exploration
DIAYN	[7]	Uniform Sample	$I(s; z)$
DSP	[25]	Uniform Sample	$I(s, a; z)$
DGPO	[4]	Uniform Sample	$\min_{z' \neq z} D_{KL}(\rho^{\pi_\theta}(s\|z) \|\| \rho^{\pi_\theta}(s\|z'))$
Our work		Bandit Selection	Any form mentioned above

4 Methodology

In this section, we will provide a theoretical analysis of diversity algorithms in detail. Firstly, in Sect. 4.1, we propose a unified framework for diversity algorithms, and point out major differences between diversity algorithms in this unified framework. Then we prove the convergence of diversity algorithms in Sect. 4.2. We further formulate the diversity optimization problem as a contextual bandit problem, and propose **bandit selection** in Sect. 4.3. Finally, we provide rigorous proof for *regret* bound of **bandit selection** in Sect. 4.4.

4.1 A Unified Framework for Diversity Algorithms

Although there has been a lot of work on exploring diversity, we find that these algorithms lack a unified framework. So we propose a unified framework for diversity algorithms in Algorithm 1 to pave the way for further research.

We use *Div* to measure the diversity distance between two policies and we abbreviate policy $\pi_\theta(\cdot|s, z_i)$ as π^i. Vector z_i can be thought of as a skill unique to each policy π^i. Moreover, we define $U \in \mathbb{R}^{N\times N}$ as diversity matrix where $U_{ij} = Div(\pi^i, \pi^j)$ and N denotes the number of policies.

For each episode, we first sample z_i to decide which policy to update. Then we interact the chosen policy with the environment to get trajectory τ, which

Algorithm 1. A Unified Framework for Diversity Algorithms

Initialize: $\pi_\theta(\cdot|s,z); U \in \mathbb{R}^{N \times N}(U_{ij} = Div(\pi^i, \pi^j))$
for each episode **do**
  Sample $z_i \sim SelectZ(U)$;
  Get trajectory τ from π^i;
  Get $r^{in} = CalR(\tau)$ and update U;
  Store tuple (s, a, s', r^{in}, z_i) in replay buffer $\mathcal{D}$;
  Update π^i with $\mathcal{D}$;
end for

is used to calculate intrinsic reward r^{in} and update diversity matrix U. We then store tuple (s, a, s', r^{in}, z_i) in replay buffer $\mathcal{D}$ and update π^i through any reinforcement learning algorithm.

Here we abstract the procedure of selecting z_i and calculating r^{in} as $SelectZ$ and $CalR$ functions respectively, which are usually the most essential differences between diversity algorithms. We summarize the comparison of some diversity algorithms in Table 1. Now we describe these two functions in more detail.

Policy Selection. Note that we denote by $p(z)$ the distribution of z. We can divide means to select z_i into three categories in general, namely **iteration fashion**, **uniform sample** and **bandit selection**:

(1) **Iteration fashion.** Diversity algorithms such as RSPO [26] and SIPO [9] obtain diverse policies in an iterative manner. In the k-th iteration, policy π^k will be chosen to update, and the target of optimization is to make π^k sufficiently different from previously discovered policies $\pi^1, ..., \pi^{k-1}$. This method doesn't ensure optimal performance and is greatly affected by policy initialization.
(2) **Uniform sample.** Another kind of popular diversity algorithm such as DIAYN [7] and DGPO [4], samples z_i uniformly to maximize the entropy of $p(z)$. Due to the method's disregard for the differences between policies, it often leads to slower convergence.
(3) **Bandit selection.** We frame obtaining diverse policies as a contextual bandit problem. Sampling z_i corresponds to minimizing regret in this context. This approach guarantees strong performance and rapid convergence.

Reward Calculation. Diversity algorithms differ in intrinsic reward calculation. Some, like [4,7,19], use mutual information theory and a discriminator ϕ to distinguish policies. DIAYN [7] emphasizes deriving skill z from the state s, while [19] suggests using state-action pairs. On the other hand, algorithms like [15,26] aim to make policies' action or reward distributions distinguishable, known as behavior-driven and reward-driven exploration. DGPO [4] maximizes the minimal diversity distance between policies.

4.2 Convergence Analysis

In this section, we will show the convergence of diversity algorithms under a reasonable diversity target. We define $\mathcal{P} = \{\pi^1, \pi^2, ..., \pi^N\}$ as the set of independent policies, or policy population.

Definition 1. $g: \{\pi^1, \pi^2, ..., \pi^N\} \rightarrow \mathbb{R}^{N \times N}$ is a function that maps population $\mathcal{P}$ to diversity matrix U which is defined in Sect. 4.1. Given a population $\mathcal{P}$, we can calculate pairwise diversity distance under a certain diversity metric, which indicates that g is an injective function.

Definition 2. Note that in the iterative process of the diversity algorithm, we update $\mathcal{P}$ directly instead of U. So if we find a valid U that satisfies the diversity target, then the corresponding population $\mathcal{P}$ is exactly our target diverse population. We refer to this process of finding $\mathcal{P}$ backward as g^{-1}.

Definition 3. $f: \mathbb{R}^{N \times N} \rightarrow R$ is a function that maps U to a real number. While U measures the pairwise diversity distance between policies, f measures the diversity of the entire population $\mathcal{P}$. As the diversity of the population increases, the diversity metric calculated by f will increase as well.

Definition 4. We further define δ*-target population set* $\mathcal{T}_\delta = \{g^{-1}(U) | f(U) > \delta, U \in \mathbb{R}^{N \times N}\}$. δ is a threshold used to separate target and non-target regions. The meaning of this definition is that, during the training iteration process, when the diversity metric closely related to U exceeds a certain threshold, or we say $f(U) > \delta$, the corresponding population $\mathcal{P}$ is our target population.

Note two important points: (1) The population meeting the diversity requirement should be a set, not a fixed point. (2) Choose a reasonable threshold δ that ensures both sufficient diversity and ease of obtaining the population.

Theorem 1. $(\frac{\partial f}{\partial U})_{ij} = \frac{\partial f}{\partial U_{ij}} = \frac{\partial f}{\partial Div(\pi^i, \pi^j)} > 0$, *where* $i, j \in \{1, 2, 3, ..., N\}$.
Proof. f *measures the diversity of the entire population* $\mathcal{P}$*. When the diversity distance between two policies in a population* π^i *and* π^j *increases, the overall diversity metric* $f(U)$ *will obviously increase.*

Theorem 2. *We can find some special continuous differentiable* f *that,* $\exists \varepsilon > 0$*, s.t.* $(\frac{\partial f}{\partial U})_{ij} > \varepsilon$*, where* $i, j \in \{1, 2, 3, ..., N\}$.
Proof. For example, we can simply define $f(U) = \sum_{i \neq j} U_{ij}$*, where* $(\frac{\partial f}{\partial U})_{ij} = 1$*. So we can choose threshold* $0 < \varepsilon < 1$*, then we can find* $(\frac{\partial f}{\partial U})_{ij} > \varepsilon$ *obviously. Of course, we can also choose other relatively complex* f *as the diversity metric.*

Theorem 3. *There's a diversity algorithm and a threshold* $\nu > 0$*. Each time the population* $\mathcal{P}$ *is updated, several elements in* U *will increase by at least* ν *in terms of mathematical expectation.*
Proof. In fact, many existing diversity algorithms already have this property. Suppose we currently choose π^i *to update. For DIAYN [7],* $Div(\pi^i, \pi^j)$ *and* $Div(\pi^j, \pi^i)(\forall j \neq i)$ *are increased in the optimization process. And for DGPO [4], suppose policy* π^j *is the closest to policy* π^i *in the policy space, then* $Div(\pi^i, \pi^j)$

and $Div(\pi^j, \pi^i)$ are increased as well in the optimization process. Apart from these two, there are many other existing diversity algorithms such as [15,19,26] that share the same property. Note that we propose Theorem 3 from the perspective of mathematical expectation, so we can infer that, $\exists \nu > 0, j \neq i$, s.t. $Div(\pi'^i, \pi^j) - Div(\pi^i, \pi^j) > \nu$, where policy π'^i denotes the updated policy π^i. And for $k \notin \{i, j\}$, we can assume U_{ik} and U_{ki} are unchanged for simplicity.

Theorem 4. *With an effective diversity algorithm and a reasonable diversity δ-target, we can obtain a diverse population $\mathcal{P} \in T_\delta$.*

Proof. *We denote by $\mathcal{P}_0$ the initialized policy population, and we define $f_0 = f(g(\mathcal{P}_0))$. Then $\exists M \in \mathcal{N}$, s.t. $f_0 + M \cdot \nu\varepsilon > \delta$. Given Theorem 2 and Theorem 3, we define $\mathcal{P}_M$ as the policy population after M iterations, then we have $f(g(\mathcal{P}_M)) > f_0 + M \cdot \nu\varepsilon$, which means we can obtain the δ-target policy population in up to M iterations. Or we can say that the diversity algorithm will converge after at most M iterations.*

Remark. Careful selection of threshold δ is crucial for diversity algorithms. Reasonable diversity goals should be set to avoid difficulty or getting stuck in the training process. This hyperparameter can be obtained through empirical experiments or methods like hyperparameter search. In certain diversity algorithms, both δ and $\mathcal{P}$ may change during training. For instance, in **iteration fashion** algorithms (Sect. 4.1), during the k-th iteration, $\mathcal{P} = \{\pi^1, \pi^2, ..., \pi^k\}$ with a target threshold of δ_k. If policy π^k becomes distinct from $\pi^1, ..., \pi^{k-1}$, meeting the diversity target, policy π_{k+1} is added to $\mathcal{P}$ and the threshold changes to δ_{k+1}.

4.3 A Contextual Bandit Formulation

As mentioned in Sect. 4.1, we can sample z_i via **bandit selection**. In this section, we formally define K-armed contextual bandit problem [14], and show how it models diversity optimization procedure.

Algorithm 2. A Contextual Bandit Formulation

Initialize: Arm Set $\mathcal{A}$; Contextual Bandit Algorithm *Algo*
for $t = 1, 2, 3, ...$ **do**
  Observe feature vectors $x_{t,a}$ for each $a \in \mathcal{A}$;
  Based on $\{x_{t,a}\}_{a \in \mathcal{A}}$ and reward in previous iterations, *Algo* chooses an arm $a_t \in \mathcal{A}$ and receives reward r_{t,a_t};
  Update *Algo* with $(x_{t,a_t}, a_t, r_{t,a_t})$;
end for

We show the procedure of the contextual bandit problem in Algorithm 2. In each iteration, we can observe feature vectors $x_{t,a}$ for each $a \in \mathcal{A}$, which are also denoted as *context*. Note that *context* may change during training. Then, *Algo* will choose an arm $a_t \in \mathcal{A}$ based on contextual information and will receive reward r_{t,a_t}. Finally, tuple $(x_{t,a_t}, a_t, r_{t,a_t})$ will be used to update *Algo*. We further define *T-Reward* [14] of *Algo* as $\sum_{t=1}^{T} r_t$. Similarly, we define the *optimal expected T-Reward* as $\mathbf{E}[\sum_{t=1}^{T} r_{t,a_t^*}]$, where a_t^* denotes the arm with maximum expected reward in iteration t. To measure *Algo*'s performance, we define *T-regret* R_T of *Algo* by

$$R_T = \mathbf{E}[\sum_{t=1}^{T} r_{t,a_t^*}] - \mathbf{E}[\sum_{t=1}^{T} r_{t,a_t}]. \tag{1}$$

Our goal is to minimize R_T.

In the diversity optimization problem, policies are akin to arms, and *context* is represented by visited states or $\rho^{\pi}(s)$. Note that *context* may change as policies evolve. When updating a policy, the reward is the difference in diversity metric before and after the update, linked to the diversity matrix U (Sect. 4.1). Our objective is to maximize policy diversity, equivalent to maximizing expected reward or minimizing R_T in contextual bandit formulation.

Here's an example to demonstrate the effectiveness of **bandit selection**. In some cases, a policy π^i may already be distinct enough from others, meaning that selecting π^i for an update wouldn't significantly affect policy diversity. To address this, we should decrease the probability of sampling π^i. Fixed uniform sampling fails to address this issue, but bandit algorithms like UCB [2] or LinUCB [14] consider both historical rewards and the number of times policies have been chosen. This caters to our needs in such cases.

4.4 Regret Bound

In this section, we provide the *regret* bound for **bandit selection** in the diversity algorithms.

Problem Setting. We define T as the number of iterations. In each iteration t, we can observe N feature vectors $x_{t,a} \in \mathbb{R}^d$ and receive reward r_{t,a_t} with $\|x_{t,a}\| \leq 1$ for $a \in \mathcal{A}$ and $r_{t,a_t} \in [0,1]$, where $\|\cdot\|$ means l_2-norm, d denotes the dimension of feature vector and a_t is the chosen action in iteration t.

Linear Realizability Assumption. Similar to lots of theoretical analyses of contextual bandit problems [1,5], we propose linear realizability assumption to simplify the problem. We assume that there exists an unknown weight vector $\theta^* \in \mathbb{R}^d$ with $\|\theta^*\| \leq 1$ s.t.

$$\mathbf{E}[r_{t,a}|x_{t,a}] = x_{t,a}^T \theta^*. \tag{2}$$

for all t and a.

We now analyze the rationality of this assumption in practical diversity algorithms. Reward $r_{t,a}$ measures the changed value of overall diversity metric

$\triangle f(U)$ of policy population $\mathcal{P}$ after an update. Suppose π_t^i is the policy corresponding to the feature vector $x_{t,a}$ in the iteration t. While $x_{t,a}$ encodes state features of π_t^i, it can encode the diversity information of π_t^i as well. Therefore, we can conclude that $r_{t,a}$ is closely related to $x_{t,a}$. So given that $x_{t,a}$ contains enough diversity information, we can assume that the hypothesis holds.

Theorem 5. *(Diversity Reinforcement Learning Oracle $\mathcal{DRLO}$). Given a reasonable δ-target and an effective diversity algorithm, let the probability that the policy population $\mathcal{P}$ reaches δ-target in T iterations be $1-\backepsilon_{\delta,T}$. Then we have* $\lim_{T\to\infty}\backepsilon_{\delta,T}=0$.
Proof. This is actually another formal description of the convergence of diversity algorithms which has been proved in Sect. 4.2. Experimental results [4, 19] have shown that $\backepsilon_{\delta,T}$ will decrease significantly when T reaches a certain value.

Theorem 6. *(Contextual Bandit Algorithm Oracle $\mathcal{CBAO}$). There exists a contextual bandit algorithm that makes regret bounded by $O\left(\sqrt{Td\ln^3(NT\ln(T)/\eta)}\right)$ for T iterations with probability $1-\eta$.*
Proof. Different contextual bandit algorithm corresponds to different regret bound. In fact, we can use the regret bound of any contextual bandit algorithm here. The regret bound mentioned here is the regret bound of SupLinUCB algorithm [5]. For concrete proof of this regret bound, we refer the reader to [5].

Theorem 7. *For T iterations, the regret for* **bandit selection** *in diversity algorithms is bounded by $O\left(\sqrt{Td\ln^3(\frac{NT\ln(T)(1-\backepsilon_{\delta,T})}{\eta-\backepsilon_{\delta,T}})}\right)$ with probability $1-\eta$. Note that* $\lim_{T\to\infty}(\eta-\backepsilon_{\delta,T})=\eta>0$.
Proof. In diversity algorithms, the calculation of the regret bound is based on the premise that a certain δ-target has been achieved. Note that $\mathcal{DRLO}$ and $\mathcal{CBAO}$ are independent variables in this problem setting. Given $0<\eta<1$, we define

$$\eta_1=\frac{\eta-\backepsilon_{\delta,T}}{1-\backepsilon_{\delta,T}}. \tag{3}$$

Then we have

$$1-\eta=(1-\backepsilon_{\delta,T})(1-\eta_1). \tag{4}$$

The implication of Eq. 4 is that, for T iterations, with probability $1-\eta$, the regret for **bandit selection** *in diversity algorithms is bounded by*

$$O\left(\sqrt{Td\ln^3(NT\ln(T)/\eta_1)}\right)=O\left(\sqrt{Td\ln^3(\frac{NT\ln(T)(1-\backepsilon_{\delta,T})}{\eta-\backepsilon_{\delta,T}})}\right). \tag{5}$$

The right-hand side of Eq. 5 is exactly the regret bound we propose in Theorem 7.

5 Experiments

This section presents some experimental results about diversity algorithms. Firstly, from an intuitive geometric perspective, we demonstrate the process of policy evolution in the diversity algorithm. Then we compare the three policy selection methods mentioned in Sect. 4.1 by experiments, which illustrates the high efficiency of **bandit selection**.

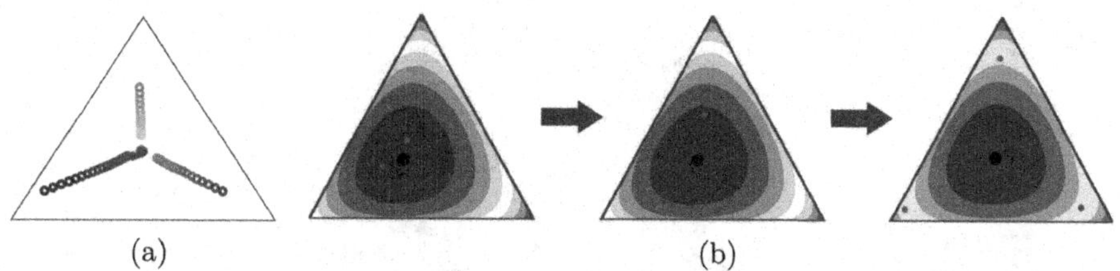

Fig. 1. (a) Policy evolution trajectory. We initialize three policies here, denoted by red, yellow, and green circles on the simplex. The darker the color of the policy, the more iterations it has gone through, and the greater the diversity distance between this policy and other policies is. Moreover, the blue circles on the simplex denote the average state marginal distribution of policies $\rho(s)$. (b) Policy evolution process. We initialize three policies here as well, denoted by red, green, and blue dots on the simplex. The black dot denotes the average state marginal distribution of policies $\rho(s)$. Moreover, the contour lines in the figure correspond to the diversity metric $I(s;z)$. (Color figure online)

5.1 A Geometric Perspective on Policy Evolution

To visualize the policy evolution process, we use DIAYN [7] as our diversity algorithm and construct a simple 3-state MDP [8] to conduct the experiment. The set of feasible state marginal distributions is described by a triangle $[(1,0,0),(0,1,0),(0,0,1)]$ in $\mathbb{R}^3$. And we use state occupancy measure $\rho^{\pi_i}(s)$ to represent policy π^i. Moreover, we project the state occupancy measure onto a two-dimensional simplex for visualization.

Let $\rho(s)$ be the average state marginal distribution of all policies. Figure 1(a) shows policy evolution during training. Initially, the state occupancy measures of different policies are similar. However, as training progresses, the policies spread out, indicating increased diversity. Figure 1(a) highlights that diversity [8] ensures distinct state occupancy measures among policies.

We use $I(\cdot;\cdot)$ to denote mutual information. The diversity metric in unsupervised skill discovery algorithms is based on the mutual information of states and latent variable z. Furthermore, the mutual information can be viewed as the average divergence between each policy's state distribution $\rho(s|z)$ and the average state distribution $\rho(s)$ [8]:

$$I(s;z) = \mathbf{E}_{p(z)}[D_{KL}(\rho(s|z) \parallel \rho(s))]. \tag{6}$$

Figure 1(b) shows the policy evolution process and the diversity metric $I(s;z)$. We find that the diversity metric increased gradually during the training process, which is in line with our expectation.

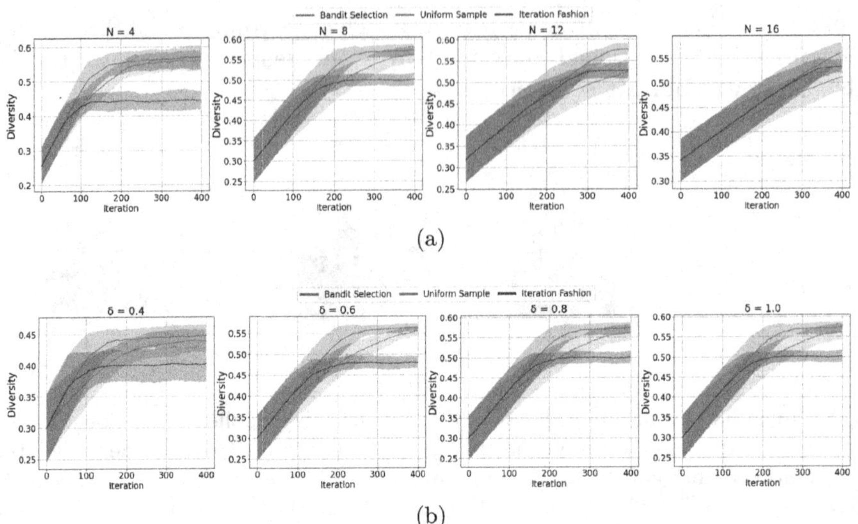

Fig. 2. Comparison of different policy selection methods. (a) Training curves for different numbers of policies with a fixed *δ-target* where $\delta = 0.8$. (b) Training curves for different *δ-target* with a fixed number of policies where $N = 8$.

5.2 Policy Selection Ablation

We continue to use 3-state MDP [8] as the experimental environment. Whereas, in order to get closer to the complicated practical environment, we set specific *δ-target* and increased the number of policies. Moreover, when a policy that hasn't met the diversity requirement is chosen to update, we will receive a reward $r = 1$, otherwise, we will receive a reward $r = 0$. We use $I(s; z)$ as the diversity metric and use LinUCB [14] as our contextual bandit algorithm.

Figure 2 shows the training curves under different numbers of policies and different *δ-target* over six random seeds. The results show that **bandit selection** not only always reaches the convergence fastest, but also achieves the highest overall diversity metric of the population when it converges. We now empirically analyze the reasons for this result:

Drawbacks of Uniform Sample. In many experiments, we observe that **uniform sample** has similar final performance to **bandit selection**, but significantly slower convergence. This is because after several iterations, some policies become distinct enough to prioritize updating other policies. However, **uniform sample** treats all policies equally, resulting in slow convergence.

Drawbacks of Iteration Fashion. In experiments, the **iteration fashion** converges quickly but has lower final performance than the other two methods. It's greatly affected by initialization. Each policy update depends on the previous one, so poor initialization can severely impact subsequent updates, damaging the overall training process.

Advantages of Bandit Selection. Considering historical rewards and balancing exploitation and exploration, **bandit selection** quickly determines if a policy is different enough to adjust the sample's probability distribution. Unlike **iteration fashion**, all policies can be selected for an update in a single iteration, making **bandit selection** not limited by policy initialization.

6 Conclusion

In this paper, we compare existing diversity algorithms, provide a unified diversity reinforcement learning framework, and investigate the convergence of training diverse policies. Moreover, we propose **bandit selection** under our proposed framework, and present the *regret* bound for it. Empirical results indicate that **bandit selection** achieves the highest diversity score with the fastest convergence speed compared to baseline methods. We also provide a geometric perspective on policy evolution through experiments. In the future, we will focus on the comparison and theoretical analysis of different reward calculation methods. And we will continually explore the application of diversity RL algorithms in more real-world decision-making tasks.

References

1. Auer, P.: Using confidence bounds for exploitation-exploration trade-offs. J. Mach. Learn. Res. **3**(Nov), 397–422 (2002)
2. Auer, P., Cesa-Bianchi, N., Fischer, P.: Finite-time analysis of the multiarmed bandit problem. Mach. Learn. **47**(2), 235–256 (2002)
3. Berner, C., et al.: Dota 2 with large scale deep reinforcement learning. arXiv preprint arXiv:1912.06680 (2019)
4. Chen, W., Huang, S., Chiang, Y., Chen, T., Zhu, J.: DGPO: discovering multiple strategies with diversity-guided policy optimization. In: Proceedings of the 2023 International Conference on Autonomous Agents and Multiagent Systems, pp. 2634–2636 (2023)
5. Chu, W., Li, L., Reyzin, L., Schapire, R.: Contextual bandits with linear payoff functions. In: Proceedings of the Fourteenth International Conference on Artificial Intelligence and Statistics, pp. 208–214. JMLR Workshop and Conference Proceedings (2011)
6. Ellis, B., et al.: SMACv2: an improved benchmark for cooperative multi-agent reinforcement learning. arXiv preprint arXiv:2212.07489 (2022)
7. Eysenbach, B., Gupta, A., Ibarz, J., Levine, S.: Diversity is all you need: learning skills without a reward function. In: International Conference on Learning Representations (2018)
8. Eysenbach, B., Salakhutdinov, R., Levine, S.: The information geometry of unsupervised reinforcement learning. In: International Conference on Learning Representations (2021)

9. Fu, W., Du, W., Li, J., Chen, S., Zhang, J., Wu, Y.: Iteratively learning novel strategies with diversity measured in state distances. Submitted to ICLR 2023 (2022)
10. Huang, S., et al.: Tikick: towards playing multi-agent football full games from single-agent demonstrations. arXiv preprint arXiv:2110.04507 (2021)
11. Huang, S., et al.: VMAPD: generate diverse solutions for multi-agent games with recurrent trajectory discriminators. In: 2022 IEEE Conference on Games (CoG), pp. 9–16. IEEE (2022)
12. Kumar, S., Kumar, A., Levine, S., Finn, C.: One solution is not all you need: few-shot extrapolation via structured maxent RL. Adv. Neural. Inf. Process. Syst. **33**, 8198–8210 (2020)
13. Lanctot, M., et al.: A unified game-theoretic approach to multiagent reinforcement learning. In: Advances in neural information processing systems, vol. 30 (2017)
14. Li, L., Chu, W., Langford, J., Schapire, R.E.: A contextual-bandit approach to personalized news article recommendation. In: Proceedings of the 19th International Conference on World Wide Web, pp. 661–670 (2010)
15. Liu, X., et al.: Unifying behavioral and response diversity for open-ended learning in zero-sum games. arXiv preprint arXiv:2106.04958 (2021)
16. Mahajan, A., Rashid, T., Samvelyan, M., Whiteson, S.: Maven: multi-agent variational exploration. arXiv preprint arXiv:1910.07483 (2019)
17. Makoviychuk, V., et al.: Isaac gym: high performance GPU-based physics simulation for robot learning. arXiv preprint arXiv:2108.10470 (2021)
18. May, B.C., Korda, N., Lee, A., Leslie, D.S.: Optimistic bayesian sampling in contextual-bandit problems. J. Mach. Learn. Res. **13**, 2069–2106 (2012)
19. Osa, T., Tangkaratt, V., Sugiyama, M.: Discovering diverse solutions in deep reinforcement learning by maximizing state-action-based mutual information. Neural Netw. **152**, 90–104 (2022)
20. Shi, J.C., Yu, Y., Da, Q., Chen, S.Y., Zeng, A.X.: Virtual-taobao: virtualizing real-world online retail environment for reinforcement learning. In: Proceedings of the AAAI Conference on Artificial Intelligence, vol. 33, pp. 4902–4909 (2019)
21. Wang, T.T., et al.: Adversarial policies beat professional-level go AIs. arXiv preprint arXiv:2211.00241 (2022)
22. Watkins, C.J.C.H.: Learning from delayed rewards. Robot. Auton. Syst. (1989)
23. Xue, W., Cai, Q., Zhan, R., Zheng, D., Jiang, P., An, B.: ResAct: Reinforcing long-term engagement in sequential recommendation with residual actor. arXiv preprint arXiv:2206.02620 (2022)
24. Yu, C., Yang, X., Gao, J., Yang, H., Wang, Y., Wu, Y.: Learning efficient multi-agent cooperative visual exploration. arXiv preprint arXiv:2110.05734 (2021)
25. Zahavy, T., O'Donoghue, B., Barreto, A., Flennerhag, S., Mnih, V., Singh, S.: Discovering diverse nearly optimal policies with successor features. In: ICML 2021 Workshop on Unsupervised Reinforcement Learning (2021)
26. Zhou, Z., Fu, W., Zhang, B., Wu, Y.: Continuously discovering novel strategies via reward-switching policy optimization. In: International Conference on Learning Representations (2021)

PruVer: Verification Assisted Pruning for Deep Reinforcement Learning

Briti Gangopadhyay(✉), Pallab Dasgupta, and Soumyajit Dey

Indian Institute of Technology Kharagpur, Kharagpur, India
briti.tana@gmail.com

Abstract. Active deployment of Deep Reinforcement Learning (DRL) based controllers on safety-critical embedded platforms require model compaction. Neural pruning has been extensively studied in the context of CNNs and computer vision, but such approaches do not guarantee the preservation of safety in the context of DRL. A pruned network converging to high reward may not adhere to safety requirements. This paper proposes a framework, PruVer, that performs iterative refinement on a pruned network with verification in the loop. This results in a compressed network that adheres to safety specifications with formal guarantees over small time horizons. We demonstrate our method in model-free RL environments, achieving 40–60% compaction, significant latency benefits (3 to 10 times), and bounded guarantees for safety properties.

Keywords: Neural Pruning · Reinforcement Learning · Verification

1 Introduction

Reinforcement learning (RL) policies are having a high penetration in embedded safety-critical domains given their capability of learning human-like control strategies [11,22]. These policies work over large continuous state spaces making Deep Neural Networks (DNN) a natural choice for policy approximation. State-of-the-art DNN architectures often contain millions of connections and neurons, making them unsuitable for edge devices. The implementation of Deep Reinforcement Learning (DRL) policies in real time embedded systems with computational limitations requires memory-optimized models. One of the popular methods for network compression is neural network pruning. Pruning refers to the selective removal of weights or connections from a pre-trained neural network to improve efficiency while retaining performance [4]. The use of sparse networks in computer vision has been thoroughly studied in [10,18], and in many cases, sparse networks are found to be just as effective as dense networks. Devising storage formats for efficient utilization of sparse neural networks is a growing body of work [7]. Although network compression is crucial for the deployment of DRL-based controllers in embedded platforms, there exists little research in this domain. In computer vision research, the performance of sparse networks is

F. Liu et al. (Eds.): PRICAI 2023, LNAI 14325, pp. 137–149, 2024.
https://doi.org/10.1007/978-981-99-7019-3_14

gauged in terms of classification accuracy. In accordance with advances in computer vision, performance comparisons for sparse networks in DRL have been made solely in terms of the maximum reward obtained [14].

One very important consideration for DRL-based controllers is *safety*. While there is a growing body of literature focusing on safe RL [13], existing literature on the effect of sparsity on safety is scarce, especially for RL. We believe that in the context of resource-constrained DRL, safety preservation is just as important as compaction. A compressed network achieving high rewards may have safety violations, as the removal of weights may undo the effect of safety-based training. To address this issue, we propose an iterative algorithm to refine a pruned network until safety specifications are guaranteed to hold.

One way to guarantee that the pruned network adheres to safety requirements is to prove safety properties over the network using formal verification. However, formal verification of DRL networks is challenging as state-of-the-art DNN verification tools [8,15–17] have scalability barriers. The scaling problem is exacerbated in the context of DRL working with environment feedback, which requires decision-making for sequential DNNs and, consequently, reasoning about recurrent DNN executions where the output of one execution can influence the input to the DNN in later invocations. In the absence of complete knowledge about the transition function in model-free RL, which further aggravates the verification problem, we propose a depth-bounded formal verification approach.

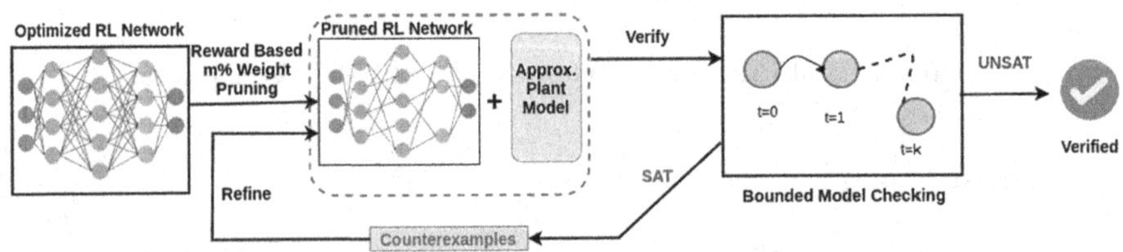

Fig. 1. Overview of the verification assisted pruning framework

We propose a novel pruning refinement and verification (*PruVer*) framework which contains the following steps:

1. To verify a reward-preserving pruned DRL network, we present a verification strategy that either guarantees or finds counterexamples for given safety specifications within a given bounded length k with monotonicity assumptions on the system dynamics.
2. For counterexamples discovered during verification, we propose an iterative refinement technique that refines the pruned DRL network while preserving rewards and inducing safety with respect to given safety specifications.

To the best of the authors' knowledge, this is the first attempt at safety-aware pruning with verification in the loop for DRL networks in a model-free setting. We implement this method on OpenAI gym environments and obtain 40–60%

network compaction with 3–10 times speedup without compromising safety on time horizons of up to 100–140 steps. An overview of the proposed PruVer framework is presented in Fig. 1.

2 Related Work

Pruning and verification are both essential for the practical realization of DNNs in embedded platforms. Hence, these fields are emerging areas of research. We discuss some of the relevant literature in this section.

2.1 Pruning in Deep Reinforcement Learning

Though neural pruning has been extensively studied and applied in computer vision tasks, it remains a neonate in the field of Deep RL. Most of the work centers around the lottery ticket hypothesis [10]. Work done by [9,24] illustrates that the success of sparse initialization mainly depends on choosing the appropriate characteristics for the input data rather than any inherent properties of the various initialization. Recent works on DRL pruning [3,14,23] focus on achieving high rewards from sparse networks. However, for safety-critical control tasks, it is also important for the sparse network to take safe actions. Our work introduces verification-assisted neural pruning, where the sparse network is iteratively revised to handle safety infractions. Other DRL pruning methods involve methods like dense to sparse training [18,21,25] where a dense neural network is reduced in size by gradually pruning the weights, and the sparse network is retrained on the given task. This method often finds the best-performing sparse network. However, continuous pruning and training induce considerable computational overhead, sometimes equivalent to training the dense network. Our method gradually incorporates the learned weights through gradient update rather than retraining the network without additional training time overhead. The benefits of safety-aware pruning of DRL networks were outlined in a 2-page student abstract in [12]. However, the formal verification approach and methodology details are presented in this work for the first time.

2.2 DRL Network Verification

DRL verification aims to establish that learned input-to-output mapping adheres to certain safety specifications. A comprehensive survey on different algorithms for DRL verification can be found in [1]. In this work, we use tools Marabou [17] and Sherlock [8], as backends that utilize search and optimization methods to falsify assertions. For a verification problem, a pre-condition P is specified on the network's input, and safety specifications are given in terms of post-condition Q on the network's output. The goal of Marabou is to solve SMT equations derived from DNN to find concrete inputs s_i such that $P(s_i) \wedge \neg Q(s_i)$ is satisfied. s_i forms the counterexample for the given safety condition. When the tool returns UNSAT, the desired property always holds. To handle the sequential nature of

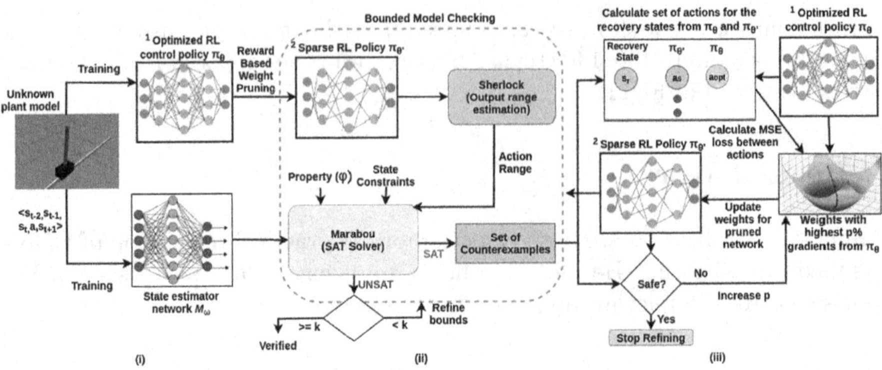

Fig. 2. Detailed overview of the PruVer framework for verification and refinement of sparse neural networks in DRL.

DRL networks where a previous output can influence the values of the following state, we use Bounded Model Checking (BMC), which is also used in recent DRL verification tools like Whirl 2.0 [1]. BMC focuses on runs with a finite length $k > 0$ for safety properties. This makes the verification algorithm tractable while ensuring any discovered counter-example is accurate. Formally the BMC query can be written as:

$$\exists s_1, \ldots, s_k . P(s_0) \wedge (\bigwedge_{i=0}^{k-1} T(s_i, s_{i+1})) \wedge (\bigwedge_{i=1}^{k} \neg Q(s_i))$$

Here $P(s_0)$ is the initial state with pre-conditions P and $T(s_i, s_{i+1})$ is the transition relation of the system, which is unknown in model-free RL.

3 Methodology

Figure 2 summarises the detailed workflow of the *PruVer* framework which comprises the following broad set of steps.

1. Given an unknown plant model (Fig. 2(i)) and an optimized safe DRL based dense policy network π_θ, with parameters θ, and average reward $\mathcal{R}(\pi_\theta)$, we first construct a sparse network $\pi_{\theta'}$ with $\theta' = m \odot \theta$, such that $\mathcal{R}(\pi_{\theta'}) \geq \lambda$ (reward greater than or equal to threshold λ). Here $m = \{0,1\}^\theta$ is the sparsity mask, $|m_1| \ll |\theta|$ (fewer parameters), and $\odot$ denotes dot product. We use the training traces of π_θ with the plant in the loop as black-box, to learn an approximate plant model $\mathcal{M}_\omega$.
2. In the next step (Fig. 2(ii)) under certain assumptions about the unknown plant dynamics, we verify the closed loop system $\mathcal{M}_\omega || \pi_{\theta'}$ against a set of safety properties φ. The safety verification problem in k-depth bounded form is given by $S_0 \in \varphi_{pre} \implies S_k \in \varphi_{post}$. Here, φ_{pre} is the set of pre-conditions, and φ_{post} is the set of post-conditions. φ_{post} are essential conditions for safe

operation. S_0 is any state satisfying the pre-conditions, $\mathcal{M}_\omega(S_i, \pi_{\theta'}(S_i)) = S_{i+1}$, and S_k is the set of states reachable after k transitions. The states in set S_k are observable. We wish to guarantee that every such S_k satisfies the post-conditions. This reduces to the underlying satisfiability query given by,

$$\exists S_0, \dots, S_k (S_0 \in \varphi_{pre}) \wedge (\bigwedge_{i=0}^{k-1} S_{i+1} = \mathcal{M}_\omega(S_i, \pi_{\theta'}(S_i))) \wedge (\bigwedge_{i=1}^{k} \neg(S_i \in \varphi_{post}))$$

3. The verification step either returns a satisfiable assignment of the input variables in some iteration i or returns UNSAT over all iterations. In the later case, $(S_0, \pi_{\theta'}) \models_k \varphi_{post}$. On encountering valid counterexamples, θ' is iteratively refined (Fig. 2(iii)) until $(S_0, \pi_{\theta'}) \models_k \varphi_{post}$ (refinement success) or $\theta' = \theta$ (refinement failure).

In the next section, we discuss the verification strategy for the pruned RL network and outline the refinement strategy. We assume that the abstract model of the dynamical system on which $\pi_{\theta'}$ acts is of the form: $\dot{s} = f(s, a)$ where $s \in \mathcal{S} \subseteq \mathbb{R}^n$ and $a \in \mathcal{A} \subseteq \mathbb{R}^m$ and f is locally Lipschitz in s and a. A flow map of the system is given by $\phi(t_k; t_0, s_k, a_k)$ denoting a state of the system at each time t_k with state s_k and action a_k. The reachability problem is as follows:

Problem 1. *(Reachability of continuous dynamical system) Given a state interval,* $[\underline{s_0}, \bar{s_0}] \subseteq \mathbb{R}^n$*, an action interval,* $[\underline{a_0}, \bar{a_0}] \subseteq \mathbb{R}^m$ *that defines the continuous action space, and a time interval* $[t_0, t_k] \subseteq \mathbb{R}$*, identify an over-approximating interval in* $\mathbb{R}^n$ *containing all states reachable from the states contained in the state interval,* $[\underline{s_0}, \bar{s_0}]$*, within* $[t_0, t_k]$*:*

$$R(t_k; t_0, [\underline{s_k}, \bar{s_k}], [\underline{a_k}, \bar{a_k}]) = \{\phi(t_k; t_0, s_k, a_k) | s_k \in [\underline{s_k}, \bar{s_k}], a_k \in [\underline{a_k}, \bar{a_k}]\}$$

If $[\underline{s_0}, \bar{s_0}] \in \varphi_{pre} \implies [\underline{s_k}, \bar{s_k}] \in \varphi_{post}$ then $(S_0, \pi_{\theta'}) \models_k \varphi_{post}$. In the model-free RL verification setting, at each timestep t_k, both the reachable state range $[\underline{s_k}, \bar{s_k}]$ and the action interval range $[\underline{a_k}, \bar{a_k}]$ are unknown. Therefore we use the following approach.

First, we estimate the action ranges from $\pi_{\theta'}$. We use the tool Sherlock [8] to estimate the maximum and minimum values of actions produced by $\pi_{\theta'}$ for input range $[\underline{s_k}, \bar{s_k}]$ at timestep k. The estimated range is guaranteed to be tight for a set of inputs forming a polyhedron ([8], Theorem 1.1).
Next, we aim to create a flow map for estimating the state range containing the reachable states within time, t_k. Since the system dynamics is not known, standard approaches for flow map construction cannot be used directly. Therefore, we prepare a state estimator network, $\mathcal{M}_\omega$, that takes $\langle s_{t-2}, s_{t-1}, s_t, a_t \rangle$ as input and estimates s_{t+1}. $\mathcal{M}_\omega$ is prepared by training a feed-forward network using $\langle s, a, s' \rangle$ pairs observed during training of the original network π_θ. $\mathcal{M}_\omega$ trains by minimizing the Mean Square Error (MSE) loss between the predicted s_{t+1} and the actual s_{t+1}. To guarantee that all reachable states in Problem 1 will be contained in the inferred state boundaries using $\mathcal{M}_\omega$ we assume the dynamics learnt by $\mathcal{M}_\omega$ is *monotonic*, as defined below:

Definition 2. *([2],Definition II.1) A dynamic control system is monotone if the following condition holds for all* $t \geq 0$*:*

$$a_1 \succeq a_2, s_1 \succeq s_2 \implies \phi(t, s_1, a_1) \succeq \phi(t, s_2, a_2) \tag{1}$$

Algorithm 1: Verification of $\pi_{\theta'}$

Input: *StateEstimator* $\mathcal{M}_\omega$, *Bound* k, $\pi_{\theta'}$,φ,ϵ_{range}

Function `Verify`($\mathcal{M}_\omega$, k, $\pi_{\theta'}$,φ,ϵ_{range}):

1 $\mathcal{M}, \xi_f = Marabou(\mathcal{M}_\omega), []$

$\varphi_{post} = [(\varphi_{post_{lower}}, \varphi_{post_{upper}})]$ //from φ

for $i = 0 \ldots k$ **do**

$\varphi_{pre} = [(\varphi_{pre_{lower}}, \varphi_{pre_{upper}})]$ //from φ

$\mathcal{A}_{range} = [(\mathcal{A}_{lower}, \mathcal{A}_{upper})]$ //from φ

2 $\mathcal{Z}_{range} = \epsilon_{range} \cup \varphi_{pre} \cup \mathcal{A}_{range}$

3 **for** $node \in \mathcal{M}_\omega.input$ **do**

$\mathcal{M}.setBound(node, \mathcal{Z}_{lower}, \mathcal{Z}_{upper})$

end

for $node \in \mathcal{M}_\omega.output$ **do**

$\mathcal{M}.addInequality(node, \varphi_{post_{lower}}, \varphi_{post_{upper}})$

end

4 $exitCode, \xi_i = \mathcal{M}.solve()$

5 **if** $exitCode == UNSAT$ **then**

$A_{lower}, A_{upper} = Sherlock(\varphi_{pre_{lower}}, \varphi_{pre_{upper}}, \pi_{\theta'})$

6 $\varphi_{pre_{lower}}, \varphi_{pre_{upper}} = \mathcal{M}_\omega(\varphi_{pre_{lower}}, \mathcal{A}_{lower}), \mathcal{M}_\omega(\varphi_{pre_{upper}}, \mathcal{A}_{upper})$

else

7 $\xi_f = \xi_f \cup \xi_i$

end

end

$Refine\_Pruned\_Policy(\pi_{\theta'}, \xi_f)$

We will make a slightly relaxed assumption, where the system only needs to be monotone with respect to the variables in the property we are verifying.

We now discuss the working of Algorithm 1, which is used to verify $\pi_{\theta'}$. We first convert the state estimator network $\mathcal{M}_\omega$ into a set of equivalent SAT formulations using the tool Marabou (line 1). We start with an initial range on states φ_{pre}, action range $\mathcal{A}_{range}$, and post conditions φ_{post}. Additionally, we are given a permissible range for history states (ϵ_{range}), which are input to $\mathcal{M}_\omega$.

The history states are copies of s_0, s_1 until $k = 2$. Since $\mathcal{M}_\omega$ has the input of the form $\langle s_{t-2}, s_{t-1}, s_t, a_t \rangle$ we combine ($\epsilon_{range}, \varphi_{pre}, \mathcal{A}_{range}$) to obtain the interval range for each input node (line 2) of $\mathcal{M}_\omega$. We set the input ranges, add inequality constraints to the SAT equations for ranges on the output nodes of $\mathcal{M}_\omega$, and solve the equations using the Marabou solver (lines 3–4). If the solver returns UNSAT for a particular iteration t, then the property holds up to t. We then propagate the interval ranges for the next time step by first calculating the action range ($\mathcal{A}_{lower}, \mathcal{A}_{upper}$) produced by $\pi_{\theta'}$ given the current bounds on the state (lines 5–6). The upper bound for the next state is obtained from $\mathcal{M}_\omega$ with inputs $\varphi_{pre_{upper}}, \mathcal{A}_{upper}$ due to the monotonicity assumption on $\mathcal{M}_\omega$. Similarly, the lower bound is obtained with inputs $\varphi_{pre_{lower}}, \mathcal{A}_{lower}$. If the solver returns SAT in any iteration with a counterexample ξ_{f_i}, then ξ_{f_i} is stored in a set ξ_f (line 7) and is used for refinement.

Since the underlying dynamic system is assumed to be monotone w.r.t φ, all the values of the property variables lie within the deduced lower and upper intervals of the states at each timestep. Hence, Algorithm 1 is sound i.e., if Algorithm 1 returns UNSAT, then $(S_0, \pi_{\theta'}) \models_k \varphi_{post}$.

3.1 Refinement of the Pruned Network $\pi_{\theta'}$

For each counterexample trajectory $\xi_{f_i} \in \xi_f$, we calculate it's recovery state using π_θ. A recovery state is defined as follows:

Definition 3. *A recovery state s_{r_i} in a counterexample trajectory $\xi_{f_i} \in \xi_f$ is defined as the last state $s_i \in \xi_{f_i}$ for which there exists some safe trajectory ξ_i', such that the prefix trajectory of $s_i \in \xi_{f_i}$ and the prefix trajectory of $s_i \in \xi_i'$ are identical, $\xi_i' \models \varphi$, and $\mathcal{R}(\xi_i') \geq \lambda$.*

We find recovery states through backtracking. It is important to note since π_θ is safe; there is at least one recovery state for each ξ_{f_i}.

Algorithm 2: Refining the pruned policy

Input: Dense Policy π_θ, Pruned Policy $\pi_{\theta'}$, Failure Trajectories ξ_f, $recovery_{set}$

Function `Refine_Pruned_Policy`($\pi_\theta, \pi_{\theta'}, \xi_f, recovery_{set}$):

  $a_{opt}, a_s, p, safe = [], [], 5, False$

  while $p \leq 100$ *and* $\neg safe$ **do**

    for *each* s_{r_i} *in* $recovery_{set}$ **do**

      $a_{opt} = \pi_\theta(s_{r_i}) \cup a_{opt_i}$

      $a_s = \pi_{\theta'}(s_{r_i}) \cup a_{s_i}$

    end

    $\mathcal{L} = MSE(a_{opt}, a_s)$

    $\pi_{\theta'}.backward(\mathcal{L})$

    $rank[layer] = max_{grad}(\pi_{\theta'}.grad, p, layer)$

    for *each* $layer \in \pi_{\theta'}$ **do**

      $\pi_{\theta'}.weight = \pi_\theta.weight[rank[layer]]$

      $safe = check\_safety(\pi_{\theta'}, \xi_f)$

      If safe **then** break

    end

    $p = p + 0.02$

  end

  return $\pi_{\theta'}$

Once the set of recovery states is identified, we use Algorithm 2 to refine the pruned network $\pi_{\theta'}$. For each recovery state in $s_{r_i} \in recovery_{set}$, the action proposed by the optimal network π_θ and the sparse network $\pi_{\theta'}$ is calculated and added to the action batches a_{opt} and a_s respectively (lines 1–2). For the recovery state s_{r_i} we aim to shift the action a_{s_i} towards a_{opt_i} so that ξ_{f_i} can be corrected. To measure the deviation of a_s from a_{opt}, we calculate the mean square error between the action batches (line 3).

$$\mathcal{L}(a_s, a_{opt}) = \frac{1}{N}\sum_{i=0}^{N}(a_{s_i} - a_{opt_i})^2$$

We calculate the first-order partial derivative for weights of each layer with respect to the Loss function, $\frac{\delta \mathcal{L}}{\delta w_{ij}}$, which is the gradient of the Loss with respect to the jth weight of the ith layer. The gradient information denotes the weight change required to shift $\pi_{\theta'}(s_{r_i})$ towards $\pi_\theta(s_{r_i})$. We select the top $p\%$ of the gradient locations from the sparsified network using the function $max_{grad}()$ and store the locations in a matrix $rank$ (line 4). The weights in $ranks$ are selected layer-wise from π_θ and reinstated in $\pi_{\theta'}$ (line 5). After each reinstatement, the refined network $\pi_{\theta'}$ is checked against all the failure traces in ξ_f using the function *check_safety*(). If all the counterexamples are corrected, then the refinement process stops. Otherwise, p is increased by a small amount, and the algorithm continues (line 6). If no sparse network exists for the given task, then $\pi_{\theta'}$ will gradually converge to π_θ.

4 Case Studies

This section presents three case studies on the continuous cart-pole, mountain car, and lunar lander environments from the OpenAI gym suite [5] and comparative studies with two state-of-the-art pruning techniques, Sparse Evolutionary Training (SET) [19] and Rigged Lottery (RigL) [9] which have been recently used for RL [14]. All experiments were performed on a workstation with AMD Ryzen 4600h six-core processor and GeForce GTX 1660 Graphics unit. We report the results of our comparative study with SET and RigL in Table 1. The SET and RigL networks are initialized at the same sparsity (provided in the Sparsity column) as the final PruVer network. We observe that training SET and RigL networks require additional hyperparameter tuning and take longer training time as they are trained from scratch. We also report that these networks converge to a lower reward than PruVer. Also, these methods provide no safety guarantees as they do not have verification in the loop like PruVer. Code contributions are available in[1]. The Specifics of case studies on each environment are discussed as follows.

Cart-pole Swing-up Environment: The continuous cart-pole swing-up environment is a benchmark problem in control systems. The goal is to balance an

[1] https://github.com/britig/PruVer.

Table 1. Comparison with SET and Rigl w.r.t to time and reward. We also show the percentage of zero parameters of the network after refinement.

Environment	SET		RigL		PruVer		%Sparsity
	Training	Reward	Training	Reward	Refinement	Reward	
Cart-pole swing-up	34.14 m	118.82 ± 80.92	47.79 m	153.47 ± 121.87	5.61 m .	194.70 ± 156.14	49.64
MountainCar	27.89 m	46.00 ± 53.24	35.38 m	43.64 ± 53.97	4.29 m	93.8 ± 3.5	59.78
Lunar Lander	34.10 m	231.91 ± 63.96	43.28 m	268.69 ± 36.33	7.70 m	283.96 ± 17.91	39.68

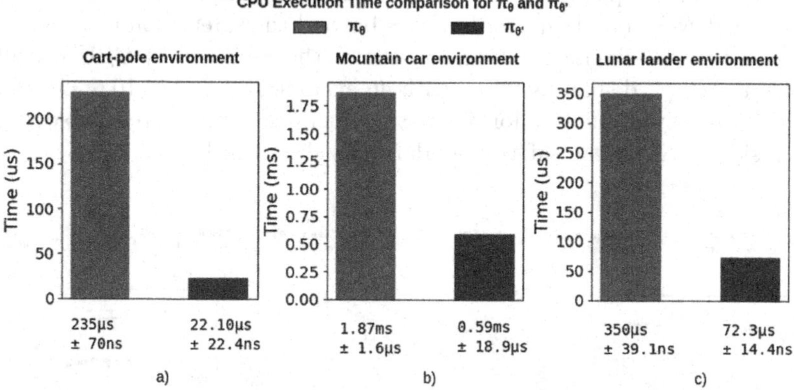

Fig. 3. Improvement in CPU execution time in $\pi_{\theta'}$, post-refinement with mean ± std. dev. of 7 runs, 100000 loops each)

unactuated pole by applying forces to a cart. The state space is described by ⟨ Cart Position (x), Cart Velocity ($\dot{x}$), Pole Angle (α), and Pole Angular Velocity ($\dot{\alpha}$) ⟩. We choose a reward threshold of $\lambda = 150$. The architecture of π_θ is $input \times 64 \times 64 \times action$ trained using PPO. We initially prune 75% of the weights based on λ and verify it against the following safety specification:

- The cart should not exceed positions −2.4 (extreme left) or +2.4 (extreme right) within 125-time units, i.e., $\varphi_{post} = [state_{range}\text{-}(-2.4, 2.4)]$ and $k = 125$.

It is essential to note that the cart pole system is monotone w.r.t the given property. The state-evolution model for cart-pole with M as the cart's mass, m, l as the mass and length of the pendulum, I as the moment of inertia, and g as the acceleration due to gravity is as follows.

$$f(x, \dot{x}, \alpha, \dot{\alpha}, a) = \begin{bmatrix} 0 & 1 & 0 & 0 \\ 0 & 0 & \frac{gm^2l^2}{I(M+m)+Mml^2} & 0 \\ 0 & 0 & 0 & 1 \\ 0 & 0 & -\frac{g(M+m)}{I(M+m)+mMl^2} & 0 \end{bmatrix} * \begin{bmatrix} x \\ \dot{x} \\ \alpha \\ \dot{\alpha} \end{bmatrix} + \begin{bmatrix} 0 \\ \frac{I+ml^2}{I(M+m)+mMl^2)} \\ 0 \\ -\frac{ml}{I(M+m)+mMl^2} \end{bmatrix} * a$$

Sign stability of Jacobian matrices of the system dynamics is a necessary and sufficient condition for monotonicity ([6], Definition 1). For the cart pole system, $\frac{\delta f(s,a)}{\delta x} \geq 0$, thus the system is monotonic with respect to the position variable. However, the system dynamics is unknown for PruVer, and monotonicity is an assumption. The starting range for each variable is x : [-1, 1], $\dot{x}$: [0, 4.16], α : [0, 0.98], $\dot{\alpha}$: [0, 0.19], ϵ_{range} : [(-0.02.0.02), (-0.01.0.01), (-0.2.0.2)/10^2, (-0.01, 0.01)] and $\mathcal{A}_{range}$: [-1, 1] . The ranges on $x, \dot{x}, \alpha, \dot{\alpha}$ together form the input range φ_{pre}. The bound k for verification depends on the prediction capacity of the State estimator model M_ω, which for cart pole gives an accuracy of 99.46% $\pm$ 0.51 on s_{t+1} up to 150 forward predictions over 1000 evaluations. The initial pruned policy reports counterexamples, as can be seen in Fig. 4a. The lower bound on position goes beyond the safety bound -2.4, which is corrected post-refinement. Figure 3a shows the decrease in CPU execution time due to achieved sparsity in $\pi_{\theta'}$ with an average speedup of 10.6. Overall we achieve a sparsity of 49.64% for $\pi_{\theta'}$ post-refinement with all reachable system states residing within the safety boundaries as shown in Fig. 4a.

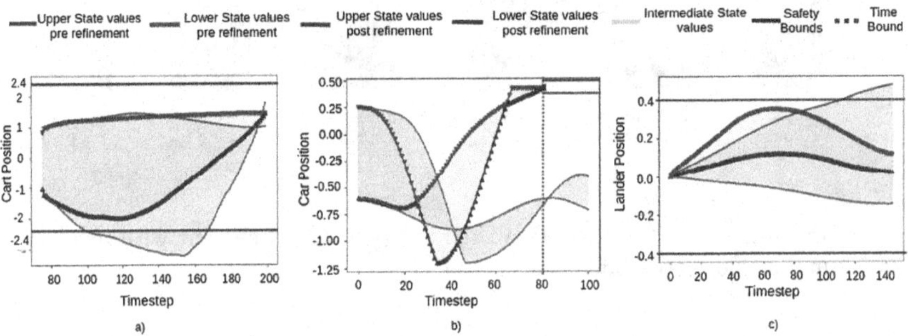

Fig. 4. Trajectories showing the upper and lower values during verification pre and post-refinement of $\pi_{\theta'}$ for a) Cartpole b) Mountain Car c) Lunar Lander environments

Mountain Car Environment: The environment has a car stochastically positioned at the bottom of a sinusoidal valley [20]. The objective is to carefully increase the car's speed to get to the top of the hill. The state information contains $\langle Position(x), Velocity(v)\rangle$ of the car. We choose a reward threshold of $\lambda = 90$ and start with a 70% pruned network based on λ. The architecture of π_θ is $input \times 400 \times 300 \times action$ trained using DDPG. We validate the following safety specifications:

- Car position between 0.4 to 0.5 (hilltop position) within 80 units of time, i.e., φ_{post} = [$state_{range}$-(0.4, 0.5)] and $80 \leq k \leq 100$.

The initial ranges for the variables in φ_{pre} are x : [$-$0.6,0.25],v : [0,0.002], ϵ_{range} : [($-$0.08,0.08),($-$0.004,0.004)] and $\mathcal{A}$: [$-$1,1]. M_ω trained with data from π_θ gives an accuracy 99.67%$\pm$0.64 on 130 forward predictions over 1000 evaluations. The initial pruned policy reports counterexamples for car position (Fig. 4b) where the lower and upper bounds do not reach the hilltop positions. Figure 4a shows the decrease in CPU execution time with an average speedup of 3.16. Overall we achieve a sparsity of 59.78% for $\pi_{\theta'}$ post-refinement with all reachable states converging to the hill position (Fig. 4b).

Lunar Lander Environment: The task in this environment is to land a lunar lander vehicle smoothly between the landing flags at coordinate (0,0). The state space is described by $\langle$ Positions (x, y), Velocity $(\dot{x}, \dot{y})$, Angle (α), Angular Velocity $(\dot{\alpha})$ $\rangle$ and two boolean variables for leg contact. We choose a reward threshold of $\lambda = 250$. The architecture of π_θ is $input \times 64 \times 64 \times action$ trained using PPO. We initially prune 55% of the weights based on λ. The network verified against the following safety specification:

- Lander position should not go beyond 0.4 to -0.4 till 140 units of time, i.e., $\varphi_{post} = [state_{range}$-(0.4,-40.4)] and $k \leq 140$.

The initial ranges for the variables in φ_{pre} are x : [0,0], y:[-1.5,1.5], $\dot{x}, \dot{y}$: [-5,5], α : [-3.14,3.14], $\dot{\alpha}$: [-5,5] ϵ_{range} : [(-0.6,0.6)/10^3,(-0.001,0.001), (-0.2,0.2)/10^5,(-0.02,0.02), (-0.6,0.6)/10^2,(-0.2,0.2)/10^5] and $\mathcal{A}$: [-1,1]*2. M_ω trained with data from π_θ gives an accuracy 98.32% $\pm$ 0.57 on 150 forward predictions over 1000 evaluations. The initial pruned policy reports counterexamples for the lander position (Fig. 4c) with the upper value going beyond bounds. Figure 3c shows the decrease in CPU execution time with an average speedup of 4.84. Overall we achieve a sparsity of 39.68% for $\pi_{\theta'}$ post-refinement with all reachable states contained within the safety bounds(Fig. 4c).

For all three environments, we observe considerable speedup with high sparsity and better reward for the PruVer networks. We also show that the upper and lower values of the states respect safety boundaries keeping the system safe.

5 Conclusions

Neural pruning and verification are important directions for developing DRL networks for embedded systems and real-time applications. In this paper, we propose a methodology for safety-aware neural pruning through an algorithm that iteratively refines a sparse network using weights from the original dense network. We discuss a verification strategy that can formally guarantee the safety of the pruned network over a finite horizon. To the best of our knowledge, this is the first work to address safety in neural pruning for DRL. Our method shows promising results in model-free RL environments with good speedup on verified policies.

References

1. Amir, G., Schapira, M., Katz, G.: Towards scalable verification of deep reinforcement learning. In: Formal Methods in Computer Aided Design, FMCAD 2021, New Haven, CT, USA, October 19–22, 2021, pp. 193–203. IEEE (2021)

2. Angeli, D., et al.: Monotone control systems. IEEE Trans. Autom. Control **48**(10), 1684–1698 (2003). https://doi.org/10.1109/TAC.2003.817920
3. Arnob, S.Y., Ohib, R., Plis, S., Precup, D.: Single-shot pruning for offline reinforcement learning. arXiv preprint arXiv:2112.15579 (2021)
4. Blalock, D., et al.: What is the state of neural network pruning? Proc. Mach. Learn. Syst. **2**, 129–146 (2020)
5. Brockman, G., et al.: Openai gym. arXiv preprint arXiv:1606.01540 (2016)
6. Coogan, S.: Mixed monotonicity for reachability and safety in dynamical systems. In: 2020 59th IEEE Conference on Decision and Control, pp. 5074–5085 (2020)
7. Deng, C., Sui, Y., Liao, S., Qian, X., Yuan, B.: GoSPA: an energy-efficient high-performance globally optimized SParse convolutional neural network accelerator. In: 2021 ACM/IEEE 48th Annual International Symposium on Computer Architecture (ISCA), pp. 1110–1123 (2021). https://doi.org/10.1109/ISCA52012.2021.00090
8. Dutta, S., Jha, S., Sankaranarayanan, S., Tiwari, A.: Output range analysis for deep feedforward neural networks. In: Dutle, A., Muñoz, C., Narkawicz, A. (eds.) NFM 2018. LNCS, vol. 10811, pp. 121–138. Springer, Cham (2018). https://doi.org/10.1007/978-3-319-77935-5_9
9. Evci, U., Pedregosa, F., Gomez, A., Elsen, E.: The difficulty of training sparse neural networks. arXiv preprint arXiv:1906.10732 (2019)
10. Frankle, J., Carbin, M.: The lottery ticket hypothesis: finding sparse, trainable neural networks. In: 7th International Conference on Learning Representations, ICLR New Orleans, LA, USA, May 6–9 (2019)
11. Gangopadhyay, B., et al.: Hierarchical program-triggered reinforcement learning agents for automated driving. IEEE Trans. Intell. Transp. Syst. **23**(8), 10902–10911 (2022). https://doi.org/10.1109/TITS.2021.3096998
12. Gangopadhyay, B., et al.: Safety aware neural pruning for deep reinforcement learning (student abstract). Proc. AAAI **37**(13), 16212–16213 (2023)
13. García, J., Fernández, F.: A comprehensive survey on safe reinforcement learning. J. Mach. Learn. Res. **16**(42), 1437–1480 (2015)
14. Graesser, L., et al.: The state of sparse training in deep reinforcement learning. In: International Conference on Machine Learning, pp. 7766–7792. PMLR (2022)
15. Huang, X., Kwiatkowska, M., Wang, S., Wu, M.: Safety verification of deep neural networks. In: Majumdar, R., Kunčak, V. (eds.) CAV 2017. LNCS, vol. 10426, pp. 3–29. Springer, Cham (2017). https://doi.org/10.1007/978-3-319-63387-9_1
16. Katz, G., Barrett, C., Dill, D.L., Julian, K., Kochenderfer, M.J.: Reluplex: an efficient SMT solver for verifying deep neural networks. In: Majumdar, R., Kunčak, V. (eds.) CAV 2017. LNCS, vol. 10426, pp. 97–117. Springer, Cham (2017). https://doi.org/10.1007/978-3-319-63387-9_5
17. Katz, G., et al.: The marabou framework for verification and analysis of deep neural networks. In: Dillig, I., Tasiran, S. (eds.) CAV 2019. LNCS, vol. 11561, pp. 443–452. Springer, Cham (2019). https://doi.org/10.1007/978-3-030-25540-4_26
18. Kusupati, A., et al.: Soft threshold weight reparameterization for learnable sparsity. In: III, H.D., Singh, A. (eds.) Proceedings of the 37th International Conference on Machine Learning, vol. 119, pp. 5544–5555. PMLR (2020)
19. Mocanu, D.C., et al.: Scalable training of artificial neural networks with adaptive sparse connectivity inspired by network science. Nat. Commun. **9**(1), 1–12 (2018)
20. Moore, A.W.: Efficient memory-based learning for robot control. Tech. Rep. University of Cambridge (1990)
21. Rusu, A.A., et al.: Policy distillation. In: 4th International Conference on Learning Representations, ICLR (2016)

22. Silver, D., et al.: Mastering the game of go without human knowledge. Nature **550**, 354–359 (2017). https://doi.org/10.1038/nature24270
23. Sokar, G., Mocanu, E., et al.: Dynamic sparse training for deep reinforcement learning. arXiv preprint arXiv:2106.04217 (2021)
24. Vischer, M.A., et al.: On lottery tickets and minimal task representations in deep reinforcement learning. arXiv preprint arXiv:2105.01648 (2021)
25. Zhang, H., et al.: Accelerating the deep reinforcement learning with neural network compression. In: International Joint Conference on Neural Networks (IJCNN), pp. 1–8 (2019)

AdaptLight: Toward Cross-Space-Time Collaboration for Adaptive Traffic Signal Control

Xintian Cai, Yilin Liu(✉), Quan Yuan, Guiyang Luo, and Jinglin Li

State Key Laboratory of Networking and Switching Technology,
Beijing University of Posts and Telecommunications, Beijing 100876, China
{caixintian,liuyilin10,yuanquan,luoguiyang,jlli}@bupt.edu.cn

Abstract. Recent multi-agent deep reinforcement learning (MADRL) approaches have shown notable benefits in traffic signal control. However, the spatial-temporal coupling, hysteresis, and heterogeneity of collaborative agents are usually ignored. States and actions among multiple intersections induce complex coupling and hysteresis in both space and time dimensions, while the actions also present spatial-temporal heterogeneity due to fluctuated traffic. These characteristics impose a critical impact on the efficiency and flexibility of coordinated control. In this paper, we propose *AdaptLight*, an MADRL-based model to achieve cross-space-time collaboration. It captures the interactions among spatial-temporal traffic components and exploits action repetition to adaptively adjust decision granularity for heterogeneous traffic. For the spatial-temporal coupling and hysteresis issue, *AdaptLight* first establishes a feature extraction network based on spatial-temporal graph Transformer. To tackle the spatial-temporal action heterogeneity problem, an action-repetition-enabled MADRL module is designed, which can decide asynchronous-cooperative actions spanning multiple timesteps. Experiments present that *AdaptLight* shows competitive performance on different datasets.

Keywords: Multi-agent deep reinforcement learning · Traffic signal control · Graph transformer · Action repetition

1 Introduction

Multi-agent deep reinforcement learning (MADRL) based multi-intersection traffic signal control (M-TSC) approaches have shown superior performance over traditional methods in improving traffic efficiency. However, there are still critical puzzles that remain unresolved. The first issue is **spatial-temporal coupling and hysteresis among states and actions**. *Coupling* is raised because the combinations of action-action, state-state, and action-state trajectories interact in different modes and result in various effects in time-space dimensions. This requires policies to identify distinct interaction modes and generate optimal coordinated behaviors accordingly. *Coupling* further prompts *hysteresis* caused by

F. Liu et al. (Eds.): PRICAI 2023, LNAI 14325, pp. 150–156, 2024.
https://doi.org/10.1007/978-981-99-7019-3_15

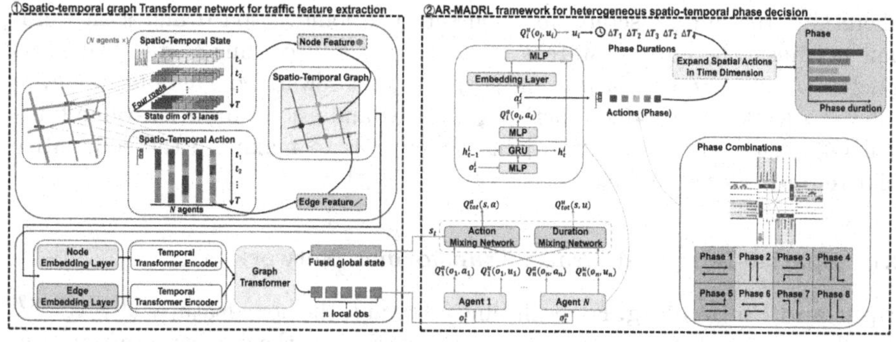

Fig. 1. The overall network structure of the proposed *AdaptLight.*

water-like traffic flows being blocked by intersections and gradually spreading to nearby regions. The second issue is **spatial-temporal heterogeneity of actions**. Actions are *heterogeneous* in space-time dimensions because the policy decision intervals should vary with the different frequencies of traffic flow change. At the same timestep, different intersections observe traffic of different fluctuation frequencies, requiring distinct decision intervals. At different timesteps, the traffic at a single intersection also presents different fluctuation frequencies, which still requires dynamic decision intervals. Existing RL-based methods usually ignore this characteristic because Dec-POMDP induces synchronous decision intervals. Neglecting these problems can result in poor efficiency and adaptability of cooperative signal control. Therefore, we propose an MADRL-based model for cross-space-time M-TSC collaboration, *AdaptLight* as shown in Fig. 1.

- We propose a spatial-temporal graph Transformer network to extract coupling and hysteresis features among multiple state-action combinations.
- We design an action repetition MADRL (AR-MADRL) framework to decide spatial-temporal heterogeneous policy decision intervals for drastic traffic.
- We evaluate *AdaptLight* on synthetic and real-world datasets. Our method outperforms both conventional and RL-based approaches, especially in dynamic and complicated environments.

2 Method

We consider M-TSC as a decentralized partially-observable SMDP problem, which is characterized by a tuple $G = \langle I, S, A, U, P, R, \Omega, O, n, \gamma \rangle$, where I is the finite set of n agents, $s \in S$ is the state, A is the finite action set. Each agent i only has access to a partial observation $o_i \in \Omega$ according to the observation function $O(s, i)$. At each step, each agent i selects an action $a_i \in A$, resulting in a joint action $\boldsymbol{a} \in A^n$. Conditioned on the observation o_i and the next action a_i, the agent also decides the corresponding duration $u_i^a \in U$ of the chosen action, where U is the finite discrete duration set. The joint action $\boldsymbol{a}$ and joint duration $\boldsymbol{u}$ transit the current state s to next state s' according to the transition function $P(s' \mid s, \boldsymbol{a}, \boldsymbol{u})$. Each agent shares a joint reward $\boldsymbol{r}$. The joint policy $\boldsymbol{\pi}$ induces a joint action-value function $\mathcal{Q}_{tot}^{\pi}(s, \boldsymbol{a})$ and a joint duration-value function $\mathcal{Q}_{tot}^{\pi}(s, \boldsymbol{u})$. The goal of the joint policy $\boldsymbol{\pi}$ is to maximize the cumulative joint rewards $\boldsymbol{r}$ of all intersections.

2.1 Spatial-Temporal Graph Transformer Network

Input and Embedding. For each time interval t, the node features $v_i^t \in \mathbb{R}^{d_n \times T}$ of node i consist of its observation history, where d_n is the dimension of concatenated observations, and T represents the window length. For edge from node i to node j, its edge features $e_{ij}^t \in \mathbb{R}^{d_e \times T}$ consist of four components: the action history of the entering intersection, the action history of the exiting intersection, the action duration transition of the entering intersection, and action duration transition of the exiting intersection. The four components are concatenated along the first dimension into a $d_e \times T$-dimensional tensor. The node features, edge features, and positional encodings are then passed through fully connected layers to get d_h-dimensional embedded node features $v_i'^t \in \mathbb{R}^{d_h}$, embedded edge features $e_{ij}'^t \in \mathbb{R}^{d_h}$, and embedded Laplacian positional encodings $\widehat{PE} \in \mathbb{R}^{d_h}$.

Temporal Transformer Layer. To handle temporal coupling and hysteresis, we use temporal Transformer to capture the time dependence of node-edge feature trajectories. Temporal Transformer learns the modes of traffic state history and intersection action history separately. For each node, the node features are permuted as a $T \times d_n$ tensor, which is then passed through a Transformer encoder layer, resulting in updated hidden features with temporal dependencies. We utilize an MLP layer as the aggregation function to output the final embedded features without the time dimension as $\hat{v}_i^t \in \mathbb{R}^{d_n}$. Similarly, the edge features are also updated with another temporal Transformer layer as $\hat{e}_{ij}^t \in \mathbb{R}^{d_e}$. Then, we add positional encodings to the input node embedding: $\widehat{h}_i^t = \widehat{v}_i^t + \widehat{PE}$. We omit the time symbol t in the following formula for the convenience of expression.

Spatial Transformer Layer. Based on the outputs of the temporal Transformer layer, we use spatial Transformer to combine temporal features with spatial features to get spatial-temporal encoded features. To solve spatial coupling and hysteresis, we specially design the attention encoding process in the spatial graph Transformer layer to extract the complex interaction information among combinations of decision intention and traffic states, which is defined as:

$$\omega_{ij}^{m,l} = Q_h^{m,l} \hat{h}_i^l K_h^{m,l} \hat{h}_j^l + Q_h^{m,l} \hat{h}_i^l K_e^{k,l} \hat{e}_{ji}^l + Q_e^{m,l} \hat{e}_{ij}^l K_h^{m,l} \hat{h}_j^l + Q_e^{m,l} \hat{e}_{ij}^l K_e^{m,l} \hat{e}_{ji}^l, \tag{1}$$

where $Q_h^{m,l}$, $Q_e^{m,l}$, $K_h^{m,l}$, $K_e^{m,l} \in \mathbb{R}^{d_m \times d_h}$ are learnable parameters, m is the number of multi-attention heads, $m = 1, \ldots, H$. This process is aimed to extract spatial interaction patterns among state-state, action-state, state-action, and action-action components in the system. The attention score $\omega_{ij}^{m,l}$ is then scaled and passed through a Softmax layer to get the final attention $\alpha_{ij}^{m,l}$. Further, node features are updated through spatial graph Transformer layers following the paradigm of vanilla graph Transformer network [1]. Edge features are also propagated to represent pairwise attention: $\widehat{e}_{ij}^{l+1} = f_{O,e}^{l}([\omega_{ij}^{m,l}]_{m=1}^{H})$, where $f_{O,e}^{l}$ is a linear function that merges concatenated head.

After L sub-layers, node features obtained at the last layer $\widehat{h}_i^L$ are treated as the local observation o_i of the followed AR-MADRL network. For providing more comprehensive global state information, all node features are fused as the global state encoding s, which is also utilized in the AR-MADRL network: $s = \frac{\sum_{i \in I} \hat{h}_i^L}{n}$.

2.2 AR-MADRL Framework for Heterogeneous Decision

AR-MADRL has a hierarchical dual-objective architecture as illustrated in Fig. 1 (right). The hierarchy consists of a higher-level policy to select asynchronous actions. To tackle temporal action heterogeneity, a lower-level policy is designed to choose timesteps for which the chosen actions will act.

For agent i at time t, given the observation o_i^t, action policy π_a outputs an action a_i^t based on the $\mathcal{Q}$-function: $\mathcal{Q}_i^a(o_i, a_i) := \mathbb{E}\left[r_t + \gamma \mathcal{Q}_i^a\left(o_i^{t+1}, a_i^{t+1}\right)\right]$. Conditioned on the observation o_i^t and chosen action a_i^t, duration policy π_u outputs a discrete duration u_i based on the n-step $\mathcal{Q}$-function: $\mathcal{Q}_i^u(o_i, u_i \mid a_i) := \mathbb{E}[\sum_{k=0}^{u_i-1} \gamma^k r_{t+k} + \gamma^{u_i} \mathcal{Q}_i^u(o_i^{t+u_i}, a_i^{t+u_i})]$, where $u_i \in \{1, \ldots, U\}$, U is the maximum duration steps. Then the chosen action will be executed for u_i steps.

To handle spatial action heterogeneity, we use multi-agent DQN to approximate both policies and coordinate agent behaviors. Policy π_a and π_u share a linear layer and a GRU to share observation context o between two policies, which is encoded as a vector δ_o and then mapped into action $a \in \mathbb{R}^{d_a}$ by action policy. Next, action a is encoded into action representation δ_a via a linear layer. Observation representation δ_o and action representation δ_a are concatenated as the input of the final linear layer, which is designed to approximate π_u and outputs the duration $u \in \mathbb{R}^{d_u}$, where we represent u as a d_u-dimension one-hot vector. To use global state features, the local $\mathcal{Q}$-values $\mathcal{Q}^a$ and $\mathcal{Q}^u$ are then mixed by mixing networks QMIX to estimate the global action-value $\mathcal{Q}_{\text{tot}}^a(s, \boldsymbol{a})$ and duration-value $\mathcal{Q}_{\text{tot}}^u(s, \boldsymbol{u})$, respectively.

The introduction of action repetition into multi-agent systems leads to asynchronous rewards since the action end time is not uniform. To solve this problem, we introduce Mac-JERTs [2] to build replay buffers. A joint reward is collected when any agent terminates an action, and agents share a joint cumulative reward $r^c = \sum_{t=t_a}^{t_{\text{end}}} r_t$, where t_a denotes the starting step of a joint action, and t_{end} refers to the timestep at which any agent ends a local action. *AdaptLight* is trained end-to-end to optimize the following objective function:

$$
\begin{aligned}
\mathcal{L}(\theta) = \mathbb{E}_D[(r^c + (\gamma \max_{\boldsymbol{a}'} \overline{\mathcal{Q}}_{\text{tot}}^a(s', \boldsymbol{a}') - \mathcal{Q}_{\text{tot}}^a(s, \boldsymbol{a})) \\
+(\gamma \max_{\boldsymbol{u}'} - \overline{\mathcal{Q}}_{\text{tot}}^u(s', \boldsymbol{u}') - \mathcal{Q}_{\text{tot}}^a(s, \boldsymbol{u})))],
\end{aligned}
\tag{2}
$$

where $\overline{\mathcal{Q}}_{\text{tot}}^a$, $\overline{\mathcal{Q}}_{\text{tot}}^u$ are target networks, θ denotes the parameters of the networks.

Table 1. Performance of different methods on 6 road networks, and *action oscillations* of *AdaptLight* and CoLight (as the baseline method) during an episode.

	Model	3 × 3-Bi	6 × 6-Uni	6 × 6-Bi	Hangzhou	Jinan-1	Jinan-2
Travel Time	Fixedtime	105.49	210.94	210.93	718.89	882.11	814.68
	MaxPressure	101.46	186.56	195.49	416.36	337.17	356.95
	IntelliLight	154.77	395.34	316.88	414.97	501.73	560.19
	CoLight	90.42	181.92	182.69	366.53	349.19	368.16
	AdaptLight	**85.46**	**167.42**	**168.00**	**312.00**	**285.57**	**299.48**
Action Oscillations	CoLight	169	178	179	177	170	172
	AdaptLight	**105**	**155**	**158**	230	209	215

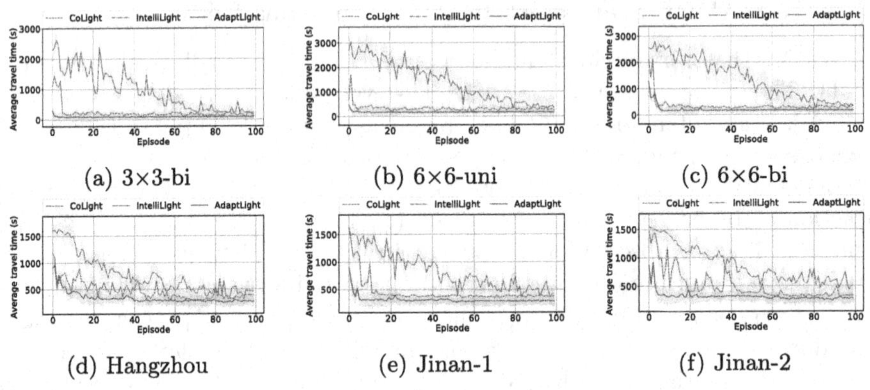

Fig. 2. Convergence curves of different methods on 6 road networks.

3 Experiments

We use CityFlow as the simulation platform. At each decision time, an agent chooses an action from 8 signal phase combinations. For our method, in addition to selecting an action, an agent also selects a phase duration that lasts for 10, 20, 30, or 40 steps. For compared methods, the phase duration is averaged as a 20-step fixed duration. Following CoLight [3], we conduct experiments on 3 synthetic grid networks (3 × 3 bi-direction, 6 × 6 uni-direction, and 6 × 6 bi-direction) and 3 real-world networks (4 × 4 in Hangzhou, 3 × 4 in Jinan, and 3 × 4 in Jinan with more dynamic traffic flows and higher throughput). We compare our method with conventional TSC methods (Fixedtime, and Maxpressure) and state-of-the-art RL-based methods (IntelliLight and Colight).

As presented in Table 1, *AdaptLight* achieves the best performance under different road networks and traffic flows. The cross-space-time collaboration is more evident on real-world datasets since these datasets have more drastic traffic flows, more complex network structures, and thus more complicated spatial-temporal dependencies among multi-intersections. Our method presents better stability. Figure 2 illustrates the convergence curves over *AdaptLight* and other approaches. The convergence speed of *AdaptLight* outperforms all the compared models, which shows the training efficiency of our method. The improvement in convergence speed is attributed to the high parallel computing efficiency of an entire attention-based Transformer mechanism without recurrence and convolutions. Meanwhile, learning to choose phase intervals as well as phase settings also improves the speed of targeting the optimal policy patterns.

In Table 1, we compare the number of action changes (the average number of switched phases for an intersection) required for one round of experiment over *AdaptLight* and CoLight. We discover that our method achieves the best performance with fewer actions in synthetic maps which have stable vehicle arrival rates, while our method requires more actions in real-world maps that have dynamic traffic. The experiments indicate that *AdaptLight* learns when it is necessary to act and decides adaptive optimal action durations for distinct flow status. This improvement can strike a balance between optimizing performance and decreasing action oscillations in TSC environments, enhancing driver experience and reducing potential safety threats.

We perform ablation experiments on the spatial-temporal graph Transformer network and AR-MADRL framework. The absence of both components leads to a loss in performance. We discover that an intersection fails to allocate proper attention scores without graph Transformer modules, which can identify spatial-temporal coupling and hysteresis features from state-action components.

4 Conclusion

In this paper, we have proposed a collaborative cross-space-time M-TSC method *AdaptLight* to handle spatial-temporal coupling, hysteresis, and heterogeneity issues. For the spatial-temporal coupling and hysteresis puzzle, we propose a spatial-temporal graph Transformer model. For the spatial-temporal action heterogeneity problem, we are the first to extend action repetition to MADRL to learn heterogeneous-asynchronous actions and decision intervals. Experiments show that our approach has strong efficiency and adaptability in various environments, especially for dynamic traffic. Experiments also give evidence that *AdaptLight* balances performance and action oscillations properly.

Acknowledgements. This paper is supported in part by the National Key Research and Development Program of China under Grant 2022YFB4300402, the Natural Science Foundation of China under Grant 62272053, Grant 62102041, and in part by the Young Elite Scientists Sponsorship Program by China Association for Science and Technology (CAST) under Grant 2022QNRC001.

References

1. Dwivedi, V.P., Bresson, X.: A generalization of transformer networks to graphs. arXiv preprint arXiv:2012.09699 (2020)
2. Xiao, Y., Hoffman, J., Amato, C.: Macro-action-based deep multi-agent reinforcement learning. In: Conference on Robot Learning, pp. 1146–1161 (2020)
3. Wei, H., Xu, N., Zhang, H., Zheng, G., Li, Z.: Colight: learning network-level cooperation for traffic signal control. In: Proceedings of the 28th ACM International Conference on Information and Knowledge Management, pp. 1913–1922 (2019)

DeepLRA: An Efficient Long Running Application Scheduling Framework with Deep Reinforcement Learning in the Cloud

Qi Si, Xuesong Lu, Weiyi Li, and Peng Pu(✉)

East China Normal University, Shanghai, China
{qsi,wyli}@stu.ecnu.edu.cn
xslu@dase.ecnu.edu.cn, ppu@cc.ecnu.edu.cn

Abstract. With the growth of cloud computing, an increasing number of *long-running applications (LRAs)* are running in the cloud, providing scalability, cost-effectiveness, and flexibility. Considering LRA interactions and resource interferences, scheduling LRAs in the cloud poses significant challenges regarding runtime performance maximization and efficient resource utilization. However, existing schedulers are usually constraint-based methods requiring priori knowledge and hard to balance LRA performance and efficient resource utilization. To address this problem, we propose DeepLRA, a novel and efficient LRA scheduling framework in the cloud. Specifically, we introduce Deep Reinforcement Learning (DRL) in LRA scheduling, where the agent learn the scheduling policy without human intervention. Furthermore, a multi-objective LRA scheduling is designed with multi-agent training. Extensive simulation experiments conducted with real-world workloads indicate that DeepLRA outperforms the state-of-the-art in the multi-objective LRA scheduling. DeepLRA shows 26.1% and 36.9% average improvement in throughput and efficient resource utilization over Kubernetes, respectively.

Keywords: Scheduling · Cloud Computing · Deep Reinforcement Learning · Long Running Applications

1 Introduction

Long-running applications (LRAs) [12] refer to applications with running times ranging from hours to months and have become an essential component of cloud computing infrastructure. The scheduling of LRAs in the cloud is the process of allocating computational resources to them, ensuring smooth execution while maximizing the overall performance and efficiency of the cloud infrastructure. Scheduling LRAs is a unique challenge that requires sophisticated algorithms to take into account various factors, such as LRA interactions and resource interferences. Unlike batch job scheduling, LRA scheduling is more complex due

F. Liu et al. (Eds.): PRICAI 2023, LNAI 14325, pp. 157–163, 2024.
https://doi.org/10.1007/978-981-99-7019-3_16

to their different characteristics such as strict Service-Level Objective (SLO) requirements and more complex interactions [13].

Existing LRA scheduling approaches typically use constraint-based methods, considering affinity and anti-affinity to satisfy as many constraints as possible [4,9,12,15]. However, constraint-based LRA scheduling methods focus on satisfying more constraints, which often does not result in better performance. Emerging scheduling methods for batch jobs usually use Deep Reinforcement Learning (DRL) methods [16], which has the benefit of setting a reward function that allows the agent to learn the scheduling policy automatically [7,8,10,11]. However, these methods are not directly applicable to LRA scheduling, since different scheduling goals lead to different environments and reward functions.

To address this challenge, this paper proposes DeepLRA, a novel and efficient LRA scheduling framework in the cloud. Specifically, we introduce DRL-based methods in LRA scheduling, where the agent can learn the scheduling policy automatically. We design the environment, state, and reward functions in DRL, model the agent and the performance predictor for instructing agent training. Furthermore, the multi-agent training is designed to consider both performance and efficient resource utilization objective. We compare the scheduling results of DeepLRA and Kubernetes to demonstrate the effectiveness of the proposed approach. DeepLRA shows 26.1% and 36.9% improvement in throughput and efficient resource utilization over Kubernetes, respectively.

2 Method

2.1 Deep Reinforcement Learning Method

We consider a cluster in the cloud with a set of m nodes denoted by $N = [N_1, N_2, ..., N_m]$. Each node provides several types of resources such as CPU, memory, and storage unit, denoted by $Res = [r_1, r_2, ..., r_n]$, where n is the number of resource types. We consider a number of LRA workloads, denoted by $W = [w_1, w_2, ..., w_k]$, where k is the number of LRA workloads.

State Space. The state space S consists of the system resource usage, the system running applications, and the current scheduling request. Specifically, at each timestamp t, the system resource usage is represented by a matrix U_t^{res}, where $u_{i,j}$ indicates the jth resource usage of the ith node. The system running applications are represented by a matrix D_t^{lra}, where $d_{i,j}$ represents the number of the jth LRA running on the ith node. The current scheduling request is represented by a one-hot vector E_t, where $e_i = 1$ represents the current scheduling request is from the ith LRA. Therefore, the state of the cluster in the cloud at timestamp t can be defined as $s_t = [s_t^U, s_t^V] = [U_t^{res}, [D_t^{lra}, E_t]]$.

Action Space. The action space refers to all possible choices of a node on which the container in the scheduling request can be launched. Based on the action made by the agent, the corresponding container is launched by the container scheduler on a specific node, and the required resources are allocated. Therefore, the action space A is defined as $A = [a_t | a_t \in \{1, 2, \cdots, m\}]$.

Reward Function. The reward function is used to measure the overall system performance after a set of scheduling requests have been processed, where a higher performance and more efficient resource utilization are rewarded with a higher score. The agent is not rewarded until a set of scheduling requests are processed. At timestamp t, we define the reward function as:

$$R_t = \begin{cases} 0 & \text{otherwise} \\ \lambda P(D_t^{lra}) + \mu B(U_t^{res}) & t = T \end{cases}. \tag{1}$$

P is a random forest prediction model which takes the current system state as input and predicts the application's performance. B is an indicator which can be chosen as variance, covariance, or entropy, allowing flexibility in assessing the balance of system resource utilization. To balance the contributions of P and B, we introduce coefficients μ and λ, which range from 0 to 1.

2.2 Model Training

Dueling DQN. Dueling DQN is an extension of the popular DQN [14] algorithm, using DNN to approximate the Q-values of state-action pairs. The advantages over standard DQN are increased stability, faster convergence, and better performance on tasks that require the agent to distinguish between actions with similar values. The main idea is to separate the estimation of the state value function and the advantage function, which allows the agent to better distinguish between actions that have similar value estimates. The reason for using Dueling DQN rather than other DRL algorithms such as rainbow, PPO is that the action space for scheduling LRA tasks is discrete.

Exploration and Experience Replay. Exploration is the process by which the agent explores the environment to discover new information and improve its decision-making capabilities. It is typically achieved using an epsilon-greedy strategy, where the agent selects a random action with probability ϵ, and otherwise selects the action with the highest predicted Q-value. The value of ϵ is gradually decreased over time, allowing the agent to explore more in the early stages of training, and exploit its learned knowledge in later stages. Experience replay is a technique used in DRL to improve the efficiency of learning by reusing past experiences. In this approach, the agent stores its experiences (i.e. the state, action, reward, and resulting state) in a replay buffer, and samples a mini-batch of experiences at each training iteration. By using experiences from the replay buffer, the agent can break the correlation between successive experiences, and more effectively learn from a wider range of scenarios.

The Predictor. The predictor is a component of the DeepLRA framework that is responsible for predicting the system's performance based on the scheduling decisions made by the agent. Specifically, the predictor receives the system's running application state D, which includes the number and type of running applications. Based on this information, the predictor uses a prediction model to estimate the expected performance of the system under different scheduling decisions. The predictor then provides this information to the agent, which uses it to select the optimal scheduling decision. To build the prediction model, we use a supervised learning approach that involves training a random forest model on historical system states and their corresponding performance metrics. Compared to deep learning models, which require a large amount of data to be effective, random forest models are more flexible and can achieve comparable performance with less data. Therefore, it is a suitable choice for our scenario where the amount of data may be limited.

Multi-agent Training. To optimize the learning objectives, we adopt a multi-agent approach to training. Multi-agent learning in DRL focuses on training multiple agents to interact and collaborate in complex environments. Each agent makes decisions to maximize its own rewards, but its actions can also impact the rewards of other agents, leading to a competitive or cooperative setting. We assign each agent a specific objective, enabling them to learn different strategies that can be combined to generate the final action. This approach facilitates exploration of a broader range of strategies and encourages collaboration among agents. Multi-agent training is particularly useful in addressing complex, multi-objective optimization problems. By dividing the problem into smaller sub-problems, multi-agent training can reduce the learning difficulty and enable agents to learn optimal strategies more consistently. To achieve this, we use agents with identical neural network structures, but train them for different objectives (i.e. performance and efficient resource utilization). In our proposed framework, each agent receives the same system state as input and scores all nodes based on its assigned objective. The combined scores are then used to determine the action that maximizes the overall objective. This approach ensures that the final action is generated by considering all relevant objectives.

3 Evaluation

3.1 Experimental Setup

We present the details of the experimental setup used to evaluate the performance of the proposed approach. The experiments were conducted on three simulated clusters with 10, 20 and 30 nodes, where each node is equipped with 16vCPUs and 64GiB memory. The cluster was used to execute 5 real-world workloads [1–3, 5, 6] in containerized environments. These workloads were carefully selected to represent a diverse range of applications, including machine learning, parallel computing, I/O and storage services.

The network architecture of Dueling DQN comprises two hidden layers, each consisting of 128 neurons. The model is trained using a batch size of 64, a learning rate of 1e−4, a discount factor γ of 0.95, and an exploration factor ϵ of 0.2. The predictor employs a random forest model, wherein the number of estimators is set to 200. To measure the overall throughput of the cluster, we used the metric of *RPS (request per second)*. A higher value of RPS indicates higher throughput and better performance. Furthermore, entropy was employed as a metric to assess the efficiency of resource allocation in the cluster. The formula are $B(X) = -\sum_{i=1}^{n} P(x_i) \log_2 P(x_i)$, where $B(X)$ represents the entropy of the random variable X and $P(x_i)$ represents the probability of the event $X = x_i$.

3.2 Scheduling Results

Varying Container and Node. Firstly, we scheduled 20, 40, and 60 application containers on 30 nodes. As shown in Fig. 1, as the number of containers increases, both DeepLRA and Kubernetes exhibit an increase in both throughput and effective resource utilization. Next, we conducted experiments with 60 application containers on 10, 20, and 30 nodes. As shown in Fig. 2, as the number of nodes increases, the action space increases, and scheduling decisions become more complex. Therefore, both DeepLRA and Kubernetes exhibit a decrease in performance. However, compared to Kubernetes, DeepLRA still improves throughput and resource utilization efficiency by an average of 26.1% and 36.9%, respectively. One reason for DeepLRA's superior performance is its sensitivity to the dynamic state of the system. While Kubernetes is not specifically designed to handle LRAs, DeepLRA leverages DRL-based methods to optimize scheduling policies based on the dynamic state of the system. This approach allows DeepLRA to take into account the unique characteristics of LRAs and make more informed scheduling decisions. Additionally, the use of DRL methods enables the agent to learn scheduling policies automatically from experience, adapting to real-time feedback and improving performance over time.

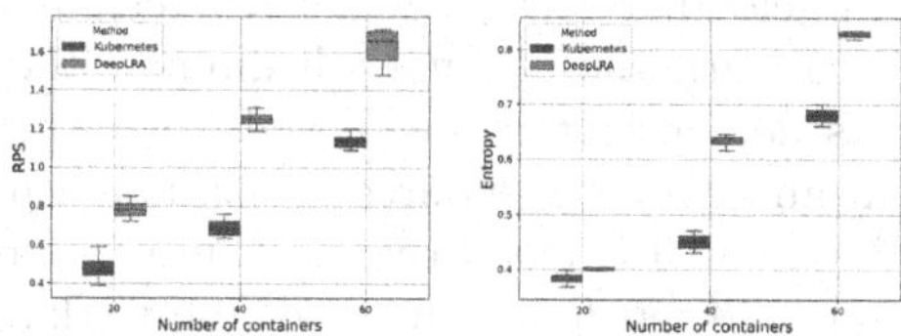

Fig. 1. Scheduling different number of containers on 30 nodes.

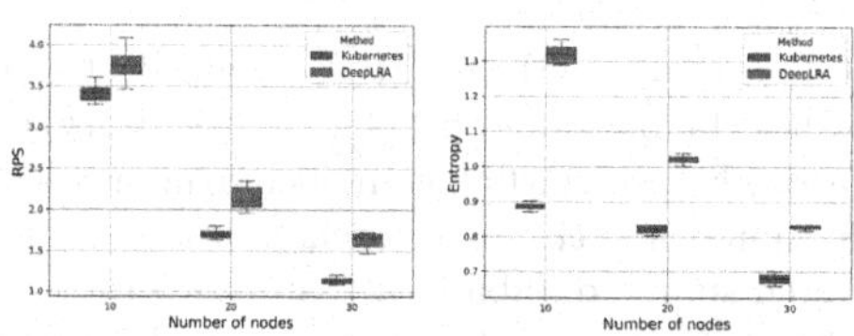

Fig. 2. Scheduling 60 containers on different number of nodes

Multi-agent vs. Single-Agent. We evaluate the effectiveness of the DeepLRA framework in both single-agent and multi-agent scenarios for multi-objective LRA scheduling in the cloud. As shown in Fig. 3, the multi-agent learning approach takes more time to find the optimal scheduling policy than the single-agent approach. However, the multi-agent approach can discover a superior performance scheduling policy. The reason behind this can be attributed to several factors. Firstly, multi-agent training allows for a more diverse exploration of the search space. This is because each agent has its own perspective on the

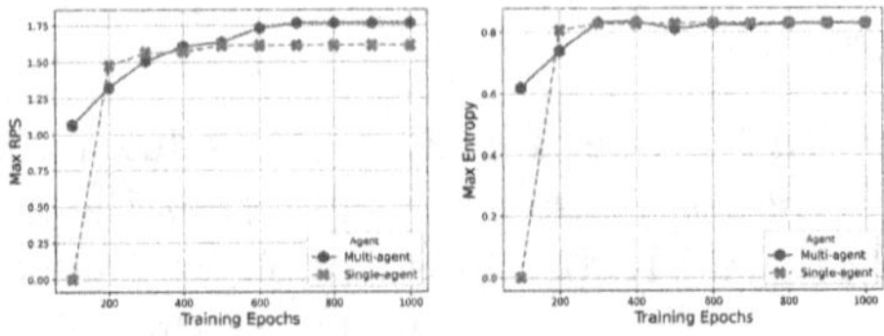

Fig. 3. Multi-agent vs. single-agent under scheduling 60 containers on 30 nodes.

problem and can explore different parts of the solution space. Secondly, multi-agent training can help to overcome the problem of local optima and allow for a more comprehensive exploration of the search space. Thirdly, multi-agent training can help to achieve a more balanced trade-off between the LRA performance and resource utilization, which are often conflicting objectives, and to identify solutions that achieve a good balance between these two objectives.

4 Conclusion

In this paper, we presented DeepLRA, a novel and efficient framework for scheduling LRAs in the cloud. By leveraging DRL techniques, we proposed a multi-agent approach to learn the optimal scheduling policy for LRAs in the cloud. Our experiments demonstrated that DeepLRA outperforms Kubernetes in terms of throughput and effective resource utilization, achieving a significant improvement of 26.1% and 36.9%, respectively. Future research should focus on scaling to larger systems and redefining the model network structure to achieve better performance.

References

1. Dask - scale the python tools you love. https://www.dask.org/
2. Hashlib - secure hashes. https://docs.python.org/3/library/hashlib.html
3. Image super-resolution. https://github.com/idealo/image-super-resolution
4. Kubernetes - production-grade container orchestration. https://kubernetes.io
5. Redis - a vibrant, open source database. https://redis.io/
6. Abadi, M., et al.: TensorFlow: a system for large-scale machine learning, vol. 16, pp. 265–283 (2016)
7. Bao, Y., Peng, Y., Wu, C.: Deep learning-based job placement in distributed machine learning clusters, pp. 505–513. IEEE, Paris, France (2019). https://doi.org/10.1109/INFOCOM.2019.8737460
8. Chen, Z., Hu, J., Min, G.: Learning-based resource allocation in cloud data center using advantage actor-critic. In: ICC 2019–2019 IEEE International Conference on Communications (ICC), pp. 1–6. IEEE (2019)
9. Delimitrou, C., Kozyrakis, C.: Paragon: QoS-aware scheduling for heterogeneous datacenters. In: ASPLOS 2013, pp. 77–88, New York, NY, USA (2013). https://doi.org/10.1145/2451116.2451125

10. Dong, H., et al.: Predictive job scheduling under uncertain constraints in cloud computing. In: Proceedings of the Thirtieth International Joint Conference on Artificial Intelligence, pp. 3627–3634, Montreal, Canada (2021). https://doi.org/10.24963/ijcai.2021/499
11. Fan, Y., Lan, O.: Deep reinforcement agent for scheduling in HPC (2021). https://doi.org/10.48550/arXiv.2102.06243
12. Garefalakis, P., Karanasos, K., Pietzuch, P., Suresh, A., Rao, S.: MEDEA: scheduling of long running applications in shared production clusters. In: Proceedings of the Thirteenth EuroSys Conference, pp. 1–13. ACM, Porto Portugal (2018). https://doi.org/10.1145/3190508.3190549
13. Luo, S., et al.: Characterizing microservice dependency and performance: Alibaba trace analysis. In: Proceedings of the ACM Symposium on Cloud Computing, pp. 412–426. ACM, Seattle, WA, USA (2021). https://doi.org/10.1145/3472883.3487003
14. Mnih, V., et al.: Playing atari with deep reinforcement learning (2013). https://doi.org/10.48550/arXiv.1312.5602
15. Mommessin, C., et al.: Affinity-aware resource provisioning for long-running applications in shared clusters (2022)
16. Sutton, R.S., Barto, A.G.: Reinforcement learning: an introduction (1999)

Guiding Task Learning by Hierarchical RL with an Experience Replay Mechanism Through Reward Machines

Jinmiao Cong, Yang Liu, and Chuanjuan Liu(✉)

School of Computer Science and Technology, Dalian University of Technology, Dalian 116024, China
cjm111@mail.dlut.edu.cn, {ly,chanjuanliu}@dlut.edu.cn

Abstract. Recently, reinforcement learning (RL) has made great progress in theory and application. Whereas, challenges remain in RL, such as low sample utilization and difficulty in designing suitable reward functions. Therefore, this paper focuses on optimizing the structure of the reward function and improving sample utilization. We propose a hierarchical reinforcement learning (HRL) algorithm based on the options framework, which incorporates a segmented reward mechanism and an experience replay mechanism. The reward mechanism can help the agent grasp the reward function's internal structure. The experience replay mechanism includes a buffer for storing typical experiences and a particular buffer for storing the special state experiences of the agent accessing the subtasks, which are conducive to training. We conducted single-task and multitask tests in multiple environments. Experimental results demonstrate that our algorithm has a better performance than baseline algorithms.

Keywords: HRL · Reward Mechanism · Experience Replay Mechanism

1 Introduction

To address low sample utilization and slow learning rate of RL [7] in large-scale problems, scholars have introduced the HRL algorithm, which decomposes intricate problems into subproblems, such as HAMs, MAXQ, and Options [5]. However, owing to the hierarchical structure, these methods may not guarantee convergence to the optimal strategy. To overcome this limitation, researchers leveraged the prior knowledge of the Reward Machines (RM) [4] to mitigate the problem of converging to suboptimal solutions. The RM has received widespread research attention, including LSRM [8], CRM [2], and HRM [2]. These works use RM to decompose tasks and to output the combination of reward functions under different conditions. In spite of solving some tasks in the environments, they are still prone to issues such as slow learning speed and poor performance.

F. Liu et al. (Eds.): PRICAI 2023, LNAI 14325, pp. 164–170, 2024.
https://doi.org/10.1007/978-981-99-7019-3_17

Our Contribution. In order to improve learning speed and problem-solving ability, this work proposes an algorithm, dubbed Hierarchy based on Options with an Experience Replay Mechanism (HOERM). HOERM adopts an option-based hierarchical structure, which is relevant to HRM [2]. However, we designed a well-structured reward mechanism and included an experience replay mechanism. We refined the segmented reward mechanism by using the value iteration method to calculate the potential values of each state in the RM (See Sect. 2 for details). The difference in potential values between states can serve as intermediate rewards. Therefore, the agent also receives appropriate rewards during the transition of intermediate states in the RM. Besides, we designed an experience replay mechanism that includes two replay buffers. *ReplayBuffer₁* is a typical buffer that normally stores various experiences during the learning process. *ReplayBuffer₂* is a special buffer that specifically stores experiences when the agent accesses task-specific states. We effectively utilized these experiences to help the agent learn the strategy and complete tasks faster. Finally, we proved the effectiveness of the proposed mechanism through experiments.

2 HOERM Through Reward Machines

This section will introduce the details of the definition of Reward Machine (RM) and how the proposed HOERM learns strategies through RM.

2.1 Reward Machine

Reward Machine (RM) [6] is a special finite state machine that takes an abstract description of the environment as input and outputs the combination of reward functions under different conditions. The formal definition of RM is below:

Definition 1. (*Reward Machine*): *Given a set of propositional symbols* ($\mathcal{P}$)*, a set of environment states* (S)*, and a set of feasible actions* (A)*, an RM can be defined as a five-tuple:* $RM = \langle U, u_0, F, \delta_u, \delta_r \rangle$*, where* U *signifies a finite set of states,* $u_0 \in U$ *is the initial state, and* F *constitutes a finite set of terminal states such that* $U \cap F = \emptyset$*.* δ_u *is the state transition function,* $\delta_u : U \times 2^{\mathcal{P}} \rightarrow U \cup F$*, and* δ_r *is the reward function outputted by the RM,* $\delta_r : U \rightarrow [S \times A \times S \rightarrow \mathbb{R}]$*.*

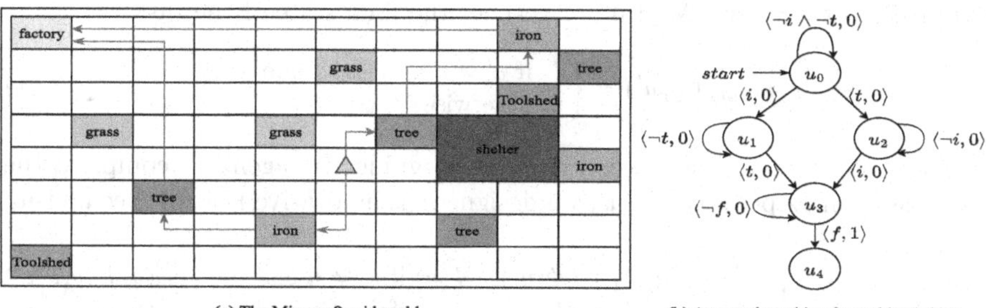

(a) The Minecraft gridworld

(b) A reward machine for making bridge

Fig. 1. The Minecraft environment and one RM for an example task

Figure 1 depicts a "make-bridge" task and its associated RM in the Minecraft environment. An RM $\mathcal{R}$ starts from an initial state u_0 and is in a certain state u_t ($u_t \in U \cup F$) after the agent moves some steps. Every edge in Fig. 1 (b) is labeled as a tuple $\langle \varphi, r \rangle$, in which φ is a logical formula composed of propositional symbols from $\mathcal{P}$ and r is the reward. When a truth assignment σ satisfies φ (i.e., $\sigma \models \varphi$), $\mathcal{R}$ transitions from state u_t to u_{t+1} and gives a reward of $r = \delta_r(u_t, u_{t+1})$. The σ is a set containing propositions in $\mathcal{P}$, which are true at the state u_t of RM.

To obtain the truth assignment σ, we introduced a labeling function $L : S \times A \times S \to 2^{\mathcal{P}}$. Given a state transition $e = (s, a, s')$, the labeling function $L(s, a, s')$ assigns truth values to the proposition symbols in $\mathcal{P}$. According to the RM definition and $L(s, a, s')$, we can formally describe how to apply RMs in RL.

Definition 2. *MDPRM: A Markov Decision Process with an RM (MDPRM) can be represented by a tuple* $\mathcal{MR} = \langle S, A, p, \gamma, \mathcal{P}, L, U, u_0, F, \delta_u, \delta_r \rangle$, *in which* S, A, p, *and* γ *are the conventional definitions of an MDP;* $\mathcal{P}$ *is the set of propositional symbols;* $L : S \times A \times S \to 2^{\mathcal{P}}$ *serves as the labeling function; and* U, u_0, F, δ_u, *and* δ_r *are the definitions of the RM.*

In $\mathcal{MR}$, the states of the environment and RM are updated after each step of the agent's execution. After the agent takes an action, then s is transitioned to s', the RM state will also transition to $u' = \delta_u(u, L(s, a, s'))$. Then, the agent receives a reward $r = \delta_r(u, L(s, a, s'))$, which is used to learn and adjust policies.

2.2 Proposed HOERM

This subsection introduces our HOERM for learning MDPRM policies. Our HOERM learns a set of options [5] for each task, focusing on causing RM to transition from one state to another. The high-level policy learns to select the most suitable option, while the low-level policy is modeled using double DQN, responsible for executing actions, and learns options to complete each subtask.

As mentioned above, our HOERM learns an option for each transition $\langle u, u_t \rangle$ between RM states. The initial set of each option is defined as $\mathcal{I}_{\langle u, u_t \rangle} = \{\langle s, u \rangle : s \in S, u \in U\}$. Since option$_{\langle u, u_t \rangle}$ can only be selected to execute when the RM state is u, its policy can be represented as $\pi_{\langle u, u_t \rangle}(a|s)$ by the environmental state s. The termination of an option$_{\langle u, u_t \rangle}$ is defined by Eq. (1), that is, when it transitions to a new RM state or reaches the final state of the task.

$$\beta_{\langle u, u_t \rangle}(s', u') = \begin{cases} 1 & \text{if } u' \neq u \text{ or } s' \text{ is terminal} \\ 0 & \text{otherwise} \end{cases} \quad (1)$$

The goal of option strategy $\pi_{\langle u, u_t \rangle}$ is to guide the agent to complete the option as soon as possible. Thus, we designed an innovative reward mechanism.

$$r_{\langle u, u_t \rangle}(s, a, s') = \begin{cases} \delta_r(u)(s, a, s') + \gamma \Phi(u_t) - \Phi(u) & \text{if } u_t \neq u \text{ and } u_t = \delta_u(u, L(s, a, s')) \\ \delta_r(u)(s, a, s') + r^{+} & \text{if } u_t \neq u \text{ and } u_t \neq \delta_u(u, L(s, a, s')) \\ \delta_r(u)(s, a, s') + r^{-} & \text{otherwise} \end{cases} \quad (2)$$

In Eq. (2), $\delta_r(u)\,(s, a, s')$ is the reward function output by RM, which outputs 1 only when it reaches the final state and 0 otherwise. $\Phi(u)$ is the potential function used to measure the proximity of the current state to the terminal state. In simple terms, the closer u is to the terminal state, the larger $\Phi(u)$ is. γ is the discount factor defined in the MDP. The hyper-parameters r^+ and r^- represent the auxiliary reward and punishment, respectively. If the transition (s, a, s') makes the RM state transition from u to u_t ($u_t = \delta_u(u, L(s, a, s'))$), agent will receive a reward of $\delta_r(u)(s, a, s')$, as well as an additional reward of $\gamma\Phi(u_t) - \Phi(u)$, to encourage the agent for completing the RM state transition.

In addition, when the RM state transitions from u to another state $\overline{u}$ ($\overline{u} \notin \{u, u_t\}$, but $\overline{u} \in U$), the agent receives a reward of $\delta_r(u)(s, a, s')$ and an additional auxiliary reward of r^+. This is because even though the transition is not the intended one, the experience is still valuable for the overall task.

For this reason, the experience replay mechanism includes a unique experience buffer, denoted as $ReplayBuffer_2$. It specifically stores the agent's experiences when triggering high-level events that lead to transition from u to another state $\overline{u} = \delta_u(u, L(s, a, s'))$, where $\overline{u} \notin \{u, u_t\}$ but $\overline{u} \in U$. The two main reasons for this design are as follows: (1) The conventional random sampling from the experience buffer often results in numerous irrelevant experiences, leading to slow training. (2) No matter whether $\overline{u}$ is equal to u_t, the experience gained when the agent triggers a high-level event is valuable, which helps to expedite the learning of policies for completing the subsequent subtask swiftly.

Finally, if the agent fails to trigger any high-level event and the RM state remains unchanged, it will receive an auxiliary punishment (r^-) in addition to the reward ($\delta_r(s, a, s')$). This negative feedback can motivate the agent to adjust its policy for the subtask as soon as possible.

3 Experiments

In this section, we perform algorithm performance tests on environments with discrete (Minecraft [1]) and continuous (Water World [3]) state spaces. These environments cover both single-task and multi-task scenarios. Three baseline algorithms were used, which are representative, state-of-the-art approaches for combining RMs with reinforcement learning. The first is Q-learning for RMs (QRM), proposed by [4]. The second and third are counterfactual experiences for RMs (CRM) and hierarchical RL for RMs (HRM), proposed by [2].

3.1 Experimental Setup

Each algorithm was run independently three times, and the average performance was reported. The results are presented uniformly in this paper, with four algorithms compared: the red line is the proposed HOERM; the green line is QRM; the sky-blue line is CRM; and the magenta line is HRM. The X-axis corresponds to the number of training steps, in millions, while the Y-axis represents the average normalized reward across all tasks. Tables 1 and 2 also provide the average and maximum reward values obtained by each algorithm.

3.2 Experiment 1: Results in Minecraft

The first experiment was conducted in the Minecraft environment with a discrete state space, introduced by [1]. As shown in Fig. 1 (a), the environment grid contains the agent and raw materials needed for the tasks, with randomly generated positions. The task set $\Omega = \{\varphi_1, \varphi_2, \ldots, \varphi_9, \varphi_{10}\}$, where $\varphi_i \in \Omega, i \in [1, 10]$ is one task in Minecraft (e.g., the "make-bridge" task).

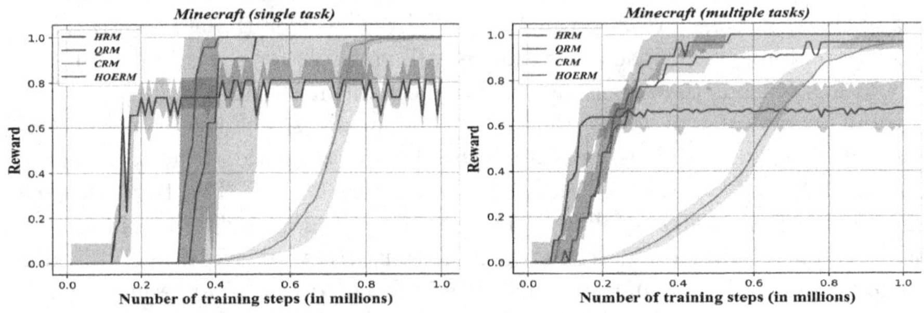

Fig. 2. Results in the Minecraft environment.

Figure 2 and Table 1 show the results obtained by each algorithm in single-task and multitask tests. According to the experimental results, the HRM algorithm has a fast initial learning speed in the two tests. In the single-task test, HRM's average reward is 0.6480, which is only slightly lower than our HOERM's 0.6712. However, HRM's maximum reward is the lowest, only 0.81. The QRM and CRM have a slower speed of obtaining rewards than HRM but result in a maximum reward of 1. The results are similar for the multitask test. On the whole, our HOERM algorithm performs best in both tests. Although the initial learning speed is slightly slower than that of HRM, it obtains the highest values for both average and maximum rewards. The maximum rewards in two types of tests are 1, indicating that HOERM can complete all tasks excellently.

Table 1. Rewards in the Minecraft environment.

Algorithm	single task		multiple tasks	
	maximum reward	average reward	maximum reward	average reward
HOERM	**1.0**	**0.6712**	1.0	**0.7746**
QRM	**1.0**	0.6218	0.9642	0.7218
CRM	**1.0**	0.6095	0.9602	0.5803
HRM	0.81	0.6480	0.6779	0.5917

3.3 Experiment 2: Results in Water World

The second experiment was conducted in "Water World", which is an environment with continuous state space and consists of a 2D box containing balls of various colors. We defined 10 tasks in this environment, including touching different specific colored balls. More detailed information can be found in [2].

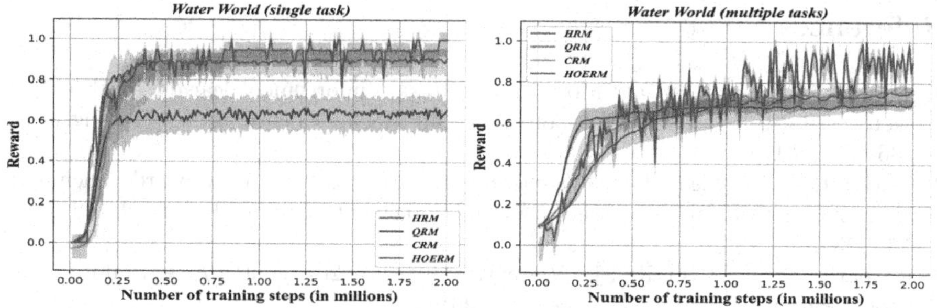

Fig. 3. Results in the Water World environment.

Figure 3 and Table 2 present the result of four algorithms in Water World. In the single-task test, the four algorithms exhibit similar initial learning speeds, but the HRM algorithm still achieves the lowest maximum reward of 0.666. In multitask test, notably, HRM's average reward is 0.6318, which is close to the value for CRM and higher than QRM thanks to its fast initial learning speed. However, HRM's maximum reward of 0.7125 still remains the lowest. Both CRM and QRM do not significantly improve their rewards compared to HRM in this complex environment. Although HOERM has a slightly slower initial learning speed than HRM, the effective sample utilization enhances its task completion capability, resulting in the highest rewards than the three baseline algorithms, demonstrating its excellent performance.

Table 2. Rewards in the Water World environment.

Algorithm	single task		multiple tasks	
	maximum reward	average reward	maximum reward	average reward
HOERM	**1.0**	**0.8571**	**0.9466**	**0.6918**
QRM	0.9137	0.8257	0.7689	0.6038
CRM	0.9553	0.8255	0.7644	0.6391
HRM	0.6660	0.5898	0.7125	0.6318

4 Discussion

In this paper, we introduced the concept of RM and proposed an HRL algorithm. The proposed algorithm effectively leverages RMs and achieves efficient sample utilization, leading to rapid strategy learning and impressive experimental results. In future work, we will explore the application of RMs in multi-agent problems to tackle more complex tasks effectively by sharing RM knowledge.

Acknowledgements. This study was supported by the National Natural Science Foundation of China (Grant Nos. 62172072).

References

1. Andreas, J., Dan, L., et al.: Modular multitask reinforcement learning with policy sketches. In: 9th International Conference on Machine Learning, Proceedings, pp. 166–175 (2017)
2. Icarte, R.T., Klassen, T.Q., Valenzano, R., McIlraith, S.A.: Reward machines: exploiting reward function structure in reinforcement learning. J. Artif. Intell. Res. **73**, 173–208 (2022)
3. Karpathy, A.: REINFORCEjs: WaterWorld demo (2015). http://cs.stanford.edu/people/karpathy/reinforcejs/waterworld.html
4. McIlraith, S., Icarte, R.T., Klassen, R.: Using reward machines for high-level task specification and decomposition in reinforcement learning. In: 10th International Conference on Machine Learning, Proceedings, pp. 2107–2116 (2018)
5. Sutton, R.S., et al.: Between MDPs and Semi-MDPs: a framework for temporal abstraction in reinforcement learning. Artif. Intell. **112**(1–2), 181–211 (1999)
6. Toro Icarte, R., Waldie, E., Klassen, T., Valenzano, R., Castro, M., McIlraith, S.: Learning reward machines for partially observable reinforcement learning. In: Advances in Neural Information Processing Systems, vol. 32 (2019)
7. Wiering, M.A., Van Otterlo, M.: Reinforcement learning. Adapt. Learn. Optim. **12**(3), 729 (2012)
8. Zheng, X., Yu, C., Zhang, M.: Lifelong reinforcement learning with temporal logic formulas and reward machines. Knowl.-Based Syst. **257**, 109650 (2022)

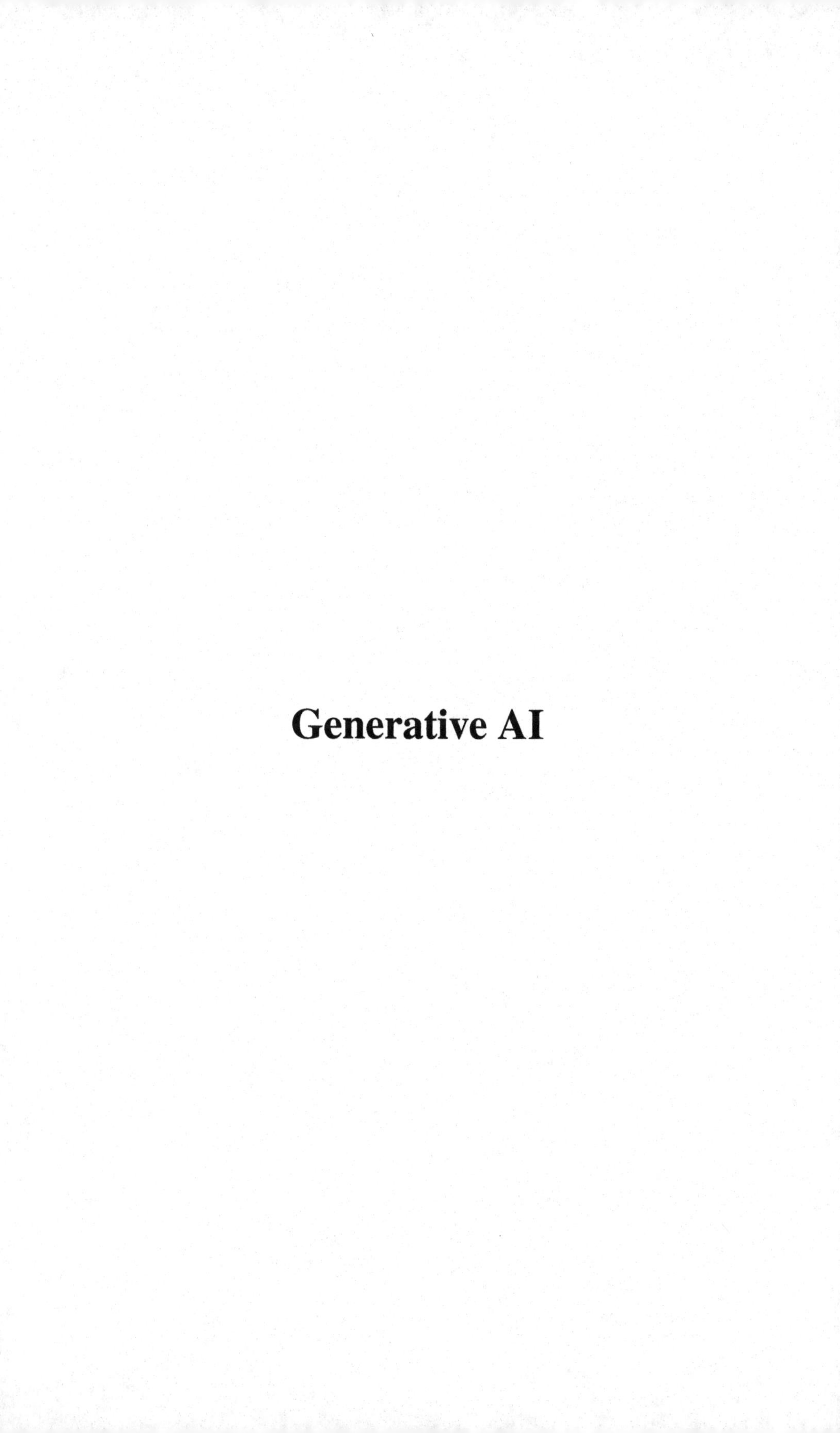

Generative AI

A Semantic Similarity Distance-Aware Contrastive Learning for Abstractive Summarization

Ying Huang[1,2] and Zhixin Li[1,2](✉)

[1] Key Lab of Education Blockchain and Intelligent Technology, Ministry of Education, Guangxi Normal University, Guilin 541004, China
[2] Guangxi Key Lab of Multi-Source Information Mining and Security, Guangxi Normal University, Guilin 541004, China
lizx@gxnu.edu.cn

Abstract. Recently, contrastive learning has been extended from visual representation to summarization tasks. Abstractive summarization aims to generate a short description for a document while retaining significant information. At present, the methods of contrastive learning summarization focus on modeling the global semantics of source documents, targets and candidate summaries to maximize their similarities. However, they ignore the influence of sentence semantics in the source document. In this paper, we propose a sentence-level semantic similarity distance-aware contrastive learning method (SSDCL), which integrates the semantic similarity distance between summaries and sentences of source documents into the contrastive loss in the form of soft weights. Therefore, our model maximize the similarity between summaries and salient information, while minimizing the similarity between summaries and noise. We conducted extensive experiments on CNN/Daily Mail and XSum datasets to verify our model. The experimental results show that the proposed method achieved remarkable performance over the baseline and many advanced methods.

Keywords: Contrastive learning · Abstractive summarization · Semantic similarity

1 Introduction

Automatic Text Summarization (ATS) [14,18,21] has attracted an increasing number of attention in the field of Natural Language Processing [1,12] in virtue of its powerful ability to handle redundant information. The purpose of ATS is to generate a short summary for a long document while retains its core content. Abstractive summarization [11,20,22] is a branch of ATS, which can be modeled as sequence-to-sequence(seq2seq) [25] problems learning to generate summaries in an autoregressive manner. With the development of pretrained language models such as BART [10], the performance of abstractive models have been significantly improved [28,33]. Recently, the contrastive learning paradigm [3] has been

F. Liu et al. (Eds.): PRICAI 2023, LNAI 14325, pp. 173–185, 2024.
https://doi.org/10.1007/978-981-99-7019-3_18

extended from unsupervised visual representation [2,29] to the text summarization [16,31,35]. It provides a new solution [15,24] to mitigate the exposure bias for abstractive summarization. However, to our knowledge, current contrastive learning studies in summarization are basically at the document or summary level [15,16], and rarely contrast the source sentences with the summary.

Furthermore, previous studies paid more attention to summaries with more co-occurrence words [32] in the source document, and less attention to the semantic similarity [7,30] between predicted sentences and source sentences. This leads to the model lacking of the ability to measure the contribution of the sentences in input document to the summary generation during training. Recent studies [8,9,28] also have attempted to use an extractive summarization model to guide the abstractive model to extract salient information. However, this form of guidance is not perfect: the number and distribution of salient content will vary from document to document, but the number of sentences output by the extractive model is fixed, and the selection process may lead to bias in the model.

Consequently, we design a contrastive learning method with sentence-level semantic similarity for abstractive summarization, which is used to improve the model's ability to distinguish salient information and denoising. This method constructs positive and negative samples according to the salience of sentences in the source document. Through contrastive learning, the generated summary can better surround the center of the input document in semantic space. The rationale for proposing this method is that we found by analyzing the CNN/Daily Mail (CNNDM) dataset [6] that some sentences of the documents largely determine the formation of summaries, and these sentences tend to be most relevant to the targets, while certain sentences do not contribute to this. Figure 1 shows an example of a document-summary pair in CNNDM. We calculate and rank the semantic similarity scores between each sentence in the source document and the target summary separately. What can be seen is that the most significant information is mainly concentrated on the three sentences with the highest similarity scores, while the sentences with low similarity may bring noise to the model.

Source sentences	score	rank
Thousands of bottles of alcohol were destroyed in Kabul this week, in what authorities described as the product of a ...	0.26	8
The bottles were confiscated over a two-year period in and around the Afghan capital, according to Kabul police ...	0.45	5
They were taken almost exclusively from "Afghan sources and not foreigners," he said.	0.73	3
The illicit items were being stored by Afghan customs officials, who burned the bottles Wednesday after receiving ...	0.34	6
Alcohol is largely banned in Afghanistan, and its sales and consumption considered a criminal offense for the country's.	0.84	2
Muslims, who constitute roughly 99% of the population.	0.33	7
Certain areas that cater to foreigners, however, are permitted to sell it.	0.99	1
Zahir said that it was in these areas -- mostly international hotels -- local sellers had come into possession of the alcohol.	0.53	4
CNN's Matiullah Mati contributed to this report.	0.18	9

Target: Official: Bottles are almost exclusively from "Afghan sources" and not foreigners. Alcohol is largely banned in Afghanistan. Certain areas, however, that cater to foreigners are permitted to sell it.

Fig. 1. An example of the relationship between similarity scores and sentences salience in CNN/Daily Mail. The sequences in green indicates coincidence with the target. (Color figure online)

What's more, the number and similarity scores of salient sentences will change according to different documents, which is related to the difficulty of distinguishing positive and negative samples in the model. If the similarity scores of sentences in a document are relatively low, or the difference between the positive and negative samples is too small, it will become a hard sample. Therefore, we further design a similarity distance-aware contrastive loss, which imposes soft weights based on the similarity distance between positive and negative samples and the targets, so that hard samples receive more attention or penalty. An overview of our method is given in Fig. 2.

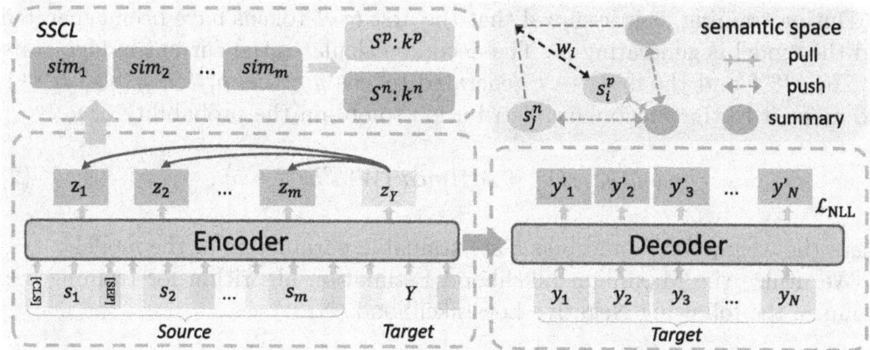

Fig. 2. Overview of our method.

Our experiments on two widely used public datasets validate that the method is simple and effective. The contributions of our work are summarized as follows:

- We propose a sentence-level semantic similarity contrastive learning method for abstractive summarization, which helps the model gain the ability to distinguish salient information from documents.
- We designed a similarity distance-aware contrastive loss to extend the similarity distance between positive and negative samples and the targets perceived by the model during training, allowing the model to pay more attention to samples that are difficult to summarize.
- Our experimental results show that our method is effective in improving the performance of large pretrained language models on ROUGE metrics.

2 Proposed Method

2.1 Problem Definition

Our generation model follow the standard Transformer architecture [26], which is composed of Encoder f and Decoder g, with long text as input and corresponding summary generated. Formally, for a source document $D = \{s_1, s_2, \cdots, s_m\}$

with m sentences and a summary $Y = \{y_1, y_2, \cdots, y_N\}$ with N tokens. Our goal is to model the conditional probability distribution $p(y_j|y_{<j}, D)$ using the Transformer architecture. We insert special tokens $[CLS]$ and $[SEP]$ at the beginning and the end of each sentence, and learn the context representation of them with the Encoder which maps the document into a series of hidden states, and treats the hidden states of the last layer as the document representation:

$$H^{enc} = \{z_1, z_2, \cdots, z_m\} = f\left(\hat{D}\right), \tag{1}$$

where z_i denotes the contextual embedding representation of the i-th sentence, and $\hat{D}$ is the input document after inserting the separator.

During training, it is assumed that the first $t-1$ tokens have been generated and the model is generating y_t. The decoder calculates the current hidden state h_t^{dec} by H^{enc} and the first $t-1$ generated tokens $y_{<t}$, i.e. $h_t^{dec} = g(y_{<t}, H^{enc})$, and maps it to the vocabulary distribution to obtain the probability of y_t:

$$p\left(y_t \middle| y_{<t}, \hat{D}\right) = softmax\left(W^{dec} h_t^{dec} + b\right), \tag{2}$$

where the weight W^{dec} and bias b are trainable parameters in the model.

We utilize the Maximum Likelihood Estimation algorithm for training, i.e. minimize the following Negative Log-Likelihood (NLL):

$$\mathcal{L}_{NLL} = -\frac{1}{N}\sum_{t=1}^{N} \log p\left(y_t \middle| y_{<t}, \hat{D}\right). \tag{3}$$

2.2 Semantic Similarity Contrastive Learning

Inspired by Zhong et al. [36], we propose a Semantic Similarity Contrastive Learning (SSCL) method, which performs semantic text matching between the summary and each sentence in the document to quantify the intrinsic gap in the degree of sentence-level contribution.

Computation of Semantic Similarity. In contrast to the way Wang et al. [27] selected salient information based on the n-gram overlap between summary and sentence, we started from the perspective of semantic similarity. Because only using n-gram overlap to judge the similarity of sentences is at the lexical level, sometimes it will not be able to accurately measure whether the real meanings between sentences are consistent. And even if two sentences contain different words, the semantic similarity can measure how similar they are.

The target summaries can be divided into single-sentence (in XSum dataset) and multi-sentence (in CNNDM dataset). Uniformly, for an summary containing n sentences, to calculate the semantic similarity scores, we also insert $[CLS]$ and $[SEP]$ tokens to separate each sentence in the summary, which are then fed separately into the Encoder to get the hidden representation $z_Y = \{z_1^Y, z_2^Y, \cdots, z_n^Y\}$.

The cosine similarity of the i-th sentence in the source document and the n sentences in the summary are calculated respectively, and n scores are obtained. As shown in Fig. 3, we consider the maximum value of the scores as the semantic similarity between the i-th source sentence and the target summary:

$$sim\left(i, Y\right) = \max_{j \in \{1,2,\cdots,n\}} \cos\left(z_i, z_j^Y\right), \tag{4}$$

where z_j^Y denotes the vector representation of the j-th sentence in the summary. Sentences with higher semantic similarity scores are more salient in documents.

Construction of the Positive and Negative Samples. One of the keys to effective contrastive learning is to construct high-quality positive and negative sample pairs. The most common way is to use data enhancement strategies to insert, replace or delete some fragments of the source document, but those methods are tends to break the structure of documents. Therefore, for each document, we select the k^p sentences with the highest similarity score as positive samples $S^p = \{z_1^p, z_2^p, ..., z_{k^p}^p\}$, and the k^n sentences with the lowest similarity score as negative samples $S^n = \{z_1^n, z_2^n, ..., z_{k^n}^n\}$ (shown in Fig. 3). During the training process, the positive and negative samples can be selected dynamically, while k^p and k^n are also varied according to the number of sentences in each document, which helps to improve the generalization ability of the model.

Contrastive Learning. Under the guidance of local semantics based on cosine similarity, contrastive learning encourages the model to capture salient information and distinguish potential noise in the documents during training, thus improving the quality of the context vector, keeping the generated summaries close to the most salient content and away from noisy information. The objective of contrastive objective is to minimize the following loss:

$$\mathcal{L}_{SSCL} = -\frac{1}{k^p} \sum_{i=1}^{k^p} \log \frac{e^{sim(i,Y)/\tau}}{\sum_{z_j \in S^n(j)} e^{sim(j,Y)/\tau} + e^{sim(i,Y)/\tau}}, \tag{5}$$

where τ is a temperature parameter. Finally, we weight the NLL objective and semantic similarity contrastive objective by a hyperparameter α as follows:

$$\mathcal{L} = \mathcal{L}_{NLL} + \alpha \mathcal{L}_{SSCL}. \tag{6}$$

2.3 Semantic Similarity Distance-Aware Contrastive Learning

The loss $\mathcal{L}_{SSCL}$ is treated the same for all documents, ignoring the relative differences between the contrastive samples of each document, which are of different quality. This is because the highlights in some documents are not always concentrated in a few sentences, and they may be scattered in most sentences. Especially for datasets with a large degree of abstraction like XSum. Even for sentences with salience information, their semantic similarity with the target summary will be relatively low. This makes it difficult for the model to distinguish between positives and negatives, which brings great challenges to contrastive learning. For such hard samples that are difficult to learn, we further propose a Semantic Similarity Distance-aware Contrastive Learning method (SSDCL).

Formally, we provide a soft weight w_i for the contrast between each positive and negative sample to reflect there relative quality differences. In other words, the semantic similarity distance-aware weights are determined by the differences between positives and negatives, as well as the quality of positive samples. The soft weight w_i is expressed as:

$$w_i = -\frac{\exp\left(1 - sim(i, Y)\right)}{\exp\left(\frac{1}{k^p}\sum_{z_i \in S^p} sim(i, Y) - \frac{1}{k^n}\sum_{z_j \in S^n} sim(j, Y) + \gamma\right)}, \tag{7}$$

where γ is a margin value, we set it to 0.01. Figure 4 illustrates how to allocate soft weights by similarity distance. For a positive sample sentence, when its similarity score with the summary is low, the molecular term of w_i is larger. For a document example, when the similarity difference between positive and negative samples is small, the denominator term of w_i is smaller. In this way, more attention can be paid to these difficult samples by applying soft weights to the contrastive loss. Therefore, the contrastive learning objective can be rewritten as:

$$\mathcal{L}_{SSDCL} = -\frac{1}{k^p}\sum_{i=1}^{k^p} \log \frac{e^{sim(i,Y)/\tau}}{w_i \sum_{z_j \in S^n(j)} e^{sim(j,Y)/\tau} + e^{sim(i,Y)/\tau}}. \tag{8}$$

The potential insight is to emphasize the contrastive effect of positive samples with low similarity scores and positive and negative samples with little difference.

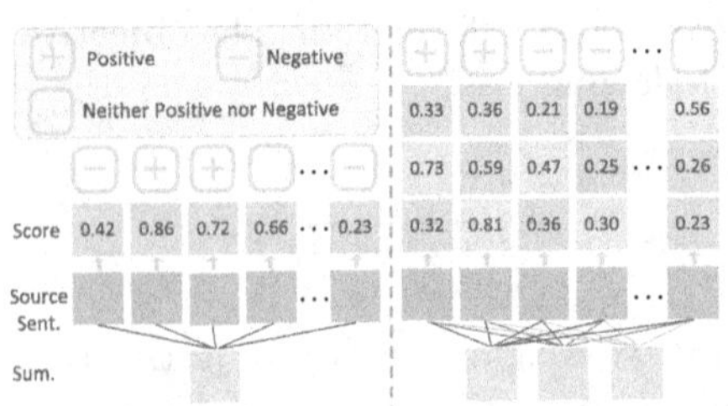

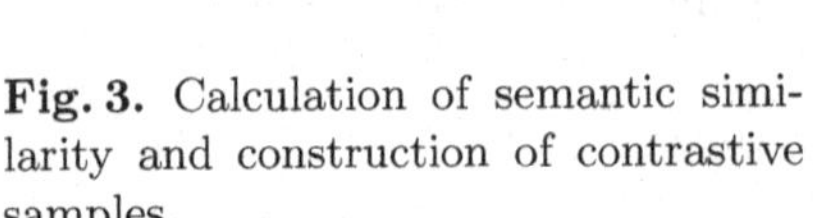

Fig. 3. Calculation of semantic similarity and construction of contrastive samples.

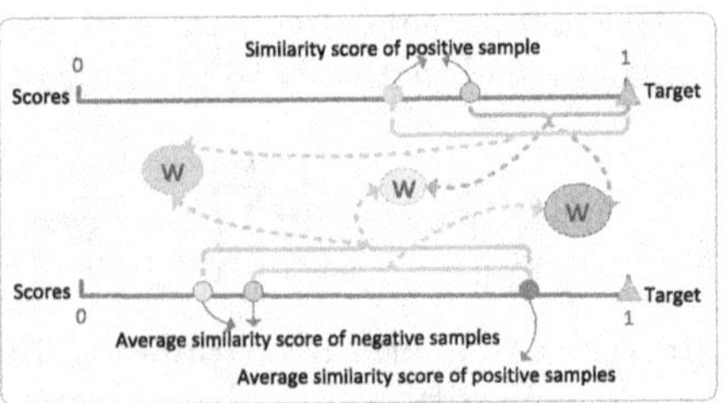

Fig. 4. Distribution of semantic similarity distance-aware soft weights.

Since our contrastive loss is sentence-level, combining it with NLL loss also solves the problem of inconsistent objective functions and evaluation metrics. Accordingly, the overall training objective combines contrastive and NLL loss:

$$\mathcal{L} = \mathcal{L}_{NLL} + \alpha \mathcal{L}_{SSDCL}, \tag{9}$$

where the hyperparameter α controls the importance of contrastive learning.

3 Experimental Results and Analysis

3.1 Datasets and Evaluation Metrics

CNN/Daily Mail (**CNNDM**) [6] come from the CNN and Daily Mail websites and includes online news articles and relevant highlights used as target summaries. **XSum** [19] is a highly abstracted dataset. Its articles come from the BBC website, while the corresponding target summaries are professionally written by human author. We follow the preprocessing steps in the work of [22] for the CNNDM, and use the official segmentation method [19] for the XSum.

ROUGE [13] is a similarity measurement method based on recall, which has two most common variants. ROUGE-N calculates the co-occurrence probability of N-gram in the target and generated summaries, and ROUGE-L measures the longest common subsequence of target and generated summary. We report the ROUGE-1, ROUGE-2 and ROUGE-L scores between reference summaries and generated summaries on two datasets, respectively.

3.2 Implementation Details

We use PEGASUS pre-training language model to initialize our proposed model, which includes 16 layer encoders and 16 layer decoders, with 16 attention headers, the dropout rate is 0.1, and the weight decay is set to $1e-8$. We insert special tokens at the beginning and end of each sentence in the training data to calculate the corresponding sentence representation. According to the document and summary length distributions of CNNDM and XSum datasets, we truncate the summaries to 128 and 64 tokens, respectively. In the contrastive loss, the temperature coefficient $\tau = 1.0$. We use Adafactor [23] to optimize the parameters of the model, and the learning rate is set to $1e-4$. The model is trained for 5 epochs. The batch size of CNNDM and XSum are 8 and 16 respectively. All our experiments are done on 2 NVIDIA GeForce RTX 3090 GPUs.

3.3 Main Results

Table 1 shows the main results of our method and the strong baseline models in recent years on CNNDM and XSum datasets.

Firstly, we compare the proposed method with the strong baseline built on the pre-training model, and our SSDCL shows obvious performance improvement. SSDCL improves by 2.07/1.05 ROUGE-1/2 than PEGASUS on the CNNDM and 0.62/0.34 on XSum, indicating that the generated summaries by our method contained more information. This demonstrates the effectiveness of our proposed contrastive learning method. On CNNDM, our performance is 2.46 ROUGE-L higher than PEGASUS, which shows that our method also shows superior performance in improving the verbal fluency of the generated summaries. SSDCL

Table 1. Main results on CNNDM and XSum, where R stands for ROUGE.

Model		CNNDM			XSum		
		R-1	R-2	R-L	R-1	R-2	R-L
Pretrain	BART [10]	44.16	21.28	40.90	45.14	22.27	37.25
	PEGASUS [34]	44.17	21.47	41.11	47.21	24.56	39.25
Extractive	MATCHSUM [36]	44.41	20.86	40.55	-	-	-
Abstractive	BIG BIRD [33]	43.84	21.11	40.74	47.12	24.05	38.80
	CaPE [4]	44.28	21.23	40.88	45.35	22.25	37.17
	RepSum [5]	44.53	21.23	41.53	44.64	21.73	36.53
	PtLAAM [17]	44.17	20.63	40.97	45.48	21.80	36.84
	GOLD-s [20]	44.82	22.09	41.81	45.85	22.58	37.65
Contrastive	SimCLS [15]	**46.67**	22.15	43.54	47.76	24.57	39.44
	ESACL [35]	44.24	21.06	41.20	44.64	21.61	36.73
	ConSum [24]	44.53	21.54	41.57	47.34	24.46	39.40
	SeqCo [31]	44.66	21.57	41.38	45.65	22.41	37.04
Ours	SSCL	45.13	22.10	42.09	47.64	**24.74**	**39.56**
	SSDCL	46.24	**22.52**	**43.57**	**47.83**	**24.90**	**39.81**

has also defeated several recent abstractive models and extractive models, and achieved better performance. The above illustrates that our SSDCL is beneficial to incorporate sentence-level contrastive learning into summarization models. Afterwards, the results on XSum compared with other baselines show that our method still shows superior performance on more abstractive dataset.

Particularly, as a contrastive learning model, our method even beats SimCLS on ROUGE-2 and ROUGE-L, achieving the best performance. This is because our model makes the summaries closer to positive samples, and at the same time, it pays more attention to the samples that are difficult to summarize by using the soft weights of the semantic similarity distance-aware of positive and negative samples. This also validates that identifying the semantic space inside the source document can effectively improve the quality of the summaries.

Finally, the second and last two rows in Table 1 are correspond to our ablation experiments, which are used to explore the influence of contrastive learning and semantic similarity distance-aware weights, where PEGASUS is the baseline. The results show that both points proposed are useful. SSDCL with semantic similarity distance-aware contrastive learning further improves SSCL with only contrastive learning, achieving even more performance gains. Especially, on CNNDM, SSDCL is 1.48 ROUGE-L higher than SSCL, and significantly outperforms the PEGASUS. The results clearly demonstrate the advantage of incorporating soft weights into the contrastive loss.

3.4 Analysis of Sentence Salience

To determine the degree of significance of the sentences, we calculated the semantic similarity scores of all sentences in the source documents with the corresponding summaries. Then we count the percentage of sentence similarity scores in each score segment for each document. Figure 5 shows the mean and standard deviation of the percentage of each score segment on the CNNDM and XSum. We considered the sentences with similarity scores higher than 0.6 as significant. On CNNDM and XSum, the average number of significant sentences per document is about 10% and 5%, respectively. The number of sentences with similarity scores below 0.4 is much higher than the number of significant sentences, indicating the necessary for us to use semantic similarity distance-aware contrastive learning to widen the gap between positives and negatives and to improve the model's ability to extract important information from positive samples. At the same time, the distribution of similarity scores provides a basis for our selection of positive and negative samples, as analyzed in the following section.

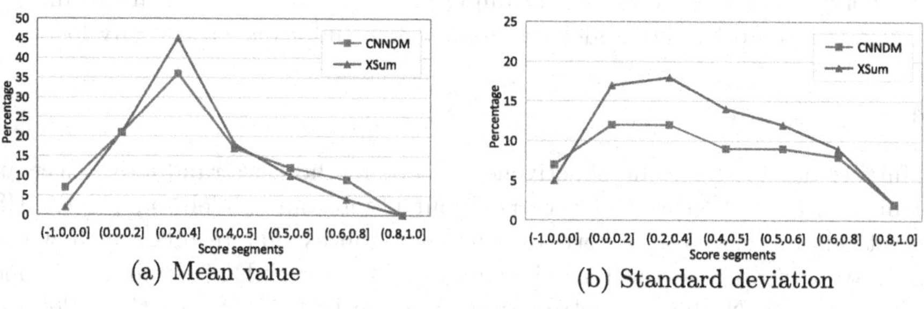

Fig. 5. The percentage statistics of each fraction in CNNDM and XSum datasets.

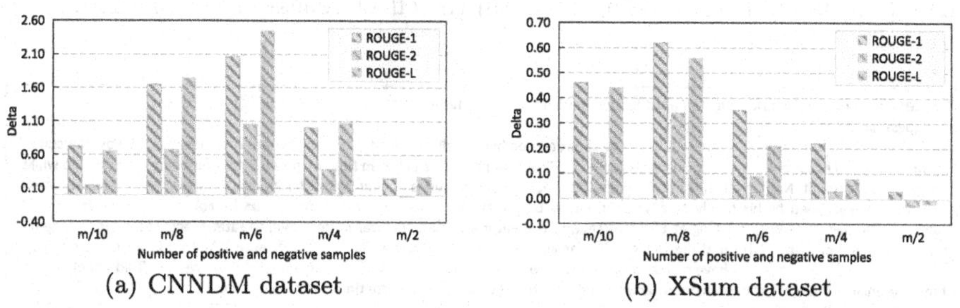

Fig. 6. Performance of different positive and negative numbers in CNNDM and XSum. The y-axis is the ROUGE delta between our SSDCL and PEGASUS. Each source document contains m sentences, the m/i means that k^p and k^n take the value of m/i.

3.5 Selection of Positive and Negative Samples

We set up an experiment to observe the influence of the selection of the number of positive samples k^p and the number of negative samples k^n on our contrastive model. Their values are related to m, the number of sentences in each document. As shown in Fig. 6(a), when we choose the $m/6$ sentences with the highest similarity scores as positive samples and the $m/6$ sentences with the lowest similarity scores as negative samples in CNNDM, the SSDCL will be improved to the best. This is because the salient information is mainly in the 10% of sentences with the highest similarity scores, while the noise is distributed in the 20% of sentences with the lowest scores. However, in XSum dataset (shown in Fig. 6(b)), SSDCL performs best when the number of positive and negative samples is $m/8$, because the documents in XSum have fewer salient sentences. Unfortunately, when more sentences are involved, performance drops significantly. It is due to the fact that the scores of some sentences are too close, and too many contrastive pairs with little discrimination may be constructed during dynamic sampling, leading to overfitting of the model. Conversely, when fewer sentences are selected, the difference between contrastive samples is too great, resulting in insufficient knowledge learned by the model and some salient information is easily lost.

3.6 Case Study

To further demonstrate the effectiveness of our method, we randomly select an document from CNNDM test set and input it into our model and PEGASUS respectively to generate the corresponding summaries. The results are shown in Fig. 7. We can observe the following findings: 1) Our SSDCL summarizes one of the causes of "Nathan's electrocution", but the PEGASUS lost these details, which suggests that our generated summary contains more salient information. 2) The summary generated by SSDCL is more linguistically coherent. 3) The words of the summary generated by PEGASUS are basically copied from the source document while our model generates new words without changing the original meaning. These findings confirm the effectiveness of our method.

Source: An apprentice electrician fell off a ladder and died in front of his father after he was electrocuted while testing lights in a factory, an inquest has heard. Nathan Brown, 19, was working with his father David, an experienced electrician, when he apparently touched a set of exposed electrical bars powering a crane. The shock caused him to fall 12ft head first onto the roof of a toilet block below the crane. He was airlifted to hospital but later died from his injuries. Tragic: Apprentice electrician Nathan Brown died after being electrocuted while testing lights . Accident: Nathan fell 12ft from a ladder after being electrocuted, and later died of his injuries . The inquest in Oldham heard that Nathan - described by his family as a 'cheeky, happy boy' - trained to become an electrician so he could follow in his father's footsteps. The pair were both working at Eurofabs UK Ltd, a sheet metal manufacturer in Rochdale, Greater Manchester, when tragedy struck in September 2013. ... He told the inquest: 'As far as I am aware the busbar should have been marked up in a sleeve with the marking "danger high voltage". I have never come across a busbar not sleeved and marked with an appropriate sign. 'Had I been aware of the presence of the busbars in such unprotected conditions then I would not have continued to take this work ...

PEGASUS: Nathan Brown, 19, was electrocuted while testing lights in a factory . He fell 12ft head first onto the roof of a toilet block below a crane . He was working with his father, an experienced electrician, at the time . Nathan had trained to become an electrician so he could follow in his father's footsteps.

SSDCL(Ours): Nathan Brown, 19, was working with father David, an experienced electrician, testing lights in a factory . He climbed up on a crane but accidentally touched exposed power supply . The shock made him fall 12ft head first and he died of his injuries . Inquest hears that the power supply was not clearly marked as dangerous .

Fig. 7. Case study on CNNDM dataset. Light purple words represent the new words generated by our model. (Color figure online)

4 Conclusions

In this work, first we focus on sentence-level contrastive learning between source document sentences and summaries, aiming to distinguish salient information from latent noise in source documents. Additionally, we innovatively integrate a soft weight of sentence semantic similarity distance-aware into the contrastive loss, and further enhance the ability of the model to capture salient information by paying more attention to the samples that are difficult to summarize. Comprehensive experiments in the abstractive summarization task demonstrate the performance of SSDCL in improving the baseline. In future work, we will consider modeling the similarity between summaries and source documents from a more fine-grained perspective, such as entity level.

Acknowledgements. This work is supported by National Natural Science Foundation of China (Nos. 62276073, 61966004), Guangxi Natural Science Foundation (No. 2019GXNSFDA245018), Innovation Project of Guangxi Graduate Education (YCSW2023141), Guangxi "Bagui Scholar" Teams for Innovation and Research Project, and Guangxi Collaborative Innovation Center of Multi-source Information Integration and Intelligent Processing.

References

1. Chen, S., Zhou, J., Sun, Y., et al.: An information minimization based contrastive learning model for unsupervised sentence embeddings learning. In: COLING, pp. 4821–4831 (2022)
2. Chen, X., Xie, S., He, K.: An empirical study of training self-supervised vision transformers. In: ICCV, pp. 9640–9649 (2021)
3. Chopra, S., Hadsell, R., LeCun, Y.: Learning a similarity metric discriminatively, with application to face verification. In: CVPR, pp. 539–546 (2005)
4. Choubey, P.K., Fabbri, A., Vig, J., et al.: CaPE: contrastive parameter ensembling for reducing hallucination in abstractive summarization. In: ACL, pp. 10755–10773 (2023)
5. Feng, J., Long, J., Han, C., et al.: RepSum: a general abstractive summarization framework with dynamic word embedding representation correction. Comput. Speech Lang. **80**, 101491 (2023)
6. Hermann, K.M., Kočiský, T., Grefenstette, E., et al.: Teaching machines to read and comprehend. In: NIPS, pp. 1693–1701 (2015)
7. Hou, C., Li, Z., Tang, Z., et al.: Multiple instance relation graph reasoning for cross-modal hash retrieval. Knowl.-Based Syst. **256**, 109891 (2022)
8. Hsu, W.T., Lin, C.K., Lee, M.Y., et al.: A unified model for extractive and abstractive summarization using inconsistency loss. In: ACL, pp. 132–141 (2018)
9. Lebanoff, L., Song, K., Dernoncourt, F., et al.: Scoring sentence singletons and pairs for abstractive summarization. In: ACL, pp. 2175–2189 (2019)
10. Lewis, M., Liu, Y., Goyal, N., et al.: BART: denoising sequence-to-sequence pretraining for natural language generation, translation, and comprehension. In: ACL, pp. 7871–7880 (2020)
11. Li, Z., Peng, Z., Tang, S., et al.: Text summarization method based on double attention pointer network. IEEE Access **8**, 11279–11288 (2020)

12. Li, Z., Sun, Y., Zhu, J., et al.: Improve relation extraction with dual attention-guided graph convolutional networks. Neural Comput. Appl. **33**, 1773–1784 (2021)
13. Lin, C.Y.: ROUGE: a package for automatic evaluation of summaries. In: Text Summarization Branches Out, pp. 74–81 (2004)
14. Liu, Y., Zhu, C., Zeng, M.: End-to-end segmentation-based news summarization. In: ACL, pp. 544–554 (2022)
15. Liu, Y., Liu, P.: SimCLS: a simple framework for contrastive learning of abstractive summarization. In: ACL, pp. 1065–1072 (2021)
16. Liu, Y., Liu, P., Radev, D., et al.: BRIO: bringing order to abstractive summarization. In: ACL, pp. 2890–2903 (2022)
17. Liu, Y., Jia, Q., Zhu, K.: Length control in abstractive summarization by pretraining information selection. In: ACL, pp. 6885–6895 (2022)
18. Nallapati, R., Zhou, B., dos Santos, C., et al.: Abstractive text summarization using sequence-to-sequence RNNs and Beyond. In: CoNLL, pp. 280–290 (2016)
19. Narayan, S., Cohen, S.B., Lapata, M.: Don't give me the details, Just the Summary! Topic-Aware convolutional neural networks for extreme summarization. In: EMNLP, pp. 1797–1807 (2018)
20. Pang, R.Y., He, H.: Text generation by learning from demonstrations. In: ICLR, pp. 1–22 (2021)
21. Rush, A.M., Chopra, S., Weston, J.: A neural attention model for abstractive sentence summarization. In: EMNLP, pp. 379–389 (2015)
22. See, A., Liu, P.J., Manning, C.D.: Get to the point: summarization with pointer-generator networks. In: ACL, pp. 1073–1083 (2017)
23. Shazeer, N., Stern, M.: Adafactor: adaptive learning rates with sublinear memory cost. In: ICML, pp. 4596–4604 (2018)
24. Sun, S., Li, W.: Alleviating exposure bias via contrastive learning for abstractive text summarization. arXiv preprint arXiv:2108.11846, pp. 1–6 (2021)
25. Sutskever, I., Vinyals, O., Le, Q.V.: Sequence to sequence learning with neural networks. In: NIPS, pp. 3104–3112 (2014)
26. Vaswani, A., Shazeer, N., Parmar, N., et al.: Attention is all you need. In: NIPS, pp. 6000–6010 (2017)
27. Wang, D., Chen, J., Zhou, H., et al.: Contrastive aligned joint learning for multilingual summarization. In: ACL, pp. 2739–2750 (2021)
28. Wang, F., Song, K., Zhang, H., et al.: Salience allocation as guidance for abstractive summarization. In: EMNLP, pp. 6094–6106 (2022)
29. Xian, T., Li, Z., Zhang, C., et al.: Dual global enhanced transformer for image captioning. Neural Netw. **148**, 129–141 (2022)
30. Xie, X., Li, Z., Tang, Z., et al.: Unifying knowledge iterative dissemination and relational reconstruction network for image-text matching. Inf. Process. Manage. **60**(1), 103154 (2023)
31. Xu, S., Zhang, X., Wu, Y., et al.: Sequence level contrastive learning for text summarization. In: AAAI, pp. 11556–11565 (2022)
32. Xu, S., Li, H., Yuan, P., et al.: Self-attention guided copy mechanism for abstractive summarization. In: ACL, pp. 1355–1362 (2020)
33. Zaheer, M., Guruganesh, G., Dubey, K.A., et al.: Big Bird: transformers for longer sequences. In: NIPS, pp. 17283–17297 (2020)
34. Zhang, J., Zhao, Y., Saleh, M., et al.: PEGASUS: pre-training with extracted gap-sentences for abstractive summarization. In: ICML, pp. 11328–11339 (2020)

35. Zheng, C., Zhang, K., Wang, H.J., et al.: Enhanced Seq2Seq autoencoder via contrastive learning for abstractive text summarization. In: IEEE Big Data, pp. 1764–1771 (2021)
36. Zhong, M., Liu, P., Chen, Y., et al.: Extractive summarization as text matching. In: ACL, pp. 6197–6208 (2020)

CCDWT-GAN: Generative Adversarial Networks Based on Color Channel Using Discrete Wavelet Transform for Document Image Binarization

Rui-Yang Ju[1,2](✉), Yu-Shian Lin[1], Jen-Shiun Chiang[1](✉), Chih-Chia Chen[1], Wei-Han Chen[1], and Chun-Tse Chien[1]

[1] Tamkang University, New Taipei City 251301, Taiwan
[2] National Taiwan University, Taipei City 106319, Taiwan
{jryjry1094791442,jsken.chiang}@gmail.com

Abstract. To efficiently extract textual information from color degraded document images is a significant research area. The prolonged imperfect preservation of ancient documents has led to various types of degradation, such as page staining, paper yellowing, and ink bleeding. These types of degradation badly impact the image processing for features extraction. This paper introduces a novelty method employing generative adversarial networks based on color channel using discrete wavelet transform (CCDWT-GAN). The proposed method involves three stages: image preprocessing, image enhancement, and image binarization. In the initial step, we apply discrete wavelet transform (DWT) to retain the low-low (LL) subband image, thereby enhancing image quality. Subsequently, we divide the original input image into four single-channel colors (red, green, blue, and gray) to separately train adversarial networks. For the extraction of global and local features, we utilize the output image from the image enhancement stage and the entire input image to train adversarial networks independently, and then combine these two results as the final output. To validate the positive impact of the image enhancement and binarization stages on model performance, we conduct an ablation study. This work compares the performance of the proposed method with other state-of-the-art (SOTA) methods on DIBCO and H-DIBCO ((Handwritten) Document Image Binarization Competition) datasets. The experimental results demonstrate that CCDWT-GAN achieves a top two performance on multiple benchmark datasets. Notably, on DIBCO 2013 and 2016 dataset, our method achieves F-measure (FM) values of 95.24 and 91.46, respectively.

Keywords: Semantic segmentation · Discrete wavelet transform · Generative adversarial networks · Document image binarization

1 Intorduction

Document image binarization is a significant research topic in Computer Vision (CV). Although the traditional image binarization methods are capable of

F. Liu et al. (Eds.): PRICAI 2023, LNAI 14325, pp. 186–198, 2024.
https://doi.org/10.1007/978-981-99-7019-3_19

extracting textual information from regular document images, they often struggle to process degraded ancient document images, including text degradation and bleed-through [16,30].

In recent years, image binarization methods based on deep learning have shown remarkable performance in addressing the problems that traditional image binarization methods [18,19,27] cannot solve. Several methods have been proposed and achieved state-of-the-art (SOTA) performance in degraded document image binarization, such as the conditional generative adversarial network-based method [35], the hierarchical deep supervised network [33], and the iterative supervised network [10], which all outperform traditional image binarization methods and other deep learning-based methods [9,32,34].

The aforementioned image binarization methods generally have superior results when applied to grayscale documents, particularly for restoring contaminated black and white scanned ancient documents. Considering that some scanned images of ancient documents are in color, we propose generative adversarial networks based on color channel using discrete wavelet transform (CCDWT-GAN), which utilize the discrete wavelet transform (DWT) on RGB (red, green, blue) split images to binarize the color degraded documents.

This paper makes the following contributions:

1) Demonstrating that applying DWT on RGB split images can improve the efficiency of the generator and the discriminator.
2) Presenting a novel method for document image binarization that achieves SOTA performance on multiple benchmark datasets.

The rest of this paper is organized as follows: Sect. 2 introduces the related work of document image binarization and GANs. Section 3 provides detailed information about the proposed method. Section 4 presents a quantitative comparison with SOTA methods on benchmark datasets. Finally, Sect. 5 concludes this paper.

2 Related Work

There are two primary categories of document image binarization methods: traditional image binarization methods and deep-learning-based semantic segmentation methods. The traditional image binarization method involves binarizing the image by calculating a pixel-level local threshold [12,15]. On the other hand, the deep learning-based semantic segmentation method utilizes U-Net [26] to capture contextual and location information. This method utilizes an encoder-decoder structure to transform the input image into the binarized representation [10,14,32,33].

Recently, generative adversarial networks (GANs) [7] have shown impressive success in generating realistic images. Zhao *et al.* [35] introduced a cascaded generator structure based on Pix2Pix GAN [13] for image binarization. This architecture effectively addresses the challenge of combining multi-scale information. Bhunia *et al.* [3] conducted texture enhancement on datasets and utilized conditional generative adversarial networks (cGAN) for image binarization. Suh *et al.* [28] employed Patch GAN [13] to propose a two-stage generative adversarial networks for image binarization. De *et al.* [4] developed a dual-discriminator framework that fuses local and global information. These methods all achieve the SOTA performance for document image binarization.

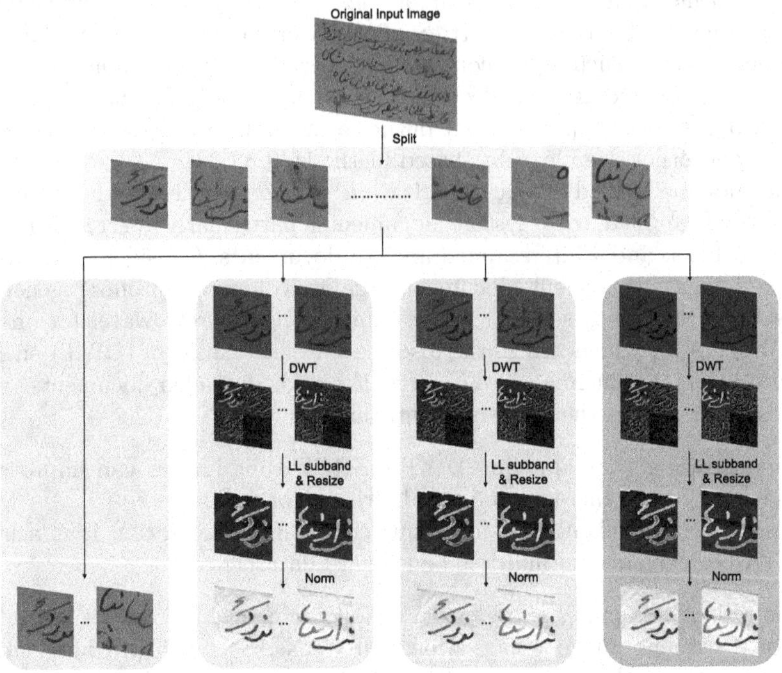

Fig. 1. The structure of the proposed model for image preprocessing. The original input image is split into multiple 224 × 224 patches. After applying DWT, the LL subband images are retained from the RGB channels split images. These images are subsequently resized to 224 × 224 pixels and perform normalization.

3 Proposed Method

This work aims to perform image binarization on color degraded document images. Due to the diverse and complex nature of document degradation, our method employs CCDWT-GAN on both RGB split images and a grayscale image. The proposed method consists of three stages: image preprocessing, image enhancement, and image binarization.

3.1 Image Preprocessing

In the first step, the proposed method employs four independent generators to extract the foreground color information and eliminate the background color from the image. To obtain different input images for four independent generators, we first split the RGB three-channel input image into three separate single-channel images and a grayscale image, as shown in Fig. 1. To preserve more information in RGB channels split images, this work applies DWT to each single-channel images to retain the LL subband images, then resizes to 224 × 224 pixels, and finally performs normalization. There are many options to process the input image of the generator and the discriminator, such as whether to perform normalization. In Sect. 4.5, we conduct comparative experiments to find the best option.

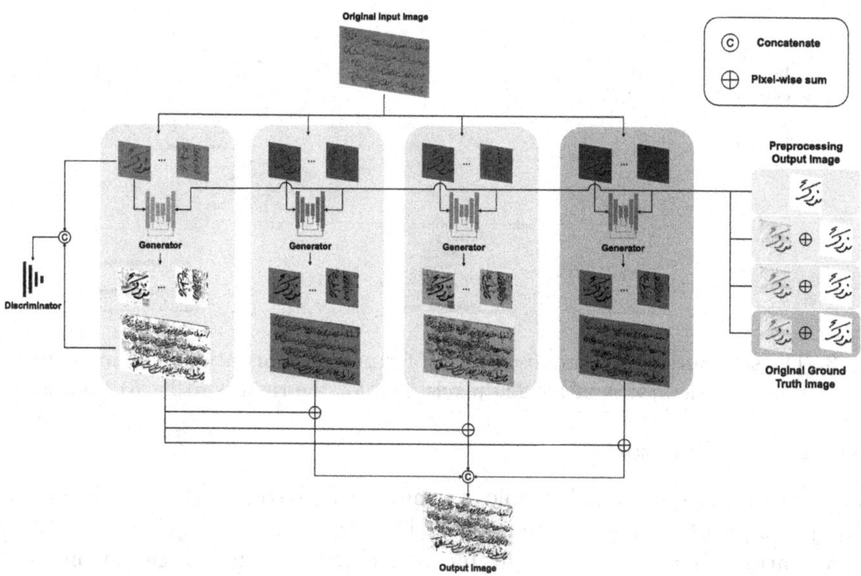

Fig. 2. The structure of the proposed model for image enhancement. The preprocessing output images and the original ground truth images are summed (pixel-wise) as the ground truth images of the generator.

3.2 Image Enhancement

In this stage, depicted in Fig. 2, the RGB input image with three channels is split into three separate single-channel images and a grayscale image. Each of these image utilizes an independent generator and shares the same discriminator to distinguish between the generated image and its corresponding ground truth image. The trained network is capable of eliminating background information from the local image patches and extracting color foreground information. To extract features, we employ U-Net++ [36] with EfficientNet [31] as the generator.

Due to the unpredictable degree of document degradation, four independent adversarial networks are used to extract text information from various color backgrounds, minimizing the interference caused by color during document image binarization. Since images with different channel numbers cannot be directly put into the same discriminator, the input of the discriminator requires a three-channel image, and the ground truth image is a grayscale (single-channel) image. As shown in the right of Fig. 2, the original ground truth image and the output image obtained from image preprocessing are summed at the pixel level to serve as the corresponding ground truth images.

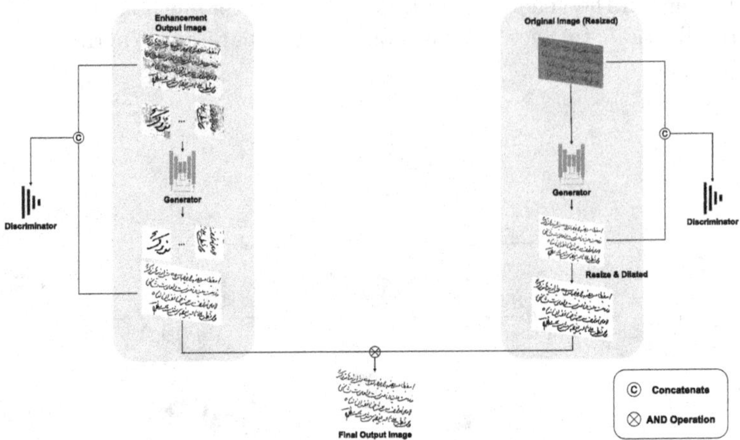

Fig. 3. The structure of the proposed model for image binarization. The input image size for the left generator is 224 × 224 pixels, and for the right is 512 × 512 pixels.

3.3 Image Binarization

Finally, the proposed method employs a multi-scale adversarial network for generating images of both local and global binarization, enabling more accurate differentiation between the background and text. We conduct global binarization on the original input images to offset any potential loss of spatial contextual information in the images caused by local prediction. Since the input image for local prediction in this stage is an 8-bit image, and the image binarization stage employs a 24-bit three-channel image, we employ two independent discriminators in the image binarization stage, respectively. As depicted in Fig. 3, the input image for local prediction corresponds to the output of the image enhancement, while the input image size for global prediction is 512 × 512 pixels.

3.4 Loss Function

In order to achieve a more stable convergence of the loss function, the proposed method utilizes the Wasserstein GAN [8] target loss function. The report of Bartusiak *et al.* [1] demonstrates that the binary cross-entropy (BCE) loss outperforms the L1 loss for binary classification tasks. Therefore, we utilize the BCE loss instead of the L1 loss employed in Pix2Pix GAN [13]. The Wasserstein GAN target loss function including the BCE loss is defined as follows:

$$\mathbb{L}_D = -\mathbb{E}_{x,y}[D(y,x)] + \mathbb{E}_x[D(G(x),x)] + \alpha\mathbb{E}_{x,\hat{y}\sim P_{\hat{y}}}[(\|\nabla_{\hat{y}}D(\hat{y},x)\|_2 - 1)^2] \quad (1)$$

$$\mathbb{L}_G = \mathbb{E}_x[D(G(x), x)] + \lambda \mathbb{E}_{G(x),y}[y \log G(x) + (1-y)\log(1-G(x))] \quad (2)$$

where the penalty coefficient is α, and the uniform sampling along a straight line between the ground truth distribution P_y and the point pairs of the generated data distribution is $P_{\hat{y}}$. λ is used to control the relative importance of different loss terms. The parameter of the generator is θ_G and the parameter of the discriminator is θ_D. In the discriminator, the generated image is distinguished from the ground truth image by the target loss function $\mathbb{L}_D$ in Eq. (1). In the generator, the distance between the generated image and the ground truth image in each color channel is minimized by the target loss function $\mathbb{L}_G$ in Eq. (2).

4 Experiments

4.1 Datasets

This work trains the model on several public datasets and compares the performance of the proposed method with other SOTA methods on benchmark datasets. Our training sets include Document Image Binarization Competition (DIBCO) 2009 [6], Handwritten Document Image Binarization Competition (H-DIBCO) 2010 [20], H-DIBCO 2012 [22], Persian Heritage Image Binarization Dataset (PHIBD) [17], Synchromedia Multispectral Ancient Document Images Dataset (SMADI) [11], and Bickley Diary Dataset [5]. The test sets comprise DIBCO 2011 [21], DIBCO 2013 [23], H-DIBCO 2016 [24], and DIBCO 2017 [25].

4.2 Evaluation Metric

Four evaluation metrics are employed to evaluate the proposed method and conduct a quantitative comparison with other SOTA methods for document image binarization. The evaluation metrics utilized include F-measure (FM), Pseudo-F-measure (p-FM), Peak signal-to-noise ratio (PSNR), and Distance reciprocal distortion (DRD).

4.3 Experiment Setup

The backbone neural network of this work is EfficientNet-B6 [31]. This paper utilizes a pre-trained model on the ImageNet dataset to reduce computational costs. During the image preprocessing stage, we divide the input images into 224×224 pixels patches, corresponding to the image size in the ImageNet dataset. The patches are sampled with scale factors of 0.75, 1, 1.25, and 1.5, and the images are rotated by 90°, 180°, and 270°. In total, the number of the training image patches are 336,702.

During the global binarization, we resize the original input image to 512×512 pixels and generate 1,890 training images by applying horizontal and vertical flips. The input images for the local binarization of the image binarization stage are obtained from the image enhancement stage, and both stages share the same training parameters. The image binarization stage is trained for 150 epochs, while the other stages are trained for 10 epochs each. This work utilizes the Adam optimizer with a learning rate of 2×10^{-4}. β_1 of the generator and β_2 of the discriminator are 0.5 and 0.999, respectively.

Table 1. Ablation study of the proposed model on benchmark datasets.

Methods	Dataset	FM↑	p-FM↑	PSNR↑	DRD↓
Enhancement	DIBCO 2011	80.32	93.93	16.02	5.19
Proposed	DIBCO 2011	94.08	97.08	20.51	1.75
Enhancement	DIBCO 2013	86.19	97.36	17.91	3.81
Proposed	DIBCO 2013	95.24	97.51	22.27	1.59
Enhancement	H-DIBCO 2016	81.60	95.65	16.82	5.62
Proposed	H-DIBCO 2016	91.46	96.32	19.66	2.94
Enhancement	DIBCO 2017	78.76	93.30	15.15	5.84
Proposed	DIBCO 2017	90.95	93.79	18.57	2.94

4.4 Ablation Study

In this section, this work presents an ablation study conducted to assess the individual contributions of each stage of the proposed method. We evaluate the output of the image enhancement stage, as "Enhancement", and compare it with the final output, as "Proposed". The evaluation and comparison of the output results are performed on four DIBCO datasets. Table 1 demonstrates that the output result of "Enhancement" is worse than the final output in terms of FM, p-FM, PSNR, and DRD values.

To further demonstrate the advantages of each stage more intuitively, we choose five images from PHIBD [17] and Bickley Diary Dataset [5] to show the step-by-step output results of image enhancement and image binarization using the proposed method. As shown in Fig. 4, (b) represents the result of retaining the LL subband image after applying DWT and normalization (the result of the image preprocessing stage), showing that the original input image is performed noise reduction. (c) is the result of image enhancement using adversarial network, and it has removed the background color and highlighted the text color. (d) is the final output image obtained using the proposed method, and it can be seen that our final output is closer to the ground truth image (e).

Fig. 4. The output images of each stage of the proposed model: (a) the original input image, (b) the LL subband image after applying DWT and normalization, (c) the enhanced image using image enhancement method, (d) the binarization image using the method combining local and global features, (e) the ground truth image.

4.5 Experimental Results

Despite mathematical theories supporting the effectiveness of applying DWT to images for storing contour information and reducing noise, we aim to comprehensively explain their impact on experimental results. To achieve this, we utilize UNet architecture [26] with EfficientNet-B5 [31] as the baseline model to conduct comparison experiments, as presented in Table 2. We formulate three options for the input images of the generator: direct input image, DWT to LL subband image, and DWT to LL subband image with normalization. Corresponding options are set up for the ground truth images. Notably, option 1: directly using the original input image as input, exhibits the worst performance on all four datasets. On DIBCO 2011 dataset, option 6: employing only DWT without normalization as the input image and corresponding to the ground truth image, demonstrate the best performance, achieving FM value of 91.95. The FM value of Option 3 reaches 94.88, achieving the top performance on DIBCO 2013 dataset by directly inputting the original image and utilizing the image processing output image as the corresponding ground truth image. Moreover, option 3 achieves the top two performance on DIBCO 2016 dataset. Based on this,

Table 2. Model performance comparison of different input images and ground truth images of the generator. Best and 2nd best performance are in red and blue colors, respectively.

(a) DIBCO 2011

Option	Input	GT	FM	p-FM	PSNR	DRD
1	\	\	86.68	89.61	19.27	4.01
2	\	DWT (LL)	88.20	90.57	19.53	3.45
3	\	DWT (LL) + Norm	87.70	90.24	19.65	3.45
4	DWT (LL)	\	87.74	89.69	18.88	3.78
5	DWT (LL) + Norm	\	89.33	91.94	19.49	3.37
6	DWT (LL)	DWT (LL)	90.53	92.82	19.68	3.11
7	DWT (LL) + Norm	DWT (LL) + Norm	89.06	92.25	19.59	3.31

(b) DIBCO 2013

Option	Input	GT	FM	p-FM	PSNR	DRD
1	\	\	92.94	94.70	21.57	2.74
2	\	DWT (LL)	94.43	95.64	21.79	2.13
3	\	DWT (LL) + Norm	94.88	96.19	22.32	1.95
4	DWT (LL)	\	93.23	94.43	20.80	2.67
5	DWT (LL) + Norm	\	93.76	95.41	21.54	2.40
6	DWT (LL)	DWT (LL)	94.39	95.34	21.91	2.26
7	DWT (LL) + Norm	DWT (LL) + Norm	94.55	95.86	22.02	2.07

(c) H-DIBCO 2016

Option	Input	GT	FM	p-FM	PSNR	DRD
1	\	\	90.74	94.46	19.39	3.30
2	\	DWT (LL)	91.76	95.74	19.67	2.93
3	\	DWT (LL) + Norm	91.49	96.46	19.68	2.92
4	DWT (LL)	\	91.86	94.95	19.62	2.99
5	DWT (LL) + Norm	\	91.28	96.03	19.47	3.04
6	DWT (LL)	DWT (LL)	91.68	95.90	19.68	2.93
7	DWT (LL) + Norm	DWT (LL) + Norm	91.95	95.87	19.75	2.84

we choose option 3 to employ UNet++ [36] with EfficientNet-B6 [31] as the generator for network design.

Due to the lack of optical character recognition (OCR) result within dataset, both the proposed method and other SOTA methods are evaluated using the four evaluation metrics described in Sect. 4.2. The evaluation results on the benchmark datasets are presented in Table 3. Our proposed method demonstrates superior performance across all four evaluation metrics on DIBCO 2016 dataset. Additionally, on DIBCO 2011 and 2013 datasets, the proposed method achieves the top two performance in each evaluation metric. Despite slightly lower FM value of 90.05 compared to the highest value of 91.33, and p-FM value of 93.79 lower than the highest value of 94.65, the PSNR and DRD values maintain top two performance on DIBCO 2017 dataset. By combining the comparison results

Table 3. Quantitative comparison (FM/p-FM/PSNR/DRD) with other state-of-the-art models for document image binarization on benchmark datasets. Best and 2nd best performance are in red and blue colors, respectively.

(a) DIBCO 2011

Methods	FM	p-FM	PSNR	DRD
Otsu [19]	82.10	85.96	15.72	8.95
Sauvola [27]	82.35	88.63	15.75	7.86
He [10]	91.92	95.82	19.49	2.37
Vo [33]	92.58	94.67	19.16	2.38
Zhao [35]	92.62	95.38	19.58	2.55
1st Place [21]	88.74	–	17.97	5.36
Yang [34]	93.44	95.82	20.10	2.25
Suh [29]	93.44	96.18	19.97	1.93
Tensmeyer [32]	93.60	97.70	20.11	1.85
Ours	94.08	97.08	20.51	1.75

(b) DIBCO 2013

Methods	FM	p-FM	PSNR	DRD
Otsu [19]	80.04	83.43	16.63	10.98
Sauvola [27]	82.73	88.37	16.98	7.34
He [10]	93.36	96.70	20.88	2.15
Vo [33]	93.43	95.34	20.82	2.26
Zhao [35]	93.86	96.47	21.53	2.32
1st Place [23]	92.70	94.19	21.29	3.10
Yang [34]	95.19	96.37	22.58	1.78
Suh [29]	94.75	97.36	21.78	1.73
Tensmeyer [32]	93.10	96.80	20.70	2.20
Ours	95.24	97.51	22.27	1.59

(c) H-DIBCO 2016

Methods	FM	p-FM	PSNR	DRD
Otsu [19]	86.59	89.92	17.79	5.58
Sauvola [27]	84.27	89.10	17.15	6.09
He [10]	91.19	95.74	19.51	3.02
Vo [33]	90.01	93.44	18.74	3.91
Zhao [35]	89.77	94.85	18.80	3.85
1st Place [24]	88.72	91.84	18.45	3.86
Guo [9]	88.51	90.46	18.42	4.13
Bera [2]	90.43	91.66	18.94	3.51
Yang [34]	90.41	94.70	19.00	3.34
Suh [29]	91.11	95.22	19.34	3.25
Ours	91.46	96.32	19.66	2.94

(d) DIBCO 2017

Methods	FM	p-FM	PSNR	DRD
Otsu [19]	77.73	77.89	13.85	15.54
Sauvola [27]	77.11	84.10	14.25	8.85
Jia [15]	85.66	88.30	16.40	7.67
Jemni [14]	89.80	89.95	17.45	4.03
Zhao [35]	90.73	92.58	17.83	3.58
1st Place [25]	91.04	92.86	18.28	3.40
Howe [12]	90.10	90.95	18.52	5.12
Bera [2]	83.38	89.43	15.45	6.71
Yang [34]	91.33	93.84	18.34	3.24
Suh [29]	90.95	94.65	18.40	2.93
Ours	90.95	93.79	18.57	2.94

from these four datasets, it is demonstrated that the images produced by our proposed method exhibit greater similarity to the ground truth images, and better binarization performance.

To compare the difference between images generated by the proposed method and other methods, two images are selected as examples. Figure 5 and Fig. 6 illustrate the results using different methods. Evidently, the proposed method preserves greater textual content while effectively eliminating shadows and noise compared to other methods.

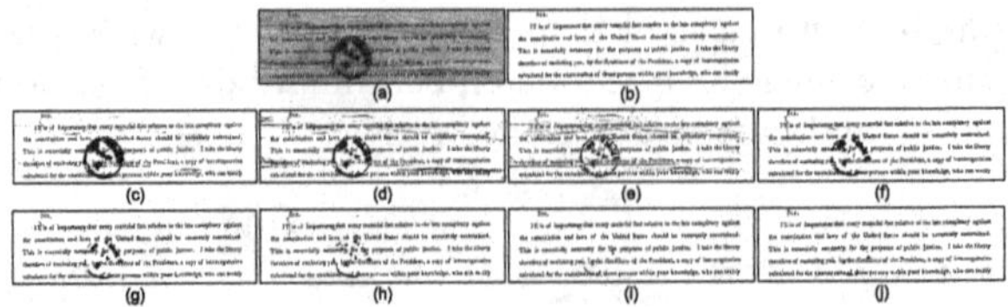

Fig. 5. Examples of document image binarization for the input image PR16 of DIBCO 2013: (a) original input images, (b) the ground truth, (c) Otsu [19], (d) Niblack [18], (e) Sauvola [27], (f) Vo [33], (g) He [10], (h) Zhao [35], (i) Suh [29], (j) Ours.

Fig. 6. Examples of document image binarization for the input image HW5 of DIBCO 2013: (a) original input images, (b) the ground truth, (c) Otsu [19], (d) Niblack [18], (e) Sauvola [27], (f) Vo [33], (g) He [10], (h) Zhao [35], (i) Suh [29], (j) Ours.

5 Conclusion

To perform image binarization on color degraded documents, this work splits the RGB three-channel input image into three single-channel images, and train the adversarial network on each single-channel image, respectively. Moreover, this work applies DWT on 224×224 patches of single-channel image in the image preprocessing stage to improve the model performance. We name the proposed generative adversarial network as CCDWT-GAN, which achieves SOTA performance on multiple benchmark datasets.

Acknowledgment. This work is supported by National Science and Technology Council of Taiwan, under Grant Number: NSTC 112-2221-E-032-037-MY2.

References

1. Bartusiak, E.R., et al.: Splicing detection and localization in satellite imagery using conditional GANs. In: 2019 IEEE Conference on Multimedia Information Processing and Retrieval (MIPR), pp. 91–96. IEEE (2019)

2. Bera, S.K., Ghosh, S., Bhowmik, S., Sarkar, R., Nasipuri, M.: A non-parametric binarization method based on ensemble of clustering algorithms. Multimed. Tools Appl. **80**(5), 7653–7673 (2021)
3. Bhunia, A.K., Bhunia, A.K., Sain, A., Roy, P.P.: Improving document binarization via adversarial noise-texture augmentation. In: 2019 IEEE International Conference on Image Processing (ICIP), pp. 2721–2725. IEEE (2019)
4. De, R., Chakraborty, A., Sarkar, R.: Document image binarization using dual discriminator generative adversarial networks. IEEE Signal Process. Lett. **27**, 1090–1094 (2020)
5. Deng, F., Wu, Z., Lu, Z., Brown, M.S.: Binarizationshop: a user-assisted software suite for converting old documents to black-and-white. In: Proceedings of the 10th Annual Joint Conference on Digital Libraries, pp. 255–258 (2010)
6. Gatos, B., Ntirogiannis, K., Pratikakis, I.: ICDAR 2009 document image binarization contest (DIBCO 2009). In: 2009 10th International Conference on Document Analysis and Recognition, pp. 1375–1382. IEEE (2009)
7. Goodfellow, I., et al.: Generative adversarial networks. Commun. ACM **63**(11), 139–144 (2020)
8. Gulrajani, I., Ahmed, F., Arjovsky, M., Dumoulin, V., Courville, A.C.: Improved training of Wasserstein GANs. In: Advances in Neural Information Processing Systems, vol. 30 (2017)
9. Guo, J., He, C., Zhang, X.: Nonlinear edge-preserving diffusion with adaptive source for document images binarization. Appl. Math. Comput. **351**, 8–22 (2019)
10. He, S., Schomaker, L.: DeepOtsu: document enhancement and binarization using iterative deep learning. Pattern Recogn. **91**, 379–390 (2019)
11. Hedjam, R., Cheriet, M.: Historical document image restoration using multispectral imaging system. Pattern Recogn. **46**(8), 2297–2312 (2013)
12. Howe, N.R.: Document binarization with automatic parameter tuning. Int. J. Doc. Anal. Recognit. (IJDAR) **16**, 247–258 (2013)
13. Isola, P., Zhu, J.Y., Zhou, T., Efros, A.A.: Image-to-image translation with conditional adversarial networks. In: Proceedings of the IEEE Conference on Computer Vision and Pattern Recognition, pp. 1125–1134 (2017)
14. Jemni, S.K., Souibgui, M.A., Kessentini, Y., Fornés, A.: Enhance to read better: a multi-task adversarial network for handwritten document image enhancement. Pattern Recogn. **123**, 108370 (2022)
15. Jia, F., Shi, C., He, K., Wang, C., Xiao, B.: Degraded document image binarization using structural symmetry of strokes. Pattern Recogn. **74**, 225–240 (2018)
16. Kligler, N., Katz, S., Tal, A.: Document enhancement using visibility detection. In: Proceedings of the IEEE Conference on Computer Vision and Pattern Recognition, pp. 2374–2382 (2018)
17. Nafchi, H.Z., Ayatollahi, S.M., Moghaddam, R.F., Cheriet, M.: An efficient ground truthing tool for binarization of historical manuscripts. In: 2013 12th International Conference on Document Analysis and Recognition, pp. 807–811. IEEE (2013)
18. Niblack, W.: An Introduction to Digital Image Processing. Strandberg Publishing Company, Birkeroed (1985)
19. Otsu, N.: A threshold selection method from gray-level histograms. IEEE Trans. Syst. Man Cybern. **9**(1), 62–66 (1979)
20. Pratikakis, I., Gatos, B., Ntirogiannis, K.: H-DIBCO 2010-handwritten document image binarization competition. In: 2010 12th International Conference on Frontiers in Handwriting Recognition, pp. 727–732. IEEE (2010)

21. Pratikakis, I., Gatos, B., Ntirogiannis, K.: ICDAR 2011 document image binarization contest (DIBCO 2011). In: 2011 International Conference on Document Analysis and Recognition, pp. 1506–1510. IEEE (2011)
22. Pratikakis, I., Gatos, B., Ntirogiannis, K.: ICFHR 2012 competition on handwritten document image binarization (H-DIBCO 2012). In: 2012 International Conference on Frontiers in Handwriting Recognition, pp. 817–822. IEEE (2012)
23. Pratikakis, I., Gatos, B., Ntirogiannis, K.: ICDAR 2013 document image binarization contest (DIBCO 2013). In: 2013 12th International Conference on Document Analysis and Recognition, pp. 1471–1476. IEEE (2013)
24. Pratikakis, I., Zagoris, K., Barlas, G., Gatos, B.: ICFHR 2016 handwritten document image binarization contest (H-DIBCO 2016). In: 2016 15th International Conference on Frontiers in Handwriting Recognition (ICFHR), pp. 619–623. IEEE (2016)
25. Pratikakis, I., Zagoris, K., Barlas, G., Gatos, B.: ICDAR 2017 competition on document image binarization (DIBCO 2017). In: 2017 14th IAPR International Conference on Document Analysis and Recognition (ICDAR), vol. 1, pp. 1395–1403. IEEE (2017)
26. Ronneberger, O., Fischer, P., Brox, T.: U-Net: convolutional networks for biomedical image segmentation. In: Navab, N., Hornegger, J., Wells, W.M., Frangi, A.F. (eds.) MICCAI 2015. LNCS, vol. 9351, pp. 234–241. Springer, Cham (2015). https://doi.org/10.1007/978-3-319-24574-4_28
27. Sauvola, J., Pietikäinen, M.: Adaptive document image binarization. Pattern Recogn. **33**(2), 225–236 (2000)
28. Suh, S., Kim, J., Lukowicz, P., Lee, Y.O.: Two-stage generative adversarial networks for binarization of color document images. Pattern Recogn. **130**, 108810 (2022)
29. Suh, S., Lee, H., Lukowicz, P., Lee, Y.O.: CEGAN: classification enhancement generative adversarial networks for unraveling data imbalance problems. Neural Netw. **133**, 69–86 (2021)
30. Sulaiman, A., Omar, K., Nasrudin, M.F.: Degraded historical document binarization: a review on issues, challenges, techniques, and future directions. J. Imaging **5**(4), 48 (2019)
31. Tan, M., Le, Q.: EfficientNet: rethinking model scaling for convolutional neural networks. In: International Conference on Machine Learning, pp. 6105–6114 (2019)
32. Tensmeyer, C., Martinez, T.: Document image binarization with fully convolutional neural networks. In: 2017 14th IAPR International Conference on Document Analysis and Recognition (ICDAR), vol. 1, pp. 99–104. IEEE (2017)
33. Vo, Q.N., Kim, S.H., Yang, H.J., Lee, G.: Binarization of degraded document images based on hierarchical deep supervised network. Pattern Recogn. **74**, 568–586 (2018)
34. Yang, Z., Xiong, Y., Wu, G.: GDB: gated convolutions-based document binarization. arXiv preprint arXiv:2302.02073 (2023)
35. Zhao, J., Shi, C., Jia, F., Wang, Y., Xiao, B.: Document image binarization with cascaded generators of conditional generative adversarial networks. Pattern Recogn. **96**, 106968 (2019)
36. Zhou, Z., Siddiquee, M.M.R., Tajbakhsh, N., Liang, J.: UNet++: redesigning skip connections to exploit multiscale features in image segmentation. IEEE Trans. Med. Imaging **39**(6), 1856–1867 (2019)

Coarse-to-Fine Response Generation for Document Grounded Conversations

Huan Zhao(✉), Shan Li, Bo Li, and Xupeng Zha

College of Computer Science and Electronic Engineering, Hunan University, ChangSha, China
{hzhao,lalisa,blee,zhaxupeng}@hnu.edu.cn

Abstract. Generating fluent and informative responses is crucial for dialogue systems. Most existing studies introduce documents as additional document to improve dialogue generation performance. However, understanding complex and multi-topic documents as well as extracting useful information related to the dialogue context from them is challenging. To solve this problem, we propose a Coarse-to-Fine Response Generation (CFRG) model with an encoder-decoder for document-grounded conversations,where the encoder is used to aware the themes of the dialogue context, and the decoder parse the semantics of replies. Specifically, the CFRG extracts coarse-grained features guided by the response from the context and documents and then uses them as input of decoder. It further interacts with the current sequence in the cross-attention layer to generate fine-grained features, on which a non-linear transformation function is trained to map to a word space. The experimental results on datasets CMU_DoG and Wizard of WikiPedia show that our model demonstrates superior performance compared to the majority of other models and achieves the best or comparable results.

Keywords: Coarse-to-fine features · Document-driven dialogue · Encoder-Decoder · Knowledge integration

1 Introduction

Dialogue systems have gained increasing attention due to their important applications in Human-bot Interaction and promising market prospects, categorized into task-oriented dialogue systems and open-domain chatbots. Task-oriented dialog systems, also referred to as closed-domain or goal-driven dialogue systems, are characterized by a clearly defined service object, such as booking airline tickets and ordering food. Conversely, open-domain chatbots without a certain topic, primarily fulfill more emotional and social needs. Depending on how they generate responses, traditional dialogue systems can be categorized into two types: retrieval-based systems and generation-based systems. The former selects the

Supported by National Natural Science Foundation of China under Grant 62076092.

F. Liu et al. (Eds.): PRICAI 2023, LNAI 14325, pp. 199–211, 2024.
https://doi.org/10.1007/978-981-99-7019-3_20

most suitable one from a series of candidate responses to answer the needs of users [11], while the latter directly generates responses based on the context.

The sequence-to-sequence (seq2seq) frameworks [14] using attention mechanism have been widely used for generating dialogue responses. However, previous research tends to generate generic and universal responses, such as "*That's fine*" and "*Sorry, I don't know*", due to the lack of background knowledge. Such bland and uninformative responses do not meet the user's needs. To overcome this challenge, recent literatures have attempted to introduce various types of background knowledge, such as common sense [23], unstructured documents [19], and knowledge graphs [18], to improve response quality. Due to the characteristics of the data and storage, unstructured knowledge is easier to obtain than structured knowledge, which largely relies on expert experience. Therefore, recent studies have used dialogue-related documents as background knowledge to enhance conversations and generate more fluent and informative responses. However, most of the current work focused on semantic parsing of the replies, but ignoring the global perception of the replies, which affects the model's ability to generate responses consistent with the dialogue context.

Our work focuses on generating conversations based on documents, which is a typical task in knowledge-based dialogue. Its goal is to use favorable information extracted from unstructured documents to constrain the scope of responses. Taking inspiration from the achievements of the transformer framework [16], we propose a coarse-to-fine dialogue generation model with an encoder-decoder based on the transformer for document-grounded dialogues. To be more precise, the encoder extracts a coarse-grained feature representation of the response by fitting the semantics of the response and the knowledge from the dialogue context and the document in training; the decoder then refines the fine-grained feature representation of each word in the response through interaction with the extracted coarse-grained features and the dialogue context so that it can be mapped to the word space. When reasoning, the encoder can independently extract knowledge about the dialogue context and the document. Our model outperforms existing state-of-the-art methods, as demonstrated by the evaluation on various widely-used metrics. To summarize, our work can be characterized by the following key contributions:

- We propose a encoder-decoder model that encodes valuable information from conversational contexts and external documents through the semantic guidance of responses, and then decodes word embeddings through the interaction of valuable information and contexts.
- Our model produces coarse- and fine-grained response features, and with the attention mechanism, it achieves feature interaction and decomposition.
- Experimental results on two publicly used datasets show that our model demonstrates superior performance compared to the baselines on multiple metrics.

2 Related Work

The construction of generative models for dialogue response generation has seen widespread use of Seq2Seq or encoder-decoder frameworks with sequential neural networks. These frameworks commonly use recurrent neural networks (RNNs), long short-term memory (LSTM), and gated recurrent units (GRUs) as kernel units to map one sequential structure to another. Qin et al. [13] utilized RNNs with memory networks as decoders to get meaningful response. Vinyals and Quoc [17] conducted research on the capabilities of LSTM networks in generating sequential multi-turn dialogues, while Zhao et al. [21] exploited GRUs as encoder to build the representation of the word sequence. However, above sequential frameworks suffer from time-consuming training due to exploding or vanishing gradients. Moreover, they struggle with resolving the issue of long-distance textual semantic dependency, which can lead to information loss.

To address the problem described above, researchers utilized attention mechanisms [16] in neural networks. Such mechanisms have advantages over traditional sequential models in terms of parallel computing, capturing long-term dependencies, not requiring sequence alignment. Cai et al. [2] developed a triple-channel encoder that utilizes an attention mechanism to learn the representation of dialogue context, documents, and the last utterance respectively, and then integrates them. Xing et al. [20] proposed a combined approach that integrates a discourse-level and a word-level attention network to extract components. All of these approaches aim to emphasize the interdependence between contexts and extract salient information for generating high-quality responses.

A variety of external knowledge resources have been introduced in the literature to expand the alternatives of information, mainly divided into structured triplets from knowledge graphs [18,23] and unstructured text from documents [1,8,19]. There were also some works [6,15] have explored the conversion of unstructured documents into structured formats or the integration of triplets and texts into graph representations. For example, Li et al. [6] identified the internal semantic relationships among sentences in documents by constructing document semantic graphs. However, they cannot avoid the problem of incomplete knowledge graphs or complex text processing. Li et al. [7] introduced a novel approach that integrates various knowledge sources to create a unified knowledge representation for knowledge-based dialogue generation tasks, which not only preserves the rich potential knowledge in unstructured documents but also utilizes the information expansion ability of structured knowledge graphs. Incorporating external knowledge is a promising approach to eliminate the gap between humans and chatbots in background information. To this, our work focuses on document-grounded dialogue systems, which are a type of knowledge-based systems that use pertinent information from unstructured text.

3 Methodology

In this study, we introduce a novel model based on transformer for document-grounded conversations. The model architecture, as illustrated in Fig. 1, follows the encoder-decoder framework and consists of two main components: 1) a coarse-grained feature extraction module that learns the semantic representation of the dialog context and document and extracts coarse-grained feature related the to response; 2) a fine-grained feature generation module that has an overall perception of the content of the response under the guidance of coarse-grained features and then produces fine-grained features of the next word interacting with the decoded sequence at every decoding time step, resulting in a response.

3.1 Task Definition

Given 1) a dialog context U presented as a sequence of utterances, 2) the corresponding document D that contains the information related to the conversation, and 3) the grounded response R, the objective of our work is to simulate the human communication process-the intention to express is generated first, then the complete utterance is output-to generate an appropriate response utterance G and let the conversation continue.

For convenience, we make the assumption that the document is a sequence of l_D tokens, denoted as $D = \{d_1, d_2, \cdots, d_{l_D}\}$. A dialog context is viewed as a series of utterances generally, the context encoder concatenates all utterances as $U = \{u_1, u_2, \cdots, u_{l_U}\}$, where u_i is the i-th word in the sequence. And $R = \{r_1, r_2, \cdots, r_{l_R}\}$ is a response in this conversation, where l_R is the length of the sequence. The CFRG accepts U and D as inputs, and generates a response G.

3.2 Coarse-Grained Feature Extraction Module

The coarse-grained feature extraction module consists of four components: a context encoder (DE) to encode U, a concatenation encoder (CE) to encode the concatenation of U and D, a response encoder (RE) encode the real response R, and a compression layer to learn the mapping from U and D to R. Next, we present the details of this module specifically.

Encoder. We adopt transformer block as the fundamental block of our encoder, the output of DE is denoted as $h_u \in R^{l_U \times d}$, where l_U represents the length of sequence, and d represents the dimension of hidden state,

$$h_u = \mathrm{DE}(U). \tag{1}$$

Similarly, CE encodes the concatenation of U and D to get a contextualized representation of knowledge:

$$h_c = \mathrm{CE}([U; D]), \tag{2}$$

where $h_c \in R^{(l_U + l_D) \times d}$. The representation of grounded response is $h_r \in R^{l_R \times d}$,

$$h_r = \mathrm{RE}(R). \tag{3}$$

Given that responses are generated from the dialog context of a conversation and knowledge documents, it is commonly assumed that they inherently contain

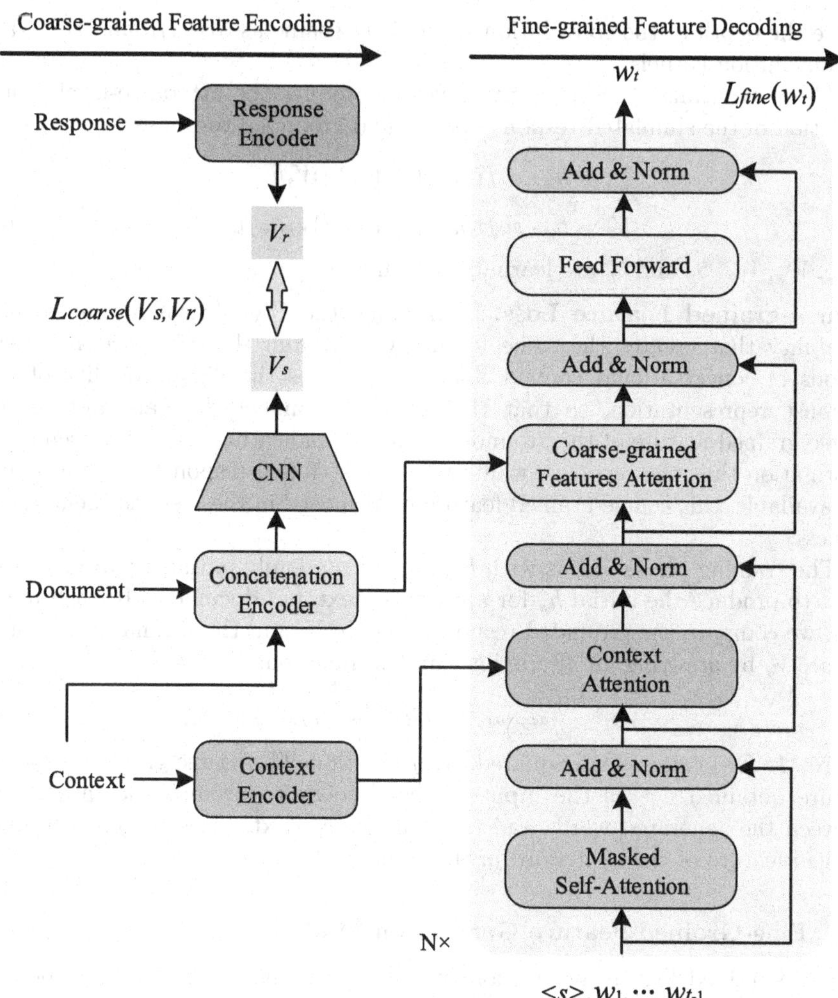

Fig. 1. The framework of the coarse-to-fine response generation (CFRG) model. The left is a coarse-grained feature encoder that matches the interlocutor's intent. The right is a fine-grained feature decoder that produces detailed responses as a result of the interaction between learned intent and context.

information that is relevant to the response. Consequently, the representation h_c is regarded as a significant resource of the response.

Compression Layer. In order to efficiently extract the coarse-grained feature of the response from the dialog context and the document, we use the grounded response to guide this extraction process during the training phase. Specifically, we obtain a simulated response vector h_s by mapping h_c to the semantic space of h_r through a convolution module:

$$h_s = \text{CNN}(h_c), \tag{4}$$

where the depth of the convolution kernel is the same as $l_U + l_D$, and there are l_R convolution kernels.

Then, we utilize a self-attentive layer to produce the utterance-level representation of the simulated response vector and grounded response,

$$V_s = h_s \cdot softmax(b_s^T \tanh(W_s h_s)), \tag{5}$$

$$V_r = h_r \cdot softmax(b_r^T \tanh(W_r h_r)). \tag{6}$$

Here, W_s, W_r, b_s and b_r are learnable parameters.

Coarse-grained Feature Loss. In training, the CNN learns a compression capability that creates the same feature vector from the combined representations of conversational context and document as the dimensionality of the response representation, so that the concatenation encoder can capture the coarse-grained feature of the grounded response, indicating the overall semantic information that the response wants to express. When response information is not available, this coarse-grained feature is then used in the response generation process.

The training phase begins with h_c, h_r and randomly initiates parameters of CNN to produce the initial h_s for a given context and document. In each iteration, we compare the grounded response feature V_r and the simulated response feature V_s by applying an approximation loss function:

$$L_{approx} = MSE(V_s, V_r), \tag{7}$$

where $MSE(\cdot)$ is the Mean Squared Error function. The coarse-grained response feature obtained act as the input of the decoder to prompt the interaction between the generated words and the dialogue context, so as to generate fine-grained feature of the next word in the response.

3.3 Fine-Grained Feature Generation Module

The fine-grained feature generation module is designed to generate responses by taking into account the dialog context and the overall representation of the response, as exemplified in the right-hand section of Fig. 1. Inspired by the cognitive processes of humans in real-world scenarios, we design a decoder that contains a multi-head attention-based hierarchical information interaction mechanism that acts within the dialogue context and decoded sequence under the prompt of the coarse-grained response feature, to produce the fine-grained feature of the next word. The decoder aims to generate more accurate and contextually relevant responses by effectively incorporating different tiers of information.

Decoder. In the architecture illustrated in Fig. 1, the decoder consists of N identical layers, with each layer containing four sub-layers. When generating t-th response word w_t, we have generated words $w_{<t}$ as input, and I_{t-1} is the representation of them. A masked self-attention is implemented as the first sub-layer, employed by a multi-head attention function (MultiHead).

$$H_1^{(n)} = MultiHead(H_0^{(n-1)}, H_0^{(n-1)}, H_0^{(n-1)}), \tag{8}$$

where $n = 1, ..., N$, $H_0^{(n-1)}$ represents the output from previous layer, and $H_0^{(0)} = I_{t-1}$. And a multi-head context attention is used as the second sub-layer:

$$H_2^{(n)} = MultiHead(H_1^{(n)}, h_u, h_u), \tag{9}$$

and a multi-head coarse-grained feature attention is the next sub-layer:

$$H_3^{(n)} = MultiHead(H_2^{(n)}, h_c, h_c). \tag{10}$$

The last sub-layer in the decoder a fully connected feed-forward network (FFN):

$$H_0^{(n)} = FFN(H_3^{(n)}). \tag{11}$$

In addition, each sub-layer has an *Add & Norm* operation the same as transformer. After N layers, the probabilities of the words is obtained through softmax:

$$P(w_t) = softmax(H_0^{(N)}). \tag{12}$$

Fine-grained Feature Loss. We adopt Negative Log Likelihood (NLL) as optimization function to train the model:

$$L_{fine} = \sum_{t=1}^{l_R} - \log P(w_t|w_{<t}, U, D). \tag{13}$$

Given a context U, a document D, and the previously generated terms($w_{<t}$), L_{fine} maximises the probability of the currently predicted word. During training, $P(w_t|w_{<t}, U, D)$ is replaced with $P(r_t|R_{<t}, U, D)$, i.e., instead of using the model's output from previous steps as input, we utilize the ground truth response as input.

Training. To create the final loss function, we assume that both loss functions have equally significant effects on the results and sum them together:

$$L = L_{coarse} + L_{fine}. \tag{14}$$

4 Experiment

4.1 Dataset

Our model was assessed on two publicly available English document-based datasets: Wizard of Wikipedia [4] and CMU_DoG [22].

Wizard of Wikipedia (Wiz). Wiz is a dialogue generation dataset based on Wikipedia. It consists of Wikipedia summaries reviewed by humans and real human conversations. The dialogue specifies a Wikipedia topic, with two people acting as the wizard and the apprentice. The apprentice can ask any questions about the topic, and the wizard answers the question based on the provided question-related information retrieved from Wikipedia. There are 22,311 dialogues with 201,999 dialogue turns in Wiz dataset. These turns are divided into a training dataset and two test datasets: a seen test set that covers topics included in the training set, and an unseen test set that includes topics that may not appears in the training set.

CMU_DoG. The present dataset consists of a collection of movie-related documents and dialogues. The documents are known to encompass pertinent details such as movie titles, ratings, descriptions, and other related information. On average, each document consists of 200 words. The dataset contains 4,221 conversations in total, each of which on average 31.79 utterances are displayed. Specifically, for training purposes, there are 72,922 utterances, while 3,626 utterances are utilized for validation, and 11,577 utterances are used for testing.

4.2 Evaluation Metrics

Following prior work [12], we choose Rouge-L [9], BLEU [10], METEOR [3] metrics and F1 as metrics.

BLEU is a metric used to measure the similarity between two sequences of text, commonly used in machine translation tasks. In dialogue systems, BLEU can also be applied to assess the generated responses by measuring the n-gram overlap between the generated response and the reference response. BLEU-n calculates the precision of n-grams (contiguous sequences of n words). METEOR is a global evaluation metric in natural language processing, which combines simple word importance (word frequency), word order and sentence length to quantify the difference between model-generated and reference utterances. Rouge-L calculates the length of the longest common subsequence between the generated and the reference sentences, taking into account lexical choice and word order to measure the similarity between the two. F1 indicates the single-group overlap between the reference and generated utterances [12].

4.3 Baselines

We compared our approach against state-of-the-art approaches: Low-Res [21], BART [5], CoDR [12], DoHA [12], and Tri-Channel [2].

Low-Res first learns separate parameters for encoding dialog context and documents through pre-training. Then, a decoding manager is trained to take the distributions of dialog context, document and decoded sequence as input to generate next token. BART is a pre-trained model that concatenates dialog context and all documents as a single sequence, and then take it as input to generate response. Both CoDR and DoHA are models based on BART. CoDR incorporates contextualized documents and dialogue context as the input of the decoder. DoHA includes an extra multi-head cross-attention mechanism for knowledge documents. Tri-Channel learns the distributed representations of document, dialog context, and the last utterance via a triple-channel encoder. All baseline results are derived from the original paper.

4.4 Implementation Details

In our experiments, we utilize the base version of BART as the foundational architecture for our model. The encoder and decoder both contain 12 stacks, with 16 attention heads. For the embedding and hidden state dimensions, we set them to 1024, while the inner size of the FFN is set to 2,048. To train the model, we use a batch size of 16. Considering the size of the data, we trained the model for 50 epochs on the CMU_DoG dataset, using a learning rate of 5e−5. Additionally, we trained the model for 25 epochs on the Wiz dataset, with a learning rate of 2e−5. In our evaluation, we focused on presenting the results for the top-performing models in each specific case.

4.5 Experimental Results

The evaluation results for our model and the baselines on the CMU_DoG and Wiz datasets are presented in Table 1 and 2, respectively. Upon analysis of the results, our model exhibits superior performance compared to all the baselines. This find indicates that our model is much better at identifying and incorporating relevant background information, so as to generate responses that align more closely with human responses.

Notably, on the dataset CMU_DoG, we see that our model improves by 20.9 BLEU-4 points compared to Low-Res. Although both Low-Res and our model use the representation of document and context as the input for encoder, our model introduces a coarse-grained feature guidance to facilitate contextual consistency and semantic relevance in fine-grained responses, enabling a more coherent continuation of the conversation. Compared to the recent best performing method Tri-Channel that takes the representations of document, dialog context, and the last utterance as input for decoder, our method still possesses overwhelming advantages. This is because the contribution of the guidance of coarse-grained feature can to some extent compensate for semantic scarcity.

Although the dialogue task on the Wiz dataset is challenging, our model still achieves a remarkable performance in terms of BLEU and METEOR scores. What's more, our model's ability to perform consistently and strongly on the Wiz unseen test data indicates that it is not only more adaptive but also has better generalization capabilities. On both datasets, we also see a significant improvement compared to the DoHA baseline (1.3 more BLEU-4 for CMU_DoG), which proves the effectiveness of the coarse-grained feature extraction module. Under the guidance of real replies, the encoder can build a more accurate representation of the content in document and dialogue context that is related to responses.

Table 4 presents a case from CMU_DoG, illustrating that our model's response not only effectively remains coherent with the context but also incorporates additional information from the document, resulting in an expanded and comprehensive response. CoDR generates a short sentence. Although DoHA generates more fluent response, but contained less information about the topic. Our model achieves more relevant and informative response.

Table 1. Automatic evaluation results on CMU_DoG.

Model	BLEU-1	BLEU-2	BLEU-3	BLEU-4	Rouge-L	Meteor	F1
Low-Res	15.00	5.70	2.50	1.20	–	–	10.7
BART	23.78	19.27	17.66	16.91	19.30	12.59	21.7
CoDR	26.86	22.75	21.30	20.68	20.41	14.47	22.7
DoHA	27.33	23.05	21.55	20.90	20.44	14.55	22.8
Tri-Channel	11.24	4.27	2.54	1.80	–	5.83	–
Ours	**28.59**	**24.26**	**22.76**	**22.11**	**20.56**	**15.12**	**33.3**

Table 2. Automatic evaluation results on Wizard of Wikipedia.

Model	BLEU-1	BLEU-2	BLEU-3	BLEU-4	Rouge-L	Meteor	F1
Test Seen							
Low-Res	21.80	11.50	7.50	5.50	–	–	18.0
BART	23.92	14.62	10.24	7.75	21.41	15.45	31.1
CoDR	24.00	14.98	10.64	8.18	21.82	15.71	31.8
DoHA	24.14	15.08	10.68	8.18	21.76	**15.89**	**31.8**
Ours	**27.36**	**17.45**	**12.36**	**9.25**	**23.99**	15.50	31.5
Test Unseen							
Low-Res	20.70	10.10	6.20	4.30	–	–	16.5
BART	21.88	12.54	8.44	6.23	19.14	14.03	28.2
CoDR	21.84	12.74	8.60	6.35	19.50	14.22	29.0
DoHA	22.31	13.04	8.89	6.60	19.62	14.47	29.0
Ours	**26.08**	**16.32**	**11.32**	**8.36**	**23.17**	**14.90**	**30.0**

4.6 Ablation Study

To verify the guiding effect of coarse-grained features on response generation, we conducted ablation experiments specifically on the CMU_DoG dataset. We remove the coarse-grained feature extraction module and only input the concatenation of the dialogue context and document into the decoding process, and we also explore the impact of the decoding order of coarse-grained features.
1) **CFRG-0:** the coarse-grained feature is removed, which ignores the guidance of ground response(the same as the DoHA in fact).
2) **CFRG-1:** the coarse-grained feature attention is exchanged with the context attention, which means that the guidance from the coarse-grained feature on generating responses is conducted before the interaction with the dialog context.

The results in Table 3 show that the CFRG model outperforms the CFRG-0 model (coarse-grained features extraction module is removec) in terms of all metrics, which indicates the guidance of coarse-grained feature used in our model is effective. In addition, it works best on the last layer. The reason is that the coarse-grained features could correct some mistakes due to misguided by the dialogue context. As we can see in Table 4, CFRG-0 and CFRG-1 generate natural and coherent response, but fail to utilize information from the documents. And the response generated by CFRG is more informative.

Table 3. Ablation study on CMU_DoG.

Model	BLEU-1	BLEU-2	BLEU-3	BLEU-4	Rouge-L	Meteor	F1
CFRG-0	27.33	23.05	21.55	20.90	20.44	14.55	22.8
CFRG-1	28.45	24.14	22.64	21.99	20.53	15.01	32.97
CFRG	28.59	24.26	22.76	22.11	20.56	15.12	33.32

Table 4. Case study.

Document	
... La la land is a 2016 American musical romantic comedy-drama film written and directed by Damien Chazelle. It stars Ryan Gosling as a jazz pianist and Emma Stone as an aspiring actress, who meet and fall in love in Los Angeles ...	
context	u1: hello, we're going to talk about la la land. Have you seen the movie? u2: no i haven't, what can you tell me about it?
Reference	it is an American movie. It is a musical comedy with some drama, staring ryan gosling and emma stone. They meet and fall in love in los angeles. He is a jazz piano player and she an aspiring actress.
CoDR	are you still there? it's a musical
DoHA	well, i don't know how you feel about romantic comedies i'm usually not a huge fan but it seemed very genuine
CFRG-1	well, it is a musical comedy with some drama, i'm usually not a huge fan but it seemed very genuine
CFRG	well, i haven't watched it either. But it seems very interesting! ryan gosling plays a jazz pianist and emma stone is an aspiring actress. They meet-up and fall in love!

5 Conclusion

In this work, we introduce a new neural model for document-grounded conversations. The model achieves an overall representation of the response through a coarse-grained feature extraction module. And then the coarse-grained feature is utilized to optimize context coherence and knowledge relevance by emulating the cognitive processes of real-world humans. Finally, we demonstrated that our model can produce responses that are more logical, accessible, and informative, which is more conducive to human-computer interaction. The model's multiple encoders, however, result in a higher computing and storage resource requirement. In the future,we will work to achieve semantic parsing of multi-source data through an encoder to improve the generalization and scalability of the model.

References

1. Bai, J., Yang, Z., Yang, J., Guo, H., Li, Z.: KINet: incorporating relevant facts into knowledge-grounded dialog generation. IEEE/ACM Trans. Audio Speech Language Process. **31**, 1213–1222 (2023)
2. Cai, Y., Zuo, M., Xiong, H.: Modeling hierarchical attention interaction between contexts and triple-channel encoding networks for document-grounded dialog generation. Front. Phys. **10**, 1019969 (2022)
3. Denkowski, M.J., Lavie, A.: Meteor 1.3: automatic metric for reliable optimization and evaluation of machine translation systems. In: WMT@EMNLP (2011)
4. Dinan, E., Roller, S., Shuster, K., Fan, A., Auli, M., Weston, J.: Wizard of wikipedia: knowledge-powered conversational agents. In: ICLR (2019)
5. Lewis, M., et al.: BART: denoising sequence-to-sequence pre-training for natural language generation, translation, and comprehension. In: ACL, pp. 7871–7880 (2020)
6. Li, S., et al.: Enhancing knowledge selection for grounded dialogues via document semantic graphs. In: NAACL, pp. 2810–2823, July 2022
7. Li, Y., et al.: Knowledge-grounded dialogue generation with a unified knowledge representation. In: NAACL, pp. 206–218 (2022)
8. Li, Z., Niu, C., Meng, F., Feng, Y., Li, Q., Zhou, J.: Incremental transformer with deliberation decoder for document grounded conversations. In: ACL, pp. 12–21 (2019)
9. Lin, C.Y.: Rouge: a package for automatic evaluation of summaries. In: ACL (2004)
10. Papineni, K., Roukos, S., Ward, T., Zhu, W.J.: Bleu: a method for automatic evaluation of machine translation. In: ACL (2002)
11. Park, Y., Ko, Y., Seo, J.: Bert-based response selection in dialogue systems using utterance attention mechanisms. Expert Syst. Appl. **209**, 118277 (2022)
12. Prabhumoye, S., Hashimoto, K., Zhou, Y., Black, A.W., Salakhutdinov, R.: Focused attention improves document-grounded generation. In: NAACL-HLT, pp. 4274–4287 (2021)
13. Qin, L., et al.: Conversing by reading: contentful neural conversation with on-demand machine reading. In: ACL, pp. 5427–5436 (2019)
14. Sutskever, I., Vinyals, O., Le, Q.V.: Sequence to sequence learning with neural networks. In: NIPS, pp. 3104–3112 (2014)
15. Varshney, D., Prabhakar, A., Ekbal, A.: Commonsense and named entity aware knowledge grounded dialogue generation. In: NAACL, pp. 1322–1335 (2022)
16. Vaswani, A., et al.: Attention is all you need. In: NINPS, vol. 30 (2017)
17. Vinyals, O., Le, Q.: A neural conversational model. Computer Science (2015)
18. Wang, H., Guo, B., Liu, J., Ding, Y., Yu, Z.: Towards informative and diverse dialogue systems over hierarchical crowd intelligence knowledge graph. ACM Trans. Knowl. Discov. Data **17**, 1–25 (2023)
19. Wu, Z., Lu, B., Hajishirzi, H., Ostendorf, M.: DIALKI: knowledge identification in conversational systems through dialogue-document contextualization. In: EMNLP, pp. 1852–1863 (2021)

20. Xing, C., Wu, Y., Wu, W., Huang, Y., Zhou, M.: Hierarchical recurrent attention network for response generation. In: AAAI, vol. 32, pp. 5610–5617 (2018)
21. Zhao, X., Wu, W., Tao, C., Xu, C., Zhao, D., Yan, R.: Low-resource knowledge-grounded dialogue generation. In: ICLR (2020)
22. Zhou, K., Prabhumoye, S., Black, A.W.: A dataset for document grounded conversations. In: EMNLP, pp. 708–713 (2018)
23. Zhou, P., et al.: Think before you speak: explicitly generating implicit commonsense knowledge for response generation. In: ACL, pp. 1237–1252 (2022)

Context-Dependent Text-to-SQL Generation with Intermediate Representation

Xuesong Gao and Junfeng Zhao(✉)

College of Computer Science, Inner Mongolia University, Hohhot, China
32009114@mail.imu.edu.cn, cszjf@imu.edu.cn

Abstract. In recent years, the Text-to-SQL task has become a research hotspot in semantic analysis. Among them, context-dependent Text-to-SQL task has received more and more attention as it meets the needs of actual scenarios. The core of the problem is how to use historical interaction information and database schema to understand the context. Most existing research ignores the structure of SQL queries and introduces low-level information such as variable names and parameters, and the mismatch problem between intents expressed in utterance and the implementation details in SQL still exists. In this paper, SemQL is applied to serve as an intermediate representation between utterance and SQL, meanwhile, the Coarse-to-Fine neural architecture is adopted to decompose decoding process of SemQL into two stages. We validated the performance of our model on SParC and CoSQL datasets, which outperforms the existing ones and achieves excellent results on both datasets.

Keywords: Semantic Parsing · Text-to-SQL · Intermediate Representation

1 Introduction

Semantic Parsing has always been a very basic and important research area, which aims to give computers the ability to understand natural language and translate it into a specified programming language. Currently, since a large amount of data is stored in structured and semi-structured knowledge bases (such as databases), the analysis and acquisition of such data requires interaction with the database through programming languages such as SQL. How to enable users without programming background to perform data analysis through natural language with zero threshold, the semantic parsing problem represented by Text-to-SQL has attracted the attention of many scholars at home and abroad.

In the early stage of research, context-independent Text-to-SQL tasks represented by datasets such as GeoQuery [1], WikiSQL [2] and Spider [3] were proposed. The setting of such datasets is that a natural language question corresponds to a SQL statement [4–8]. But in the case of complex queries, it is very

F. Liu et al. (Eds.): PRICAI 2023, LNAI 14325, pp. 212–224, 2024.
https://doi.org/10.1007/978-981-99-7019-3_21

difficult for people to describe the problem clearly in one sentence. People are more inclined to use a series of questions to interact with the database, and the model uses contextual information to gradually complete a complex query operation. Therefore, the context-dependent Text-to-SQL task that is more suitable for practical application scenarios has attracted more attention. For this task, two large datasets SParC [9] and CoSQL [10] are proposed.

However, the performance of existing research on SParC and CoSQL datasets is not satisfactory. Because SQL statements are decoded as a text sequence in most existing studies [11,12], they all ignore the semantic structure of SQL statements. Reference [13] convert SQL statements into graphs through a non-nested graph generation algorithm, which captures the semantic structure of SQL statements but introduces low-level information(such as variable names and parameters). Reference [14] think predicting detail through skeleton can obtain more full meaning representations and improves performance tasks.

So, in this paper, to alleviate these problems, based on the IGSQL [12], the SemQL intermediate representation is introduced to replace the SQL query, and a Coarse-to-Fine framework is used to divide the decoder into skeleton decoder and detail decoder two stages generate SemQL. Based on SemQL grammar rules and encoder input, research first generates a rough sketch of SemQL, where low-level information(such as variable names and arguments) is glossed over. Then, research fills in missing details by taking into account the encoder input and the sketch itself. Compared with previous SQL statements, SemQL can better reflect the semantic structure of SQL statements, and generating SemQL in stages can reduce the introduction of low-level information and better modeling the context. Finally, experimental results on datasets show that our model improves the question match accuracy and the interaction match accuracy. We also provide a detailed analysis to further study the contribution of each component to the overall framework.

2 Related Work

There are many studies on context-dependent Text-to-SQL. Reference [15–17] shows that schema linking can improve parsing performance. Moreover, related studies [6,18,19] propose graph-based linking methods to reason over the natural language question tokens and database schema entities, and to model complex inputs.

Context-dependent Text-to-SQL needs to model the context in the dialogue, and the model needs to use contextual historical information to accurately generate corresponding SQL statements. EditSQL [11] uses two independent Bi-LSTMs to encode natural language questions and table schemas respectively, and utilizes contextual information by editing previously predicted SQL to improve the quality of SQL generation. In maintaining semantic consistency, especially database semantic consistency, IGSQL [12] proposed a database schema interaction graph encoder, which utilizes the information of database schema items in previous turn. Reference [13] proposed an interactive modeling mechanism to encode and integrate different types of texts (questions, SQL, and database), which represents different types of texts as separate graphs, captures the interaction information between graphs by using heterogeneous graph aggregation, and finally aggregates the graphs into a holistic representation.

For the decoding stage of context-dependent Text-to-SQL tasks, most existing studies [11–13] use LSTM decoders with attention mechanisms to generate SQL queries. Among them, EditSQL proposes a method based on query editing. When generating the current turn of SQL statements, it copies and reuses the previous turn of SQL statements, and outputs the probability distribution.

3 Methodology

3.1 Problem Setup

In context-dependent semantic parsing tasks, the current natural language question needs to be combined with previous interaction information and database schema. Let $I = [(U_i, S_i)]_{i=1}^{n}$ is n question-query pairs in a dialogue. Let U as questions, S as SQL query. Let $D = [T_1, T_2, \ldots, T_t]$ denote the tables of a database, where t is the number of tables, and each T_t contains multiple column names, which denote as $T = [C_1, C_2, \ldots, C_m]$, m represents the number of column names in the table. The goal of the task is to generate the correct SQL statement S_i from the current natural language question U_i, the interaction history $I = [(U_{i-1}, S_{i-1})]_{i=1}^{n}$ and database schema item D.

3.2 Intermediate Representation

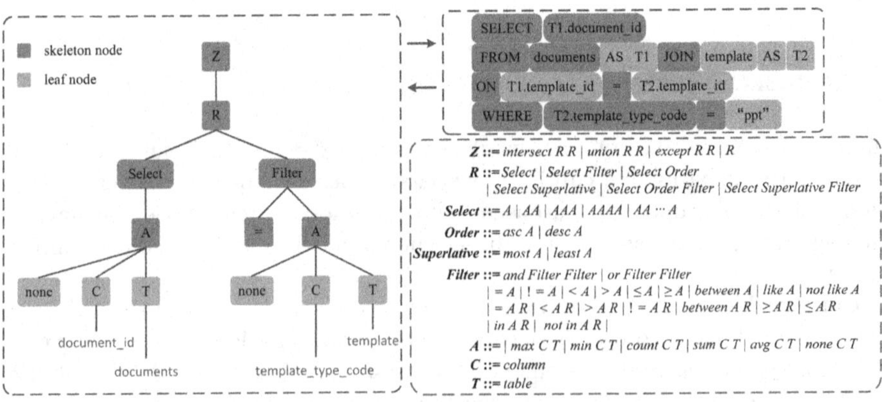

Fig. 1. An example of SemQL and SQL query.

SemQL is introduced as an intermediate representation between U and S, which can solve the mismatch problem between them. Figure 1 shows a SemQL example for a SQL query. Among them, the red blocks represent the skeleton structure of SemQL, obtained by removing all nodes under each A node. Compared with the original SQL statement, SemQL omits aliases, omits the ON clause, omits the FROM clause, and retains the semantic structure of SQL.

The red dotted frame in the Fig. 1 shows the SemQL grammar rules. Based on the grammar rules, conversion and reasoning between SQL and SemQL can be realized. Taking the *Filter* node as an example, the *Filter* node is uniformly used in the grammar rules to replace the WHERE and HAVING clauses in the SQL query.

3.3 Model

The model in this paper adopts the encoder-decoder framework with attention mechanism and uses SemQL intermediate representation instead of SQL statement. Figure 2 shows the overall structure of the model, with blocks of the same color sharing the same set of parameters. The model is divided into the following three parts: (1) Utterance Encoder, Database Schema Interaction Graph Encoder, and SemQL Encoder. (2) A Co-attention module for updating the encoder output and an interactive encoder for recording the dialogue state. (3) A SemQL decoder applying specific grammar rules to generate a SemQL intermediate representation. Finally, based on SemQL, the final SQL statement can be deduced and generated. In addition, to improve the accuracy of the model, the study also uses the BERT and Coarse-to-Fine neural network, each part will be introduced in the following chapters.

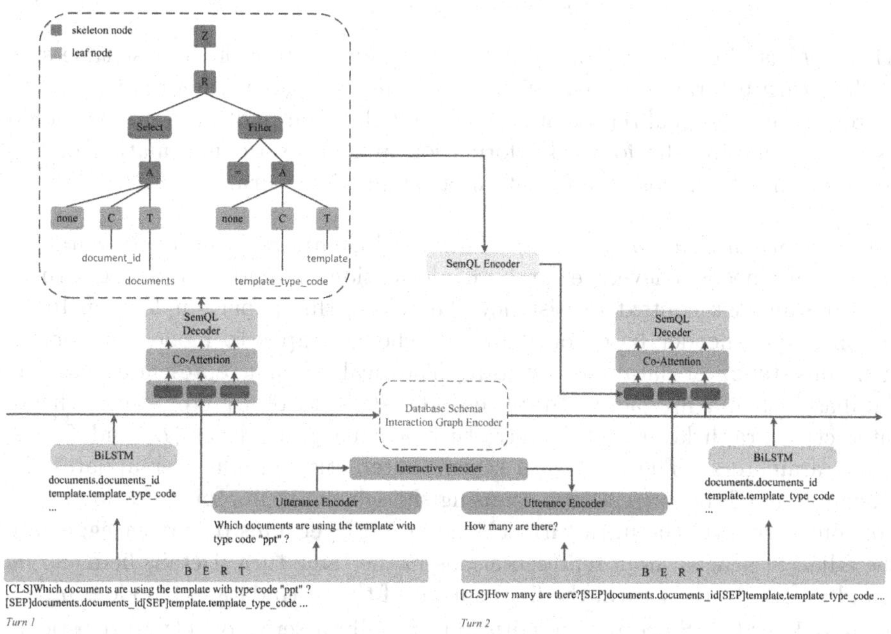

Fig. 2. An overview of the neural model.

BERT Embedding. BERT [20] is a pre-trained language representation model, which has been applied in multiple Text-to-SQL tasks, and has been significantly improved. It is currently the most widely used natural language processing algorithm. In this model, BERT needs to be used to encode natural language questions and database schema to enhance the contextual representation of question vectors and database schema vectors. Specifically, the research puts the special token [CLS] at the beginning of the sequence, and uses the [SEP] token to separate the question and the database schema [21], where the database schema is denoted by table and column names, the representation form is table.column. Finally, the sequence is fed into the pre-trained BERT model.

Encoder. The research needs to encode three types of text information to model context information, namely question interaction information, database interaction information, and historical SemQL information, which correspond to the following three encoders respectively.

Utterance Encoder. The research uses a BiLSTM to encode tokens of an question text with BERT embedding. Since in the current turn of dialogue, the user may omit the information mentioned in the previous turn, the research adds another LSTM as an interactive encoder and uses h_I to save the dialogue state during the entire dialogue process. Specifically, the calculation process of the i-th round dialogue state h_I^i is as follows.

$$h_I^i = \text{LSTM}_I\left(fh^i, h_I^{i-1}\right) \tag{1}$$

where fh^i is obtained by concatenating the hidden state of the last time step of the i turn utterance encoder, which contains the question information of the current turn. The final representation of the t-th token in utterance i is denoted as h_t^i. h_t^i contains the forward information and backward information of this sentence and the dialogue information of the previous turn.

Database Schema Interaction Graph Encoder. Like utterance encoders, database encoder also needs to leverage database information from previous dialogue turns to maintain task context consistency. Therefore, this paper employs an Interaction graph encoder based on database schema graphs to model the contextual consistency of databases by using historical schema representations. The database schema interactive graph encoder consists of L_1 cross-turn schema interaction graph layer and L_2 intra-turn schema graph layer (L_1 and L_2 are hyperparameters). The cross-turn schema interaction graph layer updates the schema item of the current turn by using the schema item representation of the previous turn, and the intra-turn schema graph layer aims to further aggregate the adjacent schema item representations in the same turn. Details here can be found in [12]. In the i turn, the final output of the m-th database node is g_m^{i,L_2}.
SemQL Encoder. Since user inquiries are usually a series of related questions, the SemQL generated by the current turn has a large overlap with the previous turn. Based on this, the study optimizes the current SemQL decoding process

by introducing the encoding information of SemQL generated in the previous turn. The SemQL structure is shown in Fig. 1. Specifically, this paper needs to encode the SemQL intermediate representation generated by the previous turn of decoding in the i turn of dialogue. p_s^i represents the encoding information of the node s in the i turn. For any node s in SemQL, its encoding information p_s^i can be calculated by LSTM from the encoding information p_{s-1}^i of its previous node and the grammar rule identification x_s^i of the current node. The grammar rules are shown in Fig. 1, and the calculation formula is as follows.

$$p_s^i = \text{LSTM}\left(p_{s-1}^i, x_s^i\right) \tag{2}$$

Co-Attention Module. To capture the relationship among three different encodings, we also add a co-attention module. The specific implementation process of natural language question vector and database vector is shown in Fig. 3. Similarly, question vectors and historical SemQL vectors, database vectors and historical SemQL vectors can also be calculated to obtain mutual representations between pairs. The database vectors, natural language question vectors, and historical SemQL vectors used by the final decoder are splicing of vectors after co-attention among the three. Expressed as $\tilde{g}_m^{i,L_2}$, $\tilde{h}_t^i$, $\tilde{p}_s^i$ after BiLSTM.

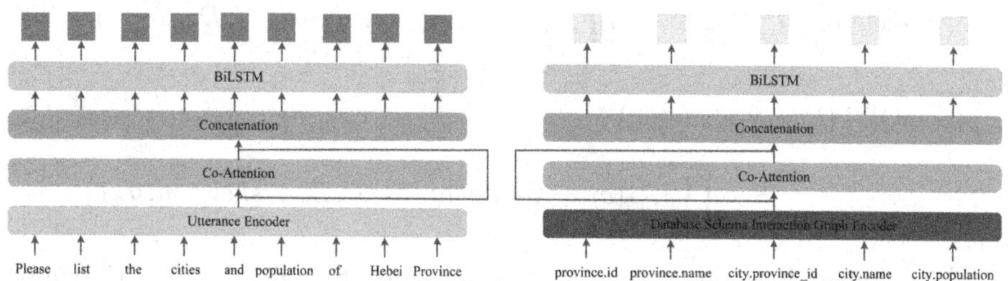

Fig. 3. Co-attention module.

Decoder. Taking SemQL in Fig. 1 as an example, Fig. 4 describes the specific process of generating SemQL by the Coarse-to-Fine neural network. The skeleton decoder and the detail decoder are responsible for generating skeleton nodes and leaf nodes respectively, and use the same encoder input.

This paper formalizes the probability of generating SemQL as the following formula.

$$p(\text{SemQL} \mid U, D, S) = p(\text{skeleton} \mid U, D, S)p(\text{SemQL} \mid U, D, S, \text{skeleton}) \tag{3}$$

Among them, U, D, S respectively represent the natural language question vector, database vector, and historical SemQL vector input by the encoder. The decomposed probability formulas correspond to the two action types of ApplyRule[r] and GenToken[v] respectively. Among them, ApplyRule[r] is responsible for applying the grammar rules r to the current derivation tree of

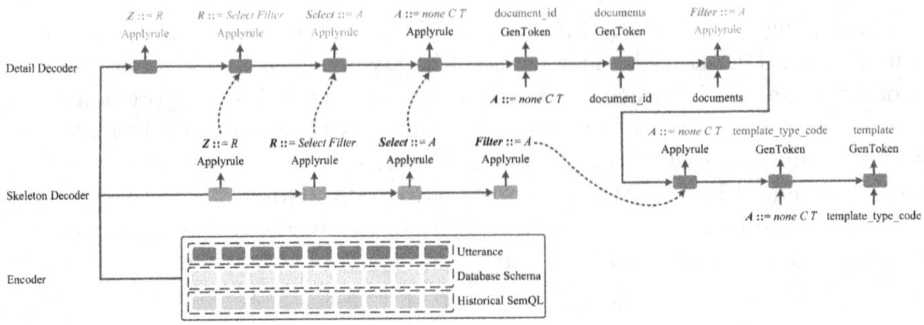

Fig. 4. Coarse-to-Fine decoding process.

SemQL, corresponding to the skeleton nodes in SemQL. The grammar rules are shown in the Fig. 1. GenToken[v] is responsible for selecting tables and columns from the database schema, corresponding to the leaf nodes in SemQL. The detailed probability calculation process is shown in the following formula, and the training goal is to maximize the log-likelihood of the generated action sequence.

$$p(\text{skeleton} \mid U, D, S) = \prod_{k=1}^{T_{\text{skeleton}}} p\left(a_k = \text{ApplyRule}\,[r] \mid U, D, S, a_{<k}\right) \tag{4}$$

$$\begin{aligned} & p(\text{SemQL} \mid U, D, S, skeleton) \\ & \quad = \prod_{k=1}^{T_{\text{skeleton}}} p\left(a_k = \text{Gentoken}\,[v] \mid U, D, S, skeleton, a_{<k}\right) \end{aligned} \tag{5}$$

The following formula is the specific implementation of the skeleton decoder based on the LSTM model.

$$s_k = \text{LSTM}\left(\left[e_{k-1}; \tilde{s}_{k-1}; p_k; n_k\right], s_{k-1}\right) \tag{6}$$

where [;] denotes vector concatenation. s_k is the hidden layer state of the decoder at step k. e_{k-1} represents the encoding of the grammar rules of the previous node, and the study maintains a corresponding embedding vector for each grammar rule. p_k is the vector representation of the parent node, which is coded and concatenated by its hidden layer vector and the corresponding grammar rule. n_k is the encoding of the current node type.

$$\tilde{s}_k = \tanh\left(W_B\left[c_k^{\text{utterance}}; c_k^{\text{column}}; c_k^{\text{semql}}; s_k\right]\right) \tag{7}$$

In order to allow the decoder to pay attention to different information in the three input vectors during decoding, the research uses the attention mechanism to obtain the context vector representation. $c_k^{\text{utterance}}$ is the attention of the previous turn of hidden state and text encoding, c_k^{column} is the attention of the previous turn of hidden state and database encoding, c_k^{semql} is the attention of the previous turn of hidden state and previous turn of SemQL.

Then, using the hidden layer state $\tilde{s}_k$ output in step k, the probability of generating the ApplyRule[r] action can be calculated, the calculation process is as follows.

$$p\left(a_k = \text{ApplyRule}\left[r\right] \mid U, D, S, a_{<k}\right) = \text{softmax}(e_r^T W_C \tilde{s}_k) \quad (8)$$

Among them, a_k is the action at step k, and $a_{<k}$ means $a_0, a_1, a_2, \ldots, a_k$ this series of actions. e is the encoding of the grammar rule r. Similarly, the detail decoder selects the encoding of database schema items and grammar rules as input, generates column names and table names and corresponding aggregation operations to populate the leaf nodes in the skeleton.

4 Experiments

4.1 DataSet and Metrics

The study conducts experiments on two large scale cross-domain context-dependent SQL generation datasets, SParC and CoSQL. The statistical data of the dataset is shown in Table 1.

Table 1. Statistics of SParC, CoSQL.

	Cross-Domain	Interaction	Train	Dev	Test	User Questions	Databases	Tables	Vocab	Avg Turn
SParC	✓	4298	3034	422	842	12726	200	1020	3794	3.0
CoSQL	✓	3007	2164	292	551	15598	200	1020	9585	5.2

We follow the evaluation metrics in reference [9] to measure the model, question match accuracy and interaction match accuracy.

4.2 Baseline Models

EditSQL. EditSQL uses a query editing mechanism. When the SQL statement of the current turn is generated, the SQL statement of the previous turn is reused at the same time. The research also uses an interactive encoding of text, database schema and historical information to better extract features.

IGSQL. Building on EditSQL leverages a database schema interaction graph encoder to model the contextual consistency of interactions.

4.3 Implementation Details

In terms of experimental settings, the model uses the Adam optimizer [22] to optimize the cross-entropy loss function. The hidden layer dimension of LSTM is 300 and the dimension is fixed, the dimension of action embedding is 128, the dimension of node type embedding is 64, and the batch size is 16. For BERT embedding, following IGSQL, the study uses the pre-trained BERT base model. The initial learning rate of the experimental model is 0.001. If the validation set loss of the current turn has increased compared with the validation set loss of the previous turn, the learning rate is multiplied by 0.8 to decay. The initial learning rate of the BERT model is 0.00001.

4.4 Experiment Results

Table 2 shows the results of model on the SParC and CoSQL datasets. Compared to state-of-the-art model IGSQL, our model achieves substantial improvement on question match accuracy by 0.7 points on SparC development sets and 1.3 points on CoSQL development sets, respectively. As for interaction match accuracy, our model improves by 0.4 points on SParC development sets and 0.7 points on CoSQL development sets.

Table 2. Results of models in SParC and CoSQL datasets.

Model	Sparc		CoSQL	
	Question Match	Interaction Match	Question Match	Interaction Match
EditSQL+BERT	47.2	29.5	39.9	12.3
IGSQL+BERT	50.7	32.5	44.1	15.8
Ours+BERT	**51.4**	**32.9**	**45.4**	**16.5**

To explore the model's ability to generate SQL queries, Fig. 5(Right) shows the performance split by hardness levels with the frequency of examples. The abscissa corresponds to the four difficulty levels, which are easy, medium, hard, and extra hard. It can be seen that the accuracy of the model decreases as the difficulty of SQL increases. But compared with the benchmark model IGSQL, the model in this paper has the highest improvement in predicting hard SQL queries, an increase of 1.1%, reaching a question matching accuracy of 40.1%. Moreover, it also has a certain improvement in predicting the other three difficulty SQLs. Similarly, Fig. 5(left) shows the performance split by turns on the dev set. The question matching accuracy of the model in this paper is always higher than that of the baseline model in all dialogue turns, which reflects the effectiveness of the model in contextual dialogue.

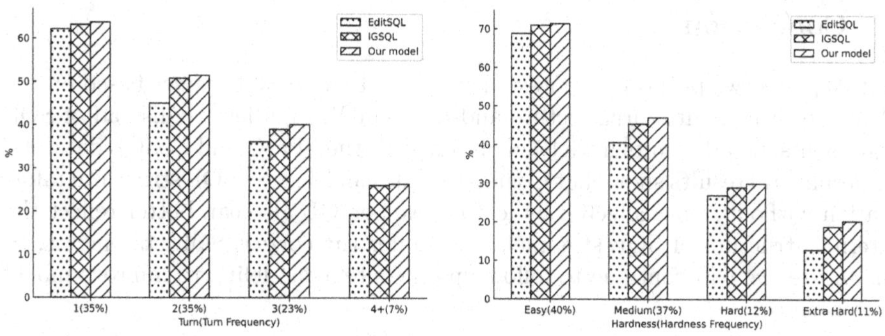

Fig. 5. Performance split by different turns (Left) and hardness levels (Right) on SParC dev set.

4.5 Ablation Study

To verify the validity of various parts of experiments, the study performed several ablation experiments: w/o Coarse-to-Fine, w/o Co-attention. The w/o representations in the experiments were removed or replaced with parts of the baseline model. Table 3 shows the results of ablation experiments. These results show that each component of the model is effective and indispensable.

Table 3. Ablation study on development sets.

Model	Sparc		CoSQL	
	Question Match	Interaction Match	Question Match	Interaction Match
Ours	51.4	32.9	45.4	16.5
w/o Coarse-to-Fine	50.1(−1.3)	32.3(−0.6)	43.7(−1.7)	15.4(−1.1)
w/o Co-attention	49.1(−2.3)	29.4(−3.5)	42.1(−3.3)	13.8(−2.7)

w/o Coarse-to-Fine. In this ablation experiment setting, the model does not generate SemQL in two stages. The experimental results in Table 3 show that the use of the Coarse-to-Fine neural network can model semantics in a fine-grained manner without being affected by leaf nodes while learning SemQL structural information.

w/o Co-attention. In this ablation experiment setting, the model does not model the relationship between the three sequences. The experimental results in Table 3 show that using co-attention can lead to better parsing performance, which is helpful for cross-domain generalization and complex SQL generation .

5 Conclusion

In this paper, we propose a context-dependent Text-to-SQL parser based on the Coarse-to-Fine neural architecture and use SemQL middleware instead of SQL statements. Good results have been obtained on the SParC and CoSQL datasets. Experimental results show that Coarse-to-Fine can learn SemQL structural information without being affected by leaf nodes. SemQL also can better reflect the internal structure of SQL statements and infer the correct SQL statements. In the future, we will continue to follow up on context modeling to improve model performance.

Acknowledgement. This work was supported by National Natural Science Foundation of China (No.61962039) and Inner Mongolia Natural Science Foundation (No.2019MS06032).

References

1. Zelle, J.M., Mooney, R.J.: Learning to parse database queries using inductive logic programming. In: Proceedings of the Thirteenth National Conference on Artificial Intelligence and Eighth Innovative Applications of Artificial Intelligence Conference, AAAI 96, IAAI 96, Portland, Oregon, USA, August 4–8, 1996, vol. 2, pp. 1050–1055. AAAI Press/The MIT Press (1996)
2. Zhong, V., Xiong, C., Socher, R.: Seq2SQL: generating structured queries from natural language using reinforcement learning. CoRR abs/1709.00103 (2017)
3. Yu, T., et al.: Spider: a large-scale human-labeled dataset for complex and cross-domain semantic parsing and text-to-SQL task. In: Proceedings of the 2018 Conference on Empirical Methods in Natural Language Processing, Brussels, Belgium, October 31 - November 4, 2018, pp. 3911–3921. Association for Computational Linguistics (2018)
4. Zhang, X., Yin, F., Ma, G., Ge, B., Xiao, W.: M-SQL: multi-task representation learning for single-table text2SQL generation. IEEE Access **8**, 43156–43167 (2020)
5. Kelkar, A., Relan, R., Bhardwaj, V., Vaichal, S., Relan, P.: Bertrand-DR: improving text-to-SQL using a discriminative re-ranker. CoRR abs/2002.00557 (2020)
6. Cao, R., Chen, L., Chen, Z., Zhao, Y., Zhu, S., Yu, K.: LGESQL: line graph enhanced text-to-SQL model with mixed local and non-local relations. In: Proceedings of the 59th Annual Meeting of the Association for Computational Linguistics and the 11th International Joint Conference on Natural Language Processing, ACL/IJCNLP 2021, (Volume 1: Long Papers), Virtual Event, August 1–6, 2021, pp. 2541–2555. Association for Computational Linguistics (2021)
7. LeClair, A., Haque, S., Wu, L., McMillan, C.: Improved code summarization via a graph neural network. In: ICPC 2020: 28th International Conference on Program Comprehension, Seoul, Republic of Korea, July 13–15, 2020, pp. 184–195. ACM (2020)
8. Huang, J., Wang, Y., Wang, Y., Dong, Y., Xiao, Y.: Relation aware semi-autoregressive semantic parsing for NL2SQL. CoRR abs/2108.00804 (2021)
9. Yu, T., et al.: SParC: cross-domain semantic parsing in context. In: Proceedings of the 57th Conference of the Association for Computational Linguistics, ACL 2019, Florence, Italy, July 28- August 2, 2019, Volume 1: Long Papers, pp. 4511–4523. Association for Computational Linguistics (2019)

10. Yu, T., et al.: CoSQL: a conversational text-to-SQL challenge towards cross-domain natural language interfaces to databases. In: Proceedings of the 2019 Conference on Empirical Methods in Natural Language Processing and the 9th International Joint Conference on Natural Language Processing, EMNLP-IJCNLP 2019, Hong Kong, China, November 3–7, 2019, pp. 1962–1979. Association for Computational Linguistics (2019)
11. Zhang, R., et al.: Editing-based SQL query generation for cross-domain context-dependent questions. In: Proceedings of the 2019 Conference on Empirical Methods in Natural Language Processing and the 9th International Joint Conference on Natural Language Processing, EMNLP-IJCNLP 2019, Hong Kong, China, November 3–7, 2019, pp. 5337–5348. Association for Computational Linguistics (2019)
12. Cai, Y., Wan, X.: IGSQL: database schema interaction graph based neural model for context-dependent text-to-SQL generation. In: Proceedings of the 2020 Conference on Empirical Methods in Natural Language Processing, EMNLP 2020, Online, November 16–20, 2020, pp. 6903–6912. Association for Computational Linguistics (2020)
13. Yu, W., Chang, T., Guo, X., Wang, M., Wang, X.: An interaction-modeling mechanism for context-dependent text-to-SQL translation based on heterogeneous graph aggregation. Neural Netw. **142**, 573–582 (2021)
14. Dong, L., Lapata, M.: Coarse-to-fine decoding for neural semantic parsing. In: Proceedings of the 56th Annual Meeting of the Association for Computational Linguistics, ACL 2018, Melbourne, Australia, July 15–20, 2018, Volume 1: Long Papers, pp. 731–742. Association for Computational Linguistics (2018)
15. Lei, W., et al.: Re-examining the role of schema linking in text-to-SQL. In: Proceedings of the 2020 Conference on Empirical Methods in Natural Language Processing, EMNLP 2020, Online, November 16–20, 2020, pp. 6943–6954. Association for Computational Linguistics (2020)
16. Guo, J., et al.: Towards complex text-to-SQL in cross-domain database with intermediate representation. In: Proceedings of the 57th Conference of the Association for Computational Linguistics, ACL 2019, Florence, Italy, July 28- August 2, 2019, Volume 1: Long Papers, pp. 4524–4535. Association for Computational Linguistics (2019)
17. Hui, B., et al.: Improving text-to-SQL with schema dependency learning. CoRR abs/2103.04399 (2021)
18. Chen, Z., et al.: ShadowGNN: graph projection neural network for text-to-SQL parser. In: Proceedings of the 2021 Conference of the North American Chapter of the Association for Computational Linguistics: Human Language Technologies, NAACL-HLT 2021, Online, June 6–11, 2021, pp. 5567–5577. Association for Computational Linguistics (2021)
19. Rubin, O., Berant, J.: SmBoP: semi-autoregressive bottom-up semantic parsing. In: Proceedings of the 2021 Conference of the North American Chapter of the Association for Computational Linguistics: Human Language Technologies, NAACL-HLT 2021, Online, June 6–11, 2021, pp. 311–324. Association for Computational Linguistics (2021)
20. Devlin, J., Chang, M., Lee, K., Toutanova, K.: BERT: pre-training of deep bidirectional transformers for language understanding. In: Proceedings of the 2019 Conference of the North American Chapter of the Association for Computational Linguistics: Human Language Technologies, NAACL-HLT 2019, Minneapolis, MN, USA, June 2–7, 2019, Volume 1 (Long and Short Papers), pp. 4171–4186. Association for Computational Linguistics (2019)

21. Hwang, W., Yim, J., Park, S., Seo, M.: A comprehensive exploration on WikiSQL with table-aware word contextualization. CoRR abs/1902.01069 (2019)
22. Kingma, D.P., Ba, J.: Adam: a method for stochastic optimization. In: 3rd International Conference on Learning Representations, ICLR 2015, San Diego, CA, USA, May 7–9, 2015, Conference Track Proceedings (2015)

CSS: Contrastive Span Selector for Multi-span Question Answering

Penghui Zhang, Guanming Xiong, and Wen Zhao(✉)

Peking University, Beijing, China
{zhangph,gm_xiong,zhaowen}@pku.edu.cn

Abstract. This study investigates the task of Multi-span Question Answering (MSQA). Currently, the MSQA task is primarily modeled as a sequence tagging problem, predicting whether each word is a part of an answer. However, this approach independently predicts words without fully utilizing a comprehensive understanding of the complexities in MSQA. In this paper, we propose a novel model, Contrastive Span Selector. Our model utilizes a multi-head biaffine attention mechanism to generate the span representations and employs a CNN block for span-wise interaction. Additionally, we incorporate the question and a global token into the encoding process, projecting all vectors into a shared representation space. To train our model, we employ contrastive learning with a dynamic threshold to control the similarity boundary between answer spans and non-answer spans. Our model outperforms the tagger model by 6.32 in F1 score for exact match on the MultiSpanQA multi-span setting and 5.69 on the expand setting, establishing it as the state-of-the-art model for MSQA. The code is available at: https://github.com/phzh24/Contrastive-Span-Selector.

Keywords: Extractive Question Answering · Multi-span Question Answering · Contrastive Learning

1 Introduction

Machine reading comprehension, which involves answering question based on a given context, has made significant strides in recent years. More challenging variants of the task have been proposed, one of which has recently gained attention is multi-span question answering (MSQA) [1,4,7]. Unlike traditional question answering task that only allows a single span as the answer [11,12], MSQA task requires extracting multiple spans from the context, making it more practical and commonly encountered.

Recent research has made notable progress in addressing the challenge of MSQA. The current state-of-the-art model [15] casts MSQA as a sequence tagging task, predicting for each context word whether it is a constituent of answering spans, which is straightforward yet effective. To further enhance the performance, multi-task module, such as answer structure predictor and span adjustment module, has been introduced [7] to capture better global information. These

F. Liu et al. (Eds.): PRICAI 2023, LNAI 14325, pp. 225–236, 2024.
https://doi.org/10.1007/978-981-99-7019-3_22

extensions improve the performance of the sequence tagging model and establish it as a robust baseline for MSQA.

However, the sequence tagging framework still has limitations. Firstly, in this framework, individual words are predicted separately, which makes it challenging to capture the associations between words and the dependencies among answer spans. Secondly, the sequence tagging models fall short of capturing comprehensive interaction between the question and context. It exclusively relies on self-attention mechanism in Transformer-based model [2,8], which are inadequate for handling the complexity of MSQA. These limitations make the sequence tagging models sub-optimal for the MSQA task.

To address these limitations, we propose Contrastive Span Selector (CSS), which conducts span-level prediction, performs span-wise interaction and utilizes contrastive learning to model the relationships between the question and candidate spans. For one thing, we utilize multi-head biaffine attention [3,16] to enumerate all candidate spans, allowing us to make predictions at span level rather than word level. Meanwhile, we observe the spatial correlations of candidate spans and employ Convolutional Neural Network (CNN) to conduct span-wise interaction. Furthermore, we use pre-trained language model like BERT [2] to encode the question and a global token. We utilize contrastive learning to pull the answer span vectors close to the question vector and push non-answer span vectors far away. In addition, the vector of the global token is used as a dynamic threshold [18] to control the boundary of answer and non-answer vectors. Our model outperforms the current SOTA model [7] by 6.32 and 5.69 on exact match F1 score on two public MSQA dataset settings [7], demonstrating its effectiveness.

In summary, the main contributions of this work are as follows:

- Our proposed model, CSS, makes span-level prediction with span-wise interaction to improve the capture of dependencies among answer spans. This approach is more appropriate than word-level sequence tagging models for the MSQA task.
- We propose utilizing a contrastive learning approach to enhance span representations and a dynamic threshold-based strategy to automatically control the boundary of answer representations.
- The CSS significantly outperforms current methods, establishing itself as the new state-of-the-art MSQA approach.

2 Related Work

2.1 Tagger Model in MSQA

In many tasks of natural language processing, it is often necessary to extract a varying number of spans from an input text. This is often formulated as a sequence tagging problem, as demonstrated in previous work [13]. The work in [15] introduced the use of a tagger schema for MSQA and employed the widely used *BIO* tagging scheme [6,14]. As shown in Fig. 1, the tags *B* and *I* denote

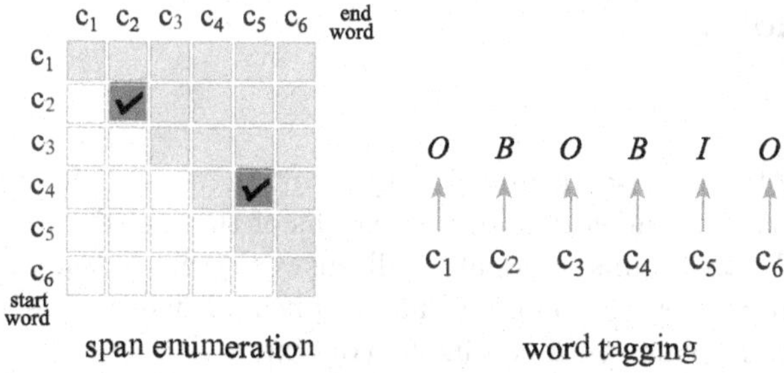

Fig. 1. The comparison between span enumeration method and word tagging method. Span enumeration method regards a span as a whole, while word tagging method predicts each word individually.

the first word and subsequent words within the spans, while the tag O indicates that the word is not within the span. However, the sequence tagging model individually predicts whether each context word is part of the answers without effectively leveraging global information.

To overcome this limitation, the work in [7] combines the tagger model with several additional components to refine the predicted spans. Specifically, this approach performs average pooling over the words in the predicted spans from the tagger model to obtain fixed-length span representations. These span representations are then concatenated with a global [CLS] token and fed into the span encoder to produce another global vector. This global vector is used to predict the answer structure and the number of spans to adjust, thereby refining the predicted spans from the tagger model. This approach effectively enhances the performance of the tagger model by incorporating global information obtained from the initial predicted spans into the span adjustment process.

However, we argue that solely abstracting global information from the initial span predictions and a global token may not provide a comprehensive model for capturing the dependencies among answer spans.

2.2 Span-Based Method in Other Extractive Task

The extractive tasks like information extraction and named entity recognition (NER) are often accomplished through span level methods. This involves the enumeration of all possible spans and their classification into various entity types. The approach naturally resolves the nested-entity issue in NER tasks. [17] enumerates all spans by the start and end position and then use a biaffine model to predict the probability of each entity type. [16] argues that previous span-based NER methods ignore spatial relations in the score matrix of spans, and proposes using Convolutional Neural Network to model these spatial relations. In [18], the authors propose a bi-encoder framework that leverages contrastive learning to project text spans and entity types into a common representation space. Additionally, they introduce a novel dynamic threshold loss to effectively discriminate entity spans from non-entity ones.

3 Methodology

3.1 Task Definition

The MSQA task comprises a question $Q = q_1, q_2, ..., q_m$, and a context $C = c_1, c_2, ..., c_n$, where m and n denote the lengths of the question and the context respectively. The task aims to identify all answer spans $s_1, s_2, ..., s_t$ within the context that are non-overlapping and non-duplicated, where t denotes the total number of answer spans contained in the context.

3.2 Model Overview

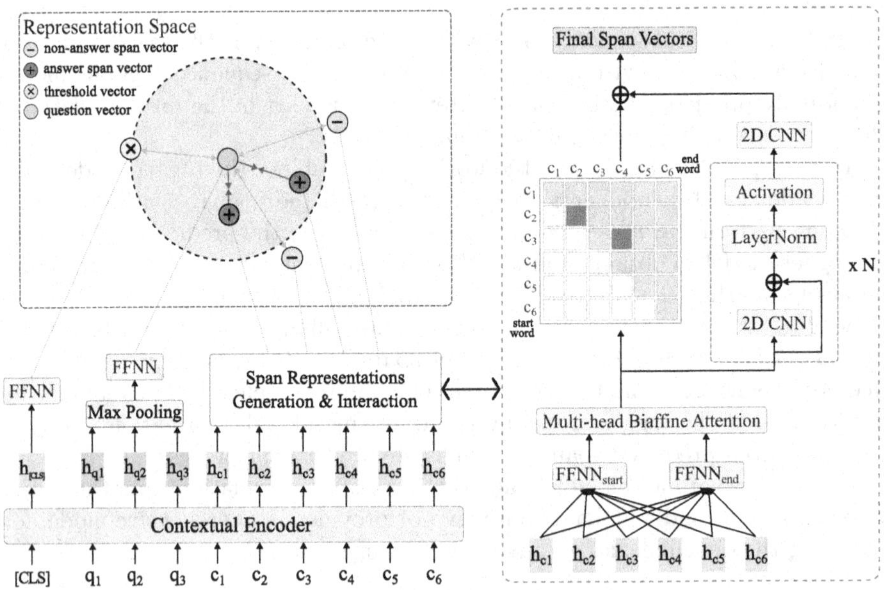

Fig. 2. The architecture of our proposed CSS model. The symbol ⊕ denotes element-wise addition. We only drew partial words and vectors for simplicity.

Our model is inspired by the named entity recognition models in [16,18]. Our model employs a contextual encoder to create the word representations of the question and context. Afterward, the representations are fed into a multi-head biaffine attention network to generate candidate span representations. Next, we utilize a stack of CNN blocks to perform span-wise interaction. Finally, we project the vectors of the question, candidate spans, and a dynamic threshold into a shared space through contrastive learning. Figure 2 shows an overview of the proposed architecture.

Word Representation. First, we employ a pre-trained language model (PLM), such as BERT [2] or RoBERTa [8], as the contextual encoder to obtain token representations for the question, context, and the prepended token [CLS]. Then, we apply max pooling to the tokens associated with each word, resulting in word-level representations for all words:

$$\mathbf{H} = \text{TokenPooling}(\text{Encoder}([\text{CLS}]\mathbf{Q}[\text{SEP}]\mathbf{C}[\text{SEP}])) \tag{1}$$

Here, $\mathbf{H} = [\boldsymbol{h}_{[\text{CLS}]}; \mathbf{H}_q; \mathbf{H}_c] = [\boldsymbol{h}_{[\text{CLS}]}; \boldsymbol{h}_{q_1}, \boldsymbol{h}_{q_2}, ..., \boldsymbol{h}_{q_m}; \boldsymbol{h}_{c_1}, \boldsymbol{h}_{c_2}, ..., \boldsymbol{h}_{c_n}]$ represents the contextual word representation of all input words, including a global token [CLS]. Special token [SEP] separates the question and context. The function TokenPooling($\cdot$) performs the max pooling operation over the tokenized word embeddings to derive a fixed-size vector representation for each word in the question and context. The vectors $\boldsymbol{h}_{[\text{CLS}]}, \boldsymbol{h}_q, \boldsymbol{h}_c \in \mathbb{R}^{d_1}$, where d_1 represents the hidden size of the encoder.

Span Representation. We employ two separate Feed Forward Neural Networks (FFNNs) to the word representations of context to create different representation for the start and end of a span, which enable the system to learn to identify the start and end independently [17].

$$\boldsymbol{x}_{s_i} = \text{FFNN}_s(\boldsymbol{h}_{c_i}) \tag{2}$$

$$\boldsymbol{x}_{e_j} = \text{FFNN}_e(\boldsymbol{h}_{c_j}) \tag{3}$$

where $\boldsymbol{x}_{s_i}, \boldsymbol{x}_{e_j} \in \mathbb{R}^{d_2}$ are position embeddings containing the start, end information of a span, i and j are indices, d_2 is the dimensionality of position representation of spans, FFNN is consist of a affine transformation and an activation function.

The representations of candidate spans are generated by multi-head biaffine attention [3,16].

$$\mathbf{R}_1(i,j) = \text{Multihead}(\boldsymbol{x}_{s_i}, \boldsymbol{x}_{e_j}) + (\boldsymbol{x}_{s_i} \oplus \boldsymbol{x}_{e_j})^\top \mathbf{W} + \boldsymbol{b} \tag{4}$$

where $\boldsymbol{R}_1(i,j) \in \mathbb{R}_{d_3}$ is the representation of the span from i-th word to j-th word of context, d_3 is the dimensionality of the span representations, $\oplus$ indicates the vector concatenation, $\mathbf{W} \in \mathbb{R}^{2d_2 \times d_3}$, $\boldsymbol{b} \in \mathbb{R}^{d_3}$ is the bias. Multihead($\cdot$) is the multi-head biaffine attention transformation, in detail as:

$$\boldsymbol{x}_{s_i}^{(1)}, \boldsymbol{x}_{s_i}^{(2)}, ..., \boldsymbol{x}_{s_i}^{(K)} = \text{Split}(\boldsymbol{x}_{s_i}) \tag{5}$$

$$\boldsymbol{x}_{e_j}^{(1)}, \boldsymbol{x}_{e_j}^{(2)}, ..., \boldsymbol{x}_{e_j}^{(K)} = \text{Split}(\boldsymbol{x}_{e_j}) \tag{6}$$

$$\boldsymbol{head}^{(k)} = {\boldsymbol{x}_{s_i}^{(k)}}^\top \mathbf{U}^{(k)} \boldsymbol{x}_{e_j}^{(k)} \tag{7}$$

$$\text{Multihead}(\boldsymbol{x}_{s_i}, \boldsymbol{x}_{e_j}) = \boldsymbol{head}^{(1)} \oplus \boldsymbol{head}^{(2)} \oplus ... \oplus \boldsymbol{head}^{(K)} \tag{8}$$

where Split($\cdot$) equally splits the position vectors, K is the number of heads, $\mathbf{U}^{(k)} \in \mathbb{R}^{d_h \times r_h \times d_h}$ is the k-th head 3D transformation tensor, $d_h \times K = d_2$, $r_h \times K = d_3$, Multihead$(\boldsymbol{x}_{s_i}, \boldsymbol{x}_{e_j})$ indicates the multi-head part of biaffine attention.

Instead of directly obtaining the candidate span representations through the second part of Eq. (4), we utilize biaffine attention over the position embeddings to derive these representations. This is because biaffine attention can caputre more comprehensive information [3]. We will empirically demonstrate this advantage in Sect. 4.3. The multi-head version of biaffine attention is employed to leverage multiple aspects of information while reducing the number of parameters.

Span-Wise Interaction. Equation (4) generates the representation of a span only from the word c_i to the wordc_j. Although the position embeddings obtain certain information from PLM encoding, they are weak for the complexity of the MSQA task. We apply 2D CNN block to conduct the span-wise interaction [16] as follows:

$$\mathbf{R}_2 = \text{Conv2d}(\text{CNNBlock}(\mathbf{R}_1)^{\times N}) \tag{9}$$

$$\text{CNNBlock}(\mathbf{x}) := \text{Activation}(\text{LayerNorm}(\mathbf{x} + \text{Conv2d}(\mathbf{x}))) \tag{10}$$

Here, Conv2d represents a 2D CNN, LayerNorm denotes layer normalization performed along the feature dimension, and Activation means a non-linearity activation function. We stack CNN block N times, the output of the former block is the input of the next. The output of the final CNN block is sent to an additional 2D CNN, then we derive the contextualized span representations that capture the interactions among spans. For the input of Conv2d, we mask the invalid spans (in which the start index is greater than the end index) with 0.

As Fig. 2, the representations of all enumerated spans after biaffine attention array as a 2D grid. The spans, whose corresponding grid points close to each other, may have a close relationship. For a span, the spans close to it, around to it, or even from a long distance with it may contain critical information and decide whether the span is one of the answers. Considering this nature, we apply 2D CNN to conduct the span-wise interaction. A CNN layer only facilitates interaction within a small grid distance. In the case of a 3×3 kernel size CNN, the central span only interacts with its surrounding spans at a distance of 1. By stacking multiple such CNN blocks, we can conduct multi-level and long-distance span-wise interactions. We show the effectiveness of this module empirically at Sect. 4.3.

3.3 Contrastive Learning for MSQA

We calculate the probability of a candidate span as one of the answers by the similarity of the span with the question. Meanwhile, we utilize the similarity of the global [CLS] with the question as the dynamic threshold.

Final Representations. First, we get the final representations of spans by adding the outputs of multi-head biaffine attention and span-wise interaction module.

$$\mathbf{R} = \mathbf{R}_1 + \mathbf{R}_2 \tag{11}$$

where $\mathbf{R} \in \mathbb{R}^{n \times n \times b_3}$, and $\mathbf{R}(i, j)$ represents the final feature vector of the span from c_i to c_j.

We utilize the representations of the question words to obtain the overall question representation:

$$\boldsymbol{q} = \text{FFNN}_q(\text{WordPooling}(\mathbf{H}_q)) \tag{12}$$

Here, WordPooling performs the max pooling operation over the word representations, and FFNN_q refers to the feed-forward neural network with the same structure as described in Eq. (2), except for the dimensionality. The resulting representation $\boldsymbol{q}$ is a vector in $\mathbb{R}^{d_3}$.

The [CLS] reads the entire input text and summarizes the contextual information, which makes it a good choice to estimate the similarity boundary to separate answer spans from non-answer spans. Similar to the question representation, we employ an FFNN to project the vector into the same dimension space of spans:

$$\boldsymbol{v}_t = \text{FFNN}_{[\text{CLS}]}(\boldsymbol{h}_{[\text{CLS}]}) \tag{13}$$

Contrastive Learning Objective. Given the representations of the question, spans, and dynamic threshold discussed above, we combine two contrastive learning objectives to train our model. The similarity is calculated using scaled dot product: $\text{sim}(q, v) = \frac{\boldsymbol{q} \cdot \boldsymbol{v}}{\tau}$, where the scaling factor τ is learnable, and $\boldsymbol{v}$ represents the vector of spans and dynamic threshold.

In the span-based objective, our goal is to ensure the similarities of answer spans (considered as positive samples) with the question are higher than these of non-answer spans (considered as negative samples) and the dynamic threshold. To achieve this, we adopt the InfoNCE loss [10] tailed for span-based objective [18] to fit the MSQA task. The span-based objective can be defined as follow:

$$l_{\text{span}} = -\frac{1}{|\mathbb{P}|} \sum_{i \in \mathbb{P}} \log \frac{e^{\text{sim}(span_i, q)}}{e^{\text{sim}(span_i, q)} + \sum_{j \in \mathbb{N} \cup \{v_t\}} e^{\text{sim}(span_j, q)}} \tag{14}$$

Here, $\mathbb{P}$ represents the collection of answer spans, $\mathbb{N}$ represents the collection of non-answer spans, and $\boldsymbol{v}_t$ is the vector controlling the dynamic threshold.

The span-based objective does not guarantee the similarities of non-answer spans with the question are lower than the dynamic threshold. To address this, we employ a similar loss function to learn a appropriate dynamic threshold [18]:

$$l_{\text{threshold}} = -\log \frac{e^{\text{sim}(v_t, q)}}{\sum_{j \in \mathbb{N} \cup \{v_t\}} e^{\text{sim}(span_j, q)}} \tag{15}$$

Combining the span-base objective and dynamic threshold objective encourages the modeling dynamic threshold to discriminate answer spans and non-answer spans properly. Our overall learning objective given by:

$$L = \beta l_{\text{span}} + (1 - \beta) l_{\text{threshold}} \tag{16}$$

Here, β is a hyperparameter that controls the trade-off between the two objectives. By optimizing this combined loss function, our model learns to generate high similarities for answer spans while ensuring non-answer spans are assigned lower than the dynamic threshold.

4 Experiments

4.1 Experiments Settings

Datasets. MultiSpanQA [7] dataset focuses on questions that require answer composed of multiple spans. We evaluate our method in two different settings of the dataset: multi-span and expand. **MultiSpanQA multi-span setting** consists of over 6,000 questions with answers involving multiple spans of context. The span count in the setting ranges from 2 to 21. Approximately 80% of the instances have 2 or 3 spans, while only about 1% of instances contain over 9 spans. **MultiSpanQA expand setting** extends the multi-span setting with both unanswerable questions and questions with single answer. It contains over 19,000 examples.

Baselines. Despite the commonality of MSQA task, there has yet to be a published span-based method. Therefore, we evaluate our CSS Model by comparing it with the start-of-the-art MSQA models, $\text{Tagger}_{\text{vanilla}}$ and $\text{Tagger}_{\text{multi-task}}$. $\textbf{Tagger}_{\textbf{vanilla}}$ [7,15] casts MSQA as a sequence tagging task, predicting for each word whether it is a part of an answer, which is straightforward. Building on this, $\textbf{Tagger}_{\textbf{multi-task}}$ [7] enhances the model with multi-task modules to capture global information. We implement the both models based on $\text{BERT}_{\text{base}}$ [2] and $\text{RoBERTa}_{\text{base}}$ [8] following the experimental setting of [7].

Evaluation Metrics. Following [7], we use exact match (EM) and partial match (PM) as the evaluation metrics. EM assigns a score of 1.0 when a prediction perfectly matches one of the ground-truth answers. On the other hand, PM calculates the level of overlap between a prediction and the ground-truth answer, with higher overlap resulting in a higher score. Both metrics rely on micro-averaged precision (P), recall (R), and F1 score (F1). All the experimental results reported are percentages.

Hyper-parameter Settings. We utilize $\text{BERT}_{\text{base}}$ and $\text{RoBERTa}_{\text{base}}$ as the encoders of our proposed method. The training is performed with a batch size of 16 for 8 epochs. We employ AdamW [9] as the optimizer with a learning rate of 4e-5. The learning rate undergoes warmup with a ratio of 0.1, followed by linear decay. A dropout probability of 0.2 is applied to all layers. The number of heads of multi-head biaffine attention is 12. The number of CNN block is 5. The kernel size of 2D CNN is 3×3. β is set to 0.5. We utilize GELU activation [5]. The model is evaluated at the end of each epoch during training, and the best-performing version is selected. The random seed is set to 2023. All experiments are conducted using two 24 GB Nvidia RTX 4090 GPUs.

4.2 Main Results

Table 1. Performance comparison between the baselines and CSS on the blind *test* datasets of two benchmark datasets. * means our implementation following the experimental setting of [7]. The best performance is in **bold**.

Method	MultiSpanQA multi-span						MultiSpanQA expand					
	Exact Match			Partial Match			Exact Match			Partial Match		
	P	R	F1	P	R	F1	P	R	F1	P	R	F1
$\text{BERT}_{\text{base}}$ as encoder												
$\text{Tagger}_{\text{vanilla}}$*	51.52	62.34	56.42	75.80	**75.16**	75.48	53.77	60.35	56.87	71.2	**70.53**	70.87
$\text{Tagger}_{\text{multi-task}}$*	55.72	58.07	56.87	76.17	71.25	73.63	57.48	58.40	57.94	74.04	68.30	71.06
CSS (our work)	**63.90**	**62.50**	**63.19**	**77.52**	74.60	**76.04**	**65.64**	**61.74**	**63.63**	**75.15**	69.71	**72.33**
$\text{RoBERTa}_{\text{base}}$ as encoder												
$\text{Tagger}_{\text{vanilla}}$*	60.40	**69.34**	64.56	78.92	**82.63**	**80.73**	62.83	**64.95**	63.87	77.52	**74.57**	**76.02**
$\text{Tagger}_{\text{multi-task}}$*	62.88	63.62	63.25	81.04	76.85	78.89	62.15	63.75	62.94	76.75	73.71	75.20
CSS (our work)	**69.76**	68.27	**69.01**	**83.03**	78.37	80.63	**71.07**	63.94	**67.32**	**80.37**	71.73	75.81

As shown in Table 1, our proposed model achieves state-of-the-art performance in the two dataset settings. Specifically, our model consistently achieves better results than baselines across almost all evaluation metrics for both multi-span setting and expand setting, as well as for both PLMs.

In the multi-span setting, where all questions have multiple answering spans, our model outperforms the baseline models on both PLMs. When using $\text{BERT}_{\text{base}}$ as encoder, our model outperforms $\text{Tagger}_{\text{vanilla}}$ and $\text{Tagger}_{\text{multi-task}}$ by 6.77 and 6.32 on the F1 score of exact match, and by 0.56 and 2.41 on F1 score of partial match, respectively. When using $\text{RoBERTa}_{\text{base}}$ as encoder, our model outperforms $\text{Tagger}_{\text{vanilla}}$ and $\text{Tagger}_{\text{multi-task}}$ by 4.45 and 5.76 on the F1 score of exact match and achieves comparable performance to $\text{Tagger}_{\text{vanilla}}$ on the F1 score of partial match while outperforming $\text{Tagger}_{\text{multi-task}}$ by 1.74. These significant improvements demonstrate the effectiveness of our model in solving the MSQA task. Moreover, our model outperforms the baseline models in the expand setting, showing that our model performs well not only in multi-span questions, but also in single-span and unanswerable questions.

4.3 Ablation Study

We conduct ablations to demonstrate the effectiveness of multi-head biaffine attention module, the span-wise interaction module and contrastive learning training in our model. Because the test dataset is blind, we conduct all ablation experiments on *validation* dataset of the MultiSpanQA multi-span setting.

Table 2. Evaluation results of the ablations on the *validation* dataset of multi-span setting. * is conducted following the setting of [7]. The best performance is in **blod**.

	EM F1	PM F1
CSS (our work)	**69.06**	**79.53**
w/o multi-head biaffine	66.83	78.76
w/o span-wise interaction	59.95	68.83
w/o contrastive learning	64.06	75.39
$\text{Tagger}_{\text{vanilla}}{}^{*}$	58.89	78.16
$\text{Tagger}_{\text{multi-task}}{}^{*}$	56.59	73.69

The ablation experiments are organized as follows:

- w/o multi-head biaffine attention. We remove the multihead part of the Eq. (4).
- w/o span-wise interaction. We remove the span-wise interaction module and use the outputs of multi-head biaffine attention as the final span representations.
- w/o contrastive learning loss. We remove contrastive learning training and dynamic threshold. We follow the span-based method [16] for NER and use linear projection to map the final span representations to logits, followed by a sigmoid function to obtain the probability that each span is one of the answer spans. During training, we used binary cross-entropy (BCE) loss. In the inference phase, we defined a span as part of answers if it have a probability greater than 0.5.

The second line of Table 2 demonstrates the effectiveness of the multi-head biaffine attention of our model. When removing it, the performance of our model drops by 2.23 on EM F1 and 0.77 on PM F1. This proves that multi-head biaffine attention can caputre more abundant information than only using affine transformation.

The third line of Table 2 shows that our model drops by 9.11 on EM F1 score and 10.7 on PM F1 score when removing the span-wise interaction module. This marked decline illustrates the effectiveness of the span-wise interaction module, indicating that the dependencies among answer spans are crucial. It also highlights the natural shortcomings of sequence tagging models in capturing these relationships, making them suboptimal for MSQA task.

When replacing contrastive learning with BCE loss, the performance of our model drops by a margin of 5.00 on EM F1 score and 4.14 on PM F1 score. The considerable performance drop shows the effectiveness of contrastive learning training. With contrastive learning and dynamic threshold, our proposed model conducts comprehensive interaction between question and candidate spans, which is also essential to the MSQA task.

Comparing the third row of Table 2 with the last two rows, we observe that without span-wise interaction modules: 1) our model outperforms the baseline models on EM F1 score, which indicates our span level biaffine model is more suitable for MSQA task than word level sequence tagging model; 2) our model performs worse on PM F1 score, which we conjecture is due to the use of contrastive learning. Specifically, the exact answer spans are treated as positive samples, while the spans with partial overlap with the ground truth are treated as negative samples. Therefore, our model is optimized for predicting exact answer spans and could be ineffective at predicting spans with partial matches.

5 Conclusion and Future Work

In this paper, we propose CSS, a novel Contrastive Span Selector model conducting span-level prediction in the MSQA task. We conduct experiments on two dataset settings and the results demonstrate our proposed model achieves state-of-the-art performance. However, the training process of CSS is more time-consuming than word-level prediction models because it involves using a stack of CNN blocks. Furthermore, while the contrastive training objective works well for exact match, it negatively impacts the performance for partial match scenarios. This is because it considers spans with partial overlap with the ground truth as negatives. In the future, our focus will be on improving efficiency and optimizing span prediction under contrastive learning.

Acknowledgments. The authors would like to thank the three anonymous reviewers for their comments on this paper. This work is supported by the National Key Research and Development Program of China (No.2020YFC0833300).

References

1. Dasigi, P., Liu, N.F., Marasović, A., Smith, N.A., Gardner, M.: Quoref: a reading comprehension dataset with questions requiring coreferential reasoning. In: Proceedings of the 2019 Conference on Empirical Methods in Natural Language Processing and the 9th International Joint Conference on Natural Language Processing (EMNLP-IJCNLP), pp. 5925–5932. Association for Computational Linguistics, Hong Kong (2019)
2. Devlin, J., Chang, M.W., Lee, K., Toutanova, K.: Bert: pre-training of deep bidirectional transformers for language understanding. In: North American Chapter of the Association for Computational Linguistics (NAACL), pp. 4171–4186 (2019)
3. Dozat, T., Manning, C.D.: Deep biaffine attention for neural dependency parsing. In: International Conference on Learning Representations (ICLR) (2017)

4. Dua, D., Wang, Y., Dasigi, P., Stanovsky, G., Singh, S., Gardner, M.: DROP: a reading comprehension benchmark requiring discrete reasoning over paragraphs. In: Proceedings of the 2019 Conference of the North American Chapter of the Association for Computational Linguistics: Human Language Technologies, vol. 1 (Long and Short Papers), pp. 2368–2378. Association for Computational Linguistics, Minneapolis (2019)
5. Hendrycks, D., Gimpel, K.: Gaussian error linear units (gelus). arXiv preprint arXiv:1606.08415 (2016)
6. Huang, Z., Xu, W., Yu, K.: Bidirectional lstm-crf models for sequence tagging. arXiv preprint arXiv:1508.01991 (2015)
7. Li, H., Tomko, M., Vasardani, M., Baldwin, T.: Multispanqa: a dataset for multi-span question answering. In: Proceedings of the 2022 Conference of the North American Chapter of the Association for Computational Linguistics: Human Language Technologies, pp. 1250–1260 (2022)
8. Liu, Y., et al.: Roberta: a robustly optimized bert pretraining approach. arXiv preprint arXiv:1907.11692 (2019)
9. Loshchilov, I., Hutter, F.: Decoupled weight decay regularization. In: International Conference on Learning Representations (2019)
10. Oord, A.V.D., Li, Y., Vinyals, O.: Representation learning with contrastive predictive coding. arXiv preprint arXiv:1807.03748 (2018)
11. Rajpurkar, P., Jia, R., Liang, P.: Know what you don't know: unanswerable questions for SQuAD. In: Proceedings of the 56th Annual Meeting of the Association for Computational Linguistics, vol. 2: Short Papers, pp. 784–789. Association for Computational Linguistics, Melbourne (2018)
12. Rajpurkar, P., Zhang, J., Lopyrev, K., Liang, P.: SQuAD: 100,000+ questions for machine comprehension of text. In: Proceedings of the 2016 Conference on Empirical Methods in Natural Language Processing, pp. 2383–2392. Association for Computational Linguistics, Austin (2016)
13. Ramshaw, L., Marcus, M.: Text chunking using transformation-based learning. In: Third Workshop on Very Large Corpora (1995)
14. Sang, E.F.T.K.: Transforming a chunker to a parser. In: Computational Linguistics in the Netherlands 2000, pp. 177–188. Brill (2001)
15. Segal, E., Efrat, A., Shoham, M., Globerson, A., Berant, J.: A simple and effective model for answering multi-span questions. In: Conference on Empirical Methods in Natural Language Processing (EMNLP), pp. 3074–3080 (2020)
16. Yan, H., Sun, Y., Li, X., Qiu, X.: An embarrassingly easy but strong baseline for nested named entity recognition. arXiv preprint arXiv:2208.04534 (2022)
17. Yu, J., Bohnet, B., Poesio, M.: Named entity recognition as dependency parsing. In: Proceedings of the 58th Annual Meeting of the Association for Computational Linguistics, pp. 6470–6476 (2020)
18. Zhang, S., Cheng, H., Gao, J., Poon, H.: optimizing bi-encoder for named entity recognition via contrastive learning. In: ICLR 2023 poster (2022)

Generative Model of Suitable Meme Sentences for Images Using AutoEncoder

Ryo Yamatomi(✉), Shahrzad Mahboubi, and Hiroshi Ninomiya

Shonan Institute of Technology (SIT), 1-1-25 Tsujido-nishikaigan, Fujisawa, Kanagawa 251-8511, Japan
23T2003@sit.shonan-it.ac.jp, {shaa,ninomiya}@info.shonan-it.ac.jp

Abstract. This paper proposes a new image caption generative model for *Meme*s called GUMI-AE. Meme denotes a humorous short sentence suitable for the given image in this paper. An Image caption generative model usually consists of an image encoder and a sentence decoder. Furthermore, most conventional models use a pre-trained neural network model for the image encoder, e.g., ResNet152 trained using ImageNet. However, pre-trained ResNet152 may not be effective as an encoder for extracting features from arbitrary images. Because the training samples for the meme generative model can be obtained from the website "Bokete" (in Japanese) which is a website that provides a system for people to post images and humorous short sentences associated with these images. Images posted on Bokete include a wide variety of images such as illustrations and text-only images which may be outside of the training images of ImageNet. This paper proposes an image caption generative model incorporating AutoEncoder (AE) as the image encoder. AE can be trained with the training samples obtained from Bokete without the image annotation. This enables the proposed method to generate short sentences with humor for memes. Finally, the proposed model is compared with the conventional one, and the evaluation of the proposed GUMI-AE will be discussed.

Keywords: Image caption generative model · Meme · Neural Networks · AutoEncoder

1 Introduction

In recent years, due to the rapid development of a generative model, it has been applied in various fields, and a wide variety of studies have been conducted. Some significant studies on generative models include Generative Adversarial Network [1], Generative Pre-trained Transformer (GPT) [2] and Meme generator using the image caption generative model [3] is attracted in this field. A meme is one of the cybercultures spreading and attracting attention worldwide, especially on social networking services (SNS), for entertainment and communication in a society where the internet has become very widespread [4]. They are images

F. Liu et al. (Eds.): PRICAI 2023, LNAI 14325, pp. 237–248, 2024.
https://doi.org/10.1007/978-981-99-7019-3_23

Fig. 1. Some meme examples generated by proposed GUMI-AE.

and videos with jokes or humorous short sentences and are meme is usually created by pasting short sentences onto an image or video. Some meme examples for images are shown in Fig. 1. These memes are generated by the proposed GUMI-AE. The data flow of the image caption generative model is shown in Fig. 2. As Fig. 2 shows, an image caption generative model usually consists of an image encoder and a sentence decoder. In the image caption generative model, an image is given as input to the image encoder and converted into a feature represented by a vector. The feature is input to a sentence decoder. The sentence decoder uses its feature vector to generate words in time series to construct a sentence. In many research and implementation, a pre-trained model, e.g. ResNet152 [5] or Inception-v3 [6], trained using ImageNet [7], is used as the image encoder [3,8,9]. ImageNet is a large dataset consisting of photographs of animals, vehicles, etc. Models pre-trained on this data are expected to have high feature extraction capability for common images. As an approach to generate memes by AI, English-based [8] and Japanese-based Neural Joking Machine (NJM) [9] have been proposed. In [8], to generate memes for images, Inception-V3 [6] which was pre-trained on ImageNet [7] is used as the image encoder for the image caption generative model to generate memes for images. In addition, as training data, $[image, meme]$ pairs obtained from "Memegenerator.net" [10], which is a website allowing users to post memes are used.

On the other hand, NJM [9] is a study on generating Japanese Memes called "Ohgiri" by using the image caption generative model with pre-trained ResNet152 [5] as the image encoder. The training dataset consists of $[image, Ohgiri]$ pairs obtained from "Bokete" [11], which is a website allowing users to post Ohgiri for images. Although the model implemented by this research is able to generate Memes for some images, it sometimes generates mistakes such as memes with unsuitable words for some images. This problem is caused by the fact that the pre-trained ResNet152 is not effective in extracting image features as the image encoder of the image caption generative model for memes. Because the training samples for the meme generative model obtain a wide variety of images from the website, such as illustration and text-only images, and these images may be outside of the images of ImageNet.

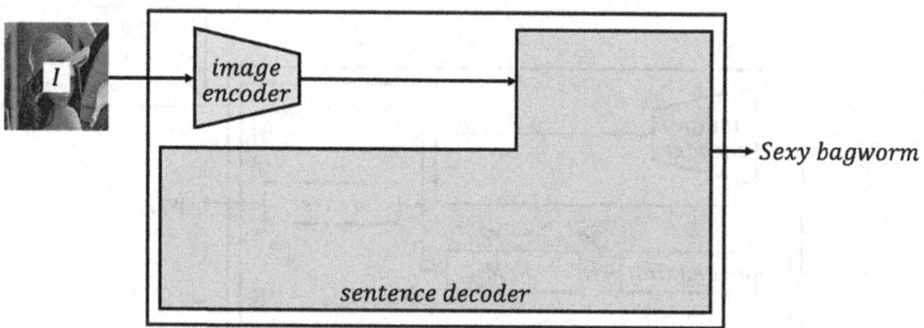

Fig. 2. The data flow of image caption generative model.

In this study, a new image caption generative model for memes, GUMI-AE, in which AutoEncoder (AE) [12] is used as an image encoder instead of pre-trained models to extract features suitable for the image is proposed. The AE is trained by the images obtained from Bokete. This means that the trained AE is suitable for extracting image features compared with the pre-trained ResNet152. The sentence decoder of GUMI-AE is composed of Long-Short Term Memory (LSTM) [13], commonly used in image caption generative models [3,8,9]. As a result, GUMI-AE increases the degree of flexibility of the model structure, which allows models to be built according to the computational resources available. Finally, the image caption generative model using ResNet152 used in NJM [9] implemented, and both of the results from GUMI-AE and NJM are compared with the proposed method. A questionnaire evaluates the sense of humor of each output meme of both of the models.

2 GUMI-AE: Generative Model of Suitable Meme Sentences for Images Using AutoEncoder

In this section, the proposed model of GUMI-AE is introduced.

2.1 Image Caption Generative Model

In an image caption generative model, an image encoder such as Convolutional Neural Network (CNN) [14] transforms an input image into its feature as a vector. The feature is used as the conditions for the generation of sentences by the sentence decoder. The structure of the image caption generative model is shown in Fig. 3, where **I** and w_t denote an input image and the $t-th$ word of the sentence, respectively. The input image of **I** is converted into the feature that is typically constructed by a vector. The word w_t is transformed into embedding the vector and processed by Recurrent Neural Network (RNN) [15] such as LSTM [13]. The RNN's internal state r_t at the time step t is also input and processed considering the time series. Both outputs of the image encoder and RNN are combined and fed into the dense layer. The number of units in this dense layer corresponds to the vocabulary of the image caption generative model, and

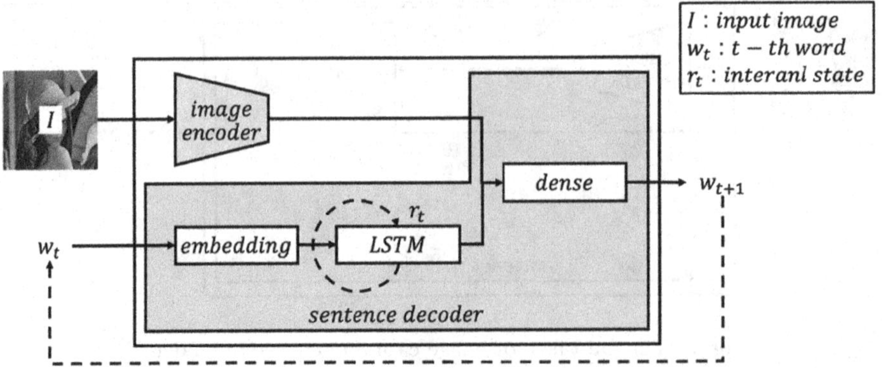

Fig. 3. The structure of the image caption generative model.

the output of this layer is converted into a probability distribution via the Softmax function. From the probability distribution produced by the image caption generative model, the $(t+1)-th$ word of the sentence is either the word with the maximum value or the word selected by the roulette selection, randomly picking a word based on a probability distribution. This procedure is recursively repeated until the token signifying the end of the sentence is selected.

2.2 AutoEncoder

AutoEncoder (AE) is proficient in feature extraction and dimensionality reduction of input data. It consists of an encoder and a decoder and is trained with the objective of (1) reconstructing the input data.

$$\min_{\mathbf{p}_e, \mathbf{p}_d} E(\mathbf{X}, decoder(encoder(\mathbf{X}))), \tag{1}$$

where $\mathbf{p}_e$, $\mathbf{p}_d$, and E denote the parameters of the encoder and the decoder and an arbitrary error function such as the mean square error (MSE) respectively, and $\mathbf{X}$ is the input to the AE, and $encoder(\mathbf{X})$ and $decoder(\mathbf{X})$ were the outputs of the encoder and decoder, respectively. Thus, data annotations are not required during the training of AE since the parameters are trained so that the input and the teacher signal of AE are the same. The encoder and decoder can be defined using arbitrary structures, such as CNN [14] for images and RNN [15] for texts.

2.3 GUMI-AE

Conventional image caption generative models generating memes for images [8,9] typically used a pre-trained image recognition model as the images encoder. However, if this pre-trained model failed to extract image features effectively during the sentence decoder training, it might not generate suitable humorous sentences for the images. One solution to this problem is to retrain the image encoder using the images for the memes, but this approach requires annotations of the images, which many datasets do not have. For example, Bokete [11] images used in the conventional model of NJM [9] have no annotations. It is difficult and time-consuming for humans to annotate such datasets. To deal with this problem, this research proposes a new image caption generative model as GUMI-AE that uses the encoder of the AutoEncoder trained with the images of meme dataset in advance as the image encoder of the image caption generative model.

The training procedure and structure of the proposed model are shown in Fig. 4 and Algorithm 1. Steps 1 through 5 in algorithm 1 train AutoEncoder, and this additional step is different from [8] and [9]. Steps 6 through 12 train the image caption generative model as in [8] and [9]. In Fig. 4, the AutoEncoder (AE) is initially trained using images from the dataset. Then, the image caption generative model uses images and sentences from the same dataset. In this process, images are converted into features by passing them through the encoder of the pre-trained AutoEncoder. During the image caption generative model training, the parameters of the pre-trained encoder of AE are frozen and not retrained, thus reducing the number of parameters used and improving training efficiency. In contrast to conventional image caption generative models that use pre-trained models [8,9], the image encoder in the proposed GUMI-AE is trained using the images of the dataset.

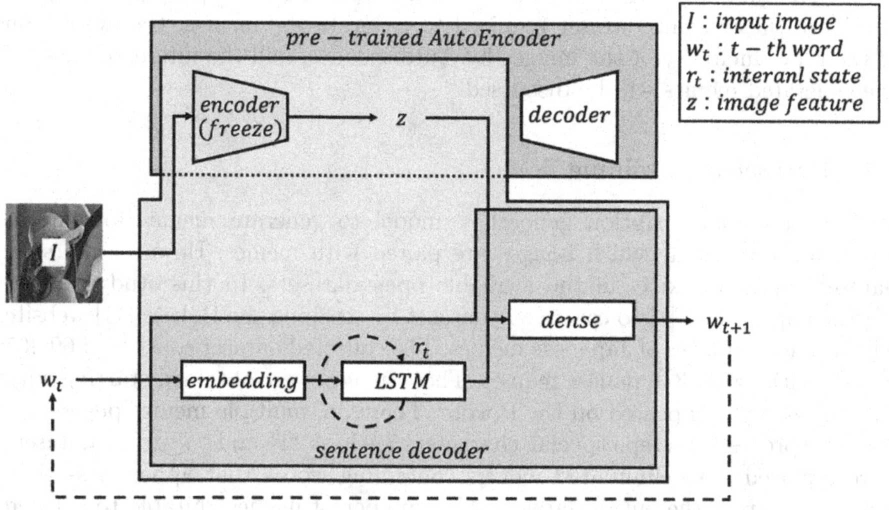

Fig. 4. The model structure of the proposed GUMI-AE.

Algorithm 1. Training procedure of proposed GUMI-AE

Require: images of meme dataset : $\mathbf{I} = \{\mathbf{I}_1, \mathbf{I}_2, ..., \mathbf{I}_N\}$, sentences meme dataset : $\mathbf{S} = \{\mathbf{S}_1, \mathbf{S}_2, ..., \mathbf{S}_N\}$, parameters of encoder : $\mathbf{w}_e$, parameters of decoder : $\mathbf{w}_d$, parameters of LSTM : $\mathbf{w}_l$, parameters of dense layer : $\mathbf{w}_f$, AutoEncoder training epoch : k_a, image caption model training epoch : k_b, loss function: E

for $i = 1$ to k_a **do**
  $\mathbf{z} = encoder_{\mathbf{w}_{e,i}}(\mathbf{I})$
  $\hat{\mathbf{I}} = decoder_{\mathbf{w}_{d,i}}(\mathbf{z})$
  update $\mathbf{w}_{e,i}, \mathbf{w}_{d,i}$ to minimize $E(\mathbf{I}, \hat{\mathbf{I}})$
end for
for $i = 1$ to k_b **do**
  $\mathbf{z} = encoder_{\mathbf{w}_e}(\mathbf{I})$
  $\mathbf{y}, \mathbf{r}_i = lstm_{\mathbf{w}_{l,i}}(\mathbf{S}, \mathbf{r}_{i-1})$
  $\mathbf{x} = Concatenate(\mathbf{z}, \mathbf{y})$
  $\mathbf{p} = dense_{\mathbf{w}_{f,i}}(\mathbf{x})$
  update $\mathbf{w}_{l,i}, \mathbf{w}_{f,i}$ to minimize $E(\mathbf{S}, \mathbf{p})$
end for

3 Experimental Results

This section demonstrates the result of the memes for the images generated by GUMI-AE compared with the conventional model of NJM [9]. In addition, the details of the training dataset required to generate the memes, the evaluation of the reproducibility of the images by AutoEncoder, and the interestingness of the generated memes will be discussed.

3.1 Dataset for Training

Training an image caption generative model to generate memes for images requires a dataset in which images are paired with memes. However, no such dataset currently exists in the available open datasets. In this study, following the approach of [9] to create our dataset by scraping the Bokete [11] website which collects images of Japanese memes. The collected dataset consists of 69,365 images with 552,613 Japanese memes. These images were obtained starting with the earliest images posted on the Bokete. There are multiple memes per image. As a preprocessing step, special characters such as "!" and "?" from datasets were removed, and eliminated memes containing words that appear less than five times across the entire dataset. The number of memes suitable to a given image varied depending on the image.

3.2 Training of AutoEncoder

This section details the training process of AutoEncoder (AE) for the image encoder of the proposed image caption generative model. The architecture of the encoder of AE used here consists of six convolution layers and one dense layer,

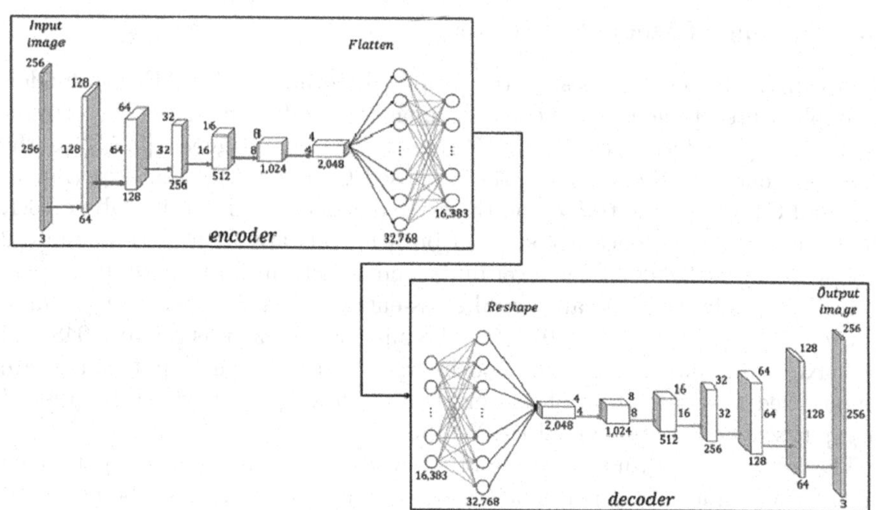

Fig. 5. The construction of AutoEncoder.

Table 1. The training result of AutoEncoder

input	output	input	output

whose output dimension is 16,384, and the decoder consists of one dense layer and six deconvolution layers. The detailed encoder and decoder construction is shown in Fig. 5. The red, orange, and blue lines indicate convolution, fully connected, and deconvolution. For each convolution and deconvolution layer, the kernel size is 3×3 and the stride is 2. The output of the decoder's output layer is input to the sigmoid function, and the outputs of all other layers are input to the LeakyReLU function. During AE training, each pixel of images is a normalized value ranging from 0 to 1. The MSE was set as the loss function and Adam ($\eta = 0.001, \beta_1 = 0.999, \beta_2 = 0.9$) [16] as the optimizer. The mini-batch size is 32, and the maximum training iterations is 150. Table 1 shows the training results of the AE. The input images in Table 1 were not used during training. The training results suggest that the implemented AE can adequately reconstruct the input image. This indicates that the AE encoder effectively extracts the image features.

3.3 Training of Meme Generator

To investigate the effectiveness of the proposed method GUMI-AE, two models are implemented to generate memes for images. The first model is the conventional NJM [9], which uses ResNet152 pre-trained on ImageNet [5,7,9] as the image encoder, and the second is the proposed GUMI-AE. In this experiment, NJM and GUMI-AE are trained on the same dataset introduced in Subsect. 3.1. The structures of sentence decoders in both models are 1,024 LSTM units, 2 total dense layers, 2,048 hidden layer units, and 48,480 output layer units, respectively. The loss function is categorical cross-entropy, and the optimizer is Adam ($\eta = 0.001, \beta_1 = 0.999, \beta_2 = 0.9$) [16]. The mini-batch size was set to 2,048 and the maximum number of training epochs was set to 100. The input images are standardized to a resolution of 224 pixels each in height and width because of the input size of the pre-trained ResNet152.

The results are shown in Figs. 6 and 7 which show the training loss per epoch and the training accuracy per epoch, respectively. In both figures, the proposed model GUMI-AE is drawn in red and the conventional model NJM is drawn in blue. These figures show that the proposed method has low training loss and high training accuracy. Therefore, it is concluded that GUMI-AE has better model performance. Since the two image caption generative models differ only in the image encoder and have the same network structure. The proposed structure namely, using AutoEncoder as a sentence decoder is suitable for the training performance of the image caption generative model.

Next, four sample memes generated by GUMI-AE and NJM and their input images are shown in Table 2. These images are not used in the training process. Each meme word is chosen by the roulette selection, which randomly selects a word according to a probability distribution output by an image caption generative model. This allows multiple sentences to be generated for a single image. Table 2(a) is the result of the illustration of Japanese Kabuki input. For this image, GUMI-AE generates the meme "Where's Wally". This meme is thought

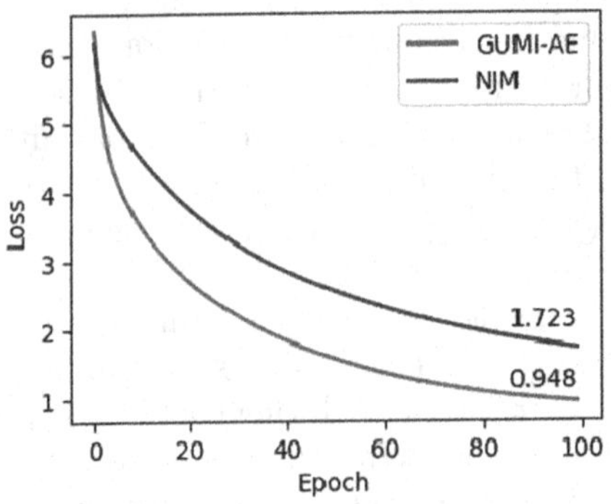

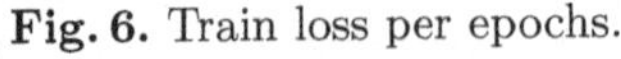
Fig. 6. Train loss per epochs.

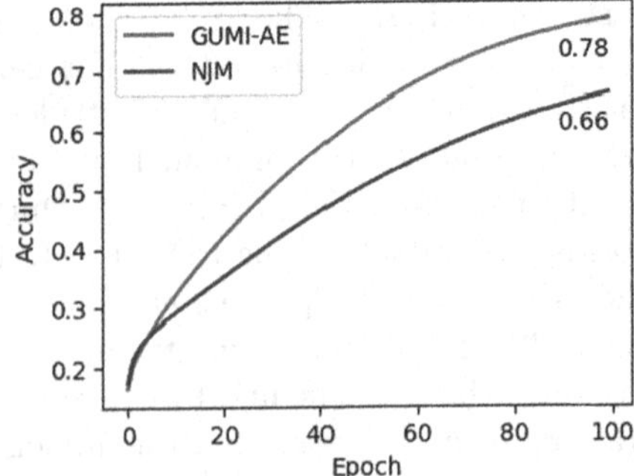

Fig. 7. Train accuracy per epochs.

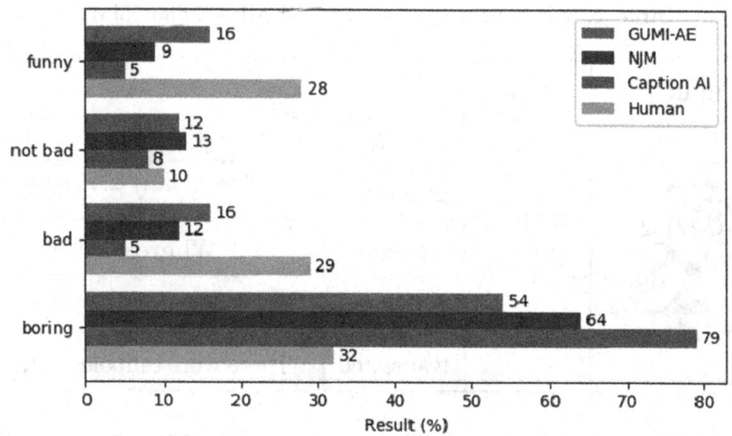

Fig. 8. The questionnaire results.

to be generated because the character in the illustration is similar in color scheme to the character in the picture book "Where's Wally?". It also can be seen that the Meme generated by NJM contains words that have no possible relevance to the image, such as "pot" and "tadpole". Table 2(b) is the result of the illustration of the baby wearing only the diaper input, and GUMI-AE generates the meme "Your zipper is open" for this image. Commenting "Your zipper is open" on the baby's diaper can cause a kind of misunderstanding or confusion since diapers usually do not have zippers. This creates a humorous surprise, an unexpected reversal, and a laugh. Contrary to this, the meme generated by NJM contains the unrelated word "sea". These two results show that GUMI-AE is able to extract features from illustration images more accurately than NJM. Table 2(c) is the result of inputting the photo of the woman. NJM fails to generate a meme that contains words that are relevant to the image, despite GUMI-AE generating a meme containing the word "Mam" and related words. This may be due to the fact that NJM's feature extractor is not highly accurate. Table 2(d) is the result of inputting the image contained in ImageNet. In response to the image of a starfish posing on land, GUMI-AE generates the sentence "Perform one last gag," which is a funny meme as it shows that the starfish is no longer able to move after being on land. NJM generated the meme "Captured jellyfish," which is also funny because it mistakes a starfish for a jellyfish. From these results, the proposed model GUMI-AE can generate more suitable memes for an image than NJM because of its higher learning accuracy, but it is considered that NJM can also generate suitable memes for the same image that has been pre-trained.

3.4 Evaluation of Humorous

Next, evaluating the proposed and conventional methods concerning humor ability is discussed. Unfortunately, at the present stage, it is impossible to automatically assess the humor ability of the generated memes. Therefore, in this study,

Table 2. The memes generated by GUMI-AE and NJM.

Input	Method		
(a)			
	GUMI-AE	generated	ウォーリーを探せ
		translated	Where's Wally
	NJM	generated	鍋にオタマジャクシが入っていた
		translated	There were tadpoles in the pot
(b)			
	GUMI-AE	generated	チャックが開いてるよぉ
		translated	Your zipper is open
	NJM	generated	海が割れるのよ
		translated	The sea will split
(c)			
	GUMI-AE	generated	ママこれ買って
		translated	Mom, buy this
	NJM	generated	100円落としたーーー
		translated	I dropped 100 yen···
(d)			
	GUMI-AE	generated	最後の一発ギャグを披露
		translated	Perform one last gag.
	NJM	generated	捕獲されたクラゲ
		translated	Captured jellyfish.

as in the conventional NJM [9] method, the humor ability of the sentences is evaluated by a questionnaire. The number of responding questionnaires was 509. As the target of the questionnaire, the sentences created by humans and uploaded in Bokete [11], and the sentences generated by the proposed method GUMI-AE,

NJM [9], and image caption generative model which uses a pre-trained model trained with STAIR caption dataset [17], the conventional research used [9]. As a questionnaire environment, one input image and one meme of each method were randomly selected and were shown on BoT which was created on one of the most particular SNS in Japan named LINE [18]. Respondents were allowed to look at the displayed image and meme and comment on them in four levels: "funny", "not bad", "bad" and "boring". Note that respondents only know whether the memes relative to the images are funny or not. The results of the questionnaire survey are shown in Fig. 8. In Fig. 8, the vertical axis is a four-level rating, and the horizontal axis is the percentage of responses. In the graph, red indicates the proposed method GUMI-AE, blue indicates NJM, green indicates caption AI, and orange indicates human. In this paper, the results "funny" and "not bad" are considered positive responses, and the items "bad" and "boring" are considered negative responses. Figure 8 shows that the caption AI trained on the STAIR Caption dataset receives more negative responses than the AI trained on the dataset combining images and memes. On the other hand, the proposed method GUMI-AE receives a 6% higher positive evaluation than the conventional method NJM. This is likely due to the higher suitability of the image encoder of the image caption generative model of the proposed method and the more accurate training of image captioning with the images in the training dataset. Comparing the proposed method GUMI-AE with humans, the percentage of positive responses to human memes is higher. One of the reasons for this result can be attributed to the fact that the proposed method uses roulette selection to select words from the probability distribution generated by the model, which sometimes results in the selection of inappropriate words. Therefore, it can be concluded that the proposed method GUMI-AE, even though it is inferior to the humor of human memes, is more accurate than the conventional model using pre-trained models for the image encoder of image caption generative model, and can generate memes that are appropriate for the images.

4 Conclusion

This paper proposed a new model, GUMI-AE, which uses the encoder of the AutoEncoder as the image encoder of the image caption generative model to generate memes appropriate for the Japanese meme "Ohgiri" for the images. Conventionally, an image caption generative model with pre-trained models as the image encoder has been used as an AI to generate memes for images. However, when using the pre-trained model, if there is domain divergence between the images for pre-training and the images for image caption training, the feature of the input image is not correctly extracted, and the meme suitable for the image cannot be created. To deal with this problem, a new model GUMI-AE, which uses the encoder of the AutoEncoder instead of pre-trained models was proposed in this paper. Experimental results show that the proposed model has higher learning accuracy than the conventional model and successfully generates memes suitable for images. In addition, since the encoder of AutoEncoder is used, the network structure can be freely configured, which has the advantage of matching the computational resources.

In future research, we will implement a generator using advanced networks such as Gated Recurrent Unit and Transformer to generate memes with higher accuracy and investigate the impact of the questionnaire on the results by taking into account the age and gender of the participants.

Acknowledgements. This work is supported by The Japan Society Promotion of Science (JSPS), KAKENHI (23K11267).

References

1. Goodfellow, I., et al.: Generative adversarial networks. Commun. ACM **63**(11), 139–144 (2020)
2. OpenAI. https://chat.openai.com, ChatGPT. Accessed 6 June 2023
3. Vinyals, O., et al.: Show and tell: a neural image caption generator. In: Proceedings of IEEE Computer Vision and Pattern Recognition (CVPR), pp. 3156–3164 (2015)
4. Akhther, N.: Internet Memes as Form of Cultural Discourse: A Rhetorical Analysis on Facebook. PsyArXiv (2021)
5. He, K., Zhang, et al.: Deep residual learning for image recognition. In: Proceedings of IEEE Computer Vision and Pattern Recognition (CVPR), pp. 770–778 (2016)
6. Szegedy, C., et al.: Rethinking the inception architecture for computer vision. In: Proceedings of IEEE Computer Vision and Pattern Recognition (CVPR), pp. 2818–2826 (2016)
7. Deng, J., et al.: ImageNet: a large-scale hierarchical image database. In: Proceedings of IEEE Computer Vision and Pattern Recognition (CVPR), pp. 248–255 (2009)
8. Peirson, V., et al.: Dank learning: generating memes using deep neural networks. arXiv preprint arXiv:1806.04510 (2018)
9. Yoshida, K., et al.: Neural joking machine: humorous image captioning. In: Proceedings of IEEE Computer Vision and Pattern Recognition Conference (CVPR) Language and Vision Workshop (2018)
10. Memegenerator.net. https://memegenerator.net. Accessed 7 June 2023
11. Omoroki INC. https://bokete.jp, Bokete. Accessed 7 June 2023
12. Hinton, G.E., et al.: Reducing the dimensionality of data with neural networks. Science **313**(5786), 504–507 (2006)
13. Graves, A., et al.: Long short-term memory. In: Supervised Sequence Labeling with Recurrent Neural Networks, vol. 385, pp. 37–45. Springer, Cham (2012). https://doi.org/10.1007/978-3-642-24797-2_4
14. LeCun, Y., et al.: Gradient-based learning applied to document recognition. Proc. IEEE **86**(11), 2278–2324 (1998)
15. Williams, R.J., et al.: A learning algorithm for continually running fully recurrent neural networks. Neural Comput. **1**(2), 270–280 (1989)
16. Kingma, D.P., et al.: Adam: a method for stochastic optimization. In: Proceedings of International Conference on Learning Representations (ICLR), pp. 1–13 (2015)
17. Yoshikawa, Y., et al.: STAIR captions: constructing a large-scale Japanese image caption dataset. In: Proceedings of Annual Meeting of the Association for Computational Linguistics (ACL), vol. 2, pp. 417–421 (2017)
18. LINE Corp. https://linecorp.com, LINE. Accessed 7 June 2023

MTMG: A Framework for Generating Adversarial Examples Targeting Multiple Learning-Based Malware Detection Systems

Lichen Jia[1,2], Yang Yang[3], Jiansong Li[6], Hao Ding[5], Jiajun Li[6], Ting Yuan[6], Lei Liu[4], and Zihan Jiang[6](✉)

[1] SKLP, Institute of Computing Technology, CAS, Beijing, China
[2] University of the Chinese Academy of Sciences, Beijing, China
[3] Institute of Technology, China University of Petroleum, Karamay Campus, Beijing, China
[4] Pukyong National University, Busan, South Korea
[5] NCMIS, Academy of Mathematics and Systems Science, CAS, Beijing, China
[6] Huawei Technologies Co., Ltd., Shenzhen, China
jiangzihan0512@gmail.com

Abstract. As machine learning technology continues to advance rapidly, an increasing number of researchers are utilizing it in the field of malware detection. Despite the fact that learning-based malware detection systems (LB-MDS) outperform traditional feature-based detection methods in terms of both performance and detection speed, recent research has shown that they are susceptible to attacks from adversarial examples. However, the adversarial examples generated thus far have only been effective against individual LB-MDS and have not been able to simultaneously attack multiple LB-MDS.

In this paper, we propose a black-box adversarial attack framework called Multi-Target Malware Generation (MTMG), which leverages reinforcement learning to simultaneously attack multiple LB-MDS. MTMG selects the obfuscation method and its corresponding parameters from the action space based on the observed state of the malware, and then applies them to generate adversarial examples that deceive multiple LB-MDS. Our results indicate that when simultaneously attacking multiple LB-MDS, including EMBER, MalConv, and six commercial antivirus software, MTMG significantly outperforms the state-of-the-art (SOTA) works, achieving an impressive attack success rate over 82%, while the SOTA works achieve a success rate of less than 6%.

Keywords: malware detection · black-box attack · reinforcement learning

1 Introduction

With the rapid advancement of machine learning, learning-based malware detection systems (LB-MDS) has demonstrated superiority in terms of both detec-

F. Liu et al. (Eds.): PRICAI 2023, LNAI 14325, pp. 249–261, 2024.
https://doi.org/10.1007/978-981-99-7019-3_24

tion speed and accuracy compared to traditional feature-based detection methods [5,12]. Notably, even mainstream commercial antivirus solutions are now integrating machine learning into their malware detection processes [1,14]. However, it is well-known that machine learning algorithms are susceptible to adversarial attacks [4,6]. Numerous studies [9,13] have provided evidence that LB-MDS is also vulnerable to adversarial examples. For instance, MalFox [17] employs adversarial generative networks (GANs) to generate adversarial examples by applying packing techniques to malwares.

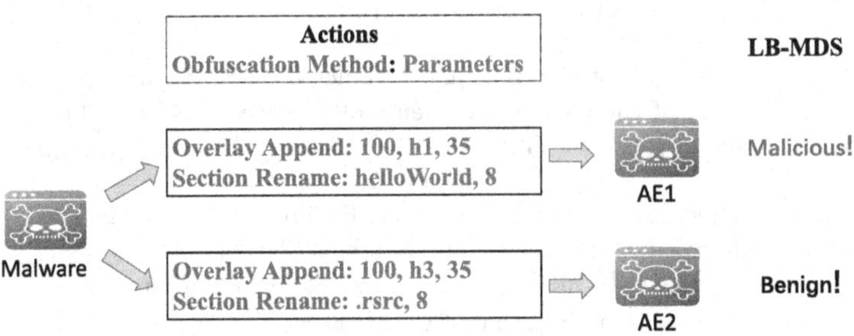

Fig. 1. We utilize the obfuscation techniques, Overlay Append and Section Rename, to obfuscate malware. These two methods are employed with distinct parameters, leading to the creation of adversarial examples AE1 and AE2, respectively. Notably, AE2 possesses the ability to mislead the LB-MDS into classifying the malware as a benign program, whereas AE1 does not achieve this feat.

However, current adversarial attacks on LB-MDS are specifically tailored to individual systems and do not possess the capability to target multiple LB-MDS simultaneously. Drawing parallels to the domain of image-based multi-target adversarial example generation [7,10], crafting adversarial examples that can compromise multiple LB-MDS carries two major implications: 1) Compared to the adversarial efforts where a separate model needs to be trained for each target, training a singular model that can attack multiple targets simultaneously can save the resources required to train additional models. 2) In military scenarios, adversarial examples need to overcome multiple adversaries to be triumphant, necessitating the ability to simultaneously attack various LB-MDS.

Through the analysis of existing LB-MDS adversarial works [4,6,13,17], we have identified two primary limitations. Firstly, the obfuscation methods used in these attacks are incapable of modifying all the features of the malware. Secondly, existing approaches primarily concentrate on selecting obfuscation methods and neglect the significance of obfuscation method parameters. As depicted in Fig. 1, even when applying the same obfuscation method to a malware sample, different parameter settings can result in distinct outcomes.

In this paper, we introduce a reinforcement learning-based adversarial attack framework named Multi-Target Malware Generation (MTMG). It selects the action, including both the obfuscation method and its corresponding parameters, based on the malware's state. MTMG generates adversarial examples capable of simultaneously attacking multiple black-box LB-MDS. When designing the action space, we meticulously considered the impact of each action on the malware's features, as depicted in Table 1 and Table 2. We ensured that by combining actions, the entire set of features of the malware can be altered. Unlike previous approaches [4,6,17] that primarily concentrate on obfuscation methods, MTMG distinguishes itself by considering both the obfuscation method and its parameters when selecting actions.

We conducted a comprehensive evaluation of MTMG's performance by targeting state-of-the-art (SOTA) LB-MDS, including EMBER [5], MalConv [12], and six commercial antivirus softwares, anonymously represented as AV1-AV6. The experimental results demonstrate that MTMG outperforms SOTA approaches in attacking both single LB-MDS and multiple LB-MDS systems. When targeting a single LB-MDS, MTMG achieves an attack success rate of over 90%. When simultaneously attacking multiple LB-MDS systems, MTMG achieves an impressive attack success rate over 82%. This paper makes the following contributions:

- This paper emphasizes the importance of the parameters associated with obfuscation methods in generating adversarial examples. It demonstrates that different parameter settings can result in distinct outcomes, even when utilizing the same obfuscation method.
- We propose MTMG, a framework that generates effective adversarial examples targeting multiple LB-MDS simultaneously by continuously selecting and applying optimal obfuscation methods and parameters based on the malware's state.
- We have demonstrated the effectiveness of MTMG in attacking LB-MDS. When attacking a single LB-MDS as well as simultaneously attacking multiple LB-MDS, MTMG achieves higher attack success rates compared to SOTA approaches.

2 Related Work

Existing black-box attacks on LB-MDS can be broadly classified into two categories: attacks based on adversarial instructions and attacks based on obfuscation actions.

Attacks Based on Adversarial Instructions. Attacks based on adversarial instructions [8,16] involve the insertion of carefully crafted instructions into malware. These adversarial instructions manipulate the malware in a way that LB-MDS misclassify the modified malware as benign. For instance, DeepMal achieves this by strategically inserting *NOP* instructions into the malicious code, ensuring that the malicious functionality remains intact while deceiving LB-MDS.

However, it is worth noting that this category of attacks is typically designed to target a single LB-MDS and lacks the ability to generate adversarial examples capable of simultaneously attacking multiple LB-MDS.

Attacks Based on Obfuscation Actions. Attacks based on obfuscation actions aim to deceive LB-MDS by applying obfuscation techniques to malware.

These methods, as described in the works by MAB and MalFox [13,17], dynamically select appropriate obfuscation techniques based on the varying states of malware, allowing the malware to be misidentified as benign by LB-MDS. For instance, MalFox employs various packing and obfuscation techniques, leveraging adversarial generative networks (GANs) to select different obfuscation methods and their combinations for malware based on its specific state.

While these methods have demonstrated that LB-MDS can still be vulnerable to adversarial examples, the generated adversarial examples are only effective against a single LB-MDS and cannot simultaneously attack multiple LB-MDS. Generating adversarial examples capable of attacking multiple LB-MDS remains a challenging task.

3 Design and Implementation

3.1 MTMG Overview

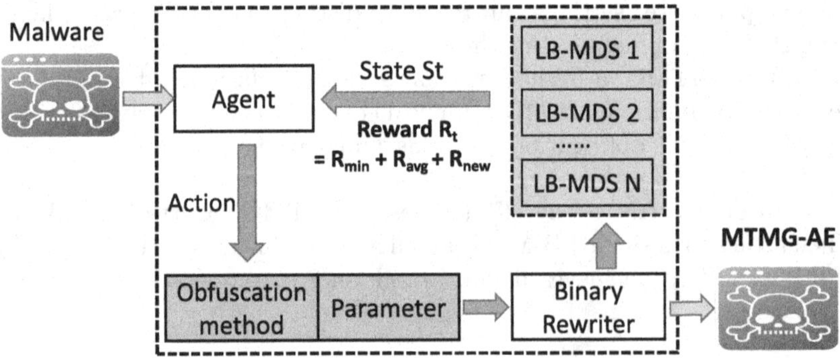

Fig. 2. The framework of MTMG.

To empower MTMG in the selection of the most suitable action (obfuscation method and the corresponding parameters) for malware, we employ a reinforcement learning (RL) algorithm [15]. The RL algorithm learns by interacting with the environment (LB-MDS 1 to LB-MDS N) and strives to maximize a cumulative reward signal. Within the framework of MTMG, the RL Agent assumes the role of a decision-maker, consistently monitoring the state of the malware and making action choices according to its policy.

The framework comprises three essential components: the Agent, Binary Rewriter, and LB-MDS, as illustrated in Fig. 2. When presented with a malware sample, the Agent chooses an action for the malware. Subsequently, the Binary Rewriter generates a modified version of the malware by applying the selected obfuscation method and its associated parameters. The detector consists of multiple LB-MDS capable of detecting malware, and it produces a tuple

$< P_{LB-MDS_1}, P_{LB-MDS_2}, ..., P_{LB-MDS_N} >$, where P_{LB-MDS_N} represents the detection outcome of the N_{th} LB-MDS, indicating whether the software is classified as benign or malicious.

When designing MTMG, we primarily consider the following questions:

- Q1) How to design the action space of the MTMG to enable its actions to modify all the features of a binary file?
- Q2) How to design the reward function of MTMG to generate adversarial examples that can effectively counter multiple LB-MDS?

3.2 Q1's Solution

When constructing the action space, as depicted in Table 1, MTMG incorporates binary-level obfuscation and packing obfuscation as its utilized obfuscation methods. Each obfuscation category encompasses multiple distinct obfuscation techniques, each of which comes with its own set of parameters. Taking *Overlay Append* as an example, this obfuscation method involves selecting content of a specified size (specified by the "Overlay Size" parameter) from a specific file (specified by the "Overlay File" parameter) and inserting it into the binary at the file offset (specified by the "Overlay Offset" parameter). The range of values for the "Overlay File" and "Overlay Size" parameters is denoted as [1:∞] because they can select any content from any file. However, the "Overlay Offset" parameter is limited to values up to the size of the file, so its range is represented as [1:N].

To ensure that all features of the malware can be modified by the obfuscation methods in our action space, we initially categorized the program features into Hash-based features, Rule-based features, and Data Distribution, as described in [13]. We also annotated which features are affected by each obfuscation method in action space. If an obfuscation method om modifies the feature set $S = \{s_1, s_2, ..., s_k\}$ of a malware sample, the impact of various obfuscation methods on the affected features can be observed in Table 2 within our framework.

For example, consider the IS obfuscation method, which replaces instructions in binary file with semantically equivalent instructions. From Table 2, it can be observed that this method affects the File Hash, Section Hash, and Code Sequence features. Since IS can replace any instructions in binary file with semantically equivalent instructions, this obfuscation method can completely modify the File Hash and Code Sequence features. Its partial modification of the Section Hash feature is due to the method's capability of modifying only the code section, without affecting the data section or other sections.

As depicted in Table 2, these obfuscation techniques in action space can modify all features of a binary file, enabling MTMG to modify all detection features of LB-MDS.

3.3 Q2's Solution

The objective of MTMG is to generate adversarial examples capable of simultaneously evading multiple LB-MDS systems. Given a malware x, it undergoes t rounds of obfuscation actions to produce x_t. The resulting x_t is then subjected to detection by multiple LB-MDS, yielding a detection result of $D_t = (P_{LB-MDS_1}, P_{LB-MDS_2}, ..., P_{LB-MDS_N})$, where P_{LB-MDS_N} represents the detection result of $LB - MDS_N$ for x_t, with 1 indicating benign program and 0 indicating malicious program.

Table 1. Obfuscation methods and their corresponding parameter ranges in the MTMG action space. The notation $[1 : N]$ denotes finite parameter ranges, while $[1 : \infty]$ represents infinite parameter ranges.

Category	Name	Abbr	Description	Parameters
Binary Obfuscation	Overlay Append	OA	Append code or data at the end of the code region in a binary file	Overlay File: [1:∞], [Overlay Offset, Overlay Size]: [1:N]
	Section Padding	SP	Append random bytes to the unused space at the end of a section in a binary file	[Random Byte Length, Random Byte Generation Method, Section Name]: [1:N]
	Section Add	SA	Add new sections to a binary file	[Section Name, Section Size, Section contents]: [1:∞], [Section Flags, Section Address]: [1:N]
	Section Rename	SR	Alter the names of sections within a binary file	New Section Name:[1:∞], Section Index:[1:N]
	Instruction Substitution	IS	Replace instructions with semantically equivalent instructions	[Original Instruction, Equivalent Instruction, Operand Mapping, Compatibility Check, Performance Considerations]:[1:N]
Packing Obfuscation	Code Encryption	CE	Transforming code into an encrypted form, decrypting the encrypted code during runtime	[Encryption Algorithm, Code Offset, Code Size, Decryption Routine]:[1:N], [Encryption Key, Key Length, Block Size, Iterations]:[1:∞]
	Code Compression	CC	Reduce the size of executable code by applying compression algorithms	[Compression Algorithm, Code Offset, Code Size, Compression Level, Decompression Routine]:[1:N]
	Binary Packing	BP	The process of Compressing or encrypting a binary and then embedding it into a self-extracting loader	**Include parameters in Code Encryption and Code Compression**, [loader]:[1:N]
	Binary Packing to Benign	BPB	Building upon Binary Packing, this technique involves the storage of the encrypted or compressed binary and loader within a benign program	**Include parameters in Binary Packing**, Benign program:[1:∞]
	Binary Packing and Encryption	BPE	Building upon binary packing, this technique encrypts the loader, resulting in a reduced size for the loader	**Include parameters in Binary Packing**, Encryption Parameters for loader:[Encryption Algorithm, Decryption Routine]:[1:N]
	Binary Packing and ROP Encryption	BPR	Building upon binary packing, this technique utilizes ROP gadgets to achieve the functionality of the decompression or decryption routine	**Include parameters in Binary Packing**, [Gadgets Selection, Gadget Chain Construction]:[1:N]
	IAT Hooking	Hook	Redirect function calls by manipulating the Import Address Table (IAT)	[Hook Function, Hook Injection Point, Hook Activation Condition, Hook Restoration]:[1:N]
	API Obfuscation	AO	Disguise the names, signatures, or usage patterns of application programming interfaces (APIs) in software code	[API Renaming, API Signature Modification, String Encryption]:[1:∞], Dynamic API Loading:[1:N]
	Dynamic Loading	DL	The process of loading software components or modules at runtime	[Module or Library Selection, Loading Location, loader]:[1:N], Loading Conditions:[1:∞]

Table 2. The affected features by obfuscation methods are indicated by ●, ◑, and ○, representing complete modification, partial modification, and slight modification of the respective feature.

		Hash-Based features		Rule-based features							Data Distribution
		File Hash	Section Hash	Section Count	Section Name	Section Padding	Debug Info	Control Flow	API Calls	Code Sequence	Data Distribution
Binary Obfuscation	OA	●	◑			○					○
	SP	●	◑			●					
	SA	●	◑	●	●						◑
	SR	●			●						
	IS	●	◑							●	
Packing Obfuscation	CE	●	●	◑	◑	◑		●	◑	◑	
	CC	●	●	◑	◑	◑		●	◑	◑	
	BP	●	●	●	●	●	●	●	◑	◑	●
	BPB	●	●	●	●	●	●	●	◑	◑	●
	BPE	●	●	●	●	●	●	●	◑	◑	●
	BPR	●	●	●	●	●	●	●	◑	●	●
	Hook	●	◑	◑				◑			
	AO	●	◑						●	◑	◑
	DL	●	◑	◑					◑	◑	

The reward function of MTMG, defined by Eq. 1, comprises three components: R_{min}, R_{avg}, and R_{new}, along with their corresponding weights W_{min}, W_{avg}, and W_{new}. R_{min} denotes the minimum value of the D_t tupple, R_{avg} denotes the average value of the D_t tuple, and R_{new} denotes the number of newly deceived LB-MDS systems compared to the (t-1) round.

$$R_t = R_{min} * w_{min} + R_{avg} * w_{avg} + R_{new} * w_{new} \tag{1}$$

$$R_{min} = min(D_t) \tag{2}$$

$$R_{avg} = sum(D_t)/N \tag{3}$$

$$R_{new} = sum(max(0, D_t - D_{t-1})) \tag{4}$$

3.4 Training Algorithm

Algorithm 1 outlines the training process of MTMG. In each training episode, the agent makes decisions on the action and its corresponding parameters to be taken based on the current malware input. Subsequently, the binary rewriter modifies the malware X_t based on the action and parameters chosen by the agent, resulting in the modified malware X_{t+1}. The modified software x_{t+1} is then subjected to detection by multiple LB-MDS, and the reward is computed according to Eq. 1. This process is repeated until the malware can be classified as benign by all LB-MDS, or the maximum number of modifications, $MAXTURN$, is reached. The detailed descriptions and settings of the parameter are shown in Table 3.

Algorithm 1: Training Algorithm.

Input: θ: network parameter θ, $EPISODES$: The total number of malware to load, $MAXTURN$: The maximum number of actions to use on a sample, LB-MDS: all LB-MDS used to detect in environment.

Output: Trained RL model

Initialize training environment with LB-MDS;
Initialize agent $agent_{MTMG}$ with parameter θ
for $episode = 1$ *to* $EPISODES$ **do**
  Select a malware sample x from the training dataset D_{train};
  S_{init} = x;
  for $t = 1$ *to* $MAXTURN$ **do**
    Choose an obfuscation method a_t and its corresponding parameters P from the action space;
    Modify x_t by obfuscation method a_t and its corresponding parameters P to x_{t+1};
    $s_{t+1} = x_{t+1}$;
    To detect s_{t+1} using LB-MDS, compute the reward r_{t+1} using Equation 1;
    Exert Adam optimizer to optimize parameter θ;
    if *Malware* x_{t+1} *can deceive all LB-MDS* **then**
      break;

4 Evaluation

Dataset. In our experiment, we collected a dataset of 35,000 malware samples from VirusShare for the year 2022. Out of these, 30,000 samples were used as the training set, while the remaining 5,000 samples were used as the testing set.

Comparison Targets. We compare our MTMG-Malware framework with SOTA attack frameworks: MAB [13] and MalFox [17]. MAB is a reinforcement learning-based black-box attack framework that uses a predefined set of actions to manipulate PE files and generates adversarial examples by adjusting the probability of each action being selected based on the reward. On the other hand, MalFox is a GAN-based attack framework that leverages packing obfuscation methods to generate adversarial malware examples.

Attack Targets. For our attack targets, we have chosen the following:

- EMBER [5] is a gradient boosted decision tree model that was trained on the EMBER dataset using LightGBM. We utilized a model provided by the Machine Learning Security Evasion Competition (MLSEC) 2019.
- MalConv [12] is a malware detection model that directly trains on the binary bytes of malwares. We utilized a model provided by the MLSEC 2019 [2].
- Commercial AVs. According to PC Magazine [3], we have selected six top commercial antivirus software.

Table 3. Implementation details of the MTMG model.

Parameter	Value	Description
EPISODES	30000	The total number of loaded malware files into environment
MAX_TURNS	30	Maximum number of actions to perform on a sample
γ	0.95	Discount factor for reward
w_{min}	0.8	Weights of elements of reward
w_{avg}	0.1	Weights of elements of reward
w_{new}	0.1	Weights of elements of reward
Learning rate	$3 * 10^{-4}$	The learning rate of Adam

Evaluation Metrices. Consistent with prior research [11], we utilize the attack success rate to evaluate the effectiveness of our adversarial attack. The definition of attack success rate is illustrated in Eq. 5, where $Targets = \{LB{-}MDS_1, LB{-}MDS_2, ..., LB - MDS_N\}$ denotes the target LB-MDS, Num_e represents the number of adversarial examples that can simultaneously attack multiple LB-MDS, and Num_A represents the total number of adversarial examples.

$$ASR = Num_M / Num_A \tag{5}$$

To facilitate future research utilizing adversarial examples produced by MTMG, we have established a GitHub repository, available at https://github.com/mtmg-malware/MTMG.

4.1 Attack on Single LB-MDS

This experiment evaluates the attack success rates of MalFox, MAB, and our MTMG when targeting a single LB-MDS. As depicted in Fig. 4, the results reveal that the success rate of utilizing raw malware against MalConv, EMBER, and commercial antivirus software AV1-AV6 is below 20%.

After undergoing MalFox's processing, the malware demonstrates a attack success rate surpassing 60% in attacking commercial antivirus software AV1-AV6. However, its attack success rate diminishes to less than 27% when targeting MalConv and EMBER. In contrast, MAB achieves a attack success rate below 47% when attacking commercial antivirus software AV1-AV6, but it surpasses 76% attack success rate against MalConv and EMBER. In our work, MTMG achieves a attack success rate exceeding 90% in attacking both commercial antivirus software AV1-AV6, MalConv, and EMBER. This is primarily due to MTMG's action space encompassing obfuscation techniques capable of modifying all the features of malware. As a result, MTMG gains the ability to manipulate all the malware features, leading to a high success rate in attacking a single LB-MDS.

Table 4. We utilize MalFox, MAB, and MTMG to launch attacks against MalConv, EMBER, and commercial antivirus software AV1-AV6.

LB-MDS	Malwares (%)	MalFox (%)	MAB (%)	MTMG (%)
AV1	2.52	65.39	23.97	90.48
AV2	6.13	60.96	30.72	94.20
AV3	3.69	68.18	35.97	91.85
AV4	2.78	67.19	46.37	93.31
AV5	7.94	73.31	41.78	95.97
AV6	3.91	68.01	36.18	96.35
MalConv	17.35	26.47	95.63	97.24
EMBER	3.76	12.69	76.18	93.72

4.2 Attack on Multiple LB-MDS

This experiment evaluates the attack success rates of MalFox, MAB, and our MTMG when simultaneously attacking multiple LB-MDS. As shown in Fig. 5, it is evident that our MTMG significantly outperforms the SOTA approaches in terms of attacking multiple LB-MDS.

Table 5. AVs refer to commercial antivirus software AV1-AV6, while MCEM represents the combined use of MalConv and EMBER for detection. Additionally, MCEM+AVs represents the combination of MCEM and AVs. We utilize MalFox, MAB, and MTMG to conduct simultaneous attacks against AVs, MCEM, as well as MCEM+AVs.

LB-MDS	Malwares (%)	MalFox (%)	MAB (%)	MTMG (%)
AVs	0	51.72	5.75	84.43
MCEM	0.79	6.42	15.96	90.32
MCEM+AVs	**0**	**5.25**	**1.93**	**82.69**

The original malware exhibited an attack success rate of less than 1% when targeting AVs, MCEM, and MCEM+AVs. MalFox achieved an attack success rate of 51.72% against AVs, but its success rate decreased to below 7% when targeting MCEM and MCEM+AVs. MAB's attack success rate against AVs, MCEM, and MCEM+AVs all remained below 16%. In contrast, our MTMG maintained an attack success rate of over 80% against AVs, MCEM, and

MCEM+AVs. This is primarily due to the reward function of MTMG, which places a greater emphasis on actions that can simultaneously influence multiple LB-MDS. This attribute of MTMG prompts it to favor obfuscation techniques and parameters that have a higher likelihood of concurrently deceiving multiple LB-MDS during its action selection process. Consequently, this characteristic leads to the generation of adversarial examples by MTMG that demonstrate superior attack performance against multiple LB-MDS.

4.3 Algorithm Efficiency Evaluation

This experiment assessed the efficiency of MTMG in attacking multiple LB-MDS. From Fig. 3a, it can be observed that both Default and Random achieve attack success rates below 30% against MCEM, but their success rates against AVs exceed 50%. This difference is primarily due to the fact that AVs predominantly rely on program features, and MTMG's obfuscation space can modify all features of the malicious software. This enables Default and Random to achieve higher attack success rates against AVs. However, some LB-MDS like MCEM, which are neural network-based, rely not only on static program features but also learn from a neural network perspective how to distinguish benign programs from malicious ones. For example, normal programs might not exhibit excessive encrypted data or specific API call sequences. Consequently, the attack success rates of Default and Random against MCEM are lower.

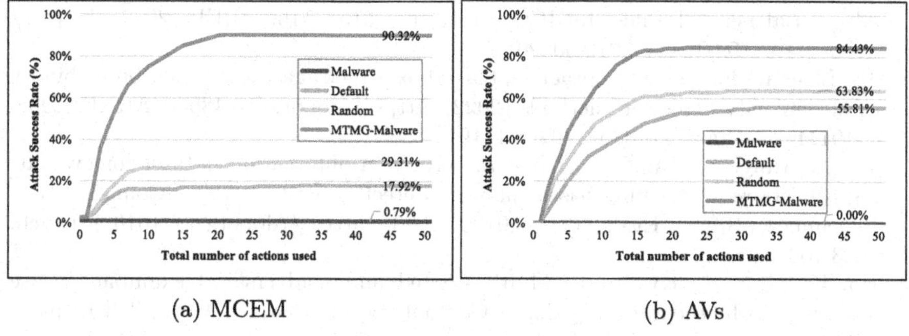

(a) MCEM (b) AVs

Fig. 3. Attack success rates of adversarial examples against multiple LB-MDS. Labels indicate: original malware rate, rate with default obfuscation parameters, rate with random obfuscation parameters, and rate achieved by MTMG.

MTMG's ability to achieve high attack success rates against both MCEM and AVs is attributed to its feedback-driven decision system, which selects appropriate parameters based on the current state of the malicious software. For instance, it hides specific APIs to evade detection based on specific API call sequences. As a result, MTMG-Malware outperforms Default and Random in terms of attack success rates as well as the number of actions used.

5 Conclusion

This paper introduces MTMG, a reinforcement learning-based attack framework. MTMG selects obfuscation methods and their associated parameters based on the current state of the malware, producing adversarial examples capable of attacking multiple LB-MDS simultaneously. Empirical results demonstrate that MTMG surpasses existing adversarial attack methodologies in attack success rate, both when targeting a single LB-MDS and when concurrently attacking multiple LB-MDS.

References

1. Avast 2018. ai & machine learning (2018). https://www.avast.com/en-us/technology/aiand-machine-learning
2. Machine learning static evasion competition 2019 (2019). https://github.com/endgameinc/malware_evasion_competition
3. The best antivirus protection (2020). https://www.pcmag.com/picks/thebest-antivirus-protection
4. Al-Dujaili, A., Huang, A., Hemberg, E., OReilly, U.M.: Adversarial deep learning for robust detection of binary encoded malware, pp. 76–82, May 2018. https://doi.org/10.1109/SPW.2018.00020
5. Anderson, H.S., Roth, P.: EMBER: An Open Dataset for Training Static PE Malware Machine Learning Models. ArXiv e-prints, April 2018
6. Anderson, H., Kharkar, A., Filar, B., Evans, D., Roth, P.: Learning to evade static pe machine learning malware models via reinforcement learning, January 2018
7. Han, J., et al.: Once a MAN: towards multi-target attack via learning multi-target adversarial network once. In: ICCV 2019, pp. 5157–5166. IEEE (2019). https://doi.org/10.1109/ICCV.2019.00526
8. Jia, L., et al.: Funcfooler: a practical black-box attack against learning-based binary code similarity detection methods (2022). https://doi.org/10.48550/ARXIV.2208.14191. https://arxiv.org/abs/2208.14191
9. Jia, L., Yang, Y., Tang, B., Jiang, Z.: Ermds: a obfuscation dataset for evaluating robustness of learning-based malware detection system. BenchCouncil Trans. Benchmarks Stand. Eval. **3**(1), 100106 (2023). https://doi.org/10.1016/j.tbench.2023.100106
10. Ko, K., Kim, S., Kwon, H.: Multi-targeted audio adversarial example for use against speech recognition systems. Comput. Secur. **128**(C), May 2023. https://doi.org/10.1016/j.cose.2023.103168
11. Mingxing, D., Li, K., Xie, L., Tian, Q., Xiao, B.: Towards multiple black-boxes attack via adversarial example generation network. In: Proceedings of the 29th ACM International Conference on Multimedia, pp. 264–272 (2021)
12. Raff, E., Barker, J., Sylvester, J., Brandon, R., Catanzaro, B., Nicholas, C.K.: Malware detection by eating a whole exe. ArXiv abs/1710.09435 (2017)
13. Song, W., Li, X., Afroz, S., Garg, D., Kuznetsov, D., Yin, H.: Mab-malware: a reinforcement learning framework for blackbox generation of adversarial malware, ASIA CCS 2022, pp. 990–1003 (2022). https://doi.org/10.1145/3488932.3497768
14. Team., M.D.A.R.: New machine learning model sifts through the good to unearth the bad in evasive malware (2019). https://www.microsoft.com/security/blog/2019/07/25/new-machine-learning-model-sifts-through-the-good-to-unearth-the-bad-in-evasive-malware/

15. Wang, Z., Schaul, T., Hessel, M., Hasselt, H., Lanctot, M., Freitas, N.: Dueling network architectures for deep reinforcement learning. In: International Conference on Machine Learning, pp. 1995–2003. PMLR (2016)
16. Yang, C., et al.: DeepMal: maliciousness-Preserving adversarial instruction learning against static malware detection. Cybersecurity **4**(1), 1–14 (2021). https://doi.org/10.1186/s42400-021-00079-5
17. Zhong, F., Cheng, X., Yu, D., Gong, B., Song, S., Yu, J.: Malfox: camouflaged adversarial malware example generation based on c-gans against black-box detectors. ArXiv abs/2011.01509 (2020)

Semantic Segmentation of Remote Sensing Architectural Images Based on GAN and UNet3+ Model

Weiwei Ding[1,2,3], Hanming Huang[1,2,3(✉)], and Yuan Wang[1,2,3]

[1] Key Lab of Education Blockchain and Intelligent Technology, Ministry of Education, Guangxi Normal University, Guilin 541004, China
{Dingww,wangyuan95}@stu.gxnu.edu.cn, huanghm@gxnu.edu.cn

[2] Guangxi Key Lab of Multi-Source Information Mining and Security, Guangxi Normal University, Guilin 541004, China

[3] School of Computer Science and Engineering, Guangxi Normal University, Guilin 541004, China

Abstract. Semantic segmentation of remote sensing building images can provide important data support for urban planning and resource management. It also plays a crucial role in assessing building density, monitoring urban expansion, and optimizing traffic planning. In recent times, with the continuous integration of computer vision and deep learning, Convolutional Neural Networks (CNNs) have achieved outstanding results in semantic segmentation tasks for remote sensing images. Although deep CNNs can significantly improve the accuracy of semantic segmentation for remote sensing images, some network models used for segmentation tasks still have limitations, such as low segmentation precision and inadequate feature extraction. In this paper, we propose an adversarial semantic segmentation network based on Generative Adversarial Networks (GANs). To better extract the features and semantics of buildings in remote sensing images, we introduce the UNet3+ network as the segmentation network of the adversarial network for the first time and make improvements to the UNet3+ network. We add the scSE (Spatial Channel Squeeze and Excitation) attention mechanism to the network, the scSE attention mechanism enhances the network's perception of different channel features by considering their correlations in the channel dimension, allowing it to capture fine-grained details and coarse-grained semantics at the full scale. In this paper, we conduct experiments on the Inria Aerial Image Labeling dataset, and the results show that our method outperforms other network models mentioned in the paper in terms of performance.

Keywords: Generate adversarial network · Remote sensing image · UNet3+ · Semantic segmentation

1 Introduction

Buildings are important components of cities, and due to their diverse forms of expression, the identification and extraction of building information are currently a hotspot and challenge in high-resolution remote sensing image applications. There has been a

F. Liu et al. (Eds.): PRICAI 2023, LNAI 14325, pp. 262–273, 2024.
https://doi.org/10.1007/978-981-99-7019-3_25

considerable amount of research on accurately and automatically extracting buildings from remote sensing images. Semantic segmentation of remote sensing building images is widely applied for various purposes, including urban planning, cartography, risk and loss assessment of natural disasters, land use, and urban modeling [1].

Semantic segmentation methods for remote sensing building images include traditional segmentation methods and methods based on convolutional neural networks (CNNs). The traditional segmentation methods can be categorized into the following five types: pixel-based segmentation methods, including thresholding methods and clustering methods; edge detection-based methods; region-based methods; mathematical theory-based methods, such as Markov random fields; and metaheuristic algorithm-based methods, including artificial neural networks [2] and genetic algorithms [3]. However, traditional segmentation methods often exhibit low efficiency and accuracy in extracting building information from remote sensing images.

With the rise of neural network models and the development of deep learning, an increasing number of researchers are applying deep neural networks to semantic segmentation tasks for remote sensing images. Compared to traditional semantic segmentation methods, the main difference lies in the fact that convolutional neural networks (CNNs) can automatically learn image features and enable end-to-end learning, thereby improving the accuracy and efficiency of semantic segmentation. In the field of semantic segmentation for remote sensing building images, Xiang Li et al. [4] proposed a segmentation method based on an enhanced multi-scale convolutional neural network. This method primarily adopts the U-Net network and introduces cascaded dilated convolutions within the U-Net network to capture objects at different scales, achieving good segmentation results. Yuting Zhu et al. [5] introduced an Edge-Detail Network (E-D-Net) for semantic segmentation, which consists of two sub-networks: The E-Net captures and preserves edge information from images, and the D-Net refines the results from the E-Net to achieve predictions with higher detail quality. Yue Qiu et al. [6] proposed an efficient network structure called MSL-Net, which focuses on multi-scale building features and multi-level image features. The network incorporates deep separable convolutions (DSC) and atrous spatial pyramid pooling (ASPP) modules to enhance the model's feature extraction capabilities for irregular-shaped buildings. Renhe Zhang et al. [7] proposed a network structure called the Shunted Dual Skip Connection UNet (SDSC-UNet), which introduces a new dual skip connection structure in the network and incorporates Vision Transformer (ViT) into the encoder to fully exploit semantic information from the image.

Although the aforementioned segmentation methods have achieved good segmentation results, they still have some limitations. For example, they employ convolution and pooling operations to aggregate contextual information. However, due to their relatively limited receptive field, they face challenges in capturing the overall global context of buildings within remote sensing images, particularly in cases of densely distributed buildings or significant variations in sizes. Their effectiveness in capturing building boundaries and textures in remote sensing data is compromised. On the other hand, the convolution and pooling operations lead to the loss of spatial details, consequently, relying solely on upsampling from deep semantic features can yield coarse and inaccurate segmentation outcomes. Therefore, in this paper, we propose an adversarial network based on Generative Adversarial Networks (GANs) for the segmentation of remote sensing building images. We utilize the U-Net3+ network as the segmentation network within the adversarial network, which is a convolutional neural network consisting of an encoder-decoder structure. Furthermore, we add the scSE attention module to the encoder part of UNet3+ to further enhance the segmentation accuracy. The scSE attention mechanism utilizes contextual information by analyzing both spatial and channel-wise relationships within the data. By combining both spatial and channel-wise information, the scSE mechanism effectively captures contextual cues present in the input data, allowing the network to adaptively emphasize informative features during various tasks such as semantic segmentation. Finally, we validate the performance of the proposed method through experiments and compare it with the methods pro-posed in references [4–7].

2 Related Work

In this section, we first review classical deep neural network models used for semantic segmentation tasks and discuss their advantages and limitations. Then, we introduce the GAN model and its application in semantic segmentation. Finally, we review the benefits of applying attention mechanisms to semantic segmentation tasks.

2.1 Deep Neural Network

Semantic segmentation is one of the fundamental tasks in computer vision, aiming to assign a category to each pixel in an image. In recent years, with the development of deep neural networks, researchers have started applying DCNNs (Deep Convolutional Neural Networks) to the field of semantic segmentation and have designed a series of excellent network models. Here, let's briefly review some classic DCNNs networks, including FCN (Fully Convolutional Network), UNet.

In 2015, Jonathan Long and Evan Shelhamer [8], among others, proposed the Fully Convolutional Network (FCN) architecture, which was the first application of a fully convolutional neural network in the field of semantic segmentation. They trans-formed the fully connected layers of the network into convolutional layers, reduced the size of image features through pooling operations to decrease computational complexity, increase the receptive field, and prevent overfitting. They also introduced upsampling through deconvolution, enabling the network to accept inputs of arbitrary image sizes. However, FCN has some limitations. When upsampling is performed through deconvolution, the results can still be blurry and less sensitive to image details.

In 2015, Olaf Ronneberger and colleagues proposed the U-Net [9], a U-shaped network architecture based on an encoder-decoder framework. The encoder, in the first half of the network, performs downsampling for feature extraction, while the decoder, in the second half, performs upsampling to increase the receptive field. The U-Net network utilizes its U-shaped structure to propagate contextual information to higher-resolution layers. U-Net has the advantage of achieving superior segmentation results with fewer training data. However, U-Net was primarily designed for medical image segmentation.

Subsequently, researchers introduced variations of U-Net, such as UNet+ and UNet3+ [10], which demonstrated improved segmentation performance compared to the original U-Net network.

Although deep learning has achieved promising results in semantic segmentation, the aforementioned deep learning models still have some limitations when it comes to segmenting remote sensing images of buildings. For instance, factors like occlusion, shadows, and scale variations that may be present in remote sensing building images can negatively impact the model's performance. Additionally, using deep learning models for segmentation requires a large amount of labeled data and do-main expertise, which can be challenging in practical applications due to the difficulty of annotating remote sensing image data. Consequently, obtaining satisfactory segmentation results with these methods may be limited by the challenges associated with labeling remote sensing data.

2.2 Generative Adversarial Network

Since the proposal of Generative Adversarial Networks (GANs) by Ian Goodfellow in 2014 [11], GANs have achieved tremendous success in the field of artificial intelligence, particularly in computer vision. They have been applied in various tasks such as face generation, object generation, and semantic segmentation [12]. GAN consists of two competing neural networks: the generator and the discriminator. Its core idea is to achieve the goal of generating realistic sample data through the adversarial training between these two networks. Reference [12] first proposed the application of GANs to the task of semantic segmentation. The core idea was to replace the generator in the GAN with a semantic segmentation network, and during training, the segmentation network was optimized using multi-class cross-entropy. In this paper, a similar approach is adopted by replacing the generator with an enhanced UNet3+ network. In recent years, numerous scholars have integrated Generative Adversarial Networks (GANs) into semantic segmentation tasks involving remote sensing imagery. However, when it comes to segmenting remote sensing images of buildings, certain limitations persist. Factors such as the inherent complexity and density of remote sensing building images, as well as significant variations in shapes, contribute to suboptimal segmentation results achieved by these networks.

2.3 Attention Mechanism

In 2014, V Mnih et al. [13] first combined recurrent neural networks (RNNs) with attention and applied them to computer vision. The basic idea of atten-tion mechanism in computer vision is to enable the model to concentrate and focus on important information while disregarding unimportant information. The essence of the attention mechanism is to learn the weight distribution using relevant feature maps and then apply the learned weights to the original feature maps for weighted summation. In the field of computer vision, attention mechanisms are typically categorized into three main domains for analysis: spatial domain, channel domain, and hybrid domain. The commonly used ones in convolutional neural networks are spatial attention and channel attention. Sometimes a hybrid attention that combines spatial and channel attention is used, with CBAM [14] and scSE [15] being representative examples of hybrid attention modules. The scSE attention module combines cSE and sSE modules and introduces both spatial and channel attention. In this paper, we combine the scSE module with UNet3+ to further improve the performance of semantic segmentation.

3 Research Method

3.1 Network Structure

In reference [25], the FISS GAN was introduced for semantic segmentation of foggy images. This approach involved the design of two segmentation networks: the Edge GAN for capturing image edges and the Semantic Segmentation GAN for full image segmentation. In reference [26], the Spine-GAN was proposed for segmenting complex spinal structures. A key innovation was the incorporation of a Long Short-Term Memory (LSTM) module into the segmentation network for image segmentation. In comparison to the aforementioned segmentation networks, this study primarily combines the attention mechanism with the UNet3+ network as the segmentation network within the adversarial framework. The overall structure of UNet3+ -GAN is illustrated in Fig. 1.

Segmentation Network Architecture In this paper, an enhanced version of the UNet3+ network is adopted for the segmentation task. This network incorporates multi-scale skip connections and deep supervision. The multi-scale skip connections directly amalgamate high-level semantic and low-level semantic information from diverse scale feature maps of remote sensing building images. Concurrently, deep supervision learns hierarchical representations from feature maps aggregated across multiple scales. Within UNet3+, this architecture adeptly captures both fine-grained details and coarse-grained semantic attributes. This leads to a more effective extraction of semantic information and features from buildings of varying sizes within remote sensing images.

Additionally, in UNet3+, we introduce the scSE (Spatial Channel Squeeze and Excitation) attention module. The scSE attention module is an attention mechanism used to enhance the performance of convolutional neural networks. It aims to adap-tively weight the feature map based on channel and spatial information to enhance the network's focus on buildings in the image. It consists of two key modules: spatial attention and channel attention. The spatial attention and channel attention com-press and excite the spatial and channel dimensions of the feature map, respectively, adaptively learning the spatial correlations and channel correlations of the feature map. Moreover, global average pooling is used to compress the spatial and channel dimensions of the feature map, generating a spatial and channel attention weight vector through a small fully connected layer. This weight vector is used to weight the original feature map, highlighting important spatial and channel locations. By combining spatial attention and channel attention, the scSE attention module enhances the network's focus on spatial and channel features, thereby improving the quality of feature representation. The overall structure of the segmentation network is shown in Fig. 2.

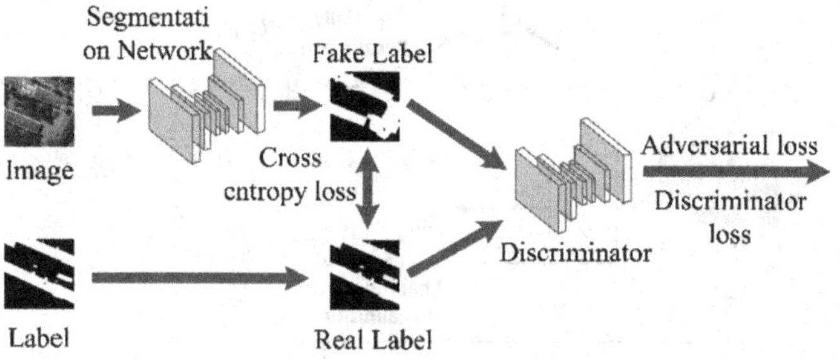

Fig. 1. UNet3+ -GAN model adapt from [16]

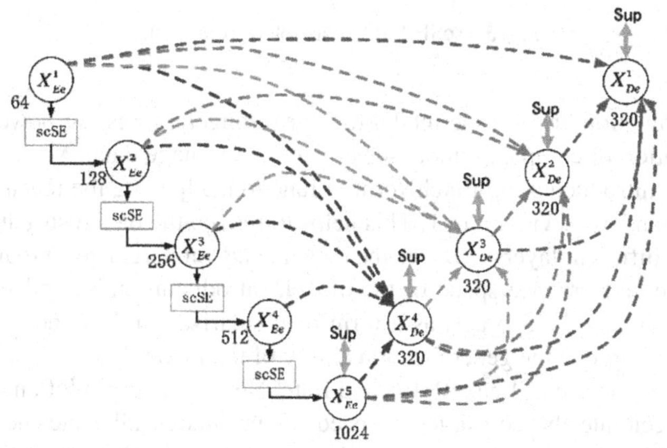

Fig. 2. Segmentation Network

As shown in the figure, we added the scSE module in the downsampling process of the UNet3+ network, as illustrated in Fig. 3. By incorporating the scSE module during downsampling, the network can pay more attention to the useful channels for building extraction tasks, thereby improving the feature expression capability. Since downsampling may result in the loss of fine-grained details, adding this module can enhance the selectivity for capturing subtle features while preserving the main features. In remote sensing building images, apart from buildings, there are various irrelevant objects such as trees, roads, lakes, as well as interference like noise. The scSE module's adaptive channel-wise weighting can help reduce the interference from unrelated objects or noise, thus improving the network's perception of buildings. Adding the scSE attention during downsampling enables the UNet3+ network to capture global contextual information in remote sensing images, leading to a more comprehensive perception capability.

Discriminator Network Architecture We use the network architecture shown in Fig. 4 as the discriminator network. In the network, we apply the LeakyReLU function and BatchNorm2d to each network layer. The LeakyReLU function helps to alleviate the problem of dead neurons, mitigates gradient vanishing, and accelerates the convergence speed of the model. Additionally, the introduction of non-linearity through the

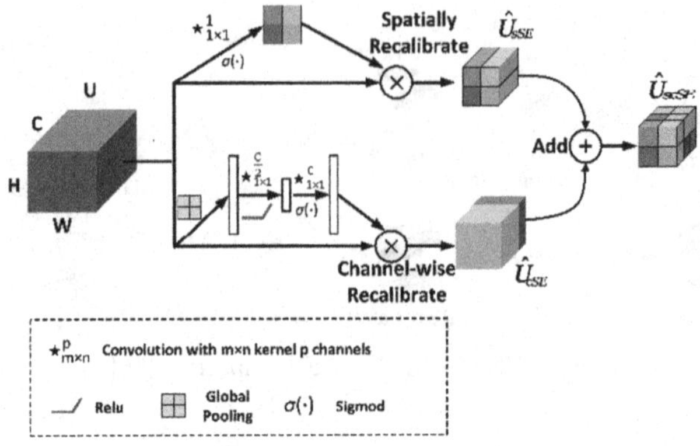

Fig. 3. scSE Module adapted from [15].

LeakyReLU function enables the model to have stronger expressive power and better fit the distribution of complex remote sensing building image data. We normalize each mini-batch by introducing the BatchNorm2d function, adjusting the mean of the input to 0 and the standard deviation to 1. This helps to reduce the data distribution discrepancy between different layers, reduces the dependency on parameter initialization, and accelerates the convergence speed of the model. Introducing noise and standardizing each mini-batch sample also acts as a form of regularization. This helps to suppress overfitting and improve the generalization ability of the model.

In summary, the use of LeakyReLU and BatchNorm2d in convolutional neural networks can accelerate the convergence speed of the model, alleviate the problem of gradient vanishing, enhance the model's expressive power, and enable the discriminator network to better distinguish real images from the generated images by the generator, thereby further improving the segmentation performance.

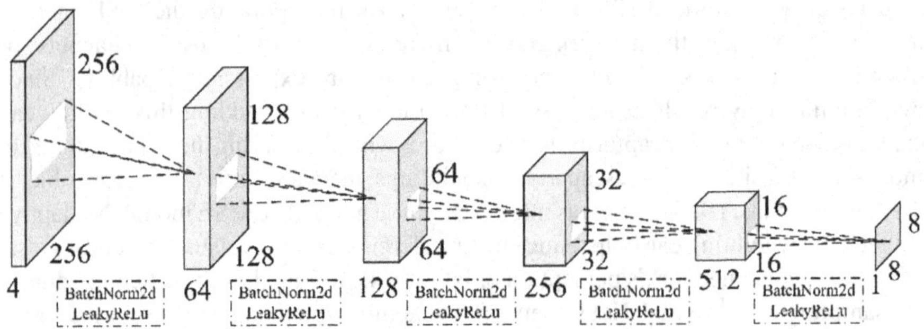

Fig. 4. Discriminator Network

3.2 Loss Function

During training, it is necessary to train the generator and the discriminator networks separately to achieve mutual adversarial training and adjustment. The cross-entropy loss function is sensitive to errors and facilitates fast convergence of the model through backpropagation. We use the *Dice* loss function to compute the segmentation loss. The *Dice* loss function takes into account the spatial relationship of buildings in remote sensing images, which promotes spatial positional accuracy in the segmentation results. It better preserves the boundaries and detail information of the targets.

The loss function for the generator is:

$$Loss_G = \lambda Loss_{dice}(X, G(Y)) + (1 - \lambda) Loss_{bce}(1, D(G(Y), Y)) \tag{1}$$

Y represents the original image, X represents the ground truth label, $G(\cdot)$ represents the generator network, $D(\cdot)$ represents the discriminator network, $Loss_G$ represents the generator loss, $Loss_{dice}$ represents the segmentation loss using the *Dice* loss, and $Loss_{bce}$ represents the discriminator loss computed using the cross-entropy loss for a batch of samples. Here, λ represents the weight.

The $Loss_{bce}$ is the cross-entropy loss function, and its formula is:

$$Loss_{bce} = \{l_1, ..., l_N\}, l_n = -\left[y_n \cdot \log(\sigma(x_n)) + (1 - y_n) \cdot \log(1 - \sigma(x_n))\right] \tag{2}$$

$\sigma(x_n)$ is the sigmoid function, which maps x to the interval (0, 1).

The discriminator loss function is:

$$Loss_D = \alpha loss_{bce}(\eta, D(X, Y)) + (1 - \alpha) loss_{bce}(\eta, D(G(Y), Y)) \tag{3}$$

α represents the weight, When the discriminator takes real images and real labels as input, the $\eta = 1$. If the input is real images and labels generated by the generator, the $\eta = 0$.

4 Research

4.1 Dataset

The experiment in this study utilized the Inria Aerial Image Dataset [17]. The original training set consists of 180 remote sensing images with dimensions of 5000 × 5000 pixels. The pixels in the ground truth are labeled into two semantic classes: buildings (pixel value 255) and non-buildings (pixel value 0). A sliding window approach was employed with a stride of 128 to divide the original images into 256 × 256 pixel images. From these images, 8262 were randomly selected as the training set, 3388 as the validation set, and 1350 as the test set.

4.2 Evaluation Metrics

In this experiment, we utilized several evaluation metrics to assess the performance, including pixel accuracy (PA), mean pixel accuracy (MPA), intersection over union (IoU), and mean intersection over union (mIoU). These metrics serve as quantitative measures to evaluate the accuracy and consistency of the segmentation results.

PA refers to the proportion of correctly classified pixels among all pixels. MPA refers to the average of pixel accuracies for each class. It is defined as:

$$PA = \frac{(TP+TN)}{(TP+TN+FP+FN)}; MPA = \frac{\sum_i^n P_i}{n} \tag{4}$$

In the equation, TP represents true positives, TN represents true negatives, FP represents false positives, and FN represents false negatives.n represents the number of classes, and P_i represents the pixel accuracy for each class.

Intersection over Union (IoU) is the ratio of the intersection to the union between the predicted results and the ground truth for a specific class. Mean Intersection over Union (mIoU) is the average of IoU values calculated for each class. It is defined as:

$$IoU = \frac{TP}{FN+FP+TP}; mIoU = \frac{1}{C} \sum_c IoU(c) \tag{5}$$

4.3 Experimental Setups

The experiment was conducted using the PyTorch framework and trained on a Tesla V100 GPU with 32GB of memory. To train both the generator and discriminator networks, Adam optimizer was utilized with a learning rate of 10^{-4} The running averages for gradient and squared gradients were set to 0.5 and 0.999, respectively. For the value of λ in Eq. 2, it was set to 0.9, and for the value of α in Eq. 6, it was set to 0.5.A batch size of 4 was used, and each model was trained for 100 epochs on the Inria Aerial Image dataset.

4.4 Experimental Results and Analysis

Four groups of experiments were conducted: UNet3+, UNet3+ -scSE, UNet3+ -GAN, and UNet3+ -scSE-GAN. By comparing the segmentation models with and without the introduction of a generative adversarial network (GAN) and scSE attention module, the effectiveness of GAN and scSE attention module was determined. The results on the Inria aerial dataset are shown in Table 1. From the table, it can be observed that the introduction of the scSE module improved the Intersection over Union (IoU) by 2.01%. When both the scSE attention module and GAN were introduced, the IoU improved by 3.13%. This indicates that the introduction of the scSE attention module and GAN led to improvements in various evaluation metrics. Furthermore, a comparison was made with references [10–13], [27], demonstrating the relative superiority of our approach. Detailed results are shown in Figure Table 2. Partial samples of the segmentation results are illustrated in Fig. 5.

Table 1. Segmentation results on Inria aerial image labeling dataset.

	PA/%	MPA/%	IoU/%	mIoU/%
UNet3+	88.75	88.50	81.40	79.20
UNet3+ -scSE	89.91	89.62	83.41	81.03
UNet3+ -GAN	89.89	89.69	80.33	78.22
UNet3+ -scSE+ -GAN	**91.77**	**91.69**	**84.53**	**84.49**

Table 2. Comparison of results on The Inria aerial image labeling dataset.

Network	IoU/%	Acc/%
Multi-scale [4]	74.24	96.12
E-D-Net [5]	79.78	96.66
MSL-Net [6]	81.1	96.80
SDSC-UNet [7]	83.01	-
GAN-SCA [18]	74.92	96.13
Ours	**84.53**	**96.95**

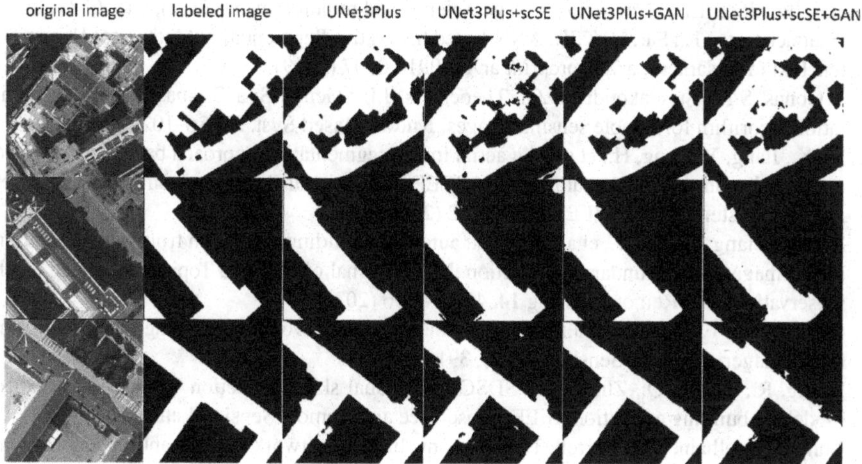

Fig. 5. Sample Result

5 Conclusion and Future Work

Introducing Generative Adversarial Networks (GANs) and attention mechanisms into the semantic segmentation task of remote sensing building images guides existing semantic segmentation models to capture binary potential function relationships between pixels, enhancing segmentation performance while keeping the segmentation model structure and parameter size unchanged. Compared to traditional seg-mentation methods, it achieves higher segmentation accuracy. Additionally, it also improves segmentation precision compared to other methods. However, utilizing Generative Adversarial Networks (GANs) for model training presents higher difficulty compared to conventional neural networks. Furthermore, due to the challenges associated with annotating remote sensing building images, we aim to incorporate semi-supervised or unsupervised learning strategies in our subsequent work. This approach seeks to enhance model segmentation efficiency and reduce dependency on the dataset.

Acknowledgement. This paper was supported by Guangxi Collaborative Innovation Center of Multi-source Information Integration and Intelligent Processing.

References

1. Maggiori, E., et al.: Convolutional neural networks for large-scale remote-sensing image classification. IEEE Transactions on geoscience and remote sensing **55**(2), 645–657 (2016)
2. Bhattacharyya, K., Sarma, K.K.: ANN-based Innovative Segmentation Method for Handwritten Text in Assamese. arXiv preprint arXiv:0911.0907 (2009)
3. Mylonas, S.K., Stavrakoudis, D.G., Theocharis, J.B.: GeneSIS: a GA-based fuzzy segmentation algorithm for remote sensing images. Knowl.-Based Syst. **54**, 86–102 (2013)
4. Li, X., Jiang, Y., Peng, H., et al.: An aerial image segmentation approach based on enhanced multi-scale convolutional neural network IEEE International Conference on Industrial Cyber Physical Systems (ICPS). IEEE, pp. 47–52 (2019)
5. Zhu, Y., Liang, Z., Yan, J., et al.: ED-Net: automatic building extraction from high-resolution aerial images with boundary information. IEEE Journal of Selected Topics in Applied Earth Observations and Remote Sensing **14**, 4595–4606 (2021)
6. Qiu, Y., Wu, F., Yin, J., et al.: MSL-Net: an efficient network for building extraction from aerial imagery. Remote Sensing **14**(16), 3914 (2022)
7. Zhang, R., Zhang, Q., Zhang, G.: SDSC-UNet: dual skip connection ViT-based U-shaped model for building extraction. IEEE Geoscience and Remote Sensing Letters (2023)
8. Long, J., Shelhamer, E., Darrell, T.: Fully convolutional networks for semantic segmentation. Proceedings of the IEEE Conference on Computer Vision and Pattern Recognition, pp. 3431–3440 (2015)
9. Ronneberger, O., Fischer, P., Brox, T.: U-net: convolutional networks for biomedical image segmentation. Medical Image Computing and Computer-Assisted Intervention–MICCAI 2015: 18th International Conference, Munich, Germany, October 5-9, 2015, Proceedings, Part III 18. Springer International Publishing, pp. 234-241 (2015)
10. Huang, H., Lin, L., Tong, R., et al.: Unet 3+: a full-scale connected unet for medical image segmentation. ICASSP 2020–2020 IEEE International Conference on Acoustics, Speech and Signal Processing (ICASSP). IEEE, pp. 1055–1059 (2020)

11. Goodfellow, I., Pouget-Abadie, J., Mirza, M., et al.: Generative adversarial networks. Commun. ACM **63**(11), 139–144 (2020)
12. Luc, P., Couprie, C., Chintala, S., et al.: Semantic Segmentation Using Adversarial Networks. arXiv preprint arXiv:1611.08408 (2016)
13. Mnih, V., Heess, N., Graves, A.: Recurrent Models of Visual Attention. Advances in Neural Information Processing Systems, **27** (2014)
14. Woo, S., Park, J., Lee, J.Y., et al.: Cbam: convolutional block attention module. Proceedings of the European Conference on Computer Vision (ECCV), pp. 3–19 (2018)
15. Roy, A.G., Navab, N., Wachinger, C.: Concurrent spatial and channel 'squeeze & excitation' in fully convolutional networks. Medical Image Computing and Computer Assisted Intervention–MICCAI 2018: 21st International Conference, Granada, Spain, September 16-20, 2018, Proceedings, Part I. Springer International Publishing, pp. 421-429 (2018). https://doi.org/10.1007/978-3-030-00928-1_48
16. Hung, W.C., Tsai, Y.H., Liou, Y.T., et al.: Adversarial Learning for Semi-Supervised Semantic Segmentation. arXiv preprint arXiv:1802.07934 (2018)
17. Maggiori, E., Tarabalka, Y., Charpiat, G., et al.: Can semantic labeling methods generalize to any city? the inria aerial image labeling benchmark. In: 2017 IEEE International Geoscience and Remote Sensing Symposium (IGARSS). IEEE, pp. 3226–3229 (2017)
18. Pan, X., Yang, F., Gao, L., et al.: Building extraction from high-resolution aerial imagery using a generative adversarial network with spatial and channel attention mechanisms. Remote Sensing **11**(8), 917 (2019)

Sparse Reconstruction Method for Flow Fields Based on Mode Decomposition Autoencoder

Jiyan Qiu[1,2], Wu Yuan[1,2](✉), Xiaoyi Hu[1,2], Jian Zhang[1,2], and Xuebin Chi[1,2]

[1] Computer Network Information Center, Chinese Academy of Sciences, Beijing, China
{qiujiyan,huxiaoyi,chi}@cnic.cn
[2] University of Chinese Academy of Sciences, Beijing, China
{yuanwu,zhangjian}@sccas.cn

Abstract. The accurate reconstruction of global flow fields from sparse measurements has been a longstanding challenge in which the quantity and positioning of measurements play a critical role. To address this issue, we propose a global flow field reconstruction method based on a mode decomposition autoencoder, which maintains interpretability while effectively handling arbitrary quantities and positioning of sensors, ensuring high accuracy in the reconstruction of flow fields and other modal data. An autoencoder is trained on global flow fields to capture the nonlinear modes of the flow. The backpropagation capability of the deep network is leveraged to transform the flow field reconstruction problem into an interpretable optimization problem, which is solved to obtain the complete flow field. In experiments carried out on a stable ocean surface temperature dataset and an unstable multi-cylinder airflow dataset, the proposed method consistently achieved high accuracy across various flow fields, surpassing the performance of current approaches.

Keywords: Neural network · Sparse measurements · Generative model · Turbulent flow

1 Introduction

Recovering high-dimensional complex flow fields from a small number of samples has been a challenge in scientific fields such as geophysics [18], astrophysics [15], atmospheric science [13], and computational fluid dynamics (CFD) [12]. Linear theory tools have traditionally been used to solve this problem because they provide a rigorous mathematical foundation and strong interpretability. One of the most famous methods, Gappy proper orthogonal decomposition (GPOD) [3], is an efficient data dimension reduction technology, which can achieve low-dimensional approximate representation and prediction of incomplete or missing value systems by feature decomposition of data [21].

However, in complex physical situations, the nonlinear relationship between variables often cannot be expressed by linear models [19]. The advent of deep

F. Liu et al. (Eds.): PRICAI 2023, LNAI 14325, pp. 274–285, 2024.
https://doi.org/10.1007/978-981-99-7019-3_26

learning has popularized the use of nonlinear methods, particularly deep neural networks (NNs), which can handle high-dimensional nonlinear data [23].

Data-driven methods are widely used in physical modeling, where supervised models can train with global flow fields. Fukami et al. [5] used a Voronoi tessellation-based convolutional neural network (CNN) to recover global flow fields, and Liu et al. [16] applied CNNs to reconstruct sparse and incomplete heat conduction data. These methods use supervised deep CNNs to reconstruct physical fields from limited measurable information. However, the interpretability of neural networks is still a challenge, which few studies have addressed [1,17], and the validity of data-driven approaches has been questioned.

To overcome this challenge, some researchers have combined reduced-order models (ROMs) with machine learning techniques and proposed methods to reconstruct flow fields based on modal reduction, where the POD [20] and DMD mode [9] are common and use long short-term memory (LSTM) networks with modal methods to reconstruct turbulent velocity fields and perform reduced-order modeling of two-dimensional unsteady flows [7]. Giannopoulos et al. [6] used GPOD with an NN to obtain the reduced-order mode of turbulent boundary layers. However, these algorithms only use machine learning methods to reconstruct the modal coefficients [11], without improving the mode itself and hence do not fully exploit the end-to-end learning capabilities of deep learning and depend too much on linear methods.

Deep neural networks have been used to enhance modal reduction in recent years. Fresca et al. [4] extended the traditional POD method to a deep learning reduced-order model, POD-DL-ROM, applying POD to reduce the dimensionality of the data and then using deep neural networks to create a low-cost and versatile reduced-dimensionality model. Murata et al. [19] used an autoencoder to extract the nonlinear modes of a flow field without supervision and applied POD to each decomposed mode. This preserves the interpretability of conventional POD modes. The accuracy of this method is comparable to that of the POD method, which inspires the use of nonlinear modes as an alternative to traditional methods. However, these methods are insufficient to reconstruct the flow field. They need an algorithm that can use the mapping of nonlinear modes to achieve modal sparsity. That is the goal of this study.

1.1 Contributions

We propose a method for global flow field reconstruction based on a mode decomposition autoencoder (MD-AE), which is an unsupervised deep learning model that can extract the nonlinear modes of the flow field from global data. MD-AE consists of an encoder that reduces the dimensionality of the data and a decoder that generates the flow field from the reduced data. A loss function is defined to ensure the consistency of the reconstructed flow field at the sparse measurement locations. This transforms the reconstruction problem into an optimization problem that can be solved efficiently using the backpropagation of deep networks and the conjugate gradient method. Experimental results show that the proposed method has better accuracy than the existing deep learning-based method and the traditional pattern-based method on different flow fields and models.

2 Problem Definition of Sparse Reconstruction

The objective of this problem is to reconstruct an N-dimensional global field with n points, represented by the variable $u \in R^n$, from r local sensor measurements $s \in R^r$ at locations $x_i \in R^N, i \in \{1, ..., r\}$ [5]. The parameter x_i denotes the positions of the measurement points on the high-resolution flow field. The variable r is the number of local sensor measurements. To achieve greater flexibility, the method accommodates any number of sensors at any position within the field, allowing for sensor positions or quantities to change over time. A machine learning model is employed to reconstruct a complete flow field without the need for retraining when sensors relocate or alter their numbers. The relationship between the global flow field and sparse measurements is represented by the measurement matrix $P \in R^{r \times n}, r \ll n$ [22], which defines r measurement positions of the global flow field, with unit values at the measured positions and zeros at unmeasured locations. P projects s onto an R-dimensional space. The sparse sampling process can be expressed as $s = Pu$, and the refactoring process as $\tilde{u} = G(s), G : R^r \to R^n$, where G represents a mapping from the dilution measurement s to the reconstructed global flow field $\tilde{u}$. In conventional methods, such as POD or DMD mode-based methods [14], G may be linear. The measurement matrix P approximates the reconstruction of the global flow field u from r measurements, as shown in the equation $s \approx P \sum_{k=1}^{r} \tilde{a}_k \psi_k$, where $\tilde{a}_k$ is the coefficient of mode ψ_k. The challenge lies in achieving maximum similarity between the reconstructed and original flow fields [24]. The optimization function is expressed as $||G(s) - u||$.

3 Framework of Model

3.1 Training Method of Mode Decomposition Autoencoder

To implement a flow field reconstruction algorithm requires the self-supervised training of a modal coefficient extractor and a global flow field generator. In this context, the decoder of an autoencoder can be viewed as the nonlinear modal decomposition of the flow field [19]. This is because the decoder learns a low-dimensional representation of the high-dimensional flow field through an unsupervised learning process. The unsupervised training is shown in Fig. 1, where the input to the deep autoencoder is the original complete global flow field u. $\mathcal{F}_{enc}$ is the encoding part of the model, and is used to encode a global vector into a latent vector, a. Then, the decoder $\mathcal{F}_{dec}$ is used to decode latent vector a into a global flow field. This process can be expressed as

$$\mathrm{a} = \mathcal{F}_{enc}(u; w_{enc}); \tilde{u} = \mathcal{F}_{dec}(u; w_{dec}). \tag{1}$$

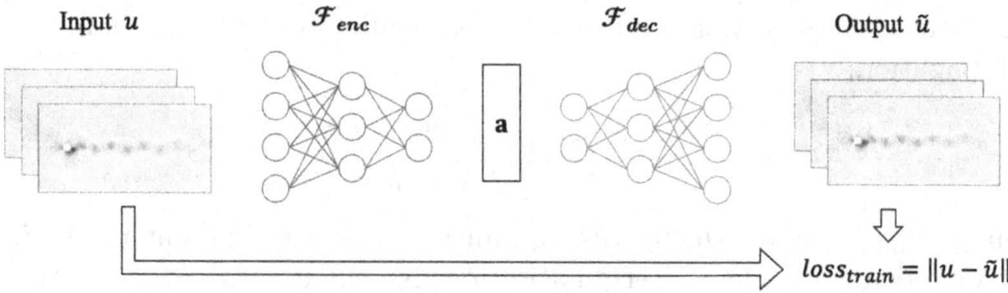

Fig. 1. Mode decomposition autoencoder is used to reconstruct flow field, in which losstrain is calculated as an error in global flow.

The function of $\mathcal{F}_{enc}$ is to extract the modal coefficients of the global flow field, which are then used as input to train $\mathcal{F}_{dec}$. Mode decomposition aims to find the optimal weights w_{enc} and w_{dec} that minimize the error norm between the input and output, given by $loss_{rec} = ||\tilde{u} - u||$. If the original data u can be restored from a, then the data are well-represented in the dimensions of a. The Adam optimizer [10] is used in training. The initial learning rate is set to 1e-3, and the stepLR scheduler is used to adjust the learning rate.

3.2 Refactoring Method

For the reconstruction of the flow field, only $\mathcal{F}_{dec}$ is needed, and $\mathcal{F}_{enc}$ is discarded. A loss function $loss_{rec}$ is constructed for reconstruction, as shown in Fig. 2, which measures the distance between the reconstructed flow field and the sensor measurements at the measurement points, using the 2-norm as the metric in this study.

Gradient descent generates a global flow field, as shown in Algorithm 1, where a_n is input to $\mathcal{F}_{dec}$ to generate $\tilde{u}$ using autoencoder modalities. Then $\tilde{u}$ is projected onto sparse measurement points, similar to P multiplied by $\tilde{u}$. The norm between the projected flow field and measured values is used to compute the reconstruction loss $loss_{rec}$, quantifying agreement with sensor measurements.

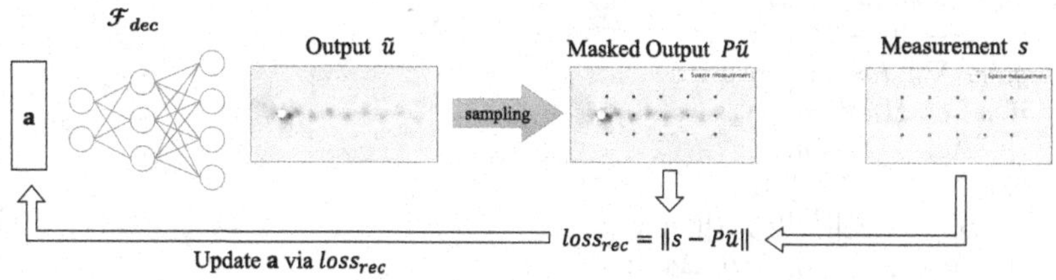

Fig. 2. $\mathcal{F}_{enc}$ is used to obtain modal coefficients of the global flow field, which are fed into $\mathcal{F}_{dec}$ for training. Mode decomposition tries to find optimal weights w_{enc} and w_{dec} that minimize the error norm between input and output, defined as $loss_{rec}$. If u can be recovered from a, then a captures the essential features of the data.

The gradient of $loss_{rec}$ with respect to a_n is calculated using the chain rule and backpropagation:

$$\nabla_{a_n} loss_{rec} = \frac{\partial loss_{rec}}{\partial a_n} = \frac{\partial ||s - P\tilde{u}||}{\partial \tilde{u}} \times \frac{\partial \tilde{u}}{\partial a_n} \tag{2}$$

Finally, a_{n+1} updates using the nonlinear conjugate gradient method, iteratively enhancing accuracy. Termination occurs when $loss_n < \epsilon$, or the max iterations are reached.

Gradient descent has several advantages for generating a global flow field, such as adaptability, convergence properties, scalability, robustness, and integration with deep learning frameworks. This method can efficiently handle nonlinear relationships and different types of problems. It can converge to a local minimum that reliably approximates the global flow field. Moreover, it can scale up to large-scale flow field reconstructions, even when the problem size increases. Gradient descent is widely used in deep learning and can be easily integrated with deep learning frameworks and tools, making it more suitable for flow field reconstruction tasks.

3.3 Mode Decomposition Autoencoder Models

We propose two models based on an automatic encoder, both suitable for the proposed flow field reconstruction method.

The first model is an MLP network that can handle unstructured grid data without requiring regular grids. However, it may have limitations in capturing

Algorithm 1: Reconstruction of the global flow field from sparse measurements.

Input: s:sparse measurements; a_0:initial value of latent vector; $\mathcal{F}_{dec}$: trained decoder; w_{dec}:weights of decoder; α:size of step

Output: $\tilde{u}$:Reconstructed flow field

initialization $n \leftarrow 0$;
do
  $\tilde{u}_n \leftarrow \mathcal{F}_{dec}(a_n; w_{dec})$;
  $loss_n \leftarrow ||s - P\tilde{u}_n||$;
  $g_n \leftarrow \nabla_{a_n} loss_n$;
  if $n = 0$ **then**
    $\Delta a_{n+1} \leftarrow -g_n$;
  else
    $\beta_n \leftarrow ||g_n||^2/||g_{n-1}||^2$;
    $\Delta a_{n+1} \leftarrow -g_n + \beta_n \Delta a_n$;
  end
  $a_{n+1} \leftarrow a_n + \alpha \Delta a_n$;
  $n \leftarrow n + 1$;
while $loss_n > \epsilon$;
return $\tilde{u}_n$

spatial correlations and local features. The architecture of this model is shown in Fig. 3 (a), where n is the number of data points in the original flow field, which depends on the dataset, and k is the number of modes in the network. The model learns nonlinear relationships in the input data, thus improving the accuracy of flow field reconstruction. The structural details and training parameters of this model, as presented in Table 1, were determined through experiments detailed in this paper. These parameters enhance the fitting performance of the model. The second model is a CNN-based network that uses strided convolutions and transposed convolutions as the main computational layers in the encoder and decoder. Figure 3(b) shows the architecture of the model, where c is the number of channels in the original data, h and w are the respective height and width of the grid data, and k is the number of modes in the network. Strided and transposed convolutions offer advantages over upsampling and downsampling, especially with respect to gradient stability (Table 2).

4 Results and Discussion

4.1 Example 1: NOAA Sea Surface Temperature

We applied the proposed method to sea surface temperature data collected by the U.S. National Oceanic and Atmospheric Administration (NOAA) from satellite and ship-based observations [8]. The sensor positions follow a uniform distribution. A single machine learning model is trained for the entire flow field and is used to reconstruct the flow field in all cases.

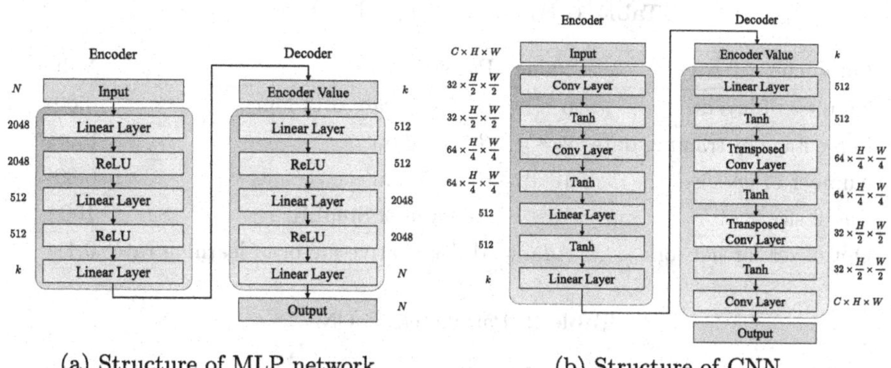

(a) Structure of MLP network

(b) Structure of CNN

Fig. 3. Networks in this paper.

The L2 norm of the error,

$$\epsilon = \frac{||u - \tilde{u}||_2}{||u||_2} = \frac{\sqrt{\sum_{i=0}^{n}(u_i - \tilde{u_i})^2}}{\sqrt{\sum_{i=0}^{n} u_i^2}} \tag{3}$$

is used as a comparison criterion [5]. The L^2 error norm has several advantages in evaluating reconstruction quality, such as computational simplicity, ease of interpretation, and sensitivity to discrepancies between the original and reconstructed data. It is calculated as the square root of the sum of squared differences between the corresponding elements of the original flow field u and its reconstruction $\tilde{u}$.

We compared the proposed method with proper orthogonal decomposition (POD), POD PLUS, shallow decoder [2], and Voronoi tessellation [5]. Performance was measured using the L2 norm of the error metric, as shown in Fig. 6(a), where the horizontal axis shows the number of random sampling points, and the vertical axis shows the L2 error values. The reconstruction problems solved by the POD, POD PLUS, and shallow decoder methods involve fixed sampling positions; therefore, we compare the fluctuating parts around the empirical mean in this context. Of these methods, only Voronoi tessellation can handle flow field reconstruction with an arbitrary number and placement of sensors, which is consistent with the problem discussed in this study.

For each number of sensor placements, we tested the average reconstruction error across 100 flow field reconstruction instances and calculated the L^2 norm of the error. With different sensor combinations, the proposed flow field reconstruction method shows stability and relatively small errors. We tested network performance with the number of modes set at 3, 8, and 32. It can be observed that as the number of sampling points or modes increases, the error in the reconstructed flow field decreases gradually. The results, as shown in Fig. 4, indicate that the model captures more data points, which can improve reconstruction sta-

Table 1. Parameters in MLP network.

Parameter	Value	Parameter	Value
Number of layers	6	Learning rate of Adam	0.001
Percentage of training data	2/3	β_1 of Adam	0.9
Number of epochs	1000	β_2 of Adam	0.99
Batch size	10	step size of StepLR	100
Optimizer for network	Adam	Multiplicative factor of learning rate	0.1

Table 2. Parameters in CNN.

Parameter	Value	Parameter	Value
Number of layers	6	Batch size	10
Conv Kernel size	3×3	Optimizer for network	Adam
Conv Kernel stride	2×2	Learning rate of Adam	0.001
Transposed Conv Kernel size	3×3	β_1 of Adam	0.9
Transposed Conv Kernel stride	2×2	β_2 of Adam	0.99
Percentage of training data	2/3	step size of StepLR	100
Number of epochs	1000	Multiplicative factor of learning rate	100

bility. This confirms that the model can adapt to different sampling situations in terms of quantity. At the same time, as the number of network modes increases, the error in the reconstructed flow field decreases, but not significantly. This means that the model's dependence on modes is relatively low, and fewer modes can yield accurate results.

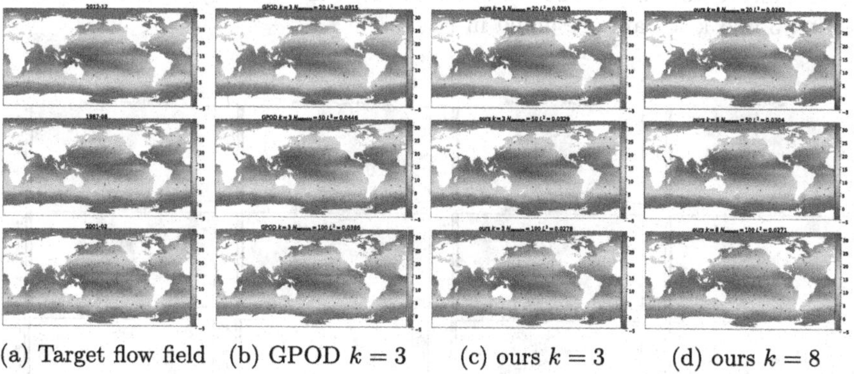

(a) Target flow field (b) GPOD $k = 3$ (c) ours $k = 3$ (d) ours $k = 8$

Fig. 4. Sparse reconstruction results for sampling with 20, 50, and 100 points. Green dots indicate measured positions. Each point has only one value in instantaneous flow field. (Color figure online)

4.2 Example 2: Dimensional Multi-cylinder Wake

The unsteady flow and vortex shedding behind an infinitely long cylinder in a uniform flow is a classic CFD problem that has been extensively studied using OpenFOAM. A more complex problem is the flow around multiple cylinders, which involves interactions between the wakes of different cylinders. The incompressible Navier-Stokes equations,

$$\nabla \cdot u = 0 \tag{4}$$

$$\frac{\partial u}{\partial t} = -(u \cdot \nabla)u - \nabla p + \frac{1}{Re}\nabla^2 u \tag{5}$$

govern both problems, where u is the velocity vector, p represents the pressure field, t is time, and Re is the Reynolds number, which in this case is set to 200.

The complexity of the flow field stems from inter-cylinder interactions, which cause vortices to merge, split, and interfere with each other, as well as fluid structure interactions between adjacent cylinders. These affect flow modes and drag and lift forces on cylinders. Therefore, this multi-cylinder case can help us to understand fluid dynamics around complex geometries, and it has important engineering applications.

The dataset has a spatial resolution of 512 × 256 and consists of 201 data samples. The division ratio of these numbers of training and validation sets and the placement of measurement points are the same as in example 1.

A widely used traditional method, GPOD, is used for comparison with k = 5 and k = 8, and it is found that the effect of the proposed method is significantly better. Moreover, as the number of modes increases, the accuracy of the reconstruction error decreases. The results are shown in Fig. 6(b). Visualized results with k = 3 and k = 8 are presented in Fig. 5.

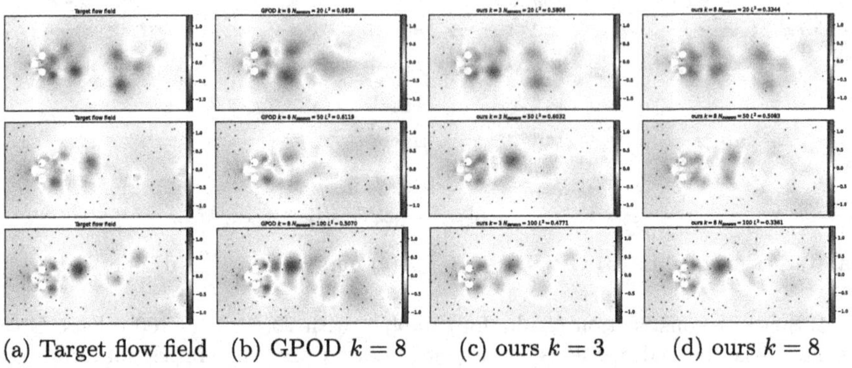

(a) Target flow field (b) GPOD $k = 8$ (c) ours $k = 3$ (d) ours $k = 8$

Fig. 5. Sparse reconstruction results for sampling with 20, 50, and 100 points. Green dots indicate measured positions. Each point has only one value in instantaneous flow field. (Color figure online)

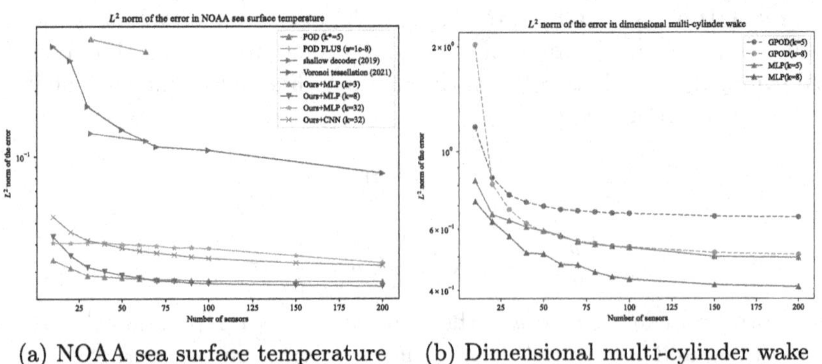

(a) NOAA sea surface temperature (b) Dimensional multi-cylinder wake

Fig. 6. Error of multiple algorithms with different numbers of sensors in multi-cylinder wake.

4.3 Discussion

The results show that the nonlinear modal approach can reconstruct the flow field with any number and location of sensors, achieving higher accuracy than other methods. The method is stable and reliable, as the reconstruction error decreases with more sampling points. The method can capture large-scale flow structures, which are the main features of the input data, and reconstruct small-scale features. The method works well with fewer modalities, indicating its effectiveness and efficiency.

In addition, MLP networks outperform CNNs in flow field reconstruction, as they can capture global information and correlations between adjacent points in flow fields, which are affected by complex physical processes. MLP networks also have shallow depths, which help avoid vanishing or exploding gradients that affect the flow field generator and can prevent overfitting by adjusting the network depth, while CNNs may suffer from overfitting due to insufficient data.

5 Conclusions

We presented a method based on a mode decomposition autoencoder for global flow field reconstruction, using two autoencoder-based neural networks to recover high-fidelity flow fields from sparse measurements with any number and location of sensors and a limited number of modes. The method requires only one training session and is robust to different sampling situations. We applied our method to a NOAA sea surface temperature dataset and 2D flow around a multi-cylinder array in OpenFOAM and compared it with POD, POD PLUS, shallow decoder, Voronoi tessellation, and GPOD methods using the L2 norm of the error. Our method achieved lower errors than other methods and could provide accurate reconstructions with fewer modes. Our code is available at https://github.com/qiujiyan/reconstruction-nonlinear.

Acknowledgements. This research was supported by the National Key Research and Development Program of China (No. 2020YFB1709500).

References

1. Dong, W., Chen, X., Yang, Q.: Data-driven scenario generation of renewable energy production based on controllable generative adversarial networks with interpretability. Appl. Energy **308**, 118387 (2022)
2. Erichson, N.B., Mathelin, L., Yao, Z., Brunton, S.L., Mahoney, M.W., Kutz, J.N.: Shallow neural networks for fluid flow reconstruction with limited sensors. Proc. R. Soc. A: Math. Phys. Eng. Sci. **476**(2238), 20200097 (2020)
3. Everson, R., Sirovich, L.: Optics InfoBase: Journal of the Optical Society of America A - Karhunen-Loève procedure for Gappy data. JOSA A **12**(8), 2–9 (1995)
4. Fresca, S., Manzoni, A.: POD-DL-ROM: enhancing deep learning-based reduced order models for nonlinear parametrized PDEs by proper orthogonal decomposition. Comput. Methods Appl. Mech. Eng. **388**, 114181 (2022)

5. Fukami, K., Maulik, R., Ramachandra, N., Fukagata, K., Taira, K.: Global field reconstruction from sparse sensors with Voronoi tessellation-assisted deep learning. Nat. Mach. Intell. **3**(11), 945–951 (2021)
6. Giannopoulos, A., Aider, J.L.: Data-driven order reduction and velocity field reconstruction using neural networks: the case of a turbulent boundary layer. Phys. Fluids **32**(9), 095117 (2020)
7. Hasegawa, K., Fukami, K., Murata, T., Fukagata, K.: CNN-LSTM based reduced order modeling of two-dimensional unsteady flows around a circular cylinder at different Reynolds numbers. Fluid Dyn. Res. **52**(6), 065501 (2020)
8. Ishii, M., Shouji, A., Sugimoto, S., Matsumoto, T.: Objective analyses of sea-surface temperature and marine meteorological variables for the 20th century using ICOADS and the Kobe Collection. Int. J. Climatol. **25**(7), 865–879 (2005)
9. Kazemi, A., Stoddard, M., Amini, A.A.: Reduced-order modeling of 4D flow MRI and CFD in stenotic flow using Proper Orthogonal Decomposition (POD) and Dynamic Mode Decomposition (DMD). In: Medical Imaging 2022: Biomedical Applications in Molecular, Structural, and Functional Imaging, vol. 12036, pp. 509–519. SPIE, April 2022
10. Kingma, D.P., Ba, J.: Adam: A Method for Stochastic Optimization, January 2017
11. Lario, A., Maulik, R., Schmidt, O.T., Rozza, G., Mengaldo, G.: Neural-network learning of SPOD latent dynamics. J. Comput. Phys. **468**, 111475 (2022)
12. Lavrinov, V.V., Lavrinova, L.N.: Reconstruction of wavefront distorted by atmospheric turbulence using a Shack-Hartman sensor. Comput. Opt. **43**, 586–595 (2019)
13. Leinonen, J., Nerini, D., Berne, A.: Stochastic super-resolution for downscaling time-evolving atmospheric fields with a generative adversarial network. IEEE Trans. Geosci. Remote Sens. **59**(9), 7211–7223 (2021)
14. Li, C.Y., Tse, T.K.T., Hu, G.: Dynamic Mode Decomposition on pressure flow field analysis: flow field reconstruction, accuracy, and practical significance. J. Wind Eng. Ind. Aerodyn. **205**, 104278 (2020)
15. Liu, N., et al.: Meshless surface wind speed field reconstruction based on machine learning. Adv. Atmos. Sci. **39**(10), 1721–1733 (2022)
16. Liu, T., Li, Y., Jing, Q., Xie, Y., Zhang, D.: Supervised learning method for the physical field reconstruction in a nanofluid heat transfer problem. Int. J. Heat Mass Transf. **165**, 120684 (2021)
17. Manfren, M., James, P.A., Tronchin, L.: Data-driven building energy modelling - an analysis of the potential for generalisation through interpretable machine learning. Renew. Sustain. Energy Rev. **167**, 112686 (2022)
18. Maulik, R., Egele, R., Lusch, B., Balaprakash, P.: Recurrent neural network architecture search for geophysical emulation. In: SC20: International Conference for High Performance Computing, Networking, Storage and Analysis, pp. 1–14, November 2020
19. Murata, T., Fukami, K., Fukagata, K.: Nonlinear mode decomposition with convolutional neural networks for fluid dynamics. J. Fluid Mech. **882**, A13 (2020)
20. Pascarella, G., Fossati, M., Barrenechea, G.: Impact of POD modes energy redistribution on flow reconstruction for unsteady flows of impulsively started airfoils and wings. Int. J. Comput. Fluid Dyn. **34**(2), 108–118 (2020)
21. Sun, S., Liu, S., Chen, M., Guo, H.: An optimized sensing arrangement in wind field reconstruction using CFD and POD. IEEE Trans. Sustain. Energy **11**(4), 2449–2456 (2020)

22. Wang, W., Wainwright, M.J., Ramchandran, K.: Information-theoretic limits on sparse signal recovery: dense versus sparse measurement matrices. IEEE Trans. Inf. Theory **56**(6), 2967–2979 (2010)
23. Wang, Z., Gong, K., Fan, W., Li, C., Qian, W.: Prediction of swirling flow field in combustor based on deep learning. Acta Astronaut. **201**, 302–316 (2022)
24. Yu, J., Hesthaven, J.S.: Flowfield reconstruction method using artificial neural network. AIAA J. **57**(2), 482–498 (2019)

StyleDisentangle: Disentangled Image Editing Based on StyleGAN2

Xuewei Li[1,2,3,4], Siyuan Ping[4], Xuzhou Fu[1,2,3], Jie Gao[1,2,3], and Zhiqiang Liu[1,2,3](✉)

[1] College of Intelligence and Computing, Tianjin University, Tianjin 300350, China
tjubeisong@tju.edu.cn

[2] Tianjin Key Laboratory of Cognitive Computing and Application, Tianjin 300350, China

[3] Tianjin Key Laboratory of Advanced Networking, Tianjin 300350, China

[4] Tianjin International Engineering Institute, Tianjin University, Tianjin 300350, China

Abstract. Thanks to the development of Generative Adversarial Networks (GANs), StyleGAN2 can generate highly realistic images by inputting a latent code and then editing them in the latent space. Disentangled image editing is crucial, where the goal is to change the desired attributes of an image while keeping the other attributes intact. As a solution, we introduce the StyleDisentangle framework for image editing. The fundamental concept of StyleDisentangle is to define attributes through two distinct sets of information: semantic segmentation coordinates - identifying the region in the image related to the attribute, and latent code coordinates - identifying the dimensions related to attributes in latent code. By utilizing these two distinct sets of coordinates, we can precisely determine the position of each attribute within the attribute editing space, resulting in disentangled image editing. We conducted extensive experiments to demonstrate the effectiveness of our method on multiple datasets and additionally compared our results with state-of-the-art methods.

Keywords: Computer Vision · Generative Adversarial Networks · Image Editing

1 Introduction

In recent years, the development of Generative Adversarial Networks (GANs) has made significant progress in high-fidelity generation modeling [2,8,11]. This progress has also driven the development of image editing. However, in current methods, disentangling image attributes still poses challenges [12–14]. The main purpose of disentangled image editing [1,5,6,9] is to change an image's desired

Supported by Tianjin Technical Export Project 20YDTPJC01570.

F. Liu et al. (Eds.): PRICAI 2023, LNAI 14325, pp. 286–297, 2024.
https://doi.org/10.1007/978-981-99-7019-3_27

attributes while keeping other attributes unchanged. Achieving this goal is not easy, especially when attributes are naturally entangled in the real world.

Some works [5,6] use an encoder-decoder architecture to manually label multiple attributes of an image for image editing. They use a loss function for specific attributes to encourage edits to specific attributes, rather than other attributes. These methods require extensive manual labeling [1,9] and can only manipulate attributes in the annotated set.

Recently, the emergence of large-scale pre-trained visual language model CLIP [17] has provided a new solution to this problem. Due to its capability to effectively measure the semantic similarity between images and texts, many methods have replaced human annotations by executing various operations through text commands and CLIP-based loss [7,16,18]. However, achieving disentangled image editing remains challenging. For instance, StyleCLIP [16] introduced three methods that require human trial and error to find the appropriate parameters to achieve the expected results.

To solve the problem of entangled attributes, this paper proposes a new framework - StyleDisentangle. The framework decomposes disentangled image editing into two subtasks. The first task is to generate semantically consistent edits in regions relevant to the given text. The second task is to constrain attribute changes in the image that are unrelated to the text.

StyleDisentangle describes each attribute from two perspectives: semantic segmentation coordinates - identifying the region in the image related to the attribute, and latent code coordinates - identifying the dimensions related to attributes in latent code. By utilizing these two distinct sets of coordinates, we can precisely determine the position of each attribute within the attribute editing space. Within the semantic segmentation region, StyleDisentangle employs a CLIP-based semantic consistency loss that encourages changes to the latent code's related dimensions to perform editing tasks. Conversely, outside the semantic segmentation region, StyleDisentangle uses image consistency loss and keeps the latent code's unrelated dimensions unchanged to perform constraint tasks. Our method can be applied to any StyleGAN2 pre-trained model. We have verified our method's effectiveness on several datasets and compared it with state-of-the-art methods.

The rest of this paper is organized as follows. Section 2 discusses related work on Generative Adversarial Networks and latent space manipulation. Section 3 presents the framework of StyleDisentangle. Section 4 conducts ablation experiments and comparison experiments with other methods, and Sect. 5 concludes the paper.

2 Related Works

2.1 Latent Space Manipulation

Latent Space Manipulation refers to the manipulation of the latent space in order to modify generated images or create new ones. Latent Space Manipulation can be classified into two categories: supervised and unsupervised methods.

Supervised methods require manual labeling of some attribute tags in order to control the variation of the latent space. Some well-known methods in this category include InterfaceGAN [19] and HiGAN [10]. InterfaceGAN maps the given attribute tags directly to the vector representation of the latent space through an end-to-end process, while HiGAN introduces an additional attribute classification task during training to better learn specific attribute information. Unsupervised methods focus on the study of the generator's latent space vector in the GAN model to achieve control over the generated images. Representative methods in this category include GANSpace [9] and SeFa [20], where the former applies Principal Component Analysis (PCA) to the randomly extracted intermediate latent vectors of BigGAN and StyleGAN models and the latter directly optimizes the intermediate weight matrix of the GAN model in a closed form.

2.2 Text-Based Image Manipulation

The goal of text-based image editing methods is to generate images that contain visual attributes corresponding to a given text input without altering irrelevant attributes. Among these methods, TediGAN [23] utilizes the inversion module of StyleGAN to invert real images and learn the correspondence between visual and language attributes. ManiGAN [15] employs a special data structure called manifold-aligned image-language embedding (MAILE) for bidirectional mapping between images and text. Most other methods use the joint text-image model CLIP to accomplish text-based image manipulation. CLIP is a multimodal contrastive learning framework with two encoder modules aimed at mapping image and text pairs to the same embedding space. Recent works such as StyleCLIP [16] utilize CLIP for image manipulation.

3 Methodology

3.1 Overview

The generator network $G(.)$ in GAN generates an image starting from a latent code $w \in W+$, i.e., $X = G(w)$, and the semantic editing of the image is done by moving its latent code along a specific direction:

$$G(w^{edit}) = G(w + \lambda n) \tag{1}$$

where λ controls the intensity of the change, and the latent direction n determines the semantic of the edit.

Our objective is to find an editing direction n, which can yield semantically meaningful edits in regions of the image relevant to the given text, while also limiting changes to image properties not associated with the text. To achieve this goal, we propose StyleDisentangle, whose process is illustrated in Fig. 1. Our model consists of two main parts: semantic segmentation coordinate calculation (green area) and latent code coordinate calculation (yellow area). Semantic segmentation coordinates are obtained from a semantic segmentation network,

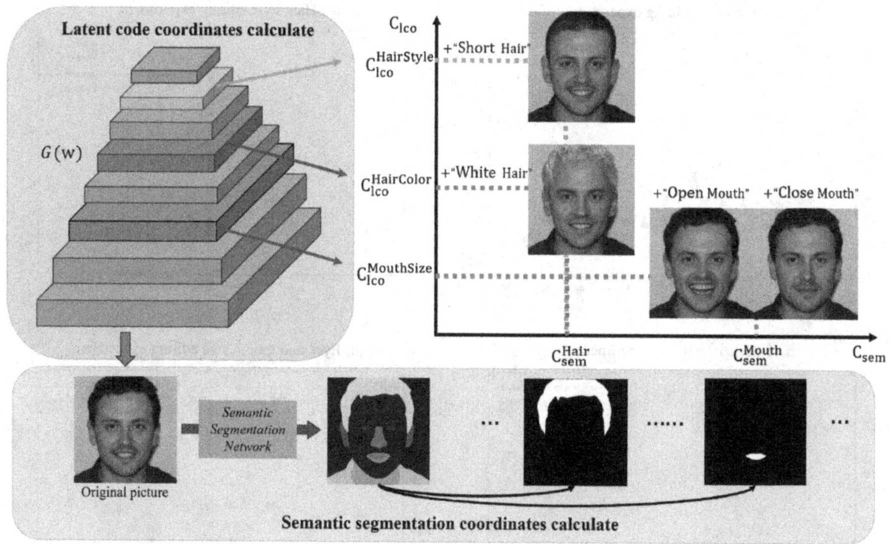

Fig. 1. Overview of StyleDisentangle Structure. Four different types of editing are shown in the figure. Among them, hairstyle editing and hair color editing have the same semantic segmentation coordinates, but different latent code coordinates. Mouth size editing has the same semantic segmentation coordinates and latent code coordinates, but different editing directions. (Color figure online)

with different target properties utilizing masks from different regions. Latent code coordinates correspond to the latent vector dimensions of target properties in the process of image generation. We will introduce the attribute coordinates and attribute editing space in Sect. 3.2, and then clarify the computation process of the loss function in Sect. 3.3.

3.2 Attribute Coordinates

Semantic Segmentation Coordinates. Semantic segmentation coordinates refer to a set of regions on the image plane that are relevant to the edit. In our experiment, we pre-trained a semantic segmentation network to divide the human face into 20 parts. The expression of semantic segmentation coordinates is as follows:

$$C_{sem} = \{r | r \in Q_{edit}\} \tag{2}$$

Where Q_{edit} is the preset segmentation label.

For example, in the process of editing the mouth, the semantic segmentation coordinates include three parts: the upper lip, the lower lip and teeth. In our experiment, the corresponding segmentation results of these three parts are 11,12,13, that is, $C_{sem}^{Mouth} = \{11, 12, 13\}$.

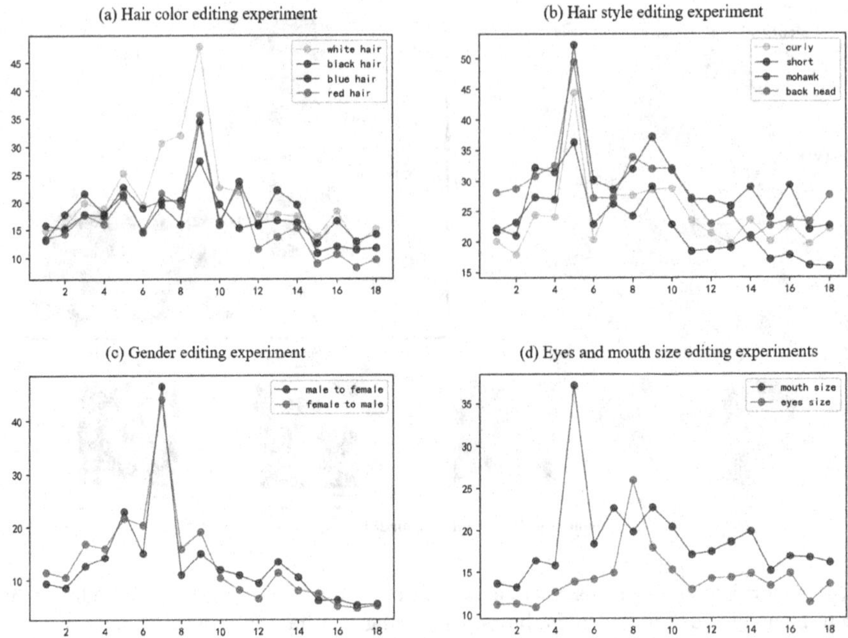

Fig. 2. Latent code coordinate determination experiments. For each subgraph, the abscissa is the dimension of the latent code w, the ordinate is the difference between the optimized latent code and the original latent code, and the dimension with the highest peak value is the latent code coordinate of the corresponding attribute.

Latent Code Coordinates. Latent code coordinates are latent code dimensions associated with target attributes. Taking StyleGAN2 as an example, the 18 dimensions of $w \in W+$ affect different resolution levels during the image generation process. As the image is progressively generated from resolution 4^2 to resolution 1024^2, each resolution layer is influenced by both dimensions of w. Corresponding to the coarse spatial resolution $(4^2 - 8^2)$, w controls the high-level information of the image, such as pose, hairstyle, face shape; corresponding to the w dimension of the medium resolution $(16^2 - 32^2)$, it controls smaller scale facial features, mouth opening/closing. Finally, the w dimension corresponding to the resolution $(64^2 - 1024^2)$ mainly controls the color scheme and microstructure. For example, the semantic segmentation coordinates of hairstyle and hair color are the same, because they are in the same region of the picture, but hairstyle and hair color are affected by different dimensions of w differently, that is, the coordinates of Latent code are different.

The latent code coordinate is the w dimension corresponding to the target attribute, and its specific expression is as follows:

$$C_{lco} = \{l | l \in K_{edit}\} \tag{3}$$

Where K_{edit} is the latent vector layer related to the target attribute, and the number of latent vector layers of different generators may be different. To determine the latent code coordinates of different attributes, we randomly generate a batch of images $G(w)$ (64 in our experiments), and for a given text t, we directly optimize the latent code by the following formula:

$$\arg\min_{\Delta w \in W} D_{CLIP}(G(w), t) \tag{4}$$

Where D_{CLIP} is the joint text-image model CLIP to measure the similarity of text and image. By taking the average of the difference between the optimized latent code and the original latent code, we can get the latent code coordinates of different attributes. As shown in Fig. 2, the ninth layer of the latent vector has the greatest impact on hair color, that is, the hair color latent code coordinate is $C_{lco}^{HairColor} = 9$. Similarly, according to the results, we can get $C_{lco}^{HairStyle} = C_{lco}^{MouthSize} = 5$, $C_{lco}^{Gender} = 7$, $C_{lco}^{EyesSize} = 8$.

3.3 Objective Function

After obtaining the semantic segmentation coordinates through the semantic segmentation network, we can obtain the attribute target region mask, denoted as M. In the experiments, M is the binary pixel mask. On this basis, we use the following formula to extract the original image target region and out-of-target region for subsequent editing.

$$I_{org}^{out} = x_{org} \odot (1 - M), I_{edit}^{out} = x_{edit} \odot (1 - M) \tag{5}$$

where I_{org}^{out} and I_{edit}^{out} represents the text-independent region of x_{org} and x_{edit}, and "$\odot$" refers to the element-wise multiplication operation.

Based on the obtained text irrelevant regions, we introduce non-target region loss,

$$L_{outside} = d(I_{org}^{out}, I_{edit}^{out}) \tag{6}$$

Non-target region loss makes the target image x_{edit} consistent with the original image x_{org} outside the target region, where d represents the similarity measure of the image, which is the sum of L_2 pixel difference and $LPIPS$. With the help of CLIP's ability to measure text and image similarity, we define the target region loss as:

$$L_{inside} = D_{CLIP}(I_{edit}^{in}, t) \tag{7}$$

Where t is the text prompt. Additionally, we also employ the identity loss:

$$L_{ID}(s) = 1 - \langle R(G(w_0)), R(G(w_{edit})) \rangle \tag{8}$$

An identity network (e.g., ArcFace [4] in the case of face recognition) denoted as R, and a cosine similarity computation, represented by $\langle \cdot, \cdot \rangle$. The purpose of the identity loss is to avoid changes to irrelevant attributes. To achieve our research objectives, we aim to solve the following optimization problem:

$$\arg\min_{w \in W} \lambda_{inside} L_{inside}(w) + \lambda_{outside} L_{outside}(s) + \lambda_{ID} L_{ID}(s) \quad (9)$$

Where λ_{inside}, $\lambda_{outside}$, and λ_{ID} are the loss coefficients of L_{inside}, $L_{outside}$, and L_{ID}, respectively. We only retain the dimension changes corresponding to the latent code coordinates, while keeping the other dimensions consistent with the original latent code w_0, to obtain the final latent code w_{final}:

$$w_{final} = \begin{cases} [w_0]_i + \alpha([w_{edit}]_i - [w_0]_i) & \text{if } i \in C_{lco} \\ [w_0]_i & \text{otherwise} \end{cases} \quad (10)$$

Where α is the editing strength. The final image $G(w_{final})$ can be generated by using the generator.

4 Experiments

We conducted evaluations on the FFHQ (260,000 images) [11], LSUN Car (260,000 images) [24], and AFHQ Dog (10,000 images) [3] datasets. We also compared our method with state-of-the-art text-based manipulation methods, including TediGAN [23], ManiGAN [15], and StyleCLIP [16]. Next, we discuss our experimental setup and present results of several StyleGAN2 models.

4.1 Experimental Setup

For manipulation experiments on real images, we use the e4e [21] method to obtain its latent code in $W+$ space. We set the coefficient λ_{CLIP} and λ_{img} to 1 for all experiments, while the coefficient λ_{id} is assigned a value between 0.1 and 1, depending on whether the character's identity is meant to change. For manipulations where the identity is significantly altered, such as gender change, a lower identity loss coefficient is used. A single 3090 RTX GPU is employed for our experiments. For the comparison algorithms, we use their official public implementation.

4.2 StyleDisentangle Manipulation Results

Our method is capable of editing in various domains. Figure 3 shows the experimental results of our model on the FFHQ dataset, where the last row is the operation on real images. Our algorithm achieves good disentangled editing results. For example, in the mouth size editing experiment, our algorithm can only change the size of the mouth without affecting other attributes (such as eyes) in the picture, which can be effectively distinguished from the "laugh"-driven editing results. For attributes that are easy to interact with each other, such as hair color and hairstyle, our method can also find out their respective precise editing directions. Figure 4(a) shows our experimental results on the AFHQ dog dataset, and Fig. 4(b) shows the experimental results on the LSUN car dataset.

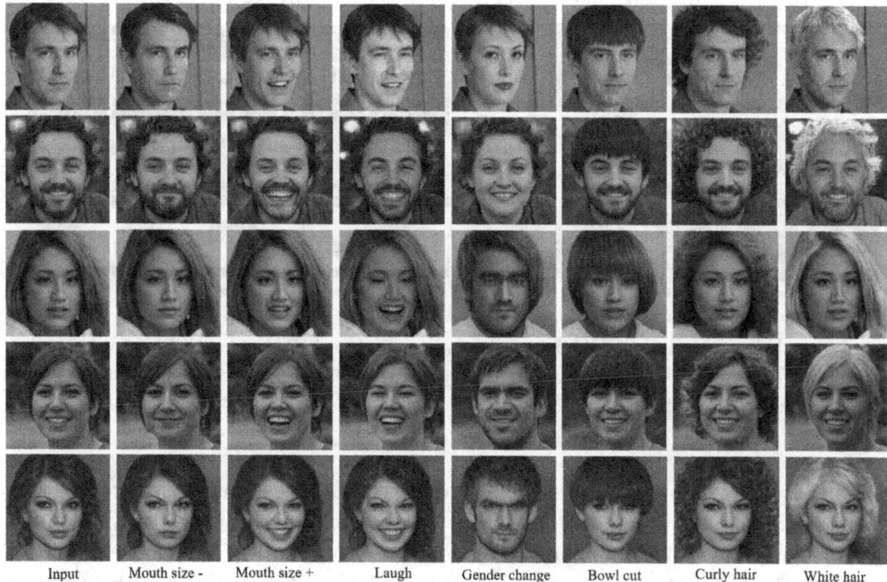

Fig. 3. A variety of manipulations on StyleGAN2 FFHQ model. Rows 1–4 illustrate manipulations performed on randomly generated images, and the last row depicts manipulations performed on real images, The text prompts used for each manipulation are located below each column.

4.3 Comparison with Text-Guided Methods

We compare our method with the state-of-the-art text-driven manipulation methods StyleCLIP, TediGAN, and ManiGAN. StyleCLIP provides three different methods, namely StyleCLIP-LO, StyleCLIP-LM and StyleCLIP-GD. For comparison, we use a StyleGAN2 model trained on FFHQ with a different set of text cues.

Qualitative Comparison. Figure 5 shows the qualitative comparison results. For the "Open Mouth" prompt, our method not only opens the character's mouth but also ensures no change in other attributes. Meanwhile, other algorithms will affect areas unrelated to the text prompt, such as TediGAN causing changes in the character's eye area. For the "Donald Trump" prompt, our method and StyleMC generate some visual features corresponding to the text prompt, such as golden hair, squinted eyes, and pursed lips. For the "Short Hair" and "White Hair" prompts, our algorithm achieved independent manipulation of a specific attribute, i.e., changing hairstyle without changing hair color and changing hair color without changing hairstyle, whereas other algorithms did not achieve this.

Quantitative Comparison. As shown in Table 1, we used five important evaluation metrics to quantitatively evaluate the results of our model. These metrics include the Inception Score (IS) and Fréchet Inception Distance (FID) for measuring image generation quality, the LPIPS image perception loss, and the

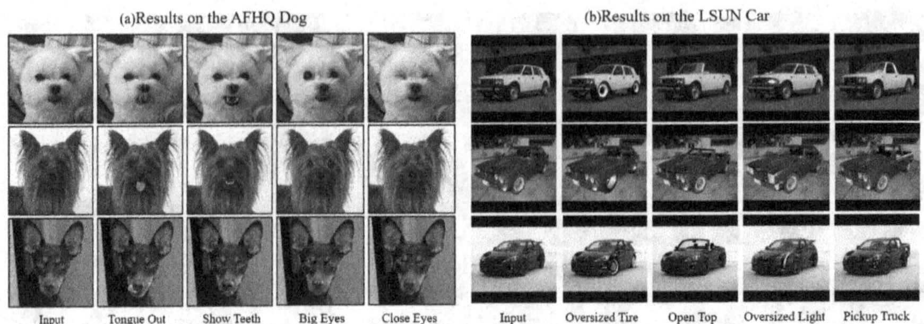

Fig. 4. (a) Edits on the AFHQ Dog. (b) Edits on the LSUN Car. The input images are located on the left-hand side, and the text prompt utilized for each manipulation is located below each column.

authenticity, text-image consistency, and attribute preservation degree of the generated images obtained through user evaluation. In the user study, we provided 20 workers with 10 images from each method, all of which were edited based on the same text prompts. We asked the workers to judge the semantic accuracy, authenticity, and preservation degree of other attributes unrelated to the text in the edited images. For each evaluation metric, the workers were asked to rate the images on a scale of 1–10, with 10 indicating the most accurate/authentic/highest degree of preservation. Our algorithm achieved the best results

Table 1. Quantitative Comparison result. We use IS, FID, LPIPS, accuracy (Acc), realism (Real), and other attribute retention degrees (Rete). ↓ means the lower the better while ↑ means the opposite.

Method	IS↑	FID↓	LPIPS↓	Acc↑	Real↑	Rete↑
StyleCLIP-LO	7.33	40.36	0.51	7.3	7.2	7.1
StyleCLIP-LM	6.16	48.35	0.49	6.2	7.3	8.1
StyleCLIP-GD	7.67	43.56	0.48	7.5	8.3	6.9
TediGAN	5.35	36.18	0.69	7.4	7.3	5.2
ManiGAN	4.16	68.35	0.71	6.2	7.3	5.1
StyleDisentangle with C_{sem}	5.65	46.38	0.51	6.9	7.5	7.2
StyleDisentangle with C_{lco}	4.54	50.22	0.54	7.6	7.9	6.4
StyleDisentangle with BigGAN	8.14	33.66	0.65	8.4	8.3	8.6
StyleDisentangle with style space	8.54	31.66	**0.39**	**9.3**	9.3	**9.7**
Ours	**8.68**	**30.98**	0.40	9.2	**9.6**	**9.7**

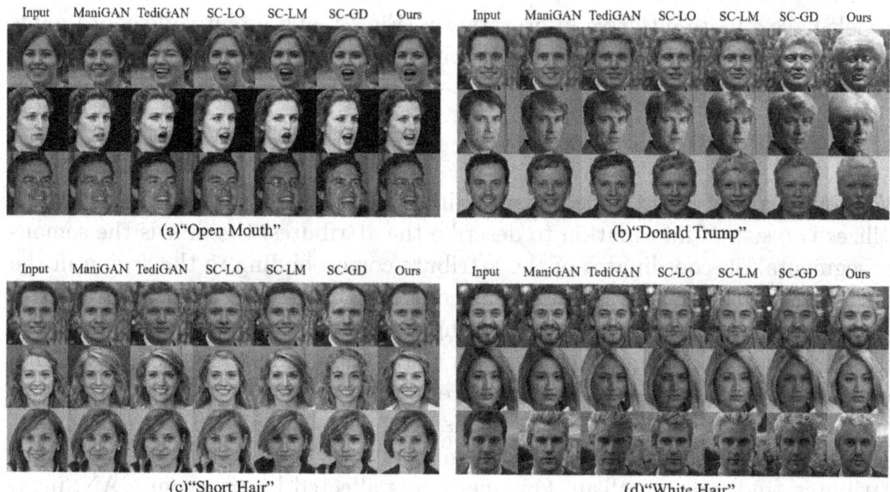

Fig. 5. Qualitative comparison results. The leftmost side of each subplot is the input image, and the text prompt used to manipulate the image is located above.

4.4 Ablation Studies

Our model achieves disentangled editing by determining the unique position of attributes in the editing space based on semantic segmentation coordinates and latent code coordinates. In this section, we name the model that only uses semantic segmentation coordinates as "StyleDisentangle with C_{sem}" and the model that only uses latent code coordinates as "StyleDisentangle with C_{lco}". Meanwhile, although BigGAN does not have a built-in hierarchical control mechanism like StyleGAN2, it has been proven that modifying the latent code of BigGAN can produce behaviors similar to StyleGAN2 [9]. Thus, we name the model that uses BigGAN as the backbone generator network as "StyleDisentangle with BigGAN". All the above ablation algorithms use StyleGAN2's $W+$ latent space. A study [22] pointed out that StyleGAN2's style space has better disentanglement characteristics than $W+$ latent space. We name the ablation model for editing in style space "StyleDisentangle with style space". In this section, we conduct ablation experiments to verify the significance and effect of each part of StyleDisentangle.

The quantitative experimental results are shown in Table 1. Both "StyleDisentangle with C_{lco}" and "StyleDisentangle with C_{sem}" produced poor experimental results, indicating that using only one coordinate is insufficient to achieve effective disentanglement control. The results generated by "StyleDisentangle with BigGAN" are also inferior to the model framework that uses StyleGAN as its main generator network, which benefits from the hierarchical characteristics of the StyleGAN generator, enabling better decoupling at the Latent code level. "StyleDisentangle with style space" produces similar results to our proposed model, with slight advantages in some indicators. But $W+$ space-based models have a more intuitive interpretation (Fig. 2), and latent code coordinates in $W+$ space are easier to record and convenient for next editing.

5 Conclusion

We propose a new disentangled image editing algorithm, StyleDisentangle, which utilizes two sets of information to describe the attributes: the first is the semantic segmentation coordinates of the attribute corresponding to the region in the source image; the second is the latent code coordinates of the attribute corresponding latent code dimension. By using these two coordinates, we can locate the unique position of each attribute in the attribute manipulation space, distinguish different attributes, and achieve attribute disentanglement. Extensive qualitative and quantitative comparisons demonstrate that our method outperforms existing methods in terms of semantic accuracy, preservation of irrelevant attributes, and image realism. Our method is affected by biases in GAN, making it difficult to add wrinkles to a child's face or apply makeup to a male face. At the same time, like other image editing algorithms, our framework is also confronted with the issue of being misused by malicious actors.

References

1. Abdal, R., Zhu, P., Mitra, N.J., Wonka, P.: StyleFlow: attribute-conditioned exploration of styleGAN-generated images using conditional continuous normalizing flows. ACM Trans. Graph. (ToG) **40**(3), 1–21 (2021)
2. Brock, A., Donahue, J., Simonyan, K.: Large scale GAN training for high fidelity natural image synthesis. arXiv preprint arXiv:1809.11096 (2018)
3. Choi, Y., Uh, Y., Yoo, J., Ha, J.W.: StarGAN V2: diverse image synthesis for multiple domains. In: Proceedings of the IEEE/CVF Conference on Computer Vision and Pattern Recognition, pp. 8188–8197 (2020)
4. Deng, J., Guo, J., Xue, N., Zafeiriou, S.: ArcFace: additive angular margin loss for deep face recognition. In: Proceedings of the IEEE/CVF Conference on Computer Vision and Pattern Recognition, pp. 4690–4699 (2019)
5. Gabbay, A., Cohen, N., Hoshen, Y.: An image is worth more than a thousand words: towards disentanglement in the wild. Adv. Neural. Inf. Process. Syst. **34**, 9216–9228 (2021)
6. Gabbay, A., Hoshen, Y.: Scaling-up disentanglement for image translation. In: Proceedings of the IEEE/CVF International Conference on Computer Vision, pp. 6783–6792 (2021)
7. Gal, R., Patashnik, O., Maron, H., Bermano, A.H., Chechik, G., Cohen-Or, D.: StyleGAN-NADA: CLIP-guided domain adaptation of image generators. ACM Trans. Graph. (TOG) **41**(4), 1–13 (2022)
8. Goodfellow, I., et al.: Generative adversarial networks. Commun. ACM **63**(11), 139–144 (2020)
9. Härkönen, E., Hertzmann, A., Lehtinen, J., Paris, S.: GANSpace: discovering interpretable GAN controls. Adv. Neural. Inf. Process. Syst. **33**, 9841–9850 (2020)
10. Hsu, W.N., et al.: Hierarchical generative modeling for controllable speech synthesis. arXiv preprint arXiv:1810.07217 (2018)

11. Karras, T., Laine, S., Aila, T.: A style-based generator architecture for generative adversarial networks. In: Proceedings of the IEEE/CVF Conference on Computer Vision and Pattern Recognition, pp. 4401–4410 (2019)
12. Karras, T., Laine, S., Aittala, M., Hellsten, J., Lehtinen, J., Aila, T.: Analyzing and improving the image quality of styleGAN. In: Proceedings of the IEEE/CVF Conference on Computer Vision and Pattern Recognition, pp. 8110–8119 (2020)
13. Kim, H., Choi, Y., Kim, J., Yoo, S., Uh, Y.: Exploiting spatial dimensions of latent in GAN for real-time image editing. In: Proceedings of the IEEE/CVF Conference on Computer Vision and Pattern Recognition, pp. 852–861 (2021)
14. Kwon, G., Ye, J.C.: Diagonal attention and style-based GAN for content-style disentanglement in image generation and translation. In: Proceedings of the IEEE/CVF International Conference on Computer Vision, pp. 13980–13989 (2021)
15. Li, B., Qi, X., Lukasiewicz, T., Torr, P.H.: ManiGAN: text-guided image manipulation. In: Proceedings of the IEEE/CVF Conference on Computer Vision and Pattern Recognition, pp. 7880–7889 (2020)
16. Patashnik, O., Wu, Z., Shechtman, E., Cohen-Or, D., Lischinski, D.: StyleCLIP: text-driven manipulation of styleGAN imagery. In: Proceedings of the IEEE/CVF International Conference on Computer Vision, pp. 2085–2094 (2021)
17. Radford, A., et al.: Learning transferable visual models from natural language supervision. In: International Conference on Machine Learning, pp. 8748–8763. PMLR (2021)
18. Roich, D., Mokady, R., Bermano, A.H., Cohen-Or, D.: Pivotal tuning for latent-based editing of real images. ACM Trans. Graph. (TOG) **42**(1), 1–13 (2022)
19. Shen, Y., Yang, C., Tang, X., Zhou, B.: InterfaceGAN: interpreting the disentangled face representation learned by GANs. IEEE Trans. Pattern Anal. Mach. Intell. **44**(4), 2004–2018 (2020)
20. Shen, Y., Zhou, B.: Closed-form factorization of latent semantics in GANs. In: Proceedings of the IEEE/CVF Conference on Computer Vision and Pattern Recognition, pp. 1532–1540 (2021)
21. Tov, O., Alaluf, Y., Nitzan, Y., Patashnik, O., Cohen-Or, D.: Designing an encoder for styleGAN image manipulation. ACM Trans. Graph. (TOG) **40**(4), 1–14 (2021)
22. Wu, Z., Lischinski, D., Shechtman, E.: Stylespace analysis: disentangled controls for styleGAN image generation. In: Proceedings of the IEEE/CVF Conference on Computer Vision and Pattern Recognition, pp. 12863–12872 (2021)
23. Xia, W., Yang, Y., Xue, J.H., Wu, B.: TediGAN: text-guided diverse face image generation and manipulation. In: Proceedings of the IEEE/CVF Conference on Computer Vision and Pattern Recognition, pp. 2256–2265 (2021)
24. Yu, F., Seff, A., Zhang, Y., Song, S., Funkhouser, T., Xiao, J.: LSUN: construction of a large-scale image dataset using deep learning with humans in the loop. arXiv preprint arXiv:1506.03365 (2015)

A Property Constrained Video Summarization Framework via Regret Minimization

Yuyao Xu[1], Jiping Zheng[1,2](✉), Yanxin Tao[1], and Kaiqin Zhu[1]

[1] College of Computer Science and Technology, Nanjing University of Aeronautics and Astronautics, Nanjing, China
{yuyaoxu,jzh,draco,xiwenz}@nuaa.edu.cn

[2] State Key Laboratory for Novel Software Technology, Nanjing University, Nanjing, China

Abstract. Video summarization has become one of the most effective solutions for quickly understanding a large amount of video data. Video properties such as importance, diversity, representativeness and storyness have been widely adopted for summarization based on kinds of features of video frames. To fully exploit these properties, in this paper we propose a property constrained video summarization framework to output fixed-size summaries based on the concept of *regret minimization* which is popular in the database community for solving multi-criteria decision making problems.

Keywords: Video summarization · Multiple properties · Regret minimization

1 Introduction

With the exponential growth of video hosting platforms and social media-sharing websites, users are often overwhelmed when facing numerous videos and increasingly inclined to get information quickly through videos in fragmented watching time. To identify the informative frames in a video, various properties are utilized to generate summaries, such as *importance*, *representativeness*, *diversity*, and *storyness*. However, it is not easy to take full advantage of all these properties [5]. The following issues still remain: (1) Enough spatial-temporal feature information should be extracted and combined [10]. (2) Training based models are always with a high cost, and non-guaranteed performance [2]. (3) It is impossible to find a summary satisfying every user due to the subjectivity in evaluating a summary [11].

In this paper, we propose a property constrained video summarization framework to output summaries with fixed-size keyframes. Our framework can combine kinds of feature information, and then find a summary satisfying every user. To avoid the drawbacks listed above [2,5,11] without any training, we borrow the

F. Liu et al. (Eds.): PRICAI 2023, LNAI 14325, pp. 298–304, 2024.
https://doi.org/10.1007/978-981-99-7019-3_28

idea of the regret minimization query [8] in the database community which can return a fixed-size result set from a multidimensional dataset without knowing user's preference to each dimension. As to the video summarization, in most scenarios, the preferences for different properties of a frame are difficult to specify. Thus, in the proposed framework, the properties of each frame are extracted to form a multidimensional point set and carry out the regret minimization query, which achieves great success in database area, to identify the representative subset to obtain the summary of a video. Experiments verify the effectiveness and priority of the proposed framework.

2 The Property Constrained Video Summarization Framework via Regret Minimization

In this section, we detail our property constrained video summarization framework via regret minimization.

2.1 Constructing the Candidate Frame Set

It is known that the neighboring frames are very similar. Thus it is wasteful and unreasonable to calculate all scores for all frames since the similar frames only need to be considered once. One common way to do this is to select the representative frames by clustering or dictionary learning to improve the efficiency. However, the selection of cluster centers or dictionary elements is not always stable and effective. To solve this issue, the following preprocessing steps are designed to construct the candidate frame set.

Removing Meaningless Frames. Before selecting the candidate frames, we set the thresholds for the handcrafted features such as colorfulness, edge distribution and contrast, etc., and the probability that a frame is a transition frame to avoid selecting meaningless frames.

Obtaining Boundary Representative Frames. Since the shots are important components of a video, the shot boundary frames are first identified to represent the shots which plays an important role in improving the accuracy of generating edited video summaries. TransNetV2 [9] is also used to predict the probability of each frame being shot boundary or being transition. We want all of the shot boundary frames of abrupt transitions rather than gradual transitions.

Obtaining Block Representative Frames via Block Sparsity.
The *block sparsity* idea from Ma et al. [7] is borrowed which is different from the clustering method. A similar regression model in [4] is used to select the block representative frames, which includes following features: motion information, colorfulness, representativeness, and edge distribution. Here, the motion information is added into the model to find the block representative frames, because users prefer to choose a stable frame as a keyframe, and it can highly represent the frames neighboring it.

First, we divide the video into uniform multiple video blocks at a fixed interval. After that, we focus on the selection of video frames within the blocks. To find the best frame of a block which is stable enough, colorful, representative, and edge clear, we use following functions to measure them: a) The stability function $S(\cdot)$ to calculate the motion information. b) The colorfulness function $C(\cdot)$ to compute the colorfulness. c) The similarity function $L(\cdot)$ to calculate the similarity. d) The edge function $E(\cdot)$ to calculate the edge distribution of the frame.

As what we want is the most stable frame, we increase the ratio of motion information, and according to [4], we set the ratio of our weights to $8:2:2:1$.

Generating the Candidate Frame Set. The block representative frames of all frame blocks are merged with the boundary representative frames to obtain the candidate frame set of the video. Meanwhile, since it is with high probability that there exist highly similar frames between candidate frames, we use the local similarity inhibition [12] to remove redundant frames which penalizes the simultaneous selection of neighboring similar frames by assigning a small weight to improve the diversity of the summary results. And we calculate the similarity between neighboring summary candidate frames based on the pHash difference [3]. Finally, we get a sequence of summary candidate frames with low redundancy.

2.2 Transforming to a Multi-dimensional Point Set

The frame candidate set obtained in the previous section is representative with low redundancy by block partitioning and similarity inhibition where a stable frame is selected from a frame block. Here, we do not consider the storyness property since the impact of storyness on the summary is usually insignificant, e.g., only 3% weighting for raw videos and 5% weighting for edited videos in [6]. Thus, we only consider it after we get an elementary summary and use it to improve the final summary quality. Besides above-mentioned properties, the importance and diversity properties are dominant for video summarization, especially the importance property. Therefore, in this section, we consider the scores of the entities of the importance property like object saliency, tracks, colorfulness, quality, and the score of the diversity property of frames. All the scores are normalized to the interval $[0, 1]$ and the higher value means the better. Finally, the 5-dimensional scores of each candidate frame are obtained.

2.3 Generating Keyframes via the Regret Minimization Query

The 5-dimensional scores of each candidate frame can be considered as 5 dimensions of a point in a space. Thus, the candidate frame set

can be considered as a 5-dimensional point set $\mathbf{P}$. The aim of our video summarization task is to find k keyframes to represent the whole video satisfying all users' preferences, i.e., our video summarization problem has been transformed into a multi-criterion problem. In the database community, the three useful tools to solve the problem are the top-k query, the skyline query and the regret minimization query [8]. Among above tools, only the top-k query and the regret minimization query can output a fixed-size summary while the skyline query output a summary with uncontrollable results which increases exponentially with dimensionality. For the top-k query, we must know the users' preferences, i.e., the preferences expressed by the weights in different dimensions should be provided. However, different users may have different preferences among the dimensions. Based on above analysis, we find the regret minimization query is able to output fixed-size summaries with unknown preferences. Generally, each user has her/his own preference function f which is called the utility function for the regret minimization query, and all the utility functions of the users compose a utility function space $\mathcal{F}$. Formally, a utility function f is expressed by $f = \langle f[1], f[2], \cdots, f[d] \rangle$ for a d-dimensional point set $\mathbf{P}$ where $f[i] \in \mathbb{R}^+$ and $\sum_{i=1}^{d} f[i] = 1$. A multi-dimensional point $p \in \mathbf{P}$ is with the form $p = (p[1], p[2], \cdots, p[d])$. The preference score or the utility of p under the utility function f is their production expressed as

$$f(p) = \sum_{i=1}^{d} f[i] \cdot p[i]. \tag{1}$$

Next, we define *gain* to capture the utility under f over a point set instead of only a point. Assume a summary with k keyframes selected from the point set $\mathbf{P}$ is denoted as $\mathbf{S}$. The gain of $\mathbf{S}$ under f is expressed by $g(\mathbf{S}, f) = \max_{p \in \mathbf{S}} f(p)$. Further, the *regret* can be defined by $r_{\mathbf{P}}(\mathbf{S}, f) = g(\mathbf{P}, f) - g(\mathbf{S}, f)$ and the *regret ratio* is defined by

$$rr_{\mathbf{P}}(\mathbf{S}, f) = \frac{r_{\mathbf{P}}(\mathbf{S}, f)}{g(\mathbf{P}, f)}. \tag{2}$$

The definition of regret ratio is reasonable since we use a summary $\mathbf{S}$ to represent the whole video denoted by $\mathbf{P}$. The value expresses how a user is unsatisfied when she/he only sees the summary expressed by $\mathbf{S}$ instead of the whole video $\mathbf{P}$. Obviously, the smaller value of the regret ratio, the better for the summary can fully delegate the whole video.

At length, we provide the notion of the *maximum regret ratio* (*mrr*) as follows:

$$mrr_{\mathbf{P}}(\mathbf{S}, \mathcal{F}) = \sup_{f \in \mathcal{F}} rr_{\mathbf{P}}(\mathbf{S}, f). \tag{3}$$

If the utility space $\mathcal{F}$ can be discretized to a finite set of utility functions, the maximum regret ratio can be expressed by:

$$mrr_{\mathbf{P}}(\mathbf{S}, \mathcal{F}) = \max_{f \in \mathcal{F}} rr_{\mathbf{P}}(\mathbf{S}, f). \tag{4}$$

The maximum regret ratio is to maximize the regret ratio over the worst case which guarantees the happiness of all users. After introducing the notion of maximum regret ratio, the aim of video summarization at this stage is to identify a point set $\mathbf{S}$ satisfying the size constraint, i.e., $|\mathbf{S}| \leq k$. The process in the database community is called the execution of a regret minimization query. It is obvious that identifying a size-k set $\mathbf{S}$ from the whole point set $\mathbf{P}$ is an NP-hard problem since there are C_n^k combinations needed to evaluate their maximum regret ratios where $|\mathbf{P}| = n$. Fortunately, the state-of-the-art approximate algorithm *Sphere* [13] with nearly optimal *mrr* has been proposed to solve our problem. In our experiments, we adopt the Sphere algorithm for the regret minimization query to compute $\mathbf{S}$ effectively and efficiently.

2.4 Adding Keyframes by Storyness

The Sphere algorithm for the regret minimization query may return a point set whose size is less than k. This is because the algorithm will not add any point to the result set when the maximum regret ratio reaches 0. To further improve the quality of the output summary, we exploit the storyness property which ensures that frames in the summary are distributed uniformly over the time sequence and form a smooth storyline where the summary content is easy to understand. Specifically, to ensure the output summary to tell a good story, we find the maximum time index interval in the summary frames and take the middle frame of the interval as the keyframe and add it to the result summary.

Table 1. Comparison of the algorithms under different metrics.

Algorithm	*Precision*(%)	*Recall*(%)	*F-score*(%)	*Redundancy*(%)	*nk*
OVP	43.21	48.41	43.10	2.81	9.70
DT	35.51	26.71	29.43	4.05	6.20
STIMO	34.73	40.03	35.75	2.70	10.00
VSUMM	47.26	42.34	43.52	**1.01**	7.70
SMRS	38.55	56.44	44.32	6.59	12.32
SOMP	38.51	61.41	45.44	4.28	13.90
MSR	36.94	57.61	43.39	12.03	13.36
AGDS	37.69	**64.76**	45.65	8.69	14.00
SBOMPc	41.40	64.27	48.46	2.78	12.58
SBOMPr	41.41	64.49	48.54	2.67	12.60
seqDPP	44.64	52.25	47.04	4.02	10.70
dppLSTM	42.67	59.40	47.91	3.17	11.80
OURS	**47.51**	57.99	**50.59**	2.62	10.84

3 Experiments

We use the dataset collected by the Open Video Project (OVP) [1]. Four quantitative evaluation metrics which are most commonly used in the literature,

Precision, *Recall*, *F-score*, and *Redundancy* are adopted to measure our summaries. We compared our method with classical and state-of-the-art methods of video summarization listed in [7], including those based on clustering, dictionary learning, deep learning, and others. In the comparison, the average summary length *nk* was also considered as a reference. The performance of each method is shown in Table 1. The best values of the metrics are highlighted in bold, and the second-best ones are underlined. The method in our paper has the best *F-score*, the best *precision*, and the second-best *Redundancy* among all the methods. The method with the second-best *F-score* is SBOMPr, which means that it is an efficient method of dividing frame blocks using the high similarity of temporally adjacent frames. In terms of *Redundancy*, it is worth noting that the VSUMM method, which is better than our method, has an average summary size of 7.7, much smaller than our method's 10.84. Hence, its summary has a low redundancy at the cost of lower summary integrity, resulting in a low *F-score* and unsatisfactory summary. In addition, the value of the *nk* metric of our method is acceptable compared with other methods.

4 Conclusion and Future Work

In this paper, we present a new property constrained video summarization framework based on the regret minimization query in the database community. The regret minimization query is carried out to get a video summary on a multi-dimensional dataset which is constructed from the properties of video frames. The experimental results prove the superiority of our framework, which gets the best performance with low redundancy. Our future work includes introducing versatile entities of the importance property and adding more properties into our framework to achieve better performance.

References

1. de Avila, S.E.F., Lopes, A.P.B., da Luz, A., de Albuquerque Araújo, A.: VSUMM: A mechanism designed to produce static video summaries and a novel evaluation method. Pattern Recogn. Lett. **32**(1), 56–68 (2011)
2. Basavarajaiah, M., Sharma, P.: Gvsum: generic video summarization using deep visual features. Multimedia Tools Appli. **80**, 14459–14476 (2021)
3. Chi Wong, H., Bern, M., Goldberg, D.: An image signature for any kind of image. In: ICIP, vol. 1, pp. 409–412 (2002)
4. Gygli, M., Grabner, H., Riemenschneider, H., Van Gool, L.: Creating summaries from user videos. In: Fleet, D., Pajdla, T., Schiele, B., Tuytelaars, T. (eds.) ECCV 2014. LNCS, vol. 8695, pp. 505–520. Springer, Cham (2014). https://doi.org/10.1007/978-3-319-10584-0_33
5. Gygli, M., Grabner, H., Van Gool, L.: Video summarization by learning submodular mixtures of objectives. In: CVPR, pp. 3090–3098 (2015)
6. Li, X., Zhao, B., Lu, X.: A general framework for edited video and raw video summarization. TIP **26**(8), 3652–3664 (2017)

7. Ma, M., Mei, S., Wan, S., Hou, J., Wang, Z., Feng, D.D.: Video summarization via block sparse dictionary selection. Neurocomputing **378**, 197–209 (2020)
8. Nanongkai, D., Sarma, A.D., Lall, A., Lipton, R.J., Xu, J.: Regret-minimizing representative databases. VLDB **3**(1), 1114–1124 (2010)
9. Souček, T., Lokoč, J.: TransNet v2: An effective deep network architecture for fast shot transition detection. arXiv preprint arXiv:2008.04838 (2020)
10. Teng, X., et al.: A multi-flexible video summarization scheme using property-constraint decision tree. Neurocomputing **506**, 406–417 (2022)
11. Tiwari, V., Bhatnagar, C.: A survey of recent work on video summarization: approaches and techniques. Multimedia Tools Appli. **80**(18), 27187–27221 (2021). https://doi.org/10.1007/s11042-021-10977-y
12. Wang, S., et al.: Scalable gastroscopic video summarization via similar-inhibition dictionary selection. Artif. Intell. Med. **66**, 1–13 (2016)
13. Xie, M., Wong, R.C., Li, J., Long, C., Lall, A.: Efficient k-regret query algorithm with restriction-free bound for any dimensionality. In: SIGMOD, pp. 959–974 (2018)

Enhancing Keyphrase Generation by BART Finetuning with Splitting and Shuffling

Bin Chen and Mizuho Iwaihara(✉)

Graduate School of Information, Production, and Systems, Waseda University, Kitakyushu 808-0135, Japan
chenbin@asagi.waseda.jp, iwaihara@waseda.jp

Abstract. Keyphrase generation is a task of identifying a set of phrases that best represent the main topics or themes of a given text. Keyphrases are dividend int present and absent keyphrases. Recent approaches utilizing sequence-to-sequence models show effectiveness on absent keyphrase generation. However, the performance is still limited due to the hardness of finding absent keyphrases. In this paper, we propose Keyphrase-Focused BART, which exploits the differences between present and absent keyphrase generations, and performs finetuning of two separate BART models for present and absent keyphrases. We further show effective approaches of shuffling keyphrases and candidate keyphrase ranking. For absent keyphrases, our Keyphrase-Focused BART achieved new state-of-the-art score on F1@5 in two out of five keyphrase generation benchmark datasets.

Keywords: keyphrase generation · deep learning · BART Finetuning · generative language model

1 Introduction

Keyphrase generation is an important task that involves identifying a set of terms or phrases that best represent the main topics or themes of a given text, having applications in information retrieval, document classification, and summarization. A **present keyphrase** is such that its word sequence appears in the document with its order preserved. Present keyphrases can be extracted from the document. An **absent keyphrase** is not present in the text but relevant to the topic of the document.

Keyphrase extraction has been extensively studied [1, 6, 9]. However, extractive methods cannot find absent keyphrases that have not appeared in the article. Recent generative methods, such as CopyRNN [5] and CatSeq [13], can directly generate candidate present and absent keyphrases from input document representations.

BART is a pre-trained generative language model based on a denoising autoencoder [7], which can directly perform sequence generation tasks through finetuning, which can be applied to keyphrase generation [6].

We point out that in most of the previous work based on generative language models, finetuning is done on present and absent keyphrases together [6]. However, we argue that there exist considerable differences in the tasks of extracting present keyphrases

F. Liu et al. (Eds.): PRICAI 2023, LNAI 14325, pp. 305–310, 2024.
https://doi.org/10.1007/978-981-99-7019-3_29

and generating absent keyphrases, which motivates us to propose splitting the absent and present keyphrase generation tasks into two parts, and train two different generative models, where different hyperparameters are used for finetuning.

The main contributions of this paper are: (1) A new model *Keyphrase-Focused BART* is proposed, in which two BART models are finetuned separately on present and absent keyphrases, with different hyperparameter settings. (2) Shuffling keyphrase lists for prompting order-independence and augmenting samples is proposed. (3) A keyphrase ranker by a BERT cross-encoder combined with TF-IDF is introduced to improve keyphrases generated by the BART models. (4) Our experimental evaluation confirms effectiveness of these approaches. Our proposed Keyphrase-Focused BART shows new state-of-the-art records on absent keyphrases, on datasets SemEval and KP20K on F1@5. The ratio of F1@5 over the previous state-of-the-art is ranging between 9 to 37%, showing a wide improvement.

2 Related Work

The following models are representative generative models, and compared against our proposed model in our evaluations:

CatSeq [13]: An RNN-based sequence-to-sequence model with copy mechanism trained under ONE2SEQ paradigm.

CatSeqTG-2RF1 [2]: Based on CatSeq with title encoding and cross-attention.

GAN$_{\mathbf{MR}}$ [10]: RL-based fine-tuning extension on CatSeq.

Fast and Constrained Absent KG [11]: Prompt-based keyphrase generation methods, with prompt created around keyword and apply mask predict decoder.

ONE2SET [12]: A sequence-to-sequence model based on transformers. ONE2SET generates a set of keyphrases, where the keyphrase order is ignored.

ONE2SET + KPDrop-a [4]: KRDrop randomly drops present keyphrases for enhancing absent keyphrase generation.

ChatGPT [8]: The large language model ChatGPT is instructed to generate keyphrases.

3 Keyphrase-Focused BART

Figure 1 shows our proposed model **Keyphrase-Focused BART**, which has two generative pretrained language models finetuned separately on present and absent keyphrases.

Language Model Separation: In the existing approaches [2, 4, 10-13] of keyphrase generation by generative language models, just a single language model is trained over the union of present and absent keyphrases. KPDrop [5] randomly masks present keyphrases to be used as augmentation for absent keyphrases, where the absent prediction could be enhanced when the absent and masked phrases are semantically similar.

But keyphrases are often topically distinct each other. Also, absent phrases need to be chosen from candidates that are vastly larger than the present phrases. The imbalanced candidate spaces for present and absent keyphrases will cause differences in the optimum training processes for both types.

To resolve the above issues, we introduce an architecture in which two separated BART models are trained independently, where one model is trained only by present keyphrases, while the other model is trained only by absent keyphrases. Different hyper-parameter settings are used for these BART models, to separately optimize the learning processes for the two tasks.

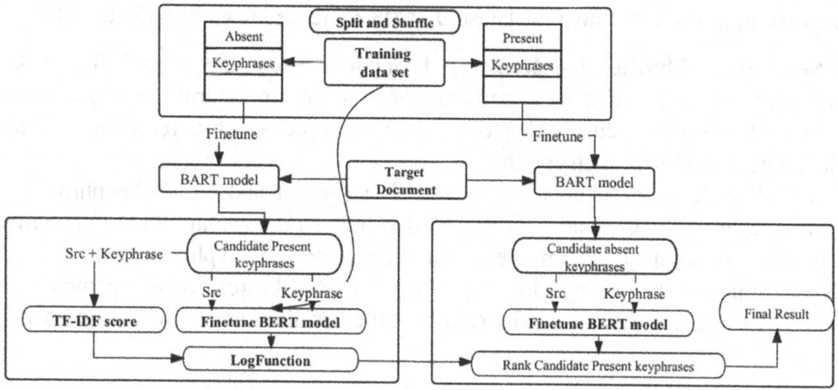

Fig. 1. Model Architecture of Keyphrase-Focused BART

Shuffling and Expanding: Keyphrase lists shall be order independent. In [12], it is mentioned that the BART model might try to generate keyphrases by considering contextual relationships between the keyphrases. To reduce contextualities in learning output sequences, we apply shuffling on the training keyphrase lists, and add the shuffled sequences to the training dataset.

Ranking by BERT Cross-Encoder: We formulate ranking candidate keyphrases as a binary classification task such that the reference keyphrases are labeled as 1, otherwise 0. The confidence score of a finetuned BERT cross-encoder [3] is is coupled with TF-IDF score as: $logScore = [\alpha * \log Cross + (1 - \alpha) * \log tf\_idf]$, where parameter α is set to 0.7 in this paper. Note that TF-IDF score is not applicable for absent keyphrases.

4 Experiments

4.1 Experimental Settings

We perform experiments on the five widely-used benchmark keyphrase datasets [12]: Inspec, Krapivin, NUS, SemEval, and KP20K. The baseline models we compared are those listed in bold fonts in Sect. 2. Below lists variations of our model, evaluated as ablations in the experiments:

Basic BART: BART model finetuned on the union of present and absent key-phrases.

A-P Separate: Two BART models are finetuned on 1) present keyphrases only, with 4 training epochs, and 2) absent keyphrases only, and 8 training epochs, where more epochs are allocated than present keyphrase model, to deal with slow convergence. The learning rate and batch size are 1e-5 and 12, respectively, for both BART models. No shuffling on keyphrase lists is done.

A-P Separate + Shuffle(1): A-P Separate, and shuffling phrase lists once and add new lists into training dataset. The final dataset KP20K increased from 514,154 to 848,684.

A-P Separate + Shuffle(2): A-P Separate, and shuffling phrase lists twice and add new lists into training dataset. The final dataset KP20K increased from 514,154 to 1,086,979.

A-P Separate + Shuffle(1) + Rank: A-P Separate + Shuffle(1), and then ranking by the BERT cross encoder. Its hyperparameter settings are: learning rate 5e-6, batch size 24, and training epochs 3. Negative filtering is used which is removing correctly predicted negatives after each epoch.

We follow [2, 4] on evaluation metrics. For present and absent keyphrases, we use macro-average $F1@5$ and $F1@M$. $F1@M$ takes into account all the keyphrases generated by the model and compares them to the reference keyphrases.

The results are shown in Table 1 and Table 2. All the results of our models are obtained by averaging four runs. The results of the baselines are from the cited papers.

4.2 Results and Analysis

Results on Present Keyphrases: From Table 1, we can see that A-P Separate that separates the training dataset shows improves over Basic BART. By adding shuffling and separating to A-P Separate, the F1 scores of present keyphrases are further improved compared to using the basic BART model directly, but there is still a gap compared to ONE2SET [12]. Then the model A-P Separate + Shuffle(1) + Rank that uses the ranking unit by BERT cross-encoder and TF-IDF is further improving performance, and achieving highest F1@5 result on the Inspec dataset. We find that shuffling twice is rather falling behind of shuffling once, so we choose A-P Separate + Shuffle(1) + Rank as our best model for present keyphrases.

Results on Absent Keyphrases: The results on absent keyphrases are shown in Table 2. We find that shuffling keyphrases once and expanding a dataset is showing improvements of 0 – 1.0% on F1 score. The ranking unit, on the other hand, shows little or no improvement of -0.3 to + 0.1% to the model without the ranking unit.

Overall, our Keyphrase-focused BART, with configuration of A-P Separate + Shuffle (1), achieved new state-of-the-art results on SemEval and KP20K on F1@5. The improvement of F1@5 over ONE2SET-KPDrop-a is ranging between 9 to 37%, achieving wide improvements. ChatGPT is showing highest score on Inspec, but the scores reported in [8] are falling behind of our proposed model on the other three datasets.

Table 1. Results on Present Keyphrases (F1-score ×100)

	Inspec		NUS		Krapivin		SemEval		KP20K	
Model	F1@5	F1@M	F1@5	F1@M	F1@5	F1@M	F1@5	F1@M	F1@5	F1@M
CatSeq [13]	22.5	26.2	32.3	39.7	26.9	35.4	24.2	28.3	29.1	36.7
CatSeqTG-2RF1 [2]	25.3	30.1	37.5	43.3	30.0	36.9	28.7	32.9	32.1	38.6
GANMR [10]	25.8	29.9	34.8	41.7	28.8	36.9	-	-	30.3	37.8
Fast and Constrained [11]	26.0	29.4	41.2	43.9	-	-	32.9	35.6	35.1	35.5
SET-TRANS (ONE 2SET) [12]	28.5	32.4	40.6	**45.1**	32.6	**36.4**	33.1	**35.7**	35.9	39.2
ONE2SET-KPDrop-a [4]	29.8	30.6	**42.6**	44.4	**34.0**	35.3	**33.6**	34.4	**38.5**	**39.6**
ChatGPT [8]	32.5	**40.3**	-	20.0	-	-	-	18.6	23.2	25.1
Proposed **Keyphrase-Focused BART** finetuned on present keyphrases										
Basic BART	29.5	29.5	27.1	27.1	19.9	19.9	21.4	21.4	30.7	30.7
A-P Separate + NoShuffle	30.9	30.9	34.7	34.7	25.2	25.2	22.7	22.7	29.9	29.9
A-P Separate + Shuffle(1)	33.1	33.1	37.9	37.9	27.8	27.8	27.6	27.8	31.5	31.5
A-P Separate + Shuffle(2)	32.9	32.9	37.2	37.2	32.3	32.3	23.9	23.9	30.3	30.3
A-P Separate + Shuffle(1) + Rank	**35.8**	35.8	41.2	41.2	29.0	29.0	28.3	28.3	33.7	33.7

Table 2. Results on Absent Keyphrases (F1-score ×100)

	Inspec		NUS		Krapivin		SemEval		KP20K	
Model	F1@5	F1@M	F1@5	F1@M	F1@5	F1@M	F1@5	F1@M	F1@5	F1@M
CatSeq [13]	0.4	0.8	1.6	2.8	1.8	3.6	1.6	2.8	1.5	3.2
CatSeqTG-2RF1[2]	1.2	2.1	1.9	3.1	3.0	5.3	2.1	3.0	2.7	5.0
GANMR [10]	1.3	1.9	2.6	3.8	4.2	5.7	-	-	3.2	4.5
Fast and Constrained [11]	1.7	2.2	3.6	4.2	-	-	2.8	3.2	3.2	4.2
SET-TRANS (ONE 2SET) [12]	2.1	3.4	4.2	6.0	4.8	**7.3**	2.6	3.5	3.6	5.8
ONE2SET-KPDrop-a [4]	3.2	3.2	**7.4**	**7.4**	**7.2**	7.2	4.6	4.7	6.5	6.6
ChatGPT [8]	**4.9**	**5.9**	-	4.2	-	-	-	2.1	4.4	5.6
Proposed **Keyphrase-Focused BART** finetuned on absent keyphrases										
Basic BART	2.4	2.4	3.8	3.8	3.8	3.8	2.9	2.9	6.5	6.5
A-P Separate + NoShuffle	2.4	2.4	5.6	5.6	6.1	6.1	4.5	4.5	7.9	7.9
A-P Separate + Shuffle(1)	2.4	2.4	5.6	5.6	6.4	6.4	4.9	4.9	**8.9**	**8.9**
A-P Separate + Shuffle(1) + Rank	2.3	2.3	5.6	5.6	6.0	6.0	**5.0**	**5.0**	8.8	8.8

5 Conclusion and Future Work

In this paper, we proposed a generative language model approach for keyphrase generation. We show that splitting the generative language model into two tasks of absent keyphrase generation and present keyphrase extraction, and training them separately bring considerable performance improvements. Overall, for absent keyphrase generation, our Keyphrase-focused BART shows improvements on F1@5 by 9 and 37% on two datasets, from the previous state-of-the-art model. In future work, we will consider integrating prompt-based approaches for ranking candidate keyphrases.

References

1. Bennani-Smires, K., Musat,C., Hossmann, A., et al.: Simple unsupervised keyphrase extraction using sentence embeddings. CoNLL, **221** (2018)
2. Chan, H.P., Chen, W., Wang, L., King, I.: Neural keyphrase generation via reinforcement learning with adaptive rewards. Proc. ACL2019, pp. 2163–2174 (2019)
3. Chen, Q., Zhuo, Z., Wang, W.: Bert for Joint Intent Classification and Slot Filling. arXiv preprint arXiv:1902.10909 (2019)
4. Chowdhury, J.R., Park S.Y., Kundu, T., Caragea, C.: KPDROP: Improving Absent Keyphrase Generation. Proc. EMNLP2022, pp. 4853–4870 (2022)
5. Gu, J., Lu, Z., Li, H., Li, V.O.K.: Incorporating copying mechanism in sequence-to-sequence learning. Proc. ACL2016, pp. 1631–1640 (2016)
6. Kulkarni, M., Mahata, D., Arora, R., et al.: Learning Rich Representation of Keyphrases from Text. arXiv preprint arXiv:2112.08547 (2021)
7. Lewis, M., Liu, Y., Goyal, N., et al.: BART: Denoising sequence-to-sequence pre-training for natural language generation, translation, and comprehension. Proc. ACL2020, pp. 7871–7880 (2020)
8. Martínez-Cruz, R., López-López, A.J., Portela, J.: ChatGPT vs State-of-the-Art Models: A Benchmarking Study in Keyphrase Generation Task. arXiv preprint arXiv:2304.14177 (2023)
9. Mihalcea, R., Tarau, P.: TextRank: Bringing order into text, Proc. 2004 Conf. Empirical Methods in Natural Language Processing, pp. 404–411 (2004)
10. Swaminathan, A., Zhang, H., Mahata, D., et al.: A preliminary exploration of GANs for keyphrase generation, Proc. 2020 Conf. Empirical Methods in Natural Language Processing (EMNLP), pp. 8021–8030 (2020)
11. Wu, H., Ma, B., Liu, W., et al.: Fast and constrained absent keyphrase generation by prompt-based learning. Proc. AAAI Conf. Artificial Intelligence **36**(10), 11495–11503 (2022)
12. Ye, J., Gui, T., Luo, Y., et al.: ONE2SET: generating diverse keyphrases as a set. Proc. ACL2021, pp. 4598–4608 (2021)
13. Yuan, X., Wang, T., Meng, R., et al.: One size does not fit all: generating and evaluating variable number of keyphrases. Proc. ACL2020, pp. 7961–7975 (2018)

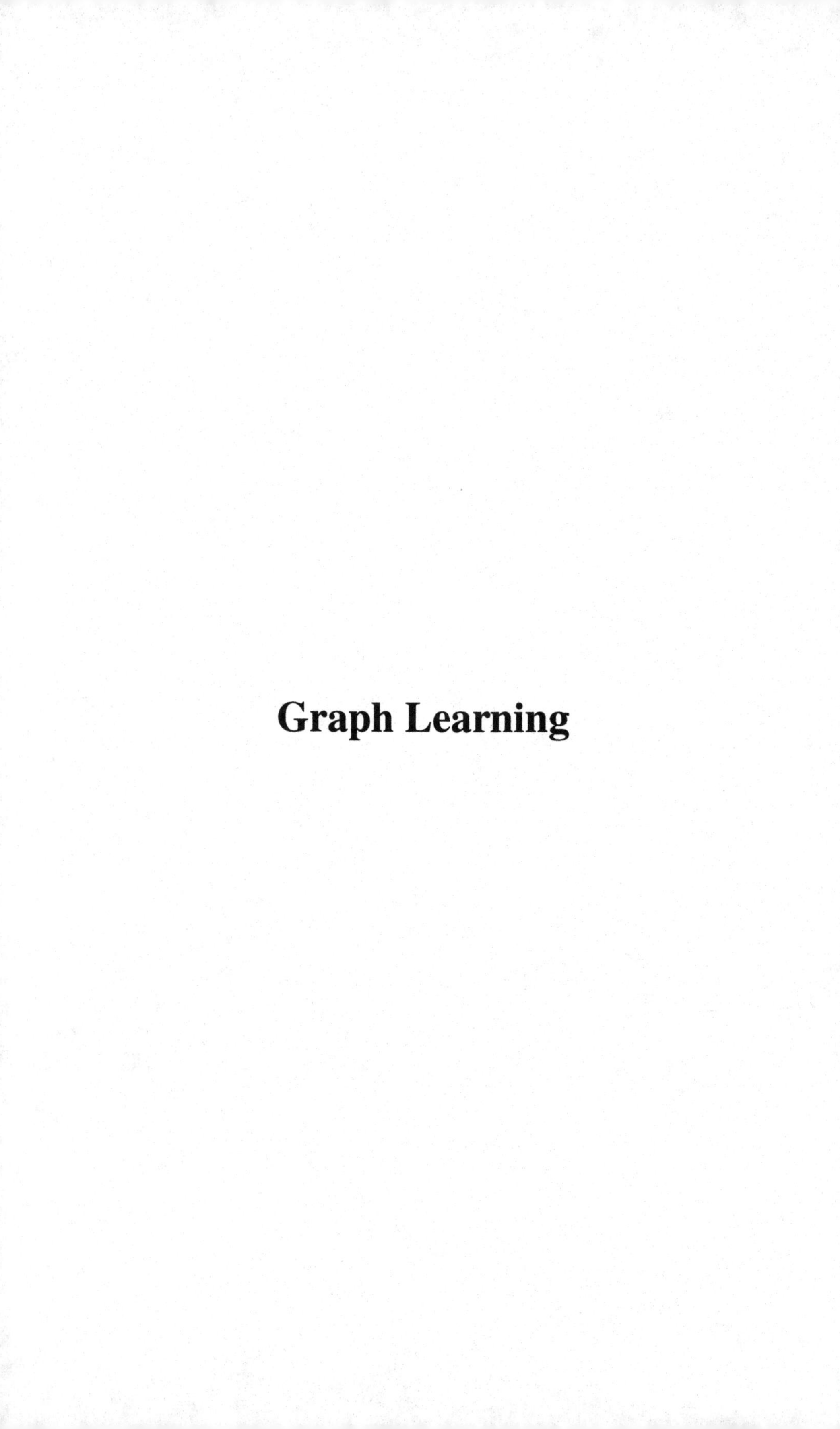

Graph Learning

A Dynamic-aware Heterogeneous Graph Neural Network for Next POI Recommendation

Tianci Wang[1,2], Yantong Lai[1,2(✉)], Gaode Chen[1,2], Ruohan Wang[1,2], Jiahui Shen[1], and Ji Xiang[1,2]

[1] Institute of Information Engineering, Chinese Academy of Sciences, Beijing, China
{wangtianci,laiyantong,wangruohan,shenjiahui,xiangji}@iie.ac.cn
[2] School of Cyber Security, University of Chinese Academy of Sciences, Beijing, China
chengaode19@gmail.com

Abstract. Next point-of-interest (POI) recommendation is of great importance for both location-based service providers and users. Current state-of-the-art methods view users and POIs as unified latent representations, and model users' transition patterns from global and local views. However, most of them still have following limitations: 1) Ignoring user's dynamic behavioral intention, which is significantly influenced by current temporal and spatial factors. 2) Insufficiently considering different activity connotations of POIs in various temporal contexts. To tackle these challenges, we propose a novel method Dynamic-aware Heterogeneous Graph Neural Network (DyHGN) for next POI recommendation, which jointly learns fine-grained representations from global and local views. In the global view, we first construct a series of dynamic-aware heterogeneous graphs, and design a fine-grained temporal enhanced graph neural network to learn users' dynamic behavioral intentions and POIs' dynamic activity connotations. In the local view, we propose a dynamic information aggregation module that employs a well-designed information enhancement layer to enhance robustness of the model. Furthermore, we improve the attention mechanism to learn important spatio-temporal factors in users' behavior. Extensive experimental results on two real-world public datasets demonstrate the effectiveness of our proposed method.

Keywords: Next POI recommendation · Heterogeneous graph neural networks · Attention mechanism

1 Introduction

In the era of information explosion, service providers are committed to developing recommender systems to alleviate information overload [1], where next point-of-interest (POI) recommendation is one of the crucial tasks of location-based social network (LBSN) service and has received widespread attention.

F. Liu et al. (Eds.): PRICAI 2023, LNAI 14325, pp. 313–326, 2024.
https://doi.org/10.1007/978-981-99-7019-3_30

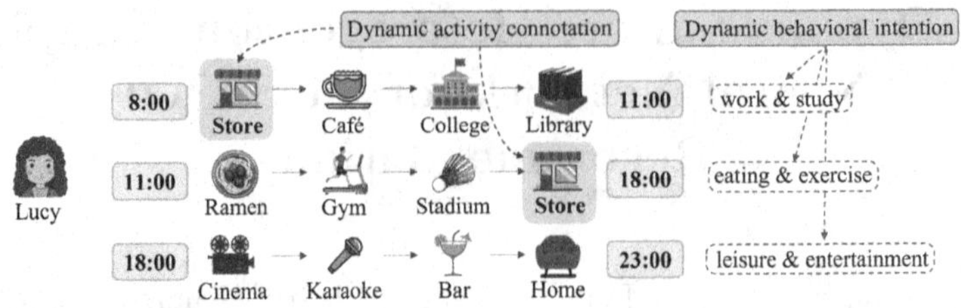

Fig. 1. A motivating example of the dynamic information in trajectories

Considering both users' current spatio-temporal contexts and historical preferences, next POI recommendation aims to suggest the subsequent locations that the user might be interested in [8,16].

Next POI recommendation is a challenging task since users' present preferences can be simultaneously influenced by some factors, e.g., sequential and spatio-temporal [14]. Early studies mainly explored the impacts of sequential and spatio-temporal factors of check-ins based on Markov chains [3] and recurrent neural networks (RNNs) [4]. For example, Zhao et al. [23] proposed a RNN-based method STGCN, which designed time and distance gates to explore spatio-temporal difference information between continuous check-ins. Recently, with the great success of attention mechanism [18] and graph neural networks (GNNs) [7], researchers have leveraged their natural flexible structures to model complex relations in next POI recommendation. For instance, to confirm the significance of non-adjacent locations and non-consecutive visits, Luo et al. [12] proposed STAN by extending the attention mechanism with spatio-temporal relation matrix and achieved considerable performance. Yu et al. [21] presented a heterogeneous graph-based method NGPR, which jointly considered the impacts of POI categories, check-in frequency, popularity and geographical distance on modeling users' preferences. Researchers [13] constructed homogeneous GNNs by utilizing distance and transition relations between POIs to capture the high-order POIs that might intrigue users.

Generally, most prior studies obtained an overall and static representation for each user and POI separately for next POI recommendation. However, they still have some notable limitations: 1) **The dynamic behavioral intentions of users have not been fully considered.** An overall user embedding only mirrors historical preferences, but is insufficient to reflect the dynamic behavioral intentions of users in different periods. As shown in Fig. 1, Lucy tends to study and work in the mornings, exercise in the afternoons, and socialize with friends at leisure venues in the evenings. 2) **Ignoring the dynamic activity connotations of POIs in various temporal contexts.** A static unified POI embedding vector could not fully reflect the activity connotations in different time slots. For instance in Fig. 1, Lucy enjoys stopping by the store in morning to buy bread for breakfast. In this case, the store is similar to POIs such as breakfast restaurants and coffee shops. Later in the day, after hearty exercising, she tends to purchase a drink in store and this time the store is close to bubble tea shops and ice cream parlors.

To solve above problems, we propose a novel method Dynamic-aware Heterogeneous Graph Neural Network (DyHGN) for next POI recommendation. Specifically, we first construct a series of heterogeneous graphs in the global view to capture dynamic relations between user and POI at different time slots, and utilize region and category as auxiliary information to enrich their representations. Then we design a novel fine-grained temporal graph neural network, which leverages flexible propagation mechanism and relation-aware graph neural network to learn dynamic representation of each node in the graphs. In the local view, we propose a dynamic information aggregation module which integrates fine-grained periodic and contextual information with a well-designed robust fusion method. Moreover, we extend the bi-attention layers by spatio-temporal relation matrices to capture the significant temporal and spatial factors in user behavior. Finally, we employ an attention scoring layer to score and rank the candidate POIs.

In summary, our main contributions are as follows:

- We propose a novel DyHGN, which explicitly considers the dynamics of POI and user representations to capture fine-grained user behavioral intentions and different activity connotations of POIs.
- Fine-grained temporal graph neural network modeling the dynamic relations among users, POIs, regions and categories is designed to enrich node representations.
- We utilize a information enhancement layer to fuse periodic and contextual fine-grained information, and improve the attention mechanism by capturing spatio-temporal correlations in users' trajectories.
- Extensive experiments on two public available datasets show that our proposed DyHGN method achieves significant improvement over existing methods.

2 Related Work

Next POI Recommendation. Next POI recommendation aims to provide users with a set of candidate POIs, where the POI that the users are most likely to visit next will be highly ranked. Early study [3] has used Markov chains to capture the sequential characteristics in user check-in records. Subsequently, many methods based on RNN and its variants emerged to make full use of the rich auxiliary information. Studies [11,23] attempted to model spatio-temporal contextual information to explore the influence of time and space on user behavior. Zang et al. [22] proposed CHA to explore the category hierarchy of POIs to help learn robust location representations even when there was insufficient data. Huang et at. [6] aimed to leverage social neighbor information to enhance the performance of next POI recommendation. Limited to contiguous visits in these RNN-based methods, study [12] started to extend attention mechanism by spatio-temporal relation matrix in an explicit or implicit way.

GNN-Based POI Recommendation. GNNs have gained attention in next POI recommendation due to the natural ability to represent complex node relations. To capture the spatio-temporal influences, GE [19] innovatively constructed four bipartite graphs to jointly learn the semantics of POIs, regions, time slots and POIs in a same low-dimensional space. STMG [13] aimed to learn POI-POI relations from a global view by constructing edges based on the difference in time and distance of check-ins. STP-UDGAT [10] constructed POI-POI relation graphs by physical distance and transition frequency between global POIs. Considering the dynamic factors in item recommendation, Chen et al. [2] enhanced the interpretability of recommendation by temporal meta-paths in Knowledge Graphs. However, few works consider the dynamic activity connotations of POIs and behavioral intentions of users affected by different spatio-temporal contexts in location recommendation.

3 Problem Formulation

Let $\mathcal{U} = \{u_1, u_2, ..., u_{|\mathcal{U}|}\}$ denote a set of users, $\mathcal{P} = \{p_1, p_2, ..., p_{|\mathcal{P}|}\}$ denote POIs. Each POI p_i has a unique geographical coordinate tuple (lon_i, lat_i) as well as an activity category label (e.g., Bar). We use GeoHash[1] to partition the POIs into regions, and let $\mathcal{R} = \{r_1, r_2, ..., r_{|\mathcal{R}|}\}$ be a set of all regions. $C = \{c_1, c_2, ..., c_{|C|}\}$ be POI categories.

Definition 1: **Check-in record.** A check-in record $l_j^{u_i} = (u_i, p_z, r_m, c_n, t_j)$ indicates user u_i has visited POI p_z in region r_m at timestamp t_j, and c_n is the category of p_z.

Definition 2: **Trajectory.** The trajectory of user u_i is a sequence that consists of all his/her check-in records sorted by timestamp. We transform each trajectory into a fixed-length sequence and denote it as $S^{u_i} = \{l_1^{u_i}, l_2^{u_i}, ..., l_L^{u_i}\}$, L represents the maximum length. The trajectories of all users can be described as $\mathcal{S} = \{S^{u_1}, S^{u_2}, ..., S^{u_{|\mathcal{U}|}}\}$.

Problem: **Next POI Recommendation.** Given users' historical check-in trajectories $\mathcal{S}$, our goal is to recommend top-K POIs for each user u_i at next timestamp t.

4 Method

In this section, we introduce the proposed DyHGN in detail, which is mainly composed of two stages in Fig. 2. We first introduce the methodology of building fine-grained temporal enhanced graph neural network and provide a detailed explanation of the well-designed dynamic information aggregation module.

[1] http://geohash.org/, we use precision 5, with each grid cell covering 4.9 km × 4.9 km.

4.1 Dynamic-Aware Heterogeneous Graphs Construction

Check-in behavior is simultaneously affected by numerous dynamic factors. For this reason, we divide a week into $|\mathcal{T}|$ time slots and construct a set of dynamic-aware heterogeneous graphs $\mathcal{G} = \{\mathcal{G}_1, \mathcal{G}_2, ..., \mathcal{G}_{|\mathcal{T}|}\}$ in the global view (Fig. 2 stage1).

We map each record in $\mathcal{S}$ to its corresponding graph $\mathcal{G}_{ts}$ by check-in time slot ts and construct edges with seven types of relation: 1) **User-POI.** Edge $e_{i,z,ts}$ means that user u_i has visited POI p_z at time slot ts, which can visually reflect user preferences during ts. 2) **POI-Region.** Edge $e_{z,m,ts}$ indicates that a user has visited POI p_z (located in region r_m) during ts. 3) **POI-Category.** Edge $e_{z,n,ts}$ means that the activity type of the POI p_z belongs to category c_n, which facilitates implicit capturing the type of activities that users are interested in during ts. 4) **Region-Category.** Edge $e_{m,n,ts}$ connects region r_m and activity category c_n if any user has left a check-in record at ts. This type of edge can capture the primary activities provided by region r_m. 5) **POI-POI.** Edge $e_{z_1,z_2,ts}$ connects p_{z_1} and p_{z_2} if any user has visited both POIs during the same period ts. 6) **Region-Region.** Edge $e_{m_1,m_2,ts}$ exists when region r_{m_1} and r_{m_2} are physically adjacent, or visited by the same user during ts. 7) **Category-Category.** Edge $e_{n_1,n_2,ts}$ indicates a user has visited the POIs of both types c_{n_1} and c_{n_2} during ts. Finally, we initialize embeddings for all nodes in each graph. For example, the initialization embeddings for user node u_i form the set $\{\mathbf{e}_{u_i}^1, \mathbf{e}_{u_i}^2, \cdots, \mathbf{e}_{u_i}^{|\mathcal{T}|}\}$, where $\mathbf{e}_{u_i}^{ts} \in \mathbb{R}^d$ and d represents the embedding dimension.

4.2 Fine-Grained Temporal Enhanced Graph Neural Network

Inspired by RGCN [15], we design a novel fine-grained network to learn nodes embeddings in heterogeneous graphs. For each relation r, we construct a trainable transition matrix $W_r^{(ts)} \in \mathbb{R}^{d \times d'}$ to capture high-dimensional features of nodes, where d' is the hidden vector dimension. Then, the message aggregation function can be described as:

$$\mathbf{e}_i^{(ts,l+1)} = \sigma\left(W_0^{(ts,l)}\mathbf{e}_i^{(ts,l)} + \sum_{r\in R}\sum_{j\in N_i^{(ts,r)}} \frac{1}{c_i^{ts,r}} W_r^{(ts,l)}\mathbf{e}_j^{(ts,l)}\right) \tag{1}$$

where $\mathbf{e}_j^{(ts,l)}$ represents the raw message propagated by neighbor node j and $\mathbf{e}_i^{(ts,l+1)}$ denotes the representation of center node i at layer $l+1$. $N_i^{(ts,r)}$ represents all neighbors of node i under relation r, and $c_i^{ts,r} = |N_i^{(ts,r)}|$ denotes the normalization constant. $\sigma(\cdot)$ represents the sigmoid activation function. To optimize our model in stage1, we design an unsupervised loss function based on negative sampling:

$$\mathcal{L}(i, ts) = -\left[\log\sigma\left(\mathbf{e}_i^{ts\mathsf{T}} \cdot \mathbf{e}_j^{ts}\right) + \sum_{n\in NEG(i,ts)} \log\sigma\left(-\mathbf{e}_i^{ts\mathsf{T}} \cdot \mathbf{e}_n^{ts}\right)\right] \tag{2}$$

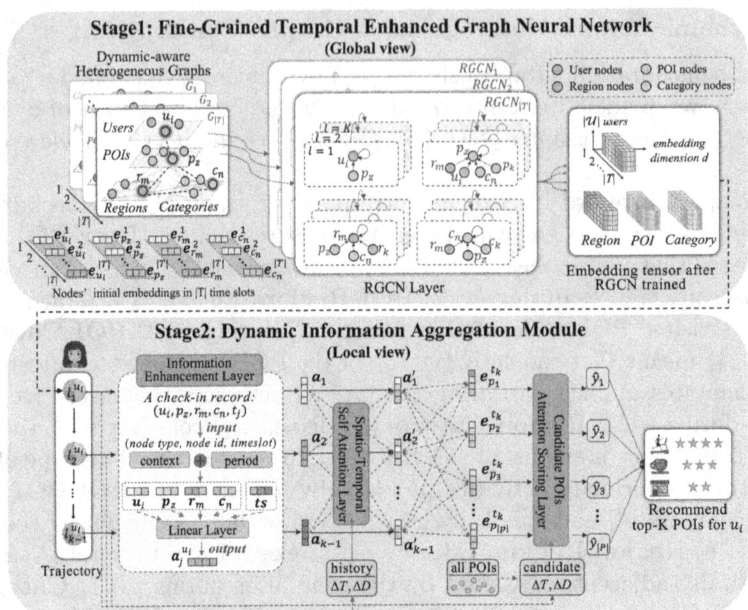

Fig. 2. Dynamic-aware Heterogeneous Graph Neural Network

where $\mathbf{e}_i^{ts}$ is the embedding of node i output by the last layer ($l = K$), j is the neighbor nodes of i, and $NEG(i, ts)$ is the set of negative samples of node i in time slot ts.

4.3 Dynamic Information Aggregation Module

Information Enhancement Layer. To reduce the impacts of check-in time fluctuations and the time slot division on node embedding representation, we fuse periodic and contextual fine-grained information for each node in time slot ts.

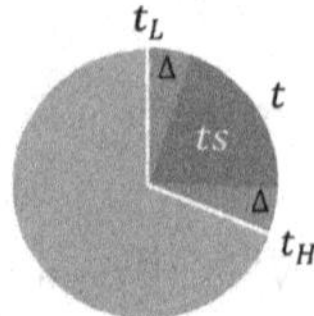

Fig. 3. Context fusion

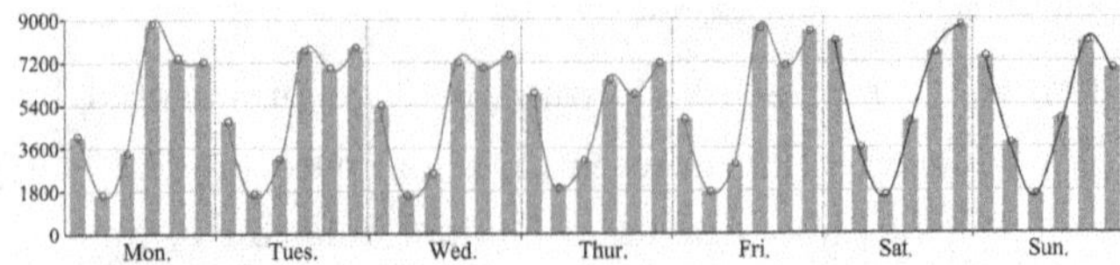

Fig. 4. Temporal periodicity of user activity signals in the NYC dataset

• *Contextual Information Fusion.* As shown in Fig. 3, each time slot consists of two parts: i) A central section which exhibits a high tolerance to check-in time jitter, and ii) Two easily disturbed end sections (e.g., splitting the check-ins at 19:59 and 20:01 into two time slots would result in significantly different node embeddings). We define the following formula to fuse the contextual information:

$$\mathbf{e}_{i,(ctxt)}^{ts} = \begin{cases} \mathbf{e}_i^{ts} & \text{if } t_L + \Delta < t < t_H - \Delta \\ [1 - \frac{(t_L+\Delta)-t}{2\Delta}] \cdot \mathbf{e}_i^{ts} + [\frac{(t_L+\Delta)-t}{2\Delta}] \cdot \mathbf{e}_i^{ts-1} & \text{if } t_L < t < t_L + \Delta \\ [1 - \frac{t-(t_H-\Delta)}{2\Delta}] \cdot \mathbf{e}_i^{ts} + [\frac{t-(t_H-\Delta)}{2\Delta}] \cdot \mathbf{e}_i^{ts+1} & \text{if } t_H - \Delta < t < t_H \end{cases} \tag{3}$$

where t is the specific check-in time of the record, and t in time slot ts. Δ is the disturbance-susceptible threshold. t_H and t_L represent the upper and lower bound time points of ts. $\mathbf{e}_i^{ts-1}$ and $\mathbf{e}_i^{ts+1}$ represent the embeddings of node i in last and next time slots. $\mathbf{e}_{i,(ctxt)}^{ts}$ denotes the representation of node i after context information fusion.

• *Periodic Information Fusion.* The activity patterns of users exhibit pronounced periodic behavior as shown in Fig. 4. Accounting for this feature, we fuse the periodic information as follows:

$$\mathbf{e}_{i,(peri)}^{ts} = \frac{1}{|WK(ts)|} \sum_{tn \in WK(ts)} \mathbf{e}_i^{tn} \tag{4}$$

where $WK(ts)$ is the set of time slots within the week that are in the same period as ts.

Then, the final expression of node i is $\mathbf{e}_i^{ts} = \mu \cdot \mathbf{e}_{i,(ctxt)}^{ts} + (1-\mu) \cdot \mathbf{e}_{i,(peri)}^{ts}$, where the parameter μ serves to balance the contextual and periodic information.

• *Local Information Aggregation Output.* For a check-in record $l_j^{u_i} = (u_i, p_z, r_m, c_n, t_j)$, we first project time t_j to the corresponding time slot ts, and obtain the embedding vector $\mathbf{ts}$. Then, we apply the above information enhancement operations to four types of nodes, yielding vectors $\mathbf{u}_i^{ts}$, $\mathbf{p}_z^{ts}$, $\mathbf{r}_m^{ts}$ and $\mathbf{c}_n^{ts}$. The final representation of $l_j^{u_i}$ is:

$$\mathbf{a}_j^{u_i} = \text{FFN}(\text{Concat}(\mathbf{u}_i^{ts}, \mathbf{p}_z^{ts}, \mathbf{r}_m^{ts}, \mathbf{c}_n^{ts}, \mathbf{ts})) \tag{5}$$

where $\text{FFN}(\cdot)$ is a feed-forward network and $\text{Concat}(\cdot)$ represents the concatenation operation on the corresponding embeddings. Then, the embedding of the history trajectory sequence S^{u_i} can be represented as $E_{(hist)} = [\mathbf{a}_1, \mathbf{a}_2 ..., \mathbf{a}_L] \in \mathbb{R}^{L \times d}$.

Spatio-Temporal Self-Attention Layer. Inspired by STAN, we improve the attention mechanism by integrating the spatio-temporal relation information between check-in records. We first define spatio-temporal relation matrices as follows:

$$\begin{cases} T_{m,n}^{(hist)} = \psi(\Delta t_{m,n}) \\ D_{m,n}^{(hist)} = \psi(\Delta d_{m,n}) \end{cases} \tag{6}$$

where m and n represent any two check-ins in trajectory S^{u_i}. Temporal weight matrix $T_{m,n}^{(hist)} \in \mathbb{R}^{L\times L}$ and $\Delta t_{m,n} = |t_m - t_n|$. Spatial weight matrix $D_{m,n}^{(hist)} \in \mathbb{R}^{L\times L}$ and $\Delta d_{m,n} = Haversine(lon_m, lat_m, lon_n, lat_n)^2$. Decay function $\psi(x) = 1/log(e + x)$ is used to convert time and distance differences into weights.

Subsequently, we employ a spatio-temporal enhanced self-attention mechanism to learn the representation $E'_{(hist)}$ of historical trajectories:

$$E'_{(hist)} = \text{softmax}\left(\frac{E_{(hist)}W^Q \cdot (E_{(hist)}W^K)^\mathsf{T} + \Delta_{TD}^{(hist)}}{\sqrt{d}}\right) \cdot E_{(hist)}W^V \quad (7)$$

where $W^Q, W^K, W^V \in R^{d\times d}$ are used to project $E_{(hist)}$ into matrices that enable the model to capture the pivotal elements of the input check-ins and allocate the appropriate weight to them. $\Delta_{TD}^{(hist)} = \rho \cdot T_{m,n}^{(hist)} + (1-\rho) \cdot D_{m,n}^{(hist)}$, and ρ represents a balance parameter. The trajectory embedding $E'_{(hist)} = [\mathbf{a}'_1, \mathbf{a}'_2 ..., \mathbf{a}'_L] \in \mathbb{R}^{L\times d}$.

Prediction and Optimization. Considering the distance between each candidate POI p_k and each history POI p_n that u_i has visited, we denote spatial matrix as $D_{k,n}^{(cand)} = \psi(\Delta d_{k,n}) \in \mathbb{R}^{|\mathcal{P}|\times L}$. And we denote the temporal matrix $T_{k,n}^{(cand)} = \psi(\Delta t_{k,n})$ in view of the difference between the current time t_k and each historical check-in time t_n. Similarly, we have the candidate spatio-temporal matrix $\Delta_{TD}^{(cand)}$.

When u_i generates a recommendation request at t_k (in time slot ts), the embedding of each candidate POI can be represented as $\mathbf{e}_{p_j}^{t_k} = \text{FFN}(\text{Concat}(\mathbf{u}_i^{ts}, \mathbf{p}_j^{ts}, \mathbf{r}_j^{ts}, \mathbf{c}_j^{ts}, \mathbf{ts}))$. All embeddings constitute the matrix $E_{(cand)} = [\mathbf{e}_{p_1}^{t_k}, \mathbf{e}_{p_2}^{t_k} ..., \mathbf{e}_{p_{|\mathcal{P}|}}^{t_k}] \in \mathbb{R}^{|\mathcal{P}|\times d}$ and we calculate the score of each candidate POI by the following formula:

$$\hat{\mathbf{y}} = \text{Sum}\left(\text{softmax}\left(\frac{E_{(cand)} \cdot {E'_{(hist)}}^\mathsf{T} + \Delta_{TD}^{(cand)}}{\sqrt{d}}\right)\right) \quad (8)$$

where $\text{Sum}(\cdot)$ denotes a weighted sum at the last dimension, $\hat{\mathbf{y}} = [\hat{y}_1, \hat{y}_2 ..., \hat{y}_{|\mathcal{P}|}] \in \mathbb{R}^{|\mathcal{P}|}$.

To fully leverage user check-ins, we set up a mask matrix $M \in \mathbb{R}^L$ to gradually train from segments to the entire sequence and consider the last visible POI $l_k^{u_i}$ as positive sample. Stage2 is optimized by minimizing the following cross-entropy loss:

$$\mathcal{J} = -\sum_{m=1}^{L-1}\left(log\sigma(\hat{y}_k) + \sum_{j\in NEG(k,u_i)} log(1 - \sigma(\hat{y}_j))\right) \quad (9)$$

where $NEG(k, u_i)$ represents a set of negative samples randomly selected from set $\mathcal{P}$.

[2] https://pypi.org/project/haversine/.

5 Experiments

This section presents the evaluation of the performance of our proposed DyHGN. We begin by describing the experimental setup, followed by a comprehensive comparison of our results against various baseline models. Finally, we provide a qualitative explanation of our model's intuitive interpretations.

5.1 Datasets and Preprocessing

We conduct experiments on two real-world datasets of Foursquare[3]: NYC and TKY, which were collected in New York City and Tokyo from Apr.2012 to Feb.2013 [20]. For preprocessing the datasets, we first eliminate unpopular POIs with less than 10 visits and sort the timestamps in chronological order, then partition them into non-overlapping sets with the first 70% visits of each user's sequence for training and the rest for testing. Furthermore, we divide each user's check-in sequence into sessions with a maximum length of $L = 30$. Table 1 gives a statistical summary for each dataset.

Table 1. Statistical information of the NYC and TKY dataset

	#Users	#POIs	#Regions	#Categories	#Check-ins
NTC	1,083	5,135	113	209	147,938
TKY	2,293	7,873	74	190	447,570

5.2 Evaluation Metrics

The model generates a recommended list for each user u_i, which contains the top-K POIs that the user might be interested in, in descending order. We adopt widely used evaluation metrics Recall@K and NDCG@K to measure the correctness of the top-k recommendations and the quality of the ranked list, respectively. In this paper, we report the metrics with $K \in \{1, 5, 10, 20\}$, each metric is calculated 10 times and averaged.

5.3 Baseline Models

To demonstrate the effectiveness of our method, we compared our framework with the following next POI recommendation methods.1) **POP:** A statistical method which recommends the most popular POIs in train dataset to users. 2) **LSTM** [5]: A type of RNN, provides a means of capturing both long- and short-term contextual influences. 3) **GRU** [4]: Another variation of RNN with fewer parameters, enabling faster computation and less risk of overfitting. 4) **ST-RNN**

[3] http://www-public.imtbs-tsp.eu/~zhang_da/pub/dataset_tsmc2014.zip.

[11]: The first model to consider incorporating spatio-temporal difference information into neural networks. 5) **LSTPM** [17]: A novel method based on LSTM that captures both long-term preferences with a non-local network and short-term preferences with a geo-dilated network. 6) **STAN** [12]: A novel method based on attention mechanism, proposing the innovative idea of incorporating non-adjacent locations and non-contiguous visits into the attention mechanism. 7) **HMT-GRN** [9]: A novel method based on GNNs that learns user region matrices at multiple granularity levels to alleviate data sparsity issues.

5.4 Parameter Settings

For baselines, settings are preserved as provided in the original papers. For our DyHGN, we pad each preprocessed data to a maximum length of $L = 30$ and divide the week into $|\mathcal{T}| = 42$ time slots, each lasting 4 h. Set the disturbance-sensitive threshold $\Delta = 1h$. The weight parameter μ (balances context and period information) is set to 0.6, while ρ (balances the spatial-temporal weight matrix) is set to 0.4. We use the Adam optimizer with a learning rate of 3e-3, weight decay of 1e-4, and dropout rate of 0.1. The embedding dimension is set to $d = 50$ and the batch size is set to 30.

5.5 Performance Comparisons

We present the evaluation results of our proposed DyHGN and the baselines in Table 2, where the relative improvement is computed between our model and the best baseline.

- Our DyHGN shows improvement over all the baselines on all the metrics for next POI recommendation. Specifically, DyHGN improves performance over the best baselines by 2.05%–16.74% and 2.97%–7.58% for NYC and TKY datasets respectively. The main reason is that our DyHGN could fully consider the dynamic behavioral intentions of users and the varying activity connotations of POIs.
- Modeling spatio-temporal correlations is crucial. Models that leveraged spatio-temporal correlations explicitly or implicitly such as ST-RNN and LSTPM outperform GRU and LSTM models that only captured sequential features. Our DyHGN captures spatio-temporal information from global and local views, providing improved performance compared to the above local-only models. For example, on NYC dataset, our DyHGN improves Recall@20 by 18.62% against LSTPM.
- Attention-based method STAN revealed that capturing non-adjacent check-in relations improves recommendation performance. However, it only learns unified, static embedding vectors for users and POIs from local view. Our DyHGN considers the user's dynamic behavior intention and varying activity connotation of POIs from global view, resulting in 16.37% improvement on Recall@10 on NYC dataset.

Table 2. Performance comparison of next POI recommendation task on two datasets

Dataset	Method	Recall@K				NDCG@K			
		K = 1	K = 5	K = 10	K = 20	K = 1	K = 5	K = 10	K = 20
NYC	POP	0.0069	0.0428	0.0497	0.0656	0.0069	0.0232	0.0254	0.0294
	LSTM	0.1216	0.2059	0.2405	0.2681	0.1216	0.1683	0.1796	0.1865
	GRU	0.1306	0.2343	0.2613	0.2937	0.1306	0.1883	0.1968	0.2049
	ST-RNN	0.1251	0.2536	0.2840	0.3027	0.1251	0.1904	0.2113	0.2160
	LSTPM	<u>0.1368</u>	0.2668	0.3193	0.3711	<u>0.1368</u>	0.2001	0.2135	0.2303
	STAN	0.1154	0.2578	0.3317	0.4077	0.1154	0.1880	0.2122	0.2315
	HMT-GRN	0.0974	<u>0.2670</u>	<u>0.3382</u>	<u>0.4146</u>	0.0974	<u>0.2014</u>	<u>0.2172</u>	<u>0.2403</u>
	DyHGN	**0.1396**	**0.3117**	**0.3860**	**0.4402**	**0.1396**	**0.2244**	**0.2454**	**0.2617**
	%Improv.	2.05%	16.74%	14.13%	6.17%	2.05%	11.42%	12.98%	8.91%
TKY	POP	0.0268	0.0991	0.1288	0.1581	0.0268	0.0642	0.0737	0.0811
	LSTM	0.1147	0.2185	0.2602	0.3063	0.1147	0.1699	0.1835	0.1952
	GRU	0.1183	0.2291	0.2701	0.3144	0.1183	0.1772	0.1906	0.2017
	ST-RNN	0.1210	0.2372	0.2826	0.3208	0.1210	0.1825	0.1972	0.2069
	LSTPM	0.1113	0.2467	0.3089	0.3594	0.1113	0.1834	0.2036	0.2166
	STAN	<u>0.1212</u>	<u>0.2625</u>	0.3245	0.3814	<u>0.1212</u>	<u>0.1959</u>	0.2160	0.2304
	HMT-GRN	0.1031	0.2516	<u>0.3364</u>	<u>0.4031</u>	0.1031	0.1801	<u>0.2235</u>	<u>0.2336</u>
	DyHGN	**0.1248**	**0.2824**	**0.3518**	**0.4153**	**0.1248**	**0.2089**	**0.2313**	**0.2448**
	%Improv.	2.97%	7.58%	4.58%	3.03%	2.97%	6.64%	3.49%	4.79%

- GNN-based method HMT-GRN statically modeled spatial hierarchies of different granularity and captured the POI-POI relation from a global view, while our DyHGN considers the auxiliary effect of geographic factors dynamically and achieves superior performance on city-level datasets.

5.6 Ablation Study

To evaluate the effectiveness of different components in our model, we create four variants by removing selected components: 1) DyHGN$_{w/o\ graphs}$ removes the process of constructing and training the heterogeneous graphs, and directly initializes a random embedding vector for all nodes in each time slot. 2) DyHGN$_{w/o\ enhance}$ is the variant that ignores the information enhance layer. 3) DyHGN$_{w/o\ st-hist}$ drops the spatio-temporal weight matrix $\Delta_{TD}^{(hist)}$ generated from historical trajectories. 4) DyHGN$_{w/o\ st-cand}$ removes the candidate spatio-temporal weight matrix $\Delta_{TD}^{(cand)}$.

The results of ablation study are shown in Fig. 5. 1) DyHGN$_{w/o\ graphs}$ only leverages the local view to optimize the fine-grained representation of all nodes and does not perform well. We believe that only using the sequence relation of nodes could not fully learn the large-scale fine-grained parameters. The rich information in heterogeneous graphs is crucial in enhancing recommendation performance. 2) DyHGN$_{w/o\ enhance}$ shows that capturing users' current behavior intentions is easily affected by the jitter check-in time. Our well-designed information enhancement layer greatly improves the model's robustness by fusing the information in adjacent and periodic time slots. 3) DyHGN$_{w/o\ st-hist}$ and DyHGN$_{w/o\ st-cand}$ show that modeling the spatio-temporal information is also vital for next POI recommendation. In summary, our proposed DyHGN benefits from these delicately designed components.

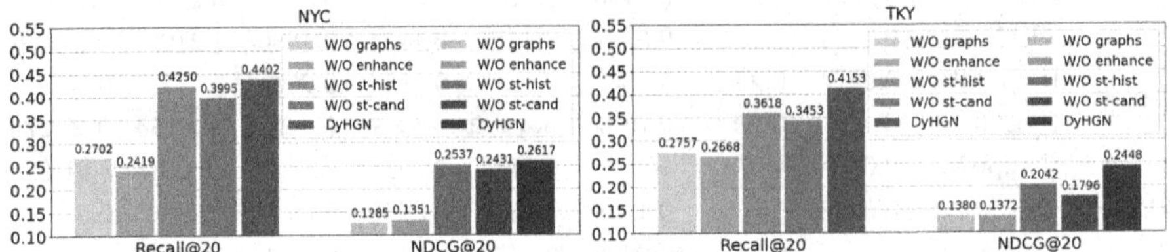

Fig. 5. Performance comparison for variants of DyHGN on two datasets

5.7 Hyperparameter Analysis

As shown in Fig. 6, we further investigate the influence of key parameters by varying each parameter while keeping others constant. 1) The dimension of node embedding d has been varied from 10 to 60 with step 10. As its shown, our model's recommendation performance is insensitive to hyperparameter d on the relatively small-sized dataset NYC. In TKY dataset with richer information, low-dimensional embedding vectors may not fully capture the similarities and differences between nodes. Overall, as d approaches 50, DyHGN performance gradually stabilizes. 2) A series number of negative neighbors $[1, 10, 20, 30, 40, 50]$ have been sampled and it has been found that the training efficiency and recommendation performance are better around 10 negative samples. 3) We vary the context-period balanced parameter μ from 0 to 1 with step 0.2 and observe that the model performs the best when $\mu = 0.6$. In particular, we find that periodic information makes a greater contribution to the model's performance. 4) Our DyHGN performs best when spatio-temporal balanced parameter $\rho = 0.4$.

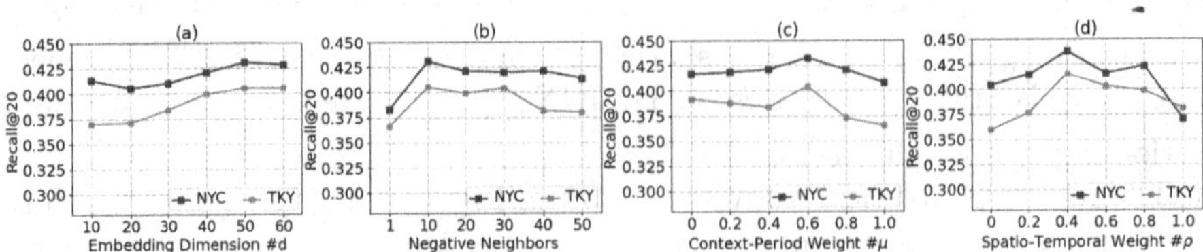

Fig. 6. Parameter sensitivity analysis

6 Conclusion

In this paper, we propose a novel network DyHGN for next POI recommendation. Through the global view, DyHGN could capture dynamic POI-POI and user-POI relations. Then the local view fully fuses fine-grained periodic-contextual information and explores the spatio-temporal correlations on user behavior. Experimental results on two datasets demonstrate the effectiveness of our DyHGN.

References

1. Chen, G., et al.: Win-win: a privacy-preserving federated framework for dual-target cross-domain recommendation. In: Proceedings of the AAAI Conference on Artificial Intelligence, vol. 37, pp. 4149–4156 (2023)
2. Chen, H., Li, Y., Sun, X., Xu, G., Yin, H.: Temporal meta-path guided explainable recommendation. In: Proceedings of the 14th ACM International Conference on Web Search and Data Mining, pp. 1056–1064 (2021)
3. Cheng, C., Yang, H., Lyu, M.R., King, I.: Where you like to go next: successive point-of-interest recommendation. In: Twenty-Third International Joint Conference on Artificial Intelligence (2013)
4. Cho, K., et al.: Learning phrase representations using RNN encoder-decoder for statistical machine translation. arXiv preprint arXiv:1406.1078 (2014)
5. Hochreiter, S., Schmidhuber, J.: Long short-term memory. Neural Comput. **9**(8), 1735–1780 (1997)
6. Huang, Z., Ma, J., Dong, Y., Foutz, N.Z., Li, J.: Empowering next poi recommendation with multi-relational modeling. In: Proceedings of the 45th International ACM SIGIR Conference on Research and Development in Information Retrieval, pp. 2034–2038 (2022)
7. Kipf, T.N., Welling, M.: Semi-supervised classification with graph convolutional networks. arXiv preprint arXiv:1609.02907 (2016)
8. Lai, Y., Su, Y., Wei, L., Chen, G., Wang, T., Zha, D.: Multi-view spatial-temporal enhanced hypergraph network for next poi recommendation. In: Wang, X., et al. (eds.) DASFAA 2023. LNCS, vol. 13944, pp. 237–252. Springer, Cham (2023). https://doi.org/10.1007/978-3-031-30672-3_16
9. Lim, N., Hooi, B., Ng, S.K., Goh, Y.L., Weng, R., Tan, R.: Hierarchical multi-task graph recurrent network for next poi recommendation. In: Proceedings of the 45th International ACM SIGIR conference on Research and Development in Information Retrieval, pp. 1133–1143 (2022)
10. Lim, N., et al.: STP-UDGAT: spatial-temporal-preference user dimensional graph attention network for next POI recommendation. In: Proceedings of the 29th ACM International Conference on Information & Knowledge Management, pp. 845–854 (2020)
11. Liu, Q., Wu, S., Wang, L., Tan, T.: Predicting the next location: a recurrent model with spatial and temporal contexts. In: Proceedings of the AAAI Conference on Artificial Intelligence, vol. 30 (2016)
12. Luo, Y., Liu, Q., Liu, Z.: STAN: spatio-temporal attention network for next location recommendation. In: Proceedings of the Web Conference 2021, pp. 2177–2185 (2021)

13. Pan, X., Cai, X., Zhang, J., Wen, Y., Zhang, Y., Yuan, X.: STMG: spatial-temporal mobility graph for location prediction. In: Jensen, C.S., et al. (eds.) DASFAA 2021. LNCS, vol. 12681, pp. 667–675. Springer, Cham (2021). https://doi.org/10.1007/978-3-030-73194-6_45
14. Rahmani, H.A., Aliannejadi, M., Baratchi, M., Crestani, F.: A systematic analysis on the impact of contextual information on point-of-interest recommendation. ACM Trans. Inf. Syst. (TOIS) **40**(4), 1–35 (2022)
15. Schlichtkrull, M., Kipf, T.N., Bloem, P., van den Berg, R., Titov, I., Welling, M.: Modeling relational data with graph convolutional networks. In: Gangemi, A., et al. (eds.) ESWC 2018. LNCS, vol. 10843, pp. 593–607. Springer, Cham (2018). https://doi.org/10.1007/978-3-319-93417-4_38
16. Su, Y., Li, X., Tang, W., Xiang, J., He, Y.: Next check-in location prediction via footprints and friendship on location-based social networks. In: 2018 19th IEEE International Conference on Mobile Data Management (MDM), pp. 251–256. IEEE (2018)
17. Sun, K., Qian, T., Chen, T., Liang, Y., Nguyen, Q.V.H., Yin, H.: Where to go next: modeling long-and short-term user preferences for point-of-interest recommendation. In: Proceedings of the AAAI Conference on Artificial Intelligence, vol. 34, pp. 214–221 (2020)
18. Vaswani, A., et al.: Attention is all you need. In: Advances in Neural Information Processing Systems, vol. 30 (2017)
19. Xie, M., Yin, H., Wang, H., Xu, F., Chen, W., Wang, S.: Learning graph-based POI embedding for location-based recommendation. In: Proceedings of the 25th ACM International on Conference on Information and Knowledge Management, pp. 15–24 (2016)
20. Yang, D., Zhang, D., Zheng, V.W., Yu, Z.: Modeling user activity preference by leveraging user spatial temporal characteristics in LBSNS. IEEE Trans. Syst. Man Cybernet. Syst. **45**(1), 129–142 (2014)
21. Yu, D., Yu, T., Wang, D., Shen, Y.: NGPR: a comprehensive personalized point-of-interest recommendation method based on heterogeneous graphs. Multimed. Tools Appl. **81**(27), 39207–39228 (2022)
22. Zang, H., Han, D., Li, X., Wan, Z., Wang, M.: CHA: categorical hierarchy-based attention for next POI recommendation. ACM Trans. Inf. Syst. (TOIS) **40**(1), 1–22 (2021)
23. Zhao, P., et al.: Where to go next: a spatio-temporal gated network for next POI recommendation. IEEE Trans. Knowl. Data Eng. **34**(5), 2512–2524 (2020)

Cross-scale Dynamic Relation Network for Object Detection

Xinfang Zhong[1,2] and Zhixin Li[1,2(✉)]

[1] Key Lab of Education Blockchain and Intelligent Technology, Ministry of Education, Guangxi Normal University, Guilin 541004, China

[2] Guangxi Key Lab of Multi-Source Information Mining and Security, Guangxi Normal University, Guilin 541004, China

lizx@gxnu.edu.cn

Abstract. The majority of object detectors only consider the features in region proposals, without taking the global context or the relationships between objects into detection. Conceivably, it would inevitably limit the improvement of performance. To tackle the problem, we introduce a Cross-Scale Dynamic Relation Network (CSDRN) that can explore the relationships between specific objects in an image, and its core components include a Cross-Scale Semantic-Aware Module (CSSAM), Dynamic Relation Graph Reasoning (DRGR), and Semantic Attention Fusion Module(SAFM). Through the CSSAM, the crucial information in feature maps of different scales achieve semantic interaction to obtain a cross-scale semantic feature. We activate the category knowledge in the image and combine the cross-scale semantic feature to create a dynamic relationship graph. Therefore, we can get more precise relation between objects. Guided by the relation, a semantic attention is generated to enrich the visual features. Experimental results on the COCO dataset show that the proposed CSDRN can effectively improve the detection performance, reaching 54.8% box AP, which is 3.9% box AP over the baseline. Moreover, 47.6% mask AP is achieved in instance segmentation, exceeding the baseline 3.6% mask AP.

Keywords: Object Detection · Semantic Relationship · Graph Convolutional Network · Attention Mechanism

1 Introduction

Object detection is a challenging task. Unlike image classification, it not only requires identifying objects in an image, but also accurately locating their position. As the cornerstone of computer vision tasks, object detection paves the way for many more complex vision tasks [32,33,38]. Driven by deep learning techniques, object detection based on the CNN framework has achieved remarkable progress [1,4,11,12,26–28]. Recently, thanks to the introduction of the Transformer [30] from Natural Language Processing into the study of image processing,

F. Liu et al. (Eds.): PRICAI 2023, LNAI 14325, pp. 327–339, 2024.
https://doi.org/10.1007/978-981-99-7019-3_31

further improved the performance of detector [2,21,24,31,39]. However, these approaches deal with each region proposals individually without considering the relation between objects which is crucial for object detection.

When confronted with a scene, humans tend to identify and localize objects based on their characteristics and the relationships they share. This has motivated scholars to explore the process of object recognition by the human visual and neural systems. Consequently, some researches attempted to model the implicit knowledge of relation learned in the human brain as a way to improve the detection capability of algorithms [15,34,35]. Due to the remarkable ability of Graph Convolutional Network (GCN) has been demonstrated in vision tasks, several studies have introduced GCN into object detection to explore the relationships between objects [5,16,34,36]. For example, Chen et al. [5] created a relation graph which used labels and co-occurrence probabilities in a dataset to construct nodes and edges for enriching visual features. However, due to the limited number of images and uneven distribution of classes in the dataset, the graph built based on the dataset is slightly biased. These could lead the model to over-learn the interdependence between common objects and ignore the uncommon objects with weaker correlations. Therefore, There would be false detection or missed detection, which limit the performance improvement. Beyond the demerit, most of the existing researches have built the relation graphs based on region proposals [15,22,34,35] or fused the obtained relationship information into region proposals [5,10,16,17]. While the region proposals obtained by Region Proposal Network (RPN) [28] may not be complete or correct. It may fundamentally leave out or incorrectly frame some targets, especially small objects, which prevent the network from accurately utilizing the relationship information.

Therefore, to precisely mine and efficiently exploit the relation between objects, we propose a cross-scale dynamic relation network (CSDRN) that combines multi-scale feature maps and global contextually significant information. We generate a dynamic relationship graph for each image and obtain a specific semantic feature, which also used for region proposals generation. As shown in Fig. 1(a), "laptop", "keyboard" and "mouse" are highly correlated in the static graph derived from the dataset. It is possible to recognize the partially obscured tiny mouse. Nevertheless, "horse" has neither a clear semantic relationship with "cat" nor any of the three objects mentioned above. In particular, "horse" is a small detail in the image, which is simple to disregard. Instead, we take into account all object classes of the image and feature maps of different scales to establish a strong connection, as illustrated in Fig. 1(b). Specifically, we present a cross-scale semantic-aware module (CSSAM) to activate crucial information in the feature maps of different scales and enhance the correlation between objects to obtain a cross-scale semantic feature for an image. Then, a dynamic relation graph reasoning (DRGR) is performed on the cross-scale semantic feature to generate a dynamic graph, and GCN is used to yield a specific object semantic representation. Finally, a semantic attention fusion module (SAFM) is proposed to enhance the corresponding visual features.

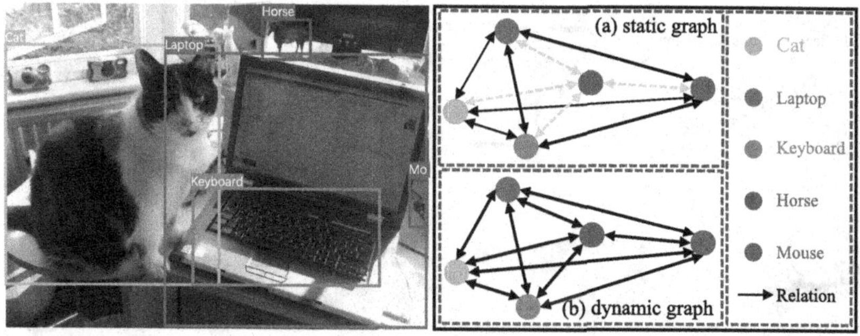

Fig. 1. An illustration of the distinction between dynamic and static graphs.

We use PVT v2 as the feature extractor and Cascade mask R-CNN as a detector to develop our CSDRN. We capture more precise semantic information for an image and improve performance. Our contributions are as follows: 1) In order to perceive semantic correlation between objects of different scales, we propose a CSSAM that allows key semantics to interact between feature maps of various scales. 2) We construct a dynamic relation graph. The nodes are generated by high-stage features with class information. In addition, we explicitly build a relationship matrix which use the perceived semantic information to mine the relationship more finely. 3) To enrich and enhance the vital information in the visual feature, we present a SAFM to achieve a better integration of semantics and visual features with the help of attention mechanism.

2 Method

In this section, we introduce CSDRN in detail. The overall architecture of the model is shown in Fig. 2. Specifically, the multi-scale feature maps extraction is implemented by PVT v2 network, in which FPN performs semantic fusion of multi-scale feature maps. CSSAM utilizes learnable convolution to accomplish significant information interaction between feature maps of different scales. DRGR performs relation reasoning to obtain the specific semantic information. SAFM well incorporate the specific semantics into the feature maps. Under the joint of these four components, the reasoning of object relationship is completed to enhance visual features and improve the ability of detection.

2.1 Multi-scale Features Extraction

Objects with considerable scale differences often appear in an image, while a single-scale feature map only contains fixed-size objects and can not fully cover objects of all scales. Therefore, we employ PVT v2 as the backbone network to extract the multi-scale feature maps $\{x_s\}_{s=1}^{S} \in \mathbb{R}^{C_s \times H_s \times W_s}$, where H_s, W_s, C_s

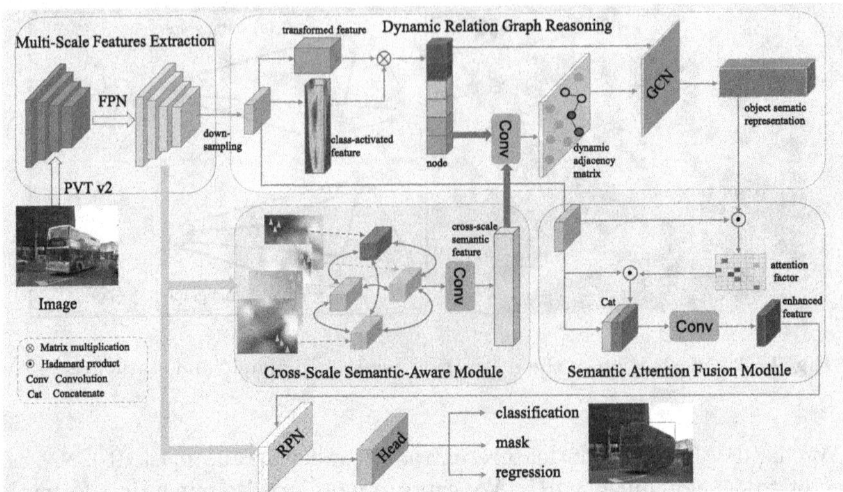

Fig. 2. The overall structure of CSDRN. CSDRN consists of a Multi-Scale Feature Extraction, a Cross-Scale Semantic-Aware Module, a Dynamic Relation Graph Reasoning, and a Semantic Attention Fusion Module.

represent the height, width and dimension of the feature map at s stage, respectively. Generally, PVT v2 has a total of four stages ($S = 4$), and each stage can generate feature maps with different height and width (i.e.different scales).

Feature Pyramid Network (FPN) [23] can fuse information in feature maps of different scales, so that each scale feature map contains more semantics. To facilitate the reasoning of semantic relation between feature maps, we use the fused features processed by FPN $\left\{x_s^{'}\right\}_{s=1}^{S} \in \mathbb{R}^{C\times H_s\times W_s}$, where H_s, W_s represents the height and width of the fused feature at s stage, respectively. The dimension of feature maps are unified into 256, making $C = 256$. In particular, FPN down-samples the feature map at the fourth stage independently to obtain the compressed feature map $x_5^{'} \in \mathbb{R}^{C\times \frac{H_4}{2}\times \frac{W_4}{2}}$, which is applicable to RPN only.

2.2 Cross-scale Semantic-Aware Module

FPN just combines the features of low-resolution and high-semantic with the features of high-resolution and low-semantic to construct a feature pyramid simply. It fails to achieve the interaction of significant information between feature maps of different scales and is likely to produce redundant information. Therefore, we propose a CSSAM to enable interaction of crucial semantics in feature maps of different scales and enhance the correlation between objects. To capture the decisive feature maps of all scales, we first flatten all pixels of the feature maps and map them to the same dimension. Then, we use global average pooling operation to calculate the statistics of the whole feature map, and generate the vector representations $\{\tilde{x}_s\}_{s=1}^{S}$, $\tilde{x}_s \in \mathbb{R}^{C\times 1}$. Formally,

$$\tilde{x}_s = \varphi_{gap}(\mu_{flatten}(x_s^{'})) \qquad s = 1, 2, 3, 4 \tag{1}$$

where $\varphi_{gap}(\cdot)$ represents global average pooling operation, and $\mu_{flatten}(\cdot)$ represents dimension flatten operation. $\{\tilde{x}_s\}_{s=1}^{S}$ not only discards confusing information and reduces distraction from critical data, but also contains global context content.

The feature map at each stages is independent. Therefore, to enhance the perception ability between feature maps of different scales and realize cross-scale information interaction, we perform the following operations on the features $\{\tilde{x}_s\}_{s=1}^{S}$. Firstly, we concatenate all feature representations in channel dimensions. We next utilize a 1×1 learnable convolution to explore semantic features of various scales to produce a new cross-scale semantic-aware vector $X_L \in \mathbb{R}^{4C\times 1}$. Finally, we reconstruct the dimension of semantic vector to derive a more comprehensive semantic feature $\hat{X}_L \in \mathbb{R}^{4C\times N}$, where N represents the number of object categories:

$$\hat{X}_L = ReLu(\chi(\psi_m(\underset{s=1}{\overset{S}{concat}}(\tilde{x}_s)))) \tag{2}$$

$\chi(\cdot)$ represents the dimension reconstruction operation, $\psi_m(\cdot)$ represents the 1×1 convolution operation, and *ReLu* represents *LeakyReLU* activation function to smooth the feature and prevent overfitting.

2.3 Dynamic Relation Graph Reasoning

Some existing works model the global connection between objects by mining the knowledge of datasets. Regretfully, because of the long tail distribution of the datasets, the graph built in this manner may incorrectly identify non-existent objects in an image and generate noise evidence. Moreover, some uncommon objects might go unnoticed, leading to erroneous detection and degrading the efficacy of detection. Accordingly, to accurately explore the relationships between objects, we use the feature maps to generate a specific semantic relation graph for an image.

Node Construction. We deploy the feature $x_5^{'}$ for semantic reasoning, enabling the nodes to perceive more semantics. We first utilize a learnable convolution for activating the category information to the maximum extent and obtain the category activation feature $\hat{x}_5^{'} \in \mathbb{R}^{N\times \frac{H_4}{2}\times \frac{W_4}{2}}$. Secondly, to guide more correlation characteristics, the feature $x_5^{'}$ is dimension transformed to obtain feature $x_5^{''} \in \mathbb{R}^{4C\times \frac{H_4}{2}\times \frac{W_4}{2}}$. Based on the feature $\hat{x}_5^{'}$, the feature $x_5^{''}$ selectively generates node representation with specific category aware $V \in \mathbb{R}^{4C\times N}$:

$$V = \sigma((\psi_c(x_5^{'}))^T)\psi_t(x_5^{'}) \tag{3}$$

where, $\sigma(\cdot)$ represents *Sigmoid* activation function, $\psi_c(\cdot)$ represents classifier that activates category feature, such as learnable convolution of 1×1, and $\psi_t(\cdot)$

represents dimension transform operation. We select the feature $x_5^{'}$ to generate the nodes because $x_5^{'}$ carries richer semantic information and it is a purer feature.

Edge Construction. In GCN, the adjacency matrix of a graph would serve as the relation knowledge. We use the cross-scale semantic feature $\hat{X}_L$ and the node representation V to construct a object-specific semantic feature, and then compress the dimension by convolution operation to generate the enhanced relation matrix $E \in \mathbb{R}^{N \times N}$:

$$E = \sigma(\phi_r(concat(\hat{X}_L, V))) \tag{4}$$

where, $\phi_r(\cdot)$ represents the dimension compression operation of 1-dimensional convolution. Consequently, we get the dynamic semantic graph $G(V, E)$.

GCN propagates information among nodes through a adjacency matrix. Therefore, we utilize GCN to update the node representation V based on the matrix E, and apply the residual connection to the original nodes. The detailed update process is as follows:

$$\hat{V} = f_{gcn}(V, E) + V = ReLu(VEW) + V \tag{5}$$

where, $\hat{V} \in \mathbb{R}^{4C \times N}$ represents the enhanced semantic object representation, $f_{gcn}(\cdot)$ represents GCN, V and E are both the input of GCN, and W represents the learnable semantic relation weight.

2.4 Semantic Attention Fusion Module

To allow the semantic feature $\hat{V}$ obtained by the previous module to participate in the generation of region proposals, we combine it with the feature map. However, the feature $\hat{V}$ is similar to textual information, which is a different modality from the visual feature. To effectively integrate these two types of features, we propose a semantic attention mechanism that combines semantics and visual feature to learn prominent regions. The attention value is calculated by the similarity of each pixel in the feature map to the specific semantic representation, and position with higher similarity may receive more score which determine the importance of the position.

We refer to the low-rank bilinear pooling method of the Hadamard product in [19] to calculate attention. The feature $\hat{V}$ first performs a dimension reduction operation to obtain a compact semantic feature $\hat{V_1} \in \mathbb{R}^{C \times N}$. Secondly, we reshape the features $\hat{V_1}$ and $x_5^{'}$ to get two new features $\hat{V_2} \in \mathbb{R}^{\frac{H_4}{2} \times \frac{W_4}{2} \times N \times C}$ and $\ddot{x}_5^{'} \in \mathbb{R}^{\frac{H_4}{2} \times \frac{W_4}{2} \times N \times C}$, and then perform the Hadamard product on these two features to get a semantic attention feature $Q \in \mathbb{R}^{\frac{H_4}{2} \times \frac{W_4}{2} \times N \times C}$. Following that, an attention factor $Q_a \in \mathbb{R}^{C \times \frac{H_4}{2} \times \frac{W_4}{2}}$ for each pixel in a specific image is calculated by class mapping. Formally,

$$Q_a = \nu(\gamma(x_5^{'}) \odot \rho(\phi_t(\hat{V}))) \tag{6}$$

where, $\nu(\cdot)$ represents the category attention function, implemented with a fully connected network. $\gamma(\cdot)$ and $\rho(\cdot)$ represent the reshape feature operation, $\phi_t(\cdot)$

represents the dimension reduction operation of 1-dimensional convolution, $\odot$ represents the Hadamard product operation. Later, we perform the Hadamard product of the attention factor and the feature $x_5^{'}$ to activate the corresponding semantic information, and then concatenate and encode with the original feature $x_5^{'}$ to obtain a enhanced feature map $\bar{x}_5^{'} \in \mathbb{R}^{\frac{H_4}{2} \times \frac{W_4}{2} \times C}$:

$$\bar{x}_5^{'} = \phi_e(concat(Q_a \odot x_5^{'}), x_5^{'}) \quad (7)$$

where, $\phi_e(\cdot)$ represents the process of 1-dimensional convolutional encode. Finally, we input the enhanced feature map $\bar{x}_5^{'}$ into the following detector for classification and regression.

3 Experimental Results and Analysis

3.1 Dataset and Evaluation Metrics

We assess our approach on the MS-COCO 2017 dataset. The dataset collects 80 different kinds of images, totaling around 160 K. To achieve a fair comparison with mainstream object detection methods, we adapt standard COCO average precision (AP) metrics to quantitatively evaluate our approach. Depending to different IOU thresholds (IOU=0.50:0.95, 0.50, 0.75) and different object scales (large, medium, small), AP metrics could be divided more finely.

3.2 Implementation Details

We implement experiments in the MMdetection library built on the PyTorch deep learning framework. To demonstrate the effectiveness and generality of the suggested method, we use two kinds of backbones for visual feature extraction: PVT v2 pre-trained on ImageNet-22K and ResNet-101 [14] trained on ImageNet-1K. Cascade mask R-CNN serves as our baseline model. All models are trained for 3× scheduler (36 epochs) and the batch size is set 16 by default, except for an additional stated. For PVT v2 as backbone, we use the AdamW optimizer with an initial learning rate of 0.0001, the weight decay is 0.5. The learning rate is reduced by a factor of 10 at the 28-th epoch and 34-th epoch, respectively. As for ResNet-101 is backbone, the Stochastic Gradient Descent (SGD) is used for training, the initial learning rate is 0.02, the weight decay is 0.0001.

3.3 Main Results

The Experimental Results with PVT v2 Backbone. We compare our results with state-of-the-arts, as present in Table 1. Our CSDRN achieves a box AP of 54.8%, and it is 3.9% greatly higher than the baseline model. We also report the FPS (frames per second) of models for speed comparison, and the FPS of our model does not drop. Compare with general methods, our CSDRN outperforms than them on all metrics. It can be simultaneously observed that our results are superior to the more powerful Transformer-based backbone (MViT v2-B [21]), which reflects the excellence of CSDRN. This is attributed to the fact that our CSDRN captures rich semantics to optimize the performance. Relation R-CNN [5] and VFNet+KROD [16] get relational knowledge from dataset, while our CSDRN focuses on the specific object relation in an image to produce a more exquisite dynamic graph, so it performs better than these methods. Moreover, our CSDRN enables the semantic information to be used in RPN to generate more accurate region proposals. Therefore, compared to RetinaNet+PCL [9], HCE Cascade R-CNN [6] and GRDN [36], our CSDRN has a better detection effect. We also report the performance of CSDRN on Mask R-CNN [13]. We can see that CSDRN improves Mask R-CNN from 44.0% box AP to 47.6% box AP, further illustrating the effectiveness of our method.

Table 1. Comparison with state-of-the-arts on MS-COCO 2017. Prefix 'X' denotes the ResNeXt network, for example X-101 denotes ResNeXt-101.

Method		Backbone	AP^b	AP^b_{50}	AP^b_{75}	AP^b_S	AP^b_M	AP^b_L	FPS
General	Cascade R-CNN [1]	PVT v2-B2-Li	50.9	69.5	55.2	33.6	54.6	65.4	10.4
	Mask R-CNN [13]	PVT v2-B2-Li	44.0	66.8	47.7	27.3	47.7	58.6	8.2
	RelationNet++ [7]	X-64x4d-101-DCN	50.3	69.0	55.0	32.8	55.0	65.8	-
	DyHead [8]	X-64x4d-101-DCN	52.3	70.7	57.2	35.1	56.2	63.4	-
	Deformable DETR [39]	X-101-DCN	50.1	69.7	54.6	30.6	52.8	64.7	-
	YSLAO [1,18]	X-101-64x4d-FPN-CFG	50.1	68.6	54.5	32.7	53.7	64.3	-
	Cascade R-CNN [1,21]	MViT v2-B	54.1	72.9	58.5	-	-	-	-
Relation	Relation R-CNN [5]	X-101-FPN	38.9	60.5	43.3	-	-	-	-
	VFNet + KROD [16]	X-101-64x4d-FPN	51.2	69.7	55.6	-	-	-	5.7
	RetinaNet + PCL [9]	X-101	44.4	61.7	44.8	28.6	45.3	54.4	-
	HCE Cascade R-CNN [6]	X-101-FPN	46.5	65.6	50.6	27.4	49.9	59.4	-
	GRDN [36]	Swin-T	52.6	71.7	56.6	36.7	55.8	67.0	-
	CSDRN (mask)	PVT v2-B2-Li	47.6	71.4	51.9	30.1	52.5	62.8	8.2
	CSDRN	PVT v2-B2-Li	**54.8**	**74.3**	**59.8**	**36.8**	**59.5**	**69.8**	10.4

The Experimental Results with ResNet-101 Backbone. In addition, we conduct experiments based on another backbone network. Our method with ResNet-101 backbone is called CSDRN*. The comparison results are displayed in Table 2. Our CSDRN* achieves a 45.3% box AP with an improvement of 2.5% box AP over the baseline. Compared with general detectors that concentrate on region proposals only, our CSDRN* achieves better performance due to incorporate the semantic information. Furthermore, compared with Reasoning-RCNN [34] and RetinaNet + KROD [16] that added static knowledge graphs, our CSDRN* has superior performance. Because our CSDRN* mines the relationship information between specific objects. Methods such as Cascade R-CNN+CODH [37], Cascade R-CNN+SA [3] and Cascade R-CNN+HCE [6] learn the contextual information between region proposals. Our CSDRN* not only allows the crucial semantics of feature maps to interact, but also uses the attention mechanism to effectively integrate semantic information into visual features. Therefore, Our increased performance is more than theirs. And the FPS of the model Cascade R-NN and Mask R-CNN are not affected.

3.4 Ablation Studies

The Effect of Different Module in CSDRN. To demonstrate that each module in our model is an integral part, we conduct the ablation experiments, as shown in Table 3. When we only add the CSSAM to the baseline, the performance is greatly improved (from 50.9% to 53.7% box AP). It confirms that our CSSAM well explores the crucial semantics of each scale feature map and accomplishes the interaction friendly. Then, we use the DRGR to mine the relation among specific objects, and the performance is further improved. Finally, we use the SAFM to add semantic information into visual features, so we get the maximum improvement of 54.8% box AP. From the results of these experiments, we can conclude that the three modules play a vital role in our model.

Table 2. Comparison with results on MS-COCO 2017 with ResNet-101 backbone. Prefix 'R' denotes the ResNet network, and R-101-FPN denotes ResNet-101 with FPN.

Method		Backbone	AP^b	AP^b_{50}	AP^b_{75}	AP^b_S	AP^b_M	AP^b_L	FPS
General	Cascade R-CNN [1]	R-101-FPN	42.8	62.1	46.3	23.9	45.4	53.6	14.5
	Mask R-CNN [13]	R-101-FPN	37.3	58.2	40.1	19.7	40.6	51.5	8.2
	DETR [2]	R-101-FPN	43.5	63.8	46.4	21.9	48.0	61.8	20
	TSP-RCNN [29]	R-101-FPN	44.8	63.8	49.2	**29.0**	47.9	57.1	9
	Conditional DETR [25]	R-101-FPN	44.5	**65.6**	47.5	23.6	48.4	63.6	-
	DN-DETR [20]	R-101-FPN	45.2	65.5	48.3	24.1	**49.1**	**65.1**	-
	YSLAO [1,18]	R-101-FPN	44.5	63.1	48.4	26.1	48.5	57.8	-
	YOLOF [4]	R-101-FPN	43.7	62.7	47.4	24.3	48.3	58.9	21
Relation	Reasoning RCNN [34]	R-101-FPN	42.9	-	-	-	-	-	13.3
	RetinaNet+KROD [16]	R-101-FPN	40.5	60.7	43.5	24.2	41.4	50.1	13.0
	Cascade R-CNN+SA [3]	R-101-FPN	44.7	63.6	48.5	25.0	47.8	57.2	-
	Cascade R-CNN+CODH [37]	R-101-FPN	43.5	62.6	47.2	24.9	46.2	55.3	6.0
	Cascade R-CNN+HCE [6]	R-101-FPN	43.0	61.6	46.9	24.6	46.6	57.4	-
	CSDRN (mask)*	R-101-FPN	39.2	60.5	42.4	20.8	43.4	53.9	8.2
	CSDRN*	R-101-FPN	**45.3**	65.4	**49.2**	26.1	48.8	56.7	14.5

Table 3. Ablation study of different module.

Methods	CSSAM	DRGR	SAFM	AP
Baseline				50.9
CSDRN	✓			53.7
CSDRN	✓	✓		54.6
CSDRN	✓	✓	✓	**54.8**

Table 4. Comparison semantics between single-scale and multi-scale.

Method	Backbone	AP^b	$mask\ AP$
Single	PVTv2-B2-Li	53.5	46.8
Multi	PVTv2-B2-Li	54.8	47.6
Single	ResNet-101	44.7	38.9
Multi	ResNet-101	45.3	39.2

The Effect of the Semantic Interaction Between Multi-scale Features. We use single-scale semantic information to conduct experiments, and the experimental results are shown in Table 4. Compared to the Cascade R-CNN baseline with different backbone (PVT v2 and ResNet-101), we only use the single-scale feature map to the semantic relation reasoning, the performance of model is boosted. It is obvious that the relational semantic information can significantly improve the detection performance. When we consider the semantics of multi-scale feature maps, all metrics are further increased. It proves that the interaction of multi-scale semantic feature maps is beneficial to enhance the correlation between objects, thus improving the detection performance.

The Effect of GCN Layer. To adequately mine the dependencies between nodes and make use of relation information, we explore the impacts of different GCN layers. We conduct experiments on Mask R-CNN with PVTv2-B2 backbone and train 1× schedule (12 epochs), as shown in Fig. 3. We can see that the best performance is achieved when the layer of GCN is one. This indicates that one layer of GCN has sufficiently exploited the correlation between nodes. However, increasing the number of layers of GCN causes over mining and gets some confusing information, so as to decrease the performance.

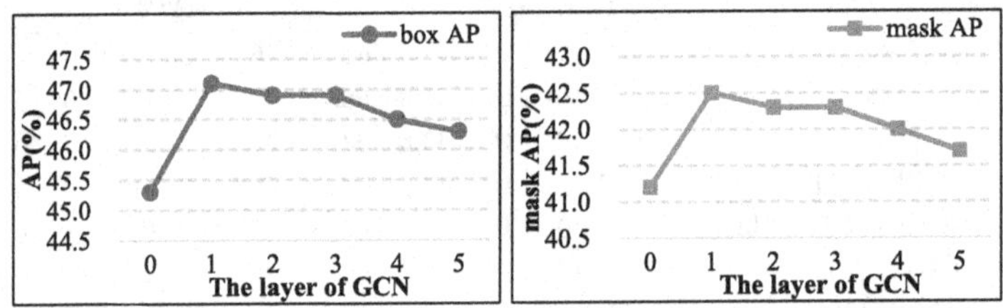

Fig. 3. The effect of GCN layers. The layer of GCN is "0" denotes that the model does not utilize GCN.

3.5 Qualitative Analysis

The visualization of results as shown in Fig. 4. Compared with the baseline model, our CSDRN could detect the persons who are blurred, smaller and blocked in Fig. 4(d). Because our CSDRN mines the contextual information (traffic scene) and learns the relation between the objects ("car" and "person"). In addition, our model is more sensitive to the tiny objects, such as "bottle" and "clock" in Fig. 4(e), "cup" in Fig. 4(f). Our model also detects the hidden "table" in Fig. 4(f). These detection results show that our approach effectively mines and fully exploits semantic knowledge, enabling our method to detect blurred, small-scale and occluded objects, and getting the better results.

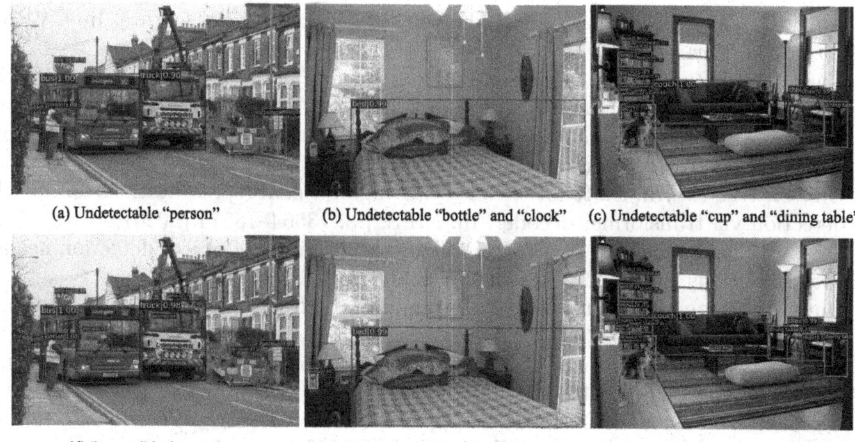

(a) Undetectable "person" (b) Undetectable "bottle" and "clock" (c) Undetectable "cup" and "dining table"

(d) "person" is detected (e) "bottle" and "clock" are detected (f) "cup" and "dining table" are detected

Fig. 4. The prediction results of baseline and our method. The top of images are the results of baseline. The bottom of images are the results of our CSDRN.

4 Conclusion

In this paper, to fully explore and better exploit the correlation between objects in images to improve the performance of object detection, we present a Cross-Scale Dynamic Relation Network that effectively mine the relation between specific objects. First, a Cross-Scale Semantic-Aware Module is proposed to achieve the interaction of multi-scale feature maps. Second, a Dynamic Relation Graph Reasoning captures the specific relation in an image. Finally, a Semantic Attention Fusion Module leverages the attention mechanism to make greater integration of semantic feature and visual feature. Experimental results demonstrate that our method can successfully contribute to the detection performance and is superior to other methods.

Acknowledgements. This work is supported by National Natural Science Foundation of China (Nos. 62276073, 61966004), Guangxi Natural Science Foundation (No.2019GXNSFDA245018), Guangxi "Bagui Scholar" Teams for Innovation and Research Project, Innovation Project of Guangxi Graduate Education (Nos. YCBZ2023055, YCBZ2022060), Guangxi Collaborative Innovation Center of Multi-source Information Integration and Intelligent Processing.

References

1. Cai, Z., Vasconcelos, N.: Cascade R-CNN: Delving into high quality object detection. In: CVPR, pp. 6154–6162 (2018)
2. Carion, N., Massa, F., Synnaeve, G., et al.: End-to-end object detection with transformers. In: ECCV, pp. 213–229 (2020)
3. Chen, C., Yu, J., Ling, Q.: Sparse attention block: aggregating contextual information for object detection. Pattern Recogn. **124**, 108418 (2022)

4. Chen, Q., Wang, Y., Yang, T., et al.: You only look one-level feature. In: CVPR, pp. 13039–13048 (2021)
5. Chen, S., Li, Z., Tang, Z.: Relation R-CNN: a graph based relation-aware network for object detection. IEEE Signal Process. Lett. **27**, 1680–1684 (2020)
6. Chen, Z.M., Jin, X., Zhao, B.R., et al.: HCE: hierarchical context embedding for region-based object detection. IEEE TIP **30**, 6917–6929 (2021)
7. Chi, C., Wei, F., Hu, H.: RelationNet++: Bridging visual representations for object detection via transformer decoder. In: NIPS, pp. 13564–13574 (2020)
8. Dai, X., Chen, Y., Xiao, B., et al.: Dynamic head: unifying object detection heads with attentions. In: CVPR, pp. 7373–7382 (2021)
9. Ding, P., Zhang, J., Zhou, H., et al.: Pyramid context learning for object detection. J. Supercomput. **76**, 9374–9387 (2020)
10. Fang, Y., Kuan, K., Lin, J., et al.: Object detection meets knowledge graphs. In: IJCAI, pp. 1661–1667 (2017)
11. Girshick, R.: Fast R-CNN. In: ICCV, pp. 1440–1448 (2015)
12. Girshick, R., Donahue, J., Darrell, T., et al.: Rich feature hierarchies for accurate object detection and semantic segmentation. In: CVPR, pp. 580–587 (2014)
13. He, K., Gkioxari, G., Dollár, P., et al.: Mask R-CNN. In: ICCV, pp. 2980–2988 (2017)
14. He, K., Zhang, X., Ren, S., et al.: Deep residual learning for image recognition. In: CVPR, pp. 770–778 (2016)
15. Hu, H., Gu, J., Zhang, Z., et al.: Relation networks for object detection. In: CVPR, pp. 3588–3597 (2018)
16. Ji, H., Ye, K., Wan, Q., et al.: Reasonable object detection guided by knowledge of global context and category relationship. Expert Syst. Appl. **209**, 118285 (2022)
17. Jiang, C., Xu, H., Liang, X., et al.: Hybrid knowledge routed modules for large-scale object detection. In: NIPS, pp. 1559–1570 (2018)
18. Jin, Z., Yu, D., Song, L., et al.: You should look atăall objects. In: ECCV, pp. 332–349 (2022)
19. Kim, J.H., On, K.W., Lim, W., et al.: Hadamard product for low-rank bilinear pooling. In: ICLR, pp. 1–8 (2017)
20. Li, F., Zhang, H., Liu, S., et al.: DN-DETR: accelerate DETR training by introducing query denoising. In: CVPR, pp. 13609–13617 (2022)
21. Li, Y., Wu, C.Y., Fan, H., et al.: MViTv2: improved multiscale vision transformers for classification and detection. In: CVPR, pp. 4794–4804 (2022)
22. Li, Z., Du, X., Cao, Y.: GAR: Graph assisted reasoning for object detection. In: WACV, pp. 1284–1293 (2020)
23. Lin, T.Y., Dollár, P., Girshick, R., et al.: Feature pyramid networks for object detection. In: CVPR, pp. 936–944 (2017)
24. Liu, Z., Lin, Y., Cao, Y., et al.: Swin transformer: Hierarchical vision transformer using shifted windows. In: ICCV, pp. 9992–10002 (2021)
25. Meng, D., Chen, X., Fan, Z., et al.: Conditional DETR for fast training convergence. In: ICCV, pp. 3631–3640 (2021)
26. Redmon, J., Divvala, S., Girshick, R., et al.: You only look once: Unified, real-time object detection. In: CVPR, pp. 779–788 (2016)
27. Redmon, J., Farhadi, A.: YOLO9000: Better, faster, stronger. In: CVPR, pp. 6517–6525 (2017)
28. Ren, S., He, K., Girshick, R., et al.: Faster R-CNN: towards real-time object detection with region proposal networks. IEEE TPAMI **39**(6), 1137–1149 (2017)
29. Sun, Z., Cao, S., Yang, Y., et al.: Rethinking transformer-based set prediction for object detection. In: ICCV, pp. 3591–3600 (2021)

30. Vaswani, A., Shazeer, N., Parmar, N., et al.: Attention is all you need. In: NIPS. pp. 5998–6008 (2017)
31. Wang, W., Xie, E., Li, X., et al.: PVT v2: improved baselines with pyramid vision transformer. In: CVM, pp. 415–424 (2022)
32. Xian, T., Li, Z., Tang, Z., et al.: Adaptive path selection for dynamic image captioning. IEEE TCSVT **32**(9), 5762–5775 (2022)
33. Xie, X., Li, Z., Tang, Z., et al.: Unifying knowledge iterative dissemination and relational reconstruction network for imagetext matching. Inf. Process. Manage. **60**(1), 103154 (2023)
34. Xu, H., Jiang, C., Liang, X., et al.: Reasoning-RCNN: Unifying adaptive global reasoning into large-scale object detection. In: CVPR, pp. 6419–6428 (2019)
35. Xu, H., Jiang, C., Liang, X., et al.: Spatial-aware graph relation network for large-scale object detection. In: CVPR, pp. 9298–9307 (2019)
36. Yang, X., Zhong, X., Li, Z.: GRDN: Graph relation decision network for object detection. In: ICME, pp. 1–6 (2022)
37. Zhang, W., Fu, C., Chang, X., et al.: A more compact object detector head network with feature enhancement and relational reasoning. Neurocomputing **499**, 23–34 (2022)
38. Zhu, J., Li, Z., Zeng, Y., et al.: Image-text matching with fine-grained relational dependency and bidirectional attention-based generative networks. In: ACM MM, pp. 39–403 (2022)
39. Zhu, X., Su, W., Lu, L., et al.: Deformable DETR: deformable transformers for end-to-end object detection. In: ICLR, pp. 1–8 (2021)

Distribution-Adaptive Graph Attention Networks for Flood Forecasting

Jun Feng(✉) and Yuanhui Mao

College of Computer and Information, Hohai University, Nanjing, China
fengjun@hhu.edu.cn

Abstract. Flood forecasting is an important task for disaster prevention and mitigation. Many recent researchers intend to utilize data-driven deep-learning models to improve their prediction accuracy. Deep-learning technology commonly assumes that the time series data is independently and identically distributed. However, as time goes on, environmental changes can cause the distribution of temporal data to change. Neglecting considerations of distribution changes can lead to a decrease in prediction accuracy. In addition to distribution changes, the accuracy of flood forecasting is also influenced by the spatiotemporal relationships among the flood factors. This paper proposes a flood forecasting model based on Distribution-Adaptive Graph Attention Networks (DAGAT). DAGAT can extract spatiotemporal information from flood data and capture the spatial relative importance among flood factors. In the meantime, it also uses the distribution adaptation mechanism of the Boosting algorithm to train weight parameters, enabling the reduction of distribution differences among different segmented periods and effectively improving the accuracy of flood forecasting. Through comparative experiments, this method's effectiveness and superiority of this method are validated, demonstrating the potential application value in flood forecasting.

Keywords: Flood forecasting · Distribution adaptation · Graph Attention Networks · Data-driven model

1 Introduction

Natural disasters are public emergencies characterized by suddenness, universality, and nonconventionality [1]. Among these, floods stand out as a significant type of natural disaster, making accurate forecasting a critical endeavor in disaster prevention and mitigation strategies. With continuous research on flood forecasting, various flood models have emerged, which can be generally classified into two main categories: physical models and data-driven models. The data-driven techniques use machine learning methods to capture statistical and causal relationships among hydrological variables, such as rainfall, to improve prediction accuracy [2].

The work is supported in part by the National Key R&D Program of China (Grant No. 2021YFB3900605 & 2021YFB3900601).

F. Liu et al. (Eds.): PRICAI 2023, LNAI 14325, pp. 340–352, 2024.
https://doi.org/10.1007/978-981-99-7019-3_32

The data-driven flood forecasting is a type of time series prediction. Deep learning methods often assume that the time series are independently and identically distributed. However, as time progresses, the statistical characteristics of temporal data change, leading to changes in the distribution of multivariate hydrological time series. This phenomenon is known as time covariate shift [3], where the distribution $P(X)$ changes over time while the conditional distribution $P(Y|X)$ remains unchanged. In flood forecasting, when the flood dataset covers a long time period, many environmental changes may occur, resulting in changes in flood-inducing factors such as rainfall intensity and frequency (i.e., changes in $P(X)$), while the conditional distribution $P(Y|X)$ for rainfall-induced floods remains unchanged. The specific distribution changes are illustrated in Fig. 1. These changes are unpredictable and can adversely affect the accuracy of flood forecasts. Therefore, we require appropriate methods to mitigate the effects of time covariate shifts and improve the accuracy of flood forecasting. Additionally, flood forecasting also needs to consider the spatial information. For example, rainfall in upstream areas can impact downstream flow, and rainfall measurements from neighboring hydrological stations exhibit a high level of correlation.

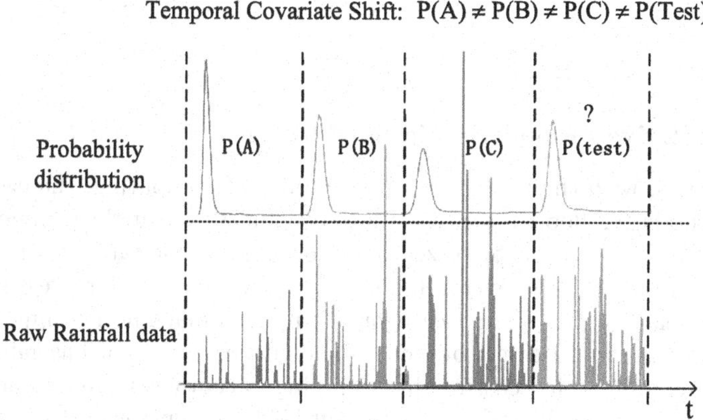

Fig. 1. The temporal covariate shift problem in flood forecasting. In the case of the original multivariate data, taking the example of the distribution change of rainfall overtime at one hydrological station, the distributions are different: $P(A) \neq P(B) \neq P(C) \neq P(Test)$

We propose Distribution-Adaptive Graph Attention Networks (DAGAT) for flood forecasting. Firstly, a hydrological spatial homogeneity graph was constructed based on the correlation of features. Building upon this graph, a Spatio-Temporal Graph Attention Network (STGAT) is introduced, which utilizes Graph Attention Networks (GAT) [4] to learn the importance weights of hydrological nodes. After spatial modeling, a Gated Recurrent Unit (GRU) [5] is employed to capture the temporal dependencies between time steps. To address the problem of multi-dimensional hydrological sequence distribution changes, we characterize the data distribution by splitting the training data into K most diverse periods with large distribution gap and employ a distribution adaptive mechanism aiming to reduce distribution mismatch in the time series and effectively improve flood forecasting accuracy.

Our main contributions can be summarized in the following manner, First of all, we successfully establish a spatiotemporal relationship model for flood forecasting with spatial attention. Secondly, by employing a distribution adaptive mechanism, we reduce the distribution differences between flood data from different periods, thereby improving the accuracy and stability of the forecasts. Compared to other models, the advantages of DAGAT are as follows: for the first time, we introduce the concept of distribution shift into flood prediction and subsequently integrate spatiotemporal relational models based on this distribution shift concept. We conducted comprehensive experiments in the Tunxi watershed, achieving the best performance compared to baseline models. This represents a completely new exploration in the field of flood prediction.

The remainder of this paper is structured as follows. Related works are introduced in Sect. 2. The specific details of our method are introduced in Sect. 3. The experiments used to analyze and affirm the efficacy of our method in Sect. 4. Section 5 concludes this paper and proposes future works.

2 Related Work

2.1 Data-Driven Flood Prediction Models

In recent years, with the improvement in intelligent computing, the use of data-driven methods for flood forecasting has become increasingly common. These methods can be broadly categorized as follows. The first category includes the traditional statistical methods for flood prediction, such as autoregressive moving average models [6]. The second category comprises machine learning methods, deep learning methods being a branch of machine learning that has gained mainstream status in flood forecasting due to its high accuracy. Common deep learning algorithms used in this field include Multilayer Perceptron (MLP) [7], Convolutional Neural Networks (CNN) [8], and Recurrent Neural Networks (RNN) [9], which offer better applicability and accuracy compared to traditional statistical methods. Ding et al. [10] propose an interpretable spatiotemporal attention Long Short-Term Memory model(LSTM) that incorporates an attention mechanism.

2.2 Application of Transfer Learning in Time Series

The goal of transfer learning is to leverage knowledge from a source domain to learn in a target domain [11]. It is often used to address the problem of different distributions between the source and target domains. The core of transfer learning is reducing the distribution differences between two domains. Distribution mismatch also exists within time series, and transfer learning can be employed to extract consistent knowledge from different distributions. Du et al. [3] introduces a distribution-adaptive recurrent neural network (AdaRnn) to address the issue of covariate shift and improve prediction accuracy. However, this model did not consider the spatial dependencies of features, making it unsuitable for direct application in the hydrological domain. In this paper, we propose for the first time the integration of the distribution adaptive concept with spatial feature information for flood forecasting, thereby improving prediction accuracy and generalization.

2.3 Graph Attention Networks

With the accumulation of spatial hydrological and meteorological data, graph neural networks have also been applied to flood forecasting. Feng et al. [12] propose a novel data-driven method that utilizes Graph Convolutional Networks (GCN) for hydrological prediction. However, this method did not consider the distribution changes in rainfall data, and GCN has higher computational complexity compared to GAT and lacks flexibility. GAT is a recently developed graph neural network structure that introduces attention mechanisms. Compared to traditional graph neural network models, GAT can more accurately capture the relationships between nodes when learning node representations, resulting in better expressiveness and predictive performance. In this study, we apply GAT to flood forecasting, leveraging the graph attention mechanism to adaptively compute weights for different hydrological stations, thereby more accurately extracting the spatial features of flood factors.

3 Methodology

This section will provide a detailed description of the proposed architecture for flood forecasting. It is primarily composed of four modules, as illustrated in the Fig. 2.

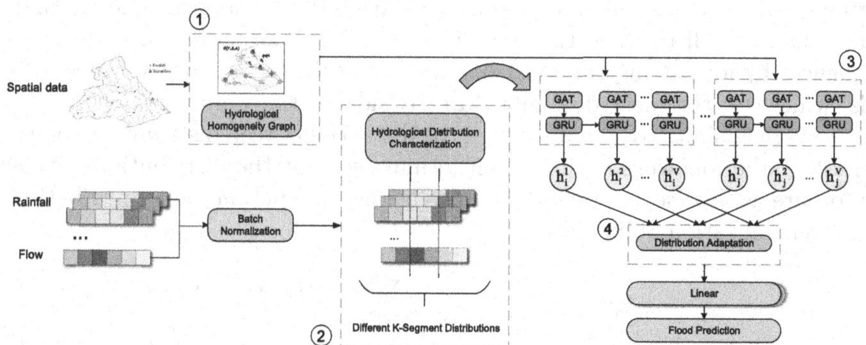

Fig. 2. After data processing through the ① hydrological spatial homogeneous graph generation module and the ② hydrological distribution characterization module, the input is fed into our established intelligent model for further processing. This model comprises the ③ STGAT model and the ④ distribution adaptation mechanism.

3.1 Hydrological Spatial Homogeneous Graph Generation Module

It is necessary to construct the topological structure of hydrological stations to investigate the spatial correlation between flood factors. From a hydrological perspective, hydrological stations that are geographically close are more likely to influence each other. We propose a hydrological spatial homogeneity graph construction method based on the Pearson correlation coefficient to capture the correlation and spatial structure between hydrological features. Equation 1 defines the adjacent matrix A_ρ of Pearson correlation coefficients between hydrological features. The module constructs a homogeneity graph $G = (V, E)$, where for consistency in the definition, we use nodes $V = \{v_1, v_2, v_3, ..., v_n\}$ to represent hydrological stations, which can be rainfall stations or flow monitoring stations. The edges E in the graph represent the strength of relationships between stations.

$$A_\rho = \begin{bmatrix} 1 & \cdots & \rho_{1,j} & \cdots & \rho_{1,n} \\ \rho_{2,1} & \cdots & \rho_{2,j} & \cdots & \rho_{2,n} \\ \vdots & & \vdots & & \vdots \\ \rho_{i,1} & \cdots & \rho_{i,j} & \cdots & \rho_{i,n} \\ \vdots & & \vdots & & \vdots \\ \rho_{n,1} & \cdots & \rho_{n,j} & \cdots & 1 \end{bmatrix} \tag{1}$$

The element $\rho_{i,j}$ in the adjacency matrix represents the final correlation between v_i and v_j. If the Pearson correlation is greater than the threshold value β, we consider this edge relationship to exist. Taking into account statistical knowledge, we set the value of β to 0.5. Based on the adjacency matrix, we eventually form the hydrological spatial homogeneity graph G.

3.2 Hydrological Distribution Characterization Module

This module characterizes the hydrological distributions by dividing time series into periods with different distributions. We utilize the principle of maximum entropy [13] to learn the shared distribution information of hydrological sequences by identifying the most dissimilar periods to each other. These periods, which are the most dissimilar, are considered the worst-case scenario for time covariate shift. We can maximize the distance between distributions of each period by the following optimization formula so that the distributions of each period are as diverse as possible and the learned prediction model has better a more generalization ability.

$$\begin{aligned} &\max_{0<K\leq K_0} \max_{n_1,\cdots,n_K} \frac{1}{K} \sum_{1\leq i\neq j\leq K} d(\mathcal{D}_i, \mathcal{D}_j) \\ &\text{s.t.} \forall i, \delta_1 < |\mathcal{D}_i| < \delta_2, \sum_i |\mathcal{D}_i| = n \end{aligned} \tag{2}$$

Here, d represents the distance metric function. In this paper, we choose the cosine distance as our distance metric formula. δ_1 and δ_2 are predefined parameters to avoid trivial solutions, and K_0 is a hyperparameter that prevents excessive splitting. K is the number of periods we set to partition. D_i refer to the i-th segmented periods.

Our dataset includes rainfall data from multiple rainfall stations and flow data from one flow station, which are only monitored during the flood season each year, with approximately equal time lengths of observations each year. To efficiently segment the multivariate time series for input, we use a greedy algorithm to solve Eq. 2. Firstly, we evenly divide the hydrological time series into n periods based on the flood seasons, with each flood season representing one period. The value of n is determined by the length of the historical dataset. Assuming the starting point of the time series is A and the endpoint is B, we iterate through $n-1$ splitting points to find a point C that maximizes the distribution distance $d(AC, CB)$. Once C is determined, we use the same strategy to select another point D.

3.3 Spatio-Temporal Graph Attention Networks Module

In this module, we propose a spatiotemporal flood forecasting model based on GAT. For hydrological stations, the degree of correlation between different nodes varies. By utilizing GAT, we can emphasize important hydrological features and handle the complex relationships between hydrological stations more flexibly. Assuming there are N hydrological sites in the hydrological site graph, the input of the F-dimensional feature set of the sites can be represented as $x = \vec{x_1}, \vec{x_2}, \ldots, \vec{x_N}, \vec{x_i} \in \mathbb{R}^F$. Petar et al. [4] propose the following method to calculate the attention coefficients of the graph neural network:

$$e_{ij} = \vec{a}^T(W\vec{x_i}||W\vec{x_j}) \tag{3}$$

$$\alpha_{ij}^k = \frac{exp\left(LeakyReLU(e_{ij})\right)}{\sum_{m \in N_i} exp\left(LeakyReLU(e_{im})\right)} \tag{4}$$

In the field of flood forecasting, x_i represents the feature of i-th hydrological site, e_{ij} represents the similarity between hydrological site node i and its neighboring site nodes, W is a weight matrix shared by all $\vec{x_i}$, $\vec{a}^T$ is a learned attention weight vector. α_{ij}^k represents the attention coefficients between x_i and x_j in the k-th attention head, *LeakyReLU* [14] is a variant of the *ReLU* activation function.

After obtaining the attention coefficients, the features of the neighboring nodes are weighted and summed, resulting in the output dimension, if we only compute attention once, it is difficult to capture all the feature information from the neighbors at one time. Therefore, we perform K rounds of self-attention operations, as shown in Formula (5):

$$\vec{x_i}' = \Big\Vert_{k=1}^{K} \sigma\left(\sum_{j \in \mathcal{N}_i} \alpha_{ij}^k \mathbf{W}^k \vec{x}_j\right) \tag{5}$$

After extracting spatial features, the output $x = \vec{x_1}', \vec{x_2}', \ldots, \vec{x_N}', \vec{x_i}' \in R^{F'}$ is obtained. The *GAT* network treats time steps as node features and performs spatial convolution on nodes. When using the *GRU*, tensors need to be transposed to exchange the dimension order between nodes and time steps. Transform the output into the following formula $x = \vec{x_1}', \vec{x_2}', \ldots, \vec{x_{F'}}', \vec{x_i}' \in R^N$.

Combined with the *GRU* formula [5], the structure of *STGAT* is shown in Fig. 3. $\vec{x_t}'$ represents the input after passing through two layers of *GAT* and adjusting the dimensions. *GRU* has two gating units: the reset gate (r_t) and the update gate (z_t). The update gate controls whether the current input should be updated in the hidden state, while the reset gate controls whether the previous hidden state should be forgotten at the current time step.

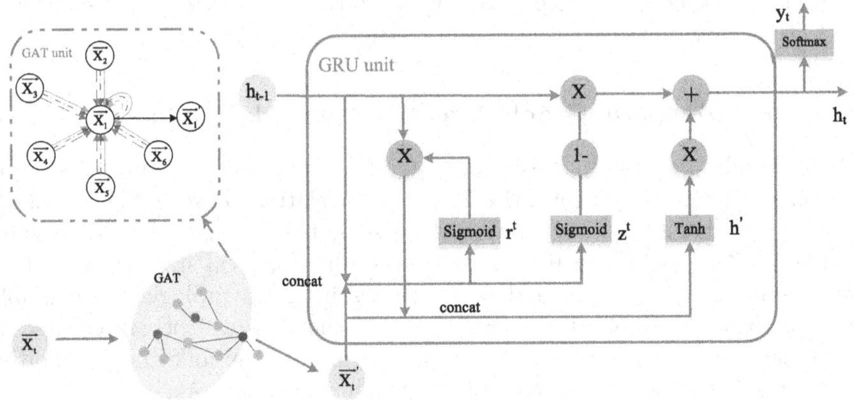

Fig. 3. The Architecture of STGAT

3.4 Distribution Adaptive Module

After hydrological distribution characterization, the hydrological dataset is divided into periods with different distributions. This module learns shared knowledge across different periods by matching their distributions. Thus, it exhibits better model generalization ability compared to methods that solely learn local distributions. The loss function is formulated as follows:

$$L(\theta, \gamma) = L_{h-pred}(\theta) + \lambda \frac{2}{K(K-1)} \sum_{i \le i \ne j \le K}^{i \ne j} L_{da}(\theta, \gamma; D_i, D_j) \tag{6}$$

Here, $L_{h-pred}(\theta)$ represents the average loss function for computing flood forecasts over multiple periods. The formula is presented as follows:

$$L_{h-pred}(\theta) = \frac{1}{K} \sum_{j=1}^{K} \frac{1}{|D_j|} \sum_{i=1}^{|D_j|} l\left(y_i^j, M\left(W\left(x_i^j\right)\right); \theta\right) \tag{7}$$

The expression (x_i^j, y_i^j) represents the i-th labeled segment from the period D_j. The module W adjusts the time step weights, and $l(...)$ denotes a loss function such as Mean Squared Error (MSE) loss. The parameter θ represents the weight parameters during training.

$L_{da}(\theta, \gamma; D_i, D_j)$ is a function designed to reduce the divergence of distribution between different periods. It introduces a weight vector γ to learn the relative importance of hidden states in the neural network. Given a period-pair (D_i,D_j), the loss of temporal distribution matching is formulated as:

$$L_{da}(\theta, \gamma; D_i, D_j) = \sum_{t=1}^{V} \gamma_{i,j}^t d(h_i^t, h_j^t; \theta) \tag{8}$$

where $\gamma_{i,j}^t$ denotes the distribution importance between the periods D_i and D_j at state t. h_i^t describes the t-th hidden state variable of the GRU at D_i.

We employ a boosting-based algorithm to learn the importance of weights γ. Prior to this, we first pre-trains the network parameters θ using $L_{h-pred}(\theta)$. This pre-training step aims to learn better representations of hidden states and facilitate learning γ. We utilize an enhancement process based on [15] to learn the importance of hidden states. We choose cross-domain distribution distance as the enhancement criterion. If the distribution distance in the $(n+1)$-th round exceeded that of the n-th round, we increased the value of $\gamma_{i,j}^{t,(n+1)}$ to enhance its effect in reducing distribution divergence. The formula (9) illustrates this process.

$$\begin{gathered}
\gamma_{i,j}^{t,(n+1)} = \begin{cases} \gamma_{i,j}^{t,(n)} \times G\left(d_{i,j}^{t,(n)}, d_{i,j}^{t,(n-1)}\right), d_{i,j}^{t,(n)} \geq d_{i,j}^{t,(n-1)} \\ \gamma_{i,j}^{t,(n)}, \text{otherwise} \end{cases} \\
\text{where,} G\left(d_{i,j}^{t,(n)}, d_{i,j}^{t,(n-1)}\right) = \left(1 + \sigma\left(d_{i,j}^{t,(n)} - d_{i,j}^{t,(n-1)}\right)\right)
\end{gathered} \tag{9}$$

Here, $d_{i,j}^{t,(n)} = D(h_i^t, h_j^t; \gamma_{i,j}^{t,(n)})$ is the distribution distance at time step t in epoch n. G is an updating function, and σ denotes the *sigmoid* function. We can learn the values of γ through the above formula.

4 Experiments

To validate the effectiveness of our models, we select eight models for comparative analysis. In this section, we will introduce the details of the experiments, including the dataset and evaluation metrics, implementation details, and performance comparisons.

4.1 DataSet and Measurements

In our experiments, we choose the Tunxi Basin as the experimental dataset. The dataset consists of 43,435 flood season records from the period between 1981 and 2003. To partition the dataset into training and testing sets, we use a ratio of 0.7 for the training set, 0.1 for the validation set, and 0.2 for the testing set.

In terms of evaluation metrics, this paper utilizes two evaluation indicators, namely, the relative mean square error (RMSE) and mean absolute error (MAE), to assess the prediction performance and measure the errors.

$$RMSE = \sqrt{\frac{\sum_{m=1}^{N}(\bar{y}_m^{pre} - y_m^{test})^2}{N}} \tag{10}$$

$$MAE = \frac{1}{N}\sum_{m=1}^{N}|\bar{y}_m^{pre} - y_m^{test}| \tag{11}$$

In the above formulas, N represents the number of test samples, $\bar{y}_m^{pre}$ represents the predicted results, and y_m^{test} represents the true values in the test set. Smaller values of RMSE and MAE indicate more accurate predictions and smaller errors.

4.2 Implementation Details

The system was implemented using the Python programming language. All experiments were conducted on a Linux server equipped with a 2.10 GHz 8-core Xeon CPU, 60 GB RAM, and Nvidia GeForce GTX 1080 Ti. For models, the batch size was set to 64, the hidden layer size was set to 128, and the learning rate was set to 0.0001. Additionally, the weight parameter for distribution divergence in DAGAT was set to 0.1, and segment K was set to 2. Our models and baselines were implemented in the PyTorch environment, utilizing error back-propagation and parameter updates. The number of iterations was set to 200, and to avoid excessive training time, an early stopping strategy was employed. If the loss did not decrease for 60 consecutive rounds, the training was stopped.

4.3 Performance Comparison

This section provides a comparison of the network performance of MLP [7], LSTM [10], GRU [4], CNN [8], Adarnn [3], ST-GCN [12], STGAT, and DAGAT. MLP is the most classic neural network with the fastest training speed. LSTM and GRU are recurrent neural network models that possess long-term memory capability, effectively preserving past information. CNN processes spatial information through convolutional layers, effectively handling spatiotemporal feature sequences. AdaRnn combines a distribution adaptive module with recurrent neural networks to alleviate distribution differences. Additionally, to highlight the effectiveness of the adaptive module, We introduced the STGAT model that does not include the distribution adaptation mechanism and independently evaluated the effectiveness of the adaptive module.

Table 1 provides a detailed comparison between our proposed DAGAT network and the other networks. In this study, we adjusted the parameters to ensure that each model achieves good performance. The first seven models are our baseline models, and at the bottom of the table is our model. We utilize the rainfall and flood features from the past 12 h to predict the flood flow for the next 9 h. As flood flow is more concerned with changes at different prediction time points, we use T as the reference time and introduce different time points such as T+1, T+3, T+6, and T+9, with a 3-h interval, to dynamically measure the changes in flood flow.

Table 1. Performance of different models at Tunxi dataset

Model	T+1		T+3		T+6		T+9		Average	
	RMSE	MAE	RMSE	MAE	RMSE	MAE	RMSE	MAE	RMSE	MAE
MLP	36.26	11.37	83.26	25.67	138.06	41.59	183.87	55.96	110.39	33.64
LSTM	59.69	19.19	82.24	26.04	120.46	37.09	175.88	52.41	109.57	33.68
GRU	44.98	12.68	75.12	21.48	119.34	33.90	177.19	50.54	104.16	29.65
CNN	76.70	26.84	94.89	32.28	135.03	42.68	187.41	57.49	123.51	39.82
AdaRnn	55.43	13.35	82.52	21.41	127.46	35.30	182.29	50.71	111.93	30.19
ST-GCN	47.84	19.95	89.20	21.44	117.24	32.61	**136.73**	**39.2**	97.75	28.30
STGAT	35.45	14.19	62.12	21.15	106.91	32.22	158.42	46.68	90.72	28.56
DAGAT	**31.74**	**10.62**	**56.28**	**16.99**	**104.83**	**30.99**	162.70	48.02	**88.88**	**26.65**

As shown in Table 1, in terms of forecasting at T+1, T+3, and T+6 time points, our model consistently achieved the best results. This effectively demonstrates that our model has improved the accuracy of short-term flood forecasting.

We conducted ablation experiments to investigate the impact of the proposed distribution adaptive module on prediction performance. Compared with the STGAT model, DAGAT showed performance improvements at different time points. Our results indicate that the distribution adaptive module significantly enhances prediction performance, providing valuable guidance for further model improvements.

4.4 Performance Analysis

As shown in Fig. 4, our model demonstrates better accuracy than other models in short-term forecasting. We found that at the T+9 time step, ST-GCN achieves higher precision compared to our model, possibly due to its stronger long-term memory capability. However, in terms of the average performance, ST-GCN is less accurate than our model. When considering the time steps, the errors of all eight models vary with the passage of time. Models perform better in shorter prediction steps and exhibit poorer performance as the prediction time increases.

To illustrate the performance of our model in flood forecasting more intuitively, we compare the representative models GRU, CNN, STGAT, and DAGAT in the T+3 and T+6 periods in terms of their actual prediction performance for flood forecasting.

Peak flow forecasting is a critically important aspect of flood prediction as it enables the early warning of the highest water levels in floods and assists relevant authorities in taking timely response measures. As shown in Fig. 5, at the T+3 time point, most models are able to fit the curve well. However, there is a slight error in peak flow estimation for the GRU and CNN models, whereas both the STGAT and DAGAT models demonstrate a better fit.

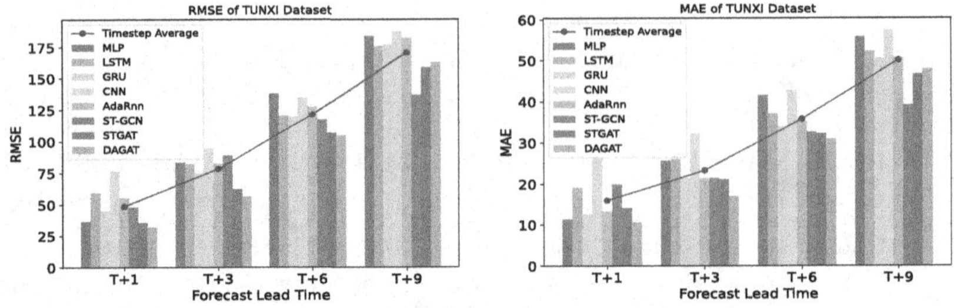

Fig. 4. Comparison of Models Performance at Tunxi

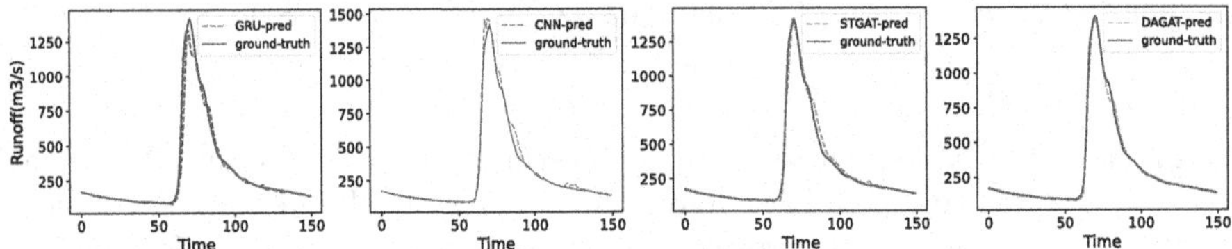

Fig. 5. Result at T+3

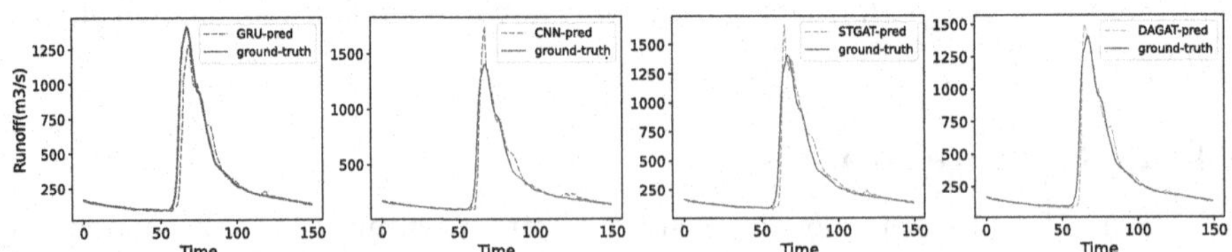

Fig. 6. Result at T+6

As shown in Fig. 6, at the T+6 time point, as the lead time increases, the prediction errors of all models generally become larger. The GRU and CNN models further amplify the forecast errors at the peak, while the STGAT model also starts to exhibit errors at the peak. However, the DAGAT model predicts more accurately. Therefore, our model demonstrates good accuracy in peak flow prediction for flood forecasting and is suitable for river flood prediction.

5 Conclusion

This paper proposes a distributed adaptive graph neural network flood forecasting method called DAGAT. It utilizes GAT to autonomously learn the spatial information of each hydrological feature and uses the GRU model to learn temporal dependencies. Introducing a distribution adaptive module to mitigate the impact of distribution differences in multivariate hydrological time series on flood forecasting accuracy. Compared to existing baseline methods, this approach demonstrates better forecasting performance at different forecast time points. For future work, We will conduct experiments in more watersheds, explore the phenomenon that different levels of distribution change in datasets, and attempt to apply this model to other natural disaster domains with temporal and spatial relationships, such as water pollution.

References

1. Shi, K., Peng, X., Lu, H., Zhu, Y., Niu, Z.: Application of social sensors in natural disasters emergency management: a review. IEEE Trans. Comput. Social Syst. (2022)
2. Hadid, B., Duviella, E., Lecoeuche, S.: Data-driven modeling for river flood forecasting based on a piecewise linear arx system identification. J. Process Control **86**, 44–56 (2020)
3. Du, Y., et al.: Adarnn: adaptive learning and forecasting of time series. In: Proceedings of the 30th ACM International Conference on Information & Knowledge Management, pp. 402–411 (2021)
4. Veličković, P., Cucurull, G., Casanova, A., Romero, A., Lio, P., Bengio, Y.: Graph attention networks. arXiv preprint arXiv:1710.10903 (2017)
5. Cho, K., et al.: Learning phrase representations using rnn encoder-decoder for statistical machine translation. arXiv preprint arXiv:1406.1078 (2014)
6. Benjamin, M.A., Rigby, R.A., Stasinopoulos, D.M.: Generalized autoregressive moving average models. J. Am. Stat. Assoc. **98**(461), 214–223 (2003)
7. Puttinaovarat, S., Horkaew, P.: Flood forecasting system based on integrated big and crowdsource data by using machine learning techniques. IEEE Access **8**, 5885–5905 (2020)
8. Miau, S., Hung, W.-H.: River flooding forecasting and anomaly detection based on deep learning. IEEE Access **8**, 198384–198402 (2020)
9. Le, X.-H., Ho, H.V., Lee, G., Jung, S.: Application of long short-term memory (LSTM) neural network for flood forecasting. Water **11**(7), 1387 (2019)
10. Ding, Y., Zhu, Y., Feng, J., Zhang, P., Cheng, Z.: Interpretable spatio-temporal attention LSTM model for flood forecasting. Neurocomputing **403**, 348–359 (2020)
11. Wang, J., Chen, Y., Feng, W., Han, Yu., Huang, M., Yang, Q.: Transfer learning with dynamic distribution adaptation. ACM Trans. Intell. Syst. Technol. (TIST) **11**(1), 1–25 (2020)
12. Feng, J., Wang, Z., Wu, Y., Xi, Y.: Spatial and temporal aware graph convolutional network for flood forecasting. In: 2021 International Joint Conference on Neural Networks (IJCNN), pp. 1–8. IEEE (2021)
13. Jaynes, E.T.: On the rationale of maximum-entropy methods. Proc. IEEE **70**(9), 939–952 (1982)

14. Xu, K., Hu, W., Leskovec, J., Jegelka, S.: How powerful are graph neural networks? arXiv preprint arXiv:1810.00826 (2018)
15. Schapire, R.E.: The boosting approach to machine learning: an overview. In: Nonlinear Estimation and Classification, pp. 149–171 (2003)

DSAM-GN: Graph Network Based on Dynamic Similarity Adjacency Matrices for Vehicle Re-identification

Yuejun Jiao[1,2], Song Qiu[1,2](✉), Mingsong Chen[1], Dingding Han[3,4], Qingli Li[2], and Yue Lu[2]

[1] MOE Engineering Research Center of Software/Hardware Co-design Technology and Application, East China Normal University, Shanghai 200062, China
sqiu@ee.ecnu.edu.cn

[2] Shanghai Key Laboratory of Multidimensional Information Processing, East China Normal University, Shanghai 200241, China

[3] School of Information Science and Technology, Fudan University, Shanghai 200433, China

[4] Shanghai Artificial Intelligence Laboratory, Shanghai 200232, China

Abstract. In recent years, vehicle re-identification (Re-ID) has gained increasing importance in various applications such as assisted driving systems, traffic flow management, and vehicle tracking, due to the growth of intelligent transportation systems. However, the presence of extraneous background information and occlusions can interfere with the learning of discriminative features, leading to significant variations in the same vehicle image across different scenarios. This paper proposes a method, named graph network based on dynamic similarity adjacency matrices (DSAM-GN), which incorporates a novel approach for constructing adjacency matrices to capture spatial relationships of local features and reduce background noise. Specifically, the proposed method divides the extracted vehicle features into different patches as nodes within the graph network. A spatial attention-based similarity adjacency matrix generation (SASAMG) module is employed to compute similarity matrices of nodes, and a dynamic erasure operation is applied to disconnect nodes with low similarity, resulting in similarity adjacency matrices. Finally, the nodes and similarity adjacency matrices are fed into graph networks to extract more discriminative features for vehicle Re-ID. Experimental results on public datasets VeRi-776 and VehicleID demonstrate the effectiveness of the proposed method compared with recent works.

Keywords: Vehicle re-identification · Graph network · Spatial attention

This work was supported by the Open Research Fund of MOE Eng. Research Center of HW/SW Co-Design Tech. and App., and the Science and Technology Commission of Shanghai Municipality (22DZ2229004).

F. Liu et al. (Eds.): PRICAI 2023, LNAI 14325, pp. 353–364, 2024.
https://doi.org/10.1007/978-981-99-7019-3_33

1 Introduction

Vehicle re-identification (Re-ID) is a task that aims to identify a target vehicle across video streams captured by different cameras. It has gained increasing importance in applications such as assisted driving systems, traffic flow management, and vehicle tracking within intelligent transportation systems. However, the presence of extraneous background information and occlusions can introduce interference and hinder the learning of discriminative features, resulting in significant feature variations of the same vehicle image in different scenarios. Therefore, it is crucial to remove extraneous information and minimize the interference of background noise in vehicle Re-ID tasks.

Various methods are proposed for fine-grained feature extraction to eliminate the interference of redundant information. These methods can be categorized into three aspects: knowledge-based methods [4,6,23], uniform spatial division methods [15,17], and part-level detection methods [13,22]. Knowledge-based methods utilize metadata such as orientation, color, car type, key points, viewpoint, and spatiotemporal information to enhance the identification of vehicle details. Uniform spatial division methods divide the feature map horizontally or vertically into multiple parts and extract features separately from each part. Part-level detection methods employ image segmentation to semantically divide vehicles into multiple regions (e.g., roof, wheels, and windows) and extract features from these segmented regions. All the aforementioned methods facilitate a comprehensive analysis of both the overall appearance and specific components of a vehicle, thereby enabling the extraction of intricate details. However, knowledge-based and part-level detection methods require additional annotations, the uniform spatial division method does not necessitate annotations but it is susceptible to partition misalignment. Additionally, the feature extraction methods employed in these approaches ignore the relationships among part regions.

In this paper, we propose a novel graph network based on dynamic similarity adjacency matrices (DSAM-GN) method for vehicle Re-ID. Our method aims to capture spatial relationships among local features and reduce background noise from the vicinity of vehicles. To achieve fine-grained feature extraction, the extracted vehicle features are divided into different patches. Unlike traditional CNN networks that overlook the correlation among local patches, we introduce a graph network to capture the spatial relationships among these patches. One challenge when applying graph networks to image representation is determining how to establish edges between nodes and which nodes to connect. In response to this challenge, we introduced a novel approach of utilizing the spatial attention mechanism to generate adjacency matrices. To overcome the issue of redundant background information, we employ a spatial attention-based similarity adjacency matrix generation (SASAMG) module to compute similarity matrices of patches. Furthermore, the SASAMG module employs dynamic erasure operation to disconnect nodes with low similarity, resulting in similarity adjacency matrices. Finally, the patches and similarity adjacency matrices are fed into graph networks to extract discriminative features for vehicle Re-ID.

The main contributions of this paper are as follows:

- We propose a novel graph network based on dynamic similarity adjacency matrices (DSAM-GN) method that combines a spatial attention mechanism to propose a new approach for constructing adjacency matrices required for the graph network. This method effectively captures spatial relationships among local features and reduces background noise from the vicinity of vehicles without any additional annotations.
- We design a spatial attention-based similarity adjacency matrix generation (SASAMG) module, which employs a spatial attention mechanism and dynamic erasure operation to optimize connections between nodes and generate a similarity adjacency matrix. By erasing attention on nodes with background noise, this module establishes a fundamental basis for the learning of discriminative features.
- Extensive experiments on public datasets VeRi-776 [8–10] and VehicleID [7] demonstrate the effectiveness of our proposed method compared with recent works.

2 Related Work

2.1 CNNs and Graph Networks

Deep learning techniques are widely adopted in vehicle Re-ID methods. Convolutional neural networks (CNNs) emerge as the dominant approach for deep feature extraction due to their exceptional capability to capture discriminative features. Several works [4,17] employ CNN architectures as feature extractors, enabling the learning of both global and local features. However, CNNs often focus only on local information and fail to capture the relationships among different regions with intricate local details. To address this limitation, graph networks (GNs) are introduced as a viable solution, allowing the exploration of interconnections among local features derived from different regions. The graph convolutional network (GCN) [5] updates node representations by aggregating information from neighboring nodes, enabling the node representation to inherit information from nearby regions. The graph attention network (GAT) [20] utilizes attention mechanism to control the influence of different neighboring nodes on the target node representation, thus reducing the impact of irrelevant nodes. GNs have been successfully applied in various domains, including computer vision [3,11,18,21,24], social networks [1], and recommendation systems [2].

2.2 Node and Edge Construction in GNs for Vehicle Re-ID

When applying graph networks to image representation, careful consideration must be given to node definition and edge construction. The local graph aggregation network with class balanced loss (LABNet) [18] defines spatial regions of the feature map as nodes and establishes edges among nodes using a simple

8-neighborhood connectivity approach. This straightforward method can introduce redundant background information, which negatively impacts model performance. The hierarchical spatial structural graph convolutional network (HSS-GCN) [21] uniformly divides the global feature map into five regions: upper-left, upper-right, middle, down-left, and down-right, and treats each of these regions as a node in a graph. Edges are formed among these regions and a global node. These regions still contain background noise. The structured graph attention network (SGAT) [24] creates nodes based on 20 selected landmarks detected by a landmark detection module, and edges among the landmarks are determined by their Euclidean distances being smaller than a predefined threshold. This method relies on expensive additional annotations for landmark detection. The parsing-guided cross-part reasoning network (PCRNet) [11] employs part-level segmentation to divide vehicles into regions, constructing a part-neighboring graph using regional features. The part-level segmentation approach also requires costly additional annotations. In this paper, the graph network based on dynamic similarity adjacency matrices (DSAM-GN) divides the extracted vehicle features into different patches as nodes. A spatial attention mechanism and dynamic erasure operation are applied to optimize connections between nodes.

3 Proposed Method

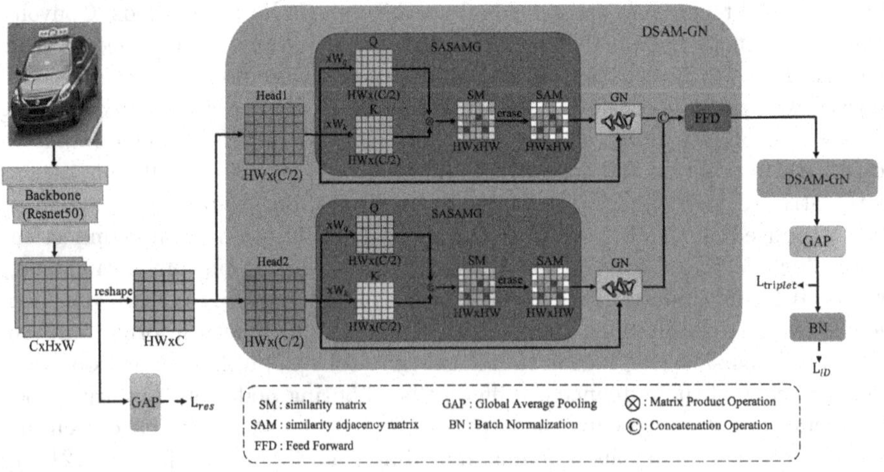

Fig. 1. The overall architecture of the proposed DSAM-GN model.

3.1 Overview

Figure 1 illustrates the proposed model's architecture. The backbone network initially processes the input image to extract fundamental vehicle features, which are divided into multiple patches before inputting into the DSAM-GN module for feature extraction. Within SASAMG, the input features are multiplied by two trainable parameter matrices, W_q and W_k, to produce the query and key matrices, respectively. The matrix product of the query and key matrices is then computed, and the resulting values are softmax-normalized to obtain the similarity matrix (SM). Then, connections between patches with low similarity are erased to obtain a similarity adjacency matrix (SAM). Each patch is treated as a node, and both the nodes and the SAM are fed into the graph network (GN), which captures feature relationships among the nodes. The Feed Forward (FFD) module consists of a multi-layer perceptron and ReLU activation function, which are used to aggregate the features extracted from the preceding two branches. The motivation for adopting two branches arises from the outstanding performance of the multi-head attention mechanism in Transformer [19]. The features are then processed through the second DSAM-GN module and undergo global average pooling (GAP) and batch normalization (BN) to produce the final output. Importantly, GAP replaces the fully connected layer, significantly reducing the number of network parameters and preventing model overfitting.

3.2 DSAM-GN

The DSAM-GN module explores the relationships among different patches while discarding redundant patches. The backbone network extracts features from the image, serving as the original appearance representation. The resulting feature is represented by a $C \times H \times W$ tensor, where C, H, and W indicate the number of feature channels, height, and width, respectively. The feature is reshaped into $N \times C$ for the subsequent similarity evaluation, with N representing the number of patches, and $N = H \times W$. The embedding features of the patches are formed as shown in Eq. (1):

$$X^{input} = [X_1, X_2, \ldots, X_i, \ldots, X_N] + P_{pos} \tag{1}$$

Here, $X^{input} \in \mathbb{R}^{N \times C}$ represents the input to the DSAM-GN module, and $P_{pos} \in \mathbb{R}^{N \times C}$ denotes the learnable positional encoding. The input features X^{input} are split along the channel dimension into two branches and fed into the SASAMG modules, respectively. Inside the SASAMG module, the input features are linearly transformed into queries $Q \in \mathbb{R}^{N \times (C/2)}$ and keys $K \in \mathbb{R}^{N \times (C/2)}$. The matrix product of them is applied to calculate the similarity matrix S, which represents the similarity among the patches according to Eq. (2):

$$S(Q, K) = \text{softmax}\left(\frac{QK^T}{\sqrt{d_k}}\right) \tag{2}$$

Furthermore, to obtain a similarity adjacency matrix, a dynamic erasure operation is applied to disconnect patches with low similarity. The similarity adjacency matrix A is computed as shown in Eq. (3):

$$A_{i,j} = \begin{cases} S_{i,j} & S_{i,j} > p(S, \beta) \\ 0 & S_{i,j} \leq p(S, \beta) \end{cases} \tag{3}$$

Here, the function p calculates the percentile value of the similarity matrix S, with the hyperparameter $\beta \in [0, 100]$ representing the percentile index for patches with low similarity. Specifically, we first flatten S into a one-dimensional array B, and sort its elements in ascending order. Let $n = N \times N$ be the length of B. For instance, if we want to calculate the 85 percentile, $p(S, 85) = B_k$, where $k = \lceil 85\% n \rceil$.

Each patch is treated as a node, and both the nodes and the similarity adjacency matrix are fed into the graph network, which captures feature relationships among the nodes. The computation of the graph network is expressed by Eq. (4):

$$\mathbf{h}'_i = \sigma \left(\sum_{j \in \mathcal{N}_i} A_{i,j} \mathbf{W} \mathbf{h}_j \right) \tag{4}$$

Here, $\mathbf{h}_j$ represents the feature vector of the i-th node's neighbor. The weight matrix $\mathbf{W}$ is a trainable parameter, and $\mathcal{N}_i$ denotes the set of neighboring nodes for the i-th node, which represents the set of nodes that remain connected to the i-th node after dynamic erasure operation. σ represents the activation function, and in this paper, the ReLU activation function is used. Finally, the output is the representation vectors of all nodes: $\mathbf{h}'_1, \mathbf{h}'_2, \ldots, \mathbf{h}'_i, \ldots, \mathbf{h}'_N$.

3.3 Loss Function

As depicted in Fig. 1, we adopt a multi-task learning approach for joint training. The output of the GAP layer (after the DSAM-GN module) is used to compute the triplet loss (L_{triplet}), while the output of the BN layer is employed to calculate the ID loss (L_{ID}), which is a cross-entropy loss. Moreover, to address the issue of large intra-class distance and small inter-class distance, we incorporate the triplet loss (L_{res}) as an auxiliary supervision for the backbone network's output. Three hyperparameters (α, β, γ) correspond to the coefficients of the aforementioned three loss functions. In order to avoid excessive fine-tuning of hyperparameters, we set $\alpha = \beta = \gamma = 1$ in the following experiments. Thus, the total loss function of the proposed method can be formulated as shown in Eq. (5):

$$L_{total} = \alpha L_{res} + \beta L_{triplet} + \gamma L_{ID} \tag{5}$$

4 Experiments

In this section, we present the experimental results and analysis of our proposed model for vehicle Re-ID. We evaluate the model on the VeRi-776 [8–10] and VehicleID [7] datasets, compare its performance with state-of-the-art methods, and conduct an ablation study to assess the effectiveness of our proposed method.

4.1 Implementation Details

Before training, we randomly applied crop, flip, and pad operations on the images with a certain probability. The images were then uniformly resized to 256 × 256 pixels. To construct our network, we employed a ResNet50 as the backbone architecture. The ResNet50 was initialized with pre-trained weights from the ImageNet dataset. The training parameters varied between the VeRi-776 and VehicleID datasets due to differences in image quality, quantity, and perspective. The VeRi-776 dataset was trained using one GPU with a batch size of 128 and SGD optimization with warm-up strategy. The learning rate increased to 0.01 after 3000 iterations and gradually decreased using cosine annealing until the 60th epoch. On the other hand, the VehicleID dataset was trained using two GPUs with a batch size of 256 and Adam optimization with warm-up strategy. The learning rate was initially set to 0.000035 and increased to 0.0002 after 2000 iterations. Then, it was reduced by a factor of 0.1 at the 30th, 70th, and 90th epochs, culminating in a total of 100 epochs. The model was implemented using the PyTorch framework and trained and tested on an NVIDIA RTX 3090.

4.2 Experimental Results and Analysis

Results on VeRi-776 Dataset. We first evaluated our model on the VeRi-776 dataset and compared its performance against various state-of-the-art methods. Table 1 presents the comparison results. Our model achieved state-of-the-art performance compared with other methods. Specifically, our method achieved a higher mAP score, surpassing the baseline by 1.12%. Moreover, the Rank-1 and

Table 1. Comparison with state-of-the-art results (%) on VeRi-776.The best result is bolded.

Method	Publicaiton	VeRi-776		
		mAP	Rank-1	Rank-5
HSS-GCN [21]	ICPR'21	44.80	64.40	86.10
DF-CVTC [6]	TETCI'22	61.06	91.36	95.77
SGAT [24]	ACMMM'20	65.66	89.69	-
KPGST [4]	Electronics'22	68.73	92.35	93.92
SAN [15]	MST'20	72.50	93.30	97.10
VGM [23]	APIN'22	73.32	92.82	95.21
PCRNet [11]	ACMMM'20	78.60	95.40	98.40
PVEN [13]	CVPR'20	79.50	95.60	98.40
LABNet [18]	Neurocput'21	79.50	95.70	-
SOFCT [22]	TITS'23	80.70	96.60	98.80
PFMN [17]	CIS'22	81.20	96.80	97.60
MRF-SAPL [14]	Entropy'23	81.50	94.70	98.70
baseline	-	81.09	96.72	98.33
DSAM-GN (ours)	-	**82.22**	**97.38**	**98.75**

Rank-5 scores showed improvements of 0.42% and 0.40%, respectively, over the baseline. These results provide strong evidence for the effectiveness of our model on the VeRi-776 dataset.

Results on VehicleID Dataset. Next, we conducted experiments on the VehicleID dataset and compared our results against state-of-the-art methods, which are presented in Table 2. Our model outperformed the baseline in terms of the mAP, Rank-1, and Rank-5 metrics. Specifically, our approach achieved the best mAP scores across all three VehicleID subsets (800, 1600, and 2400), outperforming other methods. This indicated that DSAM-GN was effective at identifying vehicles in terms of average precision. DSAM-GN has demonstrated strong performance in both Rank-1 and Rank-5 scores, with its performance being surpassed only by PCRNet. Notably, DSAM-GN achieves the best Rank-1 score on the VehicleID-2400 subset, outperforming PCRNet. Although PCRNet achieved excellent scores, its use of segmentation techniques required expensive annotation. However, DSAM-GN's results were still impressive, considering that it did not rely on costly annotations.

Table 2. Comparison with state-of-the-art results (%) on VehicleID.The best result is bolded.

Method	Publicaiton	VehicleID-800			VehicleID-1600			VehicleID-2400		
		mAP	Rank-1	Rank-5	mAP	Rank-1	Rank-5	mAP	Rank-1	Rank-5
HSS-GCN [21]	ICPR'21	77.30	72.70	91.80	72.40	67.90	87.80	66.10	62.40	84.30
DF-CVTC [6]	TETCI'22	78.03	75.23	88.11	74.87	72.15	84.37	73.15	70.46	82.13
SGAT [24]	ACMMM'20	81.49	78.12	-	77.46	73.98	-	75.35	71.87	-
SAN [15]	MST'20	-	79.70	94.30	-	78.40	91.30	-	75.60	88.30
LABNet [18]	Neurocput'21	87.50	81.20	-	84.20	78.00	-	80.80	73.50	-
MRF-SAPL [14]	Entropy'23	-	84.30	97.70	-	79.60	94.10	-	76.30	91.60
SOFCT [22]	TITS'23	89.80	84.50	96.80	86.40	80.90	95.20	84.3	78.70	93.70
PVEN [13]	CVPR'20	-	84.70	97.00	-	80.60	94.50	-	77.80	92.00
PFMN [17]	CIS'22	-	85.60	96.80	-	81.40	94.10	-	80.00	92.00
PCRNet [11]	ACMMM'20	-	**86.60**	**98.10**	-	**82.20**	**96.30**	-	80.40	**94.20**
baseline	-	75.89	66.33	89.38	69.20	58.72	82.55	64.41	53.77	76.83
DSAM-GN (ours)	-	**90.42**	85.63	96.96	**86.60**	81.62	95.22	**84.66**	**81.26**	93.89

Visualization. To visually assess the performance of our proposed model, we present the rank-5 retrieval results of an example query image from the VeRi-776 dataset, as illustrated in Fig. 2. The top five images retrieved by the Baseline and DSAM-GN approaches are displayed in the first and second rows, respectively. Correct retrieval results are indicated by red boxes, while incorrect results are highlighted with blue boxes. It is evident that our proposed model outperforms the baseline and exhibits superior ability in distinguishing similar vehicles.

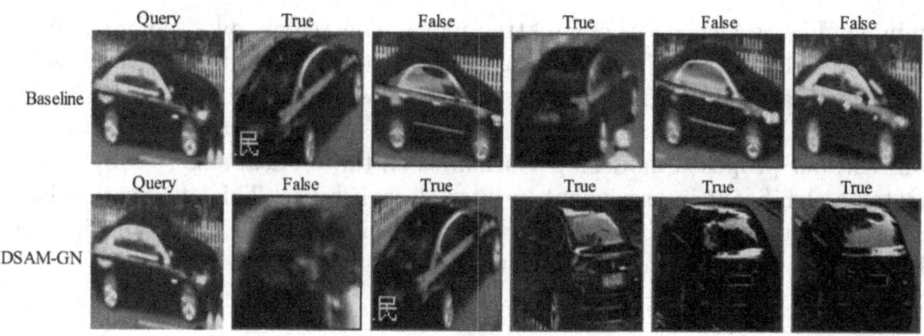

Fig. 2. Rank-5 visualization examples on VeRi-776. (Color figure online)

Additionally, we utilized Grad-CAM [16] to generate attention maps for challenging samples with background occlusions. Figure 3 shows the attention maps, illustrating the model's focus. The attention maps of the baseline model revealed a strong emphasis on the background information, negatively impacting its performance. In contrast, our proposed model exhibited a stronger focus on the vehicles themselves, effectively recalibrating the model's attention and reducing extraneous focus on the background. This visualization provides qualitative evidence of the superiority of our approach in handling background occlusions and improving the model's discriminative ability.

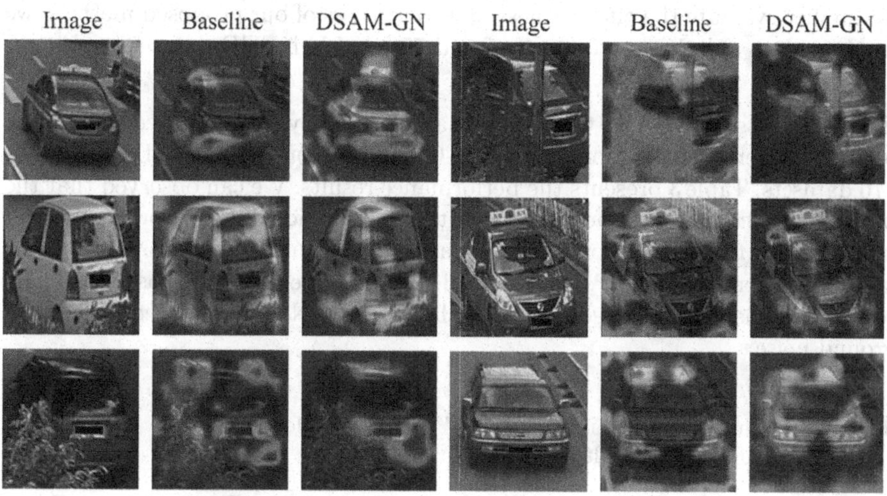

Fig. 3. Gradient-weighted Class Activation Mapping (Grad-CAM) visualization of attention maps.

Furthermore, we employed t-SNE [12] to visualize scatter plots that visualize the distribution of data points in the feature space before and after model training. Figure 4 shows these scatter plots. The scatter plot before training exhibited a disordered distribution of distinct categories. Although the baseline model facilitated clustering of different categories, it is evident from the vertical axis $(-4, 8)$ that it still had shortcomings, such as a small inter-class distance. In contrast, our proposed model's performance on the vertical axis $(-8, 8)$ demonstrated a significant improvement in inter-class distance. This observation highlights that our model can effectively learn discriminative features and improve the separation of different vehicle categories.

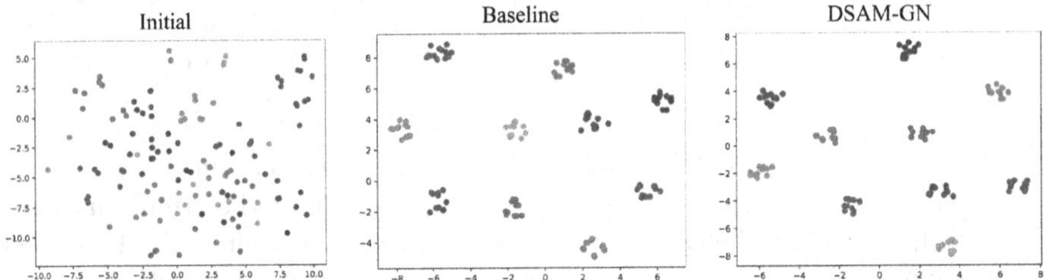

Fig. 4. t-SNE visualization of the learned feature space.

4.3 Ablation Study

To further evaluate the effectiveness and robustness of our proposed method, we conducted an ablation study on the VeRi-776 and VehicleID datasets.

Effectiveness of DSAM-GN. In this ablation study, we evaluated the impact of different percentile (β) for the DSAM-GN module on the VehicleID and VeRi-776 datasets. Table 3 presents the performance results. We can observed that the performance consistently outperformed the baseline for different percentile values. Notably, the best performance was achieved when β was set to 95, resulting in an improvement of mAP, Rank-1, and Rank-5 scores over the baseline. These results demonstrate the effectiveness of the DSAM-GN module in reducing background noise.

Table 3. Evaluation of the impact (%) of percentile β for DSAM-GN on VehicleID and VeRi-776. The best result is bolded.

Method	VehicleID-800			VehicleID-1600			VehicleID-2400			VeRi-776		
	mAP	Rank-1	Rank-5	mAP	Rank-1	Rank-5	mAP	Rank-1	Rank-5	mAP	Rank-1	Rank-5
Baseline	75.89	66.33	89.38	69.20	58.72	82.55	64.41	53.77	76.83	81.09	96.72	98.33
DSAM-GN (0 percentile)	88.64	83.22	96.13	84.19	78.08	92.54	83.06	77.36	90.39	81.15	97.08	98.63
DSAM-GN (75 percentile)	88.64	83.22	96.13	84.19	78.08	92.54	83.06	77.36	90.39	81.50	97.02	98.45
DSAM-GN (85 percentile)	90.26	85.49	96.36	85.74	79.91	93.40	83.76	78.06	91.19	81.95	97.26	98.63
DSAM-GN (95 percentile)	**90.42**	**85.63**	**96.96**	**86.60**	**81.62**	**95.22**	**84.66**	**81.26**	**93.89**	**82.22**	**97.38**	**98.75**
DSAM-GN (98 percentile)	87.85	81.89	95.78	83.73	78.02	91.56	81.70	75.90	89.03	81.42	96.90	98.57

5 Conclusion

In this paper, we propose a novel graph network based on dynamic similarity adjacency matrices (DSAM-GN) method that combines a spatial attention mechanism to propose a new approach for constructing adjacency matrices required for the graph network. This method effectively captures spatial relationships among local features and reduces background noise without any additional annotations. We design a spatial attention-based similarity adjacency matrix generation (SASAMG) module, which employs a spatial attention mechanism and dynamic erasure operation to optimize connections between nodes and generate a similarity adjacency matrix. By erasing attention on nodes with background noise, this module establishes the foundation for learning discriminative local features. Extensive experiments on the VeRi-776 and VehicleID datasets demonstrated the effectiveness of our proposed method. Visual comparisons with the baseline model showcased that our method is more focused on the vehicles themselves and demonstrated a significant improvement in inter-class distance. These results highlight the potential of our approach for vehicle re-identification tasks.

References

1. Bian, T., et al.: Rumor detection on social media with bi-directional graph convolutional networks. In: Proceedings of the AAAI Conference on Artificial Intelligence, pp. 549–556 (2020)
2. Chen, L., Wu, L., Hong, R., Zhang, K., Wang, M.: Revisiting graph based collaborative filtering: a linear residual graph convolutional network approach. In: Proceedings of the AAAI Conference on Artificial Intelligence, pp. 27–34 (2020)
3. Guo, M., Chou, E., Huang, D.-A., Song, S., Yeung, S., Fei-Fei, L.: Neural graph matching networks for Fewshot 3D action recognition. In: Ferrari, V., Hebert, M., Sminchisescu, C., Weiss, Y. (eds.) ECCV 2018. LNCS, vol. 11205, pp. 673–689. Springer, Cham (2018). https://doi.org/10.1007/978-3-030-01246-5_40
4. Huang, W., et al.: Vehicle re-identification with spatio-temporal model leveraging by pose view embedding. Electronics **11**(9), 1354 (2022)
5. Kipf, T.N., Welling, M.: Semi-supervised classification with graph convolutional networks. arXiv preprint arXiv:1609.02907 (2016)
6. Li, H., et al.: Attributes guided feature learning for vehicle re-identification. IEEE Trans. Emerg. Top. Comput. Intell. **6**(5), 1211–1221 (2022)
7. Liu, H., Tian, Y., Wang, Y., Pang, L., Huang, T.: Deep relative distance learning: tell the difference between similar vehicles. In: Proceedings of the IEEE Conference on Computer Vision and Pattern Recognition, pp. 2167–2175 (2016)
8. Liu, H., Tian, Y., Yang, Y., Pang, L., Huang, T.: Deep relative distance learning: tell the difference between similar vehicles. In: Proceedings of the IEEE Conference on Computer Vision and Pattern Recognition, pp. 2167–2175 (2016)
9. Liu, X., Liu, W., Ma, H., Fu, H.: Large-scale vehicle re-identification in urban surveillance videos. In: 2016 IEEE International Conference on Multimedia and Expo (ICME), pp. 1–6. IEEE (2016)
10. Liu, X., Liu, W., Mei, T., Ma, H.: PROVID: progressive and multimodal vehicle reidentification for large-scale urban surveillance. IEEE Trans. Multimedia **20**(3), 645–658 (2017)

11. Liu, X., Liu, W., Zheng, J., Yan, C., Mei, T.: Beyond the parts: learning multi-view cross-part correlation for vehicle re-identification. In: Proceedings of the 28th ACM International Conference on Multimedia, pp. 907–915 (2020)
12. Van der Maaten, L., Hinton, G.: Visualizing data using t-SNE. J. Mach. Learn. Res. **9**(11), 2579–2605 (2008)
13. Meng, D., et al.: Parsing-based view-aware embedding network for vehicle re-identification. In: Proceedings of the IEEE/CVF Conference on Computer Vision and Pattern Recognition, pp. 7103–7112 (2020)
14. Pang, X., Yin, Y., Zheng, Y.: Multi-receptive field soft attention part learning for vehicle re-identification. Entropy **25**(4), 594 (2023)
15. Qian, J., Jiang, W., Luo, H., Yu, H.: Stripe-based and attribute-aware network: a two-branch deep model for vehicle re-identification. Meas. Sci. Technol. **31**(9), 095401 (2020)
16. Selvaraju, R.R., Cogswell, M., Das, A., Vedantam, R., Parikh, D., Batra, D.: Grad-CAM: visual explanations from deep networks via gradient-based localization. In: Proceedings of the IEEE International Conference on Computer Vision, pp. 618–626 (2017)
17. Shen, J., Sun, J., Wang, X., Mao, Z.: Joint metric learning of local and global features for vehicle re-identification. Complex Intell. Syst. **8**(5), 4005–4020 (2022)
18. Taufique, A.M.N., Savakis, A.: LABNet: local graph aggregation network with class balanced loss for vehicle re-identification. Neurocomputing **463**, 122–132 (2021)
19. Vaswani, A., et al.: Attention is all you need. In: Advances in Neural Information Processing Systems, vol. 30 (2017)
20. Velickovic, P., Cucurull, G., Casanova, A., Romero, A., Lio, P., Bengio, Y., et al.: Graph attention networks. STAT **1050**(20), 10–48550 (2017)
21. Xu, Z., Wei, L., Lang, C., Feng, S., Wang, T., Bors, A.G.: HSS-GCN: a hierarchical spatial structural graph convolutional network for vehicle re-identification. In: Del Bimbo, A., et al. (eds.) ICPR 2021. LNCS, vol. 12665, pp. 356–364. Springer, Cham (2021). https://doi.org/10.1007/978-3-030-68821-9_32
22. Yu, Z., Huang, Z., Pei, J., Tahsin, L., Sun, D.: Semantic-oriented feature coupling transformer for vehicle re-identification in intelligent transportation system. IEEE Trans. Intell. Transp. Syst., 1–11 (2023)
23. Zhang, C., Yang, C., Wu, D., Dong, H., Deng, B.: Cross-view vehicle re-identification based on graph matching. Appl. Intell. **52**(13), 14799–14810 (2022)
24. Zhu, Y., Zha, Z.J., Zhang, T., Liu, J., Luo, J.: A structured graph attention network for vehicle re-identification. In: Proceedings of the 28th ACM International Conference on Multimedia, pp. 646–654 (2020)

Dynamic Spatial-Temporal Dual Graph Neural Networks for Urban Traffic Prediction

Li Wang[1,2], Nianwen Ning[1,2], Yihan Liu[1,2], Yining Lv[1,2], Yongmeng Tian[1,2], Yanyu Zhang[1,2], and Yi Zhou[1,2](✉)

[1] School of Artificial Intelligence, Henan University, Zhengzhou 450046, China
{wangli123,nnw,lyn,tymeng,zyy,zhouyi}@henu.edu.cn

[2] International Joint Research Laboratory for Cooperative Vehicular Networks of Henan, Zhengzhou 450046, China

Abstract. Accurate traffic prediction is a crucial aspect of intelligent transportation systems. However, existing methods typically rely on static graphs to learn correlations between different sensor in space, which ignores dynamic impact of latent factors on topology of the road network. To address this issue, we propose a traffic flow prediction method based on a dynamic spatial-temporal dual graph neural network that extracts deeper and finer-grained features from traffic data. Firstly, we propose a new data-driven strategy based on a dynamic spatial-temporal-aware graph to replace the commonly used predefined static graph in traditional graph convolutional networks. This strategy enables us to collect edge attributes (geographical proximity) and node attributes (spatial heterogeneity) between nodes. Secondly, we introduce the duality principle to construct the dual hypergraph of the traffic graph, which captures the correlations between edges of the traffic graph. In the process of dynamic graph convolutional iteration, we capture the dependencies between dynamic edge attributes and static node attributes on the basis of merging spatial relationships. Finally, an improved multi-head attention mechanism designed to represent dynamic spatial correlations. We conducted experiments on two real-world traffic prediction tasks, results demonstrate our method outperforms others.

Keywords: Spatial heterogeneity · Traffic prediction · Geographical proximity · Dynamic graph · Spatial-temporal correlation

1 Introduction

The task of traffic prediction [1] is a typical task in time series prediction, which has wide applications in machine learning. Traffic flow prediction has been widely applied, such as optimizing road use [2] and planning travel routes in advance [23].

Deep learning become a popular approach for traffic prediction. A classic approach is to use Graph Convolutional Networks (GCNs) to represent the spatiotemporal correlations of time series data in road networks with non-Euclidean

F. Liu et al. (Eds.): PRICAI 2023, LNAI 14325, pp. 365–376, 2024.
https://doi.org/10.1007/978-981-99-7019-3_34

spatial structures [4–6]. However, most existing GCN [5–8,12–22] methods use a static adjacency matrix to describe spatial correlations of road networks, which cannot reflect actual dynamics of spatial correlations within the road network.

In addition, there exist complex interactions between dynamic similar patterns and random irregular patterns in time series traffic data at both short-term and long-term time scales. At the macroscopic static level, static node attributes, such as the proximity of two schools in different regions that are far apart but share similar location attribute data patterns, the homogenous dynamic congestion during peak hours, and the deviation of stable traffic patterns. At microscopic dynamic level, traffic data exhibits dynamic and complex fluctuations. However, most existing methods [10–12] lack attention [9] to the correlation between dynamic edge attributes and static node attributes, which limits their ability to capture dynamic time dependencies within road networks (Fig. 1).

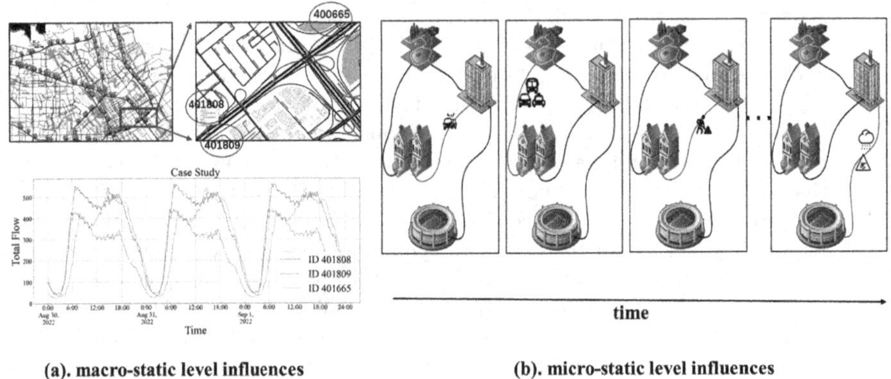

Fig. 1. Multiple influences on spatial-temporal correlation (macro-static level, micro-dynamic level).

We propose a traffic flow prediction method based on dynamic spatiotemporal dual graph neural network, as shown in Fig. 2. Unlike traditional GCN-based methods that use fixed and empirical Laplacian matrices, this method is based on a data-driven strategy using a dynamic spatiotemporal-aware graph to replace the commonly used predefined static graph in traditional graph convolutional networks. This strategy allows us to collect edge attributes (geographical proximity) and node attributes (spatial heterogeneity). Specifically, this method introduces a latent network to adaptively represent spatiotemporal relationships, which is then input into GCN to form a dynamic graph convolutional network. Paper's main contributions:

1. We propose a new dynamic graph generation algorithm that adaptively integrates adjacent nodes at different time steps and spatial heterogeneity information to obtain an adaptive dynamic graph adjacency matrix to characterize dynamic correlation, thereby improving prediction performance.

2. We introduce the duality theorem on the basis of graph neural networks and propose a new gnn method - the dynamic dual graph neural network model. Based on modeling the dynamic characteristics of traffic network nodes, the traffic map is transformed into a dual hypergraph, which uses the dual hypergraph to capture the dynamic spatiotemporal characteristics of edges to enrich the extracted features, thereby improving the accuracy of downstream prediction tasks.
3. We conducted sufficient experiments on two real datasets and it can verify the role of our model in improving the accuracy of traffic flow prediction.

2 Preliminaries and Problem Definition

2.1 Notations and Symbols

Definition 2.1 (Flow Speed). An important indicator reflecting traffic conditions is traffic speed. In this article, we first represent historical velocity data as: $\mathcal{V}_p = \{v_1, v_2, ..., v_{N_p}\}$, where $[N_p]$ is the number of road network nodes.

Definition 2.2 (Traffic Graph). The transportation network can be represented by $\mathcal{G} = (\mathcal{V}, \mathcal{E}, A)$, where road sections represent nodes, and edges represent the relationships between nodes. As shown in Fig. 3(a) and (b), $\mathcal{V}$ is set of road segment with a cardinality of $|\mathcal{V}| = N$, and $A \in R^{N \times N}$ is an adjacency matrix whose elements represent the weights of edges. These weights can initially be obtained from the connectivity and distance between nodes.

Definition 2.3 (Dual Traffic Graph). To fully leverage the spatiotemporal features of traffic data, we transform the traffic graph into its dual hypergraph, as illustrated in Fig. 3(b). This dual transformation involves mapping nodes of original graph to edges of target hypergraph, and the edges of the graph to the nodes of the target. We then apply two dynamic GCNs on the resulting sequence of graphs and hypergraphs, effectively capturing the evolving traffic patterns. Given a graph $\mathcal{G} = (\mathcal{V}, \mathcal{E}, A)$, use $\mathcal{G}_h = (\mathcal{V}_h, \mathcal{E}_h, H)$ to represent the dual hypergraph of $\mathcal{G}$.

2.2 Problem Definition and Description

The purpose of traffic speed forecasting is to use historical vehicle speeds to predict traffic speeds on various road sections over time in the future. In this paper the effect of dynamic edge attributes (geographical proximity) and static node attributes (spatial heterogeneity) are further considered. Formally, historical steps of traffic speeds and historical steps of auxiliary characteristics are given, and our objective is to learn a model to predict future traffic speed steps.

$$\widehat{X}^p_{t+1:t+Q} = f(X^p_{t-P+1:t}, X^a_{t-P+1:t}), \tag{1}$$

where $\widehat{X}$ is expected to be close to X as much as possible.

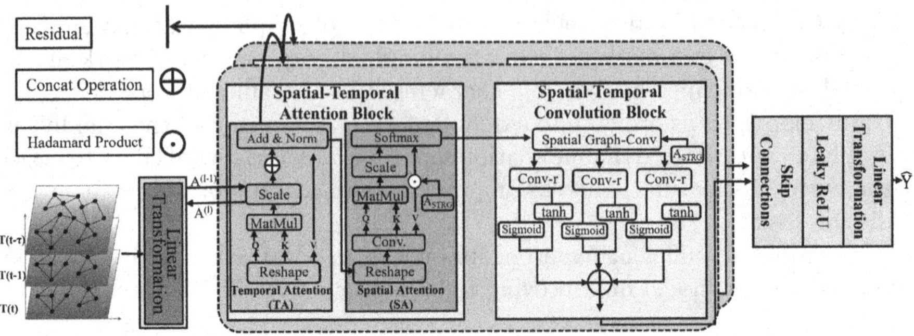

Fig. 2. Model's architecture in paper.

3 Methodology

We provide an overall framework diagram of the model, as shown in Fig. 2. From the figure, we can see that the model is mainly composed of three parts, namely the spatiotemporal attention module, spatiotemporal convolution module, and prediction module. The specific details of each module are also presented in the framework diagram. The information of the spatiotemporal attention module can be obtained from the graph. The spatiotemporal attention module consists of two parts, namely temporal attention module and spatial attention module. Spatial attention module further adjusts spatiotemporal attention through spatiotemporal correlation maps. The spatiotemporal convolution module mainly consists of graph convolution layer and multi-scale GTU. Here, we replace predefined adjacency matrix graph in traditional graph convolution with a spatiotemporal graph ($\mathbf{A}_{STAG}$) with dynamic spatial correlation information.

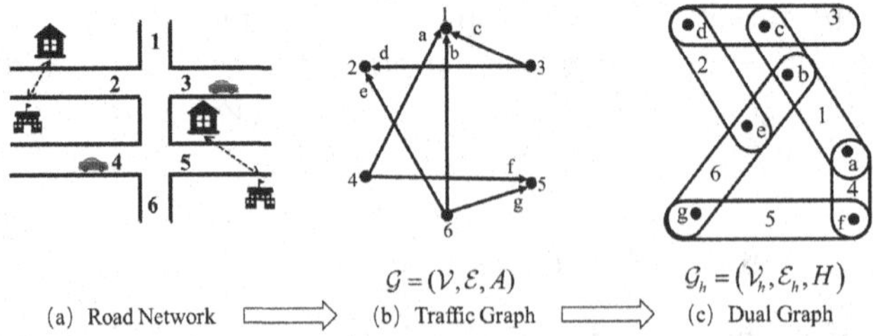

Fig. 3. Road network graph (a), traffic flow graph (b), and dual hypergraph (c)

3.1 Dynamic Spatiotemporal Graph Construction

When modeling a real road network, the spatial dependence between nodes cannot be solely reflected by the connectivity between nodes. If the spatial correlation representation during modeling is not accurate enough, it will lead to a decrease in accuracy of subsequent prediction tasks. So let's first introduce how to obtain a more accurate representation of spatial correlation.

By analyzing the factors that affect the spatial correlation between nodes, the first is the diffusion, and second is the similar attributes among nodes, that is, there may be adjacent node attributes between two nodes that are far away. Based on the above two considerations, we utilize daily and node traffic flow data in road network to represent dynamic spatial correlation between nodes by capturing similarity. Here, we use Wasserstein distance. We name this new data-driven strategy spatiotemporal perceptual distance, and define this representation obtained from spatiotemporal perceptual distance as a spatiotemporal perceptual graph.

For example, $X^f \in R^{D \times d_t \times N}$ represents the traffic flow, N represents the n-th sensor node, and D represents the number of days contained in the vector information, where d_t is the number of recording times per day (If data is recorded every 5 min, then $d_t = 288$). Treating the daily traffic data of a node as a vector, the traffic data of multiple days can be represented as a sequence of vectors. We first calculate the vector modulus and normalize it to extract daily traffic volume information for each record point:

$$m_{nd} = \frac{\|\mathbf{w}_{nd}\|_2}{Z_n}, \quad Z_n = \sum_{d=1}^{D} \|\mathbf{w}_{nd}\|_2, \tag{2}$$

where $\|\bullet\|_2$ represents Euclidean norm. We need represent difference between each probability distribution, where use cosine distance to represent it:

$$\text{cost}\left(\mathbf{w}_{n_1 i}, \mathbf{w}_{n_2 j}\right) = 1 - \frac{\mathbf{w}_{n_1 i}^{\top} \cdot \mathbf{w}_{n_2 j}}{\|\mathbf{w}_{n_1 i}\|_2 \times \|\mathbf{w}_{n_2 j}\|_2}, \tag{3}$$

where the superscript T represents performing transpose operation. Thus, the STAD can be expressed as:

$$\begin{aligned} & d_{STAD}\left(n_1, n_2\right) \triangleq \text{STAD}\left(\mathbf{X}_{n_1}, \mathbf{X}_{n_2}\right) \\ & = \inf_{\gamma \in \Pi\left[P_{n_1}, P_{n_2}\right]} \int_x \int_y \gamma(x, y)\left(1 - \frac{\mathbf{w}_{n_1 x}^{\top} \cdot \mathbf{w}_{n_2 y}}{\sqrt{\mathbf{w}_{n_1}^{\top} \mathbf{w}_{n_1 x}} \times \sqrt{\mathbf{w}_{n_2 y}^{\top} \mathbf{w}_{n_2 y}}}\right) dx dy, \\ & \text{s.t.} \int \gamma(x, y) dy = \frac{\|\mathbf{w}_{n_1 x}\|_2}{\sum_{x=1}^{D} \|\mathbf{w}_{n_1 x}\|_2}, \int \gamma(x, y) dx = \frac{\|\mathbf{w}_{n_2 y}\|_2}{\sum_{y=1}^{D} \|\mathbf{w}_{n_2 y}\|_2}. \end{aligned} \tag{4}$$

The matrix $\mathbf{A}_{STAD} \in R^{N \times N}$ that represent the correlation between nodes, where $\mathbf{A}_{STAD}[i, j] = 1 - d_{STAD}(i, j) \in [0, 1]$. Then a learnable parameter $\mathbf{W}_m \in R^{N \times N}$ to adjust influence of $\mathbf{A}_{STRG}$ on $\mathcal{P}$.

3.2 Spatial-Temporal Attention Module

In order to more accurately estimate the dependencies between nodes, we propose the definition of spatiotemporal perceptual distance. Based on this, we need to further refine the dynamics of the dependency relationships between nodes to adapt to changes in real-time generated data in application scenarios. Therefore, this paper need propose an improved spatiotemporal attention module based on the attention mechanism, specifically capturing temporal and spatial attention sequentially, and performing spatiotemporal fusion to obtain a strengthened spatiotemporal correlation representation.

Temporal Attention. The temporal attention mechanism can help us capture temporal dependencies. In order to effectively capture long-range correlations in time series data, we have entered multi head attention mechanism on basis of attention mechanism. The dynamic temporal correlation between nodes is obtained through the multi head attention mechanism. The definition of multi head attention is as follows (taking multi head attention mechanism of H head as an example):

$$X'^{(l)}\mathbf{W}_q^{(l)} \triangleq Q^{(l)}, \quad X'^{(l)}\mathbf{W}_k^{(l)} \triangleq K^{(l)}, \quad X'^{(l)}\mathbf{W}_v^{(l)} \triangleq V^{(l)}, \tag{5}$$

$$A^{(l)} = \frac{Q^{(l)} {K^{(l)}}^T}{\sqrt{d_h}} + A^{(l+1)}, \tag{6}$$

where $\mathcal{X}'^{(l)} \in R^{c^{(l-1)} \times M \times N}$ is reshaped from input of lth ST module $\mathcal{X}^{(l)} \in R^{N \times c^{(l-1)} \times M}$. We have added residual connections in the temporal attention section of each ST Block, enhancing the connection of attention between different layers. This residual attention mechanism makes the model to fuse both deep and shallow dependencies, it can avoid the disappearance of gradients and fully explore the dynamic time dependencies in the data.

$Q^{(l)}, K^{(l)}, V^{(l)}$ are projected H times with H different matrices, then stitched together, this can be expressed as a formula in the following form,

$$O^{(h)} = \text{Att}\left(Q\mathbf{W}_q^{(h)}, K\mathbf{W}_k^{(h)}, V\mathbf{W}_v^{(h)}\right), \tag{7}$$

$$Y = \text{LayerNorm}\left(\text{Linear}\left(\text{Reshape}[O^{(1)}, O^{(2)}, \ldots, O^{(H)} + X'\right)\right), \tag{8}$$

where $\mathbf{W}_{q,k,v}^{(h)} \in R^{d \times d_h}$ $(d_h = d/H)$, then $O \in R^{c^{(l-1)} \times M \times H \times d_h}$ concatenates the multi-head outputs from time attention module in the model.

Spatial Attention. The temporal attention mechanism can capture the dependencies of the temporal dimension. Based on this, we propose a self attention mechanism to calculate spatial dependence of output of temporal attention module. The improved self attention mechanism of the H head can be represented by the following formula:

$$\mathbf{P}^{(h)} = \text{Softmax} \left(\frac{\left(\mathbf{Y}_E \mathbf{W}_k'^{(h)}\right)^\top \left(\mathbf{Y}_E \mathbf{W}_q'^{(h)}\right)}{\sqrt{d_h}} + \mathbf{W}_m^{(h)} \odot \mathbf{A}_{STRG}\right), \tag{9}$$

where $\mathbf{W}_k^{\prime(h)}, \mathbf{W}_q^{\prime(h)} \in R^{d_E \times d_h}, \mathbf{W}_m^{(h)} \in R^{N \times N}$ are learnable parameters, $\mathcal{P} \in R^{H \times N \times N}$ denotes dynamic spatiotemporal attention tensor by combining outputs.

3.3 Spatial-Temporal Convolution Module

In previous research on transportation networks, the main focus was on the connectivity and globality between nodes in the network. In this process, predefined graphs were used for convolution, which aggregates information from neighboring nodes to obtain node features. On the basis of retaining the above ideas, we improve the previous method to fully utilize the topological characteristics of the transportation network. Specifically, we use Chebyshev polynomials to learn the features of nodes. The biggest difference from previous research methods is that we use spatiotemporal perception maps to replace the commonly used predefined maps in previous studies. Dynamically adjusting each term in Chebyshev polynomial to fully utilize dynamic topological features of road network.

Graph convolution is the process of aggregating neighboring node information to obtain target node information. In order to aggregate the dynamic attributes among nodes, we aggregate information from graph signal $x = \mathbf{x}_t \in R^N$ at each time slice :

$$g_\theta * Gx = g_\theta(\mathbf{L})x, \tag{10}$$

where $*G$ denotes graph convolution operation, g_θ denotes the convolution kernel,the learnable parameter $\theta \in R^K$.

4 Experiments

4.1 Datasets Used in the Experiment

The experiments were conducted on two real datasets: PEMS03 and PEMS08. The statistical information for these datasets shown in Table 1. Additional information of datasets are presented below.

Table 1. Information about datasets

Dataset	Number of Nodes	Number of Nodes Edges	Timesteps	Missing data (%)
PEMS03	358	547	26208	0.672
PEMS08	170	295	17856	0.696

PEMS03, PEMS08: It was collected by the Caltrans Performance Measurement System, published in AST-GCN [14] and includes average speeds, traffic volumes for SanFrancisco Bay Area. Then time range for data collection is from April to May 2019.

4.2 Baseline Used in the Experiment

In order to better validate performance of models, we selected several popular baseline models for comparison experiments, and the selected baseline models are as follows.

1. FC-LSTM [1]: The LSTM network is a RNN with fully linked LSTM hidden units, a special type of RNN model.
2. T-GCN [15]: effective in terms of local and global temporal relationships.
3. DCRNN [11]: diffusion convolution recurrent neural network that combining graph convolution and GRU. Combining the advantages of A and B
4. ST-GCN [16]: introduces a spatial-temporal attention mechanism into the model. To ensure fair comparisons, we reconfigured the model to use only the most recent part of the modelling cycle.
5. ASTGCN [3]: A model that applies spatial and temporal attention mechanisms prior to spatial and temporal convolution. To be fair, we only use its most recent component.
6. AGCRN [6]: makes use of the learnable embedding of nodes in graph convolution.
7. STFGNN [17]: spatial-temporal fusion graphs are used to complement spatial correlation.

The experimental results of our model on the PEMs03 and PEMS07 datasets, as well as the experimental results of seven other models (FC-LSTM, T-CN, DC-RNN, ST-GCN, etc.) on the PEMs03 and PEMS07 datasets, can be seen in Table 2. Through these experimental results, It can be seen that our model achieved the best results on all performance metrics for both datasets. The graph structure composed of spatiotemporal-aware distances proposed by us can help the model capture spatial dependencies between nodes, and the dual principle can simultaneously integrate dependencies between edges. This indicates that our model can be applied without spatial prior information and can fully utilize dependencies between two different attributes.

4.3 Setup of Experiments

When conducting comparative experiments, for fairness, we processed the data of each baseline model in the same way. For example, we divided the experimental dataset into training (7/10), validation (2/10), and testing sets (1/10). And we used one hour of historical data to predict future traffic speeds, and conducted experimental tests on each predicted time step. All training and testing were implemented on (CPU: lntel(R) Core(TM) i9-11900K, GPU: GTX 3090).

In our experiment, we selected three evaluation indicators to test the performance of our model, which will be introduced in this section. The first evaluation metric used to evaluate the model is root mean square error, the second evaluation metric is mean absolute error (MAE), and the third evaluation metric is MAPE. The three evaluation indicators are commonly used in machine learning, and the specific calculations are easy to find. Due to space limitations, they will not be elaborated on further.

Table 2. Evaluations of Our Model and Baselines on Two Real-Word Datasets

Dataset	Metrics	FC-LSTM	T-CN	DCRNN	ST-GCN	ASTGCN	AGCRN	STFGNN	**Ours**
PEMS03	MAE	21.33	19.31	18.18	17.47	17.69	15.98	16.77	**15.75**
	MAPE (%)	22.33	19.86	18.91	17.15	19.40	15.21	16.69	**14.86**
	RMSE	36.11	33.24	30.31	30.12	29.66	28.52	27.84	**27.71**
PEMS08	MAE	22.20	22.69	17.86	18.02	18.61	15.95	16.81	**15.76**
	MAPE (%)	15.02	14.04	11.45	11.40	13.08	10.12	10.62	**9.94**
	RMSE	33.06	35.79	27.83	27.38	28.16	25.22	25.97	**24.77**

4.4 Experimental Analysis

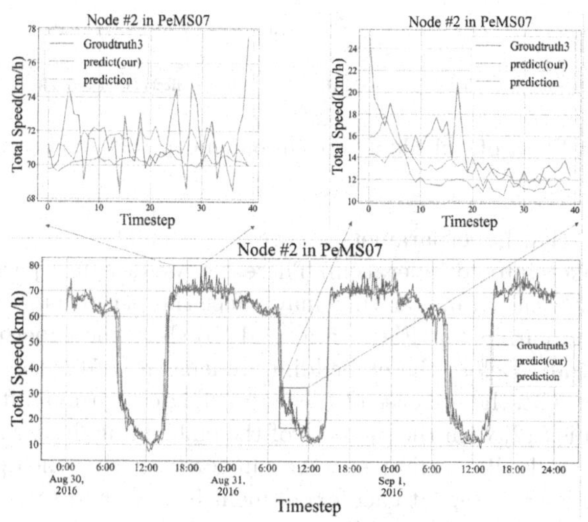

Fig. 4. Comparison between STGCN and our DSTGNN on PEMS07.

Comparison of Experimental Results. The experimental results of our model on the PEMs03 and PEMS07 datasets, as well as the experimental results of seven other models (FC-LSTM, T-CN, DC-RNN, ST-GCN, etc.) on the PEMs03 and PEMS07 datasets, can be seen in Table 2. It can be seen that our model achieved the best results on two datasets. The graph structure composed of spatial-temporal perception distances proposed by us can help the model capture the spatial dependence between nodes, which indicates that our model can be applied without spatial prior information and can well integrate node and edge information through the dual principle (Fig. 4).

Compared to the TCN and ASTGCN models, our proposed spatiotemporal attention mechanism can capture dynamic changes in the data, significantly improving the prediction performance. Moreover, the application of spatiotemporal attention mechanisms can play a good role, such as better capturing the dynamic changes of data, which is very helpful for improving prediction performance. We plotted the prediction accuracy at 12 different time steps, as shown in Fig. 6.

Parameter Sensitivity Analysis. For the sensitivity analysis of the model parameters, we did two experiments on the embedding dimension of the model, and the experimental results are as follow (Fig. 5).

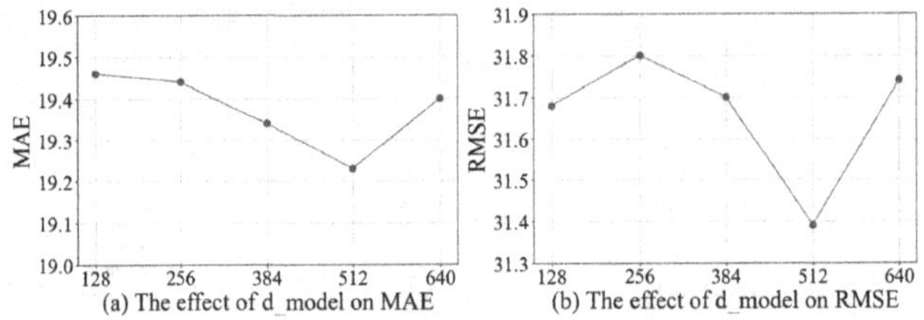

Fig. 5. Effect of embedding dimension on experimental precision

We all know that hyperparameters have an undeniable impact on the model and must be taken into consideration. Therefore, we designed parameter experiments to study each parameter that may affect the performance of the model, which is the core parameter. Figure 5(a) and (b) show the experimental results of parameter study. Before the embedding dimension is 512, the model performance improves with the increase of the embedding dimension; after the embedding dimension is 512, with the increase of the embedding dimension, the model performance is gradually declining, so we can conclude that the optimal embedding dimension is 512. Repeat each experiment 5 times and test on the test set to calculate the MAE value. In each experiment, we only change one parameter.

4.5 Ablation Experiments

The impact of dynamic information on prediction accuracy is illustrated in Fig. 5, where horizontal axis represents prediction step and vertical axis represents the mean absolute error. Yellow curve represents the experimental results obtained from the model without the feature fusion module, while the blue curve represents the total mean absolute error obtained by testing our model over 12 prediction steps. By comparing the two curves, we can conclude that the dynamic feature fusion module plays a crucial role to improving accuracy of prediction.

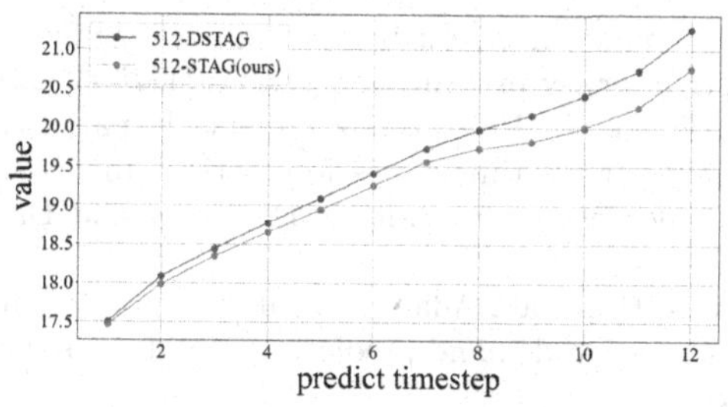

Fig. 6. Comparison of prediction curves between STGCN and DSTGNN on PEMS03.

5 Conclusion

A new traffic flow prediction model was proposed in this article. Our model is set up to encode both dynamic and static spatial dependencies, rather than relying on one predefined static adjacency matrix alone. The approach is effective in enhancing the representation of deeper dynamic association properties between road network nodes. Our model achieves state-of-the-art performance over two public datasets used for traffic flow prediction, compared to several existing state-of-the-art baseline methods.

Acknowledgments. This work was supported by National Natural Science Foundation of China (No. 62176088), the Key Science and Technology Research Project of Henan Province of China (Grant No. 22102210067, 222102210022), and the Program for Science & Technology Development of Henan Province (No. 212102210412 and 202102310198).

References

1. Liu, J., Guan, W.: A summary of traffic flow forecasting methods. J. Highw. Transp. Res. Dev. **21**(3), 82–85 (2004)
2. Han, L., Du, B., Sun, L., et al.: Dynamic and multi-faceted spatio-temporal deep learning for traffic speed forecasting. In: Proceedings of the 27th ACM SIGKDD Conference on Knowledge Discovery & Data Mining, pp. 547–555 (2021)
3. Ta, X., Liu, Z., Hu, X., et al.: Adaptive spatio-temporal graph neural network for traffic forecasting. Knowl. Based Syst. **242**(22), 180–199 (2022)
4. Lan, S., Ma, Y., Huang, W., et al.: DSTAGNN: dynamic spatial-temporal aware graph neural network for traffic flow forecasting. In: International Conference on Machine Learning, pp. 11906–11917. PMLR (2022)
5. Zheng, Q.: Dynamic spatial-temporal adjacent graph convolutional network for traffic forecasting. IEEE Trans. Big Data **21**(3), 82–85 (2022)
6. Xu, H., Zou, T., Liu, M., et al.: Adaptive spatiotemporal dependence learning for multi-mode transportation demand prediction. IEEE Trans. Intell. Transp. Syst. **23**(10), 18632–18642 (2022)
7. Kim, D., Cho, Y., Kim, D., et al.: Residual correction in real-time traffic forecasting. In: Proceedings of the 31st ACM International Conference on Information & Knowledge Management, pp. 962–971 (2022)

8. Ji, J., Wang, J., Huang, C., et al.: Spatio-temporal self-supervised learning for traffic flow prediction. arXiv preprint arXiv:2212.04475 (2022)
9. Shao, Z., Zhang, Z., et al.: Pre-training enhanced spatial-temporal graph neural network for multivariate time series forecasting. In: Proceedings of the 28th ACM SIGKDD Conference on Knowledge Discovery and Data Mining, pp. 167–177 (2022)
10. Li, F., Feng, J., Yan, H., et al.: Adaptive spatiotemporal dependence learning for multi-mode transportation demand prediction. ACM Trans. Knowl. Discov. Data **17**(1), 1–21 (2023)
11. Li, Y., Yu, R., Shahabi, C., et al.: Diffusion convolutional recurrent neural network: Data-driven traffic forecasting. arXiv preprint arXiv:1707.01926 (2017)
12. Li, Y., Shahabi, C.: A brief overview of machine learning methods for short-term traffic forecasting and future directions. SIGSPATIAL Spec. **10**(1), 3–9 (2018)
13. Zhang, J., Zheng, Y., Qi, D., et al.: DNN-based prediction model for spatio-temporal data. In: Proceedings of the 24th ACM SIGSPATIAL International Conference on Advances in Geographic Information Systems, pp. 1–4 (2016)
14. Li, Y., Yu, R., Shahabi, C., et al.: Diffusion convolutional recurrent neural network: data-driven traffic forecasting. arXiv preprint arXiv:1707.01926 (2017)
15. Zhao, L., Song, Y., Zhang, C., et al.: T-GCN: a temporal graph convolutional network for traffic prediction. IEEE Trans. Intell. Transp. Syst. **21**(9), 3848–3858 (2019)
16. Yu, B., Yin, H., Zhu, Z.: Spatio-temporal graph convolutional networks: a deep learning framework for traffic forecasting. arXiv preprint arXiv:1709.04875 (2017)
17. Li, M., Zhu, Z.: Spatial-temporal fusion graph neural networks for traffic flow forecasting. In: Proceedings of the AAAI Conference on AI, vol. 35, no. 5, pp. 4189–4196 (2021)
18. Bai, S., Kol, Z., Koltun, V.: An empirical evaluation of generic convolutional and recurrent networks for sequence modeling. arXiv preprint arXiv:1803.01271 (2018)
19. Zhou, H., Zhang, S., Peng, J., et al.: Informer: beyond efficient transformer for long sequence time-series forecasting. In: Proceedings of the AAAI Conference on Artificial Intelligence, vol. 35, no. 12, pp. 11106–11115 (2021)
20. Williams, B.M., Hoel, L.A.: Modeling and forecasting vehicular traffic flow as a seasonal ARIMA process: theoretical basis and empirical results. J. Transp. Eng. **129**(6), 664–672 (2003)
21. Lin, Z., Feng, J., Lu, Z., et al.: DeepSTN+: context-aware spatial-temporal neural network for crowd flow prediction in metropolis. In: Proceedings of the AAAI Conference on Artificial Intelligence, vol. 33, no. 01, pp. 1020–1027 (2019)
22. Yao, H., Tang, X., Wei, H., et al.: Revisiting spatial-temporal similarity: a deep learning framework for traffic prediction. In: Proceedings of the AAAI Conference on Artificial Intelligence, vol. 33, no. 01, pp. 5668–5675 (2019)
23. Xu, J.: Multi-task travel route planning with a flexible deep learning framework. IEEE Trans. Intell. Transp. Syst. **22**(7), 3907–3918 (2020)

MuHca: Mixup Heterogeneous Graphs for Contrastive Learning with Data Augmentation

Dengzhe Liang[1], Binglin Li[1], Hongxi Li[1], and Yuncheng Jiang[1,2(✉)]

[1] School of Artificial Intelligence, South China Normal University, Foshan, China
[2] School of Computer Science, South China Normal University, Guangzhou, China
jiangyuncheng@m.scnu.edu.cn

Abstract. Contrastive learning has become a highly promising learning paradigm and demonstrated significant potential when few labels are available. The effectiveness of contrastive learning on graphs is largely dependent on the quality of positive and negative pairs, which can be improved by developing data augmentation (DA). However, the majority of the current DA methods rely on homogeneous graphs while less on heterogeneous graphs. In this paper, we present a method named MuHca, a node augmentation module for the problem of heterogeneity in DA. Concretely, MuHca separately employs nodes embedding of two views, namely meta-path and network schema, into a novel contrasting generative adversarial nets structure to implement data augmentation. By adopting the contrasting generative paradigm of GANs, MuHca can generate and optimize effective negatives. To enhance the robustness of MuHca, we exploit the potential information from the original data and extend our approaches by mixing up generated negatives with original ones. The final stage involves training a generator for edges in parallel with the modeling of edge presence among nodes, culminating in contrastive learning for heterogeneous graphs. The conducted experiments on three datasets validate the effectiveness of our proposed method, surpassing various state-of-the-art and even semi-supervised methods.

Keywords: Data augmentation · Heterogeneous graph · Contrastive learning

1 Introduction

Heterogeneous Information Network (HIN) is a graph data structure for effectively representing a heterogeneous graph consisting of various types of nodes and links [15]. The majority of research on heterogeneous graphs (HGs) centers around (semi-) supervised learning situations where models are trained using well-marked manual labels to accomplish specific tasks such as node classification. Although these studies have achieved success, one drawback is the high cost associated with collecting and annotating manual labels [1], which can be

F. Liu et al. (Eds.): PRICAI 2023, LNAI 14325, pp. 377–388, 2024.
https://doi.org/10.1007/978-981-99-7019-3_35

particularly challenging for research fields that involve large datasets or require specialized knowledge [20]. Lately, to tackle the downsides of supervised or semi-supervised learning, self-supervised learning (SSL) is a promising method that decreases reliance on manual labels [9]. Contrastive learning, being a widely used SSL technique, has received notable focus.

Contrastive learning [20] requires positive and negative pairs, and the objective is to place the embeddings of positive pairs in proximity and keep those of negative pairs away from each other [19]. To enhance the effectiveness of contrastive learning, data augmentation is naturally developed to improve more challenging positive and negative samples by making minor modifications or generating new data from existing data [24]. However, generating numerous high-quality positive or negative pairs for contrastive learning is quite challenging in heterogeneous graphs [18]. Because adjacent nodes have different meanings, compressing information can occur when synthesizing minority nodes [2]. Hence the strategies of DA used for homogeneous graphs may not directly work for heterogeneous graphs [8]. Furthermore, the discrete and non-Euclidean nature of graph-structured data makes its semantics and topology closely interlinked [23]. Consequently, performing DA directly in the input space can lead to the generation of out-of-domain samples due to the inherent limitations of graph-structured data.

To address the mentioned challenges, we proposed MuHca - a novel Mixup Heterogeneous graph for contrastive learning with data augmentation. MuHca employs the weight matrix and node degrees to measure the significance of edges and node features, where the weight matrix is shared by the whole graph, reflecting the global importance of the node. MuHca learns the embedding from heterogeneous graph convolutional networks through the meta-path pairs and network schema instances captured from the HGs. Inspired by GANs [6], we first enhanced contrast-GAN and implemented it on heterogeneous graphs, which generate negatives naturally preserving schema structure in two views. Furthermore, a mixup component is built to further enhance the data, addressing the issue of heterogeneity. The contributions of the paper are summarized as follows:

- We employ contrast-GAN for data augmentation in HGs, in order to generate harder negatives by utilizing the two views after embedding. Both the generator and discriminator networks trained in cross-view improve the efficiency of producing high-quality samples.
- We propose HG-Mixup, an innovative generative augmentation strategy that utilizes interpolation to generate synthetic nodes by interpolating the existing nodes with generated ones. Furthermore, a parallel edge generator is trained to model the existence of edges connecting nodes. Combined with contrastive learning, heterogeneous graph information can be adequately utilized.
- Experiments are performed on three datasets. Results demonstrate that MuHca consistently performs better than various state-of-the-art even semi-supervised methods.

2 Related Work

Heterogeneous Graph Learning. Heterogeneous graphs are crucial data structures extensively employed to represent diverse intricate interaction systems in real-life situations [21]. NSHE [22] prioritizes both maintaining the proximity between pairs and the overall network schema. HAN [17] introduced a hierarchical attention mechanism that is capable of capturing both semantic and structural information. There is also a meta-path based work namely HAE [5] to incorporate meta-paths and meta-graphs and leverages the self-attention mechanism to explore content-based node embeddings.

Contrastive Learning. In recent times, contrastive learning has emerged as a successful method for self-supervised graph representation learning [20]. Most self-supervised contrastive learning help reduces the dependence on manual labels, in which the supervision signals are acquired from the data itself automatically [9]. A classic contrastive learning representative method is deep graph infomax [16], a widely recognized approach that employs an Infomax criterion to differentiate negative nodes, positive nodes, and global summaries. Moreover, HeCo [18] is the pioneering work that employs contrastive learning for the heterogeneous graph. However, the problem of negative sample generation is not well addressed, which can be naturally relieved by data augmentation.

Graph Data Augmentation. Graph data augmentation can significantly improve the effectiveness of contrastive learning [20]. The DA can be tailored for various graph-related tasks, resulting in multiple approaches: edge-level augmentation like DropEdge [13], graph-level augmentation such as G-Mixup [10], and node-level augmentation like GraphENS [12]. However, most DA strategies are proposed for homogeneous graphs and less for heterogeneous graphs. Applying general DA algorithms directly to heterogeneous graphs can pose challenges in capturing essential information related to different types of nodes and edges.

3 Methodology

Considering a heterogeneous graph network $G = (V, E, \mathcal{A}, \mathcal{R}, \phi, \varphi)$ is composed of a node set V and an edge set E. The function $\phi : V \rightarrow \mathcal{A}$ and $\psi : E \rightarrow \mathcal{R}$ represent the mapping of node types and edge types, respectively, where $\mathcal{A}$ denotes the set of node types and $\mathcal{R}$ denotes the set of edge types. It is important to note that $|\mathcal{A}| + |\mathcal{R}| > 2$. The objective is to learn the node representations $\mathbf{Z} \in \mathbb{R}^{|V| \times d}$, where d represents the dimension of the node representation [15].

Formally, a network schema $\mathcal{S} = (\mathcal{A}, \mathcal{R})$ is a directed graph, which is designed for a meta template of a HIN. A network schema instance $\mathcal{S}$ refers to the smallest sub-graph of a HIN that contains all the defined node types and edge types according to the network schema [15]. A meta-path $\mathcal{P}$ is defined as a path in the form of $V_1 \xrightarrow{R_1} V_2 \xrightarrow{R_2} \cdots V_t \xrightarrow{R_t} V_{t+1} \cdots \xrightarrow{R_{l-1}} V_l$, where $R = R_1 \circ R_2 \circ \cdots \circ R_{l-1}$ defines the composite relations between node types V_1 and V_l [14].

In this section, we introduce our proposed framework MuHca, a novel robust data augmentation framework based on contrast-GANs and heterogeneous graph

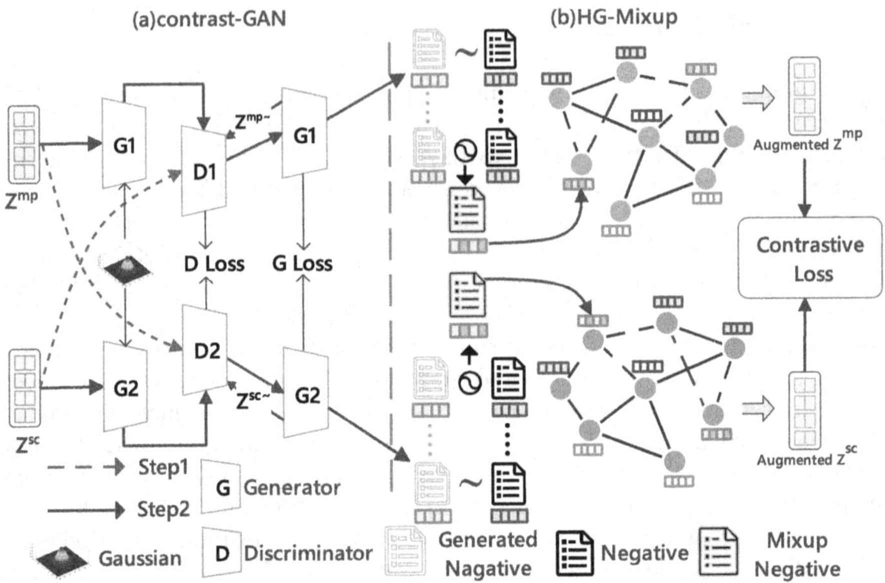

Fig. 1. The overall architecture of the proposed MuHca. Obtaining node embeddings Z^{mp} (meta-path) and Z^{sc} (network schema) from the encoders, MuHca applies data augmentation containing contrast-GAN and HG-Mixup for contrastive learning to perform the final representation of nodes.

mixup modules. Considering the inherent and essential properties of heterogeneous graph, we employ both meta-path and network schema encoders to obtain two distinct node representations for data augmentation. The DA framework comprises two parts, as shown in Fig. 1. In the contrast-GAN module, the discriminator contrasts the network schema view and generates negative samples of the meta-path view, and vice versa to generate negative samples of the network schema view. The HG-Mixup module are used for generating augmented negative samples by mixing up generated samples from contrast-GANs with original negatives. In addition, a generator for edges is trained in parallel to model the presence of connections between nodes. Those augmented data are interpolated into the embedding graph for contrastive learning.

3.1 Graph Data Augmentation

Defining positive and negative samples is the initial step toward generating more difficult negative samples in the data augmentation module. Specifically, we identify two nodes as positive samples if they are connected by numerous meta-paths set as a threshold T_p, for which we denoted the positive samples as $\mathbb{P}_i$. The remaining nodes are considered negative samples, denoted as $\mathbb{N}_i$. This positive sample strategy comprehensively considering meta-paths has the benefit of accurately reflecting the local structure of the target node.

Contrasting Generative Adversarial Nets. After obtaining positive samples $\mathbb{P}_i$ and original negative samples $\mathbb{N}_i$, we enhanced contrast-GAN and implemented it on heterogeneous graphs for $\mathbb{N}_i$. The contrast-GAN is rooted in adversarial learning, where a discriminator and a generator partake in a competition. Taking harder meta-path view generation of negatives as an example, we train D to determine the authenticity of a given node pair, distinguishing between real and fake samples while training G to produce negative sample node pairs that mimic real pairs. Both discriminators D and generators G are utilized z_i^{sc} and z_i^{mp} contrastively to improve the quality of data augmentation.

As previously stated, it is crucial to differentiate between real and fake negative samples within a given relation. With the target node i and its embedding z_i^{sc}, we can get the matrix space of the meta-path view, as shown in the upper part of Fig. 1 with red dash line. D of z_i^{sc} outputs a probability of sampling z_j from $\mathbb{N}_i$:

$$D\left(z_j \mid z_i^{sc}\right) = \left(\exp\left(-z_i^{sc\top} M_{mp}^{D} z_i\right) + 1\right)^{-1}, \tag{1}$$

where $\mathrm{M}_{mp}^{D} \in \mathbb{R}^{d\times d}$ is a matrix that projects z_i^{sc} into the space of meta-path view. If a sample belongs to the $\mathbb{N}_i$ and is linked to z_j, it should have a high probability, while a generated sample should have a low probability. The objective function of D under the network schema view is defined as follows:

$$\mathcal{L}_{i_D}^{sc} = -\left(\underset{z_j^{\widetilde{mp}} \sim G\left(z_i^{mp}\right)}{\mathbb{E}} \log\left(1 - D\left(z_j^{\widetilde{mp}} \mid z_i^{sc}\right)\right) + \underset{j\sim n_i}{\mathbb{E}} \log D\left(z_j^{mp} \mid z_i^{sc}\right)\right), \tag{2}$$

where $n_i \in \mathbb{N}_i$, which is selected at random, and $z_j^{\widetilde{mp}}$ are generated by the generator. This indicates that given z_i^{sc}, the purpose of D is to distinguish whether the negative sample comes from the meta-path view or the generator. Specifically, using z_i^{sc} as the discriminator aims to enable G to generate negatives contrastively from a different view while retaining its own characteristics. In a similar vein, we can deduce the objective function for the D based on the meta-path view $\mathcal{L}_{i_D}^{mp}$.

The objective of generator G is to generate fake samples to mimic the real ones. G continuously improves its generation quality through ongoing adversarial training with D. As shown in the upper part of Fig. 1, given a target i and its embedding z_i^{mp} initially, G employs an underlying Gaussian distribution centered on i, which are linked to the meta-path view:

$$e_j^{mp} \sim \mathcal{N}\left(z_i^{sc\top} M_{mp}^{G}, \sigma^2 \mathbf{I}\right), \tag{3}$$

where $M_{mp}^{G} \in \mathbb{R}^{d\times d}$ is a projected function to map z_i^{sc} into meta-path space, and $\sigma^2\mathbf{I} \in \mathbb{R}^{d\times d}$ is covariance for some choices of σ. To enhance the expression of the generated samples, we incorporate a two-layer multilayer perceptron:

$$z_j^{\widetilde{mp}} \sim G\left(z_i^{mp}\right) = \sigma\left(W e_j^{mp} + b\right), \tag{4}$$

where σ is non-linear activation. We train the G by minimizing the following loss:

$$\mathcal{L}_{i_G}^{mp} = \underset{z_j^{\widetilde{mp}} \sim G\left(z_i^{mp}\right)}{\mathbb{E}} - \log D\left(z_j^{\widetilde{mp}} \mid z_i^{sc}\right). \tag{5}$$

The objective function $\mathcal{L}_{iG}^{sc}$ is also similar to $\mathcal{L}_{iG}^{mp}$. So, we train the discriminator G by minimizing the following loss:

$$\mathcal{L}_{\mathcal{G}} = \frac{1}{|V|} \sum_{i \in V} [\lambda \cdot \mathcal{L}_{iG}^{mp} + (1 - \lambda) \cdot \mathcal{L}_{iG}^{sc}] . \tag{6}$$

where λ is a coefficient used to balance or equalize the impact of contrast views and V denotes the batch of nodes trained in the current epoch.

Heterogeneous Graph Mixup. To fully utilize the prospective insights contained within the original data, we present a Heterogeneous Graph Mixup (HG-Mixup) approach for synthesizing the enhanced negatives by interpolating some of the harder negatives with the original. After getting a well-trained G, we can obtain high-quality negative samples $\widetilde{z_j^{mp}}$ and $\widetilde{z_j^{sc}}$. Let $\widetilde{\mathbb{N}}_j = \{\widetilde{z}_1, \ldots, \widetilde{z}_j\}$ be the ordered set of harder negatives. We interpolate samples by using their nearest neighbors in the embedding space that also belong to the similar negatives. The harder negatives are compared to the original ones by using the k-nearest neighbor algorithm:

$$nn(j) = \underset{i}{\operatorname{argmin}} \left\| z_i - \widetilde{z}_j \right\|_2, \quad s.t. \ \mathbb{N}_i = \widetilde{\mathbb{N}}_j, \tag{7}$$

where $nn(j)$ refers to the nearest neighbor of j from the same class, and $\|\cdot\|_2$ is the ℓ_2-norm using Euclidean distance to measure. HG-mixup employs the weight matrix and node degrees to measure the significance of node features. With the nearest neighbor, a synthetic negative $z'_k \in \mathbb{N}'_i$ would be given by:

$$z'_k = \beta_k \widetilde{z}_{nn(j)} + (1 - \beta_k)\, z_i, \tag{8}$$

where $\beta_k \in (0, 0.5)$ is a randomly chosen mixing variable for the harder negatives. Note that $\beta_k < 0.5$ guarantees that the generated contribution is smaller than the one of the original negative. Let $\mathbb{N}'_i = \{z'_1 \ldots, z'_k\}$ be the set of synthetic hardest negatives to be generated.

Nevertheless, these nodes are not connected to the original graph since they do not have any edges. Therefore, we present an edge generator to model the presence of connections between nodes. The generator in our model is trained using real nodes and existing edges, and its purpose is to predict neighbor information for synthetic nodes. In order to keep the HG-Mixup model simple and enable easier analysis, we use a vanilla design with weighted inner production to implement the edge generator:

$$\mathbf{E}_{i,k} = \operatorname{softmax}\left(\sigma\left(z_i \cdot S \cdot z'_k\right)\right), \tag{9}$$

where $\mathbf{E}_{i,k}$ represents the predicted relation information between nodes z_i and z'_k, and S denotes the parameter matrix that captures the interaction among nodes. The loss function for training the edge is given by:

$$\mathcal{L}_{\text{edge}} = \|\mathbf{E} - \mathbf{A}\|_F^2, \tag{10}$$

where **E** refers to predicted connections between nodes, and **A** is the initial adjacency matrix that new nodes and edges can be added. The optimization of the generator involves the use of edge reconstruction. Eventually, the synthetic hardest negatives $\mathbb{N}_i'$ are interpolated with the original negatives $\mathbb{N}_i$ to boost contrastive learning and enhance the training.

3.2 Contrastive Loss

Given the augmented negative sample set $\mathbb{N}_i$ and positive sample set $\mathbb{P}_i$ under the above two views, we employ a two-layer Multilayer Perceptron to perform a linear transformation. In order to compute the contrastive loss function $\mathcal{L}_c$, we first need to calculate the loss function for each view. Taking the meta-path view as an example, as illustrated in Fig. 1. The target embedding is from the meta-path view (z_i^{mp}) and the embeddings of positive and negative samples are from the network schema view(z_l^{sc}, z_k^{sc}). Therefore, the contrastive loss function is presented in the meta-path view as follows:

$$\mathcal{L}_{ic}^{mp} = -\log \frac{\sum_{l\in\mathbb{P}_i} \exp\left(\cos\left(z_i^{mp}, z_l^{sc}\right)/\tau\right)}{\sum_{k\in\{\mathbb{P}_i\cup\mathbb{N}_i\}} \exp\left(\cos\left(z_i^{mp}, z_k^{sc}\right)/\tau\right)}, \tag{11}$$

where $\cos(u, v)$ represents the cosine similarity, which measures the similarity between two vectors u and v. Additionally, τ represents a temperature parameter. The contrastive loss $\mathcal{L}_{ic}^{sc}$ is comparable to $\mathcal{L}_{ic}^{mp}$, but with a distinction that the target embedding is derived from the meta-path view. The overall objective is given as follows:

$$\mathcal{L}_c = \frac{1}{|V|} \sum_{i\in V} \left(\mathcal{L}_{ic}^{mp} + \gamma \mathcal{L}_{ic}^{sc}\right), \tag{12}$$

where γ is the consistency balancing hyper-parameter. We can optimize the proposed model by utilizing backpropagation and learning the embeddings of nodes.

4 Experiments and Results

4.1 Datasets

We employ three real HG datasets to evaluate the effectiveness of graph Data Augmentation for node classification.

- **ACM** comprises 3,025 papers, 5,835 authors, and 56 subjects. The paper nodes are classified based on the conferences they are published in, serving as the target nodes for classification.
- **DBLP** is a citation network dataset comprising of 14,328 paper nodes, 4,057 author nodes, and 20 conference nodes. In this dataset, the main focus is on classifying the author nodes according to their respective research areas.
- **IMDB** is a movie dataset, which consists of 4,278 movie nodes, 5,257 actor nodes, and 2,081 director nodes. The objective here is to classify the movie nodes into three genres: comedy, action, and drama.

4.2 Baselines

We conduct a comparative analysis between the MuHca model and other heterogeneous graph neural network models to assess the respective performance:

- **DeepWalk** [7] (Deepw.) is a classical method for graph embedding that utilizes random-walk and skip-gram to learn network representations.
- **Mp2vec** [15] employs a metapath-guided random walk to generate node sequences and applies a heterogeneous skip-gram algorithm to obtain representations of nodes.
- **HERec** [14] learns meta-path embeddings to obtain the similarity between users and utilizes classic matrix factorization framework to get recommendation.
- **GAT** [9] is a semi-supervised neural network that integrates the attention mechanism for homogeneous graphs.
- **HAN** [17] trains node embedding using meta-path based neighbor nodes, excluding intermediate nodes which are incorporated in meta-paths. It generates node embeddings using an attention mechanism.
- **DMGI** [11] utilizes unsupervised learning, and GCN embedding nodes to capture the global structure of the entire graph.
- **HeCo** [18] employs self-supervised cross-view contrastive mechanism to capture both local and high-order structures, so as to learn node embeddings.
- **Magnn** [3] designs three main components for generating node embeddings by applying node content transformation, intra-metapath aggregation, and inter-metapath aggregation.
- **HAE** [5] utilizes meta-paths and meta-graphs and employs the self-attention mechanism to investigate node embeddings based on content.

4.3 Experimental Settings

We utilize the implementations of baseline methods available either from their authors or open-source libraries. Regarding other parameters, we adopt the configurations followed by their original papers. For the proposed MuHca, we employ Kaiming [4] initialization and Adam optimizer. In the DA module, we set the variance of Gaussian distribution σ^2 from 0.001 to 10. For the contrastive objective, we tune τ from 0.5 to 0.9 in intervals of 0.05. To evaluate our model more comprehensively, we opt for 20, 40, and 60 labeled nodes per class as the label rates for the training set. We train our model ten times with the same partition, and evaluate its effectiveness based on Macro-F1 and Micro-F1 scores.

4.4 Node Classification Results

The classification results for the nodes are presented in Table.1. The proposed MuHca model performs better than all other models on all datasets with all label rates. Several conclusions can be drawn from analyzing the results. Firstly, HAN and DMGI demonstrate inferior performance compared to the proposed

Table 1. Node classification results (%)

Dataset	Metrics	Training	Deepw.	Mp2vec	HERec	GAT	HAN	DMGI	HeCo	Magnn	HAE	Ours
ACM	Ma-F1	20	77.25	51.91	55.13	85.23	85.66	87.86	88.56	90.54	91.24	**93.19**
		40	80.47	62.41	61.21	87.04	87.47	86.23	87.61	90.51	91.95	**92.81**
		60	82.54	61.13	64.35	87.56	88.41	87.97	89.04	90.83	92.19	**93.70**
	Mi-F1	20	76.29	53.13	57.47	85.94	85.11	87.60	88.13	91.14	91.56	**92.86**
		40	79.45	64.43	62.62	88.31	87.21	86.02	87.45	90.16	91.73	**92.71**
		60	81.11	62.72	65.15	87.67	88.10	87.82	88.71	90.97	91.74	**92.67**
DBLP	Ma-F1	20	77.42	88.98	89.57	91.41	89.31	89.94	91.28	92.12	91.54	**94.80**
		40	81.01	88.68	89.73	91.20	88.87	89.25	90.34	92.57	92.91	**94.55**
		60	83.67	90.25	90.18	90.88	89.20	89.46	90.64	93.50	93.07	**94.29**
	Mi-F1	20	79.37	89.67	90.24	90.43	90.16	90.78	91.97	92.72	91.64	**94.78**
		40	82.43	89.14	90.15	91.16	89.47	89.92	90.76	93.63	92.40	**94.86**
		60	85.14	91.17	91.01	91.12	90.34	90.66	91.59	93.79	93.19	**94.91**
IMDB	Ma-F1	20	40.72	45.98	45.87	49.44	56.17	60.44	57.53	59.36	54.60	**61.74**
		40	45.19	47.35	46.72	50.14	56.21	60.94	57.84	60.27	56.69	**63.31**
		60	48.13	47.89	46.96	52.19	57.13	61.34	57.61	60.73	60.25	**63.68**
	Mi-F1	20	46.38	47.13	46.31	55.57	56.36	60.84	57.57	60.51	54.79	**64.03**
		40	47.99	48.06	47.78	55.91	57.14	60.64	58.30	61.54	56.73	**63.77**
		60	51.21	49.83	48.21	56.47	58.39	61.55	57.67	61.89	60.25	**64.83**

MuHca, which indicates that utilizing contrastive learning across various views is more efficient than single-view learning. Moreover, compared with cross-view module HAE and HeCo, our method achieves up to 4.6% and 3.2% improvement respectively. This shows that data augmentation plays a critical role in self-supervised learning. Finally, The performance of the Magnn module, which utilizes the label information, is nearly close to our self-supervised model. This indicates the great potential of data augmentation on heterogeneous graphs.

4.5 Performance Comparison

In this study, we perform an ablation study by removing certain design choices shown in Table 2. We use variants of MuHca, including MuHca - Mu which discards the heterogeneous graph mixup module, and MuHca - DA which removes the whole graph data augmentation module including contrast-GAN loss. The results of MuHca are consistently better than its variants across all datasets and labeled rates, indicating that the heterogeneous graph mixup module and contrast-GAN module are effective for improving node representation results for classification.

Moreover, we demonstrate the loss on the results of 60 training sets in ACM for both the generator and discriminator in contrast-GANs through their learning curves with the epochs, as shown in Fig. 2. Once the initial fluctuations in loss values subside, the generator and discriminator enter into a min-max game, steadily decreasing their individual losses over time. The results show that after about 35 epochs, the loss approaches tend to converge.

Table 2. Evaluation on ablation study

Dataset	Metrices	Training	MuHca	MuHca-Mu	MuHca-DA
ACM	Ma-F1	20	93.19	90.92	89.52
		40	92.81	91.95	90.09
		60	93.70	90.63	89.60
	Mi-F1	20	92.86	91.98	89.66
		40	92.71	91.80	89.44
		60	92.67	91.16	89.36
DBLP	Ma-F1	20	94.80	92.95	91.26
		40	94.55	91.37	90.41
		60	94.29	91.24	90.36
	Mi-F1	20	94.78	91.05	90.07
		40	94.86	91.71	89.48
		60	94.91	91.31	89.90
IMDB	Ma-F1	20	61.74	60.99	59.93
		40	63.31	61.34	60.31
		60	63.68	61.66	59.70
	Mi-F1	20	64.03	61.66	59.05
		40	63.77	61.57	58.40
		60	64.83	61.94	60.72

4.6 Parameter Sensitivity

To assess the impact of parameters, we utilize node classification Micro-F1 as a benchmark on three datasets. The Micro-F1 score is essentially the same as accuracy because it gives equal importance to each observation and guarantees that every test case is assigned to exactly one class.

Parameter λ is for the equalizing of the contrast effect in two views between the meta-path view and the network schema view used in Eq. 6. We demonstrate the Micro-F1 scores in the 3-Y line graph shown in Fig. 3. Using 3-Y line graph can better reflect the degree to which the model's results change as the parameter vary. When the parameter is raised, the model's effectiveness improves steadily until it reaches its optimal performance level, and then the performance of the model shows a drop trend. The results indicate that incorporating negative samples generated from a contrastive view is effective in GANs. A possible reason is that when λ is too small, the model inadequately captures enough information from the contrastive local graph. Although the effect of the generated samples by the contrastive view is relatively larger, having too high a proportion can interfere with the model's performance.

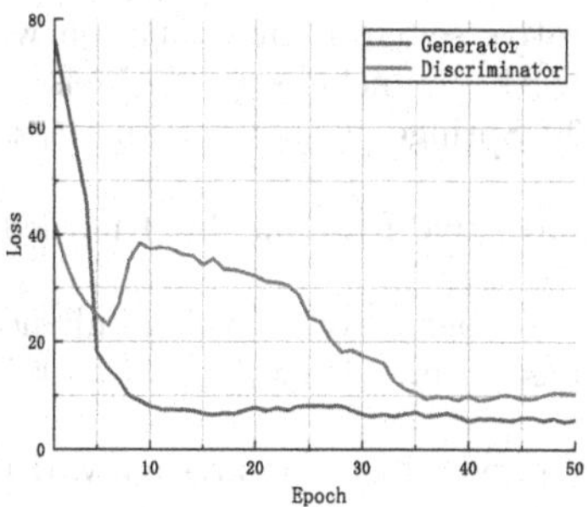

Fig. 2. Loss change

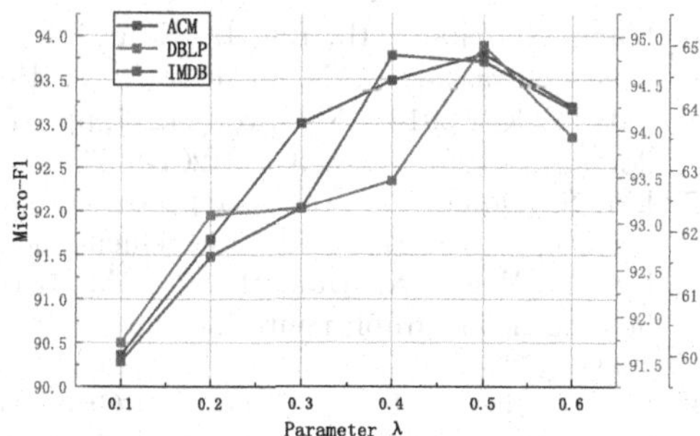

Fig. 3. Impact of parameter λ

5 Conclusion

In this paper, we propose a data augmentation strategy for HGs, which contributes to performance improvement in contrastive learning. Requiring adversarially generating negative samples by contrasting two views, it demonstrated that data augmentation on heterogeneous graphs is effective for the contrastive learning module. To further enhance the samples, we fully utilized the original data by introducing the mixup model. The conducted experiments validate the effectiveness of MuHca in the task of heterogeneous graph representation learning.

Acknowledgments. The works described in this paper are supported by The National Natural Science Foundation of China under Grant Nos. 61772210 and U1911201; The Project of Science and Technology in Guangzhou in China under Grant No. 202007040006.

References

1. Chang, Y., Chen, C., Hu, W., Zheng, Z., Zhou, X., Chen, S.: MEGNN: meta-path extracted graph neural network for heterogeneous graph representation learning. Knowl. Based Syst. **235**, 107611 (2022)
2. Chen, Y., et al.: Semi-supervised heterogeneous graph learning with multi-level data augmentation. arXiv preprint arXiv:2212.00024 (2022)
3. Fu, X., Zhang, J., Meng, Z., King, I.: MAGNN: metapath aggregated graph neural network for heterogeneous graph embedding. In: Proceedings of The Web Conference 2020, pp. 2331–2341 (2020)
4. He, K., Zhang, X., Ren, S., Sun, J.: Delving deep into rectifiers: surpassing human-level performance on ImageNet classification. In: Proceedings of the IEEE International Conference on Computer Vision, pp. 1026–1034 (2015)
5. Li, J., Peng, H., Cao, Y.: Higher-order attribute-enhancing heterogeneous graph neural networks. IEEE Trans. Knowl. Data Eng. **35**(1), 560–574 (2021)

6. Liang, X., Zhang, H., Lin, L., Xing, E.: Generative semantic manipulation with mask-contrasting GAN. In: Ferrari, V., Hebert, M., Sminchisescu, C., Weiss, Y. (eds.) ECCV 2018. LNCS, vol. 11217, pp. 574–590. Springer, Cham (2018). https://doi.org/10.1007/978-3-030-01261-8_34
7. Lin, S., Dong, C.: Cross-perspective graph contrastive learning. In: Knowledge Science, Engineering and Management, pp. 58–70 (2022)
8. Liu, N., Wang, X., Han, H., Shi, C.: Hierarchical contrastive learning enhanced heterogeneous graph neural network. IEEE Trans. Knowl. Data Eng. **35**, 10884–10896 (2023)
9. Liu, Y., Jin, M., Pan, S., Zhou, C.: Graph self-supervised learning: a survey. IEEE Trans. Knowl. Data Eng. **35**(6), 5879–5900 (2022)
10. Memmi, G., Yang, B., Kong, L., Zhang, T., Qiu, M. (eds.): 15th International Conference on Knowledge Science, Engineering and Management, vol. 13368. Springer, Cham (2022). https://doi.org/10.1007/978-3-031-10989-8
11. Park, C., Kim, D., Han, J., Yu, H.: Unsupervised attributed multiplex network embedding. In: Proceedings of the AAAI Conference on Artificial Intelligence, vol. 34, pp. 5371–5378 (2020)
12. Park, J., Song, J., Yang, E.: GraphENS: neighbor-aware ego network synthesis for class-imbalanced node classification. In: International Conference on Learning Representations (ICLR) (2021)
13. Rong, Y., Huang, W., Xu, T., Huang, J.: DropEdge: towards deep graph convolutional networks on node classification. In: International Conference on Learning Representations (ICLR) (2020)
14. Shi, C., Hu, B., Zhao, W.X.: Heterogeneous information network embedding for recommendation. IEEE Trans. Knowl. Data Eng. **31**(2), 357–370 (2018)
15. Shi, C., Wang, X., Yu, P.S.: Heterogeneous Graph Representation Learning and Applications. AIFTA, Springer, Singapore (2022). https://doi.org/10.1007/978-981-16-6166-2
16. Velickovic, P., Fedus, W., Hamilton, W.L., Liò: Deep Graph Infomax. In: International Conference on Learning Representations (ICLR) (Poster) (2019)
17. Wang, X., Ji, H., Shi, C., Wang, B., Ye, Y., Cui, P., Yu, P.S.: Heterogeneous graph attention network. In: The World Wide Web Conference, pp. 2022–2032 (2019)
18. Wang, X., Liu, N., Han, H., Shi, C.: Self-supervised heterogeneous graph neural network with co-contrastive learning. In: Proceedings of the 27th ACM SIGKDD Conference on Knowledge Discovery & Data Mining, pp. 1726–1736 (2021)
19. Wu, L., Cui, P., Pei, J., Zhao, L., Guo, X.: Graph neural networks: foundation, frontiers and applications. In: Proceedings of the 28th ACM SIGKDD Conference on Knowledge Discovery and Data Mining, pp. 4840–4841 (2022)
20. Wu, L., Lin, H., Tan, C.: Self-supervised learning on graphs: contrastive, generative, or predictive. IEEE Trans. Knowl. Data Eng. **35**(4), 4216–4235 (2021)
21. Zhang, Y., Ma, W., Jiang, Y.: MGCN: a novel multi-graph collaborative network for Chinese NER. In: Lu, W., Huang, S., Hong, Y., Zhou, X. (eds.) Natural Language Processing and Chinese Computing. NLPCC 2022. LNCS, vol. 13551. Springer, Cham (2022). https://doi.org/10.1007/978-3-031-17120-8_48
22. Zhao, J., Wang, X., Shi, C., Liu, Z., Ye, Y.: Network schema preserving heterogeneous information network embedding. In: IJCAI, pp. 1366–1372 (2020)
23. Zhao, T., Zhang, X., Wang, S.: GraphSMOTE: imbalanced node classification on graphs with graph neural networks. In: Proceedings of the 14th ACM International Conference on Web Search and Data Mining, pp. 833–841 (2021)
24. Zhou, J., Xie, C., Wen, Z., Zhao, X., Xuan, Q.: Data augmentation on graphs: a technical survey. arXiv preprint arXiv:2212.09970 (2023)

Parameter-Lite Adapter for Dynamic Entity Alignment

Meihong Xiao[1], Tingxuan Chen[1], Zidong Wang[1], Jun Long[2], Jincai Huang[2], and Liu Yang[1](✉)

[1] School of Computer Science and Engineering, Central South University, Changsha, China
{xiaomeihong,chentingxuan,zdwang,yangliu}@csu.edu.cn
[2] Big Data Institute, Central South University, Changsha, China
{jlong,huangjincaicsu}@csu.edu.cn

Abstract. Entity alignment (EA) aims to link entities referring to the same real-world identity from different knowledge graphs (KGs). Most existing EA methods focus on static KGs, while practical graphs are growing and changing over time. Although some EA methods study dynamic settings to suit the changes, they perform suboptimal as they are unaware of knowledge oblivion and the prohibitive model size. To address the above issues, we propose a **P**arameter-**L**ite dynamic **E**ntity **A**lignment model (PLEA), which leverages prior knowledge to embed entities and even represent unseen entities. We design a novel lightweight module that only trains a small number of parameters added by the adapter and keeps the original network fixed, so as to retain knowledge from previous snapshots with low computational cost. As for unseen entities, we design a regularized entity mapping mechanism to inject prior knowledge into unseen entity embeddings to improve representation ability. The experimental results on three real-world datasets demonstrate that our proposed PLEA archives up to 4% accuracy with only 50% of the number of parameters, compared with existing state-of-art methods.

Keywords: Entity Alignment · Knowledge Graph · Adapter Tune

1 Introduction

Knowledge graphs (KGs) accumulate and convey knowledge in the real world, whose nodes represent entities and edges represent potentially different relations between entities. Nowadays, KGs have been widely used in application scenarios such as search engines [1], question answering [2], and recommendation systems [3]. Different organizations build their own domain-specific KGs, resulting in data silos, heterogeneous data formats, and inconsistent data quality across different graphs [4]. In order to solve the above problems, entity alignment (EA) is proposed to align entities from distinct KGs and integrate knowledge by linking entities referring to the same real-world identity in different KGs.

Most entity alignment methods (RLEA [5], Dual-AMN [6], CycTEA [7], NeoEA [8], etc.) assume that entities and relations are fixed in KGs. However,

F. Liu et al. (Eds.): PRICAI 2023, LNAI 14325, pp. 389–400, 2024.
https://doi.org/10.1007/978-981-99-7019-3_36

real-world knowledge graphs are more complicated. For example, Wikidata currently contains over 100 million records, while it had only 20 million in 2021. That is, it has grown by about 80 million in the past two years. Obviously, real-world KGs are dynamic [9] and constantly growing at a rapid pace. In this paper, we regard the entity never appeared previously in KGs as an unseen entity [10], and the entity that appeared as a seen entity at a specific snapshot in dynamic KGs. Figure 1 demonstrates some potential scenarios for entity alignment in growing KGs. The potential alignments can be identified at each snapshot, so our goal is to utilize previously acquired knowledge rather than learn from scratch, and the prior knowledge includes entity embeddings, predicted alignments, and parameter matrix in the former model. Moreover, we can deduce that the source KG G^s and the target KG G^t grow independently and asynchronously, from Fig. 1. For example, entity e_5^t is added at snapshot 1, while its expected counterpart e_7^s is added at snapshot 2. Additionally, some unseen entities (i.e. e_5^s) in KGs have seen neighbors, while others like e_6^s and e_6^t do not. Hence, we facilitate the coexistence of both unseen and seen entities within a unified embedding space, so as to efficiently harness prior knowledge. This is based on the assumption that the closer the distance between entities in the same embedding space, the greater the possibility of alignment.

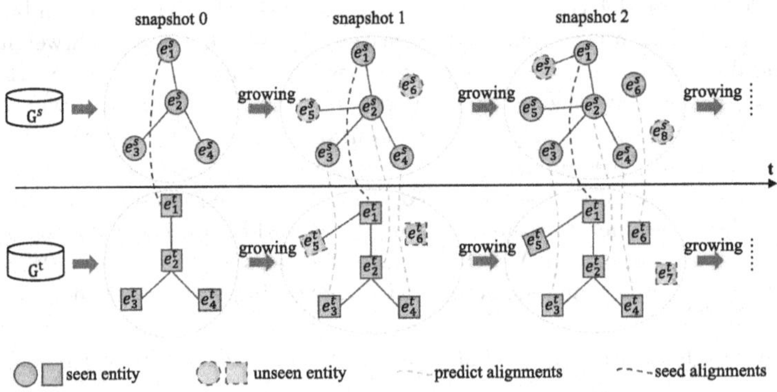

Fig. 1. Illustration of entity alignment in growing KGs. Given two dynamic KGs of the source KG $G^s = \{G_1^s, G_2^s, ..., G_n^s\}$ and the target KG $G^t = \{G_1^t, G_1^t, ..., G_n^t\}$, both KGs represent as a sequence of KG snapshots. We expect to find potential alignments for each entity at a specific snapshot. G_n^s and G_n^t denote the source KG and the target KG at snapshot n respectively.

To the best of our knowledge, the existing entity alignment methods related to dynamic settings are limited, and the models are often overly large and heavily parameterized, exhibiting inadequate performance in retaining prior knowledge [11]. To address these issues, we explore dynamic entity alignment, which seeks to identify all potential alignments in evolving KGs in this paper. A significant challenge presented by dynamic settings is how to achieve optimal alignment performance with fewer parameters. The asymmetric growth of KGs complicates the positioning of entity embeddings from different snapshots within the same embedding space. Consequently, another challenge in dynamic entity alignment is updating entity embeddings to accommodate emerging unseen entities. It is essential to maintain both unseen and seen entity embeddings within the same vector space. Otherwise, it may lead to unexpected and inaccurate alignments.

In response to these challenges, we introduce a novel and lightweight model for dynamic entity alignment, called **P**arameter-**L**ite dynamic **E**ntity **A**lignment (PLEA). PLEA effectively adapts prior knowledge to align unseen entities by fewer parameters, yielding better results than mere fine-tuning. In order to prevent rapid disruption of prior knowledge and avoid the exponential growth of the entity alignment model, we design an adapter tuning module to maintain the structural consistency of feature space by embedding entity features in a shared vector space. Specifically, we design a parameter-lite adapter and insert it into an advanced EA model, to keep the original entity alignment model fixed with a few parameters newly added by the adapter. We introduce a regularized entity mapping mechanism to boost the efficiency of the adapter, which utilizes the embeddings of seen neighbors as anchor points and projects unseen entities into the same space as their seen neighbors. The main contributions are summarized as follows:

- We propose a parameter-lite entity alignment model that integrates an adapter module to reduce the number of trainable parameters so as to achieve competitive performance with less computational cost.
- We design a regularized entity alignment mechanism to update entity embeddings by emerging unseen entity embeddings, so as to maintain the structural consistency of feature space.
- We conduct extensive experiments on the public datasets, and the experimental results show that PLEA achieves higher efficiency and accuracy than the baselines, with up to 4% accuracy improvement with only 50% of the number of parameters on average in the training process.

2 Related Work

2.1 Static Entity Alignment

Embedding-based static entity alignment methods assume that entities and relations in KGs are stationary, and they are generally categorized as translation-based models and Graph Neural Network (GNN) models. Translation-based models embed entities and relations in low-dimensional vectors, assuming that the distance between entities in vector space should be close when two entities from different KGs are aligned. TransE [12] is the first to represent entity and relation transformation as a simple vector operation, but it only copes with one-to-one relationships. To handle more complicated relationships, researchers propose enhanced TransE-based models, such as MTransE [13], IPTransE [14] and TransEdge [15]. Even though translation-based models are straightforward and effective, they are difficult to deal with complex graph structures. Hence,

GNN-based EA algorithms have been suggested as an alternative, such as GCN-Align [16], AliNet [17], RREA [25] etc. Many subsequent studies introduce other supernumerary information combined with GNN, e.g., labels for entity [18] and entity-type information [19]. Recently, researchers introduce Transformer [20,21] and Reinforcement Learning (RL) [22,23] into entity alignment to improve the accuracy and robustness of entity alignment.

2.2 Dynamic Entity Alignment

To the best of our knowledge, DINGAL [24] is the first work to study dynamic entity alignment, and its variant DINGAL-O is an inductive method that utilizes the previous parameter matrix to update the embeddings of the locally affected entities. Thus it significantly reduces the cost of space and time without updating the global graph, meanwhile, it cannot adjust or update the network to learn new knowledge. ContEA [25] fine-tunes the pre-trained model to align unseen entities, which avoids resource waste by maintaining prior knowledge. However, simple fine-tuning causes quickly prior knowledge disruption or model explosion. The dynamic settings bring new challenges, including model parameter explosion, knowledge-forgetting issues and unseen entity fusion. In this paper, we propose PLEA, a parameter-lite dynamic entity alignment model to satisfy entity alignment in dynamic settings with fewer parameters and less calculation.

3 Methodology

3.1 Overview

Given that real-world KGs continuously evolve and expand, our paper proposes a novel dynamic entity alignment model PLEA, as depicted in Fig. 2.

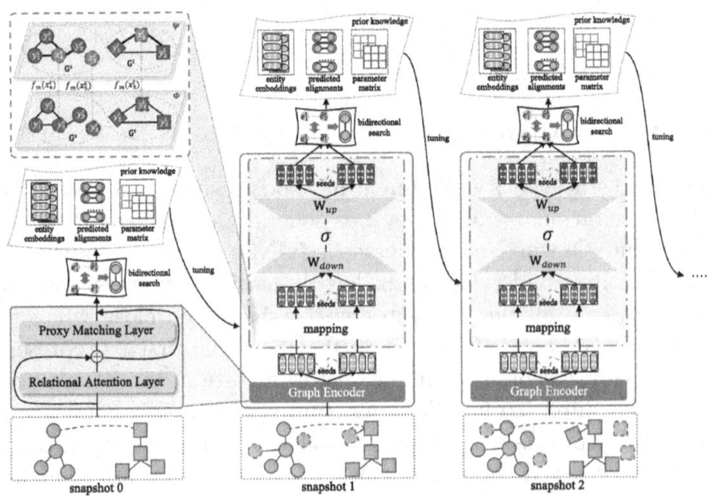

Fig. 2. Architecture of PLEA. The added adapter is shown by blocks with dashed borderlines, and the modules in gray blocks are not updated from the original model.

PLEA comprises three modules, 1) Initial Feature Generation, 2) Mapping-based Feature Fusion, and 3) Lightweight Adapter Tuning. The latter two represent our primary contributions. We utilize an advanced GNN encoder Dual-AMN to obtain rich underlying features since we don't focus on feature generation. As for mapping-based feature fusion, we design a regularized entity mapping mechanism and assimilate the features of unseen entities into the same space as seen entities to ensure consistency and stability of the embedding space. For lightweight adapter tuning, we propose a parameter-lite adapter by incorporating a small adapter into the original GNN model to handle unseen entities without modifying the original alignment model.

We leverage Dual-AMN Encoder, which contains a simplified relational attention layer and a proxy matching attention layer to capture inter-graph information and cross-graph information respectively. h_{e_i} denotes the embedding vector of entity e_i:

$$h_{e_i} = \mathcal{F}_{PML}(\mathcal{F}_{RAL}(e_i, \mathcal{N}_{e_i}), \mathcal{E}_p) \tag{1}$$

where $\mathcal{F}_{PML}(*)$ denotes the simplified relational attention layer, $\mathcal{F}_{RAL}(*)$ denotes the proxy matching attention layer, $\mathcal{N}_{e_i}$ denotes one-hop neighbor entities set of entity e_i, and $\mathcal{E}_p$ represents the proxy node. Meanwhile, we adopt a bidirectional search strategy to ensure bidirectional and consistent alignments, so as to avoid incorrect alignments. An entity pair (e_1, e_2) is considered aligned only if the predicted alignment of e_1 is e_2 and the predicted alignment of e_2 is e_1. In order to reduce the hyperparameters of the model, we use a normalization step to fix the mean and variance of the sample loss. The model alignment loss $\mathcal{L}_{align}$ is expressed as follows:

$$\mathcal{L}_{align} = \log[1 + \sum_{(e_i,e_j)\in\mathcal{T}_P} \sum_{(e_i,e'_j)\in\mathcal{T}_N} (\lambda(\gamma + sim(e_i, e_j) + sim(e_i, e'_j)) + \tau)] \tag{2}$$

where $\mathcal{T}_P$ denotes the positive sample set and $\mathcal{T}_N$ denotes the negative sample set, λ is a scale factor used to regulate sampling design and provide superior negative samples. γ and τ represent the mean and variance of the original loss respectively. We employ L2 distance to measure the similarity between entities, i.e., $sim(e_i, e_j) = ||h_{e_i} - h_{e_j}||_2^2$.

3.2 Mapping-Based Feature Fusion

The independent and asymmetric growth of dynamic KGs make it difficult to locate entity embeddings from different specific snapshots in the same space, making it inefficient to utilize pre-trained knowledge. Previous approaches exploit the average representation of seen neighbors to represent unseen entities with the assumption that all unseen entities are related to seen entities, whereas many unseen entities do not have any seen neighbors in reality. Motivated by the invariance of orthogonal transformation [26], we propose a regularized entity mapping mechanism. The key to this mechanism is to use the embeddings of seen entities as anchors to map unseen entities into the same embedding space, so as to maintain the structural consistency of the embedding space. Specifically, we employ a simple network to learn the orthogonal mapping rules from unseen entities that possess seen neighbors, and then apply the rules to unseen entities without seen neighbors.

Initially, we utilize graph convolutional networks (GCNs) to learn from unseen entities with seen neighbors. Given an unseen entity e_u, we represent it by the average representation of its seen neighbors:

$$\tilde{h}_{e_u}^{(l+1)} = \frac{1}{|\tilde{\mathcal{N}}_{e_u}|}\sigma(\sum_{e_v \in \tilde{\mathcal{N}}_{e_u}} \tilde{h}_{e_v}^{(l)} W_a^{(l)}) \tag{3}$$

$$\tilde{h}_{e_u} = f_m(h_{e_u}) = W_m h_{e_u} \tag{4}$$

where $\tilde{h}$ is the embedding vector of entity in the target embedding space, $\tilde{h}_{e_v}^{(l)}$ denotes the embedding vector of entity e_v in the target embedding space as the input to layer $l+1$, $\tilde{\mathcal{N}}_{e_u}$ represents seen neighbors set of e_u, and $W_a^{(l)}$ is the weight matrix in layer l. $f_m(*)$ denotes the mapping law and W_m is the orthogonal mapping matrix to be learned. h is the embed vector of the entity in the random initial embedding space. To obtain the optimal mapping rules, we learn the following orthogonal mapping matrix:

$$W_m = \arg \min_{W_m \in \mathcal{O}_d} ||HW_m W_a - \tilde{H}||_F^2 \tag{5}$$

where $|| * ||_F$ denotes the Frobenius norm, H denotes the input matrix to be mapped, $\tilde{H}$ denotes the matrix of anchors in the target embedding space, and $\mathcal{O}_d$ denotes a set of d-dim orthogonal matrices. Equation (5) measures the difference between actual and predicted feature matrices of unseen entities. The optimal mapping matrix W_m can be obtained by minimizing the objective function using optimization methods such as gradient descent. Finally, we apply the learned mapping rules to unseen entities by Eq. (4), and then map them into the target embedding space to retain the original structural information.

3.3 Parameter-Lite Adapter Tuning

Previous studies introduce fine-tuning to utilize prior knowledge for dynamic entity alignment. However, even a simple fine-tuning of the original entity alignment model may cause a significant increase in model scale as KG grows, resulting in computational cost and performance loss. Therefore, our goal is to achieve good performance by minimizing model parameters, making the tuning process lightweight. Inspired by the idea of parameter-efficient fine-tuning in transfer learning [27], we propose a parameter-lite adapter with a few trainable parameters to align unseen entities, and adapt prior knowledge to align unseen entities.

More specifically, we adopt a bottleneck structure to design the adapter with a small number of trainable parameters. Firstly, we feed unseen entities and prior knowledge into the adapter and map unseen entities to the target embedding space with prior knowledge. Then, we project the entity embeddings X to a specified low-dimensional space to reduce the dimension of entity embedding vector, followed by an activation function $\sigma(*)$, which is $ReLU(*)$. Finally, we restore the dimension of feature vector, to capture entity characteristics better, leading to the final form X'.

$$X' = W_{up}\sigma(W_{down}X) \tag{6}$$

where W_{up} and W_{down} denote the mapping weight matrix of $W_{down} \in \mathbb{R}^{(k\times d)\times r}$ and $W_{up} \in \mathbb{R}^{r\times d}$ respectively. k is the number of network layers, d is the feature dimension, and r is the specified low-dimensional space dimension.

We use L2 regularization loss to constrain the parameter norm of the adapter layer:

$$\mathcal{L}_{tuning} = \mu_1||W_{up}||_2^2 + \mu_2||W_{down}||_2^2 \tag{7}$$

where μ_1 and μ_2 are the regularization hyper-parameters. $\mathcal{L}_{tuning}$ is to minimize the tuning loss function by tuning the parameters in the model.

The overall loss of PLEA is defined in Eq. (8).

$$\mathcal{L} = \mathcal{L}_{align} + \theta\mathcal{L}_{tuning} \tag{8}$$

where $\mathcal{L}_{align}$ is the alignment loss, and $\mathcal{L}_{tuning}$ is the tuning loss introduced by the adapter. The hyperparameter θ is used to balance the impact on tuning and is 0 at snapshot 0.

4 Experiments

We conduct extensive experiments to verify the effectiveness of our proposed PLEA.

4.1 Experimental Setup

Datasets. To comprehensively evaluate our proposed PLEA, we conduct experiments on the dynamic entity alignment dataset DBP15K-dynamic (DBP(d) for short) [25]. DBP(d) includes three cross-language datasets to be aligned, and each dataset simulates the growth of KG by constructing 6 snapshots. They are generated from DBP15k with 20% for training, 10% for validation and 70% for testing. The detailed statistics of these datasets are shown in Table 1.

Compared Methods. As mentioned in Sect. 2, dynamic entity alignment methods can be divided into three categories: Retraining methods, Inductive methods and Fine-tuning methods. For each category, we select some entity alignment methods as baselines, and all the methods we choose only consider knowledge graph structure. Retraining methods only retrain the model to handle dynamic entity alignment. We adopt the following typical entity alignment methods as baselines, including GCN-Align [16], AliNet [17] and Dual-AMN [6]. Inductive methods aggregate neighborhood information to update the network, e.g., LAN+ [28] and DINGAL-O [24]. The only fine-tuning entity alignment method ContEA [25] uses the existing adjacent relationships to generate embeddings for unseen entities and only trains part of the parameters.

Table 1. Statistic of three datasets. S_n represents snapshot n, $|\mathcal{T}|$ denotes the number of triples in the current snapshot, $|\mathcal{E}_{un}|$ denotes the number of newly added entities in the current snapshot, and $\mathcal{P}$ denotes the percentage of unseen entities with no seen neighbors to all unseen entities in the current snapshot.

Snapshot	DBP(d)$_{ZH-EN}$				DBP(d)$_{JA-EN}$				DBP(d)$_{FR-EN}$			
	$\|\mathcal{T}_{ZH}\|$	$\|\mathcal{T}_{EN}\|$	$\|\mathcal{E}_{un}\|$	$\mathcal{P}$	$\|\mathcal{T}_{ZH}\|$	$\|\mathcal{T}_{EN}\|$	$\|\mathcal{E}_{un}\|$	$\mathcal{P}$	$\|\mathcal{T}_{ZH}\|$	$\|\mathcal{T}_{EN}\|$	$\|\mathcal{E}_{un}\|$	$\mathcal{P}$
S_0	70,414	95,142	0	NA	77,214	93,484	0	NA	10,598	115,722	0	NA
S_1	103,982	154,833	37,748	0.908	11,268	150,636	36,596	0.885	148,274	184,132	42,603	0.911
S_2	137,280	213,405	34,790	0.418	147,097	207,056	33,725	0.384	191,697	251,591	38,737	0.444
S_3	173,740	278,076	34,325	0.315	185,398	270,469	33,213	0.316	239,861	326,689	37,787	0.357
S_4	213,814	351,659	35,096	0.286	227,852	341,432	33,728	0.276	293,376	411,528	38,237	0.329
S_5	258,311	434,683	35,887	0.269	274,884	421,971	34,808	0.269	352,886	507,793	39,667	0.323

Metrics and Hyperparameters. We use precision (P), recall (R), and $F1$ to evaluate the performance of PLEA. P and R are calculated by the accuracy of top-1 and $F1 = (2 * P * R)/(P + R)$, and higher values of these indicators indicate better performance. For all datasets, we use the same hyperparameters. The embedding dimension d is 100, the depth of GNN is 2, and the dropout rate is 0.3 during the training. To ensure the reliability of the results, we report the average performance over 5 independent training runs.

4.2 Main Results

The results of all approaches are shown in Table 2, Table 3, and Table 4. We never compare the performances at snapshot 0 since the entity alignment of snapshot 0 can be regarded as static entity alignment, which is not our focus.

Table 2. Results of entity alignment on DBP(d)$_{ZH-EN}$. The best results are written in bold. S_n represents snapshot n.

Method	S_0			S_1			S_2			S_3			S_4			S_5		
	P	R	F1	P	R	F1	P	R	F1	P	R	F1	P	R	F1	P	R	F1
GCN-Align	0.550	0.249	0.343	0.212	0.152	0.177	0.133	0.115	0.123	0.096	0.091	0.094	0.076	0.075	0.076	0.062	0.062	0.062
AliNet	0.641	0.358	0.459	0.285	0.311	0.297	0.195	0.279	0.230	0.146	0.244	0.183	0.129	0.232	0.166	0.105	0.199	0.128
Dual-AMN	0.834	0.596	0.695	0.482	0.443	0.462	0.357	0.356	0.356	0.285	0.286	0.286	0.249	0.254	0.251	0.227	0.227	0.227
LAN+	0.827	0.576	0.679	0.488	0.426	0.455	0.360	0.345	0.352	0.274	0.271	0.272	0.231	0.229	0.230	0.205	0.199	0.202
DINGAL-O	0.497	0.195	0.280	0.370	0.158	0.222	0.315	0.135	0.189	0.251	0.111	0.154	0.229	0.093	0.132	0.209	0.080	0.116
ContEA	0.844	**0.606**	0.705	0.555	**0.539**	0.546	0.441	**0.475**	0.458	0.363	**0.422**	0.390	0.323	0.372	0.346	0.294	0.333	0.312
PLEA	0.846	0.595	0.699	**0.591**	0.526	**0.557**	**0.471**	0.469	**0.470**	**0.402**	0.416	**0.409**	**0.357**	**0.375**	**0.365**	**0.325**	**0.335**	**0.330**
PLEA$_{(w/o\,M)}$	**0.847**	0.601	0.703	0.569	0.525	0.546	0.450	0.465	0.457	0.381	0.412	0.396	0.338	0.368	0.353	0.308	0.329	0.318
PLEA$_{(w/o\,A)}$	0.846	0.604	**0.705**	0.560	0.528	0.544	0.442	0.466	0.453	0.371	0.411	0.390	0.328	0.366	0.346	0.296	0.325	0.310

PLEA vs. Retraining Methods. Compared with retraining methods, PLEA outperformers existing state-of-the-art methods on all datasets, with up to 10% average improvement in all metrics. Although Dual-AMN outperforms the previous SOTA on the three cross-lingual datasets due to its dual attention matching network, our PLEA still achieves superior performance, exceeding retraining Dual-AMN by at least 10% in all metrics. The performance of all retraining methods declines sharply over time without using prior knowledge, while PLEA improves by utilizing prior knowledge from past snapshots.

Table 3. Results of entity alignment on DBP(d)_{JA-EN}. The best results are written in bold. S_n represents snapshot n.

Method	S_0			S_1			S_2			S_3			S_4			S_5		
	P	R	F1	P	R	F1	P	R	F1	P	R	F1	P	R	F1	P	R	F1
GCN-Align	0.594	0.279	0.379	0.263	0.183	0.216	0.177	0.142	0.158	0.140	0.117	0.127	0.116	0.099	0.107	0.099	0.084	0.091
AliNet	0.661	0.364	0.469	0.305	0.312	0.308	0.216	0.270	0.240	0.167	0.231	0.194	0.149	0.215	0.176	0.126	0.189	0.151
Dual-AMN	0.861	0.606	0.711	0.517	0.437	0.474	.0398	0.347	0.370	0.348	0.292	0.318	0.313	0.251	0.278	0.300	0.231	0.261
LAN^+	0.845	0.575	0.684	0.528	0.424	0.470	0.410	0.333	0.368	0.335	0.265	0.296	0.296	0.226	0.257	0.274	0.200	0.231
DINGAL-O	0.540	0.227	0.320	0.391	0.174	0.241	0.328	0.137	0.194	0.271	0.113	0.159	0.249	0.092	0.134	0.231	0.078	0.116
ContEA	0.863	**0.615**	**0.718**	0.575	0.526	0.550	0.459	0.445	0.452	0.403	0.380	0.391	0.364	0.335	0.349	0.338	0.299	0.317
PLEA	**0.865**	0.604	0.711	**0.627**	**0.526**	**0.572**	**0.512**	**0. 448**	**0.477**	**0.448**	**0.384**	**0.414**	**0.406**	**0.338**	**0.369**	**0.372**	**0.300**	**0.332**
$\text{PLEA}_{(\text{w/o M})}$	0.861	0.598	0.706	0.611	0.519	0.561	.0497	0.441	0.467	0.432	0.377	0.403	0.392	0.330	0.358	0.364	0.293	0.325
$\text{PLEA}_{(\text{w/o A})}$	0.860	0.605	0.710	0.601	0.524	0.559	0.485	0.445	0.465	0.419	0.381	0.399	0.379	0.334	0.354	0.351	0.297	0.322

Table 4. Results of entity alignment on DBP(d)_{FR-EN}. The best results are written in bold. S_n represents snapshot n

Method	S_0			S_1			S_2			S_3			S_4			S_5		
	P	R	F1	P	R	F1	P	R	F1	P	R	F1	P	R	F1	P	R	F1
GCN-Align	0.561	0.262	0.357	0.233	0.161	0.190	.148	0.111	0.127	.113	0.086	0.098	0.089	0.066	0.076	0.077	0.056	0.065
AliNet	0.653	0.361	0.465	.275	0.289	0.282	0.187	0.226	0.205	0.144	0.180	0.160	0.124	0.155	0.138	0.115	0.138	0.126
Dual-AMN	0.862	0.629	0.727	0.503	0.443	0.471	.394	0.331	0.359	0.351	0.273	0.307	0.322	0.237	0.273	0.313	0.214	0.254
LAN^+	0.845	0.594	0.697	.506	0.410	0.453	.379	0.300	0.335	.304	0.227	0.260	.269	0.188	0.222	.247	0.162	0.195
DINGAL-O	0.540	0.224	0.317	0.381	0.165	0.231	0.329	0.124	0.180	0.258	0.092	0.136	0.247	0.073	0.112	0.227	0.061	0.096
ContEA	0.863	0.627	0.727	0.558	0.515	0.536	0.455	0.418	0.436	0.391	0.351	0.370	0.350	0.300	0.323	0.321	0.265	0.290
PLEA	**0.869**	0.628	0.729	**0.597**	0.518	**0.555**	**0.484**	**0.420**	**0.450**	**0.426**	0.349	**0.384**	**0.394**	**0.300**	**0.340**	**0.371**	0.263	**0.308**
$\text{PLEA}_{(w/o\ M)}$	0.867	**0.630**	**0.730**	0.587	**0.519**	0.551	0.474	0.420	0.445	0.418	**0.351**	0.381	0.387	0.300	0.338	0.360	**0.265**	0.305
$\text{PLEA}_{(w/o\ A)}$	0.863	0.623	0.723	0.586	0.516	0.549	0.469	0.420	0.442	0.407	0.349	0.376	0.368	0.299	0.330	0.340	0.263	0.296

PLEA vs. Inductive Methods. PLEA surpasses inductive methods in all metrics by at least 10%. For instance, on dataset DBP(d)_{ZH-EN}, PLEA improves the accuracy by 30% at snapshot 1. The experimental results show that inductive methods are inadequate in dynamic entity alignment because they only consider local information without updating the alignment network. While PLEA leverages prior knowledge and adapts the alignment network to deal with dynamic changes, contributing to better performance.

PLEA vs. Fine-Tuning Methods. Compared with the fine-tuning method ContEA, PLEA outperforms the fine-tuning baselines by an average of 4% in all metrics. Specifically, PLEA achieves 62.7% precision on dataset DBP(d)_{JA-EN}, which is 5.2% higher than the second-best method ContEA at snapshot 1. Meanwhile, PLEA also reaches an average of 4.5% precision improvement compared to ContEA. Besides, the performance of all methods tends to decline over time, while PLEA exhibits a slower decline. This can be attributed to the designed adapter that keeps the original model frozen and only tunes the parameters on the lightweight adapter, which helps to slow the speed of knowledge forgetting and keep the model stable.

Efficiency Analysis. As shown in Fig. 3, it can be observed that PLEA outperforms the fine-tuning method in terms of parameter numbers and storage usage on all three datasets. PLEA only trains with an average of 0.678% parameters compared to ContEA, which is the second-best model in dynamic entity alignment. Moreover, as the knowledge graph grows, the parameters that the original

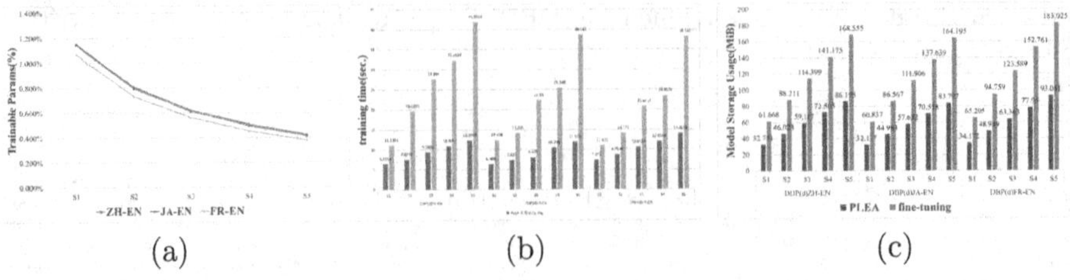

(a) (b) (c)

Fig. 3. Performance of PLEA vs. tuning the original GNN model. Subgraph (a) depicts the number of trainable parameters vs. the fine-tuning method on three datasets, and subgraph (b) shows the memory usage of PLEA and fine-tuning method.

model required to train increase even faster, but our model avoids this problem. Taking DBP(d)_{ZH-EN} as an example, the number of parameters in PLEA is just 0.413% of the fine-tuning method at snapshot 5. Furthermore, with the growth of KGs, the memory requirements of the fine-tuning method increase linearly at snapshot 5, while our method slows down this trend, reducing the requirement by almost 50%. These results demonstrate that our method is lightweight with less calculation.

In summary, the efficiency of PLEA exceeds all competitors, achieving better results by tuning fewer parameters, and its lightweight design enables real-time dynamic entity alignnment on large-scale KGs.

4.3 Ablation Study

$\text{PLEA}_{(\text{w/o,M})}$. The first variation of PLEA is $\text{PLEA}_{(\text{w/o,M})}$, which removes regularized entity mapping mechanism. Most of the unseen entities shown in Table 1 do not have seen neighbors, so it is inefficient to express the unseen entity by the average embedding of seen neighbors. The experimental results show that the accuracy drops 1% on average when the regularized entity mapping mechanism is removed as shown in Table 2, Table 3, and Table 4. This demonstrates the effectiveness of our proposed regularized entity mapping mechanism. Furthermore, compared with the second-best method, $\text{PLEA}_{(\text{w/o,M})}$ outperforms with 3% improvement of accuracy on DBP(d)_{FR-EN} and $\text{DBP(d)}_{\text{JA-EN}}$, as well as 2% on DBP(d)_{ZH-EN} on average. This improvement is brought about by the adapter designed by PLEA.

$\text{PLEA}_{(\text{w/o,A})}$. The second variation of PLEA is represented as $\text{PLEA}_{(\text{w/o,A})}$, without updating the adapter. Table 2 shows that $\text{PLEA}_{(\text{w/o,A})}$ achieves a precision that is 5% higher than the best baseline. Table 3 and Table 4 show that $\text{PLEA}_{(\text{w/o,A})}$ outperforms other baselines by 1.5% on precision. The improvement on $\text{DBP}_{\text{ZH-EN}}$ is small due to the gaps between Chinese and English embedding spaces. These results demonstrate the effectiveness of the mapping mechanism. Compared with the second-best method, $\text{PLEA}_{(\text{w/o,A})}$ reaches 1.7% precision improvement on average for each dataset, which is because of the mapping mechanism.

5 Conclusion

This paper addresses the challenge of entity alignment in real-world dynamic knowledge graphs. We propose a novel model PLEA that leverages prior knowledge to align unseen entities without rerunning or retraining alignment algorithms of static KGs. Our experiments demonstrate the effectiveness of PLEA under dynamic entity alignment tasks. For future work, we plan to explore the versatility of the adapter in our entity alignment model and develop a general framework for inserting the adapter into various static alignment models, enabling it to handle entity alignment of KGs with different properties.

References

1. Zhu, X., et al.: Multi-modal knowledge graph construction and application: a survey. IEEE Trans. Knowl. Data Eng. (2022)
2. Jiang, L., Usbeck, R.: Knowledge graph question answering datasets and their generalizability: are they enough for future research? In: 2022 Proceedings of the 45th International ACM SIGIR Conference on Research and Development in Information Retrieval, pp. 3209–3218 (2022)
3. Yang, Y., Huang, C., Xia, L., Li, C.: Knowledge graph contrastive learning for recommendation, In: 2022 Proceedings of the 45th International ACM SIGIR Conference on Research and Development in Information Retrieval, pp. 1434–1443 (2022)
4. Zhang, R., Trisedya, B.D., Li, M., Jiang, Y., Qi, J.: A benchmark and comprehensive survey on knowledge graph entity alignment via representation learning. VLDB J. **31**(5), 1143–1168 (2022)
5. Guo, L., Han, Y., Zhang, Q., Chen, H.: Deep reinforcement learning for entity alignment. arXiv preprint arXiv:2203.03315 (2022)
6. Mao, X., Wang, W., Wu, Y., Lan, M.: Boosting the speed of entity alignment 10×: dual attention matching network with normalized hard sample mining, In: 2021 Proceedings of the Web Conference, pp. 821–832 (2021)
7. Xin, K., et al.: Ensemble semi-supervised entity alignment via cycle-teaching. In: Proceedings of the AAAI Conference on Artificial Intelligence, vol. 36, no. 4, pp. 4281–4289 (2022)
8. Guo, L., Zhang, Q., Sun, Z., Chen, M., Hu, W., Chen, H.: Understanding and improving knowledge graph embedding for entity alignment, In: 2022 International Conference on Machine Learning. PMLR, pp. 8145–8156 (2022)
9. Wu, T., Khan, A., Yong, M., Qi, G., Wang, M.: Efficiently embedding dynamic knowledge graphs. Knowl. Based Syst. **250**, 109124 (2022)
10. Chen, M., Zhang, W., Geng, Y., Xu, Z., Pan, J.Z., Chen, H.: Generalizing to unseen elements: a survey on knowledge extrapolation for knowledge graphs. arXiv preprint arXiv:2302.01859 (2023)
11. Rieger, L., Singh, C., Murdoch, W., Yu, B.: Interpretations are useful: penalizing explanations to align neural networks with prior knowledge, In: 2020 International Conference on Machine Learning. PMLR, pp. 8116–8126 (2020)
12. Bordes, A., Usunier, N., Garcia-Duran, A., Weston, J., Yakhnenko, O.: Translating embeddings for modeling multi-relational data. In: Advances in Neural Information Processing Systems, vol. 26 (2013)

13. Ji, S., Pan, S., Cambria, E., Marttinen, P., Philip, S.Y.: A survey on knowledge graphs: representation, acquisition, and applications. IEEE Trans. Neural Netw. Learn. Syst. **33**(2), 494–514 (2021)
14. Christophides, V., Efthymiou, V., Palpanas, T., Papadakis, G., Stefanidis, K.: An overview of end-to-end entity resolution for Big Data. ACM Comput. Surv. (CSUR) **53**(6), 1–42 (2020)
15. Sun, Z., Huang, J., Hu, W., Chen, M., Guo, L., Qu, Y.: TransEdge: translating relation-contextualized embeddings for knowledge graphs. In: Ghidini, C., et al. (eds.) ISWC 2019. LNCS, vol. 11778, pp. 612–629. Springer, Cham (2019). https://doi.org/10.1007/978-3-030-30793-6_35
16. Wang, Z., Lv, Q., Lan, X., Zhang, Y.: Cross-lingual knowledge graph alignment via graph convolutional networks. In: 2018 Proceedings of the 2018 Conference on Empirical Methods in Natural Language Processing, pp. 349–357 (2018)
17. Sun, Z., et al.: Knowledge graph alignment network with gated multi-hop neighborhood aggregation. In: Proceedings of the AAAI Conference on Artificial Intelligence, vol. 34, no. 01, pp. 222–229 (2020)
18. Tang, W., et al.: Weakly supervised entity alignment with positional inspiration. In: 2023 Proceedings of the Sixteenth ACM International Conference on Web Search and Data Mining, pp. 814–822 (2023)
19. Ge, X., Wang, Y.C., Wang, B., Kuo, C.-C.J., et al.: TypeEA: type-associated embedding for knowledge graph entity alignment. APSIPA Trans. Sig. Inf. Process. **12**(1), 1–23 (2023)
20. Xin, K., Sun, Z., Hua, W., Hu, W., Zhou, X.: Informed multi-context entity alignment, In: 2022 Proceedings of the Fifteenth ACM International Conference on Web Search and Data Mining, pp. 1197–1205 (2022)
21. Li, Y., Li, J., Suhara, Y., Doan, A., Tan, W.-C.: Effective entity matching with transformers. VLDB J., 1–21 (2023). https://doi.org/10.1007/s00778-023-00779-z
22. Zeng, W., Zhao, X., Tang, J., Lin, X., Groth, P.: Reinforcement learning-based collective entity alignment with adaptive features. ACM Trans. Inf. Syst. (TOIS) **39**(3), 1–31 (2021)
23. Guo, L., Han, Y., Zhang, Q., Chen, H.: Deep reinforcement learning for entity alignment. arXiv preprint arXiv:2203.03315 (2022)
24. Yan, Y., Liu, L., Ban, Y., Jing, B., Tong, H.: Dynamic knowledge graph alignment. In: Proceedings of the AAAI Conference on Artificial Intelligence, vol. 35, no. 5, pp. 4564–4572 (2021)
25. Wang, Y., et al.: Facing changes: continual entity alignment for growing knowledge graphs. In: Sattler, U., et al. (eds.) The Semantic Web, ISWC 2022. LNCS, vol. 13489, pp. 196–213. Springer, Cham (2022). https://doi.org/10.1007/978-3-031-19433-7_12
26. Cotsakis, S., Klaoudatou, I., Kolionis, G., Miritzis, J., Trachilis, D.: The conformal cosmological potential. Astron. **1**(1), 17–35 (2022)
27. He, J., Zhou, C., Ma, X., Berg-Kirkpatrick, T., Neubig, G.: Towards a unified view of parameter-efficient transfer learning. arXiv preprint arXiv:2110.04366 (2021)
28. Wang, P., Han, J., Li, C., Pan, R.: Logic attention based neighborhood aggregation for inductive knowledge graph embedding. In: 2019 Proceedings of the AAAI Conference on Artificial Intelligence, vol. 33, no. 01, pp. 7152–7159 (2019)

Zoom-Based AutoEncoder for Origin-Destination Demand Prediction

Xiaojian Ma[1], Liangzhe Han[1(✉)], Gang Wang[2,3], Xu Liu[2], and Tongyu Zhu[1]

[1] State Key Laboratory of Software Development Environment, Beihang University, Beijing 100191, China
{xiaojianma,liangzhehan,zhutongyu}@buaa.edu.cn

[2] Highway Monitoring and Emergency Response Center, Ministry of Transport of the P.R.C, Beijing 100029, China
wang.gang@hmrc.net.cn

[3] School of Vehicle and Mobility, Tsinghua University, Beijing 100084, China

Abstract. The use of deep neural networks for traffic demand forecasting has garnered significant attention from both academic and industrial communities. Compared with the traditional traffic flow forecasting task, the Origin-Destination(OD) demand prediction task is more valuable and challenging, and several methods have been proposed for OD demand prediction. However, most existing methods follow a general technical route to aggregate historical information spatially and temporally. This paper proposes an alternative approach to predict Origin-Destination demand, named Zoom-based AutoEncoder for Origin-Destination demand prediction (ODZAE). The main objective of our research is to enhance the integration of diverse inherent patterns in real-world OD demand data in a more efficient manner. Besides, we proposed a zoom operation to learn spatial relationships between traffic nodes and 3DGCN to simultaneously model spatial and temporal dependencies. We have conducted experiments on two real-world datasets from Beijing Subway and New York Taxi, and the results demonstrate the superiority of our model against the state-of-art approaches.

Keywords: Origin Destination Demand Prediction · Autoencoder · Spatio-Temporal Data Mining · Graph Neural Network · Intelligent Transportation System

1 Introduction

Deep learning techniques have been widely applied in intelligent transportation systems (ITS) in recent years, such as traffic controlling and autopilot. Among all

This work was supported by the National Natural Science Foundation of China (No. 62272023) and the Fundamental Research Funds for the Central Universities (No. YWF-23-L-1203).

F. Liu et al. (Eds.): PRICAI 2023, LNAI 14325, pp. 401–412, 2024.
https://doi.org/10.1007/978-981-99-7019-3_37

these applications, traffic prediction has demonstrated its significance in urban construction, traffic control, and route planning, making it the most attractive problem.

However, most of the existing research has focused on predicting the inflow and outflow of a region, which provides a relatively rough estimate of traffic states. With the abundance of large-scale traffic data available, many scholars have started to investigate forecasting Origin-Destination demand to provide a more detailed traffic demand forecast. Although there are some attempts on OD demand prediction, three crucial issues have rarely been discussed. First, most previous methods for OD demand prediction based on spatio-temporal graph neural networks predict future demand by aggregating historical information without fully exploring the intrinsic patterns in historical OD demand data. Second, most existing models rely on graph neural network (GNN) to learn the spatial relationships between transportation nodes, using adjacency matrices constructed based on geographic proximity or POI similarity relationships. However, this approach based on manual predefined rules may introduce noise. Third, most methods model spatial and temporal patterns separately without considering their interactions, which significantly restricts the representation ability of the models a lot.

To address the above challenges, this paper proposes a novel autoencoder-based framework for Origin-Destination demand prediction, named Zoom-based AutoEncoder for Origin-Destination demand prediction (ODZAE). First, we use an encoder which consists of zoom operation and 3DGCN, to get historical hidden states from historical Origin-Destination demand data and use a decoder to reconstruct the input data in pretrain. Then we use a projection function to get future hidden states from historical hidden states and another decoder for future Origin-Destination demand prediction. Our main contributions are as follows:

- We propose a novel framework for Origin-Destination demand prediction, which uses an autoencoder to learn intrinsic patterns from historical Origin-Destination demand data and predicts future Origin-Destination demand by projected hidden states.
- We propose zoom operation to model complex spatial dependencies of traffic nodes. By zooming and enlarging, state change of one node can affect those nodes that are geographically neighboring or functionally similar to it.
- We proposed a 3DGCN which can perform graph convolution operations simultaneously on both origin dimension, destination dimension, and time dimension, allowing the model to handle spatial and temporal dependencies at the same time.
- We conducted experiments on two real world datasets, and the results demonstrate the advantages of our approach compared with baselines.

The remaining of this paper is organized as follows: Sect. 2 introduces related works, and Sect. 3 describes the preliminaries and definitions. Section 4 presents our method in detail, and the experiments are conducted in Sect. 5. Finally, we summarize this work in Sect. 6.

2 Related Work

2.1 Origin-Destination Demand Prediction

Origin-Destination demand prediction is a challenging task which aims to forecast the demand between any two traffic nodes. Basically, there are two directions to solve this problem. In the first direction, researchers divide an area into grids and then use convolutional neural network (CNN) to learn the spatial dependency between adjacent grids [4]. For instance, Chu *et al.* [3] regard localized travel demands as image pixels and then not only multiply the input and hidden states with the weights but perform convolution with weights. Duan *et al.* [10] use the discrete wavelet transform (DWT) and three CNN layers to learn the spatial dependencies from OD demand in different resolutions. Liu *et al.* [9] propose a model named CSTN, which consists of a CNN-based module to model local spatial context and another CNN-based module to model global correlation context.

The methods mentioned above divide an area into grids. However, in most cases, the distribution of traffic nodes is uneven, making it challenging to model the spatial relationship between traffic nodes using CNN. Researchers in the second direction treat the area as a graph whose vertices are traffic nodes, then use graph neural network (GNN) to model spatial dependencies of traffic nodes [15]. For instance, Wang *et al.* [13] design node embedding network via graph convolutions among defined node neighborhoods (geographical and semantic neighbors). Zhang *et al.* [16] develop a new layer named k–hop temporal node-edge attention layer which learns the representations for both nodes and edges by adaptively adjusting the relationships between each OD pair at different time intervals. Shi *et al.* [11] conduct graph convolution on both the origin dimension and the destination dimension of OD tensor, and design a dynamic graph for representing the dynamic correlations of regions as origins or destinations calculated by the historical OD flow data.

2.2 Autoencoder

Autoencoder is a classical method for representation learning, which was first introduced in [1]. Some traditional machine learning methods are autoencoders, such as PCA and k-means.

One variant of autoencoders is variational auto-encoding model, which assumes that data are generated from underlying latent representation. Kingma *et al.* [8] are pioneers in using variational inference, which assumes the prior $p(z)$ and the approximate posterior $q(z|x)$ both follow Gaussian distributions. Oord *et al.* [12] propose a novel and powerful variational AE model called VQ-VAE which relies on vector quantization (VQ) to learn the posterior distribution of discrete latent variables.

Recently, denoising autoencoders are wildly used in computer vision (CV) and natural language processing (NLP). Bert randomly masks some of the tokens from the input and then predicts them based on context information. He *et al.*

[6] develop an asymmetric encoder-decoder architecture for visual representation learning, with an encoder that operates only on the visible subset of patches (without mask tokens), along with a lightweight decoder that reconstructs the original image from the latent representation and mask tokens.

3 Problem Formulation

In this section, we will first introduce some preliminaries used throughout this paper, and then we will define the problem of Origin-Destination demand prediction.

3.1 Definitions

Definition 1 *(Traffic Nodes): The goal of the Origin-Destination demand prediction task is to predict the Origin-Destination demand value within a certain period of time between any two traffic nodes. For transportation modes with fixed stations such as buses and subways, we directly use their stations as traffic nodes. For transportation modes such as taxis or dockless bike-sharing systems, where the station locations are not predetermined, the divisions of the city (such as streets or blocks) are used as traffic nodes.*

Definition 2 *(OD Graph): An OD Graph is denoted as* $\mathcal{G} = (\mathbb{V}, \mathbb{E})$, *where* $\mathbb{V} = \{v_1, v_2, \dots v_n\}$ *is a finite set of N traffic nodes;* $\mathbb{E} = \{e_{ij}\}_{i,j=1}^{N}$ *indicates whether two nodes are geographically adjacent to each other: for transportation with fixed stations, two nodes are adjacent when they are in the same bus line or subway line; for transportation without fixed stations, two nodes are adjacent when the distance between them is less than a certain threshold. Then* e_{ij} *will be one when* v_i *is adjacent to* v_j *otherwise will be zero.*

Definition 3 *(OD Demand Matrix): The OD demand matrix records the OD demand in a fixed time interval between all OD pairs. Formally, the OD demand matrix between* t *and* $t+\tau$ *is denoted as* $\mathbf{M}_t \in \mathbb{R}^{N \times N}$ *where* τ *is the time interval of certain period of time. The* (i, j)*-entry of* $\mathbf{M}_t$ *represents how many passengers travel from* v_i *to* v_j *between* t *and* $t + \tau$.

3.2 Problem Definition

OD Demand Prediction. For a traffic system, given OD Graph and all OD Demand matrix $\{\mathbf{M}_t\}_{t=1}^{T}$, our goal is to predict the OD matrix of the next time interval $\mathbf{M}_{T+1}$.

4 Methodology

This section presents the proposed Zoom-based AutoEncoder for Origin-Destination demand prediction (ODZAE). We first present the motivation and overview of our method, and then we will introduce the proposed method step by step.

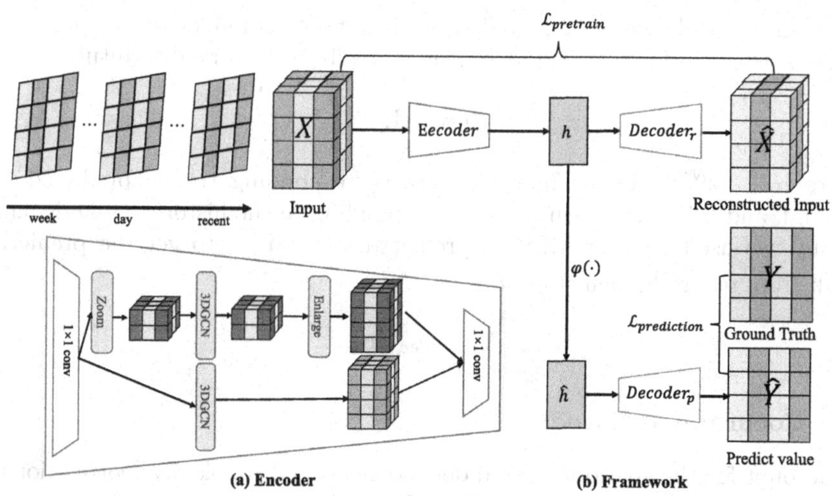

Fig. 1. The overall framework of ODZAE. It uses a Zoom-based AutoEncoder to mine the spatial and temporal dependencies of historical OD demand data to obtain hidden states, then uses a projection function to project hidden states from history to future, and finally uses another decoder to get the prediction result from future hidden states.

4.1 Motivation and Overview

Our framework aims to learn hidden states for traffic nodes that contain the intrinsic pattern features of original historical Origin-Destination demand matrix, which can be projected to the future hidden states and used to reconstruct the future OD demand matrix. The framework overview is shown in Fig. 1. First, we design an encoder δ_{enc} based on Zoom Operation and 3DGCN to extract the hidden states $\mathbf{h} \in \mathbb{R}^{3p\times N^2\times d}$ of historical OD Demand data as:

$$\mathbf{h} = \delta_{enc}(\mathbf{X}). \tag{1}$$

To account for temporal dependencies, the input variable $\mathbf{X} \in \mathbb{R}^{3p\times N^2}$ includes the OD demand from the previous p time slices, as well as the OD demand from the same time slices yesterday and last week:

$$\mathbf{X} = [\mathbf{M}_{t-7\Gamma-p+1}, \dots, \mathbf{M}_{t-7\Gamma}, \mathbf{M}_{t-\Gamma-p+1}, \dots, \mathbf{M}_{t-\Gamma}, \mathbf{M}_{t-p+1}, \dots, \mathbf{M}_{t}], \tag{2}$$

where Γ is the number of time intervals within a day. This approach captures both the trend and periodicity of the OD demand. Second, we used a Multi-layer Perceptron (MLP) as recovery decoder δ_{dec_r} to reconstruct the history OD demand matrix $\hat{\mathbf{X}} \in \mathbb{R}^{3p\times N^2}$:

$$\hat{\mathbf{X}} = \delta_{dec_r}(\mathbf{h}). \tag{3}$$

The above procedure is pretrained to assure the encoder can extract essential spatio-temporal features from original input and preserve as much information as possible into hidden states.

Then, after the encoder is well trained, a MLP as hidden states projection function $\psi(\cdot)$ is added to project hidden states from historical to future:

$$\hat{\mathbf{h}} = \psi(\mathbf{h}), \tag{4}$$

where $\hat{\mathbf{h}} \in \mathbb{R}^{N^2 \times d}$ is the hidden states corresponding to the predicted OD demand, and $\mathbf{h}$ is the hidden states corresponding to the historical OD demand. Finally, we used another MLP as predict decoder δ_{dec_p} to get the prediction result from future hidden state $\hat{h}$:

$$\hat{\mathbf{Y}} = \delta_{dec_p}(\hat{\mathbf{h}}). \tag{5}$$

4.2 Zoom Based Encoder

To account for the spatio-temporal dependencies and topological correlations in OD demand data, we developed a Zoom-Based Encoder to extract hidden states with significant pattern features to facilitate historical OD demand reconstruction. Our encoder uses a zoom operation to learn various spatial dependencies and 3DGCN to learn spatio-temporal dependencies simultaneously.

In encoder, the input $\mathbf{X}$ will first go through 1×1 convolutional layer, then will be split into two branches: the first branch will first go through zoom for compression, then use 3DGCN to deal with spatio-temporal dependencies, and then use enlarge to restore; the second branch only passes through the 3DGCN layer. After that, the results of the two branches will be concatenated together, and the output of the encoder will be obtained after another 1×1 conv layer.

Zoom Operation. Existing models for predicting OD demand often rely on graph neural networks based on adjacent matrices to capture the spatial dependencies between adjacent traffic nodes. However, the spatial dependencies of OD demand extend beyond adjacent relationships and also include functional similarities. For instance, during morning rush hour, many people in the city travel from residential to work areas. In this case, there is a spatial dependency relationship between the traffic stations located in the residential areas and those located in the work areas. However, this type of spatial dependency relationship is difficult to design manually.

To solve this problem, we propose the zoom operation. The core idea is to compress the state of N traffic nodes into M cluster states and then use the enlarge operation to restore the cluster states to the states of traffic nodes. Formally, zoom operation is computed as:

$$\mathbf{h}_{zoom} = Zoom(\mathbf{h}_{input}) = \mathbf{W}_{Zoom} \times \mathbf{h}_{input}, \tag{6}$$

where $\mathbf{h}_{input} \in \mathbb{R}^{3p \times N^2 \times d}$ is output of input X after passing through 1×1 conv layer, and $\mathbf{W}_{Zoom} \in \mathbb{R}^{N^2 d \times M^2 d}$ is the weight matrix of Zoom. Then we use

3DGCN which will be described in detail in the next section to learn spatial and temporal dependencies of cluster states.

$$\mathbf{h}_{st} = 3DGCN(\mathbf{h}_{zoom}). \tag{7}$$

Finally, we will use a MLP as enlarge operation to get nodes states $\mathbf{h}_{out} \in \mathbb{R}^{3p \times N^2 \times d}$ from cluster states:

$$\mathbf{h}_{out} = Enlarge(\mathbf{h}_{st}) = \mathbf{W}_{Enlarge} \times \mathbf{h}_{st}, \tag{8}$$

where $\mathbf{W}_{Enlarge} \in \mathbb{R}^{M^2 d \times N^2 d}$ is the weight matrix of Enlarge.

3DGCN. Graph convolutional network (GCN) has achieved the unprecedented success on a series of problems. Given a graph $\mathcal{G} = (\mathbb{V}, \mathbb{E}, \mathbf{A})$ where $\mathbb{V}$ is a set of vertices, $\mathbb{E}$ is a set of edges and $\mathbf{A} \in \mathbb{R}^{N \times N}$ is the connectivity matrix. Then, the graph Laplacian is

$$\mathbf{L} = \mathbf{I} - \mathbf{D}^{-1/2}\mathbf{A}\mathbf{D}^{-1/2}, \tag{9}$$

where $\mathbf{D}$ is the degree matrix and $\mathbf{I}$ is an identity matrix. GCN generalizes the convolution operation from CNN on graph based on graph Laplacian, which generates a signal from lth layer, i.e., $\mathbf{H}_l$, to $(l+1)$th layer by

$$\mathbf{H}_{l+1} = \sigma(\sum_{k=0}^{K-1} \alpha_k \mathbf{T}_k(L)\mathbf{H}_l), \tag{10}$$

where $\mathbf{T}_k(\cdot)$ denotes the Chebyshev polynomial of degree k. Mofnti *et al.* [11] propose 2DGCN which extends GCN to 2D graph signals. Different from traditional GCN, 2DGCN operates on a matrix that both rows and columns can be regarded on as features, i.e., the raw index is corresponding to a node as well as the column index. Thus, the 2DGCN can be defined as

$$\mathcal{H}^{(l+1)} = \sigma(\sum_{i=0}^{N-1}\sum_{j=0}^{N-1} \mathcal{H}^l \times_1 \mathbf{T}_i(L_1) \times_2 \mathbf{T}_j(L_2) \times_3 \mathbf{W}^l_{ij}, \tag{11}$$

where $\times_n$ means the matrix multiplication on the n th dimension of the tensor, $\mathbf{L}$ is the Laplacian matrix obtained by Eq. 9, $\mathbf{W}^l_{ij}$ is the learnable weight matrix for the l-th layer, and $\sigma(\cdot)$ is the activation function. MPGCN use 2DGCN to conduct GCN for both origins and destinations, using the temporal features extracted by LSTM. This method of dealing with spatial patterns and temporal patterns separately does not consider the interaction between them, which restricts the representation ability of the model a lot. To solve this problem, we extend 2DGCN to 3DGCN by adding time dimension:

$$\mathcal{H}^{(l+1)} = \sigma(\sum_{t=0}^{T-1}\sum_{i=0}^{N-1}\sum_{j=0}^{N-1} \mathcal{H}^l \times_1 \mathbf{A}_1 \times_2 \mathbf{T}_i(L_1) \times_3 \mathbf{T}_j(L_2) \times_4 \mathbf{W}^l_{ijk}. \tag{12}$$

Motivated by GraphWavenet [14], we treat the different time slices as different time nodes and calculable time nodes relationship matrix $\mathbf{A}_1$ by

$$\mathbf{A}_1 = SoftMax(\sigma(\mathbf{E}_1\mathbf{E}_2^T)), \tag{13}$$

where $\mathbf{E}_1 \in \mathbb{R}^{3p\times d_e}$ is the source time node embedding, and $\mathbf{E}_2 \in \mathbb{R}^{3p\times d_e}$ is the target time node embedding.

4.3 Training Strategy

To enhance the performance and precision of our model, we first use the ODZAE to pretrain for data reconstruction on the training set. That is, the input is historical Origin-Destination demand $\mathbf{X}$, and the output is the reconstructed historical Origin-Destination demand $\hat{\mathbf{X}}$. Then we load the parameter of the encoder in pretrained model and combine it with the projection function and prediction decoder δ_{dec_p} for supervised learning. We do not fix the parameters of the encoder, allowing them to be fine-tuned during training since the encoder have the ability to learn spatio-temporal dependencies. The loss functions for pretraining and prediction are formally defined as:

$$\mathcal{L}_{pretrain}(\mathbf{X}, \hat{\mathbf{X}}) = (\mathbf{X} - \hat{\mathbf{X}})^2, \tag{14}$$

$$\mathcal{L}_{prediction}(\mathbf{Y}, \hat{\mathbf{Y}}) = (\mathbf{Y} - \hat{\mathbf{Y}})^2. \tag{15}$$

5 Experiment

5.1 Datasets

We conduct experiment on two real-world traffic datasets to verify the effectiveness of ODZAE, namely BJSubway and NYTaxi:

1. **BJSubway** collects all transaction data of the Beijing Subway from June 1, 2017 to July 31, 2017, using the first 42 days for train, the next 7 days for validation and the last 7 days for test. We use subway stations as traffic nodes and the number of subway stations is 268.
3. **NYTaxi** collects data on taxi transactions in the Manhattan district of New York City from January 1, 2019 to June 30, 2019, using the first 139 days for train, the next 21 days for validation and the last 21 days for test.[1] We use Manhattan neighborhoods as traffic nodes and the number of neighborhoods is 63.

5.2 Baselines and Metrics

We compare our model with following methods:

[1] Data is available at https://www1.nyc.gov/site/tlc/about/tlc-trip-record-data.page.

- **HA** (Historical Average) simply takes the average value of historical OD demand for a given OD pair as the prediction result.
- **LR** (Linear Regression) uses the same input as our model, exploiting linear correlations between the input and the target value.
- **XGBoost** [2] is an improved algorithm for the original Gradient Boosting Decision Tree method.
- **GEML** [13] is an earlier work to study OD prediction. It uses semantic neighbors and geographical neighbors to model spatial relations, and uses skip LSTM to model temporal relations.
- **DNEAT** [16] uses dynamic node-edge attention from demand generation and attraction perspectives.
- **MPGCN** [11] is a model which utilizes LSTM to extract temporal features for each OD pair and two-dimensional graph convolutional network to learn the spatial dependency of origins and destinations.
- **CMOD** [5] uses a continuous-time dynamic graph representation learning framework for OD demand forecasting, which update traffic nodes representation when traffic transaction happens.
- **ODformer** [7] present a spatial-temporal transformer for OD Demand forecasting, using OD Attention mechanism and the 2D graph neural network to capture spatial dependencies in multiple scenarios.

We use three metrics to measure and evaluate the performance of baseline methods and our method, Mean Absolute Error *(MAE)*, Root Mean Squared Error *(RMSE)* and Pearson's Correlation Coefficient *(PCC)*.

5.3 Experimental Settings

The proposed method is implemented with Pytorch 1.8.1 on a machine with Intel Xeon Glod 6130 CPU and 4 T T4 GPUs. For both datasets, τ is set as 30 min and the number of previous time slices p is 3. The hidden dimension d is set as 16, and the time node embedding dimension d_e is set as 10. Adam Optimizer with initial learning rate 0.0001 and early stopping strategy with patience 5 are utilized to train the proposed model. The learning rate of all deep learning methods is chosen from [0.01, 0.001, 0.0001, 0.00001] according to the best performance on the validation set. All deep learning methods are repeated with different seeds for 5 times and the average value and the standard deviation are reported.

5.4 Comparison Results

Table 1 show the comparison with baselines. It can be observed that (1) For most methods, MAE and $RMSE$ are smaller and PCC is higher in NYTaxi than in BJSubway. This is because the average demand of each OD pair in BJSubway is larger than that in NYTaxi. (2) Traditional machine learning methods perform worse than deep learning based methods. Deep learning methods have more expressive power which can better learn the spatial and temporal dependencies

Table 1. Comparison Results with Baselines.

Dataset	Method	MAE ↓	RMSE ↓	PCC ↑
BJSubway	HA	2.9003	8.1266	0
	LR	1.9396	5.3547	0.7521
	XGBoost	1.8048	5.7709	0.7040
	GEML	1.7291 ± 0.0123	4.6018 ± 0.1138	0.8279 ± 0.0075
	DNEAT	1.4706 ± 0.0099	5.7384 ± 0.0311	0.7237 ± 0.0033
	MPGCN	1.4625 ± 0.0183	4.5716 ± 0.1054	0.8343 ± 0.0081
	CMOD	1.4475 ± 0.0202	3.6890 ± 0.0319	0.8911 ± 0.0020
	ODFormer	1.4558 ± 0.0023	3.9723 ± 0.0242	0.8523 ± 0.0073
	ODZAE	**1.3480 ± 0.0076**	**3.4866 ± 0.0187**	**0.9032 ± 0.0011**
NYTaxi	HA	1.4593	2.6569	0
	LR	0.6907	1.3611	0.8586
	XGBoost	0.6881	1.3555	0.8599
	GEML	0.6476 ± 0.0033	1.3432 ± 0.0093	0.8662 ± 0.0015
	DNEAT	0.6495 ± 0.0025	1.5179 ± 0.0172	0.8252 ± 0.0040
	MPGCN	0.6247 ± 0.0014	1.2471 ± 0.0094	0.8863 ± 0.0022
	CMOD	0.5926 ± 0.0026	1.1795 ± 0.0023	0.8959 ± 0.0004
	ODFormer	0.6068 ± 0.0057	1.3224 ± 0.0342	0.8943 ± 0.0042
	ODZAE	**0.5771 ± 0.0035**	**1.1340 ± 0.0056**	**0.9041 ± 0.0010**

in historical OD demand, thus perform better. (3) The model we propose achieves the best performance and lowest MAE and $RMSE$, and has the highest PCC on all comparison experiments, which indicates that our proposed novel framework is effective to deal with Origin-Destination demand prediction task.

5.5 Ablation Study

To demonstrate the effectiveness of each proposed component, an ablation study is conducted on BJSubway dataset with four variants:

- **ODZAE w/o zoom** removes zoom operation in the encoder.
- **ODZAE w/o 3DGCN** removes 3DGCN in the encoder.
- **ODZAE w/o projection** removes projection function, uses historical hidden states **h** as the input of prediction decoder.
- **ODZAE w/o finetune** fixes the parameters of the pretrained autoencoder and won't update them during training.

Figure 2 shows ablation results; it can be observed that (1) ODZAE performs better than ODZAE w/o zoom, which demonstrates that the proposed zoom operation can leverage spatial dependencies for better prediction; (2) the prediction performance of ODZAE w/o 3DGCN is significantly inferior to that

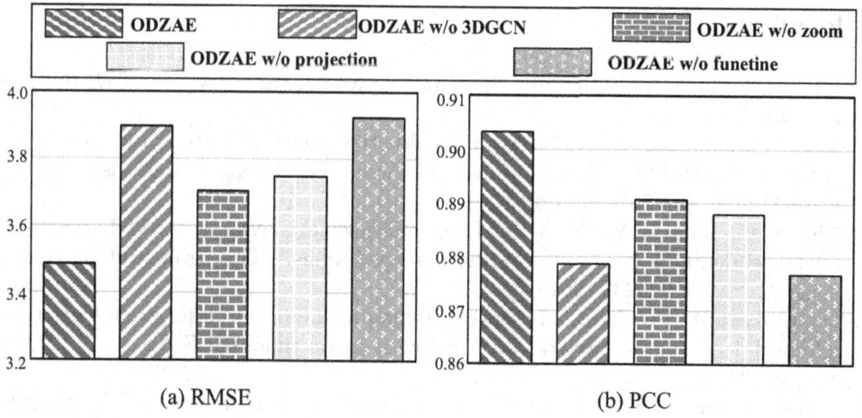

Fig. 2. Ablation study on BJSubway

of ODZAE. This outcome suggests that the future demand for OD is closely dependent on the spatio-temporal patterns of past OD demand, and 3DGCN is effective in capturing these patterns. (3) the prediction error is significantly increased after fixing the parameters during training, which indicates that the encoder of ODZAE can model temporal dependencies; (4) ODZAE performs much better than ODZAE w/o projection shows that the projection function is crucial for improving prediction accuracy.

6 Conclusion

This study proposed a novel framework for Origin-Destination demand prediction problem based on autoencoder. We propose a specially designed encoder which consists of zoom operation and 3DGCN to learn intrinsic patterns of historical Origin-Destination demand data and use a projection function to get future hidden states from historical hidden states. Finally, we use a decoder to get the prediction result. We conduct experiments on two real-world datasets, and ODZAE achieved the best performance, demonstrating its superiority for OD demand prediction. Although the use of autoencoder can achieve good prediction results, due to space constraints, we did not explore what information hidden states contain. This work bonds autoencoder and OD demand prediction for the first time, and the idea could also be further applied on more applications such as mutli-time series forecasting.

References

1. Ballard, D.H.: Modular learning in neural networks. In: AAAI, vol. 647, pp. 279–284 (1987)
2. Chen, T., Guestrin, C.: XGBoost: a scalable tree boosting system. In: Proceedings of the 22nd ACM SIGKDD International Conference on Knowledge Discovery and Data Mining, pp. 785–794 (2016)
3. Chu, K.F., Lam, A.Y., Li, V.O.: Deep multi-scale convolutional LSTM network for travel demand and origin-destination predictions. IEEE Trans. Intell. Transp. Syst. **21**(8), 3219–3232 (2019)
4. Duan, Z., et al.: Prediction of city-scale dynamic taxi origin-destination flows using a hybrid deep neural network combined with travel time. IEEE Access **7**, 127816–127832 (2019)
5. Han, L., et al.: Continuous-time and multi-level graph representation learning for origin-destination demand prediction. In: Proceedings of the 28th ACM SIGKDD Conference on Knowledge Discovery and Data Mining, pp. 516–524 (2022)
6. He, K., Chen, X., Xie, S., Li, Y., Dollár, P., Girshick, R.: Masked autoencoders are scalable vision learners. In: Proceedings of the IEEE/CVF Conference on Computer Vision and Pattern Recognition, pp. 16000–16009 (2022)
7. Huang, B., Ruan, K., Yu, W., Xiao, J., Xie, R., Huang, J.: ODformer: spatial-temporal transformers for long sequence origin-destination matrix forecasting against cross application scenario. Exp. Syst. Appl. **222**, 119835 (2023)
8. Kingma, D.P., Welling, M.: Auto-encoding variational Bayes. arXiv preprint arXiv:1312.6114 (2013)
9. Liu, L., Qiu, Z., Li, G., Wang, Q., Ouyang, W., Lin, L.: Contextualized spatial-temporal network for taxi origin-destination demand prediction. IEEE Trans. Intell. Transp. Syst. **20**(10), 3875–3887 (2019)
10. Noursalehi, P., Koutsopoulos, H.N., Zhao, J.: Dynamic origin-destination prediction in urban rail systems: a multi-resolution spatio-temporal deep learning approach. IEEE Trans. Intell. Transp. Syst. **23**(6), 5106–5115 (2021)
11. Shi, H., et al.: Predicting origin-destination flow via multi-perspective graph convolutional network. In: 2020 IEEE 36th International Conference on Data Engineering (ICDE), pp. 1818–1821. IEEE (2020)
12. Van Den Oord, A., Vinyals, O., et al.: Neural discrete representation learning. In: Advances in Neural Information Processing Systems, vol. 30 (2017)
13. Wang, Y., Yin, H., Chen, H., Wo, T., Xu, J., Zheng, K.: Origin-destination matrix prediction via graph convolution: a new perspective of passenger demand modeling. In: Proceedings of the 25th ACM SIGKDD International Conference on Knowledge Discovery & Data Mining, pp. 1227–1235 (2019)
14. Wu, Z., Pan, S., Long, G., Jiang, J., Zhang, C.: Graph WaveNet for deep spatial-temporal graph modeling. arXiv preprint arXiv:1906.00121 (2019)
15. Xiong, X., Ozbay, K., Jin, L., Feng, C.: Dynamic origin-destination matrix prediction with line graph neural networks and kalman filter. Transp. Res. Rec. **2674**(8), 491–503 (2020)
16. Zhang, D., Xiao, F., Shen, M., Zhong, S.: DNEAT: a novel dynamic node-edge attention network for origin-destination demand prediction. Transp. Res. Part C Emerg. Technol. **122**, 102851 (2021)

Healthcare and Wellbeing

A Stagewise Deep Learning Framework for Tooth Instance Segmentation in CBCT Images

Ke Cao, Lihua Tian(✉), Qiwei Li, Hao Chen, Chen Li, Yu Fan, Jianwei Ye, and Weimin Yu

Sioux Technology, Xi'an Jiaotong University, Xi'an, China
{caoke123,liqiwei}@stu.xjtu.edu.cn, {lhtian,cclidd}@xjtu.edu.cn, {hao.chen,yu.fan,jianwei.ye,weimin.yu}@sioux.asia

Abstract. Computer-assisted modeling of patient-specific 3D teeth is a clinically important technology for the development of dental diagnosis and treatment. This technology often relies on accurately segmenting the target tooth and its surrounding tissues from CBCT images. Most of the previous methods consume extensive memory for generating bounding box proposals in a detection manner, while in this paper, we propose a novel stagewise tooth instance segmentation framework from localization to segmentation. Specifically, our method follows the process of tooth centroid prediction, candidate centroid analysis, and mapping of centroids to accurately localize the ROI of individual teeth, instead of generating bounding box proposals for tooth positioning regression. To improve the segmentation quality, we propose a new loss function referred to as potential energy loss, which measures the feature similarity among voxels in a neighborhood to focus more on local information, regulating potential energy to obtain optimal segmentation. Moreover, the proposed fine segmentation network introduces a dual-branch structure and spectrum filter connections to enhance hierarchical features and anti-noise capability. Experimental results demonstrate that the proposed method surpasses state-of-the-art methods with improvements of 1.05%, 5.77%, and 16.67% on average DSC, HD95, and ASSD, respectively.

Keyword: Tooth Instance Segmentation · Potential Energy Loss · CBCT · Dental Surgery · Pre-operative Planning

1 Introduction

Computer-assisted dental diagnosis and treatment have undergone rapid development due to patient-specific modeling of 3D teeth from cone-beam computed tomography (CBCT). These dental models are crucial for clinical diagnosis and treatment planning as they provide quantitative information on 3D spatial and morphological features. In addition, during routine dental surgeries such as root canal treatment and apicoectomy, a 3D teeth model-guided navigation system dynamically tracks surgical instruments such as handpieces, enabling visualization of the difference between the predefined pathway

F. Liu et al. (Eds.): PRICAI 2023, LNAI 14325, pp. 415–425, 2024.
https://doi.org/10.1007/978-981-99-7019-3_38

and intra-operative situation. This system can improve surgical precision and minimize wound areas. However, extracting complete teeth from dental CBCT data is challenging due to difficulties in separating the target tooth from its surrounding alveolar bone, as well as boundary ambiguity among adjacent teeth. Therefore, this paper focuses on instance segmentation of all teeth from CBCT data to facilitate model-guided dental diagnosis and treatment.

Previous studies have relied on traditional methods such as thresholding [1], level-set [2], and clustering [3] for tooth segmentation, all of which have a common drawback of being difficult to generalize for diverse data due to the need for parameter tuning. Recently, new methods have emerged with the rise of deep learning. For example, Cui et al. [4] improved 3D Mask RCNN for tooth instance segmentation, while Jang et al. [5] detected bounding boxes in 2D panoramic images and mapped them onto 3D images to extract the region of interest (ROI), achieving an average DSC of 94.79%. These methods formulate the segmentation task as an object detection problem, and inevitably introduce bounding box regression errors and a significant amount of computational consumption. On the other hand, Ezhov et al. [6] proposed a method based on weakly supervised, coarse-to-fine label optimization training. CHEN et al. [7] used tooth surface probability and gradient maps to determine tooth boundaries, but performance is sometimes limited by tooth occlusion or adhesion. Li et al. [8] segmented the four quadrants of the dental area using a graph convolutional network to eliminate the effect of symmetrical and adjacent teeth, resulting in an average DSC of 91.13%. Moreover, Cui et al. [9] proposed a method that extracts ROIs with two individual networks and uses an additional network to segment the alveolar region, achieving an average DSC of 94.5% at the cost of heavy memory consumption. However, these methods concentrate on the positioning and boundary of each tooth but ignore the effect of adjacent teeth and surrounding tissues. In CBCT images, the contrast between teeth and their surroundings is low, which greatly affects the accuracy of segmentation, therefore, effectively using neighborhood information is necessary in this task.

This paper proposes a fully automatic tooth instance segmentation framework, which comprises the steps from localization to segmentation of each tooth by coarse segmentation network (CSN), ROI extraction module, and fine segmentation network (FSN). Both CSN and FSN are constructed based on the encoder-decoder structure with the same backbone, to achieve better training effect, we use the well-trained CSN network model to initialize the isomorphic part of the FSN. The CSN performs foreground separation and centroid prediction with a multi-task head. To generate the ROI of each individual tooth, the results from CSN are utilized to partition centroids connected components and mapping to foreground voxels of each tooth. Besides, a dual-branch and a spectrum filter connection are uniquely designed for FSN to enhance and make full use of edge-feature of teeth. And the FSN is used for segmenting each individual tooth in final. Note that the method decouples the ROI extraction and segmentation, allowing each tooth to be segmented independently of others. Meanwhile, we propose a new loss function based on potential energy, i.e., PE loss, which formulates the process of finding optimal segmentation as the problem of potential energy regularization, enabling models to segment edges of targets more accurately by incorporating neighborhood information.

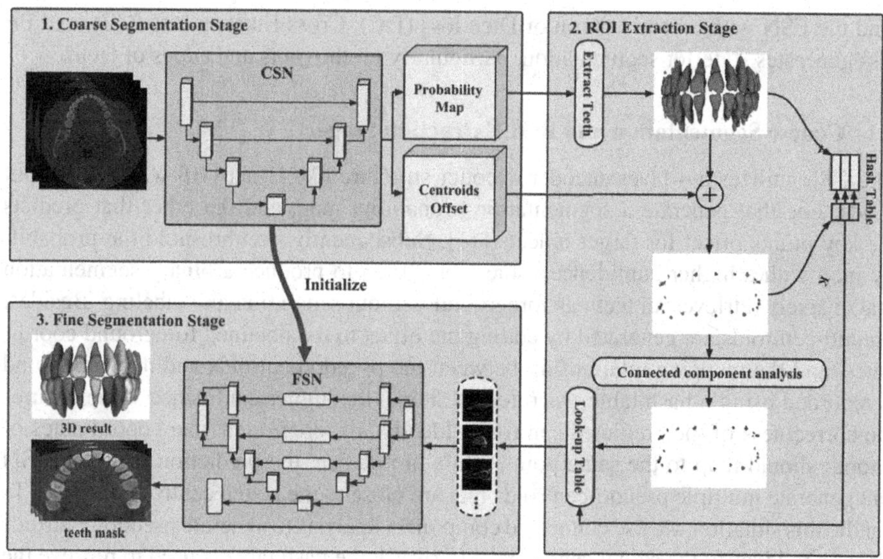

Fig. 1. Overview of the proposed tooth instance segmentation workflow with three hierarchical stages for teeth extraction and segmentation

In our study, the proposed method can detect all teeth on the CBCT images for validation and achieves an average DSC of 96.89%, outperforming state-of-the-art (SOTA) methods in comprehensive experiments.

In summary, the main contributions of this paper are three-fold:

1. We propose a novel stagewise framework for tooth instance segmentation, which uses the centroid prediction and analysis to extract ROIs but no proposal generation.
2. We propose the potential energy loss function, which use the neighborhood information and the feature similarity of different voxels to optimize the segmentation, especially on the boundary of teeth.
3. We compared FSN with the current SOTA method for semantic segmentation on the existing dataset, the experimental results showed that we outperformed other methods in metrics of DSC, HD95, and ASD.

2 Methodology

The complete workflow is illustrated as Fig. 1. Firstly, the CSN coarsely segments all teeth as foreground objects and predicts their respective centroids. In the second stage, we design a novel ROI exaction process, which fully utilizes the mapping relationship between foreground voxels and centroids and obtains individual tooth ROIs through connected component analysis and mapping of teeth centroids. In the third stage, these ROIs are fed into the FSN for accurate segmentation and results from FSN are concatenated sequentially according to the position of ROIs to form the final instance segmentation. Our ROI extraction strategy requires only one network, simplifying the calculation process and reducing memory for inference, while performing well on tooth localization.

And the FSN with a combination of Dice loss (DC), Cross Entropy loss (CE), and PE loss generates superior segmentation, particularly on the roots and edges of teeth.

2.1 Coarse Segmentation and ROI Extraction Stage

The CSN utilizes a 4-layer encoder-decoder structure like U-net [10] with two output heads: one that generate a segmentation probability map, and the other that predicts the key points offset for target objects [11]. Subsequently, we threshold the probability map with a higher confidence value (e.g., 0.95) to produce a binary segmentation that coarsely retrieves all teeth as foreground without separation and labeling. Besides, pseudo-centroids are generated by adding the offset to the obtained foreground coordinates, and the mapping relationship between the pseudo-centroids and the foreground is recorded using a hash table. As referred above, the higher confidence value ensures the correctness of the predicted centroids. Ideally, all foreground voxel coordinates of a tooth should map to the same point, while in practice, the prediction from the CSN can generate multiple pseudo-centroids that are close to the actual centroid in space. To handle this situation, we use connected component analysis to generate pseudo-centroids clusters to identify the actual centroids. Afterward, the hash table is used to retrieve the corresponding foreground voxels for each cluster, followed by the elimination of scattered points. Finally, the ROI of each tooth can be determined by the minimum bounding rectangle calculated from the foreground voxels.

Compared with region proposal network which widely used in segmentation tasks, we treat the predicted centroids as anchors and directly locate ROIs from the original image size, cleverly avoiding the introduction of bounding box regression errors. In addition, our method does not rely on proposal generation, which can greatly reduce the time and spatial complexity of the algorithm.

2.2 Fine Segmentation Stage

The FSN adopts two parallel branches for multi-level feature extraction, as shown in Fig. 2. One branch consists of two dilated convolution blocks [12], while the other utilizes an encoder-decoder structure that is identical to CSN with spectrum filter connections on the top layers. The feature maps generated by both branches are concatenated along the channel direction and then passed through a full convolution block for voxel-level classification. During training, we initialized the isomorphic parts of the FSN using the well-trained CSN model, which makes it easier for the FSN to learn semantic features and accelerate loss convergence, reducing training time. Due to the presence of implants or other tissues with similar intensities as teeth, some ROIs with "fake" tooth as negative samples may be extracted. To address that, we introduce a ROI classifier with cross-entropy loss to filter them. Specifically, we flatten the high-dimensional features output by the encoder and used a fully connected network for binary classification to judge whether the ROI contains tooth. During training, we only calculate the segmentation loss exclusively for positive samples, and for inference, we discard ROIs which are classified as negative samples.

Spectrum Filter Connection. To enhance the edge information at the top-level of the FSN while filtering out noise and enriching the features generated by the encoder, we

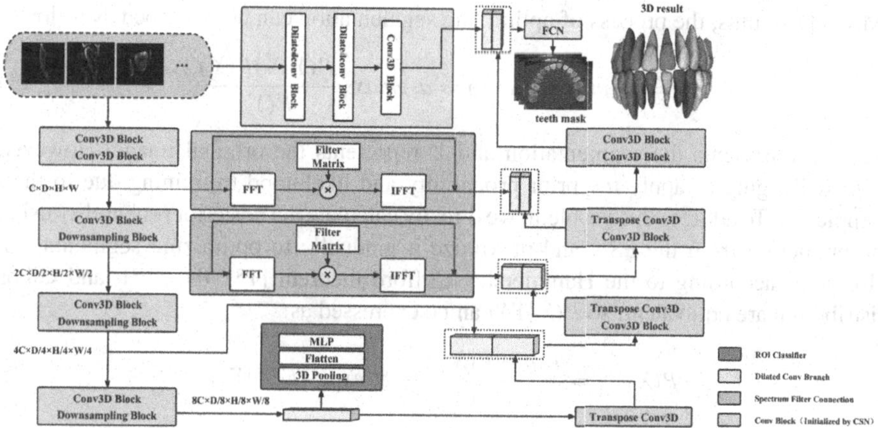

Fig. 2. As illustrated, the FSN has a dual-branch structure with spectrum filter connection, the blue block indicates the encoder-decoder, which is isomorphic to CSN and is initialized by the well-trained CSN model, while the others are unique to FSN. (Color figure online)

introduce a spectrum filter. This filter takes the spectrum diagram of the feature map obtained by Fourier transform as input and performs element-wise multiplication with a learnable weight matrix. The weight matrix is initialized as a standard Gaussian distribution in a complex form. Subsequently, the filtered feature map is obtained by performing an inverse Fourier transform. Then, we add the output to the original feature map using a residual connection. In general, the spectrum filter connection can preserve and enhance local features in high levels, especially for blurred tooth boundaries, enabling effective integration of the features from the decoder.

Dilated Convolution Branch. Due to the conical shape of most teeth, their size in axial view differs significantly from sagittal and coronal views. Furthermore, our statistical analysis shows that the majority of teeth have a height exceeding 24 mm, while their cross-sections are no more than 12*12 mm^2. To maintain isotropic resolution and compensate for information loss caused by down sampling, we design a branch that includes two dilated convolution blocks [12]. Each block is stacked by three convolutions of dilation rates 1, 2, and 5, respectively, as recommended in [13]. The kernel size is 3*3*3, which expands the receptive field to 24*24*24, which covers a significant portion of the cross-section of teeth in axial view without reducing spacing.

This design enables the feature maps to effectively retain the neighborhood information and local details of each tooth, facilitating tooth edge segmentation.

2.3 Potential Energy Loss

The category of each voxel in tooth segmentation is highly dependent on its adjacent ones, especially there are blurred boundaries between teeth and surrounding tissues, therefore, the neighborhood information plays a crucial role in accurate segmentation. Based on the neighborhood correlation, the mask can be considered as a Markov Random Field

(MRF) [14], thus, the process of optimizing segmentation can be described as follows:

$$\widehat{X} = argmax_X P(X|Y) = argmax_X \frac{P(Y|X)P(X)}{P(Y)} \quad (1)$$

Here, X represents the segmentation and Y represents the original image. However, it is challenging to apply the prior probability and likelihood to training due to their complexity. To address this problem, we directly calculate the posterior probability using the prediction from the FSN and maximize it gradually to optimizing segmentation. Moreover, according to the Hammersley-Clifford theorem [15], the MRF and Gibbs distribution are equivalent, so $P(X|Y)$ can be expressed as:

$$P(X|Y) = \frac{exp(-E(X|Y))}{Z(Y)} \propto exp(-E(X|Y)) \quad (2)$$

$Z(Y)$ is a normalization factor related to the input image, which can be disregarded, and $E(X|Y)$ is the potential energy (PE) defined on the segmentation prediction. Therefore, Eq. (2) enables the posterior probability to be represented by the PE. Following the Gibbs distribution, the PE measures the stability within a neighborhood and is calculated based on the feature similarity among voxels. Usually, the PE becomes more stable when there is higher similarity among voxels within the same category and lower similarity among voxels from different categories, leading to better segmentation results. Thus, we propose the PE loss to train the FSN by stabilizing local potential energy, which leads to optimal segmentation with accurate tooth boundaries.

Based on the properties of MRF, it is known that the category of a voxel is only related to its surrounding ones, so the expectation of its category can be expressed as:

$$E(X_i) = \sum\nolimits_{c=0}^{n} L_c \times \frac{\sum_{j \in T_i} (mask_j \odot L_c)}{size(T_i)} \quad (3)$$

Here, L is the label for segmentation, specifically 0 represents the background and the rest correspond to n foreground categories respectively, T_i represents the 3D neighborhood of voxel i and $mask_j$ is the ground truth of voxel j. To solve the problem of blurred boundaries, more attention should be paid to the feature similarity between different categories of voxels, therefore, we define the sensitivity of voxel to neighborhood for binary segmentation, which can be represented as:

$$Sensitivity(X_i) = 1 - [mask_i \times E(X_i) + (1 - mask_i) \times (1 - E(X_i))] \quad (4)$$

According to the above formulas, when the categories of voxels in a neighborhood are all the same, the sensitivity of the central voxel is 0, indicating that it is not boundary. For voxel i, we consider the segmentation prediction as the feature F_i, and define the PE of it as:

$$PE_i = \begin{cases} 1 - \frac{\sum_{j \in T_i} (mask_i \oplus mask_j) \times Euclidean\ distance(F_i, F_j)}{size(T_i) \times Sensitivity(X_i)}, & Sensitivity(X_i) > 0 \\ 0, & Sensitivity(X_i) = 0 \end{cases} \quad (5)$$

For a voxel with the sensitivity greater than 0, we calculate the difference among the voxels from different categories and use the sensitivity to scale it, therefore, the higher the PE, the closer the segmentation is to ground truth. We then define the PE loss as follows:

$$L_{PE} = exp\left[-\frac{\alpha}{N} \times \sum_{i=1}^{N}(1 - PE_i)\right] \quad (6)$$

Here, N is the number of voxels with a sensitivity greater than 0 and α is a temperature parameter, which is 1 in our study, and the size of neighborhood is 3*3*3.

In general, the PE loss reduce the feature similarity of voxels from different categories via backpropagation, thereby enabling accurate segmentation of voxels at the edge of teeth. Its working mechanism can be understood as mutual constraint and regularization among neighboring voxels. As a complement to the Dice loss which focuses on global information, the proposed PE loss regulates local behavior in a neighborhood, allowing the FSN model to pay more attention to neighborhood information and making it more conducive to edge segmentation.

3 Experiment

3.1 Data Preprocessing

The dataset used for the quantitative study includes 148 labeled CBCT images[1] with 3675 teeth, which have been de-identified for use. First, we resampled each CBCT image using linear interpolation and neighborhood interpolation for images and labels, respectively, to an isotropic resolution of 0.4mm. Next, we truncated the intensity of each resampled CBCT data to a range of 500 to 2500 and normalized it to [0, 1]. Before training the CSN, we cropped each pre-processed CBCT image to a size of 256*256*256 that only contains the region of teeth. Additionally, we calculated the centroid location of each tooth from the ground truth and then subtracted the centroid coordinates from the other foreground voxels to obtain offsets, which are used for centroid regression learning. Before training the FSN, we extracted each tooth from the CBCT images as positive samples with a shape of 96*96*96. Meanwhile, we selected 300 patches with similar teeth intensities as negative samples and augmented them to 2100 samples by rotation, translation, shear, and flip to balance the number of positive and negative samples.

3.2 Training and Results

Our quantitative evaluation includes experiments that compare our method with state-of-the-art methods, as well as an ablation study using cross-validation. The CSN model was trained for 100 epochs with a batch size of 1 and the FSN model was initialized by the well-trained CSN model and trained only for 30 epochs with a batch size of 16. All experiments were optimized by Adam and the initial learning rate was set to 0.001, which was exponentially decayed with a factor of 0.97. The training process was conducted on three NVIDIA 3090 GPUs, each with 24 GB of memory. For the comparative experiments, we used 120 CBCT images for training and the remaining ones for test. For the ablation study, we separated the 148 labeled CBCT images into five groups and conducted a 5-fold validation.

[1] This dataset is available in public from [9] only for research use.

Comparative Experiment. We detected all teeth on the test data using the CSN and the ROI extraction module, which means that the instance segmentation accuracy only depends on the FSN. In this study, we compared our method with some state-of-the-art methods, including CNN-based [16], Transformer-based [17], and DDPM-based [18] networks by keeping the other parts of the pipeline unchanged. As shown in Table 1, our method achieved the best performance among these state-of-the-art methods, with a DSC and ASD exceeding 0.96% and 15.38%, respectively, and a smaller HD95 compared to the suboptimal method, i.e., nnUnet.

Table 1. Segmentation results compared between our framework and SOAT methods.

Methods	Metrics		
	DCS	HD95 (mm)	ASD (mm)
TransUnet [19]	83.94	1.23	0.47
VT-Unet [20]	92.66	0.84	0.26
MedSegDiff [21]	90.85	0.77	0.24
SegDiff [22]	92.61	0.79	0.21
U-net [10]	95.42	0.66	0.15
nnUnet [23]	95.97	0.62	0.13
Ours	**96.89**	**0.54**	**0.11**

Ablation Experiment. To explore the individual effects of the FSN and the PE loss, we used the U-net [10] and nnUnet [23] as baselines. It is important to note that we tested individual teeth rather than the ROIs detected in the comparative experiments to avoid errors introduced by the other modules of the proposed framework. As shown in Table 2, where G1 through G5 corresponds to the different groups in the 5-fold cross validation, our method using the FSN and the combination of all three loss functions (i.e., the DC, CE, and PE losses) outperformed the base method by 1.13%, 9.62%, and 25.00% based on DSC, HD95, and ASD, respectively.

Qualitative Evaluation. We qualitatively compared the 3D teeth meshes extracted from the segmentation results by the nnUnet and our proposed method (see Fig. 3a). Our method closely conforms to the ground truth and generates smoother results, showing better preservation of the root apex and the edge of teeth. On the other hand, in Fig. 3b, we demonstrate the robustness of our method, accurately segmenting all teeth, including wisdom teeth, and handling missing teeth, malocclusion, and metal artifacts.

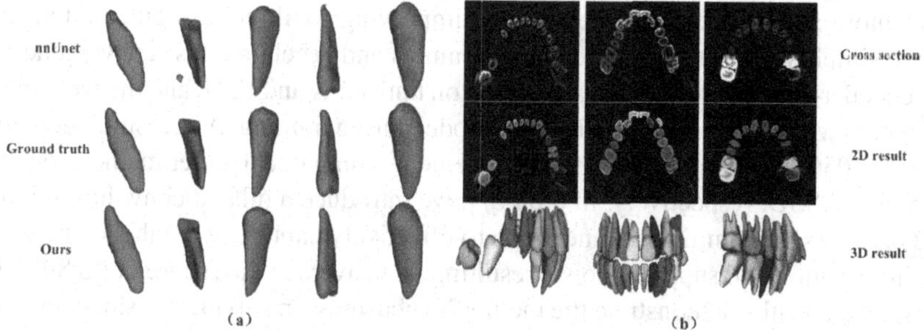

Fig. 3. Segmentation results achieved by our proposed method and nnUnet [23].

Table 2. Results of ablation experiments (the bold indicates the best performance of all the methods, and the underline indicates the best performance of baselines)

Methods		Groups					
		G1	G2	G3	G4	G5	Avg
DSC	U-net / DC + CE	96.01	95.96	94.34	95.86	95.57	95.53
	nnUnet / DC + CE	96.49	95.91	95.37	96.18	95.59	95.90
	U-net / DC + CE + PE	97.04	96.48	95.75	96.85	96.56	96.53
	FSN / DC + CE	97.03	96.54	95.83	96.82	96.56	96.55
	FSN / DC + CE + PE	**97.06**	**96.60**	**95.91**	**96.92**	**96.61**	**96.61**
HD95(mm)	U-net / DC + CE	0.53	0.48	0.61	0.47	0.49	0.52
	nnUnet / DC + CE	0.50	0.48	0.54	0.48	0.49	0.50
	U-net / DC + CE + PE	0.46	**0.47**	0.56	0.47	0.48	0.49
	FSN / DC + CE	0.46	**0.47**	0.54	**0.45**	0.47	0.48
	FSN / DC + CE + PE	**0.45**	**0.47**	**0.52**	**0.45**	**0.46**	**0.47**
ASD (mm)	U-net / DC + CE	0.13	0.10	0.14	0.10	0.11	0.12
	nnUnet / DC + CE	0.10	0.11	**0.12**	0.10	0.12	0.11
	U-net / DC + CE + PE	0.09	0.10	**0.12**	0.09	0.10	0.10
	FSN / DC + CE	0.09	0.10	**0.12**	0.08	0.10	0.10
	FSN / DC + CE + PE	**0.08**	**0.09**	**0.12**	**0.08**	**0.09**	**0.09**

4 Conclusion and Discussion

This study is significant as it proposes a novel stagewise framework for tooth instance segmentation in CBCT images. This method uses the predictions of the foreground and centroids from the CSN to localize individual teeth, avoiding bounding box regression errors and high computational consumption while achieving a detection rate of 100% on the dataset. Furthermore, the proposed PE loss constrain different categories of voxels to each other through mutually exclusive features in a neighborhood, allowing the model to pay more attention to local details and improving tooth edge segmentation accuracy. To simplify the learning of semantic features and accelerate loss convergence, the same encoder-decoder structure was utilized on both CSN and FSN, and the well-trained CSN model was used to initialize the FSN model during training. As a result, our method achieves 1.05%, 5.77%, and 16.67% improvements compared to other methods on DSC, HD95, and ASSD, respectively. In the FSN, we introduce a dilated convolution branch together with spectrum filter connections to effectively capture and enhance neighborhood information and suppress noise, resulting in an average dice score of 96.89%. Our experimental results demonstrate the method's robustness in solving missing teeth, malocclusion, and metal artifacts, which is clinically significant for assisting doctors with preoperative diagnosis and providing intraoperative navigation. In the future, we will continue to improve the segmentation of the pulp cavity to better integrate with clinical practice.

References

1. Majanga, V., Viriri, S.: Dental images' segmentation using threshold connected component analysis. Computational Intelligence and Neuroscience 2021 (2021)
2. Syuhada, F., et al.: Multi-projection segmentation on dental cone beam computed tomography images using level set method. J. Computer Science and Informatics Eng. (J-Cosine). **5**, 130–139 (2021)
3. Qaddoura, R., Manaseer, W.A., Abushariah, M.A.M., et al.: Dental radiography segmentation using expectation-maximization clustering and grasshopper optimizer. Multimedia Tools and Appl. **79**, 22027–22045 (2020)
4. Cui, Z., Li, C., Wang, W.: ToothNet: automatic tooth instance segmentation and identification from cone beam CT images. Proceedings of the IEEE/CVF Conference on Computer Vision and Pattern Recognition, pp. 6368–6377 (2019)
5. Jang, T.J., Kim, K.C., Cho, H.C., et al.: A fully automated method for 3D individual tooth identification and segmentation in dental CBCT. IEEE Trans. Pattern Anal. Mach. Intell. **44**(10), 6562–6568 (2021)
6. Ezhov, M., Zakirov, A., Gusarev, M.: Coarse-to-fine volumetric segmentation of teeth in cone-beam ct. 2019 IEEE 16th International Symposium on Biomedical Imaging (ISBI 2019). IEEE, pp. 52–56(2019)
7. Chen, Y., Du, H., Yun, Z., et al.: Automatic segmentation of individual tooth in dental CBCT images from tooth surface map by a multi-task FCN. IEEE Access. **8**, 97296–97309 (2020)
8. Li, P., Liu, Y., Cui, Z., et al.: Semantic graph attention with explicit anatomical association modeling for tooth segmentation from CBCT images. IEEE Trans. Med. Imaging **41**(11), 3116–3127 (2022)
9. Cui, Z., Fang, Y., Mei, L., et al.: A fully automatic AI system for tooth and alveolar bone segmentation from cone-beam CT images. Nat. Commun. **13**(1), 2096 (2022)
10. Ronneberger, O., Fischer, P., Brox, T.: U-net: convolutional networks for biomedical image segmentation. Medical Image Computing and Computer-Assisted Intervention–MICCAI 2015: 18th International Conference, Munich, Germany, October 5–9, 2015, Proceedings, Part III 18. Springer International Publishing, pp. 234–241 (2015)
11. Geng, Z., Sun, K., Xiao, B., et al.: Bottom-up human pose estimation via disentangled keypoint regression. Proceedings of the IEEE/CVF Conference on Computer Vision and Pattern Recognition, pp. 14676–14686 (2021)

12. Yu, F., Koltun, V.: Multi-Scale Context Aggregation by Dilated Convolutions. arXiv preprint arXiv:1511.07122 (2015)
13. Wang, P., Chen, P., Yuan, Y., et al.: Understanding convolution for semantic segmentation. 2018 IEEE Winter Conference on Applications of Computer Vision (WACV). IEEE, pp. 1451–1460 (2018)
14. Park, J.S., Fadnavis, S., Garyfallidis, E..: EVC-Net: Multi-scale V-Net with Conditional Random Fields for Brain Extraction. arXiv preprint arXiv:2206.02837 (2022)
15. Strauss, D.J.: Hammersley–clifford theorem. Encyclopedia of Statistical Sciences **5** (2004)
16. LeCun, Y., Bottou, L., Bengio, Y., et al.: Gradient-based learning applied to document recognition. Proc. IEEE **86**(11), 2278–2324 (1998)
17. Vaswani, A., Shazeer, N., Parmar, N., et al.: Attention is all you need. Advances in Neural Information Processing Syst. **30** (2017)
18. Ho, J., Jain, A., Abbeel, P.: Denoising diffusion probabilistic models. Adv. Neural. Inf. Process. Syst. **33**, 6840–6851 (2020)
19. Chen, J., Lu, Y., Yu, Q., et al.: Transunet: Transformers make Strong Encoders for Medical Image Segmentation. arXiv preprint arXiv:2102.04306 (2021)
20. Peiris, H., Hayat, M., Chen, Z., et al.: A robust volumetric transformer for accurate 3d tumor segmentation. Medical Image Computing and Computer Assisted Intervention–MICCAI 2022: 25th International Conference, Singapore, September 18–22, 2022, Proceedings, Part V. Cham: Springer Nature Switzerland, pp: 162–172 (2022). https://doi.org/10.1007/978-3-031-16443-9_16
21. Wu, J., Fang, H., Zhang, Y., et al.: MedSegDiff: Medical Image Segmentation with Diffusion Probabilistic Model. arXiv preprint arXiv:2211.00611 (2022)
22. Amit, T., Nachmani, E., Shaharbany, T., et al.: Segdiff: Image Segmentation with Diffusion Probabilistic Models. arXiv preprint arXiv:2112.00390 (2021)
23. Isensee, F., Petersen, J., Klein, A., et al.: nnu-net: Self-Adapting Framework for u-Net-based Medical Image Segmentation. arXiv preprint arXiv:1809.10486 (2018)

Hierarchical Pooling Graph Convolutional Neural Network for Alzheimer's Disease Diagnosis

Wenya Liu, Zhi Yang(✉), Haitao Gan, Zhongwei Huang, Ran Zhou, and Ming Shi

School of Computer Science, Hubei University of Technology Wuhan, Hubei, China
zyang631@hbut.edu.cn

Abstract. Deep learning techniques have found extensive applications in utilizing magnetic resonance imaging (MRI) to support the diagnosis of Alzheimer's disease (AD). However, existing research primarily focuses on the pathological changes in brain regions affected by the disease, while overlooking the intrinsic correlations among these regions. This disregard may lead to inaccurate disease predictions. Graph data, represented in the form of nodes and their connecting edges, effectively describe the relationships between nodes. However, constructing representative brain connectivity graphs remains a notable task. To solve the above problems, we come up a layered pooling graph convolutional classification network based on MRI to learn differential features between samples in the MRI data for AD diagnosis. Our innovation lies in utilizing two layers of classification networks, processing brain connectivity graphs with self-attention convolutions to obtain brain feature structure graphs at different granularities. By integrating data at different scales, we can comprehensively and accurately capture feature information in brain magnetic resonance images. Our method further utilizes global pooling to aggregate learned brain structural features and generate gradually evolving topic-level representations for AD diagnosis. Experimental validation on the openly accessible ADNI dataset demonstrates the competitive performance of our method in multiple AD-related classification tasks. Compared to existing methods, our method better captures brain structural features and exhibits stronger generalization capability.

Keywords: Alzheimer's disease · Magnetic resonance imaging · Graph Convolutional Neural Networks

1 Introduction

Alzheimer's disease (AD) is a severe neurodegenerative disorder affecting millions worldwide [17], with a projection that 300 million patients will be affected by 2050 [5]. The main factors inducing death in elderly people with Alzheimer's disease [21], is characterized by early amnesia and subsequent cognitive decline.

F. Liu et al. (Eds.): PRICAI 2023, LNAI 14325, pp. 426–437, 2024.
https://doi.org/10.1007/978-981-99-7019-3_39

Despite the absence of a definitive cure, treatments can alleviate symptoms and delay progression. Early diagnosis, particularly in initial stages like mild cognitive impairment (MCI), is crucial [14], as timely detection aids in slowing disease progression and improving patient health.

Recently, brain imaging techniques have made significant advancements in the early diagnosis of AD [1]. Magnetic resonance imaging (MRI) is a non-invasive technique that generates detailed 3D anatomical brain images, accurately depicting changes in the brain affected by AD [3]. Over the past few years, convolutional neural networks (CNNs) have demonstrated significant achievements in the field of computer vision, including medical image classification. They can significantly improve the performance of AD diagnosis based on MRI images compared to conventional methods. [11]. However, existing CNN-based methods for AD diagnosis using MRI scans are highly complex, requiring substantial computational resources and time. To enhance diagnostic accuracy, it is crucial to use simpler networks and efficient methods. Current methods primarily focus on extracting brain region features associated with AD while often overlooking positional information and potential interactions among brain regions. Constructing a brain structural connectivity graph on MRI scan images that adequately reflect complementary spatial correlations and possess flexible and efficient topological information remains a formidable undertaking.

To address the above issues, We come up a layered pooling graph convolutional classification method for AD diagnosis using MRI data, using two different layers of convolutional pooling networks. This enables early, accurate, and efficient auxiliary diagnosis, assisting medical professionals. The effectiveness of our proposed method is evaluated on the publicly available dataset, and the experimental results showcase its strong performance in various classification tasks related to Alzheimer's disease. Our research brings forth the following noteworthy contributions:

1. Our come up approach is a hierarchical pooling graph convolutional classification network that addresses the AD diagnosis task as a graph classification problem. By utilizing MRI data, it enhances the diagnostic performance of AD and enables rapid and accurate assessment of patients' disease conditions.
2. We innovatively construct brain connectivity graph by segmenting MRI data from brain regions, get the subgraph by truncating SVD, enabling our model to analyze and diagnose Alzheimer's disease on a smaller scale.
3. We introduce a new global pooling method that combines multiple pooling methods to overcome the limitations of a single pooling method.

2 Related Work

2.1 Graph Convolutional Neural Networks

GNN [6] are models used for handling data structured as graphs, which describe the irregular structure of data by considering their dependencies. As one of the most popular models, GNNs have been widely applied to handle and analyze data with graph structures. Among them, Graph Convolutional Networks (GCNs) is a type of deep learning model specifically designed for performing convolution operations on graphs, inspired by CNNs. The GCN model was initially proposed by Kipf and Welling in 2017 [9] and incorporates spectral graph convolution theory by utilizing Fourier transform and Taylor series expansion to improve the filters. Assuming a graph $G = (V, E, S)$ with N nodes, where V denotes the node set, E denotes the edge set, and S denotes the adjacency matrix consisting of edge weights, the GCN propagation rule can be expressed as shown in Eq.(1):

$$H^{l+1} = \sigma\left(\widehat{S}H^{l}W^{l}\right) \tag{1}$$

In the above equation, $\hat{S} = \widetilde{D}^{-\frac{1}{2}}\tilde{S}\widetilde{D}^{-\frac{1}{2}}$. H^l represents the feature matrix of all nodes at layer l , W^l represents the trainable weight matrix at layer l, and σ denotes the activation function. $\widetilde{S} = S + I$, I is an identity matrix, where $\widetilde{D}_{ii} = \Sigma_j \tilde{S}_{ij}$, is used to incorporate graph convolution theory into the construction of $\widehat{S}$. This process, $\widetilde{D}_{ii} = \Sigma_j \tilde{S}_{ij}$ first transforms $\tilde{S}$ into the Fourier domain, performs graph convolution using Chebyshev polynomials, and then transforms it back to the original domain. Using the aforementioned propagation rule, for input data H^0, a two-layer GCN architecture can be represented as shown in Eq.(2):

$$Z = \text{softmax}(\widehat{S}\text{ReLU}(\widehat{S}H^{0}W^{0})W^{1}) \tag{2}$$

2.2 Graph Classification Tasks

Graph classification is a task that involves [19] assigning different categories or labels to given graph data. The primary goal of this task is to utilize sophisticated computational techniques , to establish the correlation between input graphs and output categories. This enables effective classification of new unlabeled graph data, thereby facilitating accurate categorization. In graph classification, we treat each sample as graph-structured data and utilize graph convolutional neural networks for classification. Graph classification finds wide applications in various domains, including social network analysis, bioinformatics, and recommendation systems etc. [20].

2.3 Graph Pooling

Graph pooling preserves and integrates important structural information from the entire graph using specific pooling methods. Existing graph pooling methods can be roughly divided into two categories: global pooling and local pooling. Global pooling methods include MaxPooling, MeanPooling, and AddPooling [13], while local pooling methods include TopKPooling, SAGPooling, and SortPooling [15]. Local pooling enhances classification performance by aggregating information from the immediate neighborhood of the graph, capturing valuable details and refining the results. In contrast, global pooling overlooks local context by pooling over the entire graph, potentially missing important information.

3 Method

In Fig. 1, we illustrate the general structure of the hierarchical pooling graph convolutional neural network framework proposed in this study. This framework can be divided into three key components. Firstly, based on the MRI images of each subject, we construct the corresponding graph-structured data and perform sparsification of the constructed graph edges. Next, we input all the graph data into the pooling convolutional network consisting of up and down layers. Finally, the pooled data from the up and down layers are fused and fed into fully connected layers to obtain scores for each subject in their respective categories, enabling classification.

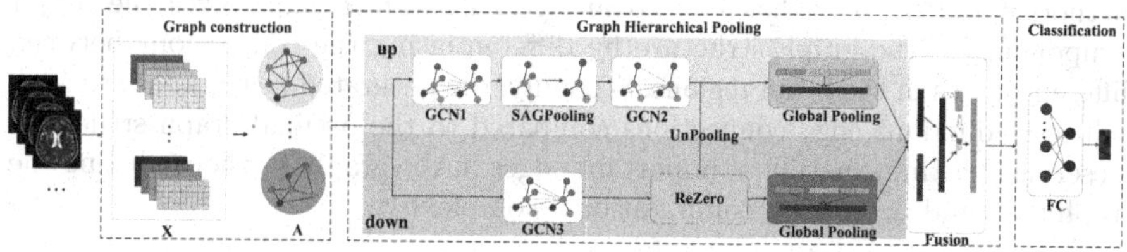

Fig. 1. Hierarchical Pooling Graph Convolutional Neural Network.

3.1 Graph Construction

To construct the graph, we first preprocess the MRI image data to obtain a brain connectivity graph for each subject. In this graph data, each node represents a brain region in the subject's brain. Assuming each graph has n nodes and each node has m features, the feature matrix is represented as $X \in \mathbb{R}^{n \times m}$. For derive the adjacency matrix $A \in \mathbb{R}^{n \times n}$ of the brain connectivity graph, by computing the pairwise distances between each pair of nodes x_i and x_j ,we create a similarity matrix that serves as the basis for constructing the adjacency matrix. This process is described by the equation presented in Eq.(3):

$$A_{i,j} = \text{sim}\left(x_i, x_j\right) = \exp\left(-\frac{\left[\rho\left(x_i, x_j\right)\right]^2}{2\sigma^2}\right) \tag{3}$$

where $\rho(\cdot)$ represents the distance function, and σ is a parameter controlling the scale of the similarity.

The resulting adjacency matrix captures the pairwise similarities between nodes, indicating the strength of connections in the brain connectivity graph. Next, the similarity matrix is normalized and symmetrized. The binarization process is shown in Eq.(4):

$$A_{i,j} = \begin{cases} 1 & A_{i,j} > \gamma \\ 0 & A_{i,j} \leq \gamma \end{cases} \tag{4}$$

γ in the formula is a threshold.

In graph data, the existence or absence of edges between nodes has a profound impact on the representation of the overall graph structure. Therefore, it is crucial to optimize the constructed graph structure to make it more representative, especially for graph classification tasks. In this study, we use a simple graph structure optimization method based on the idea of singular value decomposition (SVD) [8]. We perform truncated SVD on the adjacency matrix A and reconstruct a new adjacency matrix $\widetilde{A}$. Specifically, we first perform SVD on the adjacency matrix A as $A = U\Lambda V^T$, where Λ is a singular value matrix. We perform truncated SVD on A by retaining the top q singular values, i.e., truncating the rows of the matrix Λ. Then, we reconstruct the new adjacency matrix $\widetilde{A} = U_q\Lambda_q V_q^T$ using the truncated matrices. The graph structure optimization method based on SVD has two advantages. Firstly, it emphasizes the major components of the graph structure by differentiating the connections between different nodes in the brain regions. Secondly, the generated new graph structure reduces redundant edge connections compared to the original graph structure, preserving the information of important edges in the graph, further reducing the graph size, and decreasing computational complexity.

3.2 Graph Hierarchical Pooling

Layered Graph Convolution. Our hierarchical pooling graph convolutional network consists of two sub-networks: the up and down layers. In the up-layer network, we first use a single-layer GCN network(GCN_1) to aggregate feature information from the one-hop neighbors of each node, the feature matrix from $X \in \mathbb{R}^{n\times m}$ to $X_{up} \in \mathbb{R}^{n\times d}$, where d signifies the out channel dimensionality of the node features. Then apply the SAGPooling method [10] to the output of the aforementioned GCN, SAGPooling calculates scores for each node using the GCN network and retains high-scoring nodes while removing low-scoring nodes and their associated edges to obtain the corresponding subgraph. This SAGPooling process transforms the feature matrix from $X_{up} \in \mathbb{R}^{n\times d}$ to $X'_{up} \in \mathbb{R}^{k\times d}$,the adjacency matrix from $\widetilde{A} \in \mathbb{R}^{n\times n}$ to $A'_{up} \in \mathbb{R}^{k\times k}$, where $k = n * p$, p represents the proportion of nodes removed by SAGPooling. Next, we use a l-layer graph convolutional network(GCN_2) to transform the feature matrix from $X'_{up} \in \mathbb{R}^{k\times d}$ to $X_{up}^{(l)} \in \mathbb{R}^{k\times e}$,where e represents the dimensions of the feature vector after the l-th layer graph convolution(GCN_2) operation.

The structure of SAGPooling is show in Fig. 2, and its functionality can be expressed using Eq.(5):

$$\begin{aligned} y = \text{GCN}\big(X_{up}, \widetilde{A}\big), idx = \text{topk}(y), X_{up} = X_{up}[idx, :], \\ X'_{up} = X_{up} \odot \tanh(y), A'_{up} = \widetilde{A}(idx, idx) \end{aligned} \tag{5}$$

where y represents the scores for each node, idx represents the index of nodes selected after topk selection,$X_{up}[idx, :]$indicates that the nodes corresponding to idx are taken out to form a new matrix, that is, the mask operation, $\odot$ is

Hadamard product, and $X_{up}\odot\tanh(y)$ represents the element-wise multiplication of node features and the scores of the corresponding nodes after applying a nonlinear activation function. We then retain the top *idx* nodes to obtain X'_{up} and remove the edges connected to the removed nodes to obtain A'_{up}.

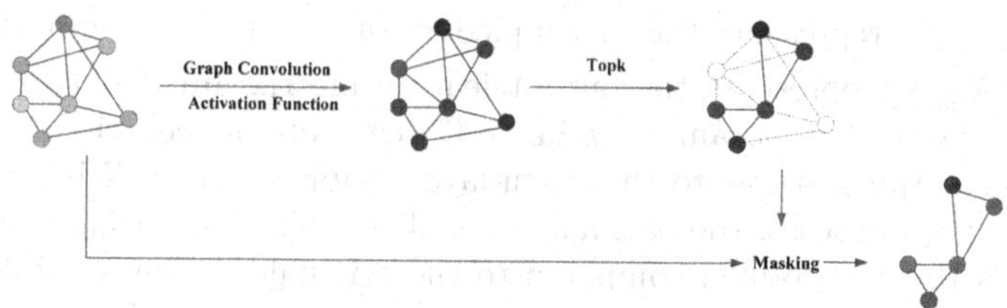

Fig. 2. Self-Attention Graph Pooling.

In the down-layer network, we directly employ the l-layer graph convolutional network(GCN_3) to transform the feature matrix from $X \in \mathbb{R}^{n\times m}$ to $X_{down}^{(l)} \in \mathbb{R}^{n\times e}$,where e represents the dimensions of the feature vector after the l-th layer graph convolution(GCN_3) operation. It is worth noting that the number of input nodes in the up-graph convolutional network(GCN_2) is smaller than that in the down-layer graph convolutional network(GCN_3). Therefore, the input channels of the up graph convolutional network(GCN_2) are smaller, but the output channels are the same.

Graph Unpooling and ReZero. To integrate feature information from graphs at different scales, we come up a method called graph unpooling and graph adaptive fusion. The concept of graph unpooling is to recover the lost nodes from the subgraphs after pooling, thereby restoring the pooled graph to the same structural size as before pooling, enabling the fusion of graphs at different scales. In this work, we employ a technique similar to Graph U-Net [4], where the preserved nodes retain their original features, the unavailable nodes are populated with zero vectors of matching dimensions. This process is represented by Eq.(6):

$$X_{unpooling} = \text{UnPooling}\left(0, X_{up}^{(l)}, \widetilde{idx}\right) \tag{6}$$

where $\widetilde{idx}$ represents the index of the node deleted in the aforementioned SAG-Pooling, $X_{up}^{(l)}$ denoted the result of the up-layer GCN_2, and $X_{unpooling}$ represents the upsampled feature matrix. The graph unpooling process effectively supplements the missing node information, thereby achieving maximum graph information integrity with minimal noise.

In classical hierarchical graph fusion methods, the feature information from different levels of graphs is simply concatenated. Despite its simplicity and efficiency, it fails to consider the varying contributions of graphs at different levels, which can significantly impact the final classification results. To address this issue, we draw inspiration from the residual connection module in ResNet [7] and propose to utilize ReZero [2] that enables the adaptive fusion of two graphs by introducing a learnable parameter η. This is formulated as Eq.(7):

$$X_{re} = X_{down}^{(l)} + \eta X_{unpooling} \tag{7}$$

where $X_{unpooling}$ represents the upsampled feature matrix in the up-layer network, and $X_{down}^{(l)}$ represents the output feature matrix after l-layers of GCN_3 in the down layer. The parameter η in Eq.(7) controls the contribution ratio of the up-layer graph features to the down-layer graph features. While the entire network training process, the optimal value of α is learned through backpropagation. This Rezero module, compared to the original residual module, adds a weight before the residual connection, so that the model can better accept the gradient signal and accelerate the convergence speed.

Global Pooling. In our work, the incorporation of graph pooling and unpooling enables effective feature learning from graphs across various scales. Nonetheless, previous research has indicated that diverse datasets may necessitate features from graphs at distinct scales to attain improved classification performance [12]. Unfortunately, existing single-scale graph pooling methods fail to meet this requirement. To ensure that our method performs well on different datasets, we propose a global pooling method to address this issue. We apply the Global Pooling module to the up-layer output $X_{up}^{(l)}$ and the down-layer after the ReZero connection X_{re} respectively, the global pooling includes three different pooling operations: MaxPooling, MeanPooling, and AddPooling. The outcomes of these operations are concatenated along a specific dimension to increase the feature dimension of the samples. Following that, a two-layer MLP network is utilized for data feature extraction. The process of global pooling is depicted in Eq.(8):

$$Z_i = \text{MLP}(\text{Concat}(\text{MaxPooling}(X_{out}), \text{MeanPooling}(X_{out}), \text{AddPooling}(X_{out}))) \tag{8}$$

where, in the global pooling module of the up-layer network, X_{out} is $X_{up}^{(l)}$ and the output is Z_1, in the global pooling model of the down-layer network, X_{out} is X_{re} and the output is Z_2. In this method, three different pooling methods, namely MaxPooling, MeanPooling, and AddPooling, are simultaneously applied. The pooling results are concatenated to obtain complementary graph feature information, which is then input into an MLP network for further extraction of each graph's feature representation.

Self-attention Feature Fusion and Classification. To perform classification, it is necessary to fuse the global pooling results from the up and down layers using a self-attention-based feature fusion method. As shown in Fig. 3, the global pooling feature vectors obtained from the up and down layers represent two different scales of graphs. Here, we first concatenate the global pooling results Z_1 and Z_2 and input them into a bias-free fully connected layer and two output channels to learn weights (α, β). The attention weights (α, β) are computed using the softmax function as specified in Eq.(9):

$$(\alpha, \beta) = \text{softmax}(W_a * \text{Concat}(Z_1, Z_2)) \tag{9}$$

where W_a is a trainable attention weight matrix, two matrices W_a and Concat(Z_1, Z_2) multiplied together. α and β are two scalars.

Then, the attention weights are multiplied element-wise with feature vectors and concatenated to obtain the fused feature vector, as shown in Eq.(10):

$$Z_{result} = \text{Concat}(\alpha * Z_1, \beta * Z_2) \tag{10}$$

Finally, the Z_{result} is passed through a connected layer, and we use the cross-entropy loss function to evaluate the classification performance. For the unlabeled samples, we assign labels based on the maximum softmax

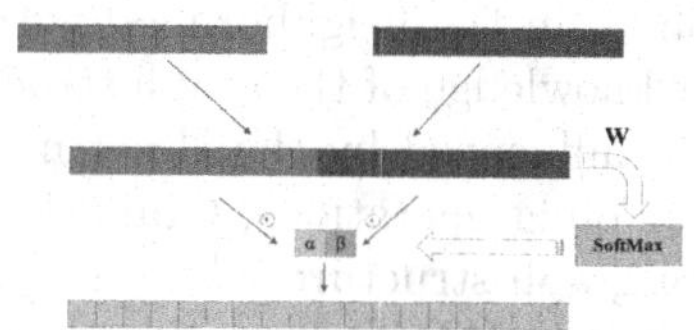

Fig. 3. Self-Attention Feature Fusion.

4 Experiments

4.1 Data Acquisition and Preprocessing

We utilized T1-weighted MRI images with a field strength of 1.5T from the ADNI dataset, which underwent preprocessing using SPM8 and DPABI toolboxes. Image preprocessing included non-brain tissue removal, motion and temporal correction, registration, filtering, smoothing, and segmentation. Using the AAL template, by segmenting the brain into 116 regions, we acquired the corresponding ROIs. Our study involved 1292 samples (338 AD, 422 MCI, 532 CN(control samples)), and classification performance was assessed on four datasets (AD vs CN, AD vs MCI, CN vs MCI, and AD vs MCI vs CN). The number of samples of four datasets is summarized in Table 1.

Table 1. The number of samples in the ADNI dataset.

Dataset	Samples	Dataset	Samples
AD-CN	338:532	CN-MCI	532:422
AD-MCI	338:422	AD-MCI-CN	338:422:532

4.2 Experimental Setup

Our experiment was completed on NVIDIA GeForce 3060 (12GB VRAM). The implementation utilized the PyTorch and PyTorch Geometric frameworks. We conducted multiple random tests on four distinct datasets and reported the average scores obtained from these tests.We adopt the method of stratified sampling to deal with the unbalance of data sets, which ensures the balance of samples in each category by drawing the same number of samples in each category. Our method was compared with baseline methods evaluation of all methods was based on three widely-used metrics: classification accuracy, recall, and F1 score. The following is a description of the comparison methods we used:

GCN [9] uses the graph's Laplacian matrix to integrate structural and feature information of central and neighboring nodes, providing a structured representation for efficient and accurate classification of irregular graph-structured data. GAT [18] is a GNN based on attention mechanisms, which aggregates neighborhood features for each node through stacked network layers. It assigns different weights to different nodes in the neighborhood without the need for costly matrix operations or prior knowledge of the graph structure. Graph U-Net [4] is an encoder-decoder model, influenced by the U-net model in CNNs. By utilizing TopK pooling and unpooling operations, Graph U-Net effectively ex-tracts and recovers features from graph-structured data, suitable for graph data classification and recognition tasks. SAGPooling [10], an end-to-end graph pooling method, employs self-attention mechanisms and graph convolutions to compute attention scores, considering node features and graph topology. By dynamically selecting representative nodes, it preserves structural information, enhancing graph neural network performance and achieving excellent results in classification and generation tasks. Dir-GNN [16] is a novel and versatile framework for deep learning on graphs. It extends the capabilities of Message Passing Neural Networks by incorporating edge directionality information. Dir-GNN achieves this by performing separate aggregations of incoming and outgoing edges.

Table 2. The Classification Performance on AD vs CN and CN vs MCI Datasets.

Method	AD vs CN			CN vs MCI		
	Accuracy	Recall	F1-score	Accuracy	Recall	F1-score
SVM	0.6144	0.6144	0.6145	0.5545	0.5545	0.5546
ResNet	0.6153	0.741	0.7272	0.7428	0.4285	0.5714
GAT	0.8007	0.6637	0.7133	0.6998	0.6950	0.6878
GCN	0.8295	0.7258	0.7550	0.6162	0.5855	0.5864
Graph U-Net	0.8218	0.7287	0.7556	0.7029	0.7093	0.7075
SAGPooling	0.8383	**0.8407**	0.8371	0.7361	0.7361	0.7340
DirGNN	0.8528	0.8300	0.8229	0.7371	0.7612	0.7489
Our	**0.8606**	0.7512	**0.8433**	**0.7638**	**0.7638**	**0.7756**

Table 3. The Classification Performance on AD vs MCI and AD vs MCI vs CN Datasets.

Method	AD vs MCI			AD vs MCI vs CN		
	Accuracy	Recall	F1-score	Accuracy	Recall	F1-score
SVM	0.5625	0.5625	0.5620	0.4076	0.3333	0.5787
ResNet	0.6538	0.2500	0.4000	0.6400	0.6400	0.6186
GAT	0.6360	0.5855	0.5190	0.5517	0.5379	0.4836
GCN	0.6162	0.5855	0.5864	0.5995	0.5707	0.5621
Graph U-Net	0.6447	0.5846	0.5247	0.6098	0.5599	0.5063
SAGPooling	0.6542	0.6542	0.6514	0.6102	0.6102	**0.6514**
DirGNN	0.5947	0.5997	0.6427	0.6403	0.6059	0.6004
Our	**0.6990**	**0.6990**	**0.6921**	**0.6500**	**0.6500**	0.5839

Table 4. The Classification Performance on AD vs CN and CN vs MCI Datasets.

Ablation	AD vs CN	CN vs MCI	AD vs MCI	AD vs MCI vs CN
No GlobalPooling	0.8407	0.7361	0.6766	0.6384
No SVD	0.8383	0.7420	0.6616	0.6451
Our	**0.8606**	**0.7638**	**0.6990**	**0.6500**

4.3 Hyperparameter Settings

We optimized hyperparameters for each method based on the literature. For our method, we set batch size to 128,epochs to 500, learning rate to 0.001, using Adam optimizer, cross-entropy loss, GCN layers l to 2, kernel value σ to 2.5,$\rho(\cdot)$ to Euclidean distance function, adjacency matrix threshold γ to 10^{-3}. Maximum retained singular values q were set to 10. SAGPooling ratio p was set to 0.8. In four sets of experiments, we divided the dataset using 7:1:2.

4.4 Analysis of Experimental Results

The results are shown in Table 2 and Table 3. Our method achieves excellent results in classifying between AD and CN, we achieved a high accuracy rate of 0.8606, and in the most challenging task of classifying AD vs. MCI vs. CN, our method still reached the highest accuracy of 0.65. Meanwhile, SAGPooling exhibits relatively high performance in some experiments, such as with an accuracy of 0.7361 in the classification between CN and MCI. Across all experiments, our method consistently achieves superior results in accuracy and F1-score compared to other approaches. The extracted features from the model were reduced to two dimensions using t-SNE and visualized in Fig. 4. In the figure, the individual points represent the samples, with each class denoted by a different color. Demonstrating the remarkable performance of our approach in enhancing the diagnostic accuracy for Alzheimer's disease. Removing the SVD method and

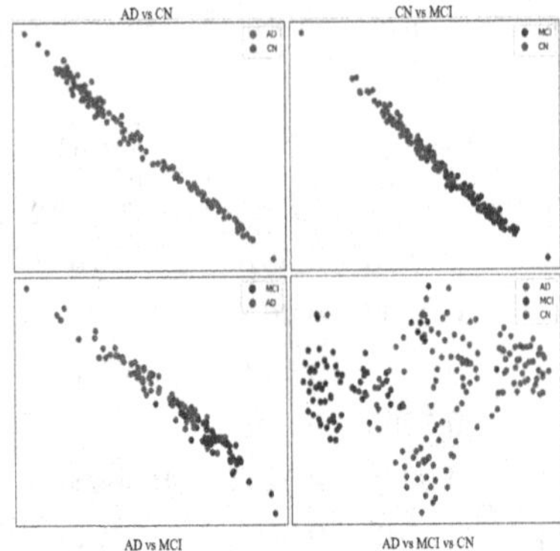

Fig. 4. Visual presentation of model extraction features.

global pooling model from the original model had a significant impact on its performance, as evident from the results in Table 4, highlighting their overall beneficial contribution.

5 Conclusion

This study proposes a novel hierarchical pooling convolutional graph classification method aimed at improving the diagnostic performance of Alzheimer's dis-ease based on magnetic resonance imaging (MRI). By extracting and fusing features of brain region nodes, combining global pooling and multi-scale feature fusion techniques, it ultimately achieves the diagnostic classification of Alzheimer's disease. The proposed model architecture exhibits outstanding classification performance on Several different datasets when compared to advanced methods. It should be indicated that this study only utilizes MRI as the medical data, which may limit the model's representational capacity and impact its performance. Future research will explore the classification performance of multi-view medical data, such as PET,fMRI, and DTI.

References

1. Abuhmed, T., El-Sappagh, S., Alonso, J.M.: Robust hybrid deep learning models for alzheimer's progression detection. Knowl.-Based Syst. **213**, 106688 (2021)
2. Bachlechner, T., Majumder, B.P., Mao, H., Cottrell, G., McAuley, J.: Rezero is all you need: fast convergence at large depth. In: Uncertainty in Artificial Intelligence. pp. 1352–1361. PMLR (2021)
3. Frisoni, G.B., Fox, N.C., Jack, C.R., Jr., Scheltens, P., Thompson, P.M.: The clinical use of structural mri in alzheimer disease. Nat. Rev. Neurol. **6**(2), 67–77 (2010)
4. Gao, H., Ji, S.: Graph U-Nets. In: International Conference on Machine Learning, pp. 2083–2092. PMLR (2019)
5. Joseph, G., Bryan, J., Tricia, J., Allison, M., Jennifer., W.: 2021 alzheimer's disease facts and figures. Alzheimer's Dementia. J. Alzheimer's Assoc. (15–3) (2019)

6. Gori, M., Monfardini, G., Scarselli, F.: A new model for learning in graph domains. In: Proceedings, 2005 IEEE International Joint Conference on Neural Networks, vol. 2, pp. 729–734. IEEE (2005)
7. He, K., Zhang, X., Ren, S., Sun, J.: Deep residual learning for image recognition. In: Proceedings of the IEEE Conference on Computer Vision and Pattern Recognition, pp. 770–778 (2016)
8. Kanada, T., Onuki, M., Tanaka, Y.: Low-rank sparse decomposition of graph adjacency matrices for extracting clean clusters. In: 2018 Asia-Pacific Signal and Information Processing Association Annual Summit and Conference (APSIPA ASC), pp. 1153–1159. IEEE (2018)
9. Kipf, T.N., Welling, M.: Semi-supervised classification with graph convolutional networks. arXiv preprint arXiv:1609.02907 (2016)
10. Lee, J., Lee, I., Kang, J.: Self-attention graph pooling. In: International conference on machine learning, pp. 3734–3743. PMLR (2019)
11. Lian, C., Liu, M., Wang, L., Shen, D.: End-to-End Dementia Status Prediction from Brain MRI Using Multi-task Weakly-Supervised Attention Network. In: Shen, D., Liu, T., Peters, T.M., Staib, L.H., Essert, C., Zhou, S., Yap, P.-T., Khan, A. (eds.) MICCAI 2019. LNCS, vol. 11767, pp. 158–167. Springer, Cham (2019). https://doi.org/10.1007/978-3-030-32251-9_18
12. Lin, L., Gao, Y., Gong, K., Wang, M., Liang, X.: Graphonomy: universal image parsing via graph reasoning and transfer. IEEE Trans. Pattern Anal. Mach. Intell. **44**(5), 2504–2518 (2020)
13. Liu, C., et al.: Graph pooling for graph neural networks: Progress, challenges, and opportunities. arXiv preprint arXiv:2204.07321 (2022)
14. Liu, M., et al.: A multi-model deep convolutional neural network for automatic hippocampus segmentation and classification in alzheimer's disease. Neuroimage **208**, 116459 (2020)
15. Ortega, A., Frossard, P., Kovačević, J., Moura, J.M., Vandergheynst, P.: Graph signal processing: Overview, challenges, and applications. Proc. IEEE **106**(5), 808–828 (2018)
16. Rossi, E., Charpentier, B., Giovanni, F.D., Frasca, F., Günnemann, S., Bronstein, M.: Edge directionality improves learning on heterophilic graphs (2023)
17. Tiwari, S., Atluri, V., Kaushik, A., Yndart, A., Nair, M.: Alzheimer's disease: pathogenesis, diagnostics, and therapeutics. Int. J. Nanomed. 5541–5554 (2019)
18. Veličković, P., Cucurull, G., Casanova, A., Romero, A., Lio, P., Bengio, Y.: Graph attention networks. arXiv preprint arXiv:1710.10903 (2017)
19. Wang, Y., Wang, W., Liang, Y., Cai, Y., Hooi, B.: CurGraph: curriculum learning for graph classification. In: Proceedings of the Web Conference 2021, pp. 1238–1248 (2021)
20. Ying, R., He, R., Chen, K., Eksombatchai, P., Hamilton, W.L., Leskovec, J.: Graph convolutional neural networks for web-scale recommender systems. In: Proceedings of the 24th ACM SIGKDD International Conference on Knowledge Discovery & Data Mining, pp. 974–983 (2018)
21. Zhu, X., Suk, H.-I., Zhu, Y., Thung, K.-H., Wu, G., Shen, D.: Multi-view Classification for Identification of Alzheimer's Disease. In: Zhou, L., Wang, L., Wang, Q., Shi, Y. (eds.) MLMI 2015. LNCS, vol. 9352, pp. 255–262. Springer, Cham (2015). https://doi.org/10.1007/978-3-319-24888-2_31

Learning Cross-Modal Factors from Multimodal Physiological Signals for Emotion Recognition

Yuichi Ishikawa[1(✉)], Nao Kobayashi[2], Yasushi Naruse[3], Yugo Nakamura[1], Shigemi Ishida[4], Tsunenori Mine[1], and Yutaka Arakawa[1]

[1] Kyushu University, Fukuoka, Japan
ishikawa_yuichi@yahoo.co.jp
[2] KDDI Research Inc., Saitama, Japan
[3] Center for Information and Neural Networks (CiNet), National Institute of Information and Communications Technology, Hyougo, Japan
[4] Future University Hakodate, Hokkaido, Japan

Abstract. Understanding user emotion is essential for Human-AI Interaction (HAI). Thus far, many approaches have been studied to recognize emotion from signals of various physiological modalities such as cardiac activity and skin conductance. However, little attention has been paid to the fact that physiological signals are influenced by and reflect various factors that have little or no association with emotion. While emotion is a cross-modal factor that triggers responses across multiple physiological modalities, features used in existing approaches also reflect modality-specific factors that affect only a single modality and have little association with emotion. To address this, we propose an approach to extract features that exclusively reflect cross-modal factors from multimodal physiological signals. Our approach introduces a multilayer RNN with two types of layers: multiple *Modality-Specific Layers* (*MSL*s) for modeling physiological activity in individual modalities and a single *Cross-Modal Layer* (*CML*) for modeling the process by which emotion affects physiological activity. By having all MSLs update their hidden states using the CML hidden states, our RNN causes the CML to learn cross-modal factors. Using real physiological signals, we confirmed that the features extracted by our RNN reflected emotions to a significantly greater extent than the features of existing approaches.

Keywords: EEG · ECG · GSR · LSTM · Multilayer RNN

1 Introduction

Understanding user emotions is extremely important for various human-AI interaction (HAI) scenarios including goal and non-goal oriented dialogue [6,8], user-adapted content creation [1], and content recommendation [2]. While most researchers collect ground truth of emotions by explicitly asking users what their

F. Liu et al. (Eds.): PRICAI 2023, LNAI 14325, pp. 438–450, 2024.
https://doi.org/10.1007/978-981-99-7019-3_40

emotions are, it is impractical to do so in real-world scenarios because doing so interferes with users and degrades the user experience. Therefore, there has been a great demand for recognizing user emotions from data that users generate.

Among various types of user-generated data, we focus on users' physiological signals such as electroencephalogram (EEG), electrocardiogram (ECG), and galvanic skin response (GSR). Using wearable devices (e.g., watches, earphones), these signals can be collected in a less constrained context compared to other types of data such as texts, vocal tone, and facial expressions, which are available only when users write or say something or stay in front of a camera. In addition, unlike these data, physiological signals provide robust signs of emotion even when users exhibit their social masks to hide their true emotions [3].

Thus far, researchers have studied many approaches to recognize emotion from physiological signals and have confirmed their significant utility for emotion recognition [6]. However, little attention has been paid to the fact that physiological signals are influenced not only by emotion but also by various factors that have little or no association with emotion. Among them are factors that influence only a single physiological modality, i.e., a modality-specific factors. For example, heart muscle strength influences ECG signals, but has little influence on modalities other than cardiac activity such as brain activity and skin conductance. In contrast, emotion is a cross-modal factor, which triggers responses across multiple physiological modalities, e.g., anger increases heart rate and skin conductance level. Others are long-term factors such as body size and gender. These factors also influence physiological activity, but they are very different from emotion in a sense that they change very slowly or do not change, whereas emotion changes over short periods of time, i.e., a short-term factor.

As such, while emotion is a cross-modal and short-term factor, physiological signals are also influenced by and reflect factors that are modality-specific and/or long-term. Although they have little utility for emotion recognition, existing approaches extract and use features without distinguishing these factors, instead mixing them into the features. We posit this has degraded emotion recognition.

In light of the above, we propose an approach to extract features that exclusively reflect cross-modal and short-term factors. To achieve this, our approach distinguishes factors reflected in physiological signals along two axes: long- or short-term and modality-specific or cross-modal, and learns four types of factors that are distinct from each other. By adopting RNN, our approach separately models long- and short-term factors.

What is novel is that to model modality-specific and cross-modal factors, we introduce a multilayer RNN that consists of two types of layers: multiple *Modality-Specific Layers* (*MSL*s) that model physiological activity in individual modalities; and a single *Cross-Modal Layer* (*CML*) that learns cross-modal factors, among which is emotion. Our RNN takes sequences of multimodal physiological signals as input (e.g., ECG and GSR signals). Each MSL takes physiological signals of its corresponding modality (e.g., MSL1 takes ECG signals, MSL2 takes GSR signals) and reflects physiological states in its hidden state. When updating the hidden state, the MSL uses not only its own hidden state but also the CML's hidden state. Since this is done in all the MSLs, it makes the CML's hidden state affect physiological state in all the modalities the MSLs correspond to. In effect, therefore, this enables the CML to learn factors that affect physiological activities across multiple modalities, i.e., cross-modal factors.

To evaluate our approach, we recruited participants and measured their EEG, ECG, and GSR signals while presenting them with musical pieces and movie clips (i.e., stimuli). We trained our RNN by these signals and, using the CML's hidden states, evaluated how accurately we could recognize emotions that the participants reported after each stimulus.

Our main contributions are as follows. 1) We propose a multilayer RNN that separates the RNN layer to learn factors that affect physiological activities across multiple modalities from the other layers designated to model modality-specific physiological activities. This enables our approach to extract features that exclusively reflect a cross-modal nature of emotion, which existing research has not focused on. 2) Using real physiological data, we demonstrate our RNN extracts features that reflect emotion to a greater extent than existing approaches.

2 Related Work

Similar to our approach, many existing approaches recognize emotion from multimodal physiological signals. Subramanian et al. [11] and Miranda et al. [7] used ECG, GSR, and EEG signals. Using feature extraction techniques that are widely used for each modality, they extracted features from each modality (*physiological features*; e.g., standard deviation of heartbeat intervals from ECG signals, mean skin conductance level from GSR signals). They then concatenated these physiological features and fed them into a classifier (i.e., early fusion). However, modality-specific factors reflected in the physiological features could not be removed by simple concatenation, thus limiting recognition accuracy. In addition, short- and long-term factors were not distinguished in the features. While they also tested late fusion, in which they combined recognition results in individual modalities to derive final results, the same issues remained because they used the same physiological features as in the early fusion, whose modality-specific factors hindered emotion recognition in each modality.

There are also multimodal approaches that adopt deep learning techniques. However, they have the same issues. Liu et al. [5] and Yin et al. [12] used deep autoencoders to learn shared representations of physiological features of multiple modalities (e.g., EEG and Electrooculogram) and recognized emotions by feeding the shared representations into classifiers. They trained the autoencoders so that the physiological features of each modality could be reproduced from the shared representations. This made the shared representations reflect not only cross-modal factors but also modality-specific factors. In addition, the use of the autoencoders did not help to distinguish between short- and long-term factors.

On the other hand, the approach proposed by Li et al. [4] can extract features that exclusively reflect short-term factors. Using the dataset built in [7], they fed time-series sequences of physiological features into LSTM, whose hidden states were then fed into an attention network. These steps enabled them to focus on

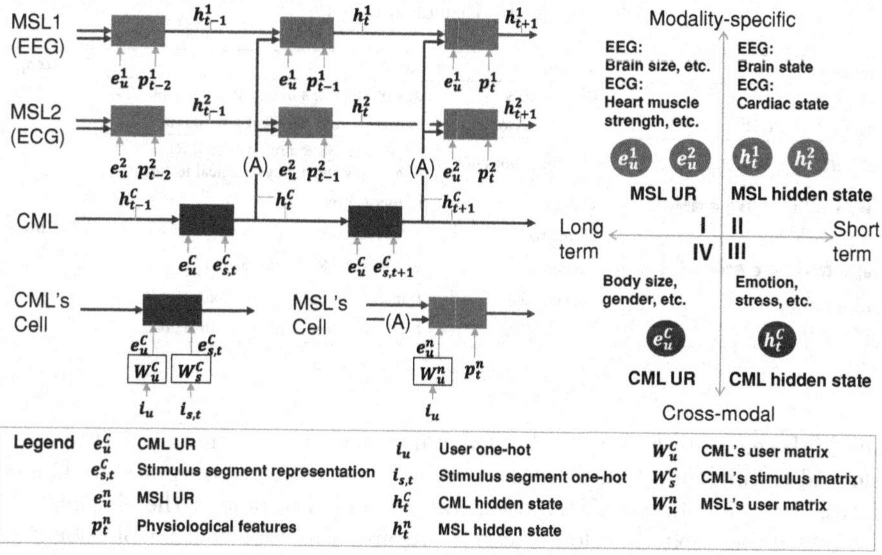

Fig. 1. An example of our multi-layered LSTM.

emotionally salient parts of the sequences, from which they extracted the hidden states and fed them into a multilayer perceptron (MLP) to recognize emotions. However, they performed these steps in each physiological modality and derived final results by combining the results of individual modalities (i.e., late fusion). Therefore, as in [7,11], emotion recognition in individual modalities was hindered by modality-specific factors, which also degraded the final recognition results.

3 Proposed Approach

In contrast to the existing approaches, our RNN explicitly distinguishes the four types of factors that influence physiological activity. Figure 1 exemplifies our RNN (left) and shows how the four types, I–IV, are mapped to its variables (right). Modality-specific factors, I and II, are modeled by the MSLs. Each MSL corresponds to a single modality, e.g., MSL1 to EEG, MSL2 to ECG. It takes sequences of 1) physiological features of the corresponding modality, which are extracted in the same way as existing approaches (e.g., [7,11]), and 2) one-hot vectors of user ID, by which a user representation (UR) is retrieved from the user matrix. Since the physiological features fed to the MSL are limited to the corresponding modality, its URs and hidden states reflect factors specific to this modality (I and II). In addition, while the hidden states are updated sequentially, the user matrix (set of URs) stays the same. This causes the MSL URs to reflect long-term factors (I) and its hidden states to reflect short-term factors (II).

On the other hand, cross-modal factors, III and IV, are modeled by the CML. As shown by link (A) in the figure, the CML sends its hidden states to the MSLs.

Table 1. List of notations

Notation	Meaning	Subscript	Superscript
N_u, N_s	# of users/SS	u: # of users, s: # of stimulus segments (SS)	-
$\boldsymbol{i}_u \in \mathbb{R}^{N_u}, \boldsymbol{i}_{s,t} \in \mathbb{R}^{N_s}$	One hot vector of …	u: user ID, s, t: SS ID of t-th action	
$d^C_{\mathrm{ue}}, d^n_{\mathrm{ue}}, d^C_{\mathrm{se}}, d^C_h, d^n_h, d^n_p$	# of dimensions of …	ue: UR, se: SS Representation (SR), h: hidden state, p: physiological features	
$\boldsymbol{W}^C_u \in \mathbb{R}^{d^C_{\mathrm{ue}} \times N_u}$, $\boldsymbol{W}^n_u \in \mathbb{R}^{d^n_{\mathrm{ue}} \times N_u}$	User matrix	u: user matrix	
$\boldsymbol{W}^C_s \in \mathbb{R}^{d^C_{\mathrm{se}} \times N_s}$	SS matrix	s: SS matrix	C: CML n: MSL n
$\boldsymbol{e}^C_u \in \mathbb{R}^{d^C_{\mathrm{ue}}}$, $\boldsymbol{e}^n_u \in \mathbb{R}^{d^n_{\mathrm{ue}}}$, $\boldsymbol{e}^C_{s,t} \in \mathbb{R}^{d^C_{\mathrm{se}}}$	UR/SR	u: UR, s, t: SR of t-th action	
$\boldsymbol{h}^C_t \in \mathbb{R}^{d^C_h}, \boldsymbol{h}^n_t \in \mathbb{R}^{d^n_h}$	Hidden state	t: hidden state after t-th action	
$\boldsymbol{p}^n_t \in \mathbb{R}^{d^n_p}$	Physiological features	t: physiological features in t-th action	

The MSL cell uses these CML hidden states together with its input (the physiological features and URs) and its previous hidden states to update its hidden states. Because updated MSL hidden states are used to predict the physiological features at the next timeslot, it can be regarded as representing physiological state. Updating such MSL hidden states using the CML hidden states means that the CML hidden states affect physiological activity of individual modalities. Because all the MSLs update their hidden states in this way, the CML learns factors that affect physiological activity across multiple modalities, i.e., cross-modal factors (III and IV). As in the MSL, the CML also reflect short-term factors (III) in its hidden states and long-term factors (IV) in its URs, but the difference being they are cross-modal.

In addition to modeling I∼IV, our RNN also models the process by which individual physiological differences moderate the relationship between emotion and physiological activity. For example, users with different heart muscle strength would have different ECG signals even when their emotions are the same. Our RNN models such moderating effect of individual differences by updating the MSL hidden states (reflecting physiological state) using both the CML hidden states (emotion) and the MSL URs (individual differences, e.g., heart muscle strength). This also differentiates our RNN from the existing approaches discussed in Section 2, all of which do not consider this moderating effect.

The next section describes in detail the hidden state updating in our RNN and its training process. See Table 1 for the notations and their descriptions.

3.1 Updating the Hidden States

Input to the CML and MSL are formatted as

$$\mathrm{CML}: \; data^C_a = [x^C_{a,1}, x^C_{a,2}, ..., x^C_{a,t}, ..., x^C_{a,T}] \text{ and} \tag{1}$$

$$\mathrm{MSL}\ n: \; data^n_a = [x^n_{a,1}, x^n_{a,2}, ..., x^n_{a,t}, ..., x^n_{a,T}], \tag{2}$$

where $x^C_{a,t} = (\boldsymbol{i}_u, \boldsymbol{i}_{s,t})$ denotes user a's t-th action (e.g., viewed t-th segment of a movie clip M); and $x^n_{a,t} = (\boldsymbol{i}_u, \boldsymbol{p}^n_t)$ denotes his physiological features extracted from signals during t-th action. Once $x^C_{a,t}$ is input to the CML, it first retrieves a UR and stimulus segment (SS) representation (SR) from the user and SS matrices, i.e., $\boldsymbol{e}^C_u = \boldsymbol{W}^C_u \boldsymbol{i}_u$ and $\boldsymbol{e}^C_{s,t} = \boldsymbol{W}^C_s \boldsymbol{i}_{s,t}$, respectively. It then updates its hidden state $\boldsymbol{h}^C_t$ as follows:

$$\boldsymbol{h}^C_t = f^C(\, \boldsymbol{h}^C_{t-1},\, \boldsymbol{e}^C_u,\, \boldsymbol{e}^C_{s,t}\,), \tag{3}$$

where f^C is a function implemented by LSTM. See the supplementary material at https://osf.io/mj3nr/ for detail.

After updating the hidden state, the CML sends it to all MSLs via link (A), which is done every time the CML updates its hidden state. When the MSL receives $\boldsymbol{h}^C_t$, it retrieves a UR from its user matrix ($\boldsymbol{e}^n_u = \boldsymbol{W}^n_u \boldsymbol{i}_u$) and uses them together with input physiological features ($\boldsymbol{p}^n_{t-1}$) to update its hidden state $\boldsymbol{h}^n_t$ as follows:

$$\boldsymbol{h}^n_t = f^n(\, \boldsymbol{h}^n_{t-1},\, \boldsymbol{h}^C_t,\, \boldsymbol{e}^n_u,\, \boldsymbol{p}^n_{t-1}), \tag{4}$$

where f^n is a function implemented by LSTM (see the supplementary material).

3.2 Model Training

When $data^n_a$ is fed, each MSL predicts physiological features in each timeslot, e.g., if the input is $data^n_a = [x^n_{a,t}, x^n_{a,t+1}, ..., x^n_{a,T-1}]$, the output is $[\hat{\boldsymbol{p}}^n_{t+1}, \hat{\boldsymbol{p}}^n_{t+2}, ..., \hat{\boldsymbol{p}}^n_T]$. The predicted physiological features are compared with the actual features to calculate the loss that is used to learn the parameters of the MSL and CML cells and the user and SS matrices ($\boldsymbol{W}^n_u$, $\boldsymbol{W}^C_u$, and $\boldsymbol{W}^C_s$). Figure 2 shows how the prediction and loss calculation are performed. The MSL predicts physiological features using its hidden state as follows: $\hat{\boldsymbol{p}}^n_{t+1} = f^n_{\text{MLP}}(\boldsymbol{h}^n_{t+1})$, where f^n_{MLP} is an MLP with ReLu activation. Then, the MSL calculates the residual sum of squares between actual and predicted physiological features as the loss.

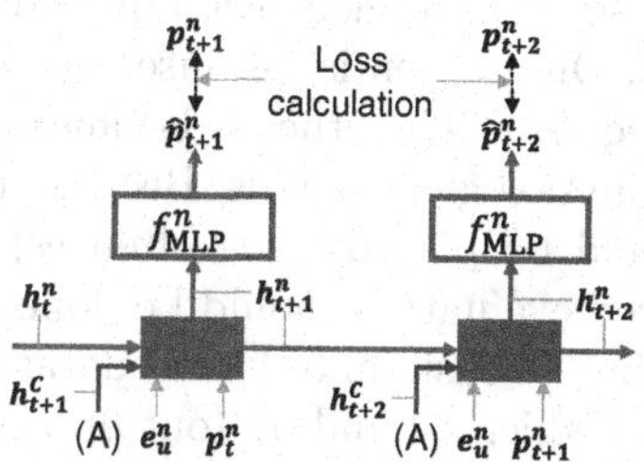

Fig. 2. Loss calculation

4 Experiment

We built datasets and evaluated the extent to which the CML hidden states reflect emotion. We performed the following three steps: (1) Feature extraction - from the physiological features stored in our datasets, we extracted another set of features for emotion recognition (*emotion features*). In our RNN, the CML hidden states were used as the emotion features; (2) feature selection - we then performed LASSO regression to select the emotion features; and (3) linear regression - using the selected emotion features, we built models to predict emotions and evaluated their model fit and prediction accuracy.

We performed (1)–(3) for our RNN and three approaches to compare. The first approach, which was implemented following [7,11], did not distinguish between the four types of factors at all when extracting the emotion features (hereafter "baseline"). The second one distinguished between long and short-term factors but not between cross-modal and modality-specific factors as in [4]; and the third one distinguished the four types of factors, but did not model the moderating effect of individual physiological differences. The last two were implemented by removing key features from our RNN (will be explained in 4.4 Ablation Study).

We built two different datasets and performed (1)-(3) for each dataset. In addition, because combinations of physiological modalities available in real-world scenario would be different depending on the devices users wear, we performed (1)-(3) for all possible modality combinations available in our datasets. That is, A) EEG+ECG+GSR, B) EEG+ECG, C) EEG+GSR, and D) ECG+GSR.

4.1 Dataset

Due to page limitations, only a brief summary of the datasets is described below. See the supplementary material (https://osf.io/mj3nr/) for detail. Although several datasets are publicly available today (e.g., [7,11]), we built and used our own datasets. One reason is because the contacts of these datasets did not respond to our requests. The other is because they used only videos as stimuli when collecting physiological signals. Because music is another popular type of stimulus that would be played more often especially while working, studying, etc., we considered evaluation should be done for both music and video.

We built Music and Movie datasets by conducting data collection experiments, in which 54 and 52 (out of 54) subjects participated, respectively. They were presented with multiple stimuli, each of which was 60 s long, while their EEG, ECG, and GSR signals were measured. In total, 2,336 and 2,119 trials were performed for the music and movie datasets, respectively (one trial denotes one subject listening to/viewing one stimulus). After listening to/viewing each stimulus, they reported emotions according to the six dimensions whose scores ranged 0–15, (a) sad-happy, (b) nervous-relaxed, (c) fear-relieved, (d) lethargic-excited, (e) depressed-delighted, and (f) angry-serene. Although Russel's circumplex model [10] has been widely used to determine emotion, we did not use it because it is not easy for lay participants to report "arousal" and "valence" defined in the model. We selected the six dimensions so that the participants can easily report their emotions and the dimensions cover the Russel's circumplex as much as possible.

After collecting the physiological signals, we extracted the physiological features from the raw signals by feature extraction techniques that are widely used for each modality as in [7,11]. We extracted two types of features: window and stimulus features, which are summarized in Table 2. For the window features, we applied sliding window to the raw signals measured during one stimulus and extracted features from each window. We set the window size to ten seconds and used two different slide sizes, three and five seconds. That is, we had 17 and 11 windows for each stimulus, respectively. The stimulus features were extracted from entire signals measured during a stimulus. We stored the physiological features in the datasets after performing z-standardization for each dimension.

Table 2. Physiological features. Bold numbers denote dimension.

Modality	Window features	Stimulus features
EEG	**29**: Power within individual frequency bands ($\delta, \theta, \alpha, \beta$) and composite score ($S$) at each electrode; power asymmetricity of individual frequency bands for one pair of electrodes	**116**: Statistics (mean, min, max, and standard deviation) of 29 window features
ECG	**7**: SDNN, pNN50, RMSSD, and HR statistics (mean, min, max, and standard deviation)	**10**: SDNN, pNN50, RMSSD, and HR statistics (mean, min, max, and standard deviation) and power within HF, LF and power ratio (HF/LF)
GSR	**8**: SCL related features (slope, mean) and SCR related features (peak, skew, kurtosis, max, min, mean)	**11**: SCL related features (slope and mean) and SCR related features (the number of peaks, max and min of peaks, skew, kurtosis, max, min, and mean)

SDNN: Standard Deviation of Normal-to-Normal intervals, pNN50: The proportion of NN50 divided by the total number of NN intervals, RMSSD: Root Mean Square of the Successive Differences, HR: Hear Rate, HF/LF: High/Low Frequency, SCL: Skin Conductance Level, SCR: Skin Conductance Response

4.2 Step1 - Extraction of Emotion Features

Proposed Approach. Of the two types of the physiological features, we used the window features as the input to our RNN. That is, an input sequence to the CML and MSL n ($data_a^C$ and $data_a^n$) corresponds to a trial. An element of $data_a^C$ (i.e., $\boldsymbol{i}_{s,t}$) and $data_a^n$ (i.e., $\boldsymbol{p}_t^n$) correspond to t-th window of a stimulus and the physiological features extracted from the raw signals in t-th window of the stimulus, respectively. The total number of input sequences was equal to the number of trials, out of which 80% were used for training and 20% for validation. We did not use the stimulus features because $\boldsymbol{i}_{s,t}$ corresponds to a stimulus if we do so and thus the number of input sequences, which is equal to the number of participants, was too small for training our RNN.

The hyper parameters were as follows: slide size of the sliding window = [3sec, 5sec], learning rate = $[5 \times 10^{-4}, 1 \times 10^{-3}]$, dimension of hidden layers of the MSL's MLP (i.e., f_{MLP}^n) = $[(16, 8), (32, 16)]$ (from input to output layer), batch size = $[16, 32]$, and dimension of UR, SR, and hidden state of the CML and MSL = $[8, 16]$. For all possible combinations of the hyper parameters, we conducted training and validation for 100 epochs and extracted the CML hidden states of the validation samples when we observed the minimum validation loss. We repeated this changing training and validation samples so that we could obtain the CML hidden states for all trials. Because the prediction target is emotion after each trial, we used the last CML hidden state of each trial as the emotion features, i.e., if the last element of $data_a^C$ was $\boldsymbol{i}_{s,T}$, we used $\boldsymbol{h}_T^C$.

Baseline. Following [7,11], we first concatenated the physiological features across modalities. This was done for both the stimulus and window features. For example, if the modality combination was A) EEG+ECG+GSR, we built

137 (116 + 10 + 11) dimension features from the stimulus features and 748 $((29+7+8) \times 17)$ dimension features from the window features (if there are 17 windows in a stimulus) for each trial. We then reduced their dimension by performing PCA and extracted top n features in terms of their contribution ratio so that their cumulative contribution ratio is maximum below a threshold. We used these features as the emotion features. We set three different thresholds, 0.85, 0.90, and 0.95. In the following, S and W denote the emotion features extracted from the stimulus and window features, respectively. Because Miranda et al. [7] reported that recognition by unimodal features outperformed multimodal features, we also extracted S and W for each physiological modality.

4.3 Step 2 and 3 - Feature Selection and Linear Regression

After extracting the emotion features, we performed feature selection and linear regression. These were done for each of the six emotion dimensions.

We performed the feature selection because dimension of the emotion features of the baseline was large relative to the sample size (i.e., the number of trials). For fair comparison, this was done for both the baseline and our approach. We first finetuned the LASSO parameter λ, which controls the strength of the imposed regularization based on the number of selected features. Over a set of λ values, we sought the value that output the most accurate prediction (i.e., minimum mean squared error between the actual and predicted emotion scores) performing five-fold cross-validation multiple times. Second, we conducted the LASSO regression again using the value of λ determined in the previous step and selected features for which the regression coefficients were not zero.

After the feature selection, we performed two types of linear regression. One is model fit evaluation using all samples. The other is prediction evaluation by performing five-fold cross validation.

4.4 Ablation Study

To determine the effectiveness of the key features of our RNN, we evaluated its variants without the key features, which are shown in Fig. 3. One is a single layer RNN (AB1) that takes concatenated multimodal physiological features ($\boldsymbol{p}_{s,t}$ in the figure) as input and the other is a multilayer RNN without the MSL URs (AB2). We extracted their hidden states (the CML hidden states in AB2) as the emotion features and evaluated them in the same way as our RNN.

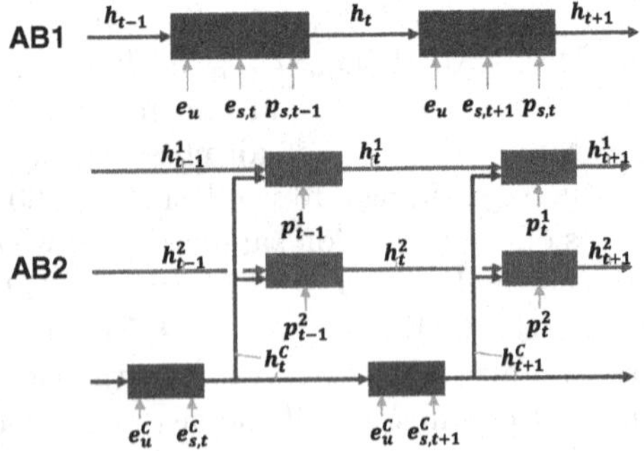

Fig. 3. Variants for ablation study.

Similar to [4], while AB1 can extract emotion features that exclusively reflect short-term factors, it cannot distinguish between modality-specific and cross-modal factors, mixing both into the features. While the emotion features of AB2 would exclusively reflect short-term and cross-modal factors, the MSL in AB2 cannot model the moderating effect of individual physiological differences due to lack of the MSL URs.

Table 3. Emotion recognition results. A–D represent the modality combinations (ref. section 4). Shaded cells denote results inferior to our RNN (ours) in the same columns. Cells with hatched lines indicate that LASSO selected no emotion feature. Black cells denote the best results for the emotion dimensions. For the baseline, BL and U-BL, the table shows the best results of the three PCA thresholds. U-BL uses a single physiological modality in BL and the table shows the result of the best modality in a corresponding combination (e.g., U-BL in column B show better of EEG and ECG).

		(a) sad-happy				(b) nervous-relaxed				(c) fear-relieved				(d) lethargic-excited				(e) depressed-delighted				(f) angry-serene			
		A	B	C	D	A	B	C	D	A	B	C	D	A	B	C	D	A	B	C	D	A	B	C	D
Results of Music dataset (n=2,336)																									
AIC ↓	BL(S)	11231	11235	11235	11234	11495	11501	11495	11503	11145	11145	11145	11162	11553	11553	11554	11544	12205	12205	12205		10416	10426	10408	10430
	BL(W)	11235			11234		11503	11503	11505	11150	11150	11151		11521	11547	11533	11534	12191	12206	12181	12201	10414	10420		10426
	U-BL(S)	11237	11237	11237	11237	11499	11499	11499	11503	11145	11145	11145	11160	11551	11551	11554	11551	12205	12205	12205	12211	10415	10415	10415	10428
	U-BL(W)	11234	11236	11234	11234	11503	11503	11503	11504	11151	11151	11151	11154	11543	11549	11543	11543	12198	12201	12198	12198	10416	10416	10416	10426
	AB1	11197	11128	11160	11206	11486	11439	11474	11486	11119	11113	11121	11142	11508	11493	11478	11499	12170	12044	12138	12182	10402	10380	10394	10429
	AB2	11130	11107	11166	11133	11431	11426	11454	11463	11097	11076	11088	11129	11421	11390	11495	11398	12086	12084	12116	12097	10350	10344	10350	10403
	Ours	**11017**	11059	11078	11077	**11363**	11398	11381	11411	11068	11060	**11039**	11094	11346	**11343**	11437	11378	11989	**11961**	12050	12057	**10318**	10376	10337	10346
RMSE ↓	BL(S)	2.232	2.232	2.235	2.233	2.422	2.430	2.423	2.434	2.159	2.159	2.159	2.149	2.392	2.391	2.392	2.401	2.925	2.926	2.926		1.856	1.865	1.851	1.860
	BL(W)	2.232			2.232		2.433	2.433	2.435	2.157	2.157	2.159		2.386	2.387	2.394	2.395	2.910	2.923	2.902	2.925	1.854	1.858		1.857
	U-BL(S)	2.231	2.233	2.231	2.231	2.428	2.428	2.428	2.434	2.154	2.154	2.159	2.154	2.392	2.392	2.392	2.397	2.923	2.923	2.923	2.928	1.859	1.860	1.859	1.859
	U-BL(W)	2.229	2.229	2.229	2.229	2.433	2.433	2.433	2.435	2.151	2.156	2.151	2.151	2.388	2.388	2.388	2.395	2.921	2.921	2.921	2.925	1.858	1.858	1.858	1.859
	AB1	2.218	2.158	2.199	2.217	2.410	2.371	2.396	2.414	2.159	2.150	2.155	2.160	2.389	2.357	2.364	2.376	2.889	2.778	2.850	2.895	1.847	1.841	1.838	1.858
	AB2	2.185	2.167	2.197	2.196	2.363	2.355	2.384	2.391	2.144	2.125	2.164	2.158	2.339	2.321	2.386	2.321	2.833	2.829	2.834	2.842	1.827	1.822	1.833	1.841
	Ours	**2.135**	2.136	2.161	2.158	**2.318**	2.342	2.330	2.367	2.135	2.131	**2.121**	2.146	**2.271**	2.286	2.331	2.312	2.752	**2.743**	2.797	2.815	**1.797**	1.808	1.806	1.828
Results of Movie dataset (n=2,119)																									
AIC ↓	BL(S)	8782	8782	8782				9227			9192	9193			9807	9825	9821	9698	9699	9699		9251	9282	9283	9274
	BL(W)	8781	8782	8781	8786	9228		9228	9229	9195		9194	9197	9812	9799		9814	9694	9693	9699	9690	9290	9290	9287	9284
	U-BL(S)	8782	8782	8782	8790	9227	9227	9227	9235	9192	9192	9192		9801	9801	9829	9801	9689	9689	9699	9689	9268	9268	9283	9268
	U-BL(W)	8780	8782	8780	8780	9214	9228	9214	9214	9171	9194	9171	9171	9795	9795	9823	9795	9686	9686	9695	9686	9264	9286	9264	9264
	AB1	8778	8777	8763	8776	9182	9223	9214	9211	9133	9186	9135	9164	9764	9774	9821	9781	9673	9668	9695	9670	9197	9210	9225	9161
	AB2	8776	8778	8740	8780	9224	9224	9206	9216	9191	9168	9117	9162	9761	9760	9722	9738	9656	9638	9625	9604	9205	9214	9225	9148
	Ours	8753	8774	**8734**	8748	9194	9197	9203	**9125**	9134	9129	**9105**	9136	9757	**9646**	9757	9715	9651	**9505**	9590	9558	9144	**9119**	9126	9162
RMSE ↓	BL(S)	1.438	1.438	1.438				1.604			1.607	1.607			1.800	1.804	1.812	1.736	1.736	1.736		1.759	1.772	1.773	1.760
	BL(W)	1.438	1.438	1.438	1.439	1.605		1.605	1.609	1.609		1.608	1.616	1.803	1.796		1.803	1.735	1.734	1.737	1.738	1.776	1.776	1.775	1.778
	U-BL(S)	1.438	1.438	1.438	1.444	1.604	1.604	1.604	1.611	1.607	1.607	1.607		1.797	1.797	1.813	1.797	1.736	1.736	1.736	1.736	1.759	1.759	1.773	1.759
	U-BL(W)	1.436	1.438	1.436	1.436	1.605	1.605	1.605	1.613	1.608	1.608	1.608	1.620	1.790	1.790	1.809	1.790	1.733	1.733	1.736	1.733	1.759	1.774	1.759	1.759
	AB1	1.432	1.432	1.424	1.435	1.601	1.604	1.607	1.617	1.617	1.617	1.615	1.626	1.778	1.794	1.808	1.781	1.739	1.741	1.740	1.732	1.722	1.744	1.743	1.727
	AB2	1.439	1.436	1.400	1.429	1.607	1.601	1.613	1.615	1.619	1.616	1.607	1.622	1.776	1.763	1.768	1.763	1.744	1.740	1.725	1.723	1.732	1.740	1.746	1.701
	Ours	1.426	1.427	**1.400**	1.421	1.603	1.594	1.609	**1.586**	1.606	1.602	**1.599**	1.614	1.754	**1.709**	1.764	1.777	1.726	**1.678**	1.723	1.711	1.704	**1.687**	1.691	1.718

5 Results and Discussion

Table 3 shows the results. Due to page limitations, the table shows only the Akaike Information Criterion (AIC; model fit metric; the lower the better) and the Root Mean Square Error (RMSE; prediction accuracy metric). See the supplementary material (https://osf.io/mj3nr/) for the results of other metrics. As the table shows, the regression models of our RNN (ours) outperformed the baseline models (BL, U-BL), AB1, and AB2 in most conditions not limited to specific stimulus types, emotion dimensions, or modality combinations.

Compared to the baseline models, which do not distinguish between the four types of factors at all, ours outperformed them in all conditions of both datasets with only one exception (RMSE of (b)-C in the Movie dataset). The differences are significant according to the relative likelihood (RL) that are calculated from their AICs; $\mathrm{RL} = \exp((\mathrm{AIC(ours)} - \mathrm{AIC(BL\ or\ U\text{-}BL)})/2)$, where $\mathrm{AIC}(M)$ denotes the AIC of regression model M. In all conditions, the RLs between ours and the best baseline models are less than 0.05 (see the supplementary material), which means that the likelihood of the best baseline models being closer to the true model than ours is less than 0.05. This indicates that the features extracted by our RNN reflect emotions to a significantly greater extent than the baseline.

The same is true between our RNN and its variants, AB1 and AB2. Out of 24 conditions, ours outperformed them in 23 conditions in the Music dataset and 20 conditions in the Movie dataset for both AIC and RMSE. The RLs between ours and the better of AB1 and AB2 were less than 0.05 in all 23 conditions in the Music dataset and 15 out of 20 conditions in the Movie dataset. These results indicate that the following key features of our RNN, which were not implemented in AB1 and AB2, significantly contributed to causing its emotion features to reflect emotion. That is, the multilayer structure for distinguishing cross-modal and modality-specific factors and the MSL URs for modeling the moderating effect of individual physiological differences.

What is notable in our RNN is that using more modalities does not necessarily make the emotion features (i.e., the CML hidden states) reflect emotion more. As shown in the table, using all three modalities (i.e., A) performed best in only three out of 12 cases (six emotion dimensions $\times$ two datasets). This accords with the existing studies [7,11]. For example, in [11], ECG+GSR outperformed EEG+ECG+GSR for recognizing arousal. The authors considered this would be because EEG did not reflect arousal as well as the other two modalities and would be noise for the recognition.

Although our RNN differs from them in the feature extraction, we consider this is also true for our approach. In our RNN, the CML learns latent common factors that affect all input physiological modalities. While this prevents the CML from learning modality-specific factors, it would be also possible that the CML fails to learn factors that are common to only a subset of input modalities and useful for emotion recognition but do not affect the remaining input modalities. For example, in the Music dataset, C) EEG+GSR outperformed A) EEG+ECG+GSR to recognize c) fear-relieved. We consider using ECG as input would have prevented the CML from learning factors that are common only to EEG and GSR and useful for recognizing this emotion dimension.

In light of the above, as in the existing approaches, it is necessary to compare possible modality combinations to identify the best combination in our approach. Since the best modality combinations are different between emotion dimensions and stimulus types (music and movie), the comparison of modality combinations should be done for each emotion dimension and stimulus type.

6 Conclusions, Limitations and Future Direction

In this paper, we proposed a multilayer RNN to extract features from multimodal physiological signals for emotion recognition. Using a multilayer structure, our RNN models the process by which emotion affects physiological activities across multiple modalities. This enables our RNN to extract features that are cross-modal, which is one of the characteristics of emotion but has been overlooked in existing studies. The experiments conducted on EEG, ECG, and GSR signals showed that the features extracted by our RNN reflected the participants' emotions to a significantly greater extent than existing approaches.

One limitation is that our RNN only models unidirectional relationship between emotion and physiological activity, i.e., the former affects the latter. According to Roberts et al [9], perception of internal physiological state (known as interoception) would also affect emotion. Modeling this inverse relationship in our RNN would make the features reflect emotion more. This possibility should be explored. Another limitation is that we only examined physiological signals collected while the participants stayed still. In real-world scenarios, however, physiological signals would contain noise caused by body movements. Further studies are warranted to investigate how our RNN performs with such signals.

References

1. Aranha, R.V., Corrêa, C.G., Nunes, F.L.: Adapting software with affective computing: a systematic review. IEEE Trans. Affect. Comput. **12**(4), 883–899 (2019)
2. Deng, J.J., Leung, C.H., Milani, A., Chen, L.: Emotional states associated with music: Classification, prediction of changes, and consideration in recommendation. ACM Trans. Interact. Intell. Syst. (TiiS) **5**(1), 1–36 (2015)
3. Kim, J., André, E.: Emotion recognition based on physiological changes in music listening. IEEE Trans. Pattern Anal. Mach. Intell. **30**(12), 2067–2083 (2008)
4. Li, C., Bao, Z., Li, L., Zhao, Z.: Exploring temporal representations by leveraging attention-based bidirectional LSTM-RNNs for multi-modal emotion recognition. Inf. Process. Manag. **57**(3), 102185 (2020)
5. Liu, W., Zheng, W.-L., Lu, B.-L.: Emotion recognition using multimodal deep learning. In: Hirose, A., Ozawa, S., Doya, K., Ikeda, K., Lee, M., Liu, D. (eds.) ICONIP 2016. LNCS, vol. 9948, pp. 521–529. Springer, Cham (2016). https://doi.org/10.1007/978-3-319-46672-9_58
6. Ma, Y., Nguyen, K.L., Xing, F.Z., Cambria, E.: A survey on empathetic dialogue systems. Inf. Fusion **64**, 50–70 (2020)
7. Miranda-Correa, J.A., Abadi, M.K., Sebe, N., Patras, I.: Amigos: a dataset for affect, personality and mood research on individuals and groups. IEEE Trans. Affect. Comput. **12**(2), 479–493 (2018)
8. Peng, W., Hu, Y., Xing, L., Xie, Y., Sun, Y.: Do you know my emotion? emotion-aware strategy recognition towards a persuasive dialogue system. In: ECML PKDD 2022, Proceedings, Part II. pp. 724–739. Springer (2023). https://doi.org/10.1007/978-3-031-26390-3_42

9. Roberts, T.A., Pennebaker, J.W.: Gender differences in perceiving internal state: Toward a his-and-hers model of perceptual cue use. In: Advances in Experimental Social Psychology, vol. 27, pp. 143–175. Elsevier (1995)
10. Russell, J.A.: A circumplex model of affect. J. Pers. Soc. Psychol. **39**(6), 1161 (1980)
11. Subramanian, R., Wache, J., Abadi, M.K., Vieriu, R.L., Winkler, S., Sebe, N.: Ascertain: emotion and personality recognition using commercial sensors. IEEE Trans. Affect. Comput. **9**(2), 147–160 (2016)
12. Yin, Z., Zhao, M., Wang, Y., Yang, J., Zhang, J.: Recognition of emotions using multimodal physiological signals and an ensemble deep learning model. Comput. Methods Programs Biomed. **140**, 93–110 (2017)

VaeSSC: Enhanced GRN Inference with Structural Similarity Constrained Beta-VAE

Hongmin Zhang, Ming Shi(✉), Zhongwei Huang, Zhi Yang, Ran Zhou, and Haitao Gan(✉)

School of Computer Science, Hubei University of Technology, Wuhan, China
{shiming,htgan01}@hbut.edu.cn

Abstract. Gene regulatory network (GRN) encodes the intricate molecular interactions that govern the regulation of cell identity, thereby controlling the functions and characteristics of cells. With the emergence of single-cell transcriptomics, single-cell RNA sequencing has provided a powerful data foundation for the reconstruction of GRN. Consequently, the reconstruction of GRN has garnered significant attention. In recent years, deep learning has demonstrated remarkable performance across various domains, leading some researchers to apply deep learning models to the reconstruction of GRN. However, often overlooked is the correlation that exists among different cell types at different stages, resulting in ample room for improvement in the performance of GRN reconstruction. To address the need for models to capture the correlation information between cells, we propose a method called VaeSSC, which effectively captures the structural information of adjacent cells. By fully integrating the structural information of adjacent cells' GRN, our method ensures that the reconstructed GRN conform more closely to objective principles, thereby enhancing the performance of GRN reconstruction. Extensive experiments conducted against challenging GRN reconstruction methods from the past have demonstrated the effectiveness of our proposed method.

Keyword: Gene regulatory network · Beta-variational autoencoder · Structure similarity constraint

1 Introduction

Single-cell transcriptomics [15, 17] is a revolutionary technology that has sparked widespread interest and attention in biological research. The advancements in the technique have enabled researchers to gain deeper insights into cellular heterogeneity and transcriptomic dynamics within cell types, developmental processes, and disease mechanisms. Despite advances in measurement technology, a number of technical issues, including amplification bias, library size differences [20], cell cycle effects [3], and particularly low RNA capture rates [11] cause a lot of noise in scRNA-seq experiments, which can ruin the biological signal below and prevent analysis [6].

F. Liu et al. (Eds.): PRICAI 2023, LNAI 14325, pp. 451–463, 2024.
https://doi.org/10.1007/978-981-99-7019-3_41

To address these challenges, it is imperative to model them to elucidate the uncertainties arising from downstream analyses. Deep learning algorithms are currently being used to filter out noise in single-cell transcriptomic data by simulating complicated gene-gene interactions [5]. However, deep learning-based frameworks [14] for single-cell analysis have often been treated as black boxes, making it challenging to analyze the extent of learning the structure of the gene regulatory network (GRN) or any other internal structures of the data.

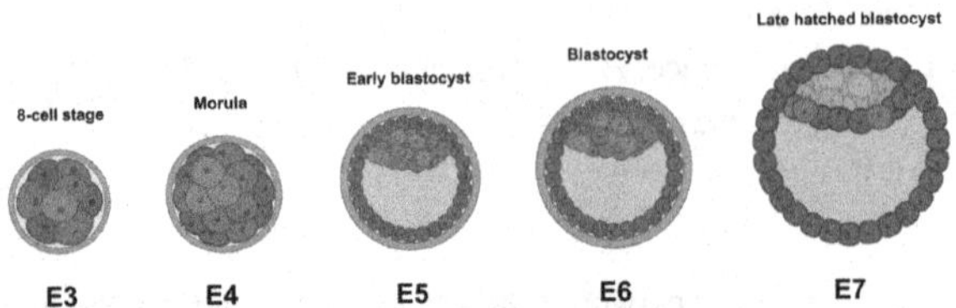

Fig. 1. The pivotal stages of human early embryonic development. Firstly, the 8-cell stage, where the fertilized egg divides into eight cells. Next is the Morula stage, characterized by a spherical embryo composed of 16 or more cells. Secondly, in the early blastocyst stage, the appearance of a cavity occurs, leading to the formation of distinct cell groups. Further development leads to the formation of a blastocyst, with the internal cavity gradually expanding. Finally, the blastocyst hatches, forming a late-hatched blastocyst, where the internal cell mass differentiates into three lineages: epiblast (EPI), primitive endoderm (PE), and trophoblast (TE).

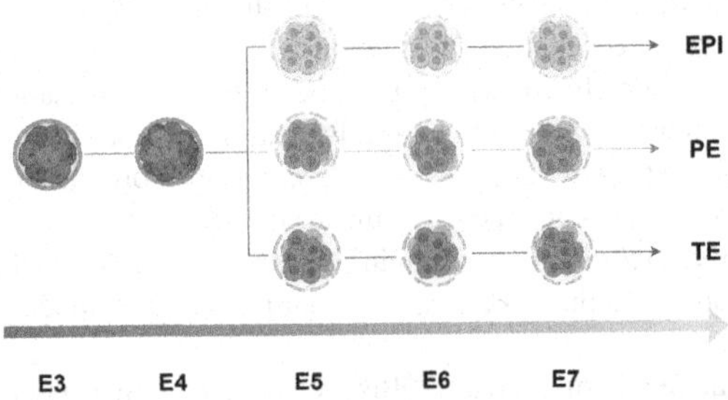

Fig. 2. The lineage tree of human embryonic development. The embryonic lineage tree is a dendrogram that encompasses a total of 11 cell types and 5 distinct stages of embryonic differentiation. It illustrates the cellular differentiation and division relationships during human embryonic development, where each node represents a specific cell type, and the connections between nodes represent the differentiation relationships between cells.

Autoencoders [13], artificial neural networks, by learning efficient data compression, force autoencoders to learn only the necessary latent features, and the reconstruction process ignores unnecessary sources of change, such as random noise. Presently, research has described the application of autoencoders in the field of GRN reconstruction. For instance, Shu et al. [19] proposed the DeepSEM structural equation model, which employs a linear model to infer causal relationships. Partial neural network architectures can be utilized to predict the GRN by including the right mathematical restrictions. Shu et al.'s earlier study showed that by building neural network layers, neural network architectures may accurately mirror the GRN structure. Within DeepSEM, nonlinear neural networks are used to solve issues with experimental noise, high-dimensional data, and scalability in single-cell data processing. The DeepSEM model allows us to analyze cellular structure, observing how multiple genes interact to influence individual gene expression levels.

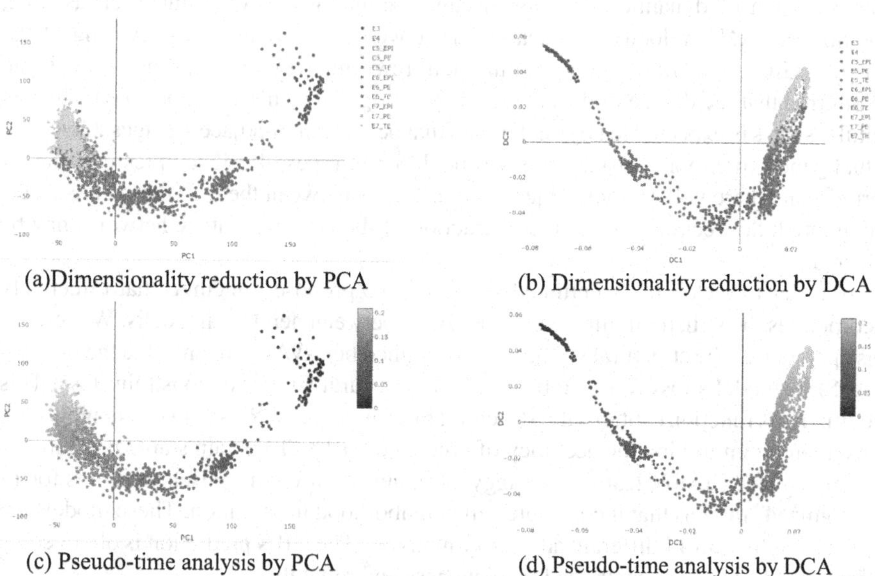

(a)Dimensionality reduction by PCA (b) Dimensionality reduction by DCA

(c) Pseudo-time analysis by PCA (d) Pseudo-time analysis by DCA

Fig. 3. Single-cell principal component analysis and Detrended correspondence analysis. Single-cell principal component analysis (PCA) (Fig a) is used to visualize the clustering results of single-cell data. This is a 2D scatterplot where the horizontal axis corresponds to major component 1 and the vertical axis corresponds to minor component 2. Each point represents a single-cell sample, and its position is determined by the calculation of the first two principal components, indicating its projection in the principal component space. Data points of different colors represent different cell populations or cell types. The single-cell pseudo-time analysis after PCA dimensionality reduction (Fig c) shows the colors of each point indicating the temporal sequence, with darker colors representing earlier time points and lighter colors representing later time points. The single-cell clustering results and pseudo-time plot after DCA dimensionality reduction are depicted in Fig b and Fig d, respectively, as shown in the figure.

However, with respect to differentiating datasets, the current known methods have neglected the intercellular correlations among distinct cell types during the process of cellular differentiation. Taking the human early embryonic development dataset as an example, the embryonic cells differentiate from a single cell type into three cellular lineages, namely EPI, PE, and TE, starting from the 3rd day after fertilization of the egg and continuing until the seventh day, as illustrated in Fig. 1 and Fig. 2. Dimensionality reduction by PCA [1] and DCA [8] on expression matrix across all cell types is illustrated in Fig. 3. As shown in the figure, the geodesic distances between cells are proportional to the degree of dissimilarity. Thus, it can be observed that the cell types vary across each stage, with smaller differences between adjacent stages and larger differences between non-adjacent stages.

Moreover, the magnitude of differences between cells in adjacent stages is smaller compared to non-adjacent stages, and these differences are related to the gene regulatory network [10]. Wang et al.'s [21] study highlight that the Dictys method enables the reconstruction of dynamic GRNs using any continuous cell ordering, such as time, pseudo-time, RNA velocity, or lineage data, unveiling the continuous rewiring of the network. Given that GRNs undergo continuous rewiring over time or pseudo time, it can be inferred that the degree of differences in gene regulatory networks between adjacent cellular stages is expected to be smaller than that between non-adjacent stages. Given the actual gene expression matrix, there will be different types of cell samples in different periods, and there will be some objective constraints between them. If these constraints are ignored, the accuracy of the reconstruction of the gene regulatory network may be affected.

In order to tackle the mentioned concerns, we propose a method that effectively incorporates the structural information of GRNs between neighboring cells. We refer to this approach as the structural similarity constrained beta-VAE. We enhance the original DeepSEM model's loss function by adding a structural similarity constraint loss. This modified loss function captures the structural information of GRNs between neighboring cells, thereby improving the accuracy of predicted GRNs. To obtain stable predictions, we employ an ensemble learning strategy, utilizing 11 different datasets as inputs for 11 "customized" models that incorporate cell neighborhood information. These models are trained, resulting in 11 different adjacency matrices. The GRN prediction is obtained by averaging 11 adjacency matrices for robustness and reliability.

In conclusion, our study makes several significant contributions:

- We propose an innovative approach that effectively integrates the structural information of gene regulatory networks (GRNs) between neighboring cells, known as the VaeSSC. By fully incorporating the structural information of gene regulatory networks between adjacent cells, we can obtain more accurate results.
- To achieve stable predictions of gene regulatory networks, we adopt an ensemble strategy. Specifically, we leverage 11 distinct datasets and train 11 different models tailored specifically to each dataset. This approach allows us to obtain 11 adjacency matrices, each derived from a model customized for its corresponding dataset. Subsequently, we compute the average of these 11 adjacency matrices to obtain the final adjacency matrix, which represents the gene regulatory network.

2 Method

In this section, we propose a network architecture called VaeSSC, aimed at enhancing the performance of GRN reconstruction. Firstly, we introduce the generalized SEM framework, which utilizes linear models to infer causal relationships and leverages a partial neural network architecture for scRNA-seq GRN prediction. Secondly, we incorporate a structural similarity constraint (SSC) in the loss function, which effectively integrates the GRN structure information of neighboring cells during different development stages. Additionally, within the VaeSSC network architecture, we provide a detailed description of the principles of this network framework. Finally, in the ensemble strategy [2], we integrate the predicted GRN results from all cell types using an ensemble approach to obtain the final GRN. The adjacency matrices of the predicted GRNs for each cell type are averaged to obtain the final adjacency matrix, thereby achieving a more accurate and comprehensive prediction.

2.1 Generalized Structural Equation Modeling

Structural equation modeling [22] stands as a potent multivariate statistical framework. It is a valuable tool for modeling relationships between observed features and hidden latent variables, enabling analysis of causal relationships, measurement errors, and structural relationships among stochastic variables within a multivariate statistical framework. SEM aids in revealing conditional associations among random variables, facilitating the anticipation of graphical arrangements in Bayesian networks and Markov random fields. DeepSEM [19] generalizes the SEM, which represents the dependent connections between random variables through a self-regression approach.

$$X = W^T X + Z \tag{1}$$

where the Eq. (1) can be modified as follows in its revised form:

$$X = \left(I - W^T\right)^{-1} Z$$
$$Z = \left(I - W^T\right) X \tag{2}$$

where $I \in R^{m \times m}$ represents the $m \times m$ identity matrix, $X \in R^{n \times m}$ denotes the gene expression matrix consisting of n cells and m genes, $W \in R^{m \times m}$ denotes the adjacency matrix of the gene regulatory network (GRN) that captures the conditional dependencies among the genes, and $Z \in R^{n \times m}$ represents the noise matrix following a Gaussian distribution. Here, we propose a modification to Eq. (2) by adopting a nonlinear version of structural equation modeling (SEM) as initially introduced by Yu et al. [22], yielding the following expression.

$$X = f_1\left(\left(I - W^T\right)^{-1} Z\right) \tag{3}$$

$$Z = \left(I - W^T\right) f_2(X) \tag{4}$$

where functions f_1 and f_2 represent multilayer neural networks, which are employed to capture complex relationships. Precisely, the expression in Eq. (3) can be broken down into the subsequent form.

$$H_Z = (I - W)^{-1} Z$$

where considering the column-wise vector representation, the matrix H_Z can be re-expressed accordingly.

$$H_Z = [h_0; h_1; \ldots; h_m], h_i \in R^{n \times 1}$$

$$
\begin{aligned}
f_1(h_i) &= \tanh(\tanh\left(\tanh(h_i W_1^T)W_2^T\right)W_3^T) \\
X &= [f_1(h_0); f_1(h_1); \ldots; f_1(h_m)] \\
W_1 &\in R^{d\times 1}, W_2 \in R^{d\times d}, W_3 \in R^{1\times d}
\end{aligned} \tag{5}
$$

where d represents the number of hidden neurons in each layer and h_i signifies the hidden latent variable for gene i, Eq. (5) possesses the interpretation of serving as a nonlinear decoding function for the stochastic variable Z. The linear weights W_1, W_2, and W_3 correspond to different layers of the neural network. Notably distinct from the traditional neural network employed in scRNA-seq modeling, f_1 exclusively accepts a single feature as input. Consequently, an encoder function with a comparable structure is formulated as follows:

$$
\begin{aligned}
X &= [x_0; x_1; \ldots; x_m], x_i \in R^{n\times 1} \\
H_X &= [f_2(x_0); f_2(x_1); \ldots; f_2(x_m)] \\
f_2(x_i) &= \tanh(\tanh\left(\tanh(x_i W_4^T)W_5^T\right)W_6^T) \\
Z &= Reparameter((I - W^{T)}H_x) \\
W_4 &\in R^{d\times 1}, W_5 \in R^{d\times d}, W_6 \in R^{2\times d}
\end{aligned} \tag{6}
$$

where x_i represents the gene i is expression level, while f_2 corresponds to an additional multilayer neural network employed to capture the noise in X. This network takes the gene expression of each individual gene as an input feature. The term 'Reparameter' refers to the utilization of the reparameterization trick [13]. The linear weights W_4, W_5, and W_6 are associated with different layers of the neural network. The layer $I - W^T$ is denoted as the GRN layer, whereas the layer $(I - W^T)^{-1}$ is referred to as the inverse GRN layer.

2.2 Loss Function Design

The loss function comprises four components. The first section denotes the reconstruction penalty, assessing the disparity between the input information and the output data produced by the decoder. It drives the generated simulated data toward approximating the real input data. Secondly, within the beta-VAE [7] framework, the transformation of X to Z is not direct. Instead of that, Z is represented as a Gaussian distribution. The mean and variance are obtained by employing a neural network, which takes X as its input characteristics. Furthermore, considering that gene regulatory networks exhibit sparsity, an $\updownarrow_1$ norm is used to constrain the adjacency matrix W, ensuring that the resulting gene regulatory network remains sparse. Lastly, as the DeepSEM method does not incorporate constraints based on the similarity of cell neighborhood information, the resulting gene regulatory network may lack proper constraints. This can lead to situations where the gene regulatory network obtained from non-adjacent periods exhibits greater similarity than the one obtained from adjacent time periods, which clearly deviates from objective reality. To ensure the accuracy of the obtained gene regulatory network, we propose a VaeSSC. The loss function utilized in the DeepSEM model, proposed by Shu et al.

[19], is defined by incorporating an additional $\updownarrow_1$ norm into a beta-VAE model for the regularization of the adjacency matrix W. Precisely, the loss function for DeepSEM is formulated in a subsequent manner:

$$l_1 = E_{q_\phi(z|x)}\left[logp_\theta(X|Z)\right] - \beta D_{KL}(q_\phi(Z|X)||p(Z)) + \lambda\alpha||W||_1 \tag{7}$$

The embryonic developmental genealogy tree is shown in Fig. 2. Assuming the tree is denoted as T, within the tree T, if an edge $e(i,j)$ belongs to T, then the adjacency matrices of the GRNs obtained from the datasets of these two cell types are represented as W_i and W_j, respectively. By imposing structural similarity constraints on the gene regulatory networks between connected cell types. The incorporation of structural similarity constraints capturing the neighborhood information among different cell-type samples can be expressed as follows:

$$l_2 = \lambda(1-\alpha)\sum_{e(i,j)}||W_i - W_j||_1 \tag{8}$$

where i represents the current task node corresponding to a cell type, j represents the neighboring cell type node connected to i. W_i denotes the adjacency matrix to be optimized for the current time period, and W_j represents the adjacency matrix of the neighboring cell type node j, which is known prior knowledge. $e(i,j)$ indicates the edge connecting node i and node j in the cell lineage tree.

Taking an example, if we are to infer the GRN of cells during the E4 period, then the variable i corresponds to the E4 node. The range of variable j includes E3, E5_EPI, E5_PE, and E5_TE. Consequently, the l_2 loss function consists of four terms, with only the nodes that have a connection with node i in the tree T being considered as j. Therefore, when inferring the GRN of each node, the loss function is not identical for all nodes. In other words, the design of the model's loss function is based on the position of the nodes within the tree T.

In summary, we have employed an approach that effectively captures the GRN information of neighboring cell types, driving the GRN of current cell types to approximate that of adjacent cell types GRN. To achieve this, we propose the incorporation of structural similarity constraints to enhance the reconstruction performance of the GRN. Furthermore, we combine this approach with the β-VAE model and apply l_1 regularization to the current cell type's gene regulatory network W_i. Ultimately, the overall loss function can be expressed as follows:

$$\begin{aligned} L &= l_1 + l_2 \\ L &= E_{q_\phi(z|x)}\left[logp_\theta(X|Z)\right] - \beta D_{KL}(q_\phi(Z|X)||p(Z)) \\ &\quad + \lambda\alpha||W_i||_1 + \lambda(1-\alpha)\sum_{e(i,j)}||W_i - W_j||_1 \end{aligned} \tag{9}$$

The expected value function E, where E stands for the expected value function, and p and q represent the probability distributions of X and Z respectively. KL refers to the KL-divergence function, while β represents hyperparameters. The expression $e(i,j)$ denotes the edge connecting cell types i and j in the cell lineage tree T, $\alpha \in (0, 1)$ and

$\lambda > 0$ are two regularization parameters. In the context of the beta-VAE framework, the direct transformation of X to Z is replaced by modeling Z as a Gaussian distribution. The mean and variance of this distribution are determined by neural networks that take X as the input features.

2.3 VaeSSC Framework

The VaeSSC model (Fig. 4), an enhancement of GRN inference with a structural similarity-constrained beta-VAE, utilizes the beta-VAE framework to jointly infer the GRN by incorporating both structural equation modeling (SEM) and the structural similarity constraint (SSC).

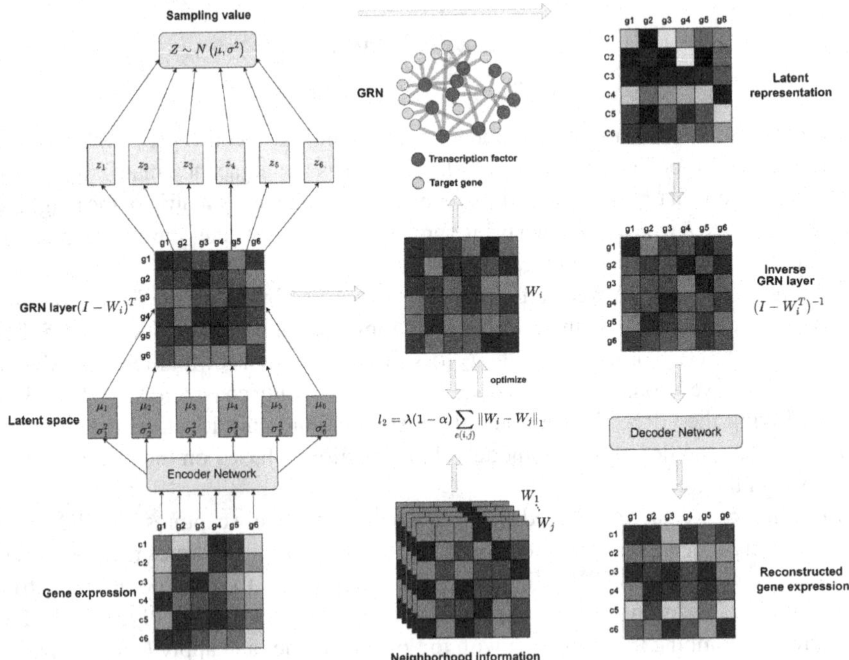

Fig. 4. The VaeSSC network model architecture. The model comprises four key components: an encoder, a GRN module, an inverse GRN module, and a decoder. Both the encoder and decoder are comprised of fully connected layers, which receive a singular gene as input. The encoder and decoder share the same set of weights across various genes. The GRN module as well as the inverse GRN module depict matrices of gene interactions, effectively capturing the GRN network and directing the flow of information within the neural network. W_i represents the currently predicted adjacency matrix. W_1 to W_j represent its neighborhood information, which serves as prior knowledge. The labels g1-g6 correspond to gene identifiers within the gene expression matrix, whereas the labels c1-c6 denote cell identifiers in the gene expression matrix.

The architecture comprises two distinct neural network modules, namely the GRN module and the inverse GRN module, which serve the explicit purpose of modeling the

GRN structure. Deviating from traditional deep learning architectures that combine gene expressions into a common latent space, the encoder mechanism of VaeSSC exclusively focuses on employing the expression of an individual gene as the input characteristic for the neural network. The results produced by these separate networks are then transformed into the posterior mean and standard deviation of a multivariate Gaussian distribution by two more fully connected neural networks. The pivotal aspect of VaeSSC lies in the decoupling of nonlinear operations and gene interactions, which enables the simultaneous attainment of more robust and interpretable hidden representations. Finally, by imposing a constraint relationship between the adjacency matrix W_i and the contextual information W_j, the optimized W_i is made more similar to the W_j of neighboring cell types, enabling the model to capture the GRN structural information of contextual cells and enhance the performance of GRN reconstruction.

2.4 Ensemble Strategy

In the task of inferring gene regulatory networks (GRNs), the key elements of each model lie in its capacity to deduce the structure of gene regulatory networks through probabilistic modeling of scRNA-seq data. The adjacency matrix $w_i(i = 1 \bullet\bullet\bullet k)$ represents the learned GRN for each model. To obtain stable predictions of the GRN, we employ an ensemble strategy [2]. As shown in Fig. 5, we train k different VaeSSC models using k distinct training approaches on datasets from k cell types. These models are tailored specifically to each dataset. Subsequently, we compute the average of the k adjacency matrices to obtain the final adjacency matrix, which corresponds to the final gene regulatory network.

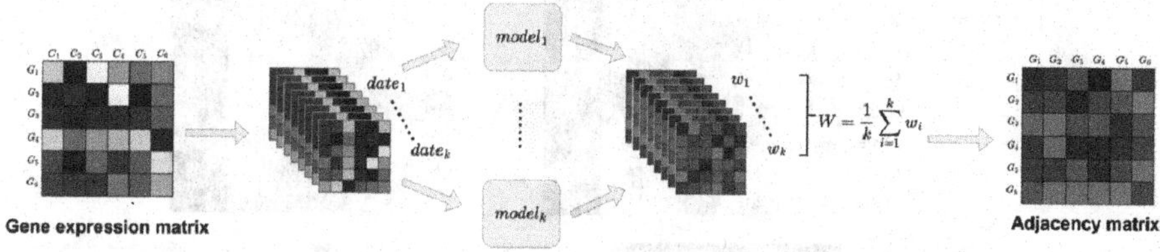

Fig. 5. The ensemble strategy. The input gene expression matrices of early human embryos are divided into different gene expression matrices according to the cell sample types. $model_1$ to $model_k$ are k VaeSSC models with different constraint relationships "tailored" for these different datasets. w_1 to w_k are the outputs of these models, and the final adjacency matrix W is obtained by averaging these k adjacency matrices.

3 Experiments and Results

3.1 Data Preprocessing

Our data were derived from the hESC[16] dataset, which Utilizing single-cell RNA sequencing, a total of 1,529 cells were isolated from 88 preimplantation human embryos spanning the developmental period from embryonic day 3 to 7. In this study, we initially partitioned the human embryonic cell dataset into 11 subsets based on 5 distinct periods and 11 different cell types. Each subset represents a specific category of cell samples. Following the data preprocessing principles provided by the BEELINE [18] framework. For each subset, we selected all transcription factors and either 500 or 1000 highly variable genes. Subsequently, using the Non-specific ChIP-seq dataset as the ground truth labels, we generated corresponding labels for each subset to evaluate the performance.

3.2 Experimental Result

To evaluate the efficacy of our approach, we followed the evaluation approach outlined in the BEELINE [18] framework for assessing the predictive performance of gene regulatory network (GRN) inference methods, specifically the early precision ratio (EPR) and AUPRC ration metric. We have a total of 11 different cell data sets during the human embryo development process. In accordance with the suggestions by Pratapa et al. [18], we exclusively investigated transcription factors (TFs) and the top M (M = 500 or 1000) most variable genes. We compared the VaeSSC method with four baseline algorithms, including DeepSEM [19], GENIE3 [9], PIDC [4], and PPCOR [12]. The

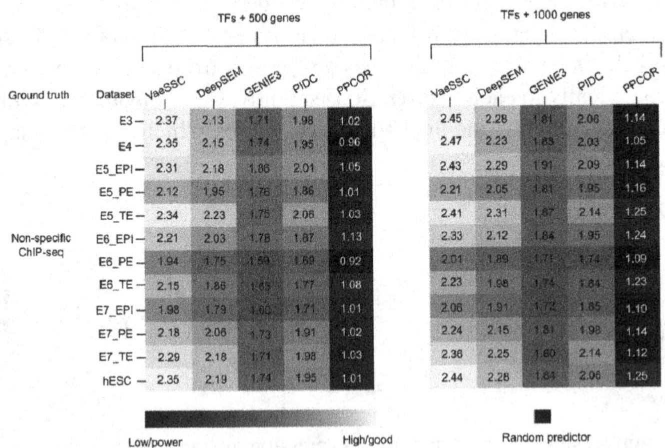

Fig. 6. Results of the hESC dataset's performance on EPR metrics. The left panel (TFs + 500 genes) illustrates the results of the dataset composed of all significantly variable transcription factors and the top 500 genes with the highest degree of variability. The right panel (TFs + 1000 genes) displays the results of the dataset comprising all significantly variable TFs and the top 1000 genes with the highest degree of variability. Every row depicted in the illustration corresponds to a scRNA-seq dataset, while each column represents a method for gene regulatory network reconstruction. Each cell in the figure displays the EPR value. The last row represents the cumulative results of all the previous datasets, denoted as the hESC dataset. The EPR values for the VaeSSC method corresponding to the hESC dataset were obtained through an ensemble learning approach. For every dataset, the color within each cell corresponds to the respective value, which is adjusted to range between 0 and 1. EPR is determined by the odds ratio of authentic positives among the foremost K forecasted connections between the model and random predictions, with K representing the count of edges in the actual GRN.

VaeSSC method excelled in the BEELINE evaluation framework, with results shown in Fig. 6 and Table 1.

Table 1. Accuracy of GRN Inference Using Challenging Approaches on the hESC Dataset

Method	TFs + 500 genes	TFs + 1000 genes
	EPR AUPRC ration	EPR AUPRC ration
PIDC	1.95 1.15	2.06 1.18
GENIE3	1.74 1.03	1.84 1.05
PPCOR	1.01 0.91	1.25 0.93
DeepSEM	2.19 1.22	2.28 1.23
DeepSEM*	2.08 1.13	2.16 1.17
VaeSSC	**2.35 1.29**	**2.44 1.32**

The method (VaeSSC) demonstrates a significant performance advantage in gene regulatory network prediction. Across subsets of hESC datasets, the EPR and AUPRC ration metric of the VaeSSC method outperforms other benchmark algorithms. To compare the performance of using a single model for all datasets versus the ensemble learning strategy. The approach where we compute the average of adjacency matrices obtained from the unconstrained DeepSEM model across all datasets, without incorporating SSC constraints, is referred to as DeepSEM*. The methodology involving the direct input of the entire hESC dataset into the model is denoted as DeepSEM. As shown in Table 1, in comparison to the unconstrained single model approach using DeepSEM*, the VaeSSC method, which integrates SSC constraints, achieves superior performance on the hESC dataset. Meanwhile, these experimental results indicate that incorporating more highly variable genes or considering all key variable transcription factors leads to improved EPR performance. However, the impact on the AUPRC ratio metric is relatively marginal, thus further validating the findings of Pratapa et al. [18]. In summary, our approach has demonstrated commendable performance in the metrics of both EPR and AUPRC ratios, thereby offering novel perspectives and insights into Gene Regulatory Network (GRN) inference.

4 Conclusion

In this paper, we primarily discuss the issue of gene regulatory network (GRN) reconstruction based on the beta-VAE model. Shu et al. [19] suggested the DeepSEM model based on the beta-VAE model, which utilizes neural networks to model the gene regulatory network. Built upon prior success in GRN reconstruction, we introduce the structural similarity constrained beta-VAE (VaeSSC). This approach leverages neighboring cells' GRN structural information, enhancing reconstruction performance. To obtain the final GRN, we adopt an ensemble strategy by averaging the adjacency matrices obtained from each cell dataset to obtain the final adjacency matrix and consequently the final

GRN. The empirical findings illustrate that compared to the DeepSEM method without the structural similarity constraint, the inclusion of the SSC significantly enhances the model's prediction of the GRN.

However, due to the fact that the structure of the GRN is modeled as a specialized layer of a neural network, it serves as a biological constraint to limit the parameter space. In other words, the parameter matrix W of the neural network, which represents the adjacency matrix, is determined by the number of input genes. A complete gene expression matrix often consists of tens of thousands of genes. Furthermore, considering that this study involves multiple custom models jointly determining the predictive outcomes, there will be multiple adjacency matrices W. This will significantly increase the number of parameters in the neural network, subsequently augmenting the time complexity and affecting computational efficiency. This also represents a limitation of the approach proposed in this study. Following the recommendations of Shu et al. [19], the selection of highly variable genes by users will substantially enhance the operational efficiency of the model.

In our future research endeavors, we will be dedicated to exploring the issues related to structural similarity constraints using different methods and strive to provide new insights and ideas for GRN reconstruction.

References

1. Abdi, H., Williams, L.J.: Principal component analysis. Wiley interdisciplinary reviews: computational statistics. **2**(4), 433–459 (2010)
2. Breiman, L.: Bagging predictors. Mach. Learn. **24**, 123–140 (1996)
3. Buettner, F., et al.: Computational analysis of cell-to-cell heterogeneity in single-cell RNA-sequencing data reveals hidden subpopulations of cells. Nat. Biotechnol. **33**(2), 155–160 (2015)
4. Chan, T.E., et al.: Gene regulatory network inference from single-cell data using multivariate information measures. Cell Syst. **5**(3), 251–267 (2017)
5. Eraslan, G., et al.: Single-cell RNA-seq denoising using a deep count autoencoder. Nat. Commun. **10**(1), 390 (2019)
6. Hicks, S.C., et al.: Missing data and technical variability in single-cell RNA-sequencing experiments. Biostatistics **19**(4), 562–578 (2018)
7. Higgins, I., et al.: Beta-vae: Learning basic visual concepts with a constrained variational framework. In: International Conference on Learning Representations (2017)
8. Hill, M.O., Gauch, H.G.: Detrended correspondence analysis: an improved ordination technique. In: Classification and Ordination: Symposium on Advances in Vegetation Science, Nijmegen, The Netherlands, May 1979, pp. 47–58. Springer (1980)
9. Huynh-Thu, V.A., et al.: Inferring regulatory networks from expression data using tree-based methods. PloS One **5**(9), e12776 (2010)
10. Kamimoto, K., et al.: Dissecting cell identity via network inference and in silico gene perturbation. Nature **614**(7949), 742–751 (2023)
11. Kharchenko, P.V., et al.: Bayesian approach to single-cell differential expression analysis. Nat. Methods **11**(7), 740–742 (2014)
12. Kim, S.: Ppcor: an R package for a fast calculation to semi-partial correlation coefficients. CSAM. **22**(6), 665–674 (2015)
13. Kingma, D.P., Welling, M.: An introduction to variational autoencoders. FNT in Machine Learn. **12**(4), 307–392 (2019)

14. Li, X., et al.: Deep learning enables accurate clustering with batch effect removal in single-cell RNA-seq analysis. Nat. Commun. **11**(1), 2338 (2020)
15. Macosko, E.Z., et al.: Highly parallel genome-wide expression profiling of individual cells using nanoliter droplets. Cell **161**(5), 1202–1214 (2015)
16. Petropoulos, S., et al.: Single-cell RNA-seq reveals lineage and x chromosome dynamics in human preimplantation embryos. Cell **165**(4), 1012–1026 (2016)
17. Picelli, S., et al.: Smart-seq2 for sensitive full-length transcriptome profiling in single cells. Nat. Methods **10**(11), 1096–1098 (2013)
18. Pratapa, A., et al.: Benchmarking algorithms for gene regulatory network inference from single-cell transcriptomic data. Nat. Methods **17**(2), 147–154 (2020)
19. Shu, H., et al.: Modeling gene regulatory networks using neural network architectures. Nature Comput. Sci. **1**(7), 491–501 (2021)
20. Vallejos, C.A., et al.: Normalizing single-cell RNA sequencing data: challenges and opportunities. Nat. Methods **14**(6), 565–571 (2017)
21. Wang, L., et al.: Dictys: dynamic gene regulatory network dissects developmental continuum with single-cell multi-omics. bioRxiv, pp. 2022–09 (2022)
22. Yu, Y., et al.: Dag-gnn: dag structure learning with graph neural networks. In: International Conference on Machine Learning, pp. 7154–7163. PMLR (2019)

Knowledge Representation and Reasoning

Parallel Construction of Knowledge Graphs from Relational Databases

Shaoyu Wang, Jingsheng Yan, Yang Liu, Pan Hu(✉), Hongming Cai, and Lihong Jiang

Shanghai Jiao Tong University, Shanghai, China
pan.hu@sjtu.edu.cn

Abstract. Knowledge graphs have recently seen a wide range of applications in various domains. In many such applications data stored in relational databases constitutes an important source for the construction of knowledge graphs. R2RML is a mapping language that can be used to specify mappings from relational to RDF data, and so it naturally suits the purpose of knowledge graph construction from relational data. In this paper, we present Fingr, a concurrent dictionary aided parallel R2RML engine that achieves fine-grained parallelization at the database tuple level. Our experiments show that our prototypical system parallelizes well, and it yields better performance than existing R2RML engines.

Keywords: RDF · R2RML · Knowledge Graph Construction

1 Introduction

Knowledge graphs have seen many applications for numerous purposes such as question-answering systems, recommender systems and information retrieval in various domains including medicine, cyber security, finance, education and news [11]. Its ability to integrate large volumes of information into a graph allows for topological interpretation and analysis such as ontological reasoning of structured knowledge. However, in recent years, as increasing volumes of data are poured into knowledge graphs from heterogeneous data sources, the demand for efficient construction of massive knowledge graphs from other standardized data sources has attracted much attention.

Approaches for standardized conversion from heterogeneous data sources to RDF[1] knowledge graphs enable knowledge graph based reasoning and have proven useful in numerous Semantic Web applications. Relevant standards include R2RML[2] and RML [5]. An R2RML mapping document specifies the mapping from a source relational database to a target RDF graph. An R2RML engine implements this conversion. RML extends the R2RML standard so that

S. Wang and J. Yan—Both authors contributed equally.

[1] https://www.w3.org/TR/rdf11-concepts/.

[2] https://www.w3.org/TR/r2rml/.

F. Liu et al. (Eds.): PRICAI 2023, LNAI 14325, pp. 467–479, 2024.
https://doi.org/10.1007/978-981-99-7019-3_42

other forms of input data sources can be supported, such as CSV and JSON. R2RML and RML engines provide access to target RDF graphs mainly in two ways, materialization and virtualization. Materialization-based approaches straightforwardly generate the target RDF graph using the input database and the mapping document. In contrast, virtualization-based approaches translate queries over the RDF graph into SQL queries over the relational database according to the mapping document, thereby avoiding the explicit storage of the target RDF graph.

R2RML engines such as Ontop [3] and Morph-RDB [8] adopt the virtualization approach and exploit several optimizations. In contrast, db2triples[3] and R2RML-F [4] are R2RML engines that adopt the materialization approach, the latter being an extension of the former. The development of RML engines has attracted a lot of attention as well. The W3C RML Implementation Report[4] listed a few of them: RMLMapper[5], SDM-RDFizer [7], Chimera [9], RocketRML [10], CARML[6], RMLStreamer [6] and Morph-KGC [2]. Among these engines, RMLStreamer utilizes a Producer-Consumer framework to achieve data record level parallel generation of RDF triples. However, their system could produce duplicate triples. Morph-KGC, SDM-RDFizer, and Chimera adopt parallelization to different extents, with Morph-KGC displaying a clear focus on improving its performance regarding throughput via parallelization. It adopts a rule partitioning strategy that assigns rules into groups such that no triple could be generated from two distinct groups, thus minimizing the amount of information exchange between parallelly executing processes. According to their experiments [1,2], Morph-KGC outperforms other engines on the GTFS^{rdb} [13] benchmark by up to an order of magnitude in terms of time, making it potentially the fastest R2RML (RML) engine to date. However, splitting workloads on a group basis may not be optimal as suggested later in our experiments: some groups can be required to deal with a much larger number of triples compared with others, resulting in imbalanced workload distribution between processes. To this end, we propose Fingr, a prototype R2RML engine that parallelizes the process of RDF graph construction at the level of database rows. Our experiments show that Fingr consistently outperforms the state-of-the-art engine by a large margin. Our system and source code can be found on github[7].

2 Preliminaries

We briefly recapitulate the most relevent concepts, RDF, R2RML and RML.

RDF (Resource Description framework) is a framework that models entities and their relationships in its core structure of a triple, comprising of a subject, a predicate, and an object. Viewing the subjects and objects as nodes, and the

[3] https://github.com/CNGL-repo/db2triples.
[4] https://rml.io/implementation-report/#rml-processor.
[5] https://github.com/RMLio/rmlmapper-java.
[6] https://github.com/carml/carml.
[7] https://github.com/ShadowNearby/R2RML.

predicates of triples as directed edges between subjects and objects, a set of triples form a graph. RDF graphs assume set semantics and do not allow for duplicate triples.

```
@prefix rr: <http://www.w3.org/ns/r2rml#>.
@prefix ex: <http://example.com/ns#>.

<#TriplesMap1>
    rr:logicalTable [ rr:tableName "EMP" ];
    rr:subjectMap [
        rr:template "http://data.ex.com/emp/{EMPNO}";
        rr:class ex:Employee;
    ];
    rr:predicateObjectMap [
        rr:predicate ex:name;
        rr:objectMap [ rr:column "ENAME" ];
    ].
```

Fig. 1. Example of an R2RML mapping document

R2RML is a mapping language from relational databases to RDF defined in Turtle[8], a syntax for RDF. This means that an R2RML mapping document is itself also an RDF graph. A mapping document of R2RML contains one or more triples maps. A triples map specifies how to translate a row in a relational table into RDF triples. Its specification includes a logical table, a subject map, and one or more predicate-object maps. A logical table specifies the data source of the triples map, the source usually being a relational database table or a query specifying a table. A subject map dictates the value of the subject of the triples that are to be generated. A predicate-object map consists of one or more predicate maps and one or more object maps (referencing object maps). Predicate maps and object maps define the values of the predicates and the objects, respectively, in a similar way as subject maps. A referencing object map specifies a join relation between two logical tables. For each row from the source table, each possible pair of these predicate and object maps defined in one single predicate-object map will be used in conjunction with the subject map, to generate corresponding RDF triples. Each of such combinations of a subject, a predicate and an object map constitute a mapping rule. Subject, predicate and object maps are all RDF term maps. An RDF term map maps a logical table row to an RDF term, which can be one of the following three forms: an IRI (Internationalized Resource Identifier), a Blank Node or a Literal. An RDF term map is a constant-valued term map, a column-valued term map, or a template-valued term map. A constant-valued term map generates constants regardless of inputs. A column-valued term map uses the content of a column of a row as its value. A template-valued term map generates strings by replacing each curly

[8] https://www.w3.org/TR/turtle/.

brace enclosed column name in the template string with the content from the corresponding column.

Example 1. Figure 1 shows an example of an R2RML mapping document, which is adapted from the W3C standard for R2RML[9]. If the table "EMP" contains a row (EMPNO:10001, ENAME:Bob), the mapping rule entailed by the R2RML document derives a triple ("http://data.ex.com/emp/10001", name, "Bob").

RML is an extension to R2RML that allows other data sources such as CSV and JSON. The counterpart to logical table of R2RML in RML is logical source.

3 The Fingr Engine

We begin by defining our main task: given a valid relational database connection, an R2RML mapping document written in Turtle, we need to generate all the triples according to the transformation specified by the document. In the remainder of this paper, we will refer to this task as **knowledge graph construction**. Specifically, we deal with this task in three stages.

- R2RML mapping resolution stage where we parse the input R2RML mapping document into triples maps.
- Triple generation stage where we apply mapping rules obtained from the triples maps to rows fetched from the database to generate required triples.
- Triple storing stage where the generated triples are stored after duplicates are removed from them.

R2RML mapping documents are generally miniscule compared to the input databases and the output RDF graphs. As such, parallelization of the first stage will merely yield negligible improvement to the overall performance. Therefore, to achieve better performance through parallelization in knowledge graph construction, we focus on parallelizing the second and third stages of the process.

3.1 R2RML Mapping Resolution

We transform a R2RML mapping document into an RDF graph, from which we extract the triples maps. For cases where the referencing object map references its own subject map, we adopt the self-join elimination technique in [2] to avoid producing redundant join queries.

3.2 Triple Generation

Before we dive into the details of how to generate triples based on the given database and the triples maps, we shall first outline the design of our concurrent dictionary, which is used extensively in the remaining procedures.

[9] https://www.w3.org/TR/r2rml/.

Algorithm 1. GetID(s)

Input: string s
Output: id of s

```
if D contains an entry for s then
    return D.stringtoid[s];
else
    i = hash(s) mod D.k;
    D.locks[i].lock();
    if D contains an entry for s then
        D.locks[i].unlock();
        return D.stringtoid[s];
    else
        id ← D.nextids[i];   D.nextids[i] ← D.nextids[i] + 1;
        D.stringtoid[s] ← id;   D.idtostring[id] ← s;
        D.locks[i].unlock();
        return id;
```

Concurrent Dictionary. Database tuples can contain duplicate values that are of varying length, most of which take up at least as much space in memory as an integer. Thus, we adopt a concurrent dictionary to assign each of these values a unique integer *id*, and replace each occurrence of these values with their respective *ids* so that we only need to operate with *ids*.

Our dictionary is composed of two hash maps that convert strings to *ids* and *ids* to strings, respectively. A dictionary of such functionality should be trivial to design in the serial execution context. It suffices to assign a fresh *id* to each newly encountered string. However, when strings are processed in parallel, more careful treatment is required: two different threads could interfere with each other when updating the dictionary. To tackle this, we adopt a concurrent hash map that can handle concurrent insertions and look-ups.

However, this was insufficient to ensure correct behavior of the dictionary since when two strings are to be allotted *ids* simultaneously by two different threads, the same *id* can potentially be allotted to two distinct strings, and two identical strings can acquire different *ids* in a similar manner.

A naive approach to addressing this problem would be to protect the current *id* with a lock. However, this approach would seriously impair parallelization since insertion of new strings into the dictionary becomes serial when every thread is competing for the same lock. A smaller lock granularity at per string level seems ideal for maximizing parallelization, but such a scheme requires a lot of memory and dynamically allocating new locks, which induces another source of workloads. Moreover, locks for each string cannot relieve us of the necessity of protecting *id* with a lock. As such, we adopted a locking scheme that achieves a reasonable trade-off between lock granularity and lock maintenance cost.

The idea is to partition the range of *id* into disjoint intervals so that we can maintain multiple *ids*, each starting from the smallest natural number in its

Algorithm 2. ProcessQuery(C, q, D)

Input: Database Connection C, Query q, Dictionary D
Output: Processed query result relation R', datatype information I of R'

```
R ← C.execute(q);
n ← R.rowcnt();
m ← R.colcnt();
R' ← an n x m array;
for i ← 0, 1, ..., n − 1 do
    for j ← 0, 1, ..., m − 1 do
        \* The following runs in parallel *\
        if R.content[i][j] ≠ null then
            R'[i][j] = D.GetID(R.content[i][j].tostring());
        else
            R'[i][j] = 0;
        \* The above runs in parallel *\
I ← R.getcolumntypes();
return ⟨R', I⟩;
```

respective interval, and each *id* is protected by its own lock. The strings to be inserted into the dictionary are in turn to be assigned, ideally evenly, to each interval so that races for the locks are minimal. Intuitively, this is viable since we only need to ensure that two different strings have different *id*s, and the order in which they are inserted is irrelevant. Let the range of *id*, $[1, Max]$, be partitioned into k almost equally large intervals starting at id_0, id_1, ..., and id_{k-1}, respectively, and let these *ids* be protected by $lock_0$, $lock_1$, ..., and $lock_{k-1}$, respectively. For a string s to be inserted into our dictionary D, we first use a hash function $hash : String \rightarrow \mathbb{N}$ to acquire an index i to an interval:

$$i = hash(s) \bmod k. \tag{1}$$

We next acquire $lock_i$, assign id_i to s, increase id_i by 1 and release $lock_i$. Notice that determining when to best acquire and release the lock is not trivial either. Since we encounter many identical strings, acquiring the lock before checking whether the string is already in the dictionary could potentially be quite costly, especially if these identical strings appear in batches, rendering the whole process nearly serial. This is remedied by checking twice for the strings' *ids*, once before acquiring the lock so that locking can be avoided if unnecessary, once after acquiring the lock to ensure that the *id* indeed needs to be assigned afresh. Algorithm 1 formalizes the above ideas. *stringtoid* and *idtostring* are the two hash maps in the dictionary D; *nextids* and *locks* are two arrays that store id_0, id_1, ..., id_{k-1} and $lock_0$, $lock_1$, ..., $lock_{k-1}$. Lines 1–2 check whether the string is already present, and if so returns the corresponding *id*. Lines 4–5 acquire the lock. Lines 6–8 check for the string's presence in the dictionary again. Finally, lines 9–13 allot a new *id* for the string.

Algorithm 3. ApplyRules(Π, C, S, L, D)

Input: A Set of rules Π, a database connection C, a hash map S mapping logical table names to their respective contents, a hash map L mapping logical table names to their column type information, Dictionary D
Output: All triples T specified by Π given connection C

```
for each rule r in Π do
    if r has a referencing object map then
        q ← generatejoinquery(Π, r);
        ⟨R′, I⟩ ← ProcessQuery(C, q, D);
    else
        R′ ← S[r.logicalTable];
        I ← L[r.logicalTable];
    n ← R′.rowcnt();
    for i ← 0, 1, ..., n − 1 do
        \* The following runs in parallel *\
        if isvalid(R′[i], r) then
            t ← derivetriple(R′[i], r);
            T ← T ∪ {t};
        \* The above runs in parallel *\
return T;
```

RDB Retrieval and Processing. From the triples maps generated in the mapping resolution stage we extract their logical tables and send corresponding queries to the input database. Each query result, which is an array of database rows, is parallelly translated into a matrix of *ids* with the help of the dictionary, and its type information is extracted. Algorithm 2 describes the above process. Line 1 executes the query. Lines 2–4 initializes the matrix of *ids*, R'. Lines 5–12 translates the query result into R'. Finally, line 13 extracts the type information.

Rule Application. For each triples map, we combine its subject map with each of its predicate-object maps to form the mapping rules. Each of these rules is transformed into a template specifying the format of the resulting triples. In each field of the template may exist column names specifying the columns whose values will be used to supplant them in the resulting triples.

We then take one mapping rule's template and one row from its logical table each time and give them to a worker thread to generate the corresponding triple. All worker threads run in parallel. In this way, parallelization is achieved at the fine-grained level of a database row.

3.3 Triple Storage

After the triples are generated, storing them could potentially become a performance bottleneck if parallelization is not properly supported. To this end, we employ a concurrent hash set that can adequately shoulder the burden of storing triples concurrently while eliminating duplicates.

Algorithm 3 describes the process of rule application and triple storage. We omit the trivial detail of combining the three types of maps of each triples map to form all mapping rules and assume that the set of all mapping rules, Π, is already given. The algorithm additionally takes as arguments S and L. We assume that S and L have already been populated with the processed content and type information, respectively, of all relevant logical tables. Finally, D is the concurrent dictionary. The output T of the algorithm is a concurrent hash set of triples. As can be seen in line 2, the two cases where the object map is or is not a referencing object map are treated differently. A rule r with referencing object map would need to execute a join query to fetch the results and generate the corresponding triples, which is depicted in lines 3–4. For rules without a referencing object map, their logical tables can be directly accessed from S and L, as depicted in lines 6–7. Function *isvalid*() in line 11 checks whether any of the columns of $R'[i]$ referenced by the current mapping rule r has null value. Function *derivetriple*() in line 12 first translates the *ids* in $R'[i]$ back into strings and replaces the corresponding part of the rule template by values from the relevant columns; it then adds type and language information to the elements of the triple if necessary; the new triple is then translated into a triple of *ids* using the dictionary (allotting new *ids* if necessary). Finally, the generated triple t is added to set T in line 13.

3.4 Overview

In all, the operating mechanism of our Fingr engine can be summarized into Algorithm 4. The algorithm first parses the mapping file in line 1, removing self-joins where applicable. Then, S, the hash map containing the content of the relevant logical tables, and L, the hash map containing type information for the logical tables, are both initialized to be empty; the dictionary D is initialized to map string *null* to 0; all *ids* are initialized to the smallest natural number of their corresponding intervals. The number of groups that *id* is partitioned into, k, is configurable. After the initialization phase, the content of the logical tables is retrieved and processed, and S, L, and D are modified accordingly, as shown in lines 4–6. Subsequently, rules are applied to their respective processed RDB tuples and triples are generated and deduplicated in line 7. Finally, the result is returned for further operations in line 8.

4 Experiments

We implemented Fingr in C++ and evaluated it on two benchmarks against Morph-KGC with Mysql 8.0. We chose Morph-KGC as the only baseline since it significantly outperforms other existing systems, sometimes even by an order of magnitude [2]. There was no available performance comparison between RML-Streamer and Morph-KGC, but the former does not support duplicate elimination. The hash maps in Algorithms 3 and 4 are implemented with Concur-

Algorithm 4. KGConstruction(M, C)

Input: A mapping file M, a database connection C.
Output: The set of output triples T

$\Pi \leftarrow parse(M)$;
Initialize S, L, D;
for each logical table q appearing in Π **do**
    $\langle R', I\rangle \leftarrow$ ProcessQuery(C, q, D);
    $S[q] \leftarrow R'$;
    $L[q] \leftarrow I$;
$T \leftarrow$ ApplyRules(Π, C, S, L, D);
return T

rent Hashmap from folly (Facebook Open-source Library)[10]. When implementing RDB retrieval and processing phase, queries are rewritten to cast all values to strings, and type information is retrieved separately.

In addition to the GTFS benchmark [13] considered in [2], we also ran both engines on the well known BSBM's (the Berlin SPARQL Benchmark) [12] datasets. The mapping files used are obtained from GTFS's[11] and morph-rdb's[12] repositories, respectively. Note that the mapping file we found for GTFS is different from that used in [2] so that the numbers of generated triples are not exactly the same. We additionally performed experiments over BSBM with varying thread numbers to examine the effect of parallelization for both engines.

Each engine was tasked to accept a valid database connection and a mapping as inputs and output the triples to disks in our experiments. For correctness we verified the outputs of the two engines and made sure they were equal. Every experiment was run at least 3 times and the average execution time was computed. We used C++ std::chrono::steady_clock to record the running time of our system and adopted the output of Morph-KGC as their running time. The experiments were performed on a Windows 11 PC with 64 GB RAM, an Intel i9-12900k CPU with 16 cores, and a Samsung MZVL21T0HCLR-00B00 SSD with 7000MB/s sequential read.

4.1 Evaluation over the GTFS Benchmark

The results for GTFS are displayed in Table 1. The running time in seconds of each setup is recorded in this table. GTFS10 means the dataset is generated with scale 10 by the GTFS benchmark. GTFS1000 caused both engines to run out of memory and therefore was not included. As the running time of different setups vary greatly, we compute the performance ratio as shown in the table to illustrate the relative performance of the two as recorded in the row Perf Ratio. As can be observed from the table, Fingr outperforms Morph-KGC by

[10] https://github.com/facebook/folly.
[11] https://github.com/oeg-upm/gtfs-bench.
[12] https://github.com/oeg-upm/morph-rdb.

at least 80% in terms of speed. We observe the advantage of Fingr dwindling as the size of dataset increases. After close examination of the running process, we discovered that the cause of this disproportionate surge in running time is the largest join query in terms of time cost. Specifically, the time taken for the Mysql Connector/C++ to execute the query and the time taken to free up the memory storing the rows dominate the query time cost. The running time of this query can be erratic, especially in the latter stage when the memory is to be freed. We deduce that this results from the Mysql Connnector/C++'s implementation of mysqlx::Row. By reviewing its source code we had the impression that the records in each row is not stored contiguously in memory. Although we parallelly clear these Rows as we transform their records into *ids*, our parallel clearing of rows collapses into an almost serial one.

Table 2 shows a dissected sample run for GTFS100. As can be seen from this table, the time taken performing interactions with the database (querying & pre-processing) in total comprises 62.07% of the total time cost. Conversion of the rows from tuples of strings to tuples of *ids* constitutes 35.01% of the database interaction time cost. The largest query's conversion time as shown in the table dominates the total conversion cost, making up 87.48% of the total conversion time. This conversion was observed to be executed almost serially, with CPU utilization persistently less than 10%. It is perceivable from this sample run that RDB retrival and processing can be an outstanding bottleneck of our engine.

Table 1. GTFS Running Time(s) Results

	GTFS1	GTFS10	GTFS20	GTFS50	GTFS100
Morph-KGC	7.469	27.469	50.369	118.970	235.961
Fingr	1.758	9.970	20.056	55.525	130.837
Perf Ratio	4.249	2.755	2.511	2.143	1.803

Table 2. A Dissected(s) Sample Run With GTFS100

	Join	Non-join	Query	Conversion	Conv. #1	Total
Fingr	63.192	17.542	80.734	28.265	24.725	130.060

4.2 Evaluation over the Berlin SPARQL Benchmark

Comparison. As reported in Table 3, which is structured homogeneously as Table 1, Fingr outperforms Morph-KGC by up to 6.28 times. Contrary to the GTFS benchmark results, Fingr's advantage becomes bigger as the size of datasets increases. This advantage in performance can be attributed to two main reasons. The first is that BSBM contains large amount of comments that are long strings. The dictionary in Fingr transforms these into *ids*, whereby laborious operations on varying length long strings are replaced by generic operations on fixed size relatively small integers. The second is that the groups the mapping rules are partitioned into by Morph-KGC are skewed in terms of workloads. Some groups dominate the total workloads meaning the parallelizaton scheme of Morph-KGC to some extent collapses into a serial one. In the case of BSBM, the mapping rules were partitioned into 10 groups by Morph-KGC so that the workloads can be parallelly processed by at most 10 cores. Even worse, The triples output by 2 groups accounts for 72.90% of the total workload, one taking up 38.06%, the other 34.84%, which means that even if the ten groups are evenly spread across 10 cores, the actual workload of each core still differs greatly. In contrast, Fingr's performance is more independent both from the database instance's data distributions and the mapping rules' features, and our parallelization scheme is not as seriously impaired in this case.

Table 3. BSBM Running Time (s) Results

	BSBM100	BSBM1000	BSBM10000	BSBM100000
Morph-KGC	3.438	8.566	65.745	721.269
Fingr	1.141	1.777	11.370	114.860
Perf Ratio	3.013	4.820	5.782	6.280

Parallelization Showcase. We wished to know how much the deficit in performance of both engines resided in parallelization level, whereby a further experiment was conducted. Table 4 records the results of running the dataset BSBM100000 with different number of threads and processes. Note that due to our implementation, the stage of output to disk has $n+1$ threads if $n > 1$. Since in Morph-KGC each process executes its instructions serially, the number of threads maximally active is the same as the number of processes. When run with 64 processes Morph-KGC reported an error, whereby no valid data was obtained. For Fingr, we observe a close to 4 times increase in terms of speed from 1 thread to 64 threads. This is reasonable as the time consumed by interacting with the database can hardly be influenced by our parallelization scheme. For Morph-KGC, however, their parallelization scheme achieved only a 62.53% speedup, with little further improvement beyond 2 processes. This is congruous with our earlier workload analysis for Morph-KGC. Since two groups make up the majority of the workloads and allowing more than two processes does not lighten the load on the two processes tasked with these two groups, we see little improvement in overall performance for Morph-KGC beyond two processes.

Table 4. Results with various # of threads on BSBM100000

Thread#	64	32	16	8	4	2	1
Fingr	119.508	127.871	125.344	137.959	170.037	243.184	440.650
Morph-KGC		722.932	725.148	725.003	732.301	733.965	1174.998

5 Conclusion and Discussion

In this paper, we presented Fingr, a prototype concurrent dictionary assisted fine-grained parallel R2RML engine and our experiments show that our engine outperforms state-of-the-art counterparts by up to 6.28 times on well established workbenches, attesting to effectiveness of the design and implementation of our prototype engine. For future work, exploration of parallelization schemes that improve RDB query efficiency can be performed. An experiment that mask the effect of RDB query can be designed and executed. Extension of Fingr to support RML and other R2RML variants is also possible.

References

1. Arenas-Guerrero, J., et al.: Knowledge graph construction with r2rml and rml: an etl system-based overview. In: CEUR Workshop Proceedings, vol. 2873 (2021)
2. Arenas-Guerrero, J., Chaves-Fraga, D., Toledo, J., Pérez, M.S., Corcho, O.: Morph-KGC: scalable knowledge graph materialization with mapping partitions. Semantic Web (2022)
3. Calvanese, D., et al.: Ontop: answering sparql queries over relational databases. Semant. Web **8**(3), 471–487 (2017)
4. Debruyne, C., Sullivan, D.O.: R2RML-F: towards sharing and executing domain logic in r2rml mappings. In: Proceedings of LDOW (2016)
5. Dimou, A., Sande, M.V., Colpaert, P., Verborgh, R., Mannens, E., Van de Walle, R.: RML: a generic language for integrated RDF mappings of heterogeneous data. In: Proceedings of LDOW (2014)
6. Haesendonck, G., Maroy, W., Heyvaert, P., Verborgh, R., Dimou, A.: Parallel RDF generation from heterogeneous big data. In: Proceedings of SBD@SIGMOD, pp. 1:1–1:6 (2019)
7. Iglesias, E., Jozashoori, S., Chaves-Fraga, D., Collarana, D., Vidal, M.-E.: Sdm-rdfizer: an RML interpreter for the efficient creation of RDF knowledge graphs. CoRR, arXiv:2008.07176v1 (2020)
8. Priyatna, F., Corcho, O., Sequeda, J.: Formalisation and experiences of r2rml-based sparql to sql query translation using morph. In: Proceedings of WWW, pp. 479–490 (2014)
9. Scrocca, M., Comerio, M., Carenini, A., Celino, I.: Turning transport data to comply with EU standards while enabling a multimodal transport knowledge graph. In Proceedings of ISWC 2020, Part II, pp. 411–429 (2020)
10. Simsek, U., Kärle, E., Fensel, D.: Rocketrml - a nodejs implementation of a use case specific RML mapper. In: ESWC 2019, vol. 2489 of CEUR Workshop Proceedings, pp. 46–53 (2019)

11. Zou, X.: A survey on application of knowledge graph. J. Phys: Conf. Ser. **1487**(1), 012016 (2020)
12. Bizer, C., Schultz, A.: The berlin SPARQL benchmark. Int. J. Semantic Web Inf. Syst. **5**(2), 1–24 (2009)
13. Chaves-Fraga, D., Priyatna, F., Cimmino, A., Toledo, J., Ruckhaus, E., Corcho, Ó.: GTFS-madrid-bench: a benchmark for virtual knowledge graph access in the transport domain. J. Web Semant. **65**, 100596 (2020)

Knowledge Graph Augmentation with Entity Identification for Improving Knowledge Graph Completion Performance

Shuichi Chikatsuji(✉), Kenta Yamamoto, Ryu Takeda, and Kazunori Komatani

The Institute of Scientific and Industrial Research (SANKEN), Osaka University, Osaka, Japan
s-chikatsuji@ei.sanken.osaka-u.ac.jp

Abstract. A knowledge graph often lacks some existent triples. Knowledge graph completion is a technique for complementing such triples and its performance can be improved by augmenting triples from other external databases. However, entity names often differ between the original knowledge graph and an external database, which reduce the augmentation's efficiency. In this study, we identify the same entities that have different names (orthographic variants) that come from different sources, merge them into one entity, and augment the knowledge graphs. Our proposed method exploits in the original knowledge graph and the external database the similarity of triples, which were embedded using BERT. Experimental evaluation on our knowledge graph completion performance showed that our proposed method with graph information effectively outperformed two baselines.

Keywords: Knowledge graph · Knowledge graph completion · Orthographic variants

1 Introduction

Many studies have investigated knowledge graphs (KGs) as databases for dialogue systems [14,19–21,24]. A KG is represented as a set of triples (e_s, r, e_o) where e_s is a subject entity, r is a relation, and e_o is an object entity. The relations between two entities can be flexibly represented in KGs. On the other hand, it is basically impossible to represent every triple in the real world.

We can estimate the missing triples in KGs using knowledge graph completion (KGC) [2,8], which can be utilized to generate the response sentences of a dialogue system [7]. However, the more missing triples that exist, the lower is the KGC performance. To improve the KGC performance, KGs can be augmented using a different external database, as exemplified in Fig. 1. Increasing the number of relations per entity by augmenting KG will improve the KGC performance.

F. Liu et al. (Eds.): PRICAI 2023, LNAI 14325, pp. 480–486, 2024.
https://doi.org/10.1007/978-981-99-7019-3_43

A crucial problem in this augmentation is that entity names often differ between an existing KG and an external database. We call such different names having identical meanings *orthographic variants*. For example, "chocolate cake" is often abbreviated to "choco cake" in Japanese.

We identify entities whose meanings are identical and merge them, as shown in the "chocolate cake" example in Fig. 1. In our study, *entity identification* refers to associating two entities with the same meanings. If such entities are successfully merged, we can augment more relations between existing entities, which will improve the KGC performance.

Our proposed entity identification uses the similarity of feature vectors generated by BERT [5] by considering the graph information. We evaluated its effectiveness by the KGC performance obtained after augmenting a KG with entity identification.

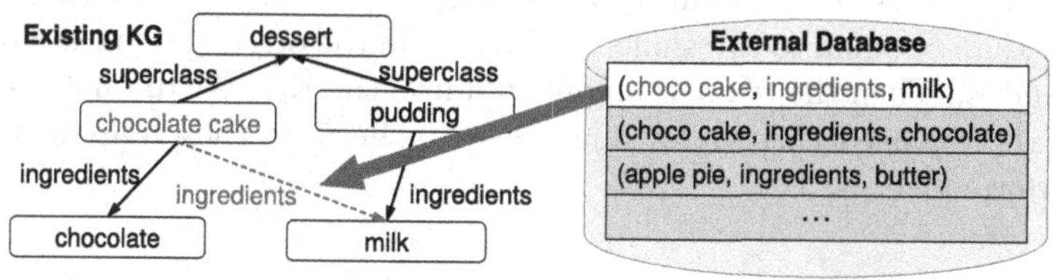

Fig. 1. Augmentation of KG using different databases

2 Related Work

Although some studies have addressed KG augmentation or construction, most did not take into account orthographic variants [1,4,9,22]. Meng et al. [10] constructed a KG from Chinese literature by merging orthographic variants using the Word2vec [11] model trained from the original literature. However, the KG and the external database considered in our study have no original literature to train a model.

Ikeda et al. [6] and Saito et al. [13] used language models to remove Japanese orthographic variants without KGs. Turson et al. [17] also studied a similar method for Uighur. Unlike our study, these works assume the availability of sufficient documents for training models.

Zhang et al. [23] and Sun et al. [15] input entity or triple information to language models to perform NLP tasks. However, both works assume that the original KG has enough relations between its entities.

3 Entity Identification Based on Graph Information

3.1 Augmentation with Entity Identification

Figure 2 shows the augmentation of a KG using entity identification, which is done on entities e_s and e_o in triples (e_s, r, e_o) of an external database used for

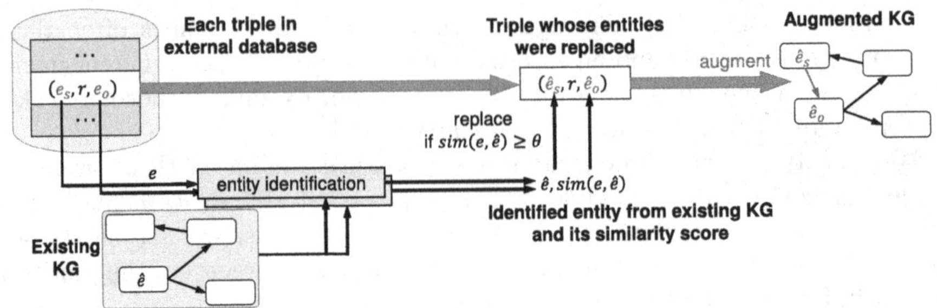

Fig. 2. Augmentation details with entity identification

augmentation. The entity identification module outputs the most similar entities, $\hat{e}_s$ and $\hat{e}_o$, in the existing KG and their similarity scores. If the similarity scores are larger than or equal to threshold θ, e_s and e_o in the original triple are replaced with $\hat{e}_s$ and $\hat{e}_o$. Then the triple is augmented into the KG. We did not use triples that have unreplaced entities for augmentation because they may degrade the KGC performance.

3.2 Feature Vectors of Entities with BERT Considering Graph Information

Entity identification calculates the cosine similarity between the feature vectors of the entities in the KG and the external database. An entity with the largest cosine similarity in the KG is identified as the most similar. The feature vectors are computed with graph information using BERT.

We use the name of each entity and the triples containing it as input to BERT. Figure 3 shows an example. The triples are grouped by relations, and the sentences about them are connected by [SEP] tokens. When computing the feature vector for entity "chocolate cake," the input is "[CLS] chocolate cake [SEP] ingredients are egg and chocolate [SEP] superclass is dessert [SEP]" based on the graph structure. A [CLS] token is always used at the beginning of the BERT input.

Mean-pooling was applied to the sequence of output vectors from BERT. The pooled vector is a feature vector of each entity. In addition, we normalized each feature vector by subtracting the mean of all the feature vectors from it to improve the KGC performance after augmentation.

4 Experiments and Evaluations

4.1 Settings

We used a food subgraph from Wikidata [18] as the original KG. We extracted a portion of it and used it as test and validation data. The remaining graph after the extraction was used as the augmentation target. The target data had 14454

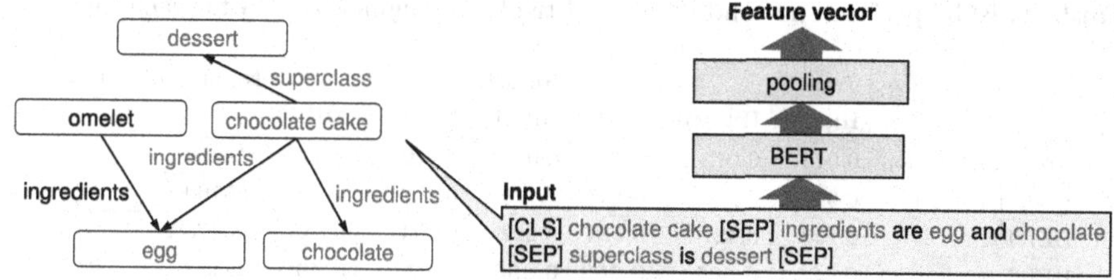

Fig. 3. Input format for BERT based on graph information

triples, the validation data had 242, and the test data had 243. They contained 8423 entities and 110 kinds of relations.

We used Rakuten Recipe from the Rakuten public data[1] for the external database. It has about 800,000 recipes. The entities to be augmented came from the names of dishes and the ingredients in the recipes.

We used TransE [3] and RotatE [16] as KGC models. Using the validation data, we set the embedding dimension to 300 for both models. For each triple (e_s, r, e_o) in the test data, we evaluated the performance of randomly predicting either e_s or e_o. Hits@$N(N = 1, 10)$ and mean reciprocal rank (MRR) were used as evaluation metrics. The BERT model was fine-tuned from a pre-trained model for Japanese[2]. Its hyperparameters are based on a previous paper [12]. Threshold θ (Fig. 2) was experimentally set to 0.4 using the validation data.

We set two baselines. One was "EditDist-based," in which similarity scores were computed by subtracting the normalized edit distance between the entity names from 1. The edit distance was normalized by the length of the longer entity name. Each entity name was treated as letters representing its Japanese pronunciation in this baseline. Entity pairs with similarity scores over 0.9 were regarded as identical. The other baseline was "BERT" without graphs, i.e., only each entity name was used to compute its feature vector by BERT.

4.2 Results and Discussion

Table 1 shows the KGC performance and the number of triples of the augmented KG for each method. Our proposed method is "BERT+graph."

Our BERT+graph method outperformed the other methods in every metric, especially the BERT baseline, and its number of triples decreased from the BERT baseline. This result indicates that the graph information reduced the triples that do not contribute to the KGC performance and positively impacted it.

Comparing the performance of each method, the increase from the BERT baseline to our BERT+graph method exceeded that from the EditDist-based baseline to the BERT baseline in all the metrics. This also confirms the effectiveness of graph information.

[1] https://rit.rakuten.com/data_release_ja/.

[2] https://huggingface.co/cl-tohoku/bert-base-japanese-whole-word-masking.

Table 1. KGC performance and number of triples of augmented KG for each method

Method	TransE			RotatE			Number of triples
	Hits@1	Hits@10	MRR	Hits@1	Hits@10	MRR	
No augmentation	0.014	0.072	0.035	0.010	0.072	0.032	14454
EditDist-based	0.072	0.327	0.157	0.121	0.377	0.209	55169
BERT	0.128	0.422	0.228	0.222	0.504	0.315	290475
BERT+graph	**0.191**	**0.531**	**0.302**	**0.383**	**0.724**	**0.497**	211168

Table 2 shows some examples of similarity scores? "Target entity" is an entity of Rakuten Recipe, and "Existing entity" is an entity of the food subgraph. We include the Japanese entity names and the pronunciations in parentheses. Our BERT+graph method successfully computed more appropriate similarity scores. For example, its similarity scores were high for similar pairs, such as 酢イカ (vinegared squid) and イカ (squid), and low for dissimilar pairs, such as 酢イカ (vinegared squid) and スイカ (watermelon) or かき揚げ (vegetable tempura) and カキ (oyster). On the other hand, even for a pair indicating exactly the same thing, such as そば(soba) and 蕎麦 (soba), the scores of another similar pair, such as そば(soba) and かけそば (kakesoba), were higher. Kakesoba is a kind of soba. While the KG augmentation improved KGC performance as demonstrated in Table 1, its negative effects were mitigated by preventing the erroneous merging of dissimilar pairs, such as 酢イカ (vinegared squid) and スイカ (watermelon).

Table 2. Examples of entity identification results

		BERT+graph	BERT	EditDist-based
酢イカ[suika]	スイカ[suika]	0.30	0.50	**1.00**
酢イカ[suika]	イカ[ika]	**0.66**	**0.70**	0.60
かき揚げ[kakiage]	カキ[kaki]	0.35	**0.71**	0.57
かき揚げ[kakiage]	から揚げ[karaage]	**0.59**	0.52	**0.71**
そば[soba]	かけそば[kakesoba]	**0.73**	0.62	0.50
そば[soba]	蕎麦[soba]	0.64	**0.79**	**1.00**

5 Conclusion

We augmented a KG with entity identification based on graph information and evaluated its KGC performance effectiveness after augmentation. Our experiment's results indicate that our proposed method outperformed the two baselines. In the future, we will verify whether our proposed method remains effective with another KG and external databases.

Acknowledgement. This work was partly supported by JST Moonshot R&D Grant Number JPMJPS2011 and JSPS KAKENHI Grant Numbers JP23H03457 and JP22H00536.

References

1. Al-Khatib, K., et al.: End-to-end argumentation knowledge graph construction. In: Proceedings of AAAI, vol. 34, pp. 7367–7374 (2020)
2. Bordes, A., et al.: Learning structured embeddings of knowledge bases. In: Proceedings of AAAI, vol. 25, pp. 301–306 (2011)
3. Bordes, A., et al.: Translating embeddings for modeling multi-relational data. In: Proceedings of NIPS, pp. 2787–2795 (2013)
4. Cannaviccio, M., et al.: Leveraging Wikipedia table schemas for knowledge graph augmentation. In: Proceedings of WebDB, pp. 1–6 (2018)
5. Devlin, J., et al.: BERT: pre-training of deep bidirectional transformers for language understanding. In: Proceedings of NAACL-HLT, pp. 4171–4186 (2019)
6. Ikeda, T., et al.: Japanese text normalization with encoder-decoder model. In: Proceedings of WNUT, pp. 129–137 (2016)
7. Komatani, K., et al.: Knowledge graph completion-based question selection for acquiring domain knowledge through dialogues. In: Proceedings of IUI, pp. 531–541 (2021)
8. Lao, N., et al.: Random walk inference and learning in a large scale knowledge base. In: Proceedings of EMNLP, pp. 529–539 (2011)
9. Luan, Y., et al.: Multi-task identification of entities, relations, and coreference for scientific knowledge graph construction. In: Proceedings of EMNLP, pp. 3219–3232 (2018)
10. Meng, F., et al.: Creating knowledge graph of electric power equipment faults based on BERT-BiLSTM-CRF model. J. Electr. Eng. Technol. **17**(4), 2507–2516 (2022)
11. Mikolov, T., et al.: Distributed representations of words and phrases and their compositionality. In: Proceedings of NIPS, pp. 3111–3119 (2013)
12. Reimers, N., et al.: Sentence-BERT: sentence embeddings using siamese BERT-networks. In: Proceedings of EMNLP-IJCNLP, pp. 3982–3992 (2019)
13. Saito, I., et al.: Improving neural text normalization with data augmentation at character-and morphological levels. In: Proceedings of IJCNLP, pp. 257–262 (2017)
14. Sarkar, R., et al.: Suggest me a movie for tonight: leveraging knowledge graphs for conversational recommendation. In: Proceedings of COLING, pp. 4179–4189 (2020)
15. Sun, T., et al.: CoLAKE: contextualized language and knowledge embedding. In: Proceedings of COLING, pp. 3660–3670 (2020)
16. Sun, Z., et al.: RotatE: knowledge graph embedding by relational rotation in complex space. In: Proceedings of ICLR, pp. 1–18 (2018)
17. Tursun, O., Cakıcı, R.: Noisy Uyghur text normalization. In: Proceedings of WNUT, pp. 85–93 (2017)
18. Vrandečić, D., et al.: Wikidata: a free collaborative knowledgebase. Commun. ACM **57**(10), 78–85 (2014)
19. Xu, L., et al.: End-to-end knowledge-routed relational dialogue system for automatic diagnosis. In: Proceedings of AAAI, vol. 33, pp. 7346–7353 (2019)
20. Yao, X., Van Durme, B.: Information extraction over structured data: question answering with freebase. In: Proceedings of ACL, vol. 1, pp. 956–966 (2014)

21. Yasunaga, M., et al.: QA-GNN: reasoning with language models and knowledge graphs for question answering. In: Proceedings of NAACL-HLT, pp. 535–546 (2021)
22. Yoo, S., Jeong, O.: Auto-growing knowledge graph-based intelligent chatbot using BERT. ICIC Express Lett. **14**(1), 67–73 (2020)
23. Zhang, Z., et al.: ERNIE: enhanced language representation with informative entities. In: Proceedings of ACL, pp. 1441–1451 (2019)
24. Zhou, H., et al.: Commonsense knowledge aware conversation generation with graph attention. In: Proceedings of IJCAI, pp. 4623–4629 (2018)

Relational Acceptability Semantics of Abstract Argumentation

Ryuta Arisaka(✉) and Takayuki Ito

Kyoto University, Kyoto 606-8317, Japan
ryutaarisaka@gmail.com, ito@i.kyoto-u.ac.jp

Abstract. We introduce *argumentation tuple relational calculus*, adapting tuple relational calculus for acceptability semantics, and derive *relational acceptability semantics* of abstract argumentation. It serves as a theoretical framework to link different types of acceptability semantics relationally. It also allows for refining existing acceptability semantics.

1 Introduction

Abstract argumentation frameworks by Dung [8] capture defeasible/conflicting information as a graph structure. Each node is an argument (information) and each edge from an argument to another argument is an attack from the source argument to the target argument. For the semantics of argumentation graphs, Dung defines several *acceptability semantics* deciding which sets of arguments are acceptable. Each of them can be derived from some of them via (1) set-theoretical operations on it and possibly also (2) the count of attacked arguments. In that sense, they are all linked in these two measures. The relationship among them is thus easy to see. However, various types of acceptability semantics exist by now and the two measures are no longer sufficient for linking them. For example, *multi-agent semantics*, *e.g.* [2,3,5], assigns a subgraph of a given argumentation graph to each agent, obtains (often) Dung acceptability semantics of each of the subgraphs (one per agent), and aggregates them in some way. This procedure is too involved to be emulated by the two measures alone. *Can we obtain a theoretical framework for recovering the linkability?* We present a *formal language for the linking* to address this question. Specifically, noting that much of the difficulty with handling multi-agent semantics is relational, we adapt tuple relational calculus [10] for acceptability semantics to derive argumentation tuple relational calculus, and formulate *relational acceptabilty semantics* which will be shown to extend the linkability to multi-agent semantics. It allows for easily specialising or generalising existing acceptability semantics, too. A fuller work is in [4].

Related Work. Identification of common constraints among different acceptability semantics is popular [1,6]. However, the constraint identification research focuses on identifying a specific set of formal constraints, and through them, a

Supported by JSPS KAKENHI Grant Number 21K12028.

F. Liu et al. (Eds.): PRICAI 2023, LNAI 14325, pp. 487–493, 2024.
https://doi.org/10.1007/978-981-99-7019-3_44

specific set of acceptability semantics. Thus, even provided there is no dependency among the constraints, they can identify at most 2^N different acceptability semantics with N being the number of them. By contrast, our proposal provides a proper formal language (a fragment of predicate logic) whose semantics is not only defined at some points but instead defined for any expression allowed in the language. Hence, by capturing acceptability semantics in the language, it becomes possible to overcome the discreteness limitation. Further, the language allows the derivation of acceptability semantics through database queries which, unlike the full predicate logic expressions, can be handled directly in SQL.

2 Technical Preliminaries

$\mathcal{A}$ is an uncountable set of entities, *arguments*. An abstract argumentation framework is normally a finite graph (A, R) with $A \subseteq \mathcal{A}$ and $R \subseteq A \times A$. Given (A, R), for any $a_1, a_2 \in A$, we say a_1 attacks a_2 just when $(a_1, a_2) \in R$. Given (A, R), $A' \subseteq A$ and $a \in A$, A' is *conflict-free* iff there is no attack (edge) in $(A', R \cap (A' \times A'))$; A' *defends* a iff, for any argument $a_1 \in A$, if a_1 attacks a, then some argument $a' \in A'$ attacks a_1; and A' is *admissible* iff it defends every member of A' and is conflict-free. We obtain 4 different - but well-linked - acceptability semantics of (A, R). The *complete semantics* of (A, R) comprises every admissible $A' \subseteq A$ that includes every argument it defends. Let Γ denote the complete semantics of (A, R), then the set comprising: every set-inclusion-wise maximal member A' of Γ is the *preferred semantics* of (A, R); every member A' of Γ such that for each $a \in (A \backslash A')$ there is some $a' \in A'$ that attacks a is the *stable semantics* of (A, R); the minimum member of Γ is the *grounded semantics* of (A, R). For each $\boldsymbol{x} \in \{\text{complete, preferred, stable, grounded}\}$, every member A' of the $\boldsymbol{x}$ semantics of (A, R) is *acceptable* under the $\boldsymbol{x}$ semantics. Now, as per [7,9], we can represent each member $A' \subseteq A$ of $\boldsymbol{x}$ semantics of (A, R) with a labelling function. Let L denote $\{\mathsf{in}, \mathsf{out}, \mathsf{und}\}$ and let Λ denote the class of all partial functions $\mathcal{A} \rightarrow L$ as labelling functions. Any member A' of the $\boldsymbol{x}$ semantics of (A, R) corresponds to some labelling function $\lambda \in \Lambda$ satisfying: (1) $\boldsymbol{dom}(\lambda) = A$ ($\boldsymbol{dom}(\lambda)$ is the domain of λ); (2) $\lambda(a) = \mathsf{in}$ just when $a \in A'$; and (3) $\lambda(a) = \mathsf{out}$ just when there is some $a' \in A'$ attacking a. Clearly, the *labelling-based* $\boldsymbol{x}$ *semantics* of (A, R) is the set of all labelling functions some member of the $\boldsymbol{x}$ semantics of (A, R) corresponds to.

One typical idea of multi-agent semantics [2,3,5] is: given an (A, R), partition A into $A_1, \ldots, A_n$ ($\bigcup_{1 \leq i \leq n} A_i = A$), each of which represents arguments put forward by an agent; each agent i ($1 \leq i \leq n$) knows some (A_x, R_x) such that $A_i \subseteq A_x \subseteq A$ and $R_x = R \cap (A_x \times A_x)$, and derives some labelling-based acceptability semantics Λ_i of (A_x, R_x). An external observer with the gods perspective aggregates these local labelling-based acceptability semantics $\Lambda_1, \ldots, \Lambda_n$ into a global labelling-based acceptability semantics Λ_g of (A, R) (where each $\lambda_g \in \Lambda_g$ satisfies $\boldsymbol{dom}(\lambda_g) = A$). Typically, each $\lambda_g \in \Lambda_g$ is such that, for each partition A_i, λ_g assigns the same labels to A_i as some $\lambda_i \in \Lambda_i$.

tbl_1	a_G	a_F	a_E	a_D	a_C	a_B	a_A
λ_1	out	in	und	und	und	und	und
λ_2	out	in	in	out	und	und	und
λ_3	out	in	out	in	out	in	out

tbl_2	a_G	a_F	a_E	a_D
λ_4	out	in	und	und
λ_5	out	in	in	out
λ_6	out	in	out	in

tbl_3	a_E	a_D	a_c	a_B	a_A
λ_7	out	in	out	in	out

Fig. 1. The tables referred to by tbl_1, tbl_2 and tbl_3 list labelling functions ($\lambda_1(a_G) = \mathsf{out}$, $\lambda_1(a_F) = \mathsf{in}$ and so on in tbl_1, similary for the others).

Example 1. 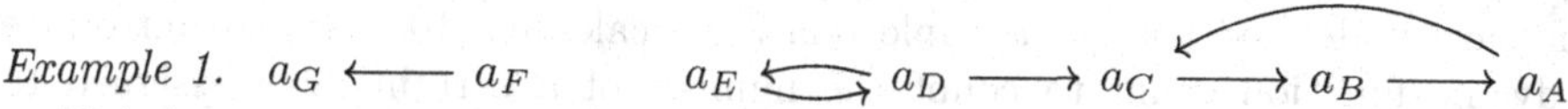

This is an argumentation graph. The labelling-based complete semantics of it comprises 3 labelling functions, as shown in (the table referred to by) tbl_1 in Fig. 1. Let us suppose 2 agents. Suppose agent 1 (resp. agent 2) puts forward $a_G, \ldots, a_E$ (resp. $a_D, \ldots, a_A$) and knows $a_G, \ldots, a_D$ (resp. $a_E, \ldots, a_A$) as well as attacks among them. Suppose agent 1 (resp. agent 2) uses the labelling-based complete semantics (resp. labelling-based stable semantics). Then, agent 1s (resp. agent 2s) local labelling-based complete (resp. stable) semantics comprises 3 (resp. 1) labelling functions as shown in tbl_2 (resp. tbl_3) in Fig. 1. Suppose the external observer uses the labelling-based complete semantics (tbl_1). Then the multi-agent semantics is a singleton set $\{\lambda_3\}$, since λ_3 is the only labelling function among $\{\lambda_1, \lambda_2, \lambda_3\}$ that can be matched by one of $\lambda_4, \lambda_5, \lambda_6$ for the labels of a_G, a_F and a_E and by λ_7 for the labels of a_D, a_C, a_B and a_A. ♣

3 Argumentation Tuple Relational Calculus and Relational Acceptability Semantics

We now formally develop *argumentation tuple relational calculus* which is a tuple relational calculus for manipulating labelling functions and formulate *relational acceptability semantics.*

Definition 1 (Arg-labelling table). An *arg-labelling table* is a tuple (A, Λ_1) with (1) $A \subseteq_{\mathsf{fin}} \mathcal{A}$, called *header* of (A, Λ_1), and $\Lambda_1 \subseteq \Lambda$ (*body* of (A, Λ_1)) with any of its member λ satisfying $\mathsf{dom}(\lambda) = A$. ♠

There is no duplicate in the body of an arg-labelling table.

Definition 2 (Relational arg-labelling database). Let $\mathcal{T}$ be a set of table names, let tbl denote its member, and let TBL denote its subset. A *relational arg-labelling database schema* is a tuple $(L, \mathsf{TBL}, \mathsf{header})$ with $\mathsf{header} : \mathsf{TBL} \to 2^{\mathcal{A}}$ associating a set of arguments to each table name. We denote the set of all relational arg-labelling database schemata by SCHM, and refer to its member by schm. A *relational arg-labelling database for* $\mathsf{schm} \equiv (L, \mathsf{TBL}, \mathsf{header})$ is db : $\mathsf{TBL} \to 2^{\Lambda}$ satisfying the following condition: for every $\mathsf{tbl} \in \mathsf{TBL}$ and every $\lambda \in db(\mathsf{tbl})$, it holds that $\mathsf{dom}(\lambda) = \mathsf{header}(\mathsf{tbl})$. ♠

Example 2 (Relational arg-labelling database). Observe in Fig. 1 that there are 3 arg-labelling tables in total. The arg-labelling database holding them is expressed with the following relational arg-labelling database schema and relational arg-labelling database with respect to it. Assume $A_1 = \{a_G, \ldots, a_A\}$, $A_2 = \{a_G, \ldots, a_D\}$, $A_3 = \{a_E, \ldots, a_A\}$, $\Lambda_1 = \{\lambda_1, \lambda_2, \lambda_3\}$, $\Lambda_2 = \{\lambda_4, \lambda_5, \lambda_6\}$, and $\Lambda_3 = \{\lambda_7\}$. Then: schm is $(L, \{\mathsf{tbl}_1, \mathsf{tbl}_2, \mathsf{tbl}_3\}, \mathsf{header} \equiv \{\mathsf{tbl}_1 \mapsto A_1, \ldots, \mathsf{tbl}_3 \mapsto A_3\})$; and db is $\{\mathsf{tbl}_1 \mapsto \Lambda_1, \ldots, \mathsf{tbl}_3 \mapsto \Lambda_3\}$. It holds that $\mathsf{dom}(\lambda_1) = A_1 = \mathsf{header}(\mathsf{tbl}_1)$, and similarly for all the others. ♣

Syntax and Semantics of Formal Query Language. The syntax of the query language is defined almost as tuple relational calculus [10], save we introduce a dyadic function count to count the number of a certain label assigned to the header arguments. This additional function helps keep formal expressions concise.

Definition 3 (Query formulas). V is an uncountable set of variables. An *atomic query formula* with respect to $\mathsf{schm} \equiv (L, \mathsf{TBL}, \mathsf{header})$ is any below. (1) $v_1.a_1 \doteq v_2.a_2$ for $v_1, v_2 \in V$ and $a_1, a_2 \in \mathcal{A}$. (2) $v_1.a_1 \doteq l$ for $v_1 \in V$, $a_1 \in \mathcal{A}$ and $l \in L$. (3) $\mathsf{tbl}[v_1]$ for $v_1 \in V$ and $\mathsf{tbl} \in \mathsf{TBL}$. (4) $\mathsf{count}(v_1, l_1) \dot{\leq} \mathsf{count}(v_2, l_2)$ for $v_1, v_2 \in V$ and $l_1, l_2 \in L$. (5) $\mathsf{count}(v_1, l_1) \dot{\leq} n$ for $v_1 \in V$, $l_1 \in L$ and $n \in \mathbb{N}$. (6) $n \dot{\leq} \mathsf{count}(v_1, l_1)$ for $v_1 \in V$, $l_1 \in L$ and $n \in \mathbb{N}$. Then, any below is a *query formula* with respect to schm. We may refer to a query formula by $\boldsymbol{F}$. (1) an atomic query formula with respect to schm. (2) $\neg \boldsymbol{F}_1$ if $\boldsymbol{F}_1$ is a query formula. (3) $\boldsymbol{F}_1 \wedge \boldsymbol{F}_2$ if $\boldsymbol{F}_1$ and $\boldsymbol{F}_2$ are query formulas. (4) $\boldsymbol{F}_1 \vee \boldsymbol{F}_2$ if $\boldsymbol{F}_1$ and $\boldsymbol{F}_2$ are query formulas. (5) $\exists v : A[\boldsymbol{F}_1]$ if v is in V, A is a set of arguments and $\boldsymbol{F}_1$ is a query formula. (6) $\forall v : A[\boldsymbol{F}_1]$ if v is in V, A is a set of arguments and $\boldsymbol{F}_1$ is a query formula. ♠

The following semantics of the language is fairly standard to the database theory.

Definition 4 (Semantics). Let $\mathsf{eval} : V \to \Lambda$ be an interpretation function such that $\mathsf{eval}(v) \in \Lambda$, and let a 'semantic structure' be a tuple $(\mathsf{schm}, db, \mathsf{eval})$ for schm and db for schm. We inductively define $(\mathsf{schm}, db, \mathsf{eval}) \models \boldsymbol{F}$ for any $(\mathsf{schm}, db, \mathsf{eval})$ and any $\boldsymbol{F}$ as follows.

- $(\mathsf{schm}, db, \mathsf{eval}) \models v_1.a_1 \doteq v_2.a_2$ iff $a_1 \in \mathsf{dom}(\mathsf{eval}(v_1))$ and $a_2 \in \mathsf{dom}(\mathsf{eval}(v_2))$ and $\mathsf{eval}(v_1)(a_1) = \mathsf{eval}(v_2)(a_2)$.
- $(\mathsf{schm}, db, \mathsf{eval}) \models v_1.a_1 \doteq l$ iff $a_1 \in \mathsf{dom}(\mathsf{eval}(v_1))$ and $\mathsf{eval}(v_1)(a_1) = l$.
- $(\mathsf{schm}, db, \mathsf{eval}) \models \mathsf{tbl}[v_1]$ iff $\mathsf{eval}(v_1) \in db(\mathsf{tbl})$.
- $(\mathsf{schm}, db, \mathsf{eval}) \models \mathsf{count}(v_1, l_1) \dot{\leq} \mathsf{count}(v_2, l_2)$ iff $|\{a \in \mathsf{dom}(\mathsf{eval}(v_1)) \mid \mathsf{eval}(v_1)(a) = l_1\}| \leq |\{a \in \mathsf{dom}(\mathsf{eval}(v_2)) \mid \mathsf{eval}(v_2)(a) = l_2\}|$
- $(\mathsf{schm}, db, \mathsf{eval}) \models \mathsf{count}(v_1, l_1) \dot{\leq} n$ iff $|\{a \in \mathsf{dom}(\mathsf{eval}(v_1)) \mid \mathsf{eval}(v_1)(a) = l_1\}| \leq n$.
- $(\mathsf{schm}, db, \mathsf{eval}) \models n \dot{\leq} \mathsf{count}(v_1, l_1)$ iff $n \leq |\{a \in \mathsf{dom}(\mathsf{eval}(v_1)) \mid \mathsf{eval}(v_1)(a) = l_1\}|$.
- $(\mathsf{schm}, db, \mathsf{eval}) \models \exists v : A[\boldsymbol{F}]$ iff there is some λ such that $\mathsf{dom}(\lambda) = A$ and that $(\mathsf{schm}, db, \mathsf{eval}') \models \boldsymbol{F}$ where eval' is almost exactly eval except $\mathsf{eval}'(v) = \lambda$.
- $(\mathsf{schm}, db, \mathsf{eval}) \models \forall v : A[\boldsymbol{F}]$ iff, for every λ, if $\mathsf{dom}(\lambda) = A$, then $(\mathsf{schm}, db, \mathsf{eval}') \models \boldsymbol{F}$ where eval' is almost exactly eval except $\mathsf{eval}'(v) = \lambda$.

Due to space, we omit the cases of $\neg \boldsymbol{F}$, $\boldsymbol{F}_1 \wedge \boldsymbol{F}_2$ and $\boldsymbol{F}_1 \vee \boldsymbol{F}_2$ which are standard. We say that $(\mathsf{schm}, db, \mathsf{eval})$ models $\boldsymbol{F}$ iff $(\mathsf{schm}, db, \mathsf{eval}) \models \boldsymbol{F}$. ♠

For atomic formulas, $v_1.a_1 \doteq v_2.a_2$ tests whether the label of a_1 assigned by $\lambda_x \equiv \mathsf{eval}(v_1)$ and that of a_2 assigned by $\lambda_y \equiv \mathsf{eval}(v_2)$ matches. The first two attached conditions force $a_1 \in \mathsf{dom}(\lambda_x)$ and $a_2 \in \mathsf{dom}(\lambda_y)$. $v_1.a_2 \doteq l$ tests whether the label of a_1 assigned by $\lambda_x \equiv \mathsf{eval}(v_1)$ is l. $\mathsf{tbl}[v_1]$ tests whether $\lambda_x \equiv \mathsf{eval}(v_1)$ is in the body of the arg-labelling table $db(\mathsf{tbl})$. $\mathsf{count}(v_1, l_1) \dot{\leq} \mathsf{count}(v_2, l_2)$ compares the number of arguments assigned l_1 by $\lambda_1 \equiv \mathsf{eval}(v_1)$ and that of arguments assigned l_2 by $\lambda_2 \equiv \mathsf{eval}(v_2)$. Similarly for the other two atomic formulas.

Definition 5 (Relational acceptability semantics). An *arg-labelling query* is an expression $\{v : A \mid \boldsymbol{F}\}$, whereby the only free variable in $\boldsymbol{F}$ is v. The semantics of a query $\{v : A \mid \boldsymbol{F}\}$ with respect to some schm and db is the set of all λ satisfying $(\mathsf{schm}, db, \mathsf{eval}) \models \boldsymbol{F}$ with $\mathsf{eval}(v) = \lambda$. Let $\|\{v : A \mid \boldsymbol{F}\}\|$ denote the set. A *relational acceptability semantics* with respect to schm and db is some $\|\{v : A \mid \boldsymbol{F}\}\|$ with respect to schm and db. ♠

Basic database queries such as selecting rows of a table, selecting columns of a table, and joining two tables, produce certain effects on arg-labelling database with associated arg-labelling tables.

Example 3 (Selecting columns). In Fig. 1, tbl_2 (or the arg-labelling table referred to by tbl_2) is the result of selecting 4 columns a_G, a_F, a_E and a_D of tbl_1. The corresponding relational acceptability semantics is $\|\{v : \{a_G, a_F, a_E, a_D\} \mid \mathsf{tbl}_1[v]\}\|$ with respect to the same schm and db in Example 2. To see to it, we firstly enumerate all λ with $(\mathsf{schm}, db, \mathsf{eval}) \models \mathsf{tbl}_1[v]$ for $\mathsf{eval}(v) = \lambda$, which are λ_1, λ_2 and λ_3; for each of them, we force the domain to $\{a_G, \ldots, a_D\}$, to obtain λ_4, λ_5 and λ_6. We saw in Sect. 2 that multi-agent semantics has the step of restricting attention to a subset of arguments. This process is *explainable* as column selection operations. The time complexity of this query is $O(n)$ for the number of rows n. ♣

Example 4 (Selecting rows). The labelling-based complete/preferred/stable/grounded semantics is explained through row selection on the labelling-based complete semantics. With tbl_1, $\|\{v : \{a_G, \ldots, a_A\} \mid \mathsf{tbl}_1[v] \wedge \neg 1 \dot{\leq} \mathsf{count}(v, \mathsf{und})\}\|$ with respect to the same schm and db is the labelling-based stable semantics. The time complexity of this query is $O(n)$ for the number of rows n. ♣

The process of aggregation of local labelling-based acceptability semantics into a multi-agent semantics is explainable with condition join. We let $\bigwedge_{i \in \{G, \ldots, A\}} v.a_i \doteq v_1.a_i$ abbreviate $v.a_G \doteq v_1.a_G \wedge \ldots \wedge v.a_A \doteq v_1.a_A$. Similarly for others.

Example 5 (Condition join). Let us join tbl_2 and tbl_3 in such a way that for any λ in the body of tbl_1, λ is in the resulting table's body iff there is some $\lambda_x \in db(\mathsf{tbl}_2)$ and some $\lambda_y \in db(\mathsf{tbl}_3)$ such that $\lambda_x(a_i) = \lambda(a_i)$ and $\lambda_y(a_j) = \lambda(a_j)$ hold for every $a_i \in \{a_G, a_F, a_E\}$ and every $a_j \in \{a_D, \ldots, a_A\}$. The relational acceptability semantics of this operation is $\|\{v : \{a_G, \ldots, a_A\} \mid \mathsf{tbl}_1[v] \wedge \exists v_1 : \{a_G, \ldots, a_D\} [\mathsf{tbl}_2[v_1] \wedge (\bigwedge_{i \in \{G, \ldots, E\}} v.a_i \doteq v_1.a_i) \wedge \exists v_2 : \{a_E, \ldots, a_A\} [\mathsf{tbl}_3[v_2] \wedge \bigwedge_{i \in \{D, \ldots, A\}} v.a_i \doteq v_2.a_i]]\}\|$ with respect to the same schm and db. This, incidentally, forms the multi-agent semantics we saw in Example 1. With the sequential two joins, the time complexity of this query is capped by $O(n^2)$ for the largest number of rows n in the 3 tables. ♣

To unify multi-agent semantics and the traditional labelling-based semantics as a relational acceptability semantics with respect to some schm and db, it suffices to let them cover the labelling-based complete semantics of (A, R) as well as $(A_i, R \cap (A_i \times A_i))$ $(1 \leq i \leq n)$ where A_i is the arguments agent i knows.

Theorem 1. *Given (A, R) and n partitions of A into $A_1, \ldots, A_n$ (representing the arguments each of the agents expressed), suppose for every $1 \leq i \leq n$ that there is some A'_i (representing the arguments each of the agents knows) such that $A_i \subseteq A'_i \subseteq A$. Let TBL denote $\{\mathsf{tbl}_{ad}, \mathsf{tbl}_{1ad}, \ldots, \mathsf{tbl}_{nad}\}$ and let $\Lambda_{ad}, \Lambda_{1ad}, \ldots, \Lambda_{nad}$ be the labelling-based complete semantics of: (A, R), $(A'_1, R \cap (A'_1 \times A'_1)), \ldots, (A'_n, R \cap (A'_n \times A'_n))$. Now, let $\mathsf{schm} \equiv (L, \mathsf{TBL}, \mathsf{header})$ and db be such that $\mathsf{header}(\mathsf{tbl}_{ad}) = A$, $\mathsf{header}(\mathsf{tbl}_{iad}) = A'_i (1 \leq i \leq n)$, $db(\mathsf{tbl}_{ad}) = \Lambda_{ad}$ and $db(\mathsf{tbl}_{iad}) = \Lambda_{iad}$ $(1 \leq i \leq n)$. Then, the labelling-based complete/preferred/stable/ grounded semantics of (A, R) and the multi-agent semantics of (A, R) are a relational acceptability semantics with respect to schm and db.*

This shows that the argumentation tuple relational calculus makes the acceptability semantics linkable in the single relational perspective. The relational perspective helps fine-tune existing acceptability semantics, too. As we saw, multi-agent semantics derives a local view (or local views) covering a part of an argumentation graph in order to compute an output. We can see it as a specialisation of the following *partial semantics.* In Fig. 1, tbl_2 is a partial semantics of tbl_1.

Proposition 1 (Partial semantics). *Given (A, R), assume some labelling-based acceptability semantics of it Λ^{sem} such that each $\lambda \in \Lambda^{sem}$ satisfies $\mathbf{dom}(\lambda) = A$. For an $\Lambda_1 \subseteq \Lambda$, we say Λ_1 is a partial semantics of Λ^{sem} iff there is some $A_1 \subseteq A$ such that all the following conditions hold. (1) For every $\lambda_x \in \Lambda_1$, $\mathbf{dom}(\lambda_x) = A_1$ holds. (2) For every $\lambda_x \in \Lambda_1$ and for every $a_1 \in A_1$, there is some $\lambda \in \Lambda^{sem}$ such that $\lambda_x(a_1) = \lambda(a_1)$. (3) For every $\lambda \in \Lambda^{sem}$ and for every $a_1 \in A_1$, there is some $\lambda_x \in \Lambda_1$ such that $\lambda_x(a_1) = \lambda(a_1)$. Assume TBL is some set of table names, then every partial semantics of Λ^{sem} is a relational acceptability semantics with respect to $\mathsf{schm} \equiv (L, \{\mathsf{tbl}_{sem}\} \cup \mathsf{TBL}, \mathsf{header})$ and db where tbl_{sem} and db satisfy the following conditions: $\mathsf{header}(\mathsf{tbl}_{sem}) = A$ and $db(\mathsf{tbl}_{sem}) = \Lambda^{sem}$. Given the schm and db, it is polynomial-time computable.*

4 Conclusions

Given a plethora of acceptability semantics being proposed in various ways, there was always a question of how they may link in what way. As we showed, it is reasonable to let a formal language take care of the linking. We formulated the relational acceptability semantics by formulating argumentation tuple relational calculus. We also showed how it assists find more general acceptability semantics from an existing one, which should complement the recent endeavour [1,6] to try to find reasonable formal constraints for characterising acceptability semantics for specialised abstract argumentations. A fuller work is in [4].

References

1. Amgoud, L., Ben-Naim, J.: Weighted bipolar argumentation graphs: axioms and semantics. In: IJCAI, pp. 5194–5198 (2018)
2. Arisaka, R., Bistarelli, S.: Defence outsourcing in argumentation. In: COMMA, pp. 353–360 (2018)
3. Arisaka, R., Dauphin, J., Satoh, K., van der Torre, L.: Multi-agent argumentation and dialogue. IfCoLog J. Logics Appl. **9**(4), 921–954 (2022)
4. Arisaka, R., Ito, T.: Relational argumentation semantics. arXiv:2104.12386 (2021)
5. Arisaka, R., Satoh, K., van der Torre, L.: Anything you say may be used against you in a court of law. In: Pagallo, U., Palmirani, M., Casanovas, P., Sartor, G., Villata, S. (eds.) AICOL 2015-2017. LNCS (LNAI), vol. 10791, pp. 427–442. Springer, Cham (2018). https://doi.org/10.1007/978-3-030-00178-0_29
6. Baroni, P., Rago, A., Toni, F.: How many properties do we need for gradual argumentation? In: AAAI, pp. 1736–1743 (2018)
7. Caminada, M.: On the issue of reinstatement in argumentation. In: JELIA, pp. 111–123 (2006)
8. Dung, P.M.: On the acceptability of arguments and its fundamental role in non-monotonic reasoning, logic programming, and n-person games. Artif. Intell. **77**(2), 321–357 (1995)
9. Jakobovits, H., Vermeir, D.: Robust semantics for argumentation frameworks. J. Log. Comput. **9**, 215–261 (1999)
10. Ramakrishnan, R., Gehrke, J.: Database Management Systems, 3rd edn. McGraw-Hill, New York (2002)

Author Index

F. Liu et al. (Eds.): PRICAI 2023, LNAI 14325, pp. 495–500, 2024.
https://doi.org/10.1007/978-981-99-7019-3

Printed in the United States
by Baker & Taylor Publisher Services

Printed in the United States
by Baker & Taylor Publisher Services